This Handbook will be of great practical importance. It does not just assemble rules, practices and clauses in order to illustrate the life of international treaties. It delivers much more: it is a manual on *good* treaty practice, designed to educate those in the front line of treaty work on how to handle everything they might come across in their job not only in a correct, but in an optimal way. The scope and depth of the Handbook are truly impressive without being intimidating; the language is clear and the many examples are well chosen. The work lives up to the – PLATO – standard it sets for treaty practice: professional, legal, assured, transparent, organised.

Bruno Simma, *Former Member of the International Law Commission and the International Court of Justice, Judge at the Iran–United States Claims Tribunal (The Hague)*

This Handbook is a collaborative effort by the authors to identify, through engagement with various stakeholders, the best practices in treaty-making. It is a comprehensive guide, providing expertise on each stage of a treaty's lifespan including reservation, ratification and amendments. It condenses highly technical information into an accessible framework, making it an indispensable resource not only for treaty experts, diplomats and administrators, but also lawyers, academics and students delving into the intricacies of treaty practice.

Gabrielle Marceau, *Professor of Law, University of Geneva and World Trade Organization Senior Counsellor*

This remarkable book provides a unique and insightful account of all aspects of treaty practice, and as such will not only be essential reading for government officials whose work relates to treaties, but of considerable interest to international law practitioners and academics.

Dan Sarooshi QC, *Essex Court Chambers and University of Oxford*

Treaty law is a very important component of international law. Diplomats, government legal advisers and legal practitioners are frequently engaged in the process of making, interpreting and implementing treaties. They will find this Handbook an indispensable guide to good treaty practice.

Tommy Koh, *Ambassador-at-Large, Ministry of Foreign Affairs, Singapore*

Centre for International Law, National University of Singapore (CIL-NUS)

The Centre for International Law (CIL) was established as a university-level research institute at the National University of Singapore (NUS) in 2009, in response to the growing need for international law thought leadership and capacity building in the Asia-Pacific region. CIL's focus areas of research and training are ocean law and policy, ASEAN law and policy, investment law and policy, and international law and practice.

The mission of CIL is to enable Singapore and the Asia-Pacific region to play a more significant role in the promotion and development of international law. CIL's vision is to become a regional intellectual hub and thought leader for research on and teaching of international law.

More information about CIL can be found at www.cil.nus.edu.sg

Handbook on Good Treaty Practice

JILL BARRETT
Queen Mary University of London

ROBERT BECKMAN
National University of Singapore

Assisted by

PAUL BARNETT

RANYTA YUSRAN

HAO DUY PHAN

CAMBRIDGE
UNIVERSITY PRESS

CAMBRIDGE
UNIVERSITY PRESS

University Printing House, Cambridge CB2 8BS, United Kingdom

One Liberty Plaza, 20th Floor, New York, NY 10006, USA

477 Williamstown Road, Port Melbourne, VIC 3207, Australia

314–321, 3rd Floor, Plot 3, Splendor Forum, Jasola District Centre,
New Delhi – 110025, India

79 Anson Road, #06–04/06, Singapore 079906

Cambridge University Press is part of the University of Cambridge.

It furthers the University's mission by disseminating knowledge in the pursuit of education, learning, and research at the highest international levels of excellence.

www.cambridge.org
Information on this title: www.cambridge.org/9781107111905
DOI: 10.1017/9781316282335

First published 2020

A catalogue record for this publication is available from the British Library.

Library of Congress Cataloging-in-Publication Data
Names: Barrett, Jill M., 1958– author. | Beckman, Robert C. (Law teacher), author.
Title: Handbook on good treaty practice / Jill Barrett, Queen Mary University of London; Robert Beckman, National University of Singapore ; assisted by Paul Barnett, Ranyta Yusran, Hao Duy Phan.
Description: Cambridge, United Kingdom ; New York, NY : Cambridge University Press, [2019] | Includes index.
Identifiers: LCCN 2019018405 | ISBN 9781107111905
Subjects: LCSH: Treaty-making power. | Treaties.
Classification: LCC K3342 .B37 2019 | DDC 341/.1–dc23
LC record available at https://lccn.loc.gov/2019018405

ISBN 978-1-107-11190-5 Hardback
ISBN 978-1-107-53068-3 Paperback

Contents

Contents

Figures

Cover image: A South African official (far left) and Paul Barnett, UK Government treaty official (far right) assist their respective ministers, Pallo Jordan, Minister for Arts and Culture of South Africa (left) and Tessa Jowell, Secretary of State for Culture Media and Sport of the UK (right), at the signing of the Film Co-production Agreement between the Government of the United Kingdom of Great Britain and Northern Ireland and the Government of the Republic of South Africa, London, 24 May 2006.

Boxes

Acknowledgements

This Handbook originated from a research collaboration on treaty law and practice between the Centre for International Law (CIL) at the National University of Singapore (NUS) and the British Institute of International and Comparative Law (BIICL). CIL continued to provide support to the authors throughout the preparation of this Handbook. We would like to thank CIL, and in particular, Professor Lucy Reed, CIL Director, for her support for this project.

As part of the project, a regional workshop on 'Treaty Law and Practice' was held in Singapore in January 2012 and another workshop on 'Treaty Management of International Organisation: Lessons Learnt and ASEAN Practice' was held at the ASEAN Secretariat in Jakarta in December 2016. The data on treaty practice gathered through a set of questionnaires in the 2012 workshop and updated in the 2016 workshop were used in the Handbook to broaden the range of the Handbook's treaty practice coverage. We thank all participants of the workshops for their co-operation and information.

The Handbook also benefits from the research conducted in visits by the authors to the treaty offices of selected governments and international organisations in several continents, and additional interviews with serving and former treaty officials; in particular:

ASEAN: Robert Beckman and CIL researchers conducted interviews at the ASEAN Secretariat in Jakarta and several ASEAN Member States, and are grateful to AKP Mochtan, ASEAN Deputy Secretary General for Community and Corporate Affairs, Un Sovannasam, Head of Legal Services and Agreements Directorate of the ASEAN Secretariat and their staff, especially Sendy Hermawaty, for information and resources provided at the interviews and in subsequent correspondence. We would also like to thank H. E. Bagas Hapsoro, Ambassador extraordinary and plenipotentiary of the Republic of Indonesia to Kingdom of Sweden and Republic of Latvia for his input and support for the project in his capacity as former ASEAN Deputy Secretary General for Community and Corporate Affairs in 2011–13.

Australia: Jill Barrett conducted interviews at the Treaties Secretariat of the Department of Foreign Affairs and Trade, Canberra, Australia, in June 2012 and is grateful to David Mason, Executive Director of the Treaties Secretariat, and his staff, for information provided at the interviews and in subsequent correspondence.

Council of Europe: Jill Barrett, assisted by Paul Barnett, conducted interviews at the Council of Europe, Strasbourg, France, in December 2011, and is grateful to Manuel Lezertua, Director of Legal Advice and Public International Law, and Elise Cornu, Head of the Treaty Office and Legal Adviser, and their staff, for information provided. We also thank Ms Cornu and her successor, Ana Gomez Heredero, Head of the Treaty Office Unit, Directorate of Legal Advice and Public International Law, for their respective contributions to the Singapore and Jakarta workshops, and for continuing to answer questions about the work of the Treaty Office by correspondence on numerous occasions from 2012 to 2018.

Indonesia: Ranyta Yusran conducted interviews at the Directorate General for Legal Affairs and International Treaties of the Ministry of Foreign Affairs, Jakarta, Indonesia, in December 2012, and is grateful to Abdulkadir Djailani, then Director for Economic and Socio-Cultural Treaties, and his staff, for information provided then and in subsequent correspondence.

Japan: Jill Barrett visited the International Legal Affairs Bureau of the Ministry of Foreign Affairs, Tokyo, Japan, in August 2013 and March 2016. She is grateful in particular to Kenichi Kobayashi and Tomohiro Mikanagi, successive Directors of the International Legal Affairs Division and Takeshi Akahori, Director of the Treaties Division, and their staff, for the information provided at these meetings.

The Netherlands: Gerard Limburg, Former Director of Treaties, Ministry of Foreign Affairs of the Kingdom of the Netherlands, provided information on the treaty practice of the Netherlands at the Singapore Workshop and in interviews and further correspondence with Jill Barrett in 2011–13. She is grateful for the information provided.

New Zealand: Jill Barrett conducted interviews with Kate Nielson, Treaty Officer, Ministry of Foreign Affairs and Trade, New Zealand, at meetings in June 2012 and by subsequent correspondence. She is grateful to Ms Nielson for the information provided.

United Kingdom: Jill Barrett, assisted by Paul Barnett, conducted interviews at the Foreign and Commonwealth Office (FCO) Treaty Section in 2012 and 2016. They are grateful to Nevil Hagon, Head of Treaty Section, and his successor Dale Harrison, and their staff, for continuing to answer questions by correspondence on numerous occasions from 2012 to 2018. Special thanks are also due to Dale Harrison for helping them beyond the call of duty with identifying and providing suitable sample texts for the annexes.

Important note: None of the officials or offices mentioned above are responsible for the way in which the authors have interpreted, analysed and summarised the information they kindly provided. The authors are solely responsible for any errors or omissions in this Handbook, including any failure to update information provided through interviews and personal contacts.

This Handbook could not have been completed without the expertise of Paul Barnett, former Head of Treaty Section, FCO, UK (2002–10). Paul provided substantial inputs on UK treaty practice at the Singapore workshop and throughout the preparation of the Handbook, including contributing first drafts of parts of Chapters 4, 5 and 7. He also provided invaluable assistance by commenting on the draft chapters prepared by Jill Barrett.

The authors are deeply indebted to the two members of the CIL research staff who saw the project through from the initial stages to its final publication. Ms Ranyta Yusran, CIL Research Fellow, co-ordinated the CIL Special Project on Treaty Law, served as CIL's point person for the Handbook, and provided examples from the treaty practice of ASEAN and Indonesia. Dr Hao Duy Phan, CIL Senior Research Fellow, worked together with Ranyta in providing support to the project, planning the events and publication schedule, conducting research, reviewing drafts, offering comments and compiling the tables of treaties, legislation and cases.

Special thanks are also owed to Ms Anais Kedgley Laidlaw, a former CIL Research Associate, who assisted in drafting Chapter 8 on continuing engagement and provided examples of the practice of New Zealand in that chapter. Thanks are also due to Hadyu Ikrami, a former CIL Research Associate, for his work in reviewing drafts and providing examples of the practice of Indonesia. We are also grateful to former Research Assistants at BIICL who provided research assistance during the earlier stages of the project, in particular Nicholas Petrie and Maria Xiouri.

Finally, thanks are owed to Ms Vanessa Lam, a student research assistant at CIL, for her work in proofreading drafts.

Table of Cases

International Court of Justice Cases

Arbitration Cases

Domestic Cases

Table of Treaties and other International Instruments

Multilateral Treaties

Bilateral Treaties

United Nations Instruments

Other International Instruments

Table of Legislation

Abbreviations

Aarhus Convention	Convention on Access to Information, Public Participation in Decision-Making and Access to Justice in Environmental Matters, 1998
ADS	ASEAN Documents Series
ASEAN	Association of Southeast Asian Nations
ASEAN Charter	Charter of the Association of Southeast Asian Nations
AustLII	Australasian Legal Information Institute
BIICL	British Institute of International and Comparative Law
CBD	Convention on Biological Diversity, 1992
CCAMLR	Convention on the Conservation of Antarctic Marine Living Resources, 1980
CIL	Centre for International Law, National University of Singapore
CITES	Convention on International Trade in Endangered Species of Wild Fauna and Flora, 1973
CoE	Council of Europe
COP	Conference of the Parties
DFAT	Department of Foreign Affairs and Trade (of Australia)
DLAPIL	Directorate of Legal Advice and Public International Law (of the Council of Europe)
DOC	Declaration on the Conduct of Parties in the South China Sea, 2002
DPRK	Democratic People's Republic of Korea
EEC	European Economic Community
EM	Explanatory Memorandum
ETS	European Treaty Series (of the Council of Europe)
EU	European Union
FCO	Foreign and Commonwealth Office (of the UK)
FTE	full-time equivalent (number of staff members)
IAEA	International Atomic Energy Agency

ICA	International Coffee Agreement
ICCPR	International Covenant on Civil and Political Rights
ICJ	International Court of Justice
ICJ Statute	Statute of the International Court of Justice, 1945
ICLQ	International and Comparative Law Quarterly
ICSID	International Centre for Settlement of Investment Disputes
ILC	International Law Commission (of the UN)
ILC Guide	International Law Commission, 'Guide to Practice on Reservations to Treaties', 2011
ILM	International Legal Materials
IMO	International Maritime Organization
IO	international organisation
Jakarta Workshop	Workshop on Treaty Management in International Organisations held in Jakarta on 2 December 2016
JSCOT	Joint Standing Committee on Treaties (of the Australian Parliament)
Kyoto Protocol	Kyoto Protocol to the United Nations Framework Convention on Climate Change, 1997
London Convention	Convention on the Prevention of Marine Pollution by Dumping of Wastes and Other Matter, 1972
London Protocol	1996 Protocol to the Convention on the Prevention of Marine Pollution by Dumping of Wastes and Other Matter of 29 December 1972
LSAD	Legal Services and Agreement Directorate (of the ASEAN Secretariat)
MARPOL 73/78	International Convention for the Prevention of Pollution from Ships 1973
MFA	Ministry of Foreign Affairs
MOP	Meeting of the Parties
NATO	North Atlantic Treaty Organization
NGO	non-governmental organisation
NIA	National Interest Analysis
NZTS	New Zealand Treaty Series
OECD	Organisation of Economic Co-operation and Development
OJ	Official Journal of the European Union
OSPAR	Convention for the Protection of the Marine Environment of the North-East Atlantic, 1992
PLATO	Professional, Legal, Assured, Transparent, Organised
REEEP	Renewable Energy and Energy Efficiency Partnership
RoK	Republic of Korea

Singapore Workshop	International Workshop on Treaty Law and Practice held in Singapore on 17–19 January 2012
SOLAS	International Convention for the Safety of Life at Sea
TPP	Trans-Pacific Partnership
UKTS	United Kingdom Treaty Series
UN	United Nations
UN Charter	Charter of the United Nations
UNCITRAL	United Nations Commission on International Trade Law
UNCLOS	United Nations Convention on the Law of the Sea, 1982
UNECE	United Nations Economic Commission for Europe
UNESCO	United Nations Educational, Scientific and Cultural Organisation
UNFCC	United Nations Framework Convention on Climate Change, 1992
UNGA	United Nations General Assembly
UNSC	United Nations Security Council
UNSG	United Nations Secretary General
UNTC	United Nations Treaty Collection
UNTS	United Nations Treaty Series
UST	United States Treaties and Other International Agreements
VCLT 1969	Vienna Convention on the Law on Treaties, 1969
VCLT 1986	Vienna Convention on the Law of Treaties between States and International Organizations or between International Organizations, 1986
WTO	World Trade Organization

1

Introduction to Good Treaty Practice

***

> *'Good practice takes time and trouble, but it is never wasted. It shows in the standing and reputation of practitioners, in the respect in which opponents and tribunals hold them, and above all in the satisfaction of doing a job well. In the end, by avoiding disasters, it also saves money.'*
>
> Lord Justice Sedley[1]

Who This Handbook Is For: Inside and Beyond the Treaty Office

Good treaty practice does not make news. It goes unnoticed by most users of treaties, who look at the finished product rather than how it was made. Poor treaty practice, on the other hand, usually does show one way or another. Over time, it tends to result in low participation in treaties and poor compliance by the State or organisation concerned, leading to lack of influence in international

[1] Foreword by Lord Justice Sedley in M Henderson et al., *Best Practice Guide to Asylum and Human Rights Appeals* (Immigration Law Practitioner's Association, 2003) xviii.

negotiations. Occasionally, a single error will have serious consequences – a State may bind itself to a treaty without intending to; bind itself to the wrong text; fail to join a treaty it intended to join; bind itself to more obligations than it intended to; make an ineffective reservation; misunderstand a treaty's effect in domestic law; or an organisation may fail to send an essential notification to treaty parties. Such errors can often be put right, if you know how. But when they come to light as a result of an international dispute, litigation or a contentious vote at a treaty meeting, the consequences can be far-reaching.

The aim of this Handbook is not only to present and explain treaty practices, but also to suggest how to do them well. It is first and foremost for people who work with treaties and treaty procedures, in governments, international organisations (IOs), legal practice and elsewhere. It is intended to provide practical guidance on how treaty procedures are and should be carried out, especially for those new to this area of work, or who are setting up a dedicated Treaty Office for the first time, or wish to consider ways in which their treaty practices could be improved.

We also have in mind that treaties are negotiated, made and dealt with by a wide range of people beyond the Treaty Office, such as diplomats and administrators across governments and IOs. There are many others whose work involves handling treaties or treaty information in an official capacity, such as international and domestic courts and tribunals, government archivists and information managers, parliamentarians and their officials. Our aim is to provide guidance and information that is useful and accessible to all of these groups, whether they encounter treaties daily or only occasionally, and whether they are experts in international law or not legally trained at all.

In addressing the needs of those in the 'front line' of treaty work, we hope also to meet the needs of other users of treaties for information on how treaties are made and operated. Legal practitioners advising and litigating on matters pertaining to treaties and treaty practice are often in the 'second line' of treaty work, advising governments, private individuals and companies on the status and effect of a treaty after things have gone wrong and a dispute is on its way to a court or tribunal. This is increasingly common in the fields of human rights and investment treaties, in which individuals and private entities are the direct holders of rights against governments. Litigation outcomes can turn on points of treaty procedure such as whether the treaty was validly ratified, whether it is in force for the State concerned, whether a particular document forms part of it, which language texts were authenticated (and how a treaty should be authenticated) or whether a reservation was effectively made. This Handbook may also be of interest to legal academics and students wishing to gain insight into the realities of treaty practice, as a complement to their study of the international law of treaties and the role of treaties in constitutional law.

We hope also that the principles of good treaty practice proposed in this book may add a new dimension to the concept of what is meant by the 'international rule of law' or 'rule of international law'. In the Southeast Asian region, this material is particularly relevant to the debate on the transformation of the

Association of Southeast Asian Nations (ASEAN) to a rules-based regional organisation, and the concrete steps that are needed to make this happen.[2]

The primary focus of this Handbook is treaty practice and procedures rather than the intricacies of legal rules, for all who deal with treaties whatever their level of legal knowledge. It presents a range of examples from the practice of States and IOs. Our examples are drawn from the Asian region, particularly Southeast Asia, as well as Europe and other Western nations. It explains the actions that need to be taken to create a new treaty, bring it into force, operate it, amend it and wind it up, both on the international plane (in relation to other States and IOs) and on the domestic plane (in relation to the other organs of the same State or IO). It also explores what constitutes *good* treaty practice, and develops generic principles or criteria against which to evaluate the examples chosen. In other words, the aim of the Handbook is not only to describe treaty practice as it is, but also to suggest what it should be and to present good examples which in our view meet the proposed criteria. In addition, the Handbook provides a useful analytical tool to enable each government and IO to identify and develop the best treaty practice for their circumstances, recognising that one size does not necessarily fit all.

What Are 'Treaties' and Why Are They so Important?

We use the term 'treaties' to mean instruments recognised as such by the international law of treaties, as reflected in the Vienna Convention on the Law of Treaties, 1969 (VCLT 1969)[3] and the Vienna Convention on the Law of Treaties between States and International Organizations or between International Organizations, 1986 (VCLT 1986).[4] In short, treaties are international agreements between States,

[2] Charter of the Association of Southeast Asian Nations (adopted 20 November 2007, entered into force 15 December 2008) 2624 UNTS 223 (ASEAN Charter), preamble. For analyses of the steps that ASEAN has taken to transform itself to a rules-based organisation, see Centre for International Law (CIL), 'ASEAN Integration through Law Project', https://cil.nus.edu.sg/research/asean-law-policy/topics/asean-integration-through-law/ accessed 21 September 2018.

[3] Vienna Convention on the Law of Treaties (adopted 23 May 1969, entered into force 27 January 1980) 1155 UNTS 331 (VCLT 1969). Article 2(1)(a) provides that for the purposes of that treaty:

> treaty means an international agreement concluded between States in written form and governed by international law, whether embodied in a single instrument or in two or more related instruments and whatever its particular designation;

[4] Vienna Convention on the Law of Treaties between States and International Organizations or between International Organizations (adopted 21 March 1986, not in force) 25 ILM 543 (VCLT 1986) http://legal.un.org/ilc/texts/instruments/english/conventions/1_2_1986.pdf accessed 9 September 2018. Article 2(1)(a) provides that for the purposes of that treaty:

> treaty means an international agreement governed by international law and concluded in written form:
>
> (i) between one or more States and one or more international organizations; or
> (ii) between international organizations,
>
> whether that agreement is embodied in a single instrument or in two or more related instruments and whatever its particular designation;

or between IOs, or between any combinations thereof, which are governed by international law.[5] We also consider treaties to include agreements where one or more party is neither a State nor an IO but some other kind of subject of international law, where these are recognised as treaties in international law. For example, some territories which are not States have been recognised as having capacity to enter into some treaties, such as Hong Kong Special Administrative Region, Taiwan and Palestine. This Handbook does not seek to analyse the legal status of non-orthodox parties to treaties, but rather to alert treaty professionals to the legal issues and possible controversies, and the need to select appropriate treaty procedures to handle them.

Various other kinds of agreements may be called *treaties* by some people in popular parlance and in some domestic legal systems. For example, Aboriginals made *treaties* with each other long before European fur traders or settlers arrived in what is now called Canada. Aboriginal nations would use oral *treaties* to settle land disputes and end other conflicts, including war.[6] Another well-known example is the Treaty of Waitangi 1840, signed on behalf of the British Crown and by various Māori chiefs.[7] Such instruments – interesting though they are – are not treaties as defined in international law, and so are outside the scope of this Handbook.

The importance of treaties can be seen in international relations as well as international law. Treaties are an indispensable tool for conducting international relations; indeed, no State can exist without using them. Every State has the capacity in international law to conclude treaties.[8] All States that are members of the United Nations (UN) are by definition party to at least one treaty, the Charter of the United Nations (UN Charter),[9] and all of them have concluded more, ranging from a handful to hundreds or thousands of treaties.[10]

The newest State to come into being, South Sudan,[11] signed and brought into force two bilateral treaties with the UN on the very day of its birth,

[5] See the fuller explanation of the meaning of treaty in the section on 'Definition of a treaty in international law' in Chapter 3 at 91–6.

[6] See Early Canadiana Online, http://eco.canadiana.ca/ accessed 21 September 2018.

[7] The Māori are indigenous people of New Zealand. For a history of the Treaty of Waitangi, see C. Orange, *The Treaty of Waitangi* (Bridget Williams Books Limited, Wellington 1987).

[8] VCLT 1969, art 6.

[9] Charter of the United Nations (adopted 24 October 1945, entered into force 24 October 1945) 1 UNTS XVI (UN Charter).

[10] Several UN Member States have registered participation in fewer than 50 treaties each, while over 70 Member States have more than 500 treaty records each (where the number exceeds 500, it is not shown). The number of treaty records gives an indication of the number of treaties they are party to, but is only approximate for several reasons: see n 14 below, and the section on 'Introduction – Why Organization of Treaty Work Matters?' in Chapter 2 at 43–4.

[11] The Republic of South Sudan formally seceded from Sudan on 9 July 2011 and was admitted as a new Member State by the United Nations General Assembly (UNGA) on 14 July 2011. United Nations 'Growth in United Nations Membership, 1945–present', www.un.org/en/sections/member-states/growth-united-nations-membership-1945-present/index.html accessed 21 September 2018.

9 July 2011.[12] During its first year, it joined five important multilateral treaties on subjects ranging from chemical weapons to the ozone layer, and concluded four new bilateral treaties – three with various parts of the UN and one with South Africa.[13] The second newest State, Montenegro, which declared independence in 2006, already has over 370 treaty actions recorded at the UN.[14] Even the world's smallest States have multiple treaty relations. For example, Tuvalu has over 50 treaty actions to its name, indicating over twenty multilateral treaties joined and sixteen bilaterals. Monaco, a much older micro-State, has over 200 UN treaty records.[15] New States or territories aspiring to be States invariably seek to conclude treaties as a top priority, both because of the functional necessity of legally binding transactions with other States and with IOs, and because being in treaty relations is considered to be an important *badge* of statehood, from both a legal and a political perspective.[16]

Treaties also play a major role in IOs that differs from their role in relations among States. Most IOs are established by a treaty, which therefore acts as its constitutional framework. The founding treaty typically indicates the purposes and objectives of the organisation, its legal personality, its membership and whether and how new members may be admitted, its constituent organs and their functions and powers. The founding treaty or treaties thus play a vital role within the organisation. Treaties are also important in the external relations of

[12] Exchange of letters between the United Nations Development Programme (UNDP) and the Republic of South Sudan concerning the interim legal measures to ensure continuity of UNDP's operations in South Sudan (with annexed Agreement), (adopted 9 July 2011, entered into force 9 July 2011) 2784 UNTS 105, and Exchange of letters between the United Nations Population Fund (UNFPA) and the Government of the Republic of South Sudan on the applicability of the Agreement between the United Nations Development Programme (UNDP) and the Government of South Sudan regarding interim legal measures to ensure continuity of UNDP operations in the Republic of South Sudan after the declaration of independence of the Republic of South Sudan (adopted 9 July 2011, entered into force 9 July 2011) 2784 UNTS 135.

[13] South Sudan has now registered its participation in thirty-three treaties: twelve bilateral and twenty-one multilateral. The multilaterals were mostly joined by accession or succession. Full information on South Sudan's treaty participation can be accessed on the United Nations Treaty Collection (UNTC) (through 'Participant search'), http://treaties.un.org/Pages/UNTSOnline.aspx?id=3 accessed 21 September 2018.

[14] Montenegro declared itself independent from Serbia on 3 June 2006. On 28 June 2006 it was accepted as a UN Member State by General Assembly resolution A/RES/60/264. A list of Montenegro's treaty registrations can be accessed on UNTC (through 'Participant search'), https://treaties.un.org/Pages/UNTSOnline.aspx?id=3 accessed 21 September 2018.

[15] See ibid. Cautionary note: the statistics referred to in this paragraph (and the preceding one) are taken from the United Nations Treaty Series (UNTS). This is a collection of treaties and international agreements registered or filed and recorded with and published by the Secretariat since 1946, pursuant to Article 102 of the Charter. Accordingly, the statistics do not include treaties that have not yet been submitted to the UN, but may include treaties that are no longer in force for that State. They may also include treaty amendments. The statistics are provided here to give a general indication of the diversity among States in terms of the volume of treaty activity, and to illustrate the fact that all States, however new or small, have entered into a range of treaty relations.

[16] See A Peters, 'Treaty Making Power' in R Wolfrum (ed), *Max Planck Encyclopedia of Public International Law* (OUP 2012).

Treaties' (ILC Guide)[31] contains a useful section on procedure, but it is specific to reservations and does not address practical matters outside the scope of the VCLTs 1969 and 1986. Some governments have published information about their treaty procedures and practices,[32] but these simply describe what they do without explaining the underlying rationale or setting out general principles. The few works published in English that look at the treaty practice of more than one country have the aim of informing and describing.[33] They do not generally aim to distinguish good practice from not so good, and do so only indirectly.[34]

There is no ready-made model set of treaty practices that is ideal for all States or all IOs. Even if there is one that is ideal for the State or IO that operates it (which is unlikely), it would not suit another without adaptation. For example, Australia's treaty practice is highly regarded around the world (including by the authors), mainly because the Australian Treaties Database[35] was one of the first to be made available to the public online, and its web interface is particularly comprehensive and user-friendly. But it does not follow that all Australian treaty practices would suit other States with very different circumstances, nor that all other aspects of Australia's treaty practice are necessarily ideal, even for Australia.

Could UN treaty practice be regarded as a universal benchmark? Many States refer to the UN Treaty Handbook. UN practice is an extremely important reference point, but it does not provide a comprehensive template for government treaty functions. For example, the UN is not normally concerned

[31] ILC, 'Guide to Practice on Reservations to Treaties' in 'Report of the International Law Commission covering the work of its sixty-third session' (UN Doc A/66/10), reproduced in ILC, *Yearbook of the International Law Commission 2011* (vol II, Part Two A/CN/SER.A.2011/Add.1 (Part 2), United Nations 2018) 26–38 http://legal.un.org/ilc/publications/yearbooks/english/ilc_2011_v2_p2.pdf accessed 21 September 2018; see also section 2 of the Guide on 'Procedure' at 27–32.

[32] See for example, information about treaty procedures and practices of the UK, Australia and New Zealand. Government of the UK, 'Guidance to the work of the Foreign and Commonwealth Office (FCO) Treaty Section' (last updated 4 October 2013) www.gov.uk/guidance/uk-treaties#practice-and-procedures accessed 21 September 2018; Australian Government Department of Foreign Affairs and Trade, 'Treaty making process' http://dfat.gov.au/international-relations/treaties/treaty-making-process/Pages/treaty-making-process.aspx accessed 21 September 2018; and New Zealand Ministry of Foreign Affairs and Trade, 'Treaties' www.mfat.govt.nz/en/about-us/who-we-are/treaties/#Treatymaking accessed 21 September 2018.

[33] See for example, *Aust* (n 22) 2, where the aim of Aust is stated as 'to inform the reader about all aspects of the law and practice by collecting the information in one convenient place'.

[34] Aust's book contains plenty of advice in passing, sometimes implicit (see for example, *Aust* (n 22) 33 on the benefits of using clear language to distinguish Memoranda of Understanding (MOUs) from treaties) and sometimes explicit (see for example, *Aust* (n 22) 8: 'it is not always wise to depart from established practice unless it is really necessary'); but no general principles for good treaty practice.

[35] Australian Government Department of Foreign Affairs and Trade of Australia, 'Australian Treaties Database' www.dfat.gov.au/treaties/index.html accessed 21 September 2018. It was Australia which led the initiative to develop the UN electronic treaty database, as set out in UNGA Res/51/158 on electronic treaty database (30 January 1997), for example.

with the procedures leading to the conclusion of bilateral treaties. Other IOs refer to UN practice as a guide, but UN practices might not always be suitable, especially for small regional or specialist organisations. Moreover, UN treaty practices date back more than sixty years. Some may have developed due to historical accident or bureaucratic habit – it is done thus because it has always been done thus – with their origins in a different technological era. A government or IO setting up treaty functions for the first time in the twenty-first century may be able to find a better starting point.

We therefore decided to develop *generic principles* that can be used to select a range of good treaty practices, from various States and IOs. These were derived from considering the purposes which treaty practice is designed to serve, as well as the needs and interests of all categories of people involved in the handling of treaties or affected by them (stakeholders)[36] at each stage of the life of a treaty. The range of treaty stakeholders were analysed both for a typical State and IO, and are listed in Boxes 1.2 and 1.3 in the sections on treaty stakeholder analysis at the end of this chapter. The tables in these boxes show how extensive the range of treaty stakeholders can be. The PLATO principles take account of the treaty services needed by all stakeholders, not only the administrative convenience of treaty officials.

Principles are standards to apply and aspire to, but this may not be easy where there are conflicting interests. For example, a government's desire for flexibility, speed and confidentiality in intergovernmental dealings may not sit easily with the demands of the legislature for consultation and transparency. Based on this functional analysis of the needs and expectations of all categories of treaty stakeholders, we extracted the common threads which seem to underpin them, consulted a number of treaty practitioners in governments and IOs on whether these principles accord with their notions of good treaty practice and revised the principles, taking account of their feedback.[37] The recurring themes were distilled into a set of generic principles that may be applicable to the treaty practice of any State or IO.

The concept of generic standards is commonly used in international contexts, in a way that is designed to accommodate a diverse range of

[36] J Bryson, 'What to Do When Stakeholders Matter: Stakeholder Identification and Analysis Techniques' (2004) 6 *Public Management Review* 21–53.

[37] On the discussions held with officials from ASEAN Member States, see CIL, 'International Workshop on Treaty Law and Practice', 10 October 2012, paras 33–47 https://cil.nus.edu.sg/wp-content/uploads/2012/12/Final-Treaty-Workshop-Report.pdf accessed 21 September 2018. Views of Treaty and Legal Officers of other governments and IOs in Europe and elsewhere have been canvassed by email and in interviews by the authors, using qualitative survey methods. On methods, see P Cane and HM Kritzer (eds), *The Oxford Handbook of Empirical Legal Research* (OUP 2010) 1–5. For particulars of the consultations conducted by the authors, see Acknowledgements at xxiv–xxv.

cultures and environments.[38] By making the selection criteria explicit, this Handbook aims to stimulate debate as to what constitutes good practice, and thereby to help generate more of it. This approach takes account of the expectation of others that internationally established procedures will be followed, but does not presume that existing practice is always the best way of doing things. It does not aim to promote standardisation or uniformity in any area of treaty practice, unless a good reason can be shown for this. There is no need to level the playing field, in the sense that there is no global competition among States to have better treaty practice than another State. States are likely to suffer harm or embarrassment if their treaty practice is poor, but they do not normally benefit from mistakes or poor practices by others (except, occasionally, where litigation turns on an error in treaty practice). On the contrary, the international community as a whole will benefit from the raising of standards in treaty practice by any of its members. The extent of consultation with treaty officials and users carried out by the authors has necessarily been limited to a few groups in selected States and IOs. The PLATO principles are presented in the hope that, however imperfect, they offer a useful starting point.[39]

The PLATO Principles for Good Treaty Practice

The analysis and consultation outlined above yielded some recurring themes, which were then distilled into five generic principles for good treaty practice: 'Professional'; 'Legal'; 'Assured'; 'Transparent'; 'Organised'. Each principle is equally important; the order in which they are placed here reflects merely the authors' preference for arranging them into a pronounceable acronym: PLATO. The term 'PLATO principles' is used from here on as a convenient abbreviation, and is not intended to imply reference to any philosopher bearing a similar sounding surname.

[38] For example, the International Organization for Standardization (ISO) is a global body which develops voluntary international standards. The ISO explains that '[a] standard is a document that provides requirements, specifications, guidelines or characteristics that can be used consistently to ensure that materials, products, processes and services are fit for their purpose'. ISO, 'Standards' www.iso.org/iso/home/standards.htm accessed 21 September 2018.

[39] Many collections of 'good' or 'best practice' on all kinds of subjects do not even define the term, or present any selection criteria, but simply present a collection of examples or invite submission of examples to a database. For example, the UN Security Council (UNSC) Counter-Terrorism Committee's directory of 'good practices, codes and standards' regarding counter-terrorism, pursuant to UNSC Resolution 1624 (2005): Counter-Terrorism Committee Executive Directorate, 'United Nations Security Council Resolution 1624 (2005) Compilation of International Good Practices, Codes and Standards' www.un.org/sc/ctc/wp-content/uploads/2016/03/res1624.pdf accessed 21 September 2018.

Box 1.1 PLATO principles

PROFESSIONAL	LEGAL	ASSURED	TRANSPARENT	ORGANISED
P	**L**	**A**	**T**	**O**

PROFESSIONAL

Professional approach to treaty work by those who do it and by their organisation

PROFESSIONAL APPROACH TO TREATY EXPERTISE

- Treaty practice is recognised by senior management (including Human Resources) as specialised work requiring expert knowledge, training and expertise.
- Senior management plans and provides resources for recruitment, training, capacity-building, career development and retention of treaty officials, and knowledge management.
- Care is taken to hire staff with the right skills for treaty work.

FLEXIBILITY WITH DISCRETION AND FAIRNESS

- Like cases are treated alike, respecting the principle of equality of States.
- Procedures allow flexibility and are adaptable to new situations.
- Treaty staff are trained to understand reasons for procedures and are able to make sensible judgments about when to be flexible, balancing legal and other requirements.

PUBLIC SERVICE ETHOS

- Providing treaty texts and treaty information to those outside the Treaty Office is run as a service with a high standard of *customer care.*

LEGAL

Legal requirements met; lawyers fully engaged

INTERNATIONAL LAW

- Treaty practice conforms to the international law of treaties, as reflected in the VCLT 1969, VCLT 1986 and Article 102 of the UN Charter. Relevant legal deadlines are observed.

DOMESTIC LAW

- Treaty practice conforms to domestic law and constitutional requirements (States and IOs).

Box 1.1 (cont.)

LEGAL

Legal requirements met; lawyers fully engaged

LAWYERS INVOLVED

- In-house lawyers are fully engaged in treaty work to ensure that procedures meet legal requirements.
- Treaties are properly drafted, interpreted and implemented.

LEGAL/NON-LEGAL DISTINCTIONS

- Distinctions between treaties and non-binding international instruments are understood and appropriately addressed in treaty procedures.

ASSURED

Accuracy, authenticity and authority are assured

ACCURACY

- All treaty texts and instruments are accurate.
- There is a culture of zero tolerance of errors, and effective mechanisms for prompt and transparent corrections where needed.

AUTHENTICITY

- It is always made clear whether a treaty document is the original text or a certified true copy, or if it is not, what its status is and where the original or a certified copy may be found.

AUTHORITY

- It is always made clear who is authorised to perform any treaty acts and there are procedures to ensure that unauthorised acts do not occur.
- Treaty users have confidence that treaty information is reliable, dependable, trustworthy and guaranteed.

TRANSPARENT

Clear, communicated, available and accessible in practice

CLEAR

- Clear written guidelines and standards are provided to treaty officials.
- Clear treaty information is provided to the public.

Box 1.1 (cont.)

TRANSPARENT

Clear, communicated, available and accessible in practice

COMMUNICATED

- Treaty practices and procedures are actively disseminated to ensure that they are widely known and understood by all who need to use them, not just kept on a shelf or obscure web page.

ACCESSIBLE

- There is easy access to treaty procedures, guidance and information for all who need it for their work, and others as appropriate.
- Publications of treaty texts are easy for the public to access, affordable and user-friendly.

ACCOUNTABLE

- Sufficient and timely information is provided to enable democratic oversight of the exercise of treaty-making powers and other treaty acts.
- There is a meaningful opportunity for elected representatives/Member States to scrutinise treaties and express views.

ORGANISED

Systematic, efficient, regular

RECORD MANAGEMENT SYSTEMS WORK

- Treaty collections and records are well organised and maintained, and can be searched and retrieved by present and future generations of staff.

WRITTEN OPERATING PROCEDURES

- Treaty procedures and practices are written down and disseminated to all staff concerned.
- Standard operating procedures are written down, regularly reviewed and updated.

CONSISTENT

- Treaty procedures are applied consistently. To facilitate knowledge management, records are kept on how particular cases are handled and why.

Box 1.1 (cont.)

ORGANISED

Systematic, efficient, regular

CENTRALISED

- There is a central contact point within the secretariat or government for treaty procedures for all internal and external contacts.
- A central authority has ultimate public responsibility for treaty information and procedures across the secretariat or government.

CO-ORDINATED

- All aspects of treaty procedure work harmoniously together across the secretariat or government, with effective co-ordination.

How Have the Examples of Good Treaty Practice in this Handbook Been Selected?

Examples of good treaty practice abound the world over. For practical reasons the authors had to limit the survey to selected governments and IOs. The idea of writing this Handbook originated from a research collaboration between CIL and the BIICL on treaty law and practice, aiming to improve treaty law and practice in Southeast Asia. The collaboration started with the 2012 International Workshop on Treaty Law and Practice (Singapore Workshop) attended by officials from the governments of the Southeast Asian region and the Secretariat of ASEAN and others.[40] Participants expressed interest in further opportunities to share experiences and compare them with those in other regions. The workshop also provided the authors with more information about treaty practices in the Asian region, including issues and problems.[41] A further workshop on Treaty Management in International Organisations (Jakarta Workshop) in 2016 provided the research team with the opportunity to collect more material and canvass a wider range of views.[42]

[40] The Singapore workshop was held jointly by CIL and British Institute of International and Comparative Law (BIICL) in 2012 as part of a Treaty Law and Practice research project. See BIICL, 'Treaty Law and Practice' https://www.biicl.org/newsitems/180/joint-research-project-on-treaty-law-and-practice accessed 21 September 2019 and CIL, 'Research Project on Treaty Law and Practice' https://cil.nus.edu.sg/research/special-projects/topics/treaty-law-and-practice/ accessed 21 September 2018.

[41] For all related documentation of the Workshop, see CIL, 'International Workshop on Treaty Law and Practice' https://cil.nus.edu.sg/event/international-workshop-on-treaty-law-and-practice/ accessed 21 September 2018 and BIICL, 'Compilation of Constitutional and Legislative Provisions on Treaty Practice of Selected States and International Organisations' http://www.biicl.org/research-treaty-online-resource accessed 21 September 2018.

[42] CIL, 'Workshop on Treaty Management in International Organisation (2016)' https://cil.nus.edu.sg/event/workshop-on-treaty-management-in-international-organisation-2016/ accessed 21 September 2018.

The initial selection of examples of treaty practice from beyond Asia were drawn mainly from Australia, the Netherlands, New Zealand, the UK, the Council of Europe (CoE) and the UN. These jurisdictions were chosen for several reasons, including the generally high international reputation of their treaty practice, their long-established and very experienced Treaty Offices, the authors' personal contacts with the Treaty Offices which facilitated the collection of information and discussion of issues, and the availability of material in the English language. In addition, the selection aimed to provide examples from both common law and civil law traditions. The authors have also acquired a variety of information and examples of particular aspects of treaty practice from a number of other governments, which feature in this Handbook where relevant. There are many more States and IOs whose practices are not presented here, and which may be exemplary in meeting all the PLATO criteria. We continue to collect information, and offers of more are always welcome.

Treaty Stakeholder Analysis for a State

The table in Box 1.2 lists in detail all major stakeholders of a State and their treaty functions and engagement. It looks at the treaty engagement from the perspective of a State, at what we consider to be a sufficiently high level of generality as to be broadly applicable to any State. The term 'stakeholders' is used in a broad sense to include all people who are involved in the handling of treaties or whose interests are affected by them. It includes both treaty actors and treaty users, as these categories are not mutually exclusive; for example, the same person may be the initiator of an action in relation to a treaty and also the recipient of another action by someone else in relation to the same treaty.

Box 1.2 Treaty stakeholder analysis for a State

I. NATIONAL STAKEHOLDERS OF STATE X A. GOVERNMENT'S TREATY PROCEDURE OFFICIALS	
Treaty functions	1. Organise and advise on treaty procedures, ensure all treaty acts are legally effective, establish domestic procedures, publish, register, and keep State treaty records. 2. Responsible for communications between the executive and the legislature about constitutional treaty processes.

Box 1.2 (cont.)

A. GOVERNMENT'S TREATY PROCEDURE OFFICIALS	
	3. Monitor all communications from treaty depositaries and secretariats (especially about amendments, new parties and reservations), and circulate them to the relevant policy leads with clear advice about required action and deadlines. 4. Perform depositary functions (if applicable).
What they need to do their job well	1. Clear treaty procedures which are observed by all officials throughout government. 2. Central control of treaty procedures within government. 3. Well-resourced and supported treaty team with experienced and knowledgeable staff who understand the policy context of treaty procedures and pay meticulous attention to detail. 4. Ability to access accurate information about own State's treaties, treaty actions, precedents for treaty documents, internal records of decision-making and legal advice on treaty procedures. 5. Reliable information and technology (IT) systems with adequate functionality. 6. Ability to access accurate information about other States' treaties and treaty actions. 7. Clear and co-ordinated policy instructions from administrators and ministers, when needed, on particular treaties. 8. Training and development in treaty law and practice for treaty staff. 9. Career structure for treaty professionals.
Constraints and issues	1. Resources: capacity, time, funding. 2. Overall human resource needs of ministry/unit. 3. Domestic legal requirements for treaty procedures and treaty publications.
B. DIPLOMATS IN FOREIGN MINISTRY (INCLUDING LEGAL ADVISERS)	
Treaty functions	1. Negotiate treaties. 2. Support home departments in treaty negotiations. 3. Set policy priorities for treaty relations with other States and IOs.

Box 1.2 (cont.)	
B. DIPLOMATS IN FOREIGN MINISTRY (INCLUDING LEGAL ADVISERS)	
	4. Decide policy questions in relation to particular treaties. 5. Request treaty officials to arrange treaty signings, ratifications, etc. 6. Ensure new treaties are compatible with international law. 7. Interpret treaties. 8. Implement treaties in domestic law or co-ordinate with other government departments/agencies to achieve this. 9. Participate in Conferences and Meetings of the Parties (COPs and MOPs), treaty bodies, working groups, compliance committees, etc. of treaties within the foreign ministry's remit or in support of the responsible home department or agency.
What they need to do their job well	1. Clear treaty procedures that are easy to access and follow. 2. Ideally one central contact point in the treaty team for co-ordinated advice on treaty matters. 3. Confidence that treaty officials will deal with procedural matters quickly and accurately. 4. Knowledge of relevant international and national law. 5. Easy and reliable access to accurate information about own State's treaties and treaty actions. 6. Clear rules on where, within government, responsibility lies for each aspect of treaty matters. 7. Mechanisms for ensuring that all government departments and agencies observe correct procedures and division of responsibilities.
Constraints and issues	1. Need to ensure that policy diplomats handling treaties have sufficient legal awareness and know when to consult lawyers and treaty officials.
C. DIPLOMATS AT POSTS ABROAD	
Treaty functions	1. Carry out treaty actions with depositary governments and secretariats (multilateral) or host government (bilateral). 2. Record and communicate the treaty acts and notifications of others to own government.

Box 1.2 (cont.)	
	C. DIPLOMATS AT POSTS ABROAD
	3. Negotiate new treaties. 4. Arrange treaty signings or the participation of representatives in ceremonies hosted by others. 5. Discuss treaty issues with host State or secretariat. 6. Manage and resolve disputes about treaties. 7. Participate in COPs and MOPs, treaty bodies, working groups, compliance committees, etc. of treaties, representing or supporting the responsible department or agency, as required.
What they need to do their job well	1. Clear instructions from government on specific treaty actions. 2. Clear treaty procedures that are easy to access and follow. 3. Effective communication with treaty officials at home – ideally one central contact point for treaty procedures. 4. Awareness of the role of other government ministries and agencies in treaty matters and effective co-ordination with them. 5. Effective communication with treaty officials in host government – ideally one central contact point. 6. Confidence that treaty officials will deal with procedural matters quickly and accurately. 7. Knowledge of relevant international and domestic law. 8. Easy access to accurate information about own State's treaties and treaty actions. 9. Ability to access accurate information about other States' treaties and treaty actions.
Constraints and issues	1. Need to ensure diplomats overseas are acting on behalf of the whole government (not only one ministry), and that all actions are within scope of authority (not freelancing).
	D. OTHER GOVERNMENT DEPARTMENTS AND AGENCIES
Treaty functions	1. Set policy priorities, negotiate and interpret treaties on matters within the departmental remit. 2. Ministers may sign treaties within remit. 3. Responsible for domestic action to implement treaties, including legislation.

Box 1.2 (cont.)

D. OTHER GOVERNMENT DEPARTMENTS AND AGENCIES	
	4. Responsible for domestic enforcement, including prosecution. 5. Responsible for periodic reporting to treaty bodies and compliance mechanisms within the departmental remit. 6. Participate in COPs and MOPs, treaty bodies, working groups, compliance committees, scientific committees etc. of treaties within the departmental remit. 7. Monitor COP and MOP decisions, especially amendments to treaty annexes subject to tacit acceptance procedures, and keep Treaty Office informed. 8. Responsible for consultation with and flow of information to relevant stakeholders, sectors of civil society, etc.
What they need to do their job well	1. Clear general treaty procedures that are easy to access and follow. 2. Ideally one central contact point in government for treaty procedural matters. 3. Confidence that treaty officials will deal with procedural matters quickly and accurately. 4. Knowledge of relevant international and domestic law. 5. Easy access to accurate information about own State's treaties and treaty actions. 6. Mechanisms for ensuring that all government departments and agencies observe correct procedures and division of responsibilities.
Constraints and issues	1. Need to ensure that all ministries and agencies fulfil responsibilities, while observing central control and supervision (i.e. the central authority needs the ability to rein in unauthorised treaty actions by single ministries or agencies, if necessary).
E. HEAD OF STATE/GOVERNMENT, MINISTERS, CABINET AND INTER-AGENCY MINISTERIAL COMMITTEES	
Treaty functions	1. Set international policy agenda. 2. Direct ministries to negotiate and conclude treaties. 3. Conduct high-level treaty negotiations with counterparts in other States.

Box 1.2 (cont.)	
E. HEAD OF STATE/GOVERNMENT, MINISTERS, CABINET AND INTER-AGENCY MINISTERIAL COMMITTEES	
	4. Decide on signature and ratification. 5. Sign treaties and instruments of ratification. 6. Sign full powers. 7. Attend treaty ceremonies. 8. Propose, explain and defend treaty actions to the legislature and the public.
What they need to do their job well	1. Awareness of own role in treaty matters, including legal powers and limits. 2. Well-trained and experienced treaty officials to ensure that the treaty actions on behalf of government are undertaken correctly, accurately and at the appropriate time with the correct advice given. 3. All ministries and agencies to take forward the policy agenda for treaties, as set by government. 4. Treaty ceremonies to be conducted correctly and presented well for the media. 5. Policy officials that have sufficient awareness of treaty procedures to refer matters to the treaty team promptly.
Constraints and issues	1. Ministers may sometimes desire a greater role in treaty decisions and public acts than is appropriate under international law or domestic law. 2. Ministers may wish treaty events or procedures to take place in a timeframe or manner that is not feasible for legal or practical reasons.
F. PROVINCIAL/STATE, REGIONAL AND LOCAL AUTHORITIES	
Treaty functions	1. Implement treaty obligations within constitutional or statutory remit. 2. Enforce implementing legislation, including prosecutions. 3. May participate in treaty negotiations within remit. 4. May be consulted on treaty signature or ratification. 5. Occasionally may be authorised to conclude treaties (where permitted by international and domestic law).
What they need to do their job well	1. Access to information about treaty negotiations and actions before the event.

Box 1.2 (cont.)	
F. PROVINCIAL/STATE, REGIONAL AND LOCAL AUTHORITIES	
	2. To be consulted by the central government on treaty negotiations and proposed actions, and have regional/local views respected. 3. May wish for facilities to negotiate own treaties with other States and regions (where permitted by international law and national constitution). 4. Access to advice and assistance from central government on treaty procedures, interpretation and implementation. 5. Constitutional means of resolving disputes with central government over treaty competences.
Constraints and issues	1. Central and regional/provincial authorities may hold differing views on the competence of regional/provincial authorities on treaty matters. Solution of such differences depends on constitutional arrangements. 2. Under international law, the State is responsible for fulfilling all treaty obligations, but under domestic law, the central government may rely on implementation by regional authorities. Therefore, securing the regional authorities' co-operation is necessary; failure to do so might result in the State being in breach of its treaty obligations.
G. NATIONAL ARCHIVES / PUBLIC RECORDS OFFICE	
Treaty functions	1. Keep permanent public records of all official treaty documents, including signed originals and certified true copies. 2. Catalogue, index and manage collections. 3. Ensure efficient retrieval and access by officials and the public. 4. Comply with domestic legislation concerning preservation of records, access to information, national security, privacy, data protection, etc.
What they need to do their job well	1. All officials to send original documents to archives promptly once action is completed. 2. Confidence that documents received in archives are the originals and come from an authentic source. 3. Confidence that documents received in archives are complete and not defaced or amended.

Box 1.2 (cont.)	
G. NATIONAL ARCHIVES / PUBLIC RECORDS OFFICE	
	4. Organised numerical system for identifying and locating archived documents. 5. Professional training for archive officials in archives management and relevant legal framework, including on treaties. 6. Archiving regulations and good practices that are known and observed throughout all government departments and agencies.
Constraints and issues	1. Domestic legal requirements for treaty records and publications.
H. NATIONAL LEGISLATURE / PARLIAMENT	
Treaty functions	1. Approve signature or ratification of treaties. 2. Scrutinise and debate treaties before or after ratification, amendment or major events. 3. Pass legislation to implement treaty obligations. 4. Scrutinise government actions through committee reports and investigations. 5. Apply political pressure on government in relation to specific treaties. 6. Inform and consult the public about treaty issues. (*Depending on national statutory or constitutional provisions*)
What they need to do their job well	1. Treaties to be sent to legislature for approval or scrutiny in good time. 2. National constitutional and legal procedures to be complied with by government. 3. Accurate information on the treaty, including *one true copy* of the text and Explanatory Memorandum (EM) or national interest assessment. 4. Sufficient resources and expertise within the legislature for proper consideration and debate. 5. Clear procedures for considering the treaty within the legislature. 6. Independent (non-government) legal advice on treaties and treaty procedures. 7. Easy access to accurate information about treaties and treaty actions of own State.

Box 1.2 (cont.)	
	H. NATIONAL LEGISLATURE / PARLIAMENT
	8. Some legislatures may be entitled to or may demand information about ongoing treaty negotiations and pre-signature scrutiny and consultation.
Constraints and issues	1. Legislature's desire for scrutiny may exceed their resources or interest, resulting in excessive delay in ratification. 2. Legislators may prevent or delay progress of a treaty for unrelated political reasons. 3. Giving the legislature information on treaty negotiations in progress might prejudice the government's international negotiating position. 4. Giving the legislature a right to pre-signature scrutiny might be impracticable and/or restrict the government's ability to participate in urgent treaties.
	I. NATIONAL COURTS
Treaty functions	1. Interpret and apply treaty obligations where relevant according to domestic law. 2. Decide on the status of treaties in national law and their relevance to particular cases. 3. Enforce national laws giving effect to treaty provisions. 4. Rule on domestic law powers to enter into treaties or undertake treaty acts.
What they need to do their job well	1. Ability to access copies of the treaty that they can be certain are the authentic text. 2. Searchable online treaty databases to find authoritative information on a treaty or a range of treaties. 3. Procedure for obtaining authoritative treaty facts from government, e.g. whether State X is a party to Y treaty. 4. Judges need awareness of the international law of treaties.
Constraints and issues	1. Judges in domestic courts may lack knowledge of the international law of treaties. 2. Judicial training may need to take this into account and senior judges may need periodic training to update their international law knowledge.

Box 1.2 (cont.)	
	J. STAKEHOLDERS IN PARTICULAR TREATIES
Treaty role or interest	1. Particular treaties may affect the interests of specific sectors, e.g. industry, professions, public services. 2. Affected sectors may be consulted or offer advice to government about proposed new treaty. 3. Non-governmental organisations (NGOs) or representative bodies may have procedural role in a treaty body, e.g. as observer or applicant. 4. Particular treaties may require the co-operation of a specific sector for domestic implementation and enforcement, e.g. professional self-regulation, industry standards.
What they need to protect their interests	1. Advance information and consultation on treaty negotiations that might affect their interests. 2. Consultation on implementation of relevant treaty obligations in domestic law. 3. Information about relevant treaties (as for general public).
Constraints and issues	1. Giving information to particular stakeholders on treaty negotiations in progress might be impracticable or prejudice the government's international negotiating position. 2. There may be tensions between particular stakeholders' interests and wider public interests which the government has to take into account.
	K. GENERAL PUBLIC
Treaty role or interest	1. The public is affected by treaty rights and obligations, e.g. human rights, air services, environment, investment, double taxation. 2. The public may wish to study treaties for academic reasons. 3. Libraries have a duty to provide documents and information. 4. The media may be interested in particular treaties relevant to news stories. 5. Pressure groups have an interest in treaties on particular subjects. 6. Lawyers advise clients on treaties affecting them and may cite them in litigation.

Box 1.2 (cont.)	
	K. GENERAL PUBLIC
What they need or want (for any purpose)	1. Ability to access copies of the treaty that they can be certain are the authentic text. 2. Searchable online treaty databases to find information on a particular treaty or a range of treaties. 3. The public, especially the media, might also want access to internal government information and policy discussions about a particular treaty (e.g. the Treaty of Lisbon amending the treaty on European Union and the Treaty Establishing the European Community 2007, the Kyoto Protocol to the United Nations Framework Convention on Climate Change (Kyoto Protocol) 1997, Treaty between the UK and Libya on the Transfer of Prisoners 2008). 4. The general public needs to understand what treaties are and why they are important domestically and internationally.
Constraints and issues	1. Public access to certain kinds of information relating to treaties might not be appropriate, e.g. information on treaty negotiations in progress, internal legal advice, confidential diplomatic communications. Domestic law and policy will determine the balance for each State. 2. The global public may also be interested in State X's treaties, while State X may consider its responsibility limited to its national public.
	II. INTERNATIONAL STAKEHOLDERS OF STATE X **A. OTHER GOVERNMENTS**
Treaty functions	1. Manage treaty relations with State X. 2. Negotiate new treaties with State X. 3. Discuss treaty matters with State X, e.g. on implementation, compliance, interpretation. 4. Arrange treaty signings with State X. 5. May have an interest in State X's treaties with third States. 6. May lobby State X to become party to a multilateral treaty. 7. May raise a dispute against State X for breach of treaty, which may lead to international litigation or arbitration. 8. Their nationals and companies may be protected under State X's treaties, e.g. if going to or investing in X.

Box 1.2 (cont.)	
	A. OTHER GOVERNMENTS
What they need to do their job well	1. Easy access to accurate information about treaties and treaty acts of State X. 2. Confidence that treaty information and documents from State X are authentic and authoritative. 3. Central contact point for treaty officials in State X. 4. Prompt information from depositaries about the treaty actions of State X. 5. Confidence that State X's treaty practice conforms to the international law of treaties. 6. Efficient, accurate and prompt handling of any bilateral treaty procedure by officials of State X.
Constraints and issues	1. Ensuring good treaty practice in relations with other States should be a high priority for any government. 2. Normally both (or all) States concerned have a mutual interest in good treaty practice on both (all) sides. 3. In the event of a treaty dispute leading to litigation, another State may seek to take advantage of poor treaty practice by State X.
	B. INTERNATIONAL ORGANISATIONS AND SECRETARIATS
Treaty functions	1. Propose, host and service negotiations for new treaties. 2. Service COPs, MOPs and other treaty bodies. 3. Administer reporting and compliance mechanisms. 4. Provide information about treaties to Member States and the public. 5. Promote membership of treaties. 6. May be party to treaties (e.g. headquarters agreement). 7. Act as depositary (see below for details).
What they need to do their job well	1. Central contact point for treaty officials in State X. 2. Prompt responses from State X to requests for action. 3. Prompt information from depositaries about treaty actions of State X. 4. Confidence that State X's treaty practice conforms to the international law of treaties. 5. Confidence that treaty information and documents from State X are authentic and authoritative. 6. Easy access to accurate information about treaties and treaty acts of State X.

Box 1.2 (cont.)	
B. INTERNATIONAL ORGANISATIONS AND SECRETARIATS	
Constraints and issues	1. Ensuring good treaty practice in direct State–IO relations should be a high priority for any State. 2. Occasionally, a particular secretariat may act outside the scope of its mandate or impose unreasonably burdensome procedures on Member States with no legal basis. In such cases, State X would be justified in challenging it.
C. DEPOSITARIES (OTHER GOVERNMENTS AND IOs)	
Treaty functions	1. Maintain record of all actions by States in relation to each treaty. 2. Communicate those actions to all other parties. 3. Provide certified true copies. 4. Receive treaty instruments from States and IOs. 5. Ensure original documents recorded and preserved. 6. Make or broker decisions about own powers, validity of treaty instruments, treaty capacity of States and other entities.
What they need to do their job well	1. Clear points of contact with State X for treaty matters. 2. State X to provide information in timely manner and in a suitable form for communication to other parties. 3. Confidence that documents received from State X are accurate, complete and authentic. 4. Its procedures to be understood and correctly observed by State X. 5. Prompt replies from State X to all communications. 6. Confidence that State X's treaty practice conforms to the international law of treaties. 7. State X's officials to understand role of the depositary, especially duty of impartiality.
Constraints and issues	1. Effective communications with depositaries and compliance with their required procedures should be high priority for any State. 2. Occasionally, a particular depositary may impose unreasonably burdensome procedures with no legal basis. In such cases, State X would be justified in challenging it.

Box 1.2 (cont.)	
	D. INTERNATIONAL COURTS AND TRIBUNALS
Treaty functions	1. Arbitrate and settle disputes between States (and sometimes IOs and individuals) on treaty matters.
What they need to do their job well	1. Where State X's treaty relations are in issue, access to certified true copies of the treaty documents may be required. 2. Searchable online treaty databases to find authoritative information on a treaty or a range of treaties for State X. 3. If State X wishes to rely on a treaty, that treaty needs to be registered under Article 102 UN Charter.
Constraints and issues	1. If State X's treaty practice is deficient, this may come to light in the context of international litigation and may have serious consequences, e.g. if State X seeks to rely on a treaty but is unable to provide authentic documents to prove the provisions in question.

In the table, the 'Treaty functions' sections list functions for which each category of stakeholders is typically responsible, but these vary from one State to another. In some States, a particular function may be assigned elsewhere or may not exist at all. For stakeholders with no official functions this is changed to 'treaty role or interest'.

The 'What they need to do their job well' sections focus on aspects of State treaty practice that are important from that stakeholder's perspective, as treaty service providers or users. Adequate resources are always needed, so this is not repeated for each category. Finally, 'Constraints and issues' refers to reasons why that category of stakeholders may not necessarily be able to have what they need or want to do their job. Inadequate resources may be a constraint for any category so is not repeated throughout the table.

Treaty Stakeholder Analysis for an IO

The table in Box 1.3 lists in detail all major stakeholders of an IO and their treaty functions and engagement. IOs are of course structured very differently from States, and their treaty practice is different and more limited in scope; this is therefore reflected in a smaller range of actors and stakeholders. The table shows in detail how the treaty management analysis of an IO might look. Any other kind of organisation wishing to reflect upon its treaty practices could adapt the table in a similar way as an aid to analysing its treaty engagement.

In the table, 'Treaty functions' lists functions for which each category of stakeholders is typically responsible, but these vary from one IO to another. In some IOs, a particular function may be assigned elsewhere or may not exist at all. For stakeholders with no official function, this is changed to 'treaty role or interest'.

The heading 'What they need to do their job well' focuses on aspects of treaty practice that are important from their perspective, as treaty service providers or other stakeholders. Adequate resources are always needed, so this is not repeated for each category. Finally, 'Constraints and issues' refers to reasons why that category of stakeholders may not have what they need or want to do their job. Inadequate resources may be a constraint for any category so is not repeated in the table.

Box 1.3 Treaty stakeholder analysis for an IO

I. INTERNAL STAKEHOLDERS OF AN INTERNATIONAL ORGANISATION (Organisation Y) A. SECRETARIAT OFFICIALS RESPONSIBLE FOR DEPOSITARY FUNCTIONS	
Treaty functions	1. Maintain record of all actions by States in relation to each treaty. 2. Communicate those actions to all other parties. 3. Provide certified true copies. 4. Receive treaty instruments from States and IOs. 5. Ensure original documents recorded and preserved. 6. Make or broker decisions about own powers, validity of treaty instruments, treaty capacity of States and other entities. (Standard depositary functions VCLT 77)
What they need to do their job well	1. To receive information from States in a timely manner and be able to communicate it to parties involved. 2. Confidence that documents received from States are accurate and come from an authentic source. 3. Clear treaty operating procedures. 4. Central control within own organisation of depositary functions or very clear division of functions. 5. Sufficient treaty staff to handle depositary responsibilities. 6. Treaty staff to have knowledge of international law and awareness of the political context of depositary issues, as well as the ability to act impartially and pay meticulous attention to detail.

Box 1.3 (cont.)

A. SECRETARIAT OFFICIALS RESPONSIBLE FOR DEPOSITARY FUNCTIONS	
	7. Ability to access accurate information about all past depositary actions, precedents for circulars and treaty documents, internal records of decision-making and legal advice on treaty procedures. 8. Reliable IT capability with adequate functionality. 9. Staff training and development in treaty matters. 10. Career structure for treaty professionals.
Constraints and issues	1. Resources of organisation Y: • capacity • personnel • time • costs/funding. (Note: these factors apply to all functions of the organisation, so are not repeated below.) 2. Occasionally, issues of independence and impartiality may arise, e.g. if a Member State attempts to exert influence over a secretariat staff member holding its nationality. The head of the Treaty Office needs to be alert to such issues and act to ensure that independence is not compromised.
B. OFFICIALS RESPONSIBLE FOR TREATIES TO WHICH THE ORGANISATION IS PARTY	
Treaty functions	1. Negotiate bilateral treaties (e.g. headquarters agreements). 2. Represent own organisation's interests in multilateral treaty negotiations. 3. Organise (or arrange with the Treaty Office) treaty procedures for own organisation's treaties. 4. Ensure all treaty acts of the organisation are legally effective and within its internal rules and mandate. 5. Report treaty actions to Member States and consult them in advance as required. 6. Oversee the implementation of treaty obligations by own organisation. 7. Publish, register and keep treaty records.

Box 1.3 (cont.)

B. OFFICIALS RESPONSIBLE FOR TREATIES TO WHICH THE ORGANISATION IS PARTY	
What they need to do their job well	1. Clear treaty procedures and guidelines for all officials throughout own organisation. 2. Clear contact point in Treaty Office for advice on procedures (where responsibility for negotiating a treaty lies with another branch of the organisation). 3. Staff with expertise in treaty negotiations. 4. Prompt advice and action from Treaty Office when required. 5. Ability to access accurate information about all the organisation's treaties and treaty actions, precedents, internal records of decision-making and legal advice on treaty procedures. 6. Clear mandates and guidance from Member States when required.
Constraints and issues	1. The secretariat's freedom to conclude treaties is constrained by the organisation's own constitutional and other rules, its capacity in international law, and the views of its Member States.
C. OFFICIALS RESPONSIBLE FOR TREATY SECRETARIAT AND ADMINISTRATIVE FUNCTIONS	
Treaty functions	1. Propose, host and service negotiations among Member States on new treaties. 2. Service COPs, MOPs and other treaty bodies. 3. Administer reporting and compliance mechanisms under treaties. 4. Provide information about treaties and their activities and programmes. 5. Promote wider membership of treaties. 6. Provide advice and (sometimes) technical assistance to Member States wishing to participate in treaties.
What they need to do their job well	1. Expertise in subject matter of treaties concerned. 2. Easy access to accurate depositary information within own organisation. 3. Knowledge of treaty procedures and law, as well as easy access to advice from treaty law experts in own organisation.

Box 1.3 (cont.)	
C. OFFICIALS RESPONSIBLE FOR TREATY SECRETARIAT AND ADMINISTRATIVE FUNCTIONS	
Constraints and issues	1. Constitutional and other rules of own organisation that govern its functions in relation to treaties concluded under its auspices. 2. Provisions in each particular treaty concerning the role of the organisation as the secretariat. 3. Views of the Member States about the proper role of the secretariat, expressed through the organisation's representative organs, or the treaty body concerned.
D. OVERSEAS REPRESENTATIVES OF THE ORGANISATION	
Treaty functions	1. Liaising with governments of Member States about the organisation's treaty matters. 2. Negotiating new treaties between the organisation and the State where its representative is based (e.g. on privileges and immunities), or discussing the operation of existing treaties. 3. Carrying out treaty actions with depositary governments and liaising with secretariats of other treaty bodies.
What they need to do their job well	1. Clear instructions from the organisation's headquarters on specific treaty actions. 2. Clear general treaty procedures that are easy to access and follow. 3. Effective communication with treaty officials at headquarters and confidence that they will act on treaty procedures promptly. 4. Effective communication with treaty officials in the government of the State of location – ideally one central contact point. 5. Knowledge of the international law of treaties. 6. Easy access to accurate information about treaties and treaty actions of the State of location.
Constraints and issues	1. The functions and positions of overseas-based representatives will normally be governed by an agreement between the organisation and the government of the State of location. (Note: not all organisations have or need representative offices overseas.)

Box 1.3 (cont.)

	E. HEAD OF THE ORGANISATION
Treaty functions	1. Sets strategic direction for the organisation within its mandate. 2. Directs officials to negotiate and conclude treaties (within the organisation's mandate). 3. Signs treaties and instruments of ratification on behalf of the organisation. 4. Carries out ceremonial functions in relation to treaties. 5. Proposes, explains and promote treaties to Member States and the public. 6. Signs Full Powers (Article 7 VCLT 1986). 7. Is publicly accountable for the organisation's performance of its treaty obligations.
What they need to do their job well	1. Awareness of own role in treaty matters including legal powers and limits. 2. Well-trained and experienced treaty officials to ensure that treaty actions on behalf of the organisation are undertaken effectively and promptly. 3. Treaty ceremonies to be conducted correctly and presented well for media. 4. Supervisory systems within the secretariat to ensure that the organisation delivers on treaty obligations undertaken by the organisation on its own behalf. 5. Enforcement machinery within the organisation to ensure that Member States deliver on any treaty obligations entered into by the organisation on behalf of its Member States (if it has competence to do so).
Constraints and issues	1. The capacity of the head of the organisation to conclude treaties on behalf of the organisation and/or its Member States is restricted by the organisation's own constitutional and other rules, as well as international law. 2. Member States may mandate the organisation to enter into treaty obligations on their behalf, yet resist effective machinery to enforce their delivery on those obligations. The head of the organisation needs to resist pressure to conclude treaties beyond its legal capacity or ability to deliver.

Box 1.3 (cont.)

F. GOVERNMENTS OF MEMBER STATES OF THE ORGANISATION	
Treaty functions	1. Manage treaty relations with the organisation and other Member States. 2. Negotiate new treaties under auspices of the organisation. 3. Discuss treaty matters at meetings hosted by the organisation, e.g. on interpretation, implementation, compliance monitoring and review, amendments, work programmes, scientific or technical committees, etc. 4. Attend treaty signings hosted by the organisation. 5. May (occasionally) raise a dispute against the organisation or another Member State for breach of treaty, which should normally be resolved within the organisation, but if not, might lead to international litigation or arbitration.
What they need to do their job well	1. Easy access to accurate information about treaties and treaty acts of the organisation. 2. Convenient direct contact with treaty officials of the organisation. 3. Prompt information from the organisation as depositary about treaty actions of other parties. 4. Confidence that the organisation's treaty practice conforms to international law of treaties. 5. Efficient secretariat servicing of treaty meetings.
Constraints and issues	1. The organisation must respect its mandate and views of its Member States, but these may conflict, e.g. on whether the organisation should promote new treaty negotiations, how much help it can offer to Member States to enable their participation in treaties, and whether the organisation should conclude treaties with third States and other IOs.
II. EXTERNAL STAKEHOLDERS **A. OTHER INTERNATIONAL ORGANISATIONS AND SECRETARIATS**	
Treaty functions	1. Manage treaty relations with Organisation Y (if any). 2. Provide information to its own Member States about treaties and treaty actions of Organisation Y. 3. Co-ordinate and exchange information with the secretariat of Organisation Y about treaties on subjects of common interest.

Box 1.3 (cont.)

A. OTHER INTERNATIONAL ORGANISATIONS AND SECRETARIATS	
What they need to do their job well	1. Easy access to accurate information about treaties and treaty actions of Organisation Y. 2. Convenient contact point for treaty officials of Organisation Y. 3. Confidence that Organisation Y's treaty practice conforms to the international law of treaties.
Constraints and issues	1. Other organisations may have broader or more flexible mandates regarding their ability to participate in treaties or co-operate with other organisations and secretariats. The officials of Organisation Y need to take care to respect the limits of their own mandate in their dealings with counterparts in other organisations.
B. STAKEHOLDERS IN A PARTICULAR TREATY	
Treaty role or interest	1. Particular treaties may affect the interests of specific sectors, e.g. industries, professions, and categories of people such as refugees, children and indigenous peoples. 2. Particular treaties may confer procedural rights on particular groups to participate in treaty bodies. 3. Particular treaties may set up processes that directly determine the rights and obligations of individuals and companies, as well as the mechanisms for individual applicants (e.g. human rights, investment).
What they need to protect their interests	1. Advance information and consultation about treaty negotiations under the auspices of the organisation that might affect their interests. 2. Easy access to accurate information about treaties and treaty actions of the organisation. 3. Impartial and efficient treatment by secretariats when seeking to exercise procedural rights under treaty.
Constraints and issues	1. The secretariat needs to take care to respect the organisation's mandate in all its dealings with stakeholders, and take account Member States' views. 2. There may be issues regarding which NGOs are entitled to represent particular groups of stakeholders.

Box 1.3 (cont.)

C. INTERNATIONAL COURTS AND TRIBUNALS	
Treaty functions	1. Arbitrate and settle disputes (concerning a treaty concluded under the auspices of Organisation Y) between: Organisation Y and a third State, Organisation Y and another organisation, or Member States of Organisation Y.
What they need to do their job well	1. Copies of the relevant treaty that they can be certain are the authentic text. 2. Searchable online treaty databases to find authoritative information on a treaty or a range of treaties of Organisation Y. 3. If applicable, treaty in question should be registered under Article 102 UN Charter.
Constraints and issues	1. If Organisation Y's treaty practice is deficient, this may come to light in the context of international litigation and may have serious consequences for the organisation and/or the States concerned.
D. NATIONAL COURTS	
Treaty functions	1. Interpret and apply domestic law in relation to Organisation Y (where the proceedings concern Organisation Y as a legal person under domestic law, e.g. of the host State or any jurisdiction where Y operates). 2. Enforce national laws giving effect to treaties for which Organisation Y is the secretariat or depositary.
What they need to do their job well	1. Ability to access copies of the treaty that they can be certain are the authentic text. 2. Searchable online treaty databases to find authoritative information on a treaty or a range of treaties. 3. Procedure for obtaining authoritative treaty facts from Organisation Y.
Constraints and issues	1. Providing accurate treaty information and contact points for national courts, especially in the host State of Organisation Y's headquarters, is very important. This may be largely satisfied by good public treaty information services.

Box 1.3 (cont.)

E. GENERAL PUBLIC IN MEMBER STATES WORLDWIDE	
Treaty role or interest	1. The public is affected by treaty rights and obligations, e.g. human rights, air services, environment, double tax. 2. The public may wish to study treaties for academic reasons. 3. Libraries have a duty to provide documents and information. 4. The media may be interested in particular treaties relevant to news stories. 5. Pressure groups may be interested in treaties on particular subjects. 6. Lawyers may advise clients on treaties affecting them and may cite them in litigation.
What they need or want (for any purpose)	1. Ability to access copies of the treaty that they can be certain are the authentic text. 2. Searchable online treaty databases to find information on a particular treaty or a range of treaties. 3. The public, especially the media, might also want access to meeting records, negotiating documents, etc. 4. The general public needs to understand what treaties are and why they are important domestically and internationally.
Constraints and issues	1. Public access to some kinds of information relating to treaties might not be appropriate, e.g. papers discussed at closed meetings, diplomatic communications. 2. Secretariats have to observe the organisation's mandate and rules, as well as guidance from Member States in dealings with the public.

2

Organising Treaty Work in Governments and International Organisations

***

'The most important role of the Czech Legal Adviser and their team is the oversight over the process leading to the conclusion of treaties. This is mainly because of the decentralised system where most treaties are made not by the MFA, but rather by one of the other ministries.'[1]

'Australia is an interesting example in the region, because of its unique institutional arrangements for the complex distribution of international law work across government. ... Overall, these arrangements mean that coordination and consultation is critical across all areas of government doing work with an international law dimension.'[2]

Introduction: Why Organisation of Treaty Work Matters

In international law, a treaty is binding on *the whole of* each State and IO that is party to it. It does not just bind the ministry, agency or directorate that was involved in negotiating or concluding it. Nor can a State or IO be excused from compliance on the basis that the treaty has not taken effect in its internal law, or is inconsistent with it. It is the responsibility of each State and IO to organise its treaty work in a way that is fully co-ordinated across the whole of its operations and personnel, is compliant with international law, and integrates with its domestic legal system and internal procedures. Each State and IO therefore needs a clear and effective allocation of responsibilities for each aspect of treaty work, and a system for co-ordinating them in a way that meets these criteria.

[1] P Válek, 'The Different Roles of the Czech Legal Adviser: From a Watchdog to a Headhunter', in A Zidar and J Gauci (eds), *The Role of Legal Advisers in International Law* (Brill, Leiden 2017) 148.

[2] S McCosker, 'The Intersecting Professions of the International Law Adviser and Diplomat in a Rising Asia: Australia, India and Malaysia' in *Zidar* and *Gauci* (n 1) 104 and 106.

This is governed not only by the international law of treaties, but also the international law rules on the responsibility of States and IOs. The following rules are fundamental:

- A State or IO may not excuse itself from complying with a treaty on the basis that the person who concluded it on its behalf was not authorised to do so under its internal law (except in exceptional circumstances).[3]
- A State or IO is not excused from complying with a treaty on the basis that its terms are incompatible with its constitution, or have no effect in its internal law (except in exceptional circumstances).[4]
- All organs of the State are bound by that State's treaty obligations. This includes governmental, legislative and judicial authorities at all levels from central to local (even in a federal State), the legislature and the courts. An equivalent rule applies to IOs.[5]
- The responsibility of a State or IO may be incurred under international law by the actions of any organ or official empowered to act in relation to a treaty, even if that official exceeds their authority.[6]

[3] VCLT 1969 art 46:

> Provisions of Internal Law Regarding Competence to Conclude Treaties
>
> 1. A State may not invoke the fact that its consent to be bound by a treaty has been expressed in violation of a provision of its internal law regarding competence to conclude treaties as invalidating its consent unless that violation was manifest and concerned a rule of its internal law of fundamental importance.

See also VCLT 1986 http://legal.un.org/ilc/texts/instruments/english/conventions/1_2_1986.pdf accessed 9 September 2018. The VCLT 1986 contains an equivalent rule.

[4] VCLT 1969 art 27. Article 27 concerns 'Internal law and observance of treaties' and stipulates: 'A party may not invoke the provisions of its internal law as justification for its failure to perform a treaty.' The VCLT 1986 contains an equivalent rule. See also ILC, 'Articles on Responsibility of States for Internationally Wrongful Acts, with commentaries 2001' reproduced in ILC, *Yearbook of the International Law Commission* (vol II, 2001 (Part 2)) arts 3 and 32:

> Article 3: Characterization of an act of a State as internationally wrongful
>
> The characterization of an act of a State as internationally wrongful is governed by international law. Such characterization is not affected by the characterization of that same act as lawful by internal law.
>
> Article 32: Irrelevance of internal law
>
> The responsible State may not rely on the provisions of its internal law as justification for failure to comply with its obligations under this part.

See also art 5.

[5] ILC (n4), art 4.

> Article 4: Conduct of organs of a State:
>
> The conduct of any State organ shall be considered an act of that State under international law, whether the organ exercises legislative, executive, judicial or any other functions, whatever position it holds in the organization of the State, and whatever its character as an organ of the central Government or of a territorial unit of the State.

See also UNGA, Res/66/100, 'Responsibility of International Organizations' 27 February 2011, Annex, art 6.

[6] VCLT 1969, art 7.

Poor Organisation of Treaty Work: What Can Go Wrong?

Poor organisation of treaty work will almost certainly result in numerous failings of a routine nature, which may go undetected for some time. Sooner or later, this will lead to a serious problem. The following sections describe the typical kinds of problems that occur.

Scenario 1: Example of Failure to Centralise or Co-ordinate the Conclusion of Treaties

Officials of the Forestry Ministry of State A attend international negotiations whose outcome is the conclusion of a treaty establishing a new forestry organisation. Without consulting any other part of government, the Ministry submits a document entitled 'Instrument of Ratification' to the new Secretariat, which acts as Depositary for the treaty. The (inexperienced) Secretariat accepts it, even though it is signed by the Minister for Forestry, and lists State A as a party to the treaty. The forestry officials of State A participate in the meetings of parties held under the treaty.

Some years later, the Forestry Ministry of State A hosts a treaty meeting. A delegate from State B is arrested in State A for a serious crime. The Ambassador of State B protests to the Ministry of Foreign Affairs (MFA) of State A that their delegates are, under the treaty, entitled to privileges and immunities while visiting State A for the meeting. The Ambassador of State B calls on State A to release the delegate immediately. The MFA of State A was not aware of this treaty. State A's Foreign Minister is also unable to require the police to release the accused, whose privileges and immunities have not been incorporated into State A's legal system, and will not be recognised by its courts.

At best, State A suffers serious public embarrassment and a claim from State B for reparations. At worst, if it cannot resolve the problem, it may be on the receiving end of international legal proceedings. The Treaty Secretariat is also criticised by State B and other States for having incorrectly accepted a purported Instrument of Ratification signed by State A's Minister of Forestry, and this leads to discord in the organisation.

Scenario 2: Example of Failure to Consult International Law Advisers

Officials from the energy ministries of States C and D meet regularly to discuss bilateral co-operation. They decide to negotiate a new Memorandum of

Article 7: Excess of authority or contravention of instructions

The conduct of an organ of a State or of a person or entity empowered to exercise elements of the governmental authority shall be considered an act of the State under international law if the organ, person or entity acts in that capacity, even if it exceeds its authority or contravenes instructions.

The VCLT 1986 contains an equivalent rule. See also 'Responsibility of International Organizations' (n 5) art 8.

Understanding (MOU) on civil nuclear energy co-operation. State C's officials assume this will be informal and non-binding, and that they therefore do not need to consult lawyers or involve their MFAs. The MOU is signed by the energy minister and filed in the Energy Ministry.

Several years later, a dispute arises regarding State C's implementation of the MOU. State D asserts that it is a treaty and that State C is in breach of its legal obligations. State C's energy officials consult the government's international lawyers (for the first time), who confirm that it is a treaty and is therefore binding on both States.

When this dispute becomes public, State C's government is severely criticised by the legislature for concluding a treaty without first submitting the text for approval according to national constitutional procedures. The Energy Minister is dismissed. State C also has to acknowledge that, if its breach of the treaty is proven, it will have legal liability to State D.

Applying the PLATO Principles to the Organisation of Treaty Work

Every State and IO will have its own way of allocating responsibilities for treaty work across its organisation, and its own methods of co-ordination. No single model can work for all. This is especially the case for governments, as the structures and workings of each one is a product of its national history, constitution and political system, and so the variations among them are endless. Whatever methods are chosen, these principles (defined in Box 1.1) are especially pertinent:

- 'Organised': some 'centralisation' of responsibility for certain treaty procedural functions, effective 'co-ordination' of treaty work across government (or the secretariat), and 'communication' of responsibilities and procedures to all who work with treaties, at all levels.
- 'Legal': treaty procedures and treaty information officials work closely with international law advisers. This means locating the centralised treaty functions within the international law directorate, or very close to it.
- 'Professional': a professional approach to the staffing of centralised treaty procedures and information work, and the provision of training in treaty law and practice for treaty officials and all who work with treaties across the government/organisation, at all levels.

Does Organisation of Treaty Work Raise Different Issues for Governments and IOs?

The PLATO principles, especially the features highlighted above, apply fully to governments and IOs. The issues raised for governments tend to be more complex, due to the larger range of treaty work and the greater institutional complexity of a State. Controlling and co-ordinating work across the various ministries and agencies of a government is typically even more challenging than co-ordinating across a secretariat, given the greater physical, political and subject-matter separation between them. The bulk of a government's treaty work is generated by its own treaty relations, and mostly concerns bilateral treaties. Depositary functions are usually a small part of government treaty work, if they feature at all. By contrast, the main focus of an IO's treaty work is on depositary functions or other secretariat roles in relation to multilateral treaties to which their Member States are party. IOs themselves do not usually enter into many treaties except, notably, the EU.

Despite these differences of focus, the organisation of treaty work in governments and IOs raises similar issues and will be discussed together in this chapter.

Overview of All Treaty Functions of a Government or IO

Bearing in mind all the ways in which treaties feature in the work of governments and IOs, the kinds of work they generate are very varied, as are the levels at which officials are engaged. Not all treaty functions can be centralised; there has to be a balance between centralisation and co-ordination. Treaty functions could be categorised very broadly as follows:

- Procedural: processing; organising; recording; producing; publishing; administration.
- Legal: interpreting; drafting; advising.
- Policy: negotiating; assessing substance of treaties in light of government/IO aims, priorities and budget; promoting treaty priorities; devising action programmes; advising political leaders; setting up domestic implementation measures.
- Political: making major decisions on treaty actions and being accountable to the legislature (or the IO's Member States) and external actors; high-level negotiating.
- Ceremonial and representational: carrying out a high-profile formal function that has public effect, such as signing, presiding, declaring; usually carrying out a mandate or political decision already made, on behalf of the State or IO.

Which Treaty Functions Can or Should Be Centralised?

Treaties feature regularly in the work of a vast range of public servants. It would not be possible to centralise all of these functions, nor would it be desirable. Getting the balance right between centralisation and decentralisation, achieving respect for the centralised roles, co-ordinating effectively with the decentralised ones – these are constant challenges for any government or IO.

Treaty procedure functions lend themselves to centralisation. They are mainly clerical and managerial functions that are removed from the content of a treaty, are essentially the same for all treaties regardless of subject matter, and are best performed by staff who are not involved with the policy on that subject. Yet these tasks are not just ordinary administration; they require knowledge of the legal framework for treaties as well as treaty practice and procedures, both international and national. These functions include document processing, organising ceremonies (protocol), recording, producing, publishing, administrating and managing external communications, including with diplomatic contacts. They need to be carried out or managed centrally to ensure consistency, professionalism, impartiality and compliance with legal requirements.

Typically, these procedural functions are centralised in a Treaty Office of some kind. Where we refer below to 'the Treaty Office', we mean any administrative unit within a ministry or secretariat which is dedicated to centralised treaty procedural functions (whatever its name). However, in some smaller governments and IOs, there may be treaty procedure officials within a larger unit where treaty work may be combined with other functions. In some contexts, our references below to 'the Treaty Office' are intended to include any officials carrying out centralised treaty procedure functions, whether or not in a dedicated unit.

Policy decisions and operational actions relating to treaties should normally be taken by those responsible for the policy on the subject matter of the treaty. This is because they have specialist knowledge of that subject and are responsible for domestic implementation of the treaty, or work closely with those who are. For example, tax treaties are normally negotiated by officials from finance ministries, and their provisions are implemented by the same ministries in their dealings with taxpayers. Air services treaties are normally negotiated by policy officials from aviation or transport ministries, which are responsible for implementing those treaties in domestic legislation and through the aviation agencies.

The same applies to *treaty decisions at the political level* where there is political accountability. For example, the government has to answer to the legislature or the public, or the IO has to answer to its Member States. This task is commonly carried out by the minister or senior official responsible for the subject. For example, if there is a political issue concerning a tax treaty, it would be more commonly dealt with by the Finance Minister than the Head of Government. Of all the treaties in which a government is typically involved, only a small proportion will be of central importance to government policy or foreign affairs, for which the political lead may be taken by the Foreign Minister or the Head of Government. These tend to include major bilateral treaties on high-level relations, membership of IOs with a broad remit such as the UN, the EU or the ASEAN; or other treaties whose significance is very broad or touches on sovereignty or territorial issues, such as the United Nations Convention on the Law of the Sea, 1982 (UNCLOS),[7] the Treaty on Principles Governing the Activities of States in the Exploration and Use of

[7] United Nations Convention on the Law of the Sea (adopted 10 December 1982, entered into force 16 November 1994) 1833 UNTS 3 (UNCLOS).

Outer Space, including the Moon and other Celestial Bodies, 1967,[8] or the Antarctic Treaty, 1959.[9]

Legal work relating to treaties – in particular, advising on and interpreting treaties, drafting treaties, drafting implementing legislation – is needed at all levels and alongside all other functions. It follows that international law advice has to be both centralised and decentralised, throughout a government or IO. The Treaty Office has to work hand-in-glove with the international lawyers in the government/IO who are versed in the law of treaties and general public international law. Those lawyers also need to be conversant with relevant aspects of internal law. Hence, government lawyers need expert knowledge of constitutional law relating to treaties, and IO lawyers need familiarity with all aspects of the IO's constitution and institutional rules.

Policy-makers and administrators in all government ministries and agencies, or all departments of an IO, need to work with international lawyers who have sufficient familiarity with their subject to understand the treaty, as well as the requirements for its domestic implementation. For many treaties, a general knowledge of international law and the domestic legal system may suffice. However, some branches of international treaty law (such as climate change, international trade, shipping and international labour law) are now so technical and specialised that practising in them can be a full-time job for the lawyers concerned. This has led to greater specialisation within the international law cadres of governments and IOs, for example through their division into teams which focus on specific subjects. It has also led to legal advisers within domestic ministries developing expertise in the international law aspects of their subject, and handling these together with the domestic law aspects. Increasing decentralisation of subject-specific international law work is thus not only inevitable but desirable, as it gives policy-makers direct access to the specialised and customised legal advice they need. It does, however, mean that those lawyers might not have the necessary expertise on the international law of treaties to deal with all aspects of treaty work, particularly those relating to treaty final clauses and treaty procedures.

It follows that legal work pertaining to treaties needs to be well co-ordinated across all parts of governments and IOs. The more it is decentralised, the greater the need for a central cadre of general international lawyers to perform a co-ordinating role to ensure the provision of training in the law and practice of treaties broadly across all the legal services, and to promote legal awareness among all policy-makers and diplomats right up to the top levels – ministers, directors, secretaries general.[10]

[8] Treaty on Principles governing the Activities of States in the Exploration and Use of Outer Space, including the Moon and other Celestial Bodies (adopted 27 January 1967, entered into force 10 October 1967) 610 UNTS 205.

[9] Antarctic Treaty (adopted 1 December 1959, entered into force 23 June 1961) 402 UNTS 71.

[10] See *Válek* (n 1) and *McCosker* (n 2).

Mixed treaty functions – in practice, there are different kinds of treaty functions that are often so closely related that it is difficult to classify them. For example, a lawyer may combine legal and policy roles when negotiating a treaty. These roles may become inseparable when the lawyer-diplomat is representing the government in an international negotiation. Some treaty functions require several different teams to play different parts to make them happen. For example, when a treaty-signing ceremony is arranged overseas, this is a treaty procedures function for the Treaty Office which could involve representational, protocol and sometimes public relations and media roles for the embassy or ministry staff.

Whether to Establish a Treaty Office

Is it Necessary to Have a Treaty Office?

Some form of centralisation of treaty procedures is unavoidable. One of the essentials for successfully managing treaty information is to have a single organised collection of all the treaties to which the government or IO concerned is a signatory, has ratified or acceded to, and to which they are a party. If there is no central point of reference such as a Treaty Office within the government or IO, maintaining such a collection is extremely difficult, although not impossible. It is also necessary to have a central point of contact for arranging treaty procedures, both for officials across the government or IO, and for external contacts, especially official ones such as (other) governments, parliamentarians, etc. This is to ensure that treaty procedures are managed consistently and in accordance with legal requirements, actions are systematically recorded and authoritative information is provided.

But does this require the establishment of a *Treaty Office*? Most governments and IOs do have a Treaty Office – a unit dedicated to the handling of treaty procedures and treaty information for the whole government or IO. It normally has 'treaty' in its title – if not 'Treaty Office', then 'Treaty Section', 'Treaty Secretariat', 'Treaties Directorate' or suchlike. Examples are listed below.[11]

States

- *Australia*: the 'Treaties Secretariat' of the Department of Foreign Affairs and Trade.
- *Brunei*: the 'Treaty Section' of the Ministry of Foreign Affairs and Trade.
- *Cambodia*: the 'Treaty Bureau' in the Legal and Consular Department, Ministry of Foreign Affairs and International Cooperation.
- *Canada*: the 'Treaty Law Division' in the Legal Affairs Bureau, Department of Foreign Affairs and International Trade.

[11] The examples listed are derived from a number of sources including personal interviews held between 2012 and 2018, updated wherever possible by email (these records are on file with the authors – see Acknowledgements at xxiii–xxv) and from the cited published sources.

- *Czech Republic*: the 'Treaty Law Unit' in the International Law Department of the Legal and Consular Section, MFA.
- *Indonesia*: the 'Directorate General of Law and International Treaties' of the MFA. The Treaty Room is a special section in the Directorate General that deals with filing and updating the status of all treaties that Indonesia is a party and/or depositary to.
- *Ireland*: the 'Treaty Office' in the Legal Division, Department of Foreign Affairs and Trade.
- *Japan*: the 'Treaties Division' in the International Legal Affairs Bureau, MFA.
- *Myanmar*: the 'Treaty Section' in the Consular and Legal Affairs Department, MFA.
- *The Netherlands*: the 'Treaties Division' in the Legal Affairs Department, MFA.
- *The Philippines*: the 'Treaties Division' in the Office of Legal Affairs, Department of Foreign Affairs.
- *Thailand*: the 'Treaty Division' in the Department of Treaties and Legal Affairs, MFA.
- *United Kingdom*: the 'Treaty Section', in the Legal Directorate, Foreign and Commonwealth Office (FCO).
- *United States of America*: the 'Office of Treaty Affairs' in the Office of the Legal Adviser, Department of State.
- *Vietnam*: the 'Treaty Division' in the Department of International Law and Treaties, MFA.

International Organisations

- *ASEAN*: the 'Legal Services and Agreements Directorate' in the Community and Corporate Affairs Department, ASEAN Secretariat.
- *CoE*: the 'Treaty Office' in the Public International Law Division and Treaty Office, Directorate of Legal Advice and Public International Law.
- *EU*: the 'Treaties Office' under the Directorate General for External Relations, European Commission.
- *International Atomic Energy Agency (IAEA)*: the 'Nuclear and Treaty Law Section' of the Office of Legal Affairs.
- *UN*: the 'Treaty Section' of the Office of Legal Affairs.

Some Treaty Offices are large (20–100 staff), some have as few as two or three staff members, while staffing levels of around eight to fifteen people would seem to be quite common.[12] However, staffing levels cannot be directly compared between ministries or secretariats, as they reflect a number of factors, including the volume of treaties handled and the functions performed by that office.

[12] Reference to numbers of staff mean FTE; two members of staff each working 0.5 time are counted as one member.

Not all governments and IOs have a specific unit dedicated to treaties. In some, centralised treaty functions are carried out by a single Treaty Officer or several officers within a larger unit, typically a legal directorate or, less commonly, an information management unit. For example:

- *New Zealand*: there is a Treaty Officer and a Treaty Support Officer, both based in the Legal Division of the Ministry of Foreign Affairs and Trade. The Legal Division oversees all treaty actions.
- *Malaysia and Singapore*: treaty procedural functions are carried out by officers in the MFA, and legal advice on treaty matters is provided by the International Affairs Division of the Attorney General's Chambers.

Is it Desirable to Establish a Treaty Office – even in a Small State or IO?

The establishment of a single Treaty Office as a separate unit is likely to have a number of advantages. It raises the profile and status of treaty procedure functions. It may give these functions higher visibility externally as the central point of contact on treaty matters. It may give it higher visibility internally and so increase its authority in relation to other parts of the administration. It may make it a more attractive posting for staff. It may be helpful in securing resources within the administration and greater autonomy over managerial and spending decisions – depending of course on how such matters work in the government or IO concerned. Whether or not these factors are advantages, and whether the amount of treaty procedures work warrants a separate unit, are matters for each government or IO. If, in practice, the designation of specific treaty officers within a larger legal unit works well and is well understood by external contacts, this may be perfectly satisfactory.

In deciding whether a Treaty Office is needed, an important factor to be taken into account by any government/IO is the extent of its depositary responsibilities, given that these require regular dealings with a wider range of external treaty actors. Looking at examples of States that have a Treaty Office, the USA is depositary for over 200 treaties,[13] the Netherlands for 116,[14] the UK for 45,[15] Australia for 8[16] and Indonesia for 2. Looking at examples of States that do not have a Treaty Office but do have treaty officers

[13] Office of the Legal Adviser, 'Depositary Information' (US Department of State) www.state.gov/s/l/treaty/depositary/index.htm accessed 21 September 2018.

[14] The Kingdom of the Netherlands, 'Treaty Database' https://treatydatabase.overheid.nl/en accessed 21 September 2018.

[15] United Kingdom FCO, 'Treaties for which the UK is Depositary' (published 11 December 2013) www.gov.uk/government/collections/treaties-for-which-the-uk-is-depositary/ accessed 21 September 2018.

[16] Australasian Legal Information Institute (AustLII), 'Multilateral Treaties for which Australia is Depository' (last updated September 2010) www.austlii.edu.au/au/other/dfat/treaty_list/depository/ accessed 21 September 2018.

within a larger unit, New Zealand is depositary for eleven treaties[17] and Malaysia for one.[18]

As for IOs, the CoE is depositary for over 220 treaties,[19] and the IAEA for 19 treaties.[20] Both have a Treaty Office. To illustrate the extent of the work involved, the CoE Treaty Office processed a total of 511 acts concerning the exercise of its depositary functions in 2017: 76 signatures, 92 ratifications, 6 denunciations and 334 reservations, declarations and objections. Furthermore, the office processed 286 notifications in relation to these acts.[21]

In contrast, IOs and treaty bodies such as the International Whaling Commission and the Antarctic Treaty Secretariat have treaty functions but no depositary role and no Treaty Office; their treaty-related functions are carried out by administrative staff. The North Atlantic Treaty Organization (NATO) has an Office of Legal Affairs with seven staff, but it has no Treaty Office.[22] NATO is not a depositary. Its Office of Legal Affairs provides advice on treaty-related issues and participates in a range of treaty-related functions, such as the preparatory work for, as well as the drafting, negotiating and reviewing of, official translations of the texts of international agreements. The current Director of NATO's Office of Legal Affairs has commented that:

> The rapidly growing number of agreements, which are done in at least two language versions … and sometimes more, has posed administrative challenges for a small office such as OLA. These have been recently addressed through a substantial project to develop OLA's in-house database of agreements.[23]

The above examples suggest that where a State or IO is depositary for a number of treaties, or where an IO performs substantial other treaty functions for its Member States, the establishment of a dedicated Treaty Office is highly desirable, if not essential.

Where Should the Treaty Office (or Centralised Treaty Procedure Functions) Be Located?

A clear pattern can be seen in the examples of Treaty Offices listed above – they are all located within a larger legal office. While the specific location and

[17] New Zealand Ministry of Foreign Affairs and Trade, 'International Treaties that New Zealand Administers' www.mfat.govt.nz/en/about-us/who-we-are/treaties-we-administer//u accessed 21 September 2018.

[18] Attorney General's Chambers of Malaysia, 'International Affair Division' www.agc.gov.my/agcportal/index.php?r=portal2/left&menu_id=dDlsN0JEL1U1Yml5L3RlZ3RqN2FzUT09 accessed 21 September 2018.

[19] Treaty Office, 'Complete list of the Council of Europe's treaties' (CoE, last updated 18 September 2018) www.coe.int/en/web/conventions/full-list accessed 21 September 2018.

[20] International Atomic Energy Agency, 'Treaties under IAEA Auspices' https://www.iaea.org/resources/treaties/treaties-under-IAEA-auspices accessed 21 September 2018.

[21] The CoE is depositary for 222 treaties as of 27 April 2018. Information and the other statistics in this paragraph are courtesy of the CoE Treaty Office.

[22] S Hill, 'The Role of NATO's Legal Adviser' in *Zidar* and *Gauci* (n 1) 221.

[23] ibid 231.

structure of a Treaty Office will be different in every administration, one thing is clear: it needs to work closely with international law advisers. This indicates one of two options: either the Treaty Office should be located *within* the legal service which provides international law advice to the whole government or IO; or it needs to be very close to it, in both an organisational and a physical sense.

Where an IO has a legal department at its headquarters, this will be the natural home for its Treaty Office, especially when it has depositary functions. The legal department of an IO will invariably include international lawyers, some of whom might work in the Treaty Office or supervise it, such as at the UN and the CoE. By contrast, in the EU, the European Commission's Treaty Office is a part of the European External Action Service. Its role is to advise on practice and procedural matters relating to the different stages of negotiation of treaties to which the EU is a party, and to provide information on those treaties; it does this by developing and maintaining an electronic database and information system known as the Treaties Office Database. It has no depositary functions.

Arrangements within a government for providing international law advice are much more varied and often less straightforward. All governments have a foreign ministry or a ministry that combines foreign affairs with other responsibilities, commonly international trade (here we refer to all of these generically as 'foreign ministries'). Most of them have an in-house legal service of some sort. There are usually international law specialists within the legal service, or engaged by it to provide advice; for example, some ministries engage international law professors to provide advice. Usually, the foreign ministry's international lawyers provide advice on international law to the whole government. Where this is the case, their unit will be the obvious choice of location for the Treaty Office. However, there are a variety of other kinds of arrangements for international law advice within governments. This may complicate the issue of whether, and if so how, to centralise treaty procedure functions, and in particular where to locate the Treaty Office.

How International Law Work Is Structured within Governments and IOs

States have different traditions in the organisation and functions of their government legal advisers in the field of public international law. They fall broadly into three categories, as follows:[24]

1. Lawyers in the office of the legal adviser at the foreign ministry are all professionally qualified lawyers, whose government career is wholly or largely spent within the legal office rather than on regular diplomatic

[24] This categorisation is based on M Wood, 'Legal Advisers' in *Zidar* and *Gauci* (n 1) 60, developed using information from J Kingston, 'Organisation and Context for the Work of Legal Advisers: The Legal Division of the Department of Foreign Affairs and Trade of Ireland' in ibid 70, *McCosker* (n 2) 96, combined with additional information obtained by Jill Barrett from other governments and IOs.

assignments (though they may have occasional postings overseas, such as to represent their government at the UN in New York or Geneva). Their career structure is in principle separate from the rest of the diplomatic service. Lawyers are typically recruited from legal practice or university law faculties, and leave to resume legal careers elsewhere.
Examples: the US, the UK, Ireland.

2. The legal adviser's office within the foreign ministry consists largely, if not entirely, of regular diplomats with some legal background or professional legal training. Some international law training is typically received in diplomat training school. These diplomats come to the legal office on a regular posting for a specific period, like any other diplomatic posting in the ministry. They may have only one legal posting in their whole career, or may return several times to the legal department, thus building up expertise. They are recruited from, and return to, regular diplomatic postings in embassies or the ministry.
Examples: Germany, Japan,[25] Canada, Czech Republic, Vietnam,[26] possibly India.[27]
3. The foreign ministry receives legal advice from a central government legal office, typically from an attorney general's chambers or justice ministry.
Examples: Cyprus, Malaysia, Malta, Singapore and, to some extent, Australia.

The first two systems may be combined. For example, in France some members of the *Quai's Direction des Affaires Juridiques* are regular diplomats, for whom a period in the legal office is much like any other posting in Paris, whereas others are recruited specifically as legal advisers, such as on secondment from the judiciary. The third system may be combined with elements of the first or second, where legal advice on certain matters is provided in the foreign ministry.

Australia has a hybrid system in that the primary unit within government that conducts international law work is the Office of International Law in the Attorney General's Department.[28] Australia's Department of Foreign Affairs and Trade (DFAT) has an IOs and Legal Division, within which is the International Law Section and the Treaties Secretariat. The Treaties Secretariat plays certain formal roles regarding treaty signature and ratification, undertaking these roles in close consultation with other departments with an interest in the substantive matters covered by the treaty.[29] Overseas

[25] Y Kita, 'The Legal Advice System of the Ministry of Foreign Affairs of Japan: Between Legal Advisers and Foreign Policy Makers' in *Zidar* and *Gauci* (n 1) 128.

[26] In the case of Vietnam, most officials at the Department of International Law and Treaties, MFA have received professional legal training. Many work for the Department for their whole government career, except when they are posted overseas.

[27] *McCosker* (n 2) p 115. [28] ibid 104.

[29] Treaties Secretariat, *Signed, Sealed and Delivered: Treaties and Treaty Making – Officials' Handbook* (15th edn, Department of Foreign Affairs and Trade, Canberra 2015) paras 19–23, cited in

postings requiring international law expertise (such as in Geneva and New York) are staffed with diplomats from DFAT who usually have prior experience in international law at DFAT.

Malaysia's system appears at first sight to be a hybrid system similar to Australia's: its principal source of advice on international law issues is the International Affairs Division in the Attorney General's Chambers. In addition, the Malaysian MFA has a Legal Division, which provides legal advice and is responsible for drafting and/or vetting bilateral and multilateral treaties which fall within the purview of the Ministry. The Legal Division is responsible for the vetting of Instruments of Ratification/Accession/Notification in respect of treaties to which Malaysia intends to become a party, as well as keeping treaty records. The Ministry's Legal Division is staffed by officers from the Attorney General's Chambers whose duties have been delegated to them by the Attorney General, which are to 'ensure that the legal advice provided is in line with the Federal Constitution, federal and other laws as well as in accordance with international law and Malaysia's existing international obligations'.[30] It has been commented that Malaysia's system seems to be more centralised than Australia's, with a greater degree of control or influence over international law advice being exerted by the International Affairs Division of the Attorney General's Chambers.[31]

It may be that all governments whose main source of international law advice is the Attorney General's Chambers (or another central government legal office) have, in reality, some kind of hybrid system in which certain international law functions, typically including some treaty procedures, are carried out by the foreign ministry.

The Committee of Legal Advisers on Public International Law of the CoE has on its website a useful database describing the organisation of international law advisory services in each of its Member and Observer States.[32]

There are naturally advantages and disadvantages of each of these systems and their variants. It is beyond the scope of this Handbook to consider these advantages and disadvantages (on which there is already a considerable

McCosker (n 2) at fn 26. The 11th edition of the Handbook issued September 2011 is on file with Jill Barrett. These complex institutional arrangements are underpinned and regulated by a formal document, 'The Commonwealth Legal Services Directions 2005' (revised in July 2015). Attorney-General's Department of Australia, 'Legal Services Directions and Guidance Notes' www.ag.gov.au/LegalSystem/LegalServicesCoordination/Pages/Legalservicesdirectionsandguidancenotes.aspx accessed 21 September 2018.

[30] Ministry of Foreign Affairs of Malaysia, 'Departments/Divisions: Legal Division' www.kln.gov.my/web/guest/dd_legal-division accessed 21 September 2018.

[31] *McCosker* (n 2) at 119–22.

[32] Committee of Legal Advisers on Public International Law, 'The Organisation and Functions of the Office of the Legal Adviser in the Ministry of Foreign Affairs' (Council of Europe) www.coe.int/en/web/cahdi/databases accessed 21 September 2018.

amount of literature).[33] The issue to be discussed here is the bearing that these systems have upon the location, structure and staffing of the Treaty Office (on which very little has been written).

Where Should the Treaty Office Be Located when the Primary Source of International Law Advice for the Government is the Foreign Ministry's Legal Advisers?

As indicated above, where the foreign ministry's legal advisers are the main source of international law advice to the whole government (whether of system 1 or 2), it makes sense to place the Treaty Office within the legal office.[34] This is in fact its location in all the examples we have looked at.

However, that is not to say that other arrangements might not be workable and reasonable in particular circumstances. For example, the UK's Treaty Section was, until 2004, located within the FCO's Information Management Directorate and, before that, in various departments with responsibility for managing the FCO's records and library. This arrangement worked well enough, as the Treaty Section always worked very closely with FCO Legal Advisers and were co-located in the same or a nearby building. In 2004, the Information Management Directorate moved out of London, forcing a review of the appropriate administrative home for the Treaty Section. Treaty officials needed their office to remain in the capital city, close to government ministers, Parliament and foreign embassies. It was decided that the Treaty Section would be moved into the FCO's Legal Directorate, where they would continue to function as a distinct team under the supervision of a Legal Councillor. The move was a good one from both the Treaty Section's and the Legal Directorate's points of view, and it is now hard to imagine that it would be changed. The previous arrangement was a product of history – the FCO started to record treaties in the 1830s,[35] but there was no internal FCO Legal Adviser at that time. Until 1876, treaties were compiled by the Librarian's Department, while all Foreign Office legal matters were referred to the Queen's Advocate or other central government law officers.[36]

[33] See for example: *Kingston* (n 24) 81–84 and *Kita* (n 25) 144–47. For earlier comparative discussions, see: G Fitzmaurice, 'Legal Advisers and Foreign Affairs' (1965) 59 *American Journal of International Law* 80–84; RSJ Macdonald, 'The Role of Legal Adviser of Ministries of Foreign Affairs' (1977) 156 *Recueil des Cours de l'Académie de Droit International* 387–88, 454–58.

[34] See the introduction to the section on 'Where Should the Treaty Office (or Centralised Treaty Procedure Functions) Be Located?' above at 53–9.

[35] FCO, 'Guidance to the work of the Foreign and Commonwealth Office (FCO) Treaty Section' (2 July 2013) www.gov.uk/guidance/uk-treaties accessed 21 September 2018.

[36] K Jones, 'Marking Foreign Policy by Justice: the Legal Advisers to the Foreign Office, 1876–1953' in R McCorquodale and J Gauci (eds), *British Influences on International Law, 1915–2015* (Brill, Leiden 2016) 28–29.

Another example of a different arrangement is the Netherlands, where the Treaty Department of the MFA was a separate department acting directly under the Secretary General of the Ministry for fifty years, until about fifteen years ago. It is now part of the legal service of the Ministry.

Where Should the Treaty Office Be Located when the Foreign Ministry Receives International Law Advice from a Central Government Legal Office?

This may make the choice of location for the Treaty Office more difficult, especially if the foreign ministry has no in-house international law advisers at all. There are different advantages and corresponding disadvantages to consider for each option.

How the balance is best struck will depend upon other factors that may be unique to each government. If there are no international law advisers within the foreign ministry, that may already be a problem which should be addressed at the same time as considering where a Treaty Office should be placed. If so, there are possible solutions to be found in the examples mentioned above – one solution is to second one or more international lawyers from the central government legal office to the foreign ministry. Their role might be to run the Treaty Office, and/or to provide international law advice to it and directly to diplomats on treaty law and procedures (the Malaysian approach). Another option is for the foreign ministry to engage international lawyers itself, for the same purpose. In the latter case, it would be very important to set out a clear division of functions between the international lawyers in the foreign ministry and those in the central government legal service, and to establish close co-ordination between the teams (the Australian approach).

How Should Treaty Work Be Organised When There Is No Centralised International Law Service and No Treaty Office?

There needs to be some other mechanism for maintaining a single, authoritative and official collection of all treaties to which the government or IO is party, all treaties for which it has depositary or other responsibilities and all treaty actions. As an alternative to assigning this function to a legal office, it could be carried out by information management specialists, for example as part of a central record-keeping, archiving or library service. Alternatively, it could be done by, or under the supervision of, a central co-ordinating agency such as a cabinet office or prime minister's office, or, in an IO, by the office of the head of the organisation.

If the treaty collection is not centralised, the work relating to it will need to be very carefully co-ordinated to avoid inconsistencies, duplication or confusion. The effort involved in co-ordinating it may however be greater than the effort needed to set up and run a single centralised treaty collection.

Box 2.1 Factors to consider in deciding whether a Treaty Office should be located in the foreign ministry or in the central government legal office

FACTORS IN FAVOUR OF LOCATING THE TREATY OFFICE IN THE FOREIGN MINISTRY

- Many treaty actions are carried out by diplomats, especially at overseas posts, e.g. depositing instruments of ratification with the depositary; attending signature ceremonies overseas; negotiating treaties; and exchanging diplomatic notes with another government. By locating the Treaty Office in the foreign ministry, it will be better placed to provide rapid and direct advice.
- The Treaty Office will be better able to keep track of treaty negotiations and actions carried out by diplomatic staff around the world, ensure that all diplomatic staff are aware of the need to involve the Treaty Office, and where necessary, insist upon correct procedures.
- The Foreign Minister is the most frequent signatory of treaties and of ratification instruments, being the only minister (other than the Head of State or Government) who has general authority to sign without Full Powers, according to the international law of treaties.
- Incoming diplomatic notes from other governments concerning treaty actions and depositary notes are normally addressed to the foreign ministry.
- Treaty Office staff based in the foreign ministry will be better versed in matters of diplomatic protocol, and more experienced in communicating effectively with foreign embassies than staff based in domestic offices.
- It would be an advantage for the Treaty Office for some of its staff to have experience of overseas diplomatic postings, or at least a good knowledge of how an overseas post works.
- Under some national constitutions, the foreign ministry may have responsibility for parliamentary procedures in relation to treaty ratifications and/or publications.

FACTORS IN FAVOUR OF LOCATING THE TREATY OFFICE IN THE CENTRAL GOVERNMENT LEGAL OFFICE

- Treaty procedure work needs to be carried out in close consultation with international lawyers. This is the most easily achieved when the Treaty Office is integrated into the same administrative structure as the government's international law advisers.
- A central government legal office will be best placed to communicate with the full range of ministries and agencies that deal with treaties, provide advice across government, and exert its authority when necessary to ensure consistency and compliance with international law.

Box 2.1 (cont.)

- A central government legal office that combines international law and national law advice will be best placed to ensure effective implementation of treaty obligations in the domestic legal system, as their remit (or oversight) will include the drafting and interpretation of domestic law.
- It will be easier for the government's international lawyers to acquire the knowledge of treaty practice and procedures that they need in order to advise effectively on treaty matters.

Constitutional and Legislative Frameworks Governing Responsibility for Treaties within Governments and IOs

How Treaty Procedure Work May Be Supported – and Constrained – by Legal Rules

Governments and IOs may not have a completely free choice as to whether and, if so, where to establish a Treaty Office. Responsibility for certain treaty functions may be assigned by existing rules. In the case of a government, there may be applicable provisions of the national constitution, legislation or regulations; in the case of an IO, there may be provisions in its constitutional treaty or organisational rules. Not all States or IOs regulate such matters by law; in many cases, responsibility is regulated solely by administrative rules, guidelines or conventions (long-established normative practices). The choice of legislative or other means to designate responsibilities varies greatly from one State to another, and is a function of various factors including constitutional, legal and political culture. Some examples are set out below to illustrate the diversity that exists.

Case Studies: States

China

In China, the central role of the MFA and the State Council in relation to treaties is prescribed by law.[37] The law is 'applicable to bilateral or multilateral treaties and agreements and other instruments of the nature of a treaty or agreement concluded between the People's Republic of China and foreign States'.[38] Agreements to be negotiated and signed in the name of a governmental department, concerning matters within the scope of functions and

[37] Law of the People's Republic of China on the Procedure of the Conclusion of Treaties 1990, adopted 28 December 1990, promulgated 28 December 1990 by Order No. 37 of the President of the People's Republic of China. Text in English translation is available at National People's Congress, 'Law of the People's Republic of China on the Procedure of the Conclusion of Treaties' http://www.npc.gov.cn/englishnpc/Law/2007-12/12/content_/u1383893.htm accessed 9 September 2018. See also BIICL, 'Compilation of Constitutional and Legislative Provisions on Treaty Practice of the People's Republic of China' www.biicl.org/documents/54_prc_treaty_report.pdf accessed 21 September 2018.

[38] ibid art 2.

powers of the department concerned, shall be decided upon by the department itself *or* after consultation with the MFA.[39]

Czech Republic

In the Czech Republic, the distribution of responsibilities among ministries for concluding treaties is governed by legal provisions. In essence, the MFA's Legal Adviser has oversight over the process leading to the conclusion of treaties, in a decentralised system where most treaties are not made by the MFA, but rather by one of the other ministries. The Government Directive on Conclusion, Internal Approval, Application and Termination of Treaties provides that a ministry that is entirely or partly competent for the issues covered by the proposed treaty may act as *manager* for that treaty.[40] Under the Competence Law, the MFA 'co-ordinates and ensures the preparation, conclusion and internal approval of treaties'. This has been described by the Czech Legal Adviser as vesting in the MFA a special *watchdog* power over treaty-making by other ministries.[41]

Indonesia

In Indonesia, the allocation of governmental responsibilities for treaties is governed by constitutional and statutory provisions. The Constitution confers power to conclude treaties on the President, subject to certain controls by the legislature.[42] Under Law No. 37 of 1999 on Foreign Relations, the President may delegate his or her powers in foreign affairs and foreign policy to the Minister of Foreign Affairs.[43] In accordance with Law No. 24 of 2000 on International Agreements, the Minister of Foreign Affairs has broad powers in relation to the process of concluding and ratifying treaties.[44]

Government agencies at national and sub-national levels which plan to enter into a treaty are obliged to consult and co-ordinate with the Minister. The Minister also leads Indonesian delegations in treaty negotiations, unless stipulated otherwise under the treaty or any applicable legislation. In negotiating the treaty, the Indonesian delegates must act in accordance with guidelines approved by the Minister, which set out the position of the Indonesian government with respect to that treaty. Where a government institution wishes for the ratification of a treaty, it must submit a proposal to the Minister of Foreign Affairs, who will

[39] ibid art 5. [40] *Válek* (n 1) 150.

[41] Competence Law No. 2/1969 of the Official Gazette, as amended. See ibid 151.

[42] Constitution of the Republic of Indonesia of 1945, 18 August 1945 (as amended in 2002) art 11(1–2) (English version) (5th edn, Office of the Registrar and the Secretariat General of the Constitutional Court of the Republic of Indonesia, Jakarta 2015) http://www.mahkamahkonstitusi.go.id/public/content/infoumum/regulation/pdf/uud45%20eng.pdf accessed 21 September 2018.

[43] Law No. 37 of 1999 on Foreign Relations, 14 September 1999, State Gazette 1999 No. 156, arts 6 (2) and 1(4) (in Indonesian).

[44] Law No. 24 of 2000 on International Agreements, 23 October 2000, State Gazette 2000 No. 185 art 2. An unofficial translation of the law is provided by the MFA of Indonesia and on file with the authors.

then submit it to the President. Other treaty functions of the Minister of Foreign Affairs include signing the instrument of ratification of a treaty, keeping custody of the original text of the treaty, transmitting a copy of the instrument of ratification to relevant government agencies, and where the Indonesian government is appointed as the depositary of that treaty, exercising depositary functions relating to the treaty.[45] With regard to the role of the Minister stipulated in the Law on International Agreements, the MFA has issued a manual on treaty procedures for its own staff and other government ministries and institutions.[46]

The Netherlands

In the Netherlands, the legal framework for the allocation of governmental responsibilities for treaties is set by the Constitution and legislation. The Constitution provides that the Cabinet (of Ministers) shall decide upon overall policy and that the Council of State should be consulted on proposals for the approval of treaties made by the States General (Parliament), unless this requirement is dispensed with by an Act of Parliament.[47] The Kingdom Act of 1994 governs the approval and publication of treaties and publication of decisions of IOs.[48] This is an Act of Parliament which imposes obligations specifically on the Minister of Foreign Affairs with regard to the legislature. The Minister of Foreign Affairs is required to submit to Parliament a list of draft treaties under negotiation, and is responsible for publication of the Treaty Series of the Kingdom of the Netherlands.[49] It follows from this legislation that when other ministers have political responsibility for the subject matter of the treaty, and therefore also for any necessary legislation and for the

[45] ibid arts 5(1–4), 12(3), 14 and 17(1 and 4–5).

[46] Directorate General of Law and International Treaty, 'Practice Manual on the Conclusion, Ratification, and Custody of Treaties, including the Preparation of Full Powers and Credentials' (Ministry of Foreign Affairs of Indonesia, Jakarta 2012). The Indonesian version of the manual is available at Directorate General of Law and International Treaty, 'Pedoman Praktis Pembuatan, Pengesahan dan Penyimpanan Perjanjian Internasional termasuk Full Powers dan Credentials' https://www.kemlu.go.id/Documents/Pedoman%20Praktis%20Pembuatan%20Pengesahan%20dan%20Penyimpanan%20Naskah%20PI/Pedoman%20Praktis%20Pembuatan%20Pengesahan%20dan%20Penyimpanan%20Naskah%20PI.pdf accessed 21 September 2018. A copy of the manual's English translation is on file with the authors, courtesy of the MFA of Indonesia.

[47] The Constitution of the Kingdom of the Netherlands 2008 (English version), arts 45 and 73. See Government of the Netherlands, 'The Constitution of the Kingdom of the Netherlands 2008' https://www.government.nl/binaries/government/documents/regulations/2012/10/18/the-constitution-of-the-kingdom-of-the-netherlands-2008/the-constitution-of-the-kingdom-of-the-netherlands-2008.pdf accessed 21 September 2018.

[48] The Kingdom Act on the Approval and Publication of Treaties (Kingdom Act), adopted 7 July 1994 and entered into force 20 August 1994. The summary is based on an unofficial English translation of the Kingdom Act prepared by the Translation Department of the MFA, which has been kindly provided to the authors. For the official Dutch language version, see Government Law Database, 'Rijkswet goedkeuring en bekendmaking verdragen' http://wetten.overheid.nl/BWBR0006799/geldigheidsdatum_24-11-2011 accessed 21 September 2018.

[49] ibid s 1 and 16.

implementation of the treaty, those ministries are required to co-operate with the Treaties Department of the MFA. The legislation is supplemented by various administrative guidance documents which contain guidance on treaty procedures.[50] The MFA has issued a Handbook containing practical guidance on legal affairs and treaties, and advises officials in other ministries to refer back to the Legal Service and the Treaties Division in case of queries.[51]

New Zealand

New Zealand has no specific constitutional or legislative provisions dealing with treaty-making powers.[52] The relevant rules and procedures are contained in a combination of Standing Orders of the House of Representatives[53] and constitutional conventions that are codified and reflected in the Cabinet Manual. This Manual states:

> In New Zealand, the power to conclude treaties rests with the Executive. Any proposal to sign a treaty or to take binding treaty action must be submitted to Cabinet for approval …
>
> Before the government takes binding treaty action on them, multilateral treaties and major bilateral treaties of particular significance are presented to the House of Representatives for examination. The requirements for parliamentary treaty examination are set out in the Standing Orders. The Minister of Foreign Affairs determines whether a bilateral treaty amounts to a major bilateral treaty of particular significance.[54]

United Kingdom

The UK does not have a codified constitution. There are statutory provisions that impose requirements on the government as a precondition for ratifying certain

[50] There are a number of guidelines such as the 'Instructions for Legislation' (*Aanwijzingen voor de Regelgeving*). This document is established by decree of the Prime Minister, amended regularly and available only electronically, in Dutch. Other guidelines are included in the 'Handbook for Legislation' (*Draaiboek voor de wetgeving*), which is issued by the Ministry of Justice. The Handbook is amended regularly and available only electronically, in Dutch.

[51] MFA, *Handbook for the Ministry of Foreign Affairs* (MFA, the Netherlands 2011) (in Dutch). The Handbook is approved by the Secretary General of the Foreign Ministry and amended regularly. The Handbook is available only in Dutch. English translations of this handbook and the documents referred to in n 50 are not currently available. Information about their contents has been kindly provided to the authors by Gerard Limburg, former Director of Treaties, Ministry of Foreign Affairs, the Netherlands.

[52] For a summary of New Zealand's Constitution, see Cabinet Office, Cabinet Manual 2017 (Department of the Prime Minister and Cabinet, Wellington 2017) 1–6 https://dpmc.govt.nz/sites/default/files/2017-06/cabinet-manual-2017.pdf accessed 21 September 2018.

[53] The full text of the Standing Orders of the House of Representatives can be accessed on the New Zealand Parliament website, 'Standing Orders of the House of Representatives 2011' (published 11 November 2012) www.parliament.nz/en-nz/pb/rules/standing-orders/00HOHPBReferenceStOrders3/standing-orders-of-the-house-of-representatives-2011 accessed 21 September 2018.

[54] *Cabinet Office* (n 52) paras 7.123–24 at p 118. See also paras 7.125–133 at pp 118–19, and paras 5.77–81 at p 84.

categories of treaties. In most cases the requirement is to consult the UK Parliament, while in a few cases it is necessary to obtain Parliament's approval in an Act of Parliament and/or the approval of the electorate in a referendum.[55] The statutory provisions do not specify a particular minister; they refer to 'a Minister of the Crown', which legally permits a minister from any ministry to exercise the powers and perform the duties. Nonetheless, in practice, those powers are exercised by particular ministers, in accordance with established practice.

Responsibility for concluding treaties lies primarily with the Secretary of State for Foreign and Commonwealth Affairs. The FCO is responsible for the foreign policy aspects of all treaties and deals with questions of form and procedure. It must also consider points of international law. This remains the case even when the negotiation of the treaty is led by another government department, that is, the department that will carry out the treaty's provisions. The FCO Treaty Section supports government departments with advice on practice and procedural matters relating to the conclusion of treaties by the UK, and provides treaty information. The Treaty Section has issued various guidance documents for its own staff and other ministries, which are now published on the 'UK Treaties' pages of the Government's website.[56]

Vietnam

Vietnam has enacted very detailed legislative provisions on the management of treaty responsibilities. In 2016, the National Assembly passed a new Law on Treaties, replacing an earlier one of 2005.[57] This law contains eighty-four subdivided articles which provide for the conclusion, reservation, amendment, supplementation, extension, termination, denunciation, withdrawal from, suspension of application, deposit, keeping custody, making of certified copies of, publication, registration and conduct of implementation of a treaty in the name of the State or the name of the Government of the Socialist Republic of Vietnam. It contains several articles assigning responsibilities to the MFA, including on treaty procedures and information, treaty drafting and diplomatic treaty procedures, and

[55] Constitutional Reform and Governance Act 2010 (as amended in 2011 and 2012) Part 2 and European Union (Amendment) Act 2008 (as amended by the European Union Act 2011). See J Barrett, 'The United Kingdom and Parliamentary Scrutiny of Treaties: Recent Reforms', International and Comparative Law Quarterly (ICLQ), Vol 60, (2011) 225–45.

[56] FCO, 'Guidance to the Work of the Foreign and Commonwealth Office (FCO) Treaty Section' (2 July 2013) www.gov.uk/guidance/uk-treaties accessed 21 September 2018. See in particular: Treaty Section, *Treaties and Memoranda of Understanding (MOUs): Guidance on Practice and Procedures* (2nd edn, FCO, updated March 2014) https://assets.publishing.service.gov.uk/government/uploads/system/uploads/attachment_data/file/293976/Treaties_and_MoU_Guidance.pdf accessed 21 September 2018.

[57] Law on Treaties, 9 April 2016, 108/2016/QH13. The full text of the law in Vietnamese can be accessed on the National Legal Normative Documents Database, http://vbpl.vn/TW/Pages/vbpq-van-ban-goc.aspx?ItemID=101899 accessed 21 September 2018. An unofficial English translation version is available on the National Legal Normative Documents Database, 'Law on Treaties' http://vbpl.vn/TW/Pages/vbpqen-toanvan.aspx?ItemID=11039 accessed 21 September 2018.

responsibilities of recommending agencies in respect of initiating the conclusion of treaties and domestic implementation.[58] Here is an example of one of these statutory provisions to show how clearly they set out ministerial responsibilities:

Article 58. Keeping custody of a treaty

1. The Ministry of Foreign Affairs shall keep custody of the original of a bilateral treaty; a copy of a multilateral treaty to which the Socialist Republic of Vietnam is a contracting party authenticated by the depository; the document of ratification, approval of or accession to a treaty; Full Powers for negotiation and signing of a treaty; credentials for participation in an international conference and other relevant documents.
2. The proposing agency shall send to the Ministry of Foreign Affairs the original or authenticated copy and the Vietnamese translation of a treaty, Full Powers of negotiation and signing of a treaty of the foreign contracting party within the time limit prescribed in Articles 26 and 46 of this Law.

Case Studies: IOs

CoE

The CoE is governed by the Statute of the Council of Europe. The 'law' of the organisation imposes obligations on the Secretary General. A range of texts, rules and resolutions relate to the treaties of the CoE and govern the activities of the Treaty Office, which is located within the Directorate of Legal Advice and Public International Law (DLAPIL). Of particular importance in this regard is the Secretary General Rule No. 1390 of 11 May 2017 defining the role of the DLAPIL within the Secretariat General of the CoE.[59]

Article 1 sets out the tasks for the DLAPIL. The ones pertaining to treaties are:

e. providing legal opinions to the various committees within the Organisation, in particular as regards draft treaties and their final clauses, with a view to ensuring the desirable harmony between international legally binding instruments prepared within the Council of Europe;
f. performing the functions of the Secretary General as depositary of Council of Europe treaties concluded in the framework of the Council of Europe as well as all the legal tasks related to the exercise of depositary functions and those deriving from the Statute of the Council of Europe Development Bank regarding notifications to the members of the Bank and the Governor;
g. upon a request from the Major Administrative Entities concerned, keeping the originals of the agreements which the Council of Europe may conclude with States as well as other entities, such as intergovernmental organisations, public entities and non-governmental organisations;

[58] ibid arts 98–99.

[59] Directorate of Legal Advice and Public International Law, 'Treaty Office' (Council of Europe) www.coe.int/en/web/dlapil/treaty-office accessed 21 September 2018.

h. keeping a register of acts notified to the Secretary General for the purposes of acceding to Partial Agreements as well as acts notifying withdrawal therefrom;

Requests for legal assistance under paragraphs b, c, d and e above shall be transmitted to the DLAPIL by the Major Administrative Entity concerned.

Article 2 requires the administrative parts of the Secretariat to consult the Legal Advice Department on all legal matters including:

d. approach Legal Advice whenever a draft treaty raises a legal issue and in any case, to ensure that all draft treaties have obtained the approval of Legal Advice before being submitted to the Committee of Ministers.

ASEAN

ASEAN is governed by the Charter of the Association of Southeast Asian Nations, 2007 (ASEAN Charter)[60] and its day-to-day activities are carried out by the ASEAN Secretariat,[61] comprising the Secretary General and his/her staff.[62] Although the Secretary General is the Chief Administrative Officer of ASEAN, the Secretary General and the ASEAN Secretariat also have a wide range of functions relating to treaties and legal matters, including:

- facilitating and monitoring progress in the implementation of ASEAN agreements and decisions;[63]
- assisting throughout the process of conclusion of international agreements by ASEAN;[64] and
- providing interpretation of the ASEAN Charter upon the request of any Member State.[65]

Within the ASEAN Secretariat, agreements and legal issues are specifically dealt with by the Legal Services and Agreements Directorate (LSAD) under the Community and Corporate Affairs Department.[66] The LSAD is further divided into three divisions:

[60] Charter of the Association of Southeast Asian Nations (adopted 20 November 2007, entered into force 15 December 2008) 2624 UNTS 223 (ASEAN Charter).

[61] ASEAN, 'ASEAN Secretariat' http://asean.org/asean/asean-secretariat/ accessed 21 September 2018.

[62] ASEAN Charter art 11(7). [63] ibid art 11(2)(b) and (3).

[64] Rules of Procedure for Conclusion of International Agreements by ASEAN (adopted 17 November 2011) r 11 www.asean.org/storage/images/archive/documents/ROP%20for%20Conclusion%20of%20International%20Agreements%20by%20ASEAN.pdf accessed 21 September 2018.

[65] ASEAN Charter art 51(1) and Rules of Procedure for the Interpretation of the ASEAN Charter (adopted 2 April 2012) r 1(1) www.asean.org/storage/images/archive/documents/ROP%20for%20Interpretation%20of%20ASEAN%20Charter.pdf accessed 21 September 2018.

[66] ASEAN, 'ASEAN Secretariat Organizational Structure' http://asean.org/storage/2012/05/ASEAN-Secretariat-Organizational-Structure-effective-1-January-2016.png accessed 21 September 2018.

- Treaty Division;
- International Economic and Trade Law Division; and
- General Legal Affairs Division.

However, there is a paucity of public data available detailing the mandate and work of LSAD and the three divisions within it.

Does Every State and IO Need a Law on Responsibility for Treaty Procedures?

It is clear from the above range of examples that some States and IOs assign responsibility for treaties by law, while others do so by administrative means. If the responsibilities are widely understood and respected by all across the government or IO, there may be no need for statutory provisions. If they are not, and serious issues arise in your government or IO, it may be useful to consider whether new legislation would help to address them. If you are establishing a Treaty Office for the first time, it would be pertinent to consider whether its role and authority would be enhanced by legislation or whether administrative means would be adequate.[67]

Designating responsibility for treaty acts *by law* has certain advantages – a legislative text is highly visible and easily accessible to all officials, and its statutory authority may help ensure that compliance is taken seriously by other departments and agencies. This may be important in a decentralised system where treaty-related activity is diffuse and central control is difficult to enforce. Unlike administrative circulars, legislative provisions cannot be lost or deleted by mistake. On the other hand, when guidance is contained in an administrative form, it is easier to update and to expand with fuller details. It is also easier to move the Treaty Office if organisational restructuring is desired. The Treaty Office itself can issue guidance on its own initiative and keep control of its review and dissemination.

Legislation and administrative guidance are of course not mutually exclusive. As shown in the examples above, some States and IOs have both. For example, in the Netherlands, the legislation is supplemented by various administrative guidance documents. Others, such as Indonesia, have a law which sets out general guidelines on treaty-making as well as more detailed administrative procedures set out in manuals or guidelines issued by the relevant government department to the relevant officials. Treaty procedures at the UN are governed by the UN Charter and UN General Assembly (UNGA) resolutions, and these are supplemented by formal administrative guidance to the Secretariat.[68] The CoE has a published rule that sets out the formal role of

[67] See discussion of problems arising from decentralisation of treaty work in the section on 'Which Treaty Functions Can and Should Be Centralised?' above at 47–50.

[68] UN Charter art 102 and UNGA Res 24 (1)-I, 'Functions and Powers belonging to the League of Nations under International Agreements' (12 February 1946); UNGA Res 97(1), 'Regulations to give effect to Article 102 of the Charter of the United Nations' (14 December 1946) 859

the Legal Directorate in treaty matters,[69] and issues detailed internal guidance to staff in the Treaty Office and elsewhere in the Secretariat.

Which Functions Belong to a Treaty Office?

In the section 'Overview of All Treaty Functions of a Government or IO' above at page 47, we looked at the whole range of treaty functions across a government or IO, considering which best lend themselves to centralisation in a Treaty Office.[70] We suggested that *treaty procedures* are best performed centrally by staff who are not responsible for the policy on that subject. These may be considered as the core functions of a Treaty Office. In this section, we outline what these are, and whether they may be combined with other functions.

The Core Functions of a Treaty Office

The core functions of a Treaty Office normally include:

- managing treaty collections (including maintenance of database records);
- providing authoritative treaty information;
- advising on treaty procedures and processes;
- publishing treaty texts;
- receiving and registering treaty instruments;
- sending treaty instruments (such as to other States, IOs or depositaries);
- checking draft treaty texts;
- preparing agreed treaty texts for signing;
- organising or officiating at ceremonies of signature or ratification;
- drafting Full Powers and ratification instruments;
- depositary functions;
- registering treaties and treaty acts with the UN under Article 102 UN Charter;
- archiving treaty texts and other instruments;
- providing training and guidance on treaty procedures for staff throughout the government or IO (and, in the case of an IO, to its Member States).

UNTS VIII (as amended by UNGA Res 364 B (IV) (1 December 1949); UNGA Res 482 (V) (12 December 1950); UNGA Res 33/141 (9 December 1978); and UNGA Res 52/153 (15 December 1997)); and United Nations Secretary General (UNSG) ST/SGB/2001/7, 'Secretary-General's Bulletin: Procedures to be Followed by the Departments, Offices and Regional Commissions of the United Nations with regard to Treaties and International Agreements' (28 August 2001).

69 Secretary General Rule No. 1390 defining the role of the Directorate Legal Advice and Public International Law within the Secretariat General of the Council of Europe (adopted 11 May 2017) https://rm.coe.int/1680781db3 accessed 21 September 2018. See also *Directorate of Legal Advice and Public International Law* (n 59) and related text.

70 See particularly the section on 'Which Treaty Functions Can or Should Be Centralised?' above at 47–50.

Although these functions are *normally* carried out by the Treaty Office, there is considerable variation from one State or IO to another. Some of these functions may be shared with or transferred to other parts of the government or IO, or even contracted out in part. For example, some publishing may be carried out by a publications department or a private contractor, while document archiving may be undertaken by a specialist facility elsewhere in the administration. However, one would expect the Treaty Office to be fully engaged with the process and exercise some form of supervision and quality control over the output.

Should the Treaty Office Provide Legal Advice on Treaties?

As discussed above, legal advice on treaties needs to be both centralised and decentralised across the whole government or IO, as it needs to be available to all staff involved in treaty work. The Treaty Office must work very closely with lawyers who are versed in the international law of treaties and relevant domestic law. Many, if not most, Treaty Offices are located within the legal service. Some combine legal advice with treaty procedures while others keep the two services distinct.

Where the Treaty Office is staffed by lawyers, or managed by a lawyer, a common arrangement is for the lawyer(s) to combine the giving of legal advice with their treaty procedure or management functions. For example, at the CoE, the Head of Treaty Office is always a lawyer who combines this function with being a legal adviser in the Public International Law Division (legal qualifications are required, as 70 per cent of the job involves giving legal advice on treaties and 30 per cent involves management of treaty procedures). In the Australian DFAT, the Head of Treaties Secretariat is normally a lawyer who combines this role with providing international law advice on treaties.

Legal advice on treaties will be routinely needed internally within the Treaty Office, and externally by legal and policy staff elsewhere in the administration. When the Treaty Office advises other staff it would be an advantage for it to be able to give fully integrated advice on law and on procedure, thereby providing a unified 'Treaty Law and Procedure' service.

Where the Treaty Office is staffed by non-lawyers, clearly they should *not* provide legal advice. They need to have rapid access to legal advice whenever they need it in carrying out their work; and they need to be able to refer any external requests for legal advice over to the legal service. Treaty Office staff need a high level of legal awareness: the ability to spot a legal issue, to understand the boundaries of their own procedural expertise and to resist any pressure to provide legal advice that they are not qualified to give. Provided that they do have this awareness, there is no reason why this arrangement should not work perfectly well, as it does, for example, in the UK.

Should the Treaty Office Perform Treaty Policy Functions?

Treaty procedures should always be kept separate from policy functions. It is important that professionalism and consistency are maintained in the way that treaty procedures are handled. In policy work, there may be other imperatives. For example, it is not uncommon for there to be pressure to cut corners on treaty formalities, whether at the international or domestic level, for political reasons or simply due to time pressure. When this occurs, the Treaty Office and its legal advisers will need to assess whether those other imperatives can be accommodated within the legal framework, and if necessary, resist the pressure or give robust advice to political leaders.

The need for impartiality is particularly important in carrying out depositary functions. This is a procedural role which entails obligations to all States and IOs involved in the treaty. Where multilateral treaties are involved, especially universal ones, there may well be parties or signatory States that do not recognise each other and/or are in dispute about matters related to the treaty or otherwise. The depositary must nevertheless apply the same rules and procedures to them, even if its own State or IO has a policy or alliance in favour of one side or the other. For example, if a government depositary receives an instrument from an entity that it does not recognise as a State, its duty is to circulate it to the treaty parties and request them to make a decision as to its status. The government, in its capacity as a treaty party, may express its view according to its policy (and this is usually best done through the policy branch). But in its depositary capacity, the Treaty Office must act impartially. Sometimes, this separation of roles is difficult for policy officials to understand, and on such occasions the Treaty Office must be prepared to defend the neutrality of its depositary actions.

In a small State or IO with an irregular flow of treaty procedure work, the Treaty Office may have part-time staff that combine their treaty roles with other roles that may include policy work. Those officials will need to take extra care that they are always clear in which capacity they are acting, and do not allow policy priorities to cloud their judgment on treaty procedures.

Should the Treaty Office Handle Other Kinds of International Instruments?

The handling of treaties should be separated from the handling of other kinds of international documents. This is because treaties are subject to the requirements of international and domestic law, such as the obligation to publish and register them with the UN, and legal consequences follow from their non-implementation. International relations generate an infinite variety of other kinds of documents.

Some of them set out commitments and may look similar to treaties. This is explained fully in Chapter 3. Should the Treaty Office process 'treaty-like documents' (which are not treaties), or should there be a separate system elsewhere?

This is a question for each IO and government to decide. If it is decided that the Treaty Office should handle non-treaty instruments which are 'treaty-like', it should keep them separate from treaties and devise a separate set of procedures for handling them that are appropriate to their status. If it is decided that the Treaty Office should not handle them, the question then is whether there should be some other centralised system for recording and handling them.

Box 2.2 Factors to consider in deciding the Treaty Office's role in handling treaty-like documents

ARGUMENTS IN FAVOUR OF THE TREATY OFFICE HANDLING TREATY-LIKE DOCUMENTS

- Written political commitments solemnly entered into should be observed, even if not legally binding.
- Record-keeping of non-treaty documents needs to be meticulous, as for treaties.
- A centralised system is important to ensure that drafts are checked, legal advice is obtained, etc.
- Similar skills and methods are needed.
- It is not always easy to distinguish treaties from non-treaty documents.
- Some non-treaty documents are closely related to treaties.

ARGUMENTS AGAINST THE TREATY OFFICE HANDLING TREATY-LIKE DOCUMENTS

- If both treaties and non-treaty documents are handled by the Treaty Office, it might blur the important distinction between them.
- Non-treaty documents do not require treaty functions.
- There is a huge variety of non-treaty documents – where is the boundary between those which are treaty-like and those which are not? How can you define a non-treaty?
- Treaty-like documents should not be centralised; they should be dealt with by each operational/policy department, and recorded with related policy papers.
- If the Treaty Office has a very tight budget, it is better to focus on its core treaty functions and not expand its remit.

If a Central Record of Treaty-Like Documents Is Maintained outside the Treaty Office, Where Should It Be?

A centralised record of treaty-like documents of a certain type could be maintained by a general record-keeping unit, such as the library, records or archiving service, or by a central co-ordinating agency such as a cabinet office or secretary general's office. Since these documents may be generated within any part of a government or secretariat that has international dealings, this arrangement would only work if all officials routinely inform the central agency of their existence. There would need to be guidance on the type of document that should be referred, and at what stage of its formation, for example in draft or after its conclusion. This would be an admirable aim but difficult to achieve in practice, without a great deal of training and explaining to officials across a wide range of administrative units.

Having no comprehensive centralised system in governments or IOs for processing and recording international instruments other than treaties seems to be more common practice. For example, the CoE maintains a clear distinction between treaties and non-binding instruments. The DLAPIL gives legal advice on the full range of instruments, but the Treaty Office only handles treaties. Operational directorates are responsible for handling and recording non-treaty documents within their remit.

In the Netherlands, the Treaty Division only deals with treaties, while the handling and recording of other documents are the responsibility of the policy units concerned. In the UK, the FCO Treaty Section has no formal role in relation to non-treaty documents, which are the responsibility of the policy units concerned. There is no official centralised government system of record-keeping for such documents. Nevertheless, Treaty Section staff maintain a list of all such instruments which are sent to them, and keep copies on file. This is a useful resource, but it is not comprehensive or systematic. In theory, it should include all documents called 'MOU' or of a similar type concluded by all government departments, as all such documents should be sent to Treaty Section in draft for checking (to ensure that they are not inadvertently worded in treaty language). In practice, their records are far from complete, as some administrators overlook this; moreover, policy departments do not necessarily send a copy of the final version to Treaty Section. The signed original document is retained by the policy department.

Staffing the Treaty Office

Applying the PLATO Principles to Staffing the Treaty Office

The key principle in this context is 'Professional'. It means that a professional approach to treaty work is taken, both by those who do it and by their senior management. In particular:

- Treaty practice is recognised by high-level authorities (including the Human Resources department) as specialised work requiring expert knowledge, training and expertise.
- The government/IO plans and provides resources for recruitment, training, capacity-building, development and retention of treaty officials, and knowledge management.
- Care is taken to hire staff with the right skills for treaty work.

What Skills are Needed for Treaty Procedures Work?

A range of skills are needed for effective treaty management. The following skills and expertise all play an important role in one or more aspects of the work:

- clerical and secretarial;
- proofreading and editing;
- information and archives management;
- webmaster, IT;
- external communications;
- publishing;
- management (human, resources, systems);
- legal (international and domestic law);
- diplomatic and protocol; and
- prior experience of treaty procedures.

Clearly, no single individual is likely to have all of these attributes. If the Treaty Office is very well-resourced, it may be fortunate enough to be able to engage staff who have, among them, all of the skills and prior experience needed. If, however, its resources only permit the hiring of a small number of staff, recruitment priorities will need to be set.

Which Skills are Essential within the Treaty Office and which Can Be Found Elsewhere?

The Treaty Office needs to have certain core skills among its own staff, but may also be able to make use of expertise elsewhere within the administration or engage external contractors for specific functions. In the personal experience of the authors, as well as of the Treaty Office heads that we have consulted, these are the essential core skills and personal qualities needed among its own staff:

- top-quality clerical skills – is methodical and accurate, and pays meticulous attention to detail;
- total commitment to 100 per cent accuracy – quality-controls own work and is ready to admit mistakes and make corrections on the record where necessary;

- ability to assimilate large amounts of complex detail;
- high integrity – is committed to impartiality, understands procedural fairness and the reasons behind procedural rules;
- information management – professionally trained or experienced, including in running databases and publishing;
- knowledge management – committed to using past knowledge and developing institutional memory for the benefit of future staff;
- legal awareness – able to spot a legal issue and know when to ask for legal advice;
- diplomatic awareness – aware of protocol and diplomatic sensitivities in external communications;
- policy awareness – understands policy context and able to adapt to fast-moving developments;
- strong customer focus; and
- commitment to training and further development.

Other skills are of course very desirable; for example, legal expertise inside the Treaty Office is an advantage. However, provided that professional legal advice is readily available to Treaty Office staff, legal awareness is sufficient for their day-to-day work. Diplomatic experience is an advantage, but if the Treaty Office staff work closely with diplomats and learn about how overseas posts work, that should suffice. It is of course desirable for a new recruit to the Treaty Office, especially its head, to have prior experience of treaty work. But given that there are not many jobs in this field, recruitment cannot be limited to those who have previously held such a position. It is more important to ensure that they have the right aptitudes, receive thorough on-the-job training and are committed to continuing professional development.

The Importance of a Career Path (or Paths) for Treaty Office Officials

It is important to consider not only where suitable recruits to the Treaty Office staff might come *from*, but also where they might wish to progress *to* after their posting. Their work in the Treaty Office needs to fit within an overall career plan, both to make it attractive to the individual and to ensure that the Treaty Office secures the best staff that it can and makes full use of their skills.

Here are some suggestions of where staff with the right mix of skills and interests are likely to be found:

- In information management positions elsewhere in the government or IO, such as library, record-keeping and archiving services. Some of them may already have professional qualifications in information management (or librarianship), and work on treaty information management might offer opportunities for them to broaden their experience in this field.

- Legal executives (quasi-legal professionals) working in a legal office in a domestic government ministry, such as on case management, assisting lawyers, etc.
- Administrators working in fields of legal regulation, such as data protection, freedom of information requests, court and tribunal administration, nationality or visa applications, notary or legalisation procedures.
- Diplomats with experience in protocol matters or various kinds of management.
- Top-level secretaries in high-profile positions, such as personal assistant to a minister, ambassador or secretary general.
- Treaty Office of another IO or government (rare but very valuable, if external recruitment or secondment is practicable).

If lawyers are recruited to staff or head the Treaty Office, thought needs to be given to the legal/managerial balance of their work compared with other positions in the legal service, to ensure that the position is attractive and that their Treaty Office experience will help their career progression.

Placing the Treaty Office on a well-thought-out career map – and promoting it as such throughout the organisation – is an important factor in attracting a strong field of applications for Treaty Office vacancies. Without this, a number of undesirable patterns can develop. For example, if it is treated as just another diplomatic posting, there may be a rapid turnover of individuals whose interest lies in policy work. Or, if the Treaty Office is perceived elsewhere in the administration as a dull backwater, it may attract people for the wrong reasons, or be used by Human Resources managers looking to 'dump' staff who are difficult to fit elsewhere. To ensure that this does not happen, the managers of the Treaty Office need to take a proactive approach to defining the skills they need and recruiting the right people.

It is helpful for the Treaty Office to be staffed by officials who are able to remain in their posts for a reasonable period of time. Many diplomats move postings on a frequent basis, perhaps only remaining in one post for as little as eighteen months or two years, and this will often not allow them to develop the broad spectrum of knowledge and expertise that is needed in a Treaty Office. The right amount of time will probably be several years, but it is also important to ensure that treaty staff do not stay in the job indefinitely simply because there is no onward career path for them. The head of a Treaty Office, if not a lawyer, needs to know that when they seek to move on, their treaty experience will be valued elsewhere in the administration. The following examples may better illustrate the different career paths for Treaty Office officials.[71]

[71] Information derived from interviews in 2012 and supplemented in 2018 with further interviews and email correspondence. Information on file with the authors. See the section on 'The Need for New Generic Principles for Good Treaty Practice' in Chapter 1 at 11–14.

In the CoE, the head of the Treaty Office is always a qualified lawyer with expertise in international law. The Office has two other full-time equivalent (FTE) members of administrative staff. In addition, the Director of Legal Advice and Public International Law and the Head of the Public International Law Division and Treaty Office supervise the work of the Treaty Office. The Head of Treaty Office is usually recruited from within the CoE legal service, while the previous Head of the Treaty Office usually progresses to another legal position within the CoE.

In the Netherlands, the Treaty Division of the MFA has twenty-three (FTE) staff. The Head is always a lawyer. Some of the staff are trained as lawyer-diplomats, while others are trained in general administration.

In the UK, the FCO Treaty Section has eight (FTE) members of staff, reduced from eleven in 2011. There is no 'typical' career path for treaty officers within the FCO. Some officers at various grades may have a diplomatic background. The majority, however, come from an administrative background within government, often from other government departments. One of the previous Heads of Treaty Section had an extensive career elsewhere in the civil service before joining the FCO, including experience in judicial administration, and remained in post for eight years. Some have had a specialist background in librarianship or information management; for example, another former Head of Treaty Section who came with an information management qualification has since moved on to a more senior post in this field. The present Head is a career diplomat with extensive experience in various kinds of management, consular and immigration work. The experience of the Treaty Section staff and their managers (in the Legal Directorate) is that the Section works best when it has at least one staff member with previous experience in information management, and when its Head is prepared and able to remain in post for a number of years.

Providing Guidance on Treaty Procedures across the Government or IO

As mentioned above, it is important for a number of reasons to develop a single set of procedures for the management of treaties that are widely known and adhered to. This applies whether or not a government or IO has a centralised Treaty Office. If there is one, developing the guidance and disseminating it across the organisation will be one of its functions. If there is not, the guidance will need to be drawn up by a central legal service or other co-ordinating department.

Providing training courses is a useful method of ensuring that all officials across government or the IO are familiar with treaty procedures and respect the central authority of the Treaty Office. Outreach is therefore an important activity for the Treaty Office. In recent years, the UK Treaty Section has increased its efforts in this area, offering training programmes in treaty procedures for diplomats and officials across government, including an online e-learning course. These courses are often delivered together with FCO legal advisers who specialise in the law of treaties. In the words of the FCO Principal Legal adviser, 'courses on treaty practice and procedure are perennially popular as so many FCO staff are involved in negotiating, implementing or lobbying on others' implementation of treaties'.[72]

The UN Secretary General issued 'Procedures to Be Followed by the Departments, Offices and Regional Commissions of the United Nations with regard to Treaties and International Agreements' in the form of a bulletin. It is administrative guidance addressed to all parts of the Secretariat, setting out officials' treaty responsibilities, especially with regard to consulting and informing the Treaty Section and the Office of Legal Affairs.[73]

The CoE's Treaty Office prepared a Nutshell booklet on the signature and ratification procedures of CoE treaties.[74] The booklet was designed mainly for the staff of the permanent representations to the CoE, to whom copies were sent. An information session on the Treaty Office, based on the booklet, also took place. The Treaty Office has also published on its website a series of model templates for legal acts related to treaties, partial agreements and model final clauses, for the guidance of Member States.[75]

In Southeast Asia, States such as Indonesia and Vietnam have also published internal guidelines pertaining to their treaty practice. The Directorate General of Law and International Treaty within the MFA of Indonesia published a 'Practical Guide to the Drafting, Adoption and Recording of International Treaties', which includes guidelines for the drafting and adoption of Full Powers and credentials.[76] The Ministry conducts workshops and conferences for government officials (in collaboration with other government ministries or institutions and regional governments), and engages national academic societies in national dialogue on treaty procedures.[77] In Vietnam, the Department of International Law and Treaties, MFA has organised several training courses

[72] I Macleod, 'The FCO's Legal Advisers and Contemporary Challenges' in *Zidar* and *Gauci* (n 1) 30.

[73] *UNSG* (n 68).

[74] CoE, 'The Treaty Office in a Nutshell' https://rm.coe.int/16802f5aff accessed 21 September 2018. See also J Polakiewicz, *Treaty-Making in the Council of Europe* (Council of Europe Publishing, Strasbourg 1999) https://book.coe.int/img/cms/Treaty-making%20GBR%203899-6.pdf accessed 21 September 2018. Although old, it is still useful.

[75] Treaty Office 'Templates' (Council of Europe) www.coe.int/en/web/conventions/templates accessed 21 September 2018.

[76] *Directorate General of Law and International Treaty* (n 46).

[77] For such workshops and academic engagements, see, for example: Pelita Harapan University, 'National Seminar: The Law on Treaties', 17 November 2014; Ministry of Finance, 'Assessment Techniques and Workshop on International Treaties Related to Customs', 7–26 May 2012; Faculty of Law of University 17 August 1945 Semarang, 'Training on the Drafting of International Treaties', Semarang (24 October 2014); and MFA, 'Training on Diplomacy Techniques and Foreign Relations for Regional Governments' (March 2017). These trainings and workshops were all delivered in Indonesian.

for government officials on treaty procedures.[78] The Department also published a Handbook on Treaties and another on International Agreements, containing guidance on the procedures to conclude and implement treaties and other kinds of international instruments.[79]

[78] See, for example, MFA, '2003 Training Workshop on Treaty and Agreements Management' (in Vietnamese) www.mofahcm.gov.vn/vi/mofa/nr040807104143/nr040807105001/ns130606015825 accessed 21 September 2018, and The World and Vietnam Report, '2013 Training Workshop on Implementation of Treaty Law' (in Vietnamese) http://baoquocte.vn/tap-huan-pho-bien-kien-thuc-ve-cong-tac-phap-ly-51422.html accessed 21 September 2018.

[79] See The World and Vietnam Report, 'The Ministry of Foreign Affairs Published Two Handbooks: Treaties and International Agreements' (in Vietnamese) http://baoquocte.vn/bo-ngoai-giao-phat-hanh-hai-an-pham-so-tay-dieu-uoc-quoc-te-va-thoa-thuan-quoc-te-1459.html accessed 21 September 2018.

3

Treaties and Other Kinds of International Instruments

***

'At no time did I consider that in signing the Minutes I was committing Bahrain to a legally binding agreement.'

Statement of Foreign Minister of Bahrain to the International Court of Justice[1]

Introduction

International affairs generate an enormous variety of documents and communications every day, from matters of war and peace, trade and economic policy, to sharing information, arranging meetings and cups of tea. The fact that people in different countries are participating in it makes it international, but does not endow it with any legal status. How does one identify, from among the blizzard of papers and emails, which documents are or potentially could be binding in international law? Which ones are treaties? Why might it matter?

Treaties are only one kind of international instrument. There are many other kinds of international instruments, some of which have legal status of some kind, and others which do not. There are several other kinds of international instruments that can contain binding obligations; for example, acts of IOs may be binding in international law, with mandatory UN Security Council (UNSC) resolutions being perhaps the most well-known type. Governments may also enter into agreements that are binding under a system of national law, and when they do so with other governments or international entities, the

[1] *Maritime Delimitation and Territorial Questions between Qatar and Bahrain (Qatar v Bahrain)* (Jurisdiction and admissibility – Judgment) [1994] ICJ Rep 112 paras 21–30 and 41. See the section on 'Case Study 1: Example of a Mistake About Whether a Document is Binding Under International Law' above at 82.

document may look like a treaty but it is not – it is probably a domestic law contract.

There is an even larger variety – perhaps infinite – of international instruments of a non-binding nature. Some of these might contain commitments, set standards for future conduct, or establish frameworks or institutions for international co-operation. They may take the form of a declaration, MOU, guidelines or arrangements, just to give a few examples. In this chapter, we use the term 'treaty-like instruments' in the widest, non-technical sense, to refer to *any* kind of international document that is not a treaty but might bear some resemblance to one. In practice, distinguishing *non-binding international instruments* from treaties, and deciding how to handle them, poses the greatest challenges for Treaty Offices. It is this distinction that is therefore the main focus of this chapter and the Top Tips at the end.

Why It Is Necessary to Distinguish Between Treaties and other kinds of International Instruments

When one is faced with any international instrument, there are two related questions to ask about its status: (1) is it legally binding? and (2) is it a treaty? If it is a treaty, it is by definition binding in international law. If it is not a treaty, however, it does not follow that it is not legally binding; as explained above, there are other kinds of international instruments that can create legal obligations both in international and domestic law. Both questions are therefore important, for different reasons. Whether the primary question for you is its treaty status, its legal effects or both, depends on your role and reason for dealing with the text.

A legal adviser in a government or IO looking at an international instrument will need to ascertain whether it contains obligations that are binding and applicable to the State or IO concerned. This matters as it determines whether the rules are mandatory for that government or IO, or whether there is discretion to apply them and what the consequences of not doing so might be. Whether that document is a treaty is only one of the questions the legal adviser will need to look at. The legal adviser needs to be concerned with the substance and legal effect of any document that is relevant to the matter at hand.

A treaty official who receives the same document might only be concerned with whether or not it is a treaty. If it is a treaty, that official will need to process it in a certain way. If it is not a treaty, treaty procedures will not apply. The treaty official might not need to process the document at all: if the Treaty Office's responsibilities are limited to treaty procedures (as they commonly are), a treaty-like instrument may be sent elsewhere and it will be for others to decide what it is and what to do with it. The treaty official, in this example, is concerned with the correct application of procedures, as mandated by international and domestic law and other administrative guidance.

Why It Matters: What Can Go Wrong

The following case studies may illustrate better why the distinction between treaties and treaty-like instruments is important, and what can go wrong if the distinction is not made correctly.

Case Study 1: Example of a Mistake about whether a Document Is Binding under International Law

At a meeting between the Foreign Minister of Qatar and the Foreign Minister of Bahrain on 25 December 1990, the two Ministers signed minutes recording what they had agreed. In 1991 Qatar instituted proceedings before the ICJ against Bahrain in relation to a dispute about sovereignty over islands and maritime delimitation. Qatar relied on the signed minutes as a binding agreement to refer the dispute to the Court. Bahrain objected to the jurisdiction of the Court, arguing that the minutes were not legally binding.

As we showed at the beginning of this chapter, the Foreign Minister of Bahrain stated that 'at no time did I consider that in signing the Minutes I was committing Bahrain to a legally binding agreement'. He believed it was a simple record of a meeting containing political commitments. The ICJ held that the minutes did constitute an international agreement creating rights and obligations for the Parties; that it did have jurisdiction to hear the case; and it went on to deliver judgment on the merits of the dispute about sovereignty and delimitation.[2]

Case Study 2: Example of a Mistake about whether a Document Is a Treaty under International Law and Domestic Law

Embassy officials of a European government signed an agreement with the Middle Eastern host government to provide training support to the latter's armed forces. Defence ministry officials in that European government, believing it to be a non-binding arrangement, did not initiate parliamentary treaty procedures. Four months later, they received a formal notice from the Middle Eastern government that its Parliament had approved the treaty and they were ready to bring it into force.

At this point, the European Foreign Ministry's Treaty Office was consulted, and it advised that the agreement was a treaty. According to that State's domestic law, it had to be sent to Parliament for scrutiny before it could be brought into force. This caused a delay of several more months before the European government could inform the other government that it was ready to bring the treaty into force. As a result, the deployment of its troops and the training programme in the Middle Eastern country had to be postponed, with

[2] ibid paras 21–30 and 41. See also the section on 'Disputes over Whether a Text is a Treaty or Non-Binding International Instrument' below at 108–111.

operational and financial detriment to the armed forces, and damage to the bilateral relationship.[3]

Lessons Learnt

In both these examples, the mistake was essentially the same and concerned the legal status of the document. In the *Qatar v Bahrain* case, the primary issue was whether the signed minutes were a treaty as defined by international law, because the question arose in international legal proceedings before the ICJ, whose function is to apply international law. Despite the belief of one of the parties that it was not binding, the ICJ decided that objectively it was a treaty that was binding on both parties. In the case of the bilateral military training agreement, there were two related issues: whether the document was a treaty in international law and whether it was a 'treaty' for the purposes of each party's respective domestic procedures for parliamentary scrutiny. The European party made a mistake about its status in international law, which led to its failure to initiate the appropriate domestic procedure for consulting the legislature prior to ratifying treaties.

The moral of both tales is clear: any document generated in an international context that contains agreements, commitments, undertakings, understandings, regulations, standards or anything of that sort *could* be legally binding. It may not be obvious from the appearance of the document. To distinguish between a legally binding text and a non-binding one, or between a treaty and a treaty-like instrument, requires knowledge of international law and sometimes also of the domestic constitutional law of a particular State. Anyone who does not have such expertise should seek specialist legal advice; without it, any decisions they make in relation to such documents could have adverse consequences that may not become apparent until much later.

Good Practice in Distinguishing between Treaties and other kinds of International Instruments: Applying the PLATO Principles

In view of the questions at issue and the consequences of errors, the most vital of the PLATO principles in this context are:

- 'Legal': all legal requirements are met, in both international and domestic law; and lawyers with the appropriate specialist knowledge are fully engaged at all stages;
- 'Professional': a professional approach to treaty work is taken by those who do it and is respected by all officials throughout the administration;

[3] The case study is a hypothetical scenario, based on a similar one within the experience of one of the authors. In the real case, this mistake was made but, fortunately, the consequences were not quite as severe (but they could easily have been).

- 'Organised': guidance on the distinction between treaties and other international instruments must be written down, and provided in systematic form to all staff concerned; and
- 'Transparent': this principle requires clarity of guidelines and for their active dissemination to all who may have an interest.[4]

Written Guidance on Distinguishing between Treaties and Non-Binding International Instruments

An area of particular difficulty for government and IO officials is how to distinguish between treaties and non-binding international instruments (documents that contain political commitments but are not legally binding under international or domestic law). Many governments and IOs recognise this problem, and some issue guidance to their officials. For example, Australia issues a treaty practice manual for internal use which includes sections on 'What is a treaty?' and 'Arrangements of less than treaty status', with advice on when to use each and how to draft them.[5] In the Netherlands, the International Law Division of the MFA has compiled internal guidance on when a non-binding instrument is more appropriate than a binding one, and how to differentiate between a treaty and a non-binding instrument.[6]

Even better are those guidelines that are also made available to the public online. The New Zealand Government's Guide on 'International Treaty Making' was written for officials and is also posted on the Ministry's public website, making it easy for all officials to find as well as interested members of the public.[7] The Guide begins with a section entitled 'An Important

[4] See the section on 'The PLATO Principles for Good Treaty Practice' in Chapter 1 at 14.

[5] Treaties Secretariat, *Signed, Sealed and Delivered – Treaties and Treaty-Making: Officials' Handbook* (Australia Department of Foreign Affairs and Trade, Canberra 2011). This is a manual issued for internal government use, containing instructions to officials on such matters as how government work on treaties is organised, mandate to negotiate, negotiation and finalisation of the text, Executive Council approval, signature, scrutiny by Parliament, entry into force, and what to do following entry into force. It is updated annually, but is not available online. A copy of the 11th edition (2011) is on file with the author, courtesy of the Department of Foreign Affairs and Trade, Canberra. See also Treaties Secretariat, *Australia and International Treaty Making Information Kit* (3rd edn, Australia Department of Foreign Affairs and Trade, Canberra 2000). The book is a public information kit which contains, among others, brief information on 'What is a treaty?'. An online version of the publication is available at Treaty Law Resources, 'Australia International Treaty Making Information Kit' (July 2000) www.austlii.edu.au/au/other/dfat/reports/infokit.html#sect1 accessed 21 September 2018.

[6] Ministry of Foreign Affairs, *Handbook for the Ministry of Foreign Affairs* (Ministry of Foreign Affairs, 2011) (in Dutch). The Handbook is only available in Dutch. Information about its contents has been provided to the authors by Gerard Limburg, Former Director of Treaties, Ministry of Foreign Affairs of the Kingdom of the Netherlands.

[7] New Zealand Ministry of Foreign Affairs and Trade, *International Treaty Making: Guidance for government agencies on practice and procedures for concluding international treaties and*

Distinction: International Treaties and Arrangements' which advises as follows:

> There is an **important legal distinction** between the two types of instruments that the New Zealand Government may conclude with other countries and international organisations:
>
> 1. **Treaties**: international instruments that are legally binding under international law;
> 2. **Arrangements**: international instruments of less-than-treaty-status (they are not intended to be legally binding but can still create important political commitments).
>
> This distinction has significant practical implications for staff involved in the negotiation and implementation of international instruments.
>
> Both **treaties** and **arrangements** are international legal documents. Proposals to enter into international treaties and arrangements require consultation with the Legal Division of MFAT at an early stage. While arrangements are not legally binding, they nevertheless require careful drafting. New Zealand takes its commitments under international arrangements seriously.[8]

The UK manual 'Treaties and Memoranda of Understanding (MOUs): Guidance on Practice and Procedures' was originally an internal document issued by the FCO's Treaty Section only to government officials, but recent editions have also been published on the UK Government website.[9] It contains guidance on 'What is a treaty?', 'What is an MOU?' and 'How do you distinguish an MOU from a treaty?' The US State Department's Office of Treaty Affairs has also published its 'Guidance on Non-Binding Documents', advising officials that 'Ambiguity as to whether or not a document is legally binding should be avoided' and offering guidance on how to do so.[10]

Concern to distinguish correctly between treaties and non-binding international instruments is not confined to common law jurisdictions. The approach of the Netherlands has already been mentioned. Spain is another example of a State with a legal system rooted in the civil law tradition which takes a similar approach. The Spanish Ministry of Foreign Affairs and Co-operation has issued instructions on the use of non-binding instruments to government officials, in the form of an Order. The preamble to the Order notes the increase

arrangements (August 2018) www.mfat.govt.nz/assets/Uploads/International-Treaty-Making-Guide-2018.pdf accessed 22 October 2018.

[8] ibid 3.

[9] Treaty Section, *Treaties and Memoranda of Understanding (MOUs): Guidance on Practice and Procedures* (Foreign and Commonwealth Office, updated March 2014) www.gov.uk/government/uploads/system/uploads/attachment_data/file/293976/Treaties_and_MoU_Guidance.pdf accessed 9 September 2018.

[10] Office of Legal Adviser, 'Guidance on Non-Binding Documents' (US Department of State) www.state.gov/s/l/treaty/guidance/ accessed 9 September 2018.

in recent years in the number of non-binding instruments (political agreements) being used in international affairs, both by the Ministry itself and by other public authorities. The Order sets out the criteria for entering into such agreements, how they should be drafted so as to distinguish them from treaties, how they should be handled within government; and establishes that it is for the Foreign Ministry to determine whether a particular document is a non-binding agreement as opposed to a treaty, regardless of which department or agency has negotiated it. The Order is a public document.[11] Similarly, the MFA of Vietnam has also issued a handbook on other kinds of international instruments which provides the criteria and procedure for the conclusion of such instruments.[12]

The provision of this kind of guidance to officials across government meets several of the PLATO criteria, in particular the 'Legal' principle (provided of course that all of the guidance is legally correct) and 'Organised' (in particular the provision of written guidance in systematic form to all staff concerned). The 'Transparent' principle is also very important, particularly the *accessibility* of the guidance to all those who need to use it and its active *dissemination* so that all concerned are aware of it. For this reason, the practice of governments such as New Zealand, Spain, the UK and the USA of posting their internal guidance on their public website is particularly to be commended. Not only does it improve the flow of information to the public and to the legislature, it also makes it easier for officials across all government departments and agencies to locate the most up-to-date version.

In the CoE, the difference between a treaty and a recommendation was established by Article 15 of the 'Statute of the Council of Europe, 1949', which provides:

a. On the recommendation of the Consultative Assembly or on its own initiative, the Committee of Ministers shall consider the action required to further the aim of the Council of Europe, including the conclusion of conventions or agreements and the adoption by governments of a common policy with regard to particular matters. Its conclusions shall be communicated to members by the Secretary General.
b. In appropriate cases, the conclusions of the Committee may take the form of recommendations to the governments of members, and the Committee may request the governments of members to inform it of the action taken by them with regard to such recommendations.[13]

[11] Ministry of Foreign Affairs and Co-operation of Spain, 'Order Circular 3,286: Rules for the processing of non-binding agreements by the organs of this Department, and in regard to monitoring and collaborating with other public authorities in this matter' 19 July 2010 (in Spanish).

[12] See The World and Vietnam Report, 'The Ministry of Foreign Affairs Published Two Handbooks: Treaties and International Agreements' (in Vietnamese) http://baoquocte.vn/bo-ngoai-giao-phat-hanh-hai-an-pham-so-tay-dieu-uoc-quoc-te-va-thoa-thuan-quoc-te-1459.html accessed 9 September 2018.

[13] Statute of the Council of Europe (adopted 5 May 1949, entered into force 3 August 1949, last amended June 2015), 87 UNTS 103, ETS 001.

The 'conventions and agreements' referred to in paragraph (a) are treaties (there is no legal distinction between a 'convention' and an 'agreement'). Recommendations are not binding. The choice of a treaty or a recommendation depends on the subject matter and the level of support among Member States for developing a binding instrument. A recommendation can precede a treaty or can follow a treaty.[14]

Multilateral treaties adopted in the CoE can be clearly differentiated from recommendations or declarations. Apart from the fact that treaties must be signed and ratified by States, the wording used is also different. Normally treaties use the verb 'shall' and recommendations 'should'. The drafting of treaties is based on the CoE's practice which is evident in the texts of over 220 published treaties, supplemented on particular points by Statutory Resolutions and Recommendations, which are all published.[15]

As for *bilateral* instruments concluded between the CoE and a single State or IO, their binding nature depends on the wording used and by the presence or absence of well-defined legal elements in the text of the document.[16] The way in which the CoE distinguishes in practice between its own binding and non-binding bilateral instruments is not as clear as its practice in relation to multilateral treaties concluded under its auspices. As there is no published guidance, it may not be easy for the public to understand which of the CoE's bilateral agreements are binding. For example, the CoE publishes on its website 'Lists of Agreements Concluded by the Council of Europe with other International Intergovernmental Organisations or Public International Institutions'.[17] It is not indicated which of these (if any) are treaties and which are non-binding. As for its bilateral agreements, the CoE has published only two agreements in its treaty series; both are between the CoE and France relating to its headquarters.[18] The CoE has also concluded around thirty seat agreements with States in whose territory it has representative offices. However, these are not published, and, it would appear, are not classified as treaties by the CoE.[19]

[14] An example of a recent recommendation is: Recommendation CM/Rec(2018)6 of the Committee of Ministers to Member States on Terrorists Acting Alone (adopted 4 April 2018).

[15] Treaty Office, 'Complete list of the Council of Europe's treaties' (Council of Europe) www.coe.int/en/web/conventions/full-list accessed 9 September 2018.

[16] According to information provided to Jill Barrett by a member of the Council of Europe Secretariat.

[17] Treaty Office, 'Bi- or Multilateral Agreements' (Council of Europe) www.coe.int//uen/web/conventions/bi-or-multilateral-agreements accessed 9 September 2018.

[18] The Special Agreement Relating to the Seat of the Council of Europe (adopted 2 September 1949, entered into force 2 September 1949) ETS 003 and the Supplementary Agreement amending certain provisions of the General Agreement on Privileges and Immunities of the Council of Europe (adopted 18 March 1950, entered into force 18 March 1950) ETS 004.

[19] This is implied by the fact that they are not mentioned in the CoE's online Glossary, under the definition of 'Treaty'. There is no explicit statement as to their legal status, or even their existence. See Treaty Office, 'Glossary' (Council of Europe) www.coe.int/en/web/conventions/glossary accessed 9 September 2018.

Centralisation: One Point of Contact for Advice about the Distinction between Treaties and other International Instruments

Centralisation is an important aspect of the 'Organised' principle. It complements the principle of 'Professionalism', by recognising that distinguishing between treaties and treaty-like instruments requires specialist legal and treaty expertise, as well as a consistent approach across the government or secretariat.

Good practice in relation to the organisation of treaty procedures work was discussed in Chapter 2. An important factor is the centralisation of treaty procedures and official treaty information in a single Treaty Office, or in designated treaty officials within a larger unit, which serves the whole government or IO.[20] The remit of the Treaty Office should state clearly what its responsibilities are in relation to treaty-like instruments, especially non-binding international instruments.[21] Some Treaty Offices carry out functions in relation to certain kinds of non-treaty instruments, for example, they may keep copies and/or lists of them, and may publish some of them. Other Treaty Offices may restrict their functions to treaties only. Either way, there needs to be clear criteria for officials to apply to determine what is and is not a treaty, and what should be done with other types of international instruments. There also needs to be clear guidance on when it is appropriate to create a new treaty and when some other kind of instrument should be used. The guidance should also emphasise that in cases of doubt, advice is available from the Treaty Office and its legal advisers. This should achieve a uniform approach across the administration to the use of treaties and other instruments. In practice it may not necessarily, in itself, achieve this aim, if the role of the Treaty Office is not widely understood and respected.

While most States and IOs designate the central authority for *treaty* procedures clearly in an official published document, whether legislation, administrative guidance or both,[22] it is less common to designate a central authority for non-binding international instruments. It is even less common to do so in legislation. Nevertheless, in some States, the responsibility for certain types of international instruments beyond the category of treaties is specified by law.

An example of the legislative approach is Vietnam, where the MFA is assigned *by legislation* as the body with central responsibility to manage and co-ordinate *both* treaties *and* certain types of international agreements of

[20] See the section on 'Where Should the Treaty Office (or Centralised Treaty Procedure Functions) Be Located?' in Chapter 2 at 53–60.

[21] See the section on 'Should the Treaty Office Handle Other Kinds of International Instruments?' in Chapter 2 at 70–1.

[22] See the section on 'Providing Guidance on Treaty Procedures across the Government or IO' in Chapter 2 at 76–8.

a non-treaty nature. According to Vietnam's Law on Treaties 2016, a 'treaty' is:

> an agreement in written form concluded in the name of the State or in the name of the Government of the Socialist Republic of Vietnam with a foreign contracting party, that gives rise to, changes or terminates rights and obligations of the Socialist Republic of Vietnam under international law.[23]

The law sets out in chapter IX the central responsibilities of the MFA for treaties, and the obligations of all relevant ministries, agencies and local authorities to co-ordinate with the MFA in the exercise of treaty-related State management.

Vietnam also has an Ordinance on Conclusion and Implementation of International Agreements 2007, which defines an international agreement as:

> a written agreement on international cooperation concluded in the name of a central state agency, a provincial-level agency or an organization's central body within the scope of its functions, tasks and powers with one or more than one foreign party.[24]

The foreign party has to be of a similar type (not a State or government) and its contents may not include certain subjects of high importance such as peace, sovereignty and human rights. The Ordinance provides that such agreements are 'only binding on the agency concluding the international agreement, without giving rise to international legal rights and obligations of the Vietnamese State or Government'. It sets out detailed rules for the conclusion and implementation of these agreements, specifying procedures that are different from, and lighter than, treaty procedures.

For example, Vietnam's Law on Treaties makes it mandatory to 'deposit, keep custody and provide certified copy of, and publish and register treaties', whereas the Ordinance requires only the 'Making of statistics on and archive of international agreements'. Central responsibility is assigned to the MFA for the conclusion and management of international agreements, and the Ordinance imposes an obligation on other ministries, agencies and authorities to co-ordinate with the MFA in these matters (similar to the obligation of co-operation in relation to treaties).[25] It has thus been made very clear to all

[23] Law on Treaties, 9 April 2016, art 2(1). This law was adopted by the XIIIth National Assembly of the Socialist Republic of Vietnam at its 11th session. The full text in its original language (Vietnamese) can be accessed at: Vietnam's National Legal Normative Documents Database http://vbpl.vn/TW/Pages/vbpq-van-ban-goc.aspx?ItemID=101899 accessed 9 September 2018. An unofficial English translation version is available at: Vietnam's National Legal Normative Documents Database http://vbpl.vn/TW/Pages/vbpqen-toanvan.aspx?ItemID=11039 accessed 9 September 2018.

[24] Ordinance No: 33/2007/PL-UBTVQH11 on Conclusion and Implementation of International Agreements, 20 April 2007, art 2(1). The Ordinance was adopted by the Standing Committee of the National Assembly of the Socialist Republic of Vietnam. The text in English translation is available at: Ministry of Justice of Vietnam www.moj.gov.vn/vbpq/en/Lists/Vn%20bn%20php%20lut/View_Detail.aspx?ItemID=3691 accessed 9 September 2018.

[25] ibid arts 2(1), 3(1), 4(4), 5, 5(4) and 6 and Chapter IV.

officials concerned that any queries or doubts about the status of a particular text must be referred to the MFA for guidance. It is worth noting, however, that even this Ordinance, detailed though it is, does not cover all types of international instruments beyond treaties. For example, it is silent on the question of non-binding arrangements entered into by the Vietnamese Government with another government. The Vietnamese Government has indicated its plan to draft a new Law on International Agreements which might cover non-binding instruments concluded by the Government and a foreign party.[26]

More commonly, governments use administrative regulations or guidance to prescribe the ministry or units responsible for treaty-like international instruments. For example, the Australian treaty handbook sets out the treaty responsibilities of the Treaties Secretariat, which is located within the DFAT's International Legal Branch.[27] It also advises that 'DFAT's International Legal Branch is responsible for, and should be consulted on, all aspects of the negotiation, conclusion, collection, formatting, tabling, publishing and interpretation of treaties *and arrangements of less than treaty status*' (emphasis added), and that 'The text of a proposed arrangement of less than treaty status should be forwarded to the Treaties Secretariat for clearance prior to its finalisation'.[28] This clearly recognises the need for treaty experts to ensure that each instrument has been correctly characterised.

The New Zealand administrative manuals set out the leading role of the Ministry of Foreign Affairs and Trade in relation to other government departments and agencies, and include the injunction: 'Proposals to enter into international treaties *and arrangements* require consultation with the Legal Division of Ministry of Foreign Affairs and Trade at an early stage.'[29] (Emphasis added; the word 'arrangements' here refers to non-binding instruments.)

The UK treaty practice manual similarly sets out the responsibility of all government departments for consulting the FCO on the drafting of non-binding international instruments (which it refers to as 'MOUs'):

> The FCO is responsible for Foreign and Commonwealth policy aspects of all treaties, as well as for dealing with questions of form and procedure. It must also consider points of international law. This remains the case even when the negotiation of the treaty is led by other government departments (OGDs) i.e. the department which will carry out the treaty's provisions. FCO Legal Advisers and FCO Treaty Section must be given the opportunity to comment on the drafts of all treaties under negotiation to ensure that

[26] See Government News, 'Proposing to Draft A Law on International Agreements' (29 January 2018) (in Vietnamese) http://baochinhphu.vn/Chinh-sach-moi/De-nghi-xay-dung-Luat-Thoa-thuan-quoc-te/328528.vgp accessed 9 September 2018.

[27] *Treaties Secretariat* (n 5) para 16. [28] ibid para 29.

[29] *New Zealand Ministry of Foreign Affairs and Trade* (n 7) 3.

they are drafted in accordance with correct international practice. The same applies to MoUs.[30]

The US Department of State's 'Guidance on Non-Binding Documents' indicates the central role of its Treaty Office in determining whether an international instrument is binding or not. This role is not itself enforceable by law, but the guidance indicates that legal consequences flow from the characterisation of a document:

> The Office of Treaty Affairs encourages agencies and offices to share the texts of proposed non-binding documents with the office, which is responsible by law for determining whether a particular document is a binding 'international agreement' for purposes of reporting to Congress. Our determination is made on the basis of a number of criteria, including the identity and mutual intention of those entities involved, rather than simply the form or title of the document.[31]

Which is the better practice – establishing centralised responsibilities for international instruments other than treaties by legislation or by administrative procedures? In Chapter 2 we looked at the relative advantages of allocating central responsibility for treaty functions by legislation or by administrative means. With regard to responsibility for non-treaty instruments, the balance of advantage will also be different for each State. It is however less common for non-treaties to be addressed in legislation. There are a number of reasons for this: for example, the difficulty of defining categories of non-treaty instruments and keeping abreast of the ever-growing range of bodies that engage in dealings with their international counterparts. Administrative guidance is more flexible and so can be more readily adapted to address new problems.

Training Programmes for all Officials with International Responsibilities

No matter how clear the legislation, circulars or guidance manuals may be, they will never be enough on their own. In a seminar or classroom environment the issues can be explained more fully, brought to life with real examples, and discussed in the way that is most relevant to treaty officials' work. All officials who may have international dealings or handle international documents should ideally receive basic training on treaties early in their career, which should include a comparison of treaties with other kinds of international instruments. It is also important for more specialised and refresher training to be available to officials as they progress through their careers, especially when moving into roles that have a greater or different international focus. As the types and uses of international instruments evolve over time,

30 *Treaty Section* (n 9) s 1.

31 US Department of State, 'Guidance on Non-Binding Documents', www.state.gov/s/l/treaty/guidance/ accessed 19 November 2018.

governments and IOs may need to devise customised training programmes that reflect new priorities for particular groups of officials. For example, in a State where regional authorities are acquiring greater autonomy, their use of non-binding international instruments may be an important area to clarify. A government whose domestic ministries and agencies are becoming more involved in multilateral standard-setting forums might need to devise training for officials in technical subject areas to help them understand the nature of the international documents they are dealing with.

Some examples of good practice can be found in, among others, the practice of the UK and its devolved regions, and Vietnam. The UK's FCO organises training programmes in international law for legal advisers across all government departments and agencies. These include workshops on the law and practice of treaties, with guidance on treaties and non-binding international instruments. In addition, FCO Treaty Section officials periodically visit other government departments to deliver training seminars to a wide range of lawyers and administrators. The Scottish Government and the Welsh Government (of devolved regions of the UK) also provide training programmes in public international law for their lawyers and policy officials. They include how to distinguish between treaties and non-binding instruments, and when they are used. As mentioned in Chapter 2, the Vietnamese MFA has issued a Handbook on Treaties and a Handbook on International Agreements, containing guidance on the procedures to conclude and implement treaties and other kinds of international instruments.[32] Several training workshops have been organised for officials at the central and local levels.[33]

These examples illustrate the PLATO principles in action:

- 'Professional': treaty practice needs to be recognised by high-level authorities as specialised work requiring expert knowledge, training and expertise.
- 'Legal': legal requirements met; lawyers fully engaged.
- 'Transparent': clear and easy to understand, available and accessible in practice, actively disseminated.
- 'Organised': written operating procedures, centralisation.

These examples are also consistent with the recommendations of the Singapore Workshop.[34] In particular, the following actions were identified by participants

[32] See *The World and Vietnam Report* (n 12). The Handbooks are, however, published in Vietnamese only and not available for access on the internet.

[33] See The World and Vietnam Report, 'Ten-Year Review of the Implementation of the Ordinance on Conclusion and Implementation of International Agreements' (in Vietnamese) http://baoquocte.vn/preview_article/b3dccd29b4556bd17c0ac691c7555636/tong-ket-10-nam-thi-hanh-phap-lenh-ve-thoa-thuan-quoc-te-59127.html accessed 9 September 2018.

[34] See the section on 'How Have the Examples of Good Treaty Practice in this Handbook been Selected?' in Chapter 1 at 18. The workshop report is on the BIICL and CIL websites. See CIL and BIICL, 'Workshop on Treaty Law and Practice: Workshop Report', (BIICL,

as ones for each ASEAN Member State to consider taking, in order to help improve its own national treaty practice:

> Recommendation 9: Distinguish clearly between treaties and non-binding international instruments; when negotiating a new international instrument clarify with other parties whether it is intended to be binding and ensure it is drafted appropriately; involve government international lawyers in drafting; ensure all officials understand the consequences and effects of concluding a treaty as opposed to a non-binding instrument; ensure appropriate handling of the instrument according to its status;
>
> Recommendation 10: Clarify the role of the treaty office in relation to non-binding treaty-like documents.[35]

Definition of a Treaty in International Law

International lawyers generally use the term 'treaties' to mean instruments recognised as such by the international law of treaties, as reflected in VCLT 1969[36] and VCLT 1986.[37] These two definitions do not exhaustively define all types of treaties recognised (or arguably recognised) by customary international law, but they set out an uncontroversial core. The two definitions most commonly referred to by international lawyers are these:

Article 2(1)(a) VCLT 1969

1. For the purposes of the present Convention:
   (a) 'treaty' means an international agreement concluded between States in written form and governed by international law, whether embodied in a single instrument or in two or more related instruments and whatever its particular designation;

Article 2(1)(a) VCLT 1986

1. For the purposes of the present Convention:
   (a) 'treaty' means an international agreement governed by international law and concluded in written form:
      (i) between one or more States and one or more international organizations; or
      (ii) between international organizations,

   whether that agreement is embodied in a single instrument or in two or more related instruments and whatever its particular designation;

19 January 2012) www.biicl.org/documents/41_singapore_treaty_workshop_full_report.pdf accessed 9 September 2018, and CIL and BIICL, 'Workshop on Treaty Law and Practice: Workshop Report Executive Summary', (BIICL) www.biicl.org/documents/40_singapore_treaty_workshop_executive_summary.pdf accessed 9 September 2018.

35 ibid 10.

36 VCLT 1969 (adopted 23 May 1969, entered into force 27 January 1980) 1155 UNTS 331.

37 VCLT 1986 (adopted 21 March 1986, not yet in force) 25 ILM 543 http://legal.un.org/ilc/texts/instruments/english/conventions/1_2_1986.pdf. accessed 9 September 2018.

Combining these two provisions, a 'treaty' could be defined as an international agreement between States, or between IOs, or between any combination thereof, governed by international law and in written form,[38] whether embodied in a single instrument or in two or more related instruments and whatever its particular designation.

While this definition is proposed here as the best definition to use for everyday working purposes, it is not a complete definition of all types of treaties. It is important to note that each definition in the VCLT 1969 and 1986 begins 'For the purposes of the present Convention'. The VCLT 1969 applies only to treaties between States; the 1986 VCLT applies only to treaties between one or more States and one or more IOs, and treaties between IOs; and both contain an important Article 3 headed 'International agreements not within the scope of the present Convention', which makes clear that the fact that the Convention does not apply to various other kinds of international agreements does not affect the legal force of those agreements. For example, Article 3 of both VCLT 1969 and 1986 expressly provides that the fact that the Convention does not apply to international agreements 'not in written form' does not affect the legal force of oral agreements under other rules of international law (customary international law).

Using these VCLT definitions of 'treaty' does not mean that under the general customary international law of treaties there cannot be other kinds of treaties, rather that there is no universal agreement on a broader definition.

Key Points in the Definition of Treaty in International Law

The following parts break down the key points in the definition of treaty in international law.

'governed by international law'

This phrase distinguishes treaties from two other kinds of international instruments – those governed by a system of national law (contracts) and non-binding international instruments.

The requirement that, to qualify as a treaty, an agreement must be 'governed by international law' can be a difficult question of legal interpretation. It is necessary to determine whether the parties intended their agreement to be governed by international law, as evidenced by the words used in the treaty itself. The first thing to look for is an 'applicable law' provision in the treaty, that is, a clause that expressly states what the applicable law of the agreement is. If it states that the agreement is governed by international law, it is a treaty (if the other elements of the definition of treaty are present). If it states that it is

[38] Treaties are normally in written form. Treaties may be concluded orally – this is not precluded by the law of treaties, rather, such agreements are outside the scope of the VCLTs. As oral treaties are apparently rare, and anyway would not be capable of being handled as treaties unless recorded in writing, it was decided unnecessary to consider them in this Handbook.

governed by the law of a particular State, it is not a treaty. If there is no applicable law provision, it is necessary to look at the whole document, as well as the context in which it was concluded, and any related acts and statements.[39]

'embodied in a single instrument or in two or more related instruments'

This phrase makes clear that the form of a treaty is flexible. It can be an exchange of notes or letters, or a series of notes or letters, or a combination of other kinds of documents. The documents do not need to be physically united, as long as the connection between them is evident. There is no technical meaning to the word 'instrument'; it is not defined in the VCLT 1969 or 1986. In ordinary English usage, 'instrument' simply means a formal or legal document.[40] Any permanent written form may be used, so it is possible to conclude a treaty by email or other electronic means. However, when the means of communication lacks formality, for example, when there is an ordinary piece of paper with no official stamp, ribbon or seal, or a series of emails, there is a greater need for clear evidence to show that the parties had reached an agreement that they intended to be binding in international law. Without this, its treaty status may be queried or overlooked at a later date.[41]

'whatever its particular designation'

This phrase makes clear that a treaty does not have to be called a treaty; it may have another name or none at all. Titles commonly used for treaties include: convention, charter, protocol, agreement, statute. Titles less commonly used include MOU, declaration, principles. This may seem like the saying 'A rose by any other name smells as sweet'. But how do we know it is a rose? Many international instruments look similar to treaties but are not treaties. A text might look international simply because it has participants from or in different States. It may look like a treaty simply because it contains some kind of agreement, understanding, undertaking, promise, formal statement or something of that kind.

It is important to note that the name given to the document under the domestic law of any of the parties has no bearing on its status in international law. In some domestic legal systems, treaties are categorised according to

[39] By analogy with the General Rule of Interpretation of a treaty set out in Article 31 VCLT 1969, and the Supplementary Means of Interpretation set out in Article 32 VCLT 1969. Strictly speaking, these rules apply to the interpretation of a document which has already been determined to be a treaty, but the method of interpretation set out in those rules are equally apt to make the prior determination as to whether the document is a treaty. See A Aust, *Modern Treaty Law and Practice* (3rd edn, CUP 2013) 17–18; R Gardiner, *Treaty Interpretation* (2nd edn, OUP 2015) 20–21; D Hollis, 'Defining Treaties' in D Hollis (ed), *The Oxford Guide to Treaties* (OUP 2012) 11–45.

[40] *Oxford Dictionary of English* (3rd edn, OUP 2010).

[41] See *Aust* (n 39) 19–20.

constitutional requirements; for example, those that require the prior approval of the legislature are called 'treaties', while those that do not are called 'executive agreements'. Executive agreements also have the status of treaty under international law if they meet the criteria in the definition set out above.

The Parties Are States and/or IOs

A treaty has (normally) to be concluded among States, or among IOs, or among one or more States and one or more IOs. If an agreement's signatories or participants include other types of entities, such as sub-State (such as provincial, regional or local) authorities, parliaments, NGOs, corporations, private persons, international associations of private entities (such as Chambers of Commerce), this normally indicates that the agreement is not a treaty.

There are a few exceptions to this. Occasionally, territorial entities that are not States may become party to a treaty. For example, the Marrakesh Agreement Establishing the World Trade Organization, 1994 provides for accession by any State or 'separate customs territory' under certain conditions.[42] Chinese Taipei and Hong Kong, China are both members of the World Trade Organization (WTO).[43] Even more occasionally, an international entity that is not generally considered to be an IO may become party to a treaty. For example, the Antarctic Treaty Consultative Meeting (which has not been recognised as an IO by the Consultative Parties to the Antarctic Treaty) concluded a headquarters agreement with the Argentine Republic. Its conclusion of this particular treaty was authorised by the Consultative Parties in a formal decision.[44] These examples are unusual exceptions to the general rule, and the important point is that they were possible only because the States concerned agreed to it. Entities that are neither a State nor an IO cannot enter into a treaty on their own authority. Any treaty in which other entities are participating, or where such participation is proposed, should always be considered very carefully by international law advisers.

[42] Marrakesh Agreement Establishing the World Trade Organization (adopted 15 April 1994, entered into force 1 January 1995) 1867 UNTS 14 art XII. For an example of a bilateral treaty to which one party is a sub-State entity acting under State authority, see n 15 in Chapter 5 at 167.

[43] World Trade Organization (WTO), 'Members and Observers' www.wto.org/english/thewto_e/whatis_e/tif_e/org6_e.htm accessed 9 September 2018.

[44] Headquarters Agreement for the Secretariat of the Antarctic Treaty (signed 10 May 2010, entered into force 10 May 2010) 2775 UNTS 321. See also Measure No. 1 (2003) on the Secretariat of the Antarctic Treaty (adopted 20 June 2003) art V. The Measure was adopted by the Secretariat of the Antarctic Treaty. Both documents are available at: Secretariat of the Antarctic Treaty, 'Key documents of the Antarctic Treaty System' www.ats.aq/e/ats_keydocs.htm accessed 9 September 2018.

Other International Instruments that Are 'Treaty-Like' but not Treaties

Treaties are only one kind of international instrument. As mentioned above, there are many other kinds of international instruments, some of which have legal status of some kind, and some of which do not. An 'instrument' could be any formal or legal document. It may look 'international' simply because it deals with matters that cross borders or involves people from more than one country. It may look 'treaty-like' because it refers to one or more governments or IOs, or it seems to set rules for conduct that require action by public authorities, or perhaps because it has some of the trappings of a treaty, such as a preamble, testimonium, official signatures or ribbons and seals. We use the term 'treaty-like' simply to indicate that the focus here is on the type of international instrument that could cross the desk of an official in government or an IO, and which could conceivably be mistaken for a treaty or handled alongside treaties. We are not concerned with any other kind of international instrument, such as an international airline ticket or a contract between private persons in different countries, where no such confusion could possibly arise. There cannot be a precise definition of 'treaty-like' because there is no outward limit to the types of document that might be generated in international affairs with the potential for being confused with a treaty.

From a legal point of view, there are broadly three categories which a treaty-like instrument may fall into:

1. instruments which are binding under international law;
2. instruments which are binding under a national legal system; and
3. instruments which are not binding under any system of law.

These categories are shown in more detail in Figure 3.1.

Most Treaty Offices deal primarily or solely with treaties. Treaty-like instruments may rarely cross their desks, but when they do, it is important that treaty officials are able to recognise what they are and forward them to the appropriate place. In practice, it is non-binding international instruments that are most likely to be confused with treaties and sent to the Treaty Office in error; or, conversely, treaties may be mistaken for non-binding instruments and not sent to the Treaty Office. There may be occasions when even the most experienced international lawyers are unsure whether a particular written commitment amounts to a treaty or not, and then careful decisions will need to be made as to how to handle it.

There is no reason why, if it is convenient for the administration concerned, a Treaty Office should not be tasked to manage other categories of international instruments alongside its treaty collection, for example by maintaining texts, lists or indexes, or carrying out publishing functions, provided that this is done with a clear understanding that they are distinct from treaties.

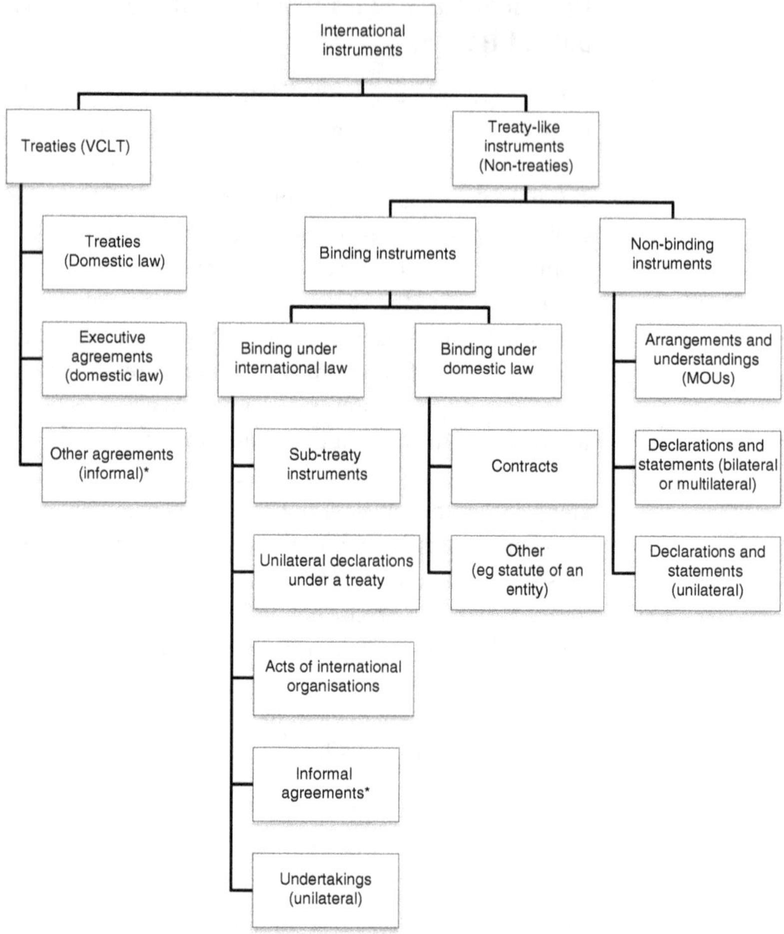

Figure 3.1 Classification of treaties and other international instruments (© Jill Barrett)
Note: The asterisk indicates where an instrument may be formally recognised as a treaty by some and not by others, but is clearly binding in international law.

Treaty-Like Instruments that Are Binding under International Law

International instruments that are not treaties may be binding in accordance with other rules of international law. For example, an act of an IO may be binding in international law if the constitution and rules of that organisation confer that effect on it. It is well known that certain resolutions of the UNSC are mandatory and binding on all UN Member States under Chapter VII of the UN Charter. Security Council resolutions are not treaties; they are not agreements concluded among the UN Member States, but rather acts of a UN organ which is empowered to adopt binding resolutions.

Unilateral acts by States can in certain circumstances be binding in international law. A State may undertake international obligations vis-à-vis other

States by means of a formal public statement or written communication. A document containing such an undertaking is another example of a type of treaty-like instrument which may be binding under international law. A high-profile example of this occurred in the *Nuclear Tests* case where the ICJ held that France was legally bound by publicly given undertakings to cease carrying out atmospheric nuclear tests.[45]

More recently, the *Chagos arbitration* illustrates another way in which undertakings can sometimes become binding in international law by virtue of rules that have nothing to do with the law of treaties.[46] An agreement was made in 1965 between the UK and the Mauritius Council of Ministers regarding the detachment of the Chagos Archipelago, in anticipation of the independence of Mauritius which took effect in 1968.[47] This agreement was not a treaty, and could not be, since it was not concluded between two sovereign States, but rather between one sovereign State and representatives of a people under its colonial governance. Nor could it be governed by international law at that time. However, when in 2015 Mauritius brought arbitral proceedings under the UNCLOS against the UK in relation to the declaration of a marine protected area around the Chagos Islands, the Arbitral Tribunal considered the status of the UK's undertakings. The Tribunal found that the UK's undertakings originally made in 1965 had subsequently become binding upon the UK.[48] This was on the basis of the international law principle of 'estoppel', which applied because of the subsequent conduct of the parties, in particular the fact that the UK had repeated the undertakings many times since independence, and Mauritius had relied upon them to its detriment. None of the documents concerned were classified as a treaty.

There are various other kinds of treaty-like instruments that may be binding or have legal effects under international law. Some of them could be mistaken for a treaty, or for a non-binding instrument, by an official who is not experienced in treaty law and practice (and even experienced officials may occasionally be caught out by this, as the above cases show). Those who engage in international dealings therefore need to be aware of them and when to seek legal advice about them. Treaty officials also need to be able to distinguish them from treaties, and, if they receive such documents for processing, know what they should do with them. Treaty procedures do not apply to them; for example, there is no ratification process and there is no registration procedure at the UN for them. Treaty Offices therefore do not usually deal with other kinds of international law instruments at all.

45 *Nuclear Tests (Australia v France)* [1974] ICJ Rep 253, 267–71; *Nuclear Test (New Zealand v France)* [1974] ICJ Rep 457, 472–75. See J Crawford, *Brownlie's Principles of International Law* (8th edn, OUP 2012) 416–18.

46 *Chagos Marine Protected Area Arbitration (Mauritius v United Kingdom)* (Award) [2015] PCA 2011-03.

47 ibid para 77. This particular paragraph in the Award deals with the Record of a Meeting held in Lancaster House at 2.30 pm on Thursday 23 September 1965. See also ibid para 418.

48 ibid Dispositif, para B(1–3).

Treaty-Like Instruments that Are Binding under a Domestic Legal System

Governments and IOs sometimes enter into agreements that are binding under a system of national law. When the only parties to such an agreement are States and/or IOs, it might easily be mistaken for a treaty. If it is an agreement concluded under domestic law, it is most likely a contract or something similar. Unlike treaties, the possible parties to a contract are not limited to States and IOs – they could (if they wished to) include any private person or legal entity that has capacity to enter into a contract under that system of domestic law. This may be one of the factors in favour of choosing a domestic law contract as the vehicle for an agreement, where it is appropriate for State agencies and private entities to participate on an equal footing. For an instrument to be binding under a system of domestic law, a particular jurisdiction must be specified in the contract or be made clear in some other way. It could specify the law of a named State, such as the law of the People's Republic of China, or the law of France, or it could specify the law of a particular jurisdiction within a State, such as the law of Scotland or the law of New York.

An example of a treaty-like instrument created under national law is the Statutes of the Renewable Energy and Energy Efficiency Partnership (REEEP). The REEEP is an association established under Austrian law, comprising 385 member organisations, which include businesses, NGOs, industry associations, financial institutions and other civil society entities, as well as 45 national governments. It has an international secretariat hosted at the offices of the United Nations Industrial Development Organization (UNIDO) in Vienna. Although it is an organisation with international characteristics in which governments participate, its governing statute is not a treaty, but rather an instrument of domestic law.[49]

The REEEP concluded a Regional Secretariat Agreement, 2011 with the General Secretariat of the Organization of American States in Washington DC. It is a bilateral agreement that in some respects resembles a treaty in the way it is set out. Its 'Final Provisions' however contain a clause on 'Governing Law and Dispute Resolutions' which provides:

> This Agreement, disputes or legal issues [arising] out of or in connection with the Agreement . . . are governed by the Austrian law, including Austria's conflict of law rules.[50]

This makes clear beyond doubt that this agreement is not a treaty, but rather a creature of domestic law, in the nature of a contract. Even though it also

[49] See REEEP, 'REEEP Legal Status' www.reeep.org/reeep-legal-status accessed 9 September 2018 and P Pattberg, K Szulecki, S Chan and A Mert, 'Assessing the Role and Relevance of the Renewable Energy and Energy Efficiency Partnership (REEEP) in Global Sustainability Governance' in D Vollmer, *Enhancing the Effectiveness of Sustainability Partnerships* (The National Academies Press, Washington DC 2009).

[50] Regional Secretariat Agreement (signed 24 May 2011, entered into force 1 April 2011) SLA 123/2011.

provides for arbitration of disputes under the United Nations Commission on International Trade Law (UNCITRAL) Arbitration Rules, the arbitrators would be obliged to apply Austrian law to the substance of the dispute, not international law. This is another example of a treaty-like instrument that is binding in domestic law.[51]

Treaty-Like Instruments that Are Not Binding under any System of Law

There is an even larger variety – perhaps infinite – of non-binding international instruments. They include bilateral and multilateral commitments, agreements, arrangements, understandings, standards, guides, declarations of intent and so forth, which the participants intend to honour but which are not intended to establish legal obligations under international law or any system of domestic law. They may be entered into in a very informal way such as by email correspondence, or with great fanfare and formality such as signature by Heads of State during a State visit. They may concern matters of high political importance or routine technical arrangements. They are normally (and should) be regarded by those who enter into them as binding in a political or moral sense. There is an expectation that the other participant(s) will do what they say they will do, unless a change of circumstances is clearly communicated. However there is no entitlement to compensation or legal remedies if another party fails to deliver.

The variety of such instruments is infinite because the range of actors has no limit. Since they are not governed by international law, the rules in the law of treaties about who has capacity to enter into treaties do not apply. Anyone can enter into a non-binding arrangement with anyone else. When the participants are from different countries or IOs, the document has an international dimension. It is common for both public and private institutions such as universities, research institutes, local authorities, libraries, museums, companies, police forces, regulatory authorities, professional associations, and so on, to make co-operative arrangements with their counterparts in other countries. A common name for such a text is MOU. When they declare common goals they might call their text a 'Declaration', 'Action Plan', 'Code of Conduct' or 'Guidelines'. Other names commonly used include Understanding, Arrangement, Minutes, Recommendation, Resolution, or the text may have no title at all.

When the participants are clearly private institutions or public authorities that are not part of central government, it is unlikely that anyone would mistake the text for a treaty or even that it would be seen by government officials. In other words, the text is unlikely to be at all 'treaty-like', but this is a question of perception, not definition.

[51] For examples of cases where the UNCITRAL arbitration rules have been used to settle a contractual dispute between a state entity and a private party, see Permanent Court of Arbitration, 'Cases' https://pca-cpa.org/en/cases/ accessed 9 September 2018.

Governments, ministries and agencies can also enter into non-binding arrangements, as can individuals who represent them, including Heads of State and government, ministers and officials. When an instrument is concluded in the name of a government or ministry or its representative, there is a risk of it being later mistaken for a treaty, especially if its content is presented in treaty-style language and format which may give the impression that the participants intended it to create legal obligations. If they do not, they need to take care to ensure that this is clear. It is always wise to run the text past the Treaty Office or international law advisers so they can check that a treaty is not being inadvertently created. The same applies to IOs when they wish to enter into non-binding arrangements with other IOs or States. The point here is that it is not only the intention of those drafting the text that counts. The general principle that applies to assess the legal effect of a text was summarised by the Tribunal in the *Chagos arbitration* as follows:

> While the Tribunal readily accepts that States are free in their international relations to enter into even very detailed agreements that are intended to have only political effect, the intention for an agreement to be either binding or non-binding as a matter of law must be clearly expressed or is otherwise a matter for objective determination. As recalled by the ICJ in *Aegean Sea Continental Shelf*, 'in determining what was indeed the nature of the act or transaction embodied in the [agreement], the [Tribunal] must have regard above all to its actual terms and to the particular circumstances in which it was drawn up' ((Greece v. Turkey), Judgment, I.C.J. Reports 1978, p. 3 at p. 39, para. 96).[52]

Moreover, even when a text is non-binding by all objective criteria, it might nevertheless give rise to legal effects. This may occur where a rule of international law comes into play due to other surrounding circumstances and the subsequent conduct of the parties. The *Chagos arbitration* shows how the principle of estoppel in international law may operate to bind a State to undertakings that were non-binding at the time they were made. The circumstances of that case were very unusual. Non-binding texts are sometimes used by courts and tribunals to interpret a related legal text. These kinds of risks should be borne in mind by anyone who is drafting or checking a non-binding international instrument.

Some Examples of Non-Binding International Instruments: Published, Reported and Unreported

The obligation in Article 102 of the UN Charter to register treaties and international agreements with the UN Secretariat, and its obligation to publish them, does not apply to non-binding instruments. It is for each State and IO to determine its own policy regarding publication, in accordance with any relevant domestic laws. In practice, while many non-binding international instruments are published, many (probably many more) are not, especially where

[52] *Chagos Arbitration* (n 46) para 426.

there are only two or a small number of participants. It is therefore impossible to have a complete overview of international practice regarding the use of these instruments, or even a complete picture of the practice of any single State or IO. The following are examples of non-binding instruments whose texts have been published:

- OSPAR Recommendation 2012/5 for a Risk-Based Approach to the Management of Produced Water Discharges from Offshore Installations, 2012;[53]
- The UN Guiding Principles on Business and Human Rights, 2011;[54]
- IMO Guidelines for Ships Operating in Polar Waters, 2010;[55]
- The Afghanistan Compact between the Islamic Republic of Afghanistan and the international community, 2006;[56]
- Memorandum of Understanding between Norway and the United Kingdom on co-operation on polar research and cultural heritage, 2017;[57]
- Memorandum of Understanding between Finland, Norway and Russia on co-operation on the Green Belt of Fennoscandia, 2010;[58] and
- Declaration on the Conduct of Parties in the South China Sea, 2002 (DOC).[59]

Governments and IOs sometimes make known the existence of non-binding texts without publishing the text itself, for example, by press release, media briefing or website summary, as in the following cases:

53 OSPAR Recommendation 2012/5 for a Risk-Based Approach to the Management of Produced Water Discharges from Offshore Installations, OSPAR 12/22/1, Annex 18 (entered into force 29 June 2012).

54 UNHRC Res 17/31, 'Report of the Special Representative of the Secretary-General on the issue of human rights, transnational corporations and other business enterprises, 'Guiding Principles on Business and Human Rights: Implementing the United Nations "Protect, Respect and Remedy" Framework', 21 March 2011.

55 IMO, *Guidelines for Ships Operating in Polar Waters* (IMO Publication, London 2010) www.imo.org/Publications/Documents/Attachments/Pages%20from%20E19E.pdf accessed 9 September 2018.

56 The Afghanistan Compact between the Islamic Republic of Afghanistan and the international community (adopted 1 February 2006) www.nato.int/isaf/docu/epub/pdf/afghanistan_compact.pdf accessed 9 September 2018.

57 Memorandum of Understanding between the Kingdom of Norway and the United Kingdom of Great Britain and Northern Ireland on Cooperation on Polar Research and Cultural Heritage (signed 23 February 2017) www.gov.uk/government/publications/uk-norway-memorandum-of-understanding-on-polar-research-and-cultural-heritage accessed 9 September 2018.

58 Memorandum of Understanding between the Ministry of the Environment of the Republic of Finland, the Ministry of the Environment of the Kingdom of Norway and the Ministry of Natural Resources and Environment of the Russian Federation on cooperation on the development of the Green Belt of Fennoscandia (adopted 17 February 2010) www.ym.fi/download/noname/%7B72447573-3434-43BB-B505-B02FBBAEDE3B%7D/104556 accessed 9 September 2018.

59 Declaration on the Conduct of Parties in the South China Sea (adopted 14 November 2002) (DOC) http://asean.org/?static_post=declaration-on-the-conduct-of-parties-in-the-south-china-sea-2 accessed 9 September 2018.

- Japan and China concluded a framework for mutual prior notification of marine scientific research in 2001. The outline of the framework was published.[60]
- India and the UK announced a range of MOUs and agreements on technology, trade and investment, on the occasion of a visit by the Indian Prime Minister to the UK in 2018. A list of the titles of these governmental and non-governmental texts was published, but not the texts themselves.[61]
- The Indian Coast Guard has published a list of titles of MOUs that it has signed with the coast guard agencies of other States for co-operation on maritime issues relevant to coast guard work. Most of these texts are not published.[62]
- The Danish and Scottish governments signed an MOU to collaborate on low carbon heat, district heat systems and energy efficiency in buildings on 31 May 2018. A signing ceremony took place at the Scottish Parliament in Edinburgh and the signing was announced to the press by both sides, but the text has not been published.[63]

Non-Binding International Instruments: Terminology and Practical Issues

Questions that commonly vex officials in governments and IOs concern the differences between treaties and treaty-like non-binding international instruments: how to distinguish them? When is it appropriate to use one type rather than another? To what extent should non-binding instruments be treated like treaties? Should they be published? Can a non-binding instrument have legal effects? What happens if different parties take different views about the status of the same document?

[60] Ministry of Foreign Affairs of Japan, 'Press release' (in Japanese), cited in J Barrett et al., *Report on the Obligations of States under Articles 74(3) and 83(3) of UNCLOS in respect of Undelimited Areas* (BIICL, London 2016) para 391.

[61] Foreign and Commonwealth Office, 'Policy paper: UK–India Memorandums of Understanding and agreements' (18 April 2018) www.gov.uk/government/publications/uk-and-india-mous-and-agreements/uk-india-announcements accessed 9 September 2018.

[62] For a list of MoUs concluded by the Indian Coast Guard, see Indian Coast Guard, 'Memorandum of Understanding', (Ministry of Defence) https://indiancoastguard.gov.in/content/1732_3_MoU.aspx?format=Print&format=Print accessed 9 September 2018. Most of the texts are unpublished. It appears to the authors that they are intended to be non-binding arrangements, but the authors are not aware of the views of the governments concerned as to their status. None of the texts have been registered with the UN under Article 102 UN Charter.

[63] Scotland is a devolved region of the UK. The signing of this MOU was announced by Denmark in a press release. See Ministry of Foreign Affairs of Denmark, 'Danish Energy Minister Signs Agreement with Scottish Government' (May 2018) http://storbritannien.um.dk/en/the-trade-council/projects/district-heating/danish-minister-of-energy-lars-christian-lilleholt-signs-energy-agreement-with-scottish-government/ accessed 9 September 2018. The signing of the MoU has received wide media attention. See for example, Network, 'Danish and Scottish governments sign heat MoU' (31 May 2018) https://networks.online/gphsn/news/1001065/danish-scottish-governments-sign-heat-mou accessed 9 September 2018.

The Name of the Document Does Not Determine its Legal Status

A document which meets the legal criteria for being a treaty is a treaty, whatever its particular designation. No matter how *non-binding* the title sounds, if the content and context make clear that it is governed by international law, it may be a treaty. Conversely, a document could be entitled 'treaty' or 'agreement', but if it is evident from its contents or context that it is not governed by international law, it is not a treaty. This can make the task of distinguishing treaties from non-binding international instruments difficult. The document signed by the Foreign Minister of Bahrain which was interpreted by the ICJ as a binding agreement to take the dispute with Qatar to the ICJ, was called 'Minutes'. Minutes of meetings do not usually have treaty status, but if an internationally binding agreement is entered into at the meeting, the record of the meeting could bind the parties.

The title 'MOU' is particularly apt to cause confusion. In the practice of many States, this title is used only for instruments which they consider to be political rather than legal. The practice of some States on this point is so consistent that the use of the title MOU may be taken as an indication of their intention that the instrument not be governed by international law. For example, Australia, Canada, New Zealand and the UK and many other States follow the same practice in this regard. However, in the practice of some other States, the title MOU is used for agreements which are treaties under international law, but which are classified for domestic law purposes as executive agreements (meaning that the approval of the legislature is not required). The United States, for example, follows this practice. When States with different practices conclude an MOU, it may be a treaty or it may not. Unsurprisingly, perhaps, some States appear to have no consistent practice, using the term MOU without regard to whether or not the document is intended to be a treaty. Some, such as New Zealand, seek to avoid using the title MOU at all because of the confusion it has generated.[64]

What Is the Best Generic Name for Non-Binding International Instruments?

The preference of the authors of this Handbook is to refer generically to non-binding international instruments, whatever their actual titles, as 'non-binding international instruments'. The word 'instrument' is neutral as to legal status; it means a legal or any other sort of document endowed with some degree of formality. 'International instruments' refers to the whole spectrum of instruments with international elements, binding and non-binding. The full range of possibilities and their relationships to one another are set out in Figure 3.1.

Some authors on treaty practice use the term 'MOU' to refer generically to all non-binding international instruments.[65] This term is also used in some

[64] *New Zealand Ministry of Foreign Affairs and Trade* (n 7) 32.

[65] See for example, *Aust* (n 39). The book's chapter 3 is entitled 'MOUs'. Aust's use of the term is explained on page 29.

government guidance manuals.[66] This Handbook does not follow this practice, as it is inconsistent with the principle that title does not determine legal status, and would risk adding to the already considerable confusion with regard to the status of an MOU.

A variety of other terms are used elsewhere. For example, the New Zealand treaty manual refers to non-binding international instruments as 'international arrangements' (in contrast to 'international agreements'). The US guidance refers to them as 'non-binding documents'. The Australian DFAT manual refers to them as 'instruments of less than treaty status'. The Australian terminology is not used in this Handbook, as it implies a legal hierarchy, whereas non-binding instruments are not in the same hierarchy as treaties at all. They are not subordinate to treaties, but a different animal altogether. (We use the term 'sub-treaty instruments' to refer to instruments adopted under treaties, which are subordinate to the parent treaty in question, and may be binding.) The Spanish circular uses the generic term *Acuerdos No Normativos* (non-binding agreements). There is no international consistency to the terminology because these instruments are not governed by international law, and have received little attention so far from legal writers. However, these practice manuals are all consistent in emphasising that it is not the name of a document which determines its legal status, but rather its contents and other factors.

How to Distinguish between Treaties and Non-Binding International Instruments

When a treaty or non-binding instrument is poorly drafted, others reading it later may find it difficult to tell what its legal status was intended to be. They will have to interpret it as best they can from its wording and related documents, and they may need to take steps to try to clarify its status. Determining whether or not the instrument is binding is an art rather than a science. These are the kinds of points to look for:

Study the Text Itself

The following points may be helpful in studying the text of an instrument to determine its status:

- *Title*: the title does not determine the status of the document and may be misleading. It should be considered as no more than an initial pointer (see below).
- *Signatories/parties/participants*: Look at the introductory sentence to see if the parties are listed, and look at the end to see if there are signatures. If they are limited to States/governments and/or IOs, it may be a treaty. If they

[66] See for example, *New Zealand Ministry of Foreign Affairs and Trade* (n 7) at 32 and UK Treaty Section (n 9) at 1.

include others such as private entities, NGOs, authorities of territories that are not States, it is probably not a treaty. If the signatories are mixed, look further at the final clauses to see if they all have the same status in the agreement. If they do, it is unlikely to be a treaty. If the parties are only States and IOs, with others participating in a more limited way, it could be a treaty.

- *Preamble*: treaties usually have a preamble that sets out the motivation and aims of the parties; non-binding instruments usually do not have a preamble but could have an introduction that serves the same purpose. If there is one, read it to see if it gives any indications. For example, '*Desiring* to clarify the law on' or '*Desiring* to establish rules to govern' would indicate a treaty, whereas '*Wishing* to encourage' or '*Aiming* to promote' might indicate a non-binding text.
- *The operative verb linked to the signatories/parties/participants' names at the beginning* (separated by the preamble if there is one): 'Have agreed as follows' or 'Undertake to perform the following obligations' indicates a treaty, whereas 'Record the following understandings' or 'Understand as follows' indicates a non-binding text.
- *Mandatory or hortatory language*: a treaty normally sets out obligations expressed in mandatory language (such as 'the parties shall/undertake to') whereas a non-binding text sets out intentions or understandings expressed in hortatory or permissive language (such as 'the participants will/intend to/may/should/will aim to'). Some treaties contain hortatory provisions mixed with mandatory ones, but it would be very unusual for a treaty to contain no mandatory provisions.
- *Specificity of obligations*: if the substance of the text is entirely aspirational, vague or unquantified (such as 'the participants will aim to co-operate to the extent possible'), it is unlikely to be a treaty. A treaty normally contains obligations or standards that are specific enough that performance against them could be assessed, although it can contain aspirational provisions as well.
- *Applicable law clause*: if there is one (there usually is not) it is likely to be found near the end with the final clauses. It may specify that the agreement is to be governed by international law (which means that it is a treaty); or that it is to be governed by the law of a particular State (which means it is a domestic law contract); or that it does not give rise to any legal rights or obligations (which means it is non-binding).
- *Settlement of disputes clause*: if there is provision for mandatory settlement of disputes by the ICJ or by an arbitral tribunal established under a treaty, it must be a treaty. If it provides only for disputes to be settled by negotiation or consultation, it could be a treaty or non-binding.
- *Consent to be bound and entry into force*: a treaty normally has provisions near the end (the 'final clauses') that specify which States or IOs may sign, ratify and/or accede to it, and how. It also normally specifies when it will enter into force. A non-binding instrument may have similar provisions, more usually expressed as 'commence operation' rather than 'enter into

force', but need not. If the text ends with signatures but no entry into force clause, or without either signatures or final clauses, it is indicative that it is non-binding.

- *Depositary*: if a depositary is specified, it indicates a treaty. If the text has a large number of signatories or participants and no depositary, it suggests it is probably non-binding.
- *Testimonium*: if the text ends with words along the following lines, it indicates a treaty:

  In witness whereof the undersigned, being duly authorised to that effect, have signed this [(Treaty/Agreement/Protocol)]; and

  Done at [place] this [day] of [month] [year] in the English and [other language] languages, both texts being equally authentic.

None of these elements can determine the status of the document alone; it is necessary to look at the totality of them. There may be contradictory indications within the same document. In that case, the next step is to look at other evidence outside the document itself.

Look at the Related Evidence

Other related evidence that can be taken into account, together with the elements above, includes the following:

- *Circumstances of conclusion*: look at how, when and where the instrument was concluded. Is there a record of the meeting at which it was adopted or signed? The meeting record may indicate how the negotiating parties viewed the legal status of the text.
- *UN registration*: look at the UN treaty website to see if that text has been registered by any party as a treaty under Article 102 UN Charter. If it has, it indicates the registering State's view that it is a treaty. If it has not been registered, however, it is not a reliable indication that it is not a treaty as there can be delays of months or years, and the requirement to register is sometimes overlooked.
- *Constitutional procedures*: if there is still doubt, it may be useful to look at what each party has done with the text in its own internal system. For example, if a State has published the text in its national treaty series, or submitted it to the legislature in accordance with constitutional treaty procedures, this provides clear evidence of that State's view that it is a treaty. If it has not done so, it may be more difficult to draw conclusions if the reason is unknown.

Disputes over whether a Text is a Treaty or Non-Binding International Instrument

If a difference of view comes to light after a dispute has arisen, the status of a document may be one of the issues that are taken to an international court or tribunal. This was vividly illustrated by the ICJ case between Qatar and Bahrain, in which a key issue was the status of the document recording their agreement to refer their dispute to the ICJ.[67] A more recent example is the case brought by the Philippines against China before an arbitral tribunal established under UNCLOS.[68] A key issue was the status of the DOC. China's position was that the DOC was a legally binding agreement, whereas the Philippines argued that it was not.[69] The Tribunal decided that it was not. It reasoned that:

> To constitute a binding agreement, an instrument must evince a clear intention to establish rights and obligations between the parties. Such clear intention is determined by reference to the instrument's actual terms and the particular circumstances of its adoption. The subsequent conduct of the parties to an instrument may also assist in determining its nature.[70]

The Tribunal observed that the DOC shared some hallmarks of an international treaty. However, after careful consideration of the elements that suggested binding obligations and those that pointed the other way, the Tribunal concluded that the DOC was not intended to create legal rights and obligations. The six paragraphs that set out the Tribunal's analysis of the legal status of the DOC are well worth reading as a guide to how to determine whether a text is binding or not, as well as how to draft one to have the desired effect:

> 213. To constitute a binding agreement, an instrument must evince a clear intention to establish rights and obligations between the parties. Such clear intention is determined by reference to the instrument's actual terms and the particular circumstances of its adoption. The subsequent conduct of the parties to an instrument may also assist in determining its nature. This test is accepted by both Parties and has been articulated in a number of international cases, including *Aegean Continental Shelf, Maritime Delimitation and Territorial Questions between Qatar and Bahrain (Qatar v. Bahrain)*, and *Land and Maritime Boundary (Cameroon v. Nigeria).*
>
> 214. Although the DOC is entitled a 'declaration' rather than a 'treaty' or 'agreement', the Tribunal acknowledges that international agreements may take a number of forms and be given a variety of names. The form or designation of an instrument is thus not decisive of its status as an agreement establishing legal obligations between the parties. The Tribunal observes that the DOC shares some hallmarks of an international treaty. It is a formal document with a preamble, it is signed by the foreign ministers of China and the ASEAN States, and the signatory States are described in the DOC as 'Parties'.

[67] See the section on 'Example of a Mistake about whether a Document is Binding in International Law' above at 82.

[68] *The South China Sea Arbitration (The Republic of Philippines v The People's Republic of China)* (Award on Jurisdiction and Admissibility) [2015] PCA Case No. 2013-19, para 213 www.pcacases.com/web/view/7 accessed 9 September 2018.

[69] For the Tribunal's summary of China's position and the Philippines' argument, see ibid paras 202–03 and 208.

[70] ibid para 213.

215. However, with respect to its terms, the DOC contains many instances of the signatory States simply 'reaffirming' existing obligations. For example, in paragraph 1, they 'reaffirm their commitment' to the UN Charter, the Convention, and other 'universally recognized principles of international law.' In paragraph 5, they 'reaffirm their respect and commitment to the freedom of navigation and overflight' as provided in the Convention. In paragraph 10, they reaffirm 'the adoption of a code of conduct in the South China Sea would further promote peace and stability in the region.' The only instance where the DOC uses the word 'agree' is in paragraph 10 where the signatory States 'agree to work, on the basis of consensus, towards the eventual attainment' of a Code of Conduct. This language is not consistent with the creation of new obligations but rather restates existing obligations pending agreement on a Code that eventually would set out new obligations. The DOC contains other terms that are provisional or permissive, such as paragraph 6, outlining what the Parties 'may explore or undertake,' and paragraph 7, stating that the Parties 'stand ready to continue their consultations and dialogues.'

216. On the other hand, some of the terms used in the DOC are suggestive of the existence of an agreement. For example, the word 'undertake', used in paragraph 4 ('undertake to resolve their ... disputes by peaceful means ... through friendly consultations and negotiations by sovereign states directly concerned') and in paragraph 5 ('undertake to exercise self-restraint'). As China mentions, the Court observed in Application of the Convention on the Prevention and Punishment of the Crime of Genocide (*Bosnia and Herzegovina v. Serbia and Montenegro*) that the word 'undertake' is 'regularly used in treaties setting out the obligations of Contracting Parties' and found the ordinary meaning of 'undertake' to be 'give a formal promise, to bind or engage oneself, to give a pledge or promise, to agree, to accept an obligation.' However, the Tribunal notes a number of differences between paragraph 4 of the DOC and Article 1 of the Genocide Convention. First, the Court was operating in the context of a treaty, whose legally binding character was not in any doubt. The examples cited by the Court—the International Convention on the Elimination of All Forms of Racial Discrimination and the International Covenant on Civil and Political Rights—were also indisputably legally binding treaties. The Court was not seeking to determine whether an agreement on the submission of disputes was binding (as it was in *Maritime Delimitation and Territorial Questions (Qatar v. Bahrain)* and *Land and Maritime Boundary (Cameroon v. Nigeria)*), but rather whether Article 1 of the Genocide Convention imposed an obligation to prevent genocide that was separate and distinct from other obligations in the Genocide Convention. Notably, the Court looked beyond the ordinary meaning of the word 'undertake' to verify its understanding. It thus gave weight to the object and purpose of the Genocide Convention and the negotiating history of the relevant provisions.

217. When a similar exercise is undertaken with respect to the DOC, it becomes apparent to this Tribunal that the DOC was not intended to be a legally binding agreement with respect to dispute resolution. The purpose and circumstances surrounding the DOC's adoption reinforce the Tribunal's understanding that

> the DOC was not intended to create legal rights and obligations. Descriptions from contemporaneous documents leading up to and surrounding the adoption of the DOC amply demonstrate that the DOC was not intended by its drafters to be a legally binding document, but rather an aspirational political document . . .
>
> 218. The Parties' subsequent conduct further confirms that the DOC is not a binding agreement. In this respect, the Tribunal notes the Parties' continuing efforts over a decade after the DOC was signed to agree upon a Code of Conduct. The Tribunal also observes that in recent years, at least before the arbitration commenced, several Chinese officials described the DOC as a 'political' document.[71]

Although the most common question arising in Treaty Offices is likely to be 'Is this document a treaty or a non-binding instrument?', the choice is not always binary. It may, occasionally, be neither a treaty nor a non-binding instrument, but rather something else, such as a contract binding under national law, or an undertaking that is binding due to other rules of international law that have nothing to do with treaties.[72]

Choosing whether to Draft a Treaty or a Non-Binding International Instrument

During a negotiation, ideally at the outset but at the latest before the text is finalised, a decision should be made about the desired outcome: a treaty or a non-binding international instrument? The choice is usually between these two options, although as outlined above, other kinds of instruments may also be possible depending on the circumstances. The following are some of the factors to consider when making a choice:

- Do both/all the proposed participants have international legal capacity to enter into a treaty? If not, a non-binding instrument may be the only option (unless, exceptionally, the States concerned agree to authorise participation by another kind of entity).
- Are there constitutional or legal requirements in domestic law for this kind of commitment to be made by treaty?
- Will the provisions need to be enforceable in the domestic legal system of any party (for example, privileges and immunities, double taxation, social security, extradition, intellectual property rights, trade)? If so, a treaty may be necessary to achieve this.
- Will the deal involve actual or potentially significant financial commitments or liability for damage? Usually the party/parties incurring financial risk will require a treaty.
- Are there any 'hard' obligations, precise enough that performance could be assessed? If so, and if you want to ensure that both/all sides are held to their

[71] ibid paras 213–18. (The footnotes to the quoted paragraphs have been omitted here.)

[72] See Figure 3.1. See also the text on *Chagos Arbitration* (n 46) quoted in n 52.

bargain, a treaty may be warranted. On the other hand, if all of the substance is vague, general, aspirational, setting the agenda for future talks, etc., there may be no point in creating legal obligations, however important the subject. In this case, a non-binding instrument would be just as effective.

- Do you want to have mandatory recourse to the ICJ, an arbitral tribunal or other form of third-party dispute settlement in the case of non-compliance by the other party/parties? And for this to be available against your side? If so, a treaty is necessary.
- Are the commitments time-limited? If they will be fully performed within a finite period (for example, they relate to an event or visit to take place in the near future), it may not be necessary or worthwhile to create a treaty.
- Is there any confidential material that needs to be in the text? All treaties should be registered with the UN (which publishes them in the UN Treaty Series), and there may be national constitutional requirements to publish treaties and present them to the legislature. If it is essential for the whole text to remain confidential, this indicates use of a non-binding instrument. Alternatively, the confidential elements could be taken out of the treaty text and included in a separate confidential document linked to the treaty, such as an implementing arrangement or understanding.
- Where the document is likely to require frequent amendment, a non-binding instrument may be a more pragmatic choice, especially if the subject matter is technical and not likely to be of particular interest to the legislature or the public.
- Is the subject matter or the occasion of high political importance? If so, this does not of itself call for a treaty. If there is no content that requires or justifies the creation of legally binding obligations, but there is political pressure to make it high-profile, there are other solutions. For example, a non-binding instrument can be given a grand title (such as MOU, Pact, Charter, Declaration, etc.), can be signed by dignitaries at a treaty-style signature ceremony, with flags, handshakes, media presence, photographs, press release, etc., as desired.
- Would you – and/or the other negotiating party/parties – be more willing to make substantial commitments if they are not binding? If so, there is a policy choice to be made between more limited binding provisions versus more substantial or more detailed non-binding ones.
- Urgency: is it more urgent to 'seal the deal' than make it legally binding? How long would the treaty process take in the executive and legislature (or in the organs of the IO)? The advantage of using a non-binding instrument that can be concluded by the executive on its own authority may be a factor to consider, especially in a case where delay might jeopardise the 'deal'.

Should Non-Binding International Instruments Be Published?

Many non-binding texts are not published at all. Their existence may be mentioned in an official text but often they are not.[73] Sometimes this is deliberate, due to the confidentiality of the contents, on grounds such as national security or commercial sensitivity. More often it is simply that governments and IOs see no need to publish them because they consider the contents routine and not likely to be of public interest. Since there is no central register of such documents at the UN, nor usually in governments or IOs, a decision to publish is normally taken by administrators responsible for the policy, and the place and manner of publication is ad hoc. This makes it difficult for the reader to know where to look for a particular text. It also means that when websites are reorganised or the document is superseded by another, it may be removed, possibly to national or organisational archives, or it may disappear from view altogether.

There is such a wide variety of types of non-binding international instruments that it is difficult to generalise about whether their full text, or information about their existence, should always be published, and if so where and how. Certainly if they affect the position of private individuals, the PLATO principles of 'Legality' and 'Transparency' point clearly in favour of full publication and accessibility. This is especially the case when a non-binding instrument may be used to aid interpretation of the provisions of a treaty that concerns individuals.

The Organisation of Economic Co-operation and Development (OECD) has led good practice in the area of tax treaties by publishing its model texts for non-binding instruments that may influence the interpretation of a treaty.[74] An example of this is the 'OECD model Memorandum of Understanding on Assistance in Tax Collection' which is intended to be used as a 'working agreement between tax administrations which are able and wish to provide each other assistance in tax collection'. This model MOU assumes that the legal instrument providing for assistance in collection of taxes is a bilateral tax treaty provision based on Article 27 of the OECD Model Tax Convention on Income and on Capital. However, despite the public availability of the OECD's model MOU texts, States making use of these models do not necessarily publish the MOUs that they conclude with other States. The unacceptability of non-publication of texts of this type was highlighted by the Court of Appeal of

[73] See the section on 'Some Examples of Non-binding International Instruments: Published, Reported And Unreported' above at 102–03 for examples of non-binding texts that are published and some whose existence is published but whose text is not.

[74] OECD, 'Manual on Assistance in the Collection of Taxes – Module 3: Model Memorandum of Understanding on Assistance in Tax collection based on Article 27 of the OECD Model Convention on Income and on Capital' www.oecd.org/tax/exchange-of-tax-information/49102492.pdf accessed 9 September 2018, and OECD, 'Manual on Assistance in the Collection of Taxes – Module 4: Model Memorandum of Understanding on the Recovery of Tax Claims based on the Convention on Mutual Administrative Assistance in Tax Matters' www.oecd.org/tax/exchange-of-tax-information/49102501.pdf accessed 9 September 2018.

England and Wales, in its judgment in a case brought by taxpayers against the UK tax authorities, based on the terms of a bilateral tax treaty between the UK and South Africa. The UK and South Africa had entered into several MOUs (based on OECD models) regarding the mode of application of their bilateral treaty. Lord Justice Jackson observed that:

> Under Article 31 of the Vienna Convention such an MOU may be taken into account as an aid to interpreting the primary instrument which the MOU supplements ... It follows from the foregoing that any taxpayer who does or did business in both South Africa and the UK has a legitimate interest in those MOUs. I was concerned to learn during argument that such MOUs are not made publicly available. The only means by which the taxpayers can ascertain what they say is by making Freedom of Information Act requests. In my view such MOUs should be placed in the public domain. This may either be done by putting them on the HMRC website or by some other means.[75]

Top Tips on Handling Treaties and other kinds of International Instruments

The top tips in Box 3.1 summarise the factors that have been discussed in this chapter that one needs to consider in determining the status of any given international instrument – whether it is a treaty or another kind of international instrument – as well as determining in which situations it is appropriate to negotiate a new treaty and when another kind of instrument might be more suitable.

Box 3.1 Top tips on handling treaties and other kinds of international instruments

TOP TIPS 1
IS THIS TEXT A TREATY OR SOMETHING ELSE?

Scenario: You're looking at an existing text and wish to know if it is a treaty or not; for example, your government has signed it and you (as a government official) need to decide how to process it; or a dispute has arisen and you need to know if there are legal consequences.

1. First study the top and the tail of the document closely.
   - Who are the parties (signatories or participants)?
   - Does the document say how it enters into force?

[75] *Ben Nevis (Holdings) Ltd & Anor v HM Revenue & Customs* [2013] EWCA Civ 578 (23 May 2013), per Lord Justice Jackson at paras 56–61. The other two Judges agreed.

Box 3.1 (cont.)

2. Look at the preamble or introductory paragraph.
3. Look for the 'final clauses'.
4. Look for any 'applicable law' clause: does it say this agreement is governed by international law or by the national law of a particular State?
5. Look at the body of the document – is the language mandatory or hortatory?
6. Look at the body of the document for the substance – are there concrete obligations?

TOP TIPS 2
THIS TEXT IS UNCLEAR WHETHER OR NOT IT IS A TREATY– WHAT TO DO NEXT?

Scenario: You've studied the text (following Top Tips 1) and it's hard to tell from the text if it is a treaty or not; for example, it contains some treaty elements but also some characteristics of a non-binding text. You still need to know if it is a treaty or not.

1. Look at the way the document was concluded.
2. At the time of conclusion, did any party make a statement that indicates its view of the status of the text?
3. Has it been registered with the UN?
4. Has it been submitted to the legislature (by your government); and if so, under what procedure?
5. Look for evidence of the views of the other government(s) involved as to whether they consider it to be a treaty or not. Have they made any subsequent statements? Have they submitted it to their legislatures in accordance with domestic treaty procedures?

TOP TIPS 3
NOT SURE IF THIS TEXT IS A TREATY OR NOT - DOES IT MATTER?

Scenario: You're not sure if the text you're looking at is a treaty or not; you're wondering if it's necessary to go to the extra effort suggested in Top Tip 2 (or you already have and are still not sure). Does it really matter if this document is a treaty or not? Does anything practical turn on the distinction?

Box 3.1 (cont.)

Yes, many practical things may turn on the distinction. For example:

1. If it is a treaty, after signature further international procedures may be required to complete your government's ratification and to bring it into force.
2. If it is a treaty, there may be constitutional or statutory procedures that must be followed by the government and the legislature, for example concerning publication and approval. If it is not a treaty, different rules (or no rules) will apply. If the correct legal procedure is not followed, there may be serious legal and political consequences, for the government, parliament and the officials involved.
3. If it is a treaty, it should be submitted to the UN for registration under Article 102 UN Charter.
4. If it is a treaty, it creates rights and obligations for the government under international law. Even if there is no compulsory dispute settlement mechanism, international obligations matter. If a government acts in breach of its treaty obligations, there will be consequences under the international law of State responsibility.
5. If it is a treaty, there might be mandatory procedures for resolving disputes relating to it. The defendant State or IO may be obliged to take part in procedures such as conciliation, mediation, arbitration, adjudication, investigation by a compliance committee and/or discussion by a meeting of all States Parties, which may result in a binding judgment or sanction.
6. If it is a treaty, even if it does not itself provide compulsory settlement of dispute procedures, an alleged breach could trigger a mandatory procedure under another treaty, for example, the Statute of the ICJ.
7. If it is a treaty, it may in some circumstances confer rights under international law on individuals or legal persons, who may have the right to bring a case against a government before an international court, tribunal or treaty body.
8. If it is a treaty, its provisions may have legal effect in the domestic legal system. Individuals and legal persons may be able to use it to bring or to strengthen a court case against the government.
9. Even if it is not a treaty, it is still important for those involved to know what kind of document it is. Other kinds of international instruments may have legal effects (see pages 96–104).

Box 3.1 (cont.)

TOP TIPS 4
IT IS UNCLEAR WHETHER OR NOT THIS TEXT IS A TREATY – IS IT POSSIBLE TO PARTICIPATE WITHOUT TAKING ON LEGAL OBLIGATIONS?

Scenario: You're advising a government that wishes to participate in a particular instrument, provided that it does NOT create binding obligations under international law. The legal status of the text is unclear. How can your government protect itself from the risk of unintended legal liability?

Consider one or more of the following possible ways to reduce the risk of unintentionally taking on legal obligations:

1. Make a formal statement at the time of signing (or completing the 'joining procedure', whatever that is) that your government does not consider this text to be legally binding.
2. Depending on the latitude available in the circumstances, if the text has to be signed, better that it is done by a minister OTHER THAN the Head of Government or Foreign Minister, or better still by an agency head, ambassador or senior official.
3. If a formal communication needs to be sent to a government or secretariat to complete the 'joining procedure', make sure it is not and does not look like a ratification instrument. Send it in the form of an ordinary letter. Do not use a treaty binder or sew it up with ribbon. Send it from a domestic ministry or agency (NOT the foreign ministry and NOT the Treaty Office). Do not refer to the addressee as 'Depositary'.
4. Do not subject the document to the same domestic procedures as a treaty. If it is appropriate to publish it and/or transmit it to the legislature, do so in a way that makes clear that it is not being done pursuant to legal requirements for treaties, but on some other basis, for example, for information only.
5. Do not submit the document to the UN for registration. If in doubt about the intentions of other participants, inform them that in your view it is not eligible for registration; and (perhaps) request confirmation that they are of the same view.

CAUTION: if according to objective criteria the instrument is a treaty, none of these steps will turn it into a non-binding instrument, but they will provide clear evidence of the intention of your government/organisation not to enter into binding legal relations. The end result might be that your government is considered not to have validly consented to be bound.

Box 3.1 (cont.)

TOP TIPS 5

IT IS UNCLEAR WHETHER OR NOT THIS TEXT IS A TREATY – IS IT POSSIBLE TO MAKE SURE IT IS A TREATY BEFORE JOINING?

Scenario: You're advising a government that wishes to participate in a particular instrument, provided that it DOES create binding obligations under international law. The legal status of the text is not as clear as you would wish. How can your government ensure that it will be recognised as a treaty?

This outcome cannot be guaranteed. Consider one or more of the following possible ways to reduce the risk of this text being interpreted as non-binding at a later date (for example, by other parties or by a court):

1. Make a formal statement at the time of signing (or completing the 'joining procedure', whatever that is) that your government considers this text to be legally binding and subject to registration with the UN under Article 102 UN Charter.
2. If the text has to be signed, ensure that it is signed by the Head of State, Head of Government or Foreign Minister, or by someone else authorised by one of those three in a formal Full Powers document. Hand over the Full Powers to the government or IO hosting the signature ceremony.
3. If the text is subject to ratification or accession or other formal notification procedure, use a formal instrument prepared in traditional form by the Treaty Office (with the trappings normally used by your government for treaty instruments). Send it from the foreign ministry via diplomatic channels.
4. Complete domestic treaty procedures, including publication of the text in the official treaty series and, if transmittal, to the legislature as required. Consider informing the other States and organisations concerned of the fact that these procedures have been undertaken.
5. If it is a bilateral treaty, submit it to the UN for registration. If it is a multilateral treaty, check that the Depositary has done so and if not, remind/request them to do it.

CAUTION: if according to objective criteria the instrument is not a treaty, taking the steps above will not turn it into one. The purpose of taking those steps is to provide clear evidence of the position of your government. If you make it known to other parties and they do not express any contrary view, this will strengthen your position in the event of a dispute arising.

Box 3.1 (cont.)

TOP TIPS 6
NEGOTIATING A NEW TEXT: SHOULD IT BE A TREATY OR SOMETHING ELSE?

Scenario: You're negotiating a new international text – bilateral or multilateral, or advising the negotiators. Should you draft a treaty or some other kind of document? How is this decided?

Factors to consider:

1. any constitutional or legal requirements for a treaty
2. whether legislative force is needed in domestic law
3. whether large financial commitments or liabilities are involved
4. whether provisions are concrete or vague/aspirational
5. whether it is confidential
6. whether it will require frequent amendments
7. whether mandatory third-party dispute settlement provisions are desired
8. balance between more substantial non-binding commitments versus more limited binding obligations
9. urgency versus duration of treaty procedures in the executive and legislature/organs of the IO.

TOP TIPS 7
NEGOTIATING A NEW TEXT: IS THERE A WAY TO COMPROMISE BETWEEN A TREATY AND A NON-BINDING INSTRUMENT?

Scenario: You're involved in negotiating a new international text – bilateral or multilateral. One side wants to conclude a treaty while the other wants a non-binding instrument (or in a multilateral negotiation, some delegations have opposing aims). How can a compromise be reached that satisfies both?

WHAT NOT TO DO – do not deliberately create a fudge or hybrid document. Do not mix treaty-like features and non-treaty features in a single text. Ambiguity as to the binding or non-binding status of the document may seem an attractive diplomatic way out of an impasse, but it is liable to lead to legal problems and disputes.
DO consider carefully the reasons advanced for and against a treaty. Try to understand the needs of the other delegation(s), and whether they are based on primarily substantive or presentational concerns. Consider whether the reasons advanced for or against a treaty apply to the entire deal or only to certain elements of it.

Box 3.1 (cont.)

POSSIBLE COMPROMISE SOLUTIONS ON THE CONTENTS OF THE TEXT:

To make a treaty more palatable to the side which prefers a non-binding text, you could offer to:

1. incorporate some leeway into certain obligations, for example: 'best endeavours', 'aim to', 'take appropriate measures', or provide a timeframe for achieving compliance;
2. omit the dispute settlement mechanism or make it optional (if there is one);
3. specify certain types of reservation which are permissible, or remove any restrictions on reservations so that the general international law of treaties applies; and/or
4. provide a limited duration or review clause.

POSSIBLE COMPROMISE SOLUTIONS ON THE FORM AND STATUS OF THE TEXT:

1. SPLIT the document into separate binding and non-binding texts. Common combinations:
   - a treaty (with operational detail) and a high-level non-binding declaration; or
   - a framework or short treaty and a set of detailed non-binding arrangements.
2. Conclude a treaty with minimum formalities; for example, use simple final clauses, such as entry into force on signature or on notification of completion of internal procedures instead of ratification. If it is bilateral, you could use an exchange of notes with no signature ceremony; or
3. Conclude a non-binding instrument with maximum formalities; for example, give the document a grand-sounding title, agree to have a 'treaty-style' signature ceremony, media presence, press release, etc.

TOP TIPS 8
THE NEW TEXT IS ADOPTED. ITS LEGAL STATUS IS AMBIGUOUS. WHAT TO DO NOW?

Scenario: You're involved in negotiating a new international text – bilateral or multilateral. Unfortunately, despite your best efforts, due to negotiating difficulties and/or poor drafting, the agreed text is a fudge, and you're not clear what its legal status is. It is too late to remedy that – political leaders are committed. What to do now?

Box 3.1 (cont.)

1. Scenario A: your government/IO does not want this to be recognised as a treaty – it did not intend to take on legal obligations.
   - See Top Tips 4.
2. Scenario B: your government/IO wants this to be recognised as a treaty.
   - See Top Tips 5.
3. Scenario C: your government/IO does not have a preference as to this document's legal status, but it is your job to handle the document correctly so you need to know what it is.
   - See Top Tips 2 and 3.
4. Scenario D: your government/IO is not sure what type of instrument is in its best interests and/or believes the ambiguity serves it well. Your political leaders hope that other parties will regard it as binding on themselves, while they avoid being held to account legally for any non-compliance by your State/IO.

ALERT: your government/IO needs to consult its international law advisers without delay. If it does not have any, or you are one of them, there are more fundamental issues to consider for the future (see Chapter 2).

TOP TIPS 9
WHEN TREATY OFFICIALS RECEIVE NON-TREATY DOCUMENTS, WHAT SHOULD BE DONE WITH THEM?

Scenario: You are an official responsible for managing treaties (in a Treaty Office or similar unit of a government or IO). You receive a variety of documents which look like treaties, but on closer examination you are clear that some of them are not treaties. What should you do with the non-treaties?

1. Your Government or IO needs a policy on whether the remit of the Treaty Office covers treaty-like international instruments that are not treaties.
2. The Treaty Office should have written guidance on distinguishing between treaties and non-binding international instruments.
3. Its remit should make clear whether it has responsibilities in relation to any international instruments other than treaties, such as maintaining texts, lists or indexes, or carrying out publishing functions. It should also provide guidance to treaty officials on where to send international instruments that fall outside its remit.

Box 3.1 (cont.)

4. If the remit of the Treaty Office includes processing or recording texts of international instruments that are not treaties, guidance needs to be issued to all officials throughout the government or IO on the kinds of texts that must be sent to the Treaty Office, when and why.

4

Managing and Using Treaty Collections

***

'Claimant contends that Respondent's claim that there exists an authentic Turkmen version of the BIT is undermined by its own, unexplained concession that no copy of such a text can be found.'[1]

Introduction: Why Good Management of Treaty Collections Matters

For any State or IO, the accurate and efficient management of treaty records is of fundamental importance. Having the ability to enter into treaty relations with other States and IOs is all very well, but if the staff of the Treaty Office, their legal advisers and those outside the office are not able to tell what their existing treaty commitments are, or with whom those relations exist, each new treaty obligation is only going to make matters worse.

This chapter looks at the hows and whys of keeping treaty records, where the information comes from and what treaty officials do with it. For any Treaty Office, the records they hold are their most valuable resource, and should be conserved and managed with the greatest of care and attention. This is true not only for the original treaty itself and the 'certified true copies' of multilateral treaties but also for the documents surrounding the treaty such as copies of Full Powers, instruments of ratification, accession, reservation, withdrawal, or certificates of exchange. Without these, a Treaty Office will quickly find that it is unable to say with any certainty which actions have definitely been taken and when they were done, and this could lead to confusion and delay.

[1] *Kilic v Turkmenistan* [2012] ICSID Case No. ARB/10/1, Decision on Article VII.2 of the Turkey–Turkmenistan Bilateral Investment Treaty (7 May 2012), para 3.10.

In this chapter, we will look at ways of managing all this information and permanently preserving treaties and associated documents, and what you need to consider when doing so. It is not just the physical documents that need to be looked after. The records of actions taken are equally vital and need to be carefully managed so that a history is created which can be researched and examined. This needs to be organised in some form of database. States and IOs need to have one for their own internal use. Some make direct access to the information available to others across government or the IO, and some may extend this facility to the public, where this can be done electronically. Electronic databases are not for everyone, however, and others find a solution in card index systems that can be regularly updated; both are discussed below.

Good management of treaty records is vital for many reasons, not least for the work that treaty officials themselves need them for: providing treaty information and publishing treaty documents. In doing so, the treaty official needs to have in mind the needs of both the internal and external users of treaty information.

In this chapter, we are going to look at what different users might need treaty information for, and the ways in which they might use it. We will look first at internal users in the Treaty Office and those closely associated with it, such as legal advisers and policy-makers within the government or IO. We will then look at those who might be called 'external users' – in effect, everyone else. Lastly, we will consider the needs of depositaries.

Use of Terms in this Chapter

We use the terms 'treaty records' and 'treaty information' to refer to things which are different but closely related, and may often overlap:

- 'Treaty records' comprise original treaty texts and official documents related to treaties. Each fact recorded in an official database about a treaty could be considered a 'treaty record', such as the date of signature, entry into force or ratification of a specific treaty by a specific government.
- 'Treaty information' is the information derived from those records, when it is collected, assembled, collated or presented in a new form. For example, a depositary may publish a list of ratifications of a particular treaty; that list is 'treaty information' which is derived from the 'treaty records' held by the depositary; in this case, the instruments of ratification it has received from States. A minister may ask which arms control treaties their State is a party to; when the Treaty Office compiles that list from records held in its database, it is producing 'treaty information'.
- 'Treaty collection' refers to the whole set of treaty documents, records and information (internal and published) held by a government or IO.
- 'Managing and using treaty collections' comprises several functions: record-keeping; archive management; information provision and publication; sending, receiving and processing formal diplomatic communications. It includes

the organisation of existing treaty records generated in the past, as well as the handling of new incoming and outgoing treaty documents. The main focus is on the handling of an existing collection; how to create a new treaty is covered in more detail in later chapters.

'Treaty records' and 'treaty information' may well overlap. For example, when a depositary sends out a notice to signatory States of a particular treaty, to inform them that it has received the requisite number of ratifications for that treaty to enter into force, that notice contains treaty information derived from its records (the facts about ratifications that have taken place) and it also generates a new treaty record about the entry into force. In this chapter, we do not intend to use these terms in an overly technical way; indeed, they may often be interchangeable. However, there will be circumstances in which the distinction matters, and so we wish the reader to be aware of it. For example, there are times when it is necessary to know whether the treaty document you are looking at is the original document or a derivative copy that might be corrupted. When you find treaty information on the internet, it is important to ascertain whether it is the official record or just recycled information whose accuracy is not guaranteed.

Is Treaty Management the same in Governments and IOs?

In general, most of the actions taken by governments and IOs in managing their treaty collections will be broadly similar. But there are some factors that affect governments and IOs differently.

The focus for most IOs will mainly be on multilateral treaties covering a particular region or subject for which they are responsible – and of course unlike a State, most IOs are themselves established by a treaty. Although they may have some bilateral treaties, these would not usually be a major feature of their treaty work.

The UN Secretariat performs a registration function in relation to bilateral treaties submitted by States, but is not involved with their conclusion. Governments, on the other hand, will be involved in treaties both bilaterally with other States and multilaterally with a range of States and organisations. These treaties will cover a broad spectrum of subjects that affect the State in question, and will involve policy-makers across government in dealing with all the issues raised. Typically, Treaty Offices in governments will be concluding and dealing with many more bilateral treaties during the course of a year than multilaterals.

IOs commonly have depositary functions (although not all do); and for some, these form a large part of the work of the Treaty Office. For example, the Secretary General of the CoE is the depositary of over 220 treaties concluded by its Member States, while the UN Secretary General is the depositary of more than 560 treaties.[2]

[2] COE, 'Complete List of the Council of Europe's Treaties' www.Coe.Int/En/Web/Conventions/Full-List accessed 21 September 2018; and UNTC, 'Multilateral Treaties Deposited with the Secretary-General' https://treaties.un.org/pages/Index.aspx accessed 21 September 2018.

Many governments also perform depositary functions, but even for those with a substantial number of treaties (for example, the UK is depositary for forty-five treaties), this is a small part of their work. Most governments are only depositary for a handful of treaties, if any. To mention some examples within the ASEAN, Indonesia is a depositary authority for at least two treaties, Malaysia for one and Vietnam for none – although Vietnam's 2016 Treaty Law provides for the MFA to perform the functions of a depositary of a multilateral treaty in case Vietnam is designated as the depositary of such multilateral treaty.[3]

Government Treaty Offices need to operate within the framework of domestic law as well as international law, and this means performing functions mandated by constitutional law and custom, such as publishing treaty documents to the legislature or in an official gazette, and may have responsibilities in relation to domestic law implementation. IO Treaty Offices are not normally concerned directly with such national procedures, though they may need an awareness of those affecting their Member States. On the other hand, they are accountable to the governing bodies of their IO.

Although some treaty management functions are more relevant to government than IO Treaty Offices, and vice versa, the principles of good management are the same and therefore this chapter will address both together.

Poor Management of Treaty Collections: What Can Go Wrong?

When treaty collections are poorly managed, it impacts most immediately on the treaty officials, who are obliged to spend their working day looking for documents that are not where they should be, or searching for other ways to try to replace the information that has been lost or cannot be retrieved. It is frustrating, tedious, inefficient, embarrassing (especially when external sources have to be consulted), and a waste of staff time and resources. It may also impede the work of policy officials and legal advisers who cannot obtain the information they need, or are given inaccurate information. This is bad enough; but occasionally a failure to manage treaty collections efficiently can lead to disastrous outcomes, as the following scenarios illustrate.

Scenario 1: Failure to Keep Records of Treaty Actions

The Foreign Ministry of a small island State engaged an international law consultant to advise it on its international environmental law obligations. On

[3] Law on Treaties, 9 April 2016, 108/2016/QH13, art 57. See the section on 'Is it Desirable to Establish a Treaty Office – Even in a Small State or IO?' in Chapter 2 at 52–3. For further information on ASEAN States' treaty practice, see CIL, 'International Workshop on Treaty Law and Practice', 10 October 2012, paras 33–47 https://cil.nus.edu.sg/wp-content/uploads/2012/12/Final-Treaty-Workshop-Report.pdf accessed 21 September 2018, or BIICL, 'Report of International Workshop on Treaty Law and Practice' www.biicl.org/documents/41_singapore_treaty_workshop_full_report.pdf?showdocument=1 accessed 21 September 2018.

arrival, the consultant asked for a list of the treaties to which that State was a party. There was no list and no official knew where to find the information. They had to start compiling a list of treaty engagements from scratch.

This task was time-consuming and resulted in embarrassment for the Foreign Ministry when it had to write to depositaries and other governments to ask for information about its own past signatures and ratifications of treaties. Only when all this information had been assembled was the consultant able to provide the legal advice that the Foreign Ministry required. As a result, that State lost a valuable opportunity to participate in a negotiation on a multilateral treaty amendment.[4]

Scenario 2: Failure to Store Original Treaty Text

A newly independent State concluded a bilateral investment treaty (BIT). Years later, a foreign investor brought a very large claim against that State before an international tribunal. The parties were in dispute over whether a specific language version of the treaty formed part of the authentic text. The defendant State wished to rely upon that language version, but the only published text of the treaty did not include it.

Neither the claimant investor nor the defendant State could produce a signed original or a certified copy of the treaty. And so, the State could not prove that the signed treaty included that language version (which would have helped its defence), and this was a factor in the judgment awarded in favour of the investor.[5]

Applying the PLATO Principles to the Management of Treaty Collections

As the management of treaty collections is one of the most important aspects of treaty work, it is no surprise that many elements of the PLATO principles apply here. Of all the principles, it is the final two – 'Transparent' and 'Organised' – that have the greatest application and underpin all the functions.

- 'Organised' stresses the importance of having *systems in place* to record and manage treaty information in a way that enables present and future generations of staff to search and retrieve it. Treaty procedures and practices should be clearly recorded and regularly reviewed to ensure they are kept up to date. While all treaty work should be co-ordinated

[4] This example is based on a real case as related by the international law consultant concerned to Jill Barrett in a private conversation.

[5] This example is based upon the facts of an ICSID investment treaty arbitration on which Jill Barrett advised, the only difference being that in the real case a settlement was eventually reached. For an example of a reported case in which a similar issue arose and the defendant State was unable to locate an original or certified copy of the treaty text that it wished to rely on, see *Kilic v Turkmenistan* (n 1) paras 3.10 and 7.11.

across government or the IO, 'Organised' also points to the need for one centralised point of contact with ultimate responsibility for the collation, retention and dissemination of all treaty records for that particular government or organisation.

- 'Transparent' emphasises the need for easy access to information and the importance of an organised system to provide for the publication of treaty information and texts. Guidelines on treaty procedures should be clear and widely communicated, and all appropriate stakeholders should be involved throughout.

There are, however, elements of the other principles that also apply here:

- 'Assured' focuses on the importance of having accurate information and authentic treaty texts available.
- 'Professional' relates to the need for those handling treaty collections – whether in a Treaty Office or elsewhere – to have the relevant skills and expertise.
- Although most of the work is clerical and can be done by non-lawyers, the 'Legal' principle is also important, in the sense that the Treaty Office must be alert to legal issues on which legal advice is needed, in particular on which documents are treaties.

Identifying the Users of Treaty Collections and How to Respond to Their Requests

The question of who the treaty collection needs to be managed for should logically precede any decision about how it is managed. Just as a library should be designed to serve its readers, not just to please the librarians who work in it, so a treaty collection should be managed to serve the needs of those who use the treaty records or the information derived from them. So we will consider the categories of treaty users next, before looking in detail at the tasks involved in treaty management. There are 'internal users', meaning those internal to the State or IO concerned, and 'external users' meaning those outside it, but these categories are fluid and may vary from one context to another. The full range of potential users were explained in Boxes 1.2 and 1.3 in Chapter 1.[6]

The Users of Treaty Collections

The Treaty Office: Manager and Primary User of the Treaty Collection

First and foremost, among the internal users are the staff of the Treaty Office themselves. The records they hold form the bedrock of everything they do, and all the staff in the office need to have rapid and direct access to all of the treaty

[6] See Chapter 1, Box 1.1 for a definition of the PLATO principles, Box 1.2 for treaty stakeholder analysis for a State and Box 1.3 for treaty stakeholder analysis for an international organisation.

records they possess. One of the most important functions of any Treaty Office is to give advice on treaty procedures and present treaty information, based on the official records. In many governments and IOs, the Treaty Office may receive such requests on a daily basis. Treaty officials therefore need constant access to a reliable source of information in which they have absolute confidence.

However much treaty information is provided online, there will be complex requests from time to time that can only be adequately handled in person, by staff with specialised knowledge of the treaty collection. This is especially the case when information is needed about a range of treaties that span a long period of time. For example, when the Union of Soviet Socialist Republics (USSR) broke up in 1991, Treaty Offices around the world were no doubt tasked by their policy-makers with providing a complete list of all treaties in which their State or IO was in treaty relations with the USSR. Their research would have needed to cover records spanning over 70 years, and perhaps more (if any pre-USSR treaties with Russia were still in force). More recently, when the UK announced its intention to leave the EU, one can imagine Treaty Offices – not only in London and Brussels – being asked to produce lists of every bilateral and multilateral treaty which could be affected by the UK's change of status. To fulfil these tasks, the Treaty Office needs to be able to search, retrieve and organise records made by their predecessors over past decades, or even centuries. In this sense, treaty officials are both the providers and primary users of the service.

Other Internal Users

The users outside the Treaty Office and its parent administrative unit (ministry, organisation or agency), but still within the same institution in its broadest sense, might be treated as internal users for some purposes but external users for others. It is desirable to treat them as internal users as far as possible, with the same access to *treaty information* as those inside the Treaty Office's own administrative unit. For example, officials across government ministries and agencies will frequently need access to treaty information for their work, and so there needs to be a system which enables them to access authoritative information and advice direct from the Treaty Office as required. For an IO, the Member States need to be treated as 'internal users' in the sense that they may likewise need direct access to authoritative information and advice, and not have to rely only on public sources of information such as the IO's website.

On the other hand, access to original *treaty records* necessarily should be restricted. Where signed original paper documents or certified copies are held, these should not be lent out of the Treaty Office, and any access to its archives must be under supervised conditions to ensure that documents are not misplaced or mishandled. Original digital records may also need to be kept in a protected database to ensure that there is one authoritative master set that cannot be amended or corrupted in error. The original raw data as received might need to be processed and inputted in a new format so as to make the *treaty information* accessible and searchable by users. To what extent it is feasible for the Treaty Office to provide access to the same information to all of these 'outer circles' of internal users in the same way will depend on the technology and systems available. Options for doing so electronically are considered below.

External Users

Beyond the government, the external users at a national level could include members of the national legislature, national judiciary, and regional or local authorities. They may be in NGOs, lawyers in arbitration firms, students, academics, the media or members of the business community. For some treaties, public interest and lobbying groups will have a strong interest, as will the media when treaties come to their attention in relation to current news issues. Lastly there is the catch-all category of the 'general public', individuals and groups who may (or may not) have an interest in, or a knowledge of, certain treaties, or for whom a particular treaty will become important as it impacts on an area of their lives.

On the international plane, external users might be officials or ministers in the government of another State or members of its national legislature. They could be a part of an international or regional organisation, whether as a Member State or in the secretariat. As a State or an organisation, they could be a depositary for the treaty concerned. Particular treaties may play a part in a hearing before an international court or tribunal. The external users of the treaties of an IO could be any member of the public, anywhere in the world.

How to Respond to Users' Requests

Considering the Needs of Users when Designing the Treaty Information Service

All of the above categories of treaty users will have differing needs for treaty information, which can range from the detailed provisions of individual treaties to the application and effect of a whole range of treaties. In each case, users, whoever they are, will need to have easy access to a reliable means of obtaining treaty information, ideally through an online database backed up if necessary by some form of treaty enquiry service.

When designing an online database for public use, it is important to consider where this is placed on the government or IO's website. It is not uncommon for such databases to be buried deep inside a website, with no clear route to get to them from the home page. This is an important consideration, and it might be worth having a link to the treaty database or information somewhere on the home page of the website, to make searching that much easier. All it needs is for one word – 'Treaties' – to be visible on the home page, with a link.

Responding to Internal Requests for Advice About Treaty Procedures

Treaty officials may also be asked for *advice* as well as information, perhaps to express an opinion or exercise a judgement about a treaty matter. For example, an administrator in another government agency might ask whether it is possible for a treaty text to be published in a day, or how a treaty signature ceremony should be organised, or what parliamentary procedures are required and how long it will take. They may wish to be able to contact a treaty official directly for an expert opinion customised to the situation at hand, based on knowledge of procedure and past practice. This kind of tailored advice cannot be obtained from a website. An important part of the Treaty Office's functions is to provide an accessible and rapid service to officials inside their organisations who need operational advice, whether by email, telephone, meetings or other means.

When a treaty official receives such a request, they may need to consider carefully whether it is appropriate to offer *advice* or whether they should confine their response to the provision of treaty *information*. This will depend upon factors such as who is asking, in what circumstances and whether the matter is within their expertise. If answering the question involves giving a legal interpretation or making a policy judgement call, they must decide if they are qualified to provide it and if not, direct the questioner to the appropriate quarters.

Responding to Public Treaty Enquiries

Some Treaty Offices provide a *public* enquiry service, for example, via an online form or a published email address or telephone number. This may be provided in addition to an online treaty database to which users are first directed, or it may be offered because there is not yet an online database. The users could be anyone and be based anywhere, but typically include law firms, academics, research students and NGOs. Treaty officials offering such a service will need to be clear about its limits. For example, it would be normal to provide a member of the public with information from official treaty records to which the public have no access, or no easy access, but reasonable to decline to provide information which is already available in the public domain. It is also wise to draw the line at providing *advice* or *opinions* about any treaty matter to a member of the public.

Managing Treaty Collections

What Information Might the Treaty Office Need when Responding to Requests?

To be able to provide a rapid, accurate and comprehensive response to requests, treaty officials will need to have certain basic facts about each treaty at their fingertips. As a minimum, they will need to be able to see whether a treaty has been signed by their government or organisation and if so, whether it has subsequently been ratified or acceded to. They will need to be able to tell whether it is in force and the precise date of entry. They will also need to be able to see whether any reservations or declarations have been tabled by their government or IO, what responses there have been, if any, and whether any responses have been made to reservations or declarations tabled by other parties to the treaty. Treaty records are also an essential means of ensuring that there is no conflict between existing treaties and those that are about to be concluded; whenever the likelihood of a new treaty is mentioned by a policy official, it is always a good idea for the Treaty Office to check the records to see what already exists on that subject, so as to enable informed decisions to be taken.

Treaty officials will also need to be able to see if their government or IO has withdrawn from the treaty in question – a vital point which means that treaty records should never be deleted! Another reason for never deleting treaty records, even when their government or IO has withdrawn from it or it has been wound up, is that it may become important at some point in the future to know what the treaty obligations were for that government or IO at a specific time in the past. For example, this could be important in the event of a claim for past wrongdoing or litigation.

These are the basics, but treaty officials will almost always want to record much more than this. In addition to whether a treaty has been signed, they will need to know where and when that action took place, and very often who the signatory was. If their government or IO has not yet consented to be bound by the treaty, they need to know what the procedure for achieving that is; for example, whether this should be by ratification or accession, or by some other means such as the mutual notification of completion of domestic procedures. If written legal advice has been provided on such matters, it would be helpful for a note of it to be kept with the treaty records, to enable retrieval by future treaty staff.

For multilateral treaties, treaty officials may also want to know about *other* signatories and parties to the treaty, including dates and places of action taken, such as signature, ratification and so on. They may also want to know whether those parties have submitted any reservations or declarations, and if so what the response of their own and other governments and organisations has been. All of this information goes towards building a comprehensive picture of the treaty actions and obligations of the government or IO concerned. Treaty officials should receive this information in the form of treaty notifications from the depositary for each treaty. These notifications are the authoritative source of information about treaty actions, and therefore must be retained and filed. They will need to consider how best to organise and retrieve this information. Ideally, on receipt, each piece of new treaty information will be entered into their own database, and linked to the entry for the treaty concerned. The manual entry of such data inevitably involves a risk of human error and therefore needs careful cross-checking. If the Treaty Office is short-staffed, officials might decide that, where there is a good depositary website for a particular treaty, it is better to rely on that as a source of information about the actions of *other* States, and to concentrate their efforts on keeping their own database up to date with their *own* government's treaty actions. If so, they will need to make sure that the source they rely on for the actions of other States is the *official* website for that treaty. For example, if they are checking the Antarctic Treaty 1959, the authoritative source of status information is the treaty website of the Depositary Government, the USA,[7] not the website of the Antarctic Treaty Secretariat, useful though its information is for other purposes.[8]

It is not enough to be able to pull up detailed information about each treaty, one at a time. Treaty officials need to be able to view the desired fields for a number of treaties at the same time. They may, for example, have to respond to a question about the number of environmental treaties in force for their government or IO, and will therefore need to see information about a range of treaties so that they can provide an accurate answer. Policy and legal officials may frequently ask for status information about treaties on a specific subject area, but it may not always be self-evident to a treaty official which treaties are relevant. For example, if they are asked a question about environmental treaties in force, should they include in their answer all treaties with the word 'emissions' in their title? It is useful to have some kind of subject classification indicated in the treaty records, in much the same way as a library uses classifications in its catalogues to help the reader sort what is relevant to a particular search. An example of a subject classification system used on a public website is the UN Treaty Collection.[9]

Sources of Treaty Information

Treaty officials may find that treaty information arrives on their desk (or in their inbox) from a vast array of sources, not all of which will be 100 per cent reliable. The primary source for treaty information is of course the original text of the treaty itself, since this can give the fundamental details needed to create any new treaty record and can be relied on to be accurate. Besides obvious

[7] Office of the Legal Adviser, 'Depositary Information' (US Department of State) www.state.gov/s/l/treaty/depositary/index.htm accessed 21 September 2018.

[8] Secretariat of the Antarctic Treaty, 'Antarctic Treaty: Parties' www.ats.aq/devAS/ats_parties.aspx?lang=e accessed 21 September 2018. This information is derived from notifications that the Secretariat receives from the Depositary Government (the United States of America), and is then rearranged and presented in a way that the Secretariat thinks helpful for their readers, with additional explanatory material. The status information is usually accurate but may not always be up to date and is not authoritative. In particular, there is explanatory wording added by the Secretariat, but its authorship is not clearly identified.

[9] UNTC, 'Multilateral Treaties Deposited with the Secretary-General: Status of Treaties' https://treaties.un.org/pages/ParticipationStatus.aspx?clang=_en accessed 21 September 2018.

factors such as the title of the treaty and whether it is bilateral or multilateral, a treaty official should be able to tell from the text where and when the treaty was signed (usually phrased as 'Done at' on a multilateral treaty, or 'Signed at' on a bilateral treaty) and who the signatories are – including the name of the individual who signed and the government or IO they represented. The testimonium, which is usually just above the signature blocks, will also state which authentic languages the treaty is in – sometimes an important factor. Officials should also be able to tell from the text of the treaty what the procedures are for communicating consent to be bound, whether this is to be by ratification or accession, or perhaps by exchanging notes confirming the completion of necessary domestic procedures.[10]

Information on a treaty action may come from elsewhere, perhaps from staff in an embassy or representative office overseas who have been handling the signature process or who have deposited an instrument of ratification or accession. In such cases, it is essential that the staff concerned know not only that they have to notify someone but precisely who should be notified and how. This also raises the question of timing, since it is important that the Treaty Office is notified as quickly as possible that the action has been taken. So as well as having procedures for handling treaty information, it is important to make sure that all those who need to know what to do are kept informed.

Treaty Offices will also pick up information on actions on a multilateral treaty from notifications circulated by the depositary. This is discussed in more detail later in this chapter from the perspective of the depositary. For the recipient Treaty Office, such notifications are a vital source of information for maintaining an up-to-date treaty record, and should be treated with care and accurately recorded. A further vital piece of information from the depositary is in relation to the entry into force of multilateral treaties. Many treaties have the provision that they will enter into force on the deposit of a specified number of instruments of ratification or accession. Depending on how high the bar has been set, it may be many years after a government has deposited its own instrument before that treaty enters into force, but recognising the importance of such notifications is a significant function of the Treaty Office and something that treaty officials need to be aware of. The entry into force of the treaty may trigger the need for actions to be taken at the domestic level, and therefore policy officials will need to be alerted promptly. An efficient depositary should alert all Contracting Parties and signatories when entry into force appears imminent, but not all depositaries can be relied upon to do so, and each State or IO concerned should keep its own count so as to avoid being taken by surprise.

[10] For more detailed discussion, see Chapter 5, specifically, the sections on 'Drafting a Treaty Text' and 'Production of Treaty Texts' at 163–76 and 176–88.

The PLATO 'Assured' Principle – Distinguishing Between Authoritative and Non-Authoritative Sources

How Can You Tell if the Text You Are Looking at Is the Original?

This should be very clear; the original text of a treaty is usually printed on a special kind of stiff paper and bound into a formal binder with ribbon, the end of which is sealed onto the binder. It will contain the original signatures. The purpose of binding and sealing the treaty is to ensure that no pages can be lost, removed or added later, thus providing guaranteed authenticity. When a bilateral treaty is concluded, it is normally signed in duplicate and each government (or IO) will keep one of the originals, which will be bound and sealed into a binder, usually bearing its own crest (See Figures 5.1 and 5.2 at page 178). A multilateral treaty will normally consist of a single signed original, kept by the depositary, who provides a certified copy to each signatory. Each certified copy will normally be bound with ribbon, sealed and signed by a senior treaty official, thus providing assurance to the recipient that it is as reliable as the original. The original and/or certified copy should always be sent to the Treaty Office, which is responsible for ensuring its permanent safekeeping.

Why Might It Be Important to Know whether a Treaty Text Is an Original or Certified Copy, or an Uncertified Copy?

If the text is an uncertified copy, there are many ways in which it may not be accurate. For example, there may be pages missing. It may not be the final version; it may be an earlier draft (which may not be apparent if the last page with the signature block is omitted). It may not show a manuscript amendment made by the signatories. It may omit one of the official language texts, or it may include an additional non-official language version that was prepared after signature. It may have been retyped with typing errors. A published copy may have had headings or punctuation changed by the publisher. If it is in digital format, the text may be corrupted. A photocopy may be of poor quality with some parts obscured. And so on.

The Treaty Office should ensure that it receives the original or a certified copy of every treaty which is part of its official collection, and use this to create its records. Before archiving the original or official certified copy, the Treaty Office will wish to make its own certified copies to store for its own use. These should ideally be an image of the signed and bound original, fixed together securely, with a clear note of the number of pages.

If the Treaty Office receives a treaty text for the first time and it is not an original (or certified copy), they should seek to ascertain its origin and status. If it is one that should be added to treaty records, they should enquire where the original is, and seek to obtain it (or a certified copy). Never trust the accuracy of a copy of a treaty that is neither certified by the depositary nor from the Treaty Office's own collection.

When Might the Original or Certified Copy of a Treaty Need To Be Consulted?

For everyday purposes, the Treaty Office will refer to its own file copies, as the original (or official certified copy) will be placed in archives. Occasionally, it will be necessary to produce the original. This may be for ceremonial purposes, or because another signature is to be added. It may also prove necessary in the event of a dispute where the other party produces a different text, especially if the dispute is taken to an international court or tribunal.

If the treaty is one that the Treaty Office's own government or IO has recently signed or ratified, then they may expect that their colleagues dealing with this treaty would inform them and send them the signed text – indeed, they may even have been dealing with the treaty themselves. But this is not necessarily always the case so there is a need for sound internal procedures for ensuring that such information is passed to the treaty official responsible for recording it. Much will depend on the size of the Treaty Office, but often something as simple as a worksheet with the action necessary at each stage of the process will ensure that the right people are notified.

How Is Treaty Information Recorded?

Precisely how the information is recorded depends to a large degree on the systems and resources available to the Treaty Office. Some Treaty Offices have online databases in which all such information is recorded on a daily basis and is therefore constantly being updated. For others, the information may be updated weekly or even less frequently. Other offices without access to online or electronic databases may have a card index system where the information is stored. The important factor in all such systems is that the information is recorded with 100 per cent accuracy and meticulous attention to detail. One simple spelling mistake in the title of the treaty may mean that an online search engine would be unable to find the treaty and retrieve the data on it. The misfiling of an index card could have the same effect.

Knowledge Management by and for the Staff of the Treaty Office

The information in the treaty records is not just used to respond to enquiries. It can be very useful as a guide for the Treaty Office's *own* work. This is especially true when an unusual procedural problem arises, and it is important to know whether this problem has ever arisen in the past and if so, how it was handled then. Setting up a 'precedents' folder with examples of different situations (for Treaty Office internal use) can save many hours of work trailing through records to find the details of a case that one treaty official can only partially remember. These precedents could relate to a range of situations, such as how an unusual request was handled; what was done when a document received from another State was not in proper order; and how a signing ceremony was organised when the treaty text was not ready. The most important aspect to a precedents folder is a regularly updated index – without this, the search could still take hours!

How to Maintain Inflow of Treaty Information to the Treaty Office

One of the most frequent problems a Treaty Office may find in managing a treaty collection is maintaining a constant flow of reliable treaty information *into* the Treaty Office. Treaty actions may be undertaken by a wide range of actors in agencies across governments and IOs, and not all will know what they are required to do with the documents they have; some may not even understand the importance of them. Junior diplomats in overseas postings may, for example, regard an exchange of notes that constitute a treaty as no different from any other exchange of diplomatic notes, and may not know the significance involved or that they have to inform the Treaty Office that the exchange has taken place.

This can also lead to problems with timing. Lack of appreciation of the importance of a document can lead to its onward transmission to the Treaty Office being given a low priority. It is not unknown for notifications of treaty actions to languish unsent in a drawer or cupboard, only to surface months (or even years) later when the official concerned moves on. One of the key factors for the successful management of treaty information is therefore strong inter-agency co-operation. This applies not only internally within different sections of an office such as a foreign ministry, but also across the whole government or IO, where a range of ministries or units may be responsible for parts of the treaty-making process. While a government's Treaty Office is often located within the foreign ministry, the policy for the subject matter of a treaty will usually be dealt with by the home ministry responsible for that subject. The treaty negotiation may be carried out by the home department's own officials, or they may send instructions directly to diplomats at the embassy who are attending the negotiation on their behalf, and if finance matters are involved they may also be liaising with the finance ministry. If all of these agencies are not co-operating closely, the opportunities for error and misinformation, as well as duplication of effort, increase considerably. Moreover, a great many of these communications may not pass through the foreign ministry at all, and in such cases a special effort needs to be made to keep the Treaty Office informed and to send the treaty documents on to them.

In some States, the responsibility for treaties on a particular matter may be delegated to a particular ministry or department. For example, the Department of Civil Aviation in the Ministry of Transportation may be given the power to negotiate and enter into bilateral air services agreements, or the Revenue Department in the Ministry of Finance may be given the power to negotiate and enter into certain types of bilateral double taxation treaties. In such cases, it is essential that the Treaty Office establishes clear procedures and ensures that they are followed, and that the original treaty documents are transmitted immediately to the Treaty Office for record-keeping purposes.

Where a government or IO has a Treaty Office, it is therefore vital that the existence of that office, and its functions, are well known to all officials. One way of promoting the activities of the Treaty Office is for officials within the Treaty Office to visit various government agencies and meet the relevant policy officials or give presentations on the work of the office. This enables treaty professionals to highlight the relevance of their work to the agency's successful achievement of its international policy aims, and to emphasise the need for close co-operation. There are many other ways of raising awareness of treaty procedures, such as providing online training to all diplomats and officials across other government departments.[11]

If there is no Treaty Office, it is even more important for a central authority to take responsibility for the management of treaties, write guidance for all officials and actively disseminate them. Officials in other parts of the government or IO should easily be able to see what they need to do with a particular piece of treaty information, and know where or to whom it should be sent.

Setting Up a Treaty Database

Factors to Consider When Choosing a Form of Database

Discussions on treaty databases can easily become embroiled in obscure technical detail and lose sight of the essential factor – the information must be stored securely and reliably, and be easy to search for and retrieve. A treaty database is essentially an organised collection of treaty records. There is a wide range of different types of databases, which are not all necessarily online or electronic. The card index system is in itself a form of database and, for those governments and IOs for whom an electronic database is not a viable proposition due to resource issues, a card index can form a workable alternative.

The first question for any organisation to ask when contemplating investing in an electronic database is – who are its users going to be? Is the main purpose of the database to organise the information for Treaty Office staff to use? Is the intention to provide direct access to other staff within the ministry or administrative unit? Is the aim (immediate or potential) to provide government-wide or IO-wide access to the information? What about public access? Identifying the intended end-users is an essential step in considering the design of the database and determining the systems it will need to connect with. The various categories of possible users of treaty information have been considered in detail above.[12] Conversely, when the technical feasibility of connecting it to IT systems in other offices and public platforms is assessed, it may reveal issues

[11] See the section on 'Providing Guidance on Treaty Procedures across the Government or IO' in Chapter 2 at 76–8.

[12] See the section on 'The Users of Treaty Collections' above at 129–31.

that limit the accessibility for end-users. In that case, the solution might be a database limited to staff use only, as well as a separate system for publishing the information online.

Technical Choices: Freestanding or Integrated with a Public Website?

Broadly, there are two types of options, each of which has advantages and disadvantages. Their suitability will depend upon the IT systems already in use across the government or secretariat, the wider IT environment and the resources available. The following text explains the possible options and some factors to consider.

Freestanding Database

A freestanding database could be set up on one standalone computer (or linked computers) in the Treaty Office, accessible to Treaty Office staff only, and other staff as desired. It has the advantage of maximum flexibility and autonomy for the Treaty Office. The Treaty Office can install it, update it, develop it, and replace it independently of the rest of the administration. It can choose software that best suits its needs, irrespective of the systems in use generally in the government or secretariat, and it need not worry about incompatibility with general system upgrades. The Treaty Office can store all of its information there, including confidential or sensitive material, in the confidence that others have no access; for example, notes about internal procedures, problems and solutions in particular cases, and legal advice. This material can be cross-referenced to the treaty it concerns. The absence of connection to a public website avoids security issues as well as compatibility with software in wider use. It is also likely to be the cheapest option. This might be the only practical option if the IT systems in use across the administration are underdeveloped, outdated or liable to be changed without consultation with the Treaty Office, or if a reliable internet service is not available.

A freestanding database does, however, have major disadvantages: provision of treaty information to other users will need to be done on another system, with manual transfer of information and the greater risk of error – or, if there is no other electronic system, by paper circulation with an email or telephone enquiry service which is labour-intensive; the ministry or secretariat's general IT support services might not be available for the database as it is not on the official system.

If there is an official internal network (intranet) that is accessible across the ministry or unit or more widely across government or the IO, connecting the database to that network might be a viable option. It offers the advantage that treaty information can be made directly accessible to a wider range of officials who need it for their work. But the disadvantages are that the system would then depend upon the efficacy of the intranet, and may be vulnerable to system-wide changes that cause incompatibilities. It may still be necessary to create a separate website for provision of treaty information to the public. Thus some of the advantages of the completely freestanding database would be lost, without the gains of a system integrated to a public website.

Database Connected to a Public Website on the Internet

A database connected to a public website on the internet has the major advantage that treaty information only needs to be entered once, and then is automatically accessible to all staff and the public. By eliminating the need for manual transfer of information, the risk of human or technical error occurring during that process is eliminated. Any errors resulting from data input will be immediately visible on the internal system, so the public website is likely to have a higher level of accuracy. Single-input also reduces the labour required and eliminates time-lag in the transfer of data from internal to public database. It provides maximum transparency and therefore public confidence. It also results in maximum accessibility by staff as they can access it via any internet-enabled device and are not reliant upon an internal intranet. The disadvantage is that only data suitable for public display can be entered. It may be possible to erect a security wall to enable certain fields of information to be visible to Treaty Office staff but not on the website, and/or to set up a password-protected area of the website for internal users only, but this may be impractical or you may consider that the risk of human or technical error makes it unwise. In that case, sensitive internal material will need to be stored separately, which might make it more difficult to index it directly to the treaty it concerns.

The following are some examples of treaty databases in States and IOs:

- The UK Treaties Online is an example of a treaty database provided directly by government. The database, which is available on the UK Government website, allows the public to search across a number of fields of data taken from the central database of treaties held by the UK Treaty Section, which is located within the FCO. The full database is, however, only available to staff within limited parts of the FCO, and the information that is searchable online is extracted from the (separate) internal database on a weekly basis, and transferred manually.
- To allow access to the full texts of treaties, the Treaty Section undertook a major project a few years ago to digitally scan the texts of all treaties published in the UK Treaty Series from 1895, and link these with treaty records contained in the database. These are now accessible through UK Treaties Online, together with the full texts of all treaties published by the UK, both before and after they have entered into force, from 1997. The database is in the process of further development.
- Vietnam also has an online treaty database publicly available on the website of the MFA, in addition to the Treaty Office's internal database. The public database, which is managed by the Ministry's Treaty Office,

includes information on all bilateral and multilateral treaties to which Vietnam is a party. It allows the public to search by the title, parties, date of signature or entry into force, keywords, leading policy agency, or the subject area of the treaty.[13]

- In Indonesia, the Directorate General of Law and International Treaties of the MFA administers an online treaty database that is available to the public. The database includes not only information on all bilateral and multilateral treaties to which Indonesia is a party, but also information on domestic legislation adopted to ratify those treaties.[14]
- The CoE Treaty Office database is linked directly to the CoE treaty website. Information entered into the database by the Treaty Office is displayed immediately on the public website.[15]
- The UN Treaty Collection has a fully searchable database of all treaties registered with the United Nations. While this is a highly useful tool, it is limited by definition to those treaties that have entered into force and have been registered by one of the parties with the UN. The Collection also includes details of the status of all multilateral treaties deposited with the Secretary General of the UN, and a range of guidance notes on treaty matters.

Technical Choices: Bespoke or Off-the-Shelf Software?

A fundamental technical question is whether to buy 'off-the-shelf' software and try to build the database around that, or instead to design a purely bespoke system. This is where a project can sometimes run into difficulties before it has even started: off-the-shelf software can sometimes prove to be unsuitable, but designing a bespoke system requires a high level of input from the Treaty Office as the software designers will not be familiar with the particular needs of treaty users. Designing a treaty database can very easily become exorbitantly expensive and consume vast amounts of time and effort, but if properly done, a fully functioning treaty database can be the most valuable tool at any Treaty Office's disposal.

To work at its peak efficiency, a treaty database needs to be fully searchable across many of its fields of data. As a minimum, those searching will want to be able to do so by the title of the treaty, the parties to the treaty and by treaty type (whether the treaty was a bilateral or multilateral). They may want to search by date if they know the date the treaty was signed, ratified or entered into force, or by a range of dates. They may also want to be able to search by the place in

[13] Treaty Office https://treaty.mofa.gov.vn/default.aspx accessed 21 September 2018. The database is only available in Vietnamese.

[14] Ministry of Foreign Affairs of Indonesia, 'Treaty Database' http://treaty.kemlu.go.id/search accessed 21 September 2018. The database is only available in Indonesian.

[15] See the section on 'Maintaining the database: the data' below at 145–47.

which the treaty was signed. Users may also be interested in searching for treaties covering a particular subject, such as extradition or investment. Other information that users may be interested in include information on treaties deposited with the Treaty Office and the status of treaties. The treaty database should be capable of providing information on all of these questions, and be able to do so in an easily readable and logical way. It is little use being able to provide the information if it is not then presented in a way that will be usable to the enquirer, who might be unfamiliar with treaty terms and expressions.[16]

This means that in addition to designing the database itself, the way in which the information is presented once it has been retrieved needs to be considered. A user faced with a list of treaties in no particular logical order may quickly find that there is too much work to do to make sense of the information, and perhaps need to turn to other sources. The information should therefore be presented in an easily readable and logical format.[17]

Providing a Database User Guide

Users of the database might find that in addition to the database, it is useful to have a User Guide. This could provide an explanation of the best way to search for information on the database and give some tips for searching. This is especially valuable when searching for treaties known largely by acronyms or the name of the place they were signed (such as Kyoto Protocol or SOLAS (International Convention for the Safety of Life at Sea, 1974)). The UK's 'UK Treaties Online' database has very useful guidance for users, which includes details of a large number of commonly used treaty acronyms to help the user find the treaty they are searching for.[18] The UN Treaty Database allows users to search by the name the treaty is popularly known by, so that for example the Convention on the Conservation of Antarctic Marine Living Resources 1980 can be searched for by its more popular title of 'CCAMLR'. Similarly, the Convention on the International Trade in Endangered Species of Wild Fauna and Flora 1973 can be searched for by 'CITES'. It may also be useful to file each treaty under certain key words such as 'environment', 'nuclear' or 'terrorism', so that a user can find it if they are searching for treaties on a particular subject but do not know the full name of the treaty or its date. The Treaties Office of the European Union External Action Service also has a very comprehensive user manual on how to search for treaty information on its database.[19] When

[16] See the section on 'What Information Might the Treaty Office Need when Responding to Requests?' above at 132–34.

[17] See 'Top Tips 1: Designing a treaty database – what can go wrong?' below at 156.

[18] FCO, 'UK Treaties Online', http://treaties.fco.gov.uk/treaties/treaty.htm accessed 21 September 2018. For a useful roadmap, see the 'Guidance for Users' section.

[19] European Union External Action Service, 'User Manual to the Treaties Office Database' (1 October 2013) http://ec.europa.eu/world/agreements/pdf/TREATIES_UMD_INTERNET.pdf accessed 21 September 2018.

writing a user manual, it is of course important to consider who its users are – is it primarily for officials or the public?

Should the Database Show the Full Text of the Treaty?

One of the other factors to consider when displaying treaty information from a database is whether it is also feasible to provide the full text of each treaty. For many users, this will no doubt be a highly valuable asset, if they are able to see and download the text of the treaty itself while viewing treaty status information. Most government and IO official treaty publications are nowadays published online. However, digital publishing may only have started recently. Treaties published more than a few years ago may be available only in a printed form. The first issue in that case is resources: are resources available to produce digital copies of all past treaties? If so, how far back in time? How should this be done?

The important factor to consider here is the accuracy and authenticity of the text. If an official treaty database contains the full text of a treaty, or access to it, that text should be the full and authentic version of the treaty concerned. So, it is essential that the text published on the database is taken from the original document (in the case of a bilateral treaty) or a certified true copy (in the case of a multilateral). Use of any other text is risky, as it may contain errors, may be incomplete or may have been edited by a third party. Even if the edits are only of a formal nature, such as adding or omitting headings to articles, it could make a difference.

The best way to present the text online is therefore to display a scanned image of the whole of the signed original (in all its languages) so that the reader can see the signatures, the original page numbers and the ribbon at the bound edge of each page. Ensuring that only this version is used, and that all its original features can be seen on the screen, will give users of the database the confidence that the version they are seeing is authentic and that its accuracy can be relied upon. However, scanning a bound treaty document can be difficult to do without damaging it or missing text close to the spine. Despite this, the original treaty binding should *never* be removed in any circumstances. A good solution is to use a scanner with a curved (convex) glass surface, of the type commonly used in libraries. However, scanning large numbers of treaties to pdf format is very time-consuming, especially as each one must be manually checked against the original. Embarking on this is a major project, so a careful assessment of resources needs to be made and categories of treaties prioritised as necessary, such as by date.

If instead a version transposed (retyped) from the original or certified true copy is displayed, it should be one that the Treaty Office has produced itself, following rigorous proofreading procedures to ensure 100 per cent accuracy. It should be retyped exactly as the original, without changes to the title, preamble, headings or style of article numberings, and with the complete final wording including the signature block. The names of signatories may be typed in place of original signatures, with an indication of this. If any element is changed or omitted deliberately, for example if other authentic language versions are omitted to save costs, this should be shown clearly on the text. Consider also the format in which the text is presented – if the text is displayed as a Word document this might allow alterations to creep in, where a PDF format is less likely to become corrupted.

The task is of course much easier when a treaty has already been published in digital format in an official series by the Treaty Office's own government or legislature (or IO, as the case may be). The digital texts can be uploaded or linked to the online treaty database. However, the online version may not be the authoritative text; typically, the sole authoritative text is the one published in printed version. Even if there is reasonable confidence in the accuracy of the displayed version, it is always important to ask: is the displayed text the authoritative version? If the digital publication has a disclaimer to the effect that only the printed version is authoritative, this disclaimer needs to be shown to the viewer of that text via the treaty database.

If it is not feasible to display any version of the original text, the database could instead provide links to an authoritative version of the text published elsewhere, if there is one. If the treaty is published by the UN in the UN Treaty Series or the Multilateral Treaties Deposited with the Secretary General series, the reader could be referred to that source. For multilateral treaties whose depositary is a government or IO other than the UN, if the depositary provides an online authoritative text, this is a good source to link to. If none of these options are available, and it is decided to provide the reader with a link or reference to a non-authoritative source of the text, such as that provided by a treaty secretariat, an NGO or academic institution, the treaty database should signpost very clearly to the reader that the link is to an unofficial text on a third-party website for which the government/IO can take no responsibility (see 'The Importance of Authenticity and Disclaimers' at page 148 below).

Maintaining the Database: The Data

The database will be one of the principal tools for officials within the Treaty Office. This will be the repository of information and the first point of reference for dealing with enquiries. So, it is vital that the database is well maintained both from a physical point of view and in terms of the information stored on it. The data stored on an electronic database must be regularly backed up and well supported by technically competent staff if the reliability and stability of the database is to be guaranteed. It is equally important that the information stored on the database is regularly reviewed and audited, to ensure that no errors have crept in when data was being inputted to the system and that information has not become corrupted.

Speed of updating information is also vital. Ideally, when each new document is received, the database should be updated immediately. An example of a Treaty Office with an exemplary track record in this regard is the CoE. The Treaty Office's Secretary/Webmaster adds information to the electronic database about each treaty act as soon as it is received, normally on the same day. When an instrument of ratification is received from a Member State, it is typically checked by the Head of Treaty Office and added to the database by the Secretary/Webmaster within fifteen minutes of receipt. The CoE treaty database is directly viewed via the public website, and each update is visible to the public as soon as it is entered.[20] The text of all CoE treaties, their explanatory reports, the status of signatures and ratifications, the declarations and reservations made by States, as well as the notifications issued by the Treaty Office since 2005, are available on this website. All documents (Full Powers, ratification instruments, *procès verbaux*, declaration, reservations, official notifications) in relation to treaty acts are digitised.[21]

The CoE database is set up to function in the five working languages of the organisation. Each treaty table on the CoE website is available for the user separately in those five languages. When treaty data is inputted by the Treaty Office, codes are used to refer to the names of countries, dates and other recurring terms, which the database software is programmed to convert instantly into the five languages. For example, the code FRA (Official code ISO–31 66) means 'France' in French; 'France' in English; 'Francia' in Italian; 'Frank' in German and 'Франция' in Russian. Non-recurring information such as the title of a new treaty has to be manually inputted in all languages by translators. The authentic text of each treaty is in English and French, the two official languages. However, translations into other languages are also published on the Treaty Office website if provided by other actors such as the States or other services within the CoE. All these translations are non-official. The uploading of unofficial translations of treaty texts to the website consequently takes a little longer than the entry of information about treaty actions.

The importance of prompt updating when new information is received applies equally to non-digital databases. If reliance is placed upon a card index system linked to treaty documents in paper files, it is also vital to review and maintain the whole system on a regular basis. This includes undertaking a risk assessment of the physical collection, and considering whether the housing in which it is stored is sufficiently protected and whether a back-up set of index cards is needed. The index cards and files should be checked regularly to ensure that they are complete and in the correct position. It is useful to have a review conducted periodically by an independent assessor (for

[20] See Treaty Office, 'Conventions' (Council of Europe) www.conventions.coe.int/ accessed 21 September 2018.

[21] The information in this and the preceding paragraph was kindly provided by the CoE Treaty Office during Jill Barrett's visit in 2012, and reconfirmed to her in November 2018. See Acknowledgements at xxiii.

example, by an information management specialist from elsewhere in the administration), including random checks.

Updating an Electronic Database: The Operating Software

Any database is likely to need a comprehensive update to its operating software every few years. This can present its own set of problems. It usually involves the migration of data from one system to another, and the opportunities for data to become corrupted in such a process are significant. Updating a database operating system, while essential, should always be regarded as a major project and might require the allocation of significant resources, not just in financial terms but also in terms of time and effort. Once migrated, the data will need to be cross-checked to ensure that it has not become corrupted in the migration process – a significant task if it has not, but an even bigger task if it has. If the data is corrupted, every treaty record will have to be manually checked to ensure its accuracy and remedied where necessary.

Maintaining the software is also a very important practical task. Given the speed at which technology evolves, it can often be the case that by the time a bespoke system has been developed, it has already become obsolete and the software on which it is based is no longer technically supported. So if a bespoke database is being considered, the requirement for ongoing development and support for the database over many years will also have to be factored in. Allied to this is the issue of whether the software chosen when the database was designed can be amended. After a database has been running for a while, it may be discovered that a particular field of information has been omitted, or that it would be useful if users could search by a topic that cannot currently be accommodated. If the software chosen does not allow such functions to be amended or added, the functionality of the database will in effect be frozen until such time as a revised operating system is installed.

Outsourcing the Treaty Database versus Running It In-House

If you are considering developing a treaty database but find that you do not have the resources necessary to do so, or that the costs of ongoing maintenance may be prohibitive, there is a possible solution. This is to enter into collaboration with an academic institution, which may be able to provide resources and support that you cannot find elsewhere. Academic institutions may for example be able to provide the means by which a treaty collection could be digitised, to enable it to be accessed electronically via the internet. They may have research staff in the legal department with sufficient expertise and interest in treaties to perform the task. But this kind of arrangement should not be undertaken lightly; it will entail a substantial ongoing commitment from both parties and transparent contractual arrangements if the collaboration is to be a success in the long term. It would be wise for the contract to specify the nature of the collaborated database, such as whether it is an official government treaty database, the types of data that can be shared and collaborated, and what will happen to the treaty collection, data and software at the end of the collaboration or in the event that the arrangement is terminated early by either side.

A good example of collaboration between governments and academic institutions to provide detailed treaty information online is that between the Australian and New Zealand Governments and the Australasian Legal Information Institute (AustLII). The AustLII, which is a joint facility of the University of Technology Sydney and University of New South Wales Faculties of Law, provides free online access to the Australian Treaties Library, to treaties since 1944 in the New Zealand Treaty Series and to New Zealand Treaties in Force. The Australian Treaties Library was developed and is maintained by the Institute with the treaty information being provided by the Australian Treaty Office, located in the DFAT. The Australian Treaties Library is a fully searchable, hypertext-linked resource that includes treaty texts from the Australian Treaty Series, indexes, status lists and explanatory material. The Treaties Library provides public access to the Australian Treaty List, which is updated on a monthly basis, together with the full texts of treaties published in the Australian Treaty Series from 1901 and those treaties not yet in force for Australia from 1983. It also provides links to a range of other documents such as National Interest Analyses, and reports and guidance on Australia's treaty-making procedures.

Useful though it is, the Australian Treaties Library is however *not* the official Australian Government treaty database. The official Australian Treaties Database is maintained by the DFAT.[22] Its functionality is more limited, but its information is the authoritative version, and so if there is any inconsistency between the two sources, the Australian Treaties Database should be used. There is an inevitable risk, with any arrangement that involves transfer of treaty information to a third party to enter into a database, that there could be human error, or interruption of the service, for technical, financial or institutional reasons beyond the control of the government. Therefore, any Treaty Office would be well advised to maintain its own official database, however basic and even if it is only internal, alongside the third-party arrangement.

The Importance of Authenticity and Disclaimers

The above examples all clearly demonstrate an important point within the PLATO 'Assured' principle that those searching for treaty information need to be able to find information whose authenticity and accuracy is assured. It is critical that users of treaty information know whether the text of the treaty they

[22] Australian Government DFAT, 'Treaties: Australian Treaties Database' http://dfat.gov.au/international-relations/treaties/Pages/treaties.aspx accessed 21 September 2018.

are viewing is the authentic full text of the treaty itself, and not an unofficial or informal version that may have been used for other purposes. In each of the examples of databases discussed above, the user can view the full official text of the treaty, published by the government or organisation responsible for it, and have the confidence that it comes from a reliable authoritative source. For the casual reader, an unofficial version may be good enough; but for others it may not, for example a lawyer who is using the text for government work or advising a client on litigation.

Where the version shown on a public website is not the authoritative text, this should be clearly stated by means of a disclaimer. For example, the CoE posts a status list for all treaties for which it is the depositary on the Treaty Office official website. There is an important disclaimer page which states, inter alia:

> Please note that it can't be guaranteed that a document available on-line exactly reproduces an officially adopted text. Only the treaties published by the Secretary General of the Council of Europe, each in a separate booklet of the 'Council of Europe Treaty Series' (CETS), are deemed authentic.[23]

Archiving Treaties: Permanent Storage, Preservation and Retrieval

The way in which treaty documents are to be stored is another factor that needs to be considered. Original copies of treaties, together with their associated documents, need to be preserved throughout the lifetime of the treaty and for some time thereafter. This invariably means several decades of storage at least – perhaps centuries. During this time they must be kept secure and preserved in their original condition. Bear in mind that this applies not just to the text of the treaty itself – all of the associated documents such as copies of Full Powers, instruments of ratification and so on, and copies of any side letters or explanatory memorandums (EMs), will also have to be kept.

This can take a lot of physical space. Initially, treaties should be kept somewhere close by to allow for easy reference – for example, when a treaty has been signed but has not yet entered into force. Even then there may be a need to keep these treaties for a number of years, so suitable storage facilities are a must-have for Treaty Offices. Ideally these facilities should permit access only by those working in the Treaty Office, to ensure that adequate security of the documents is maintained. Once a treaty is in force for the government or organisation concerned, and has been registered and published as required, then longer-term storage and preservation can be considered. This will usually be in some form of archive, whether held on the ministry or secretariat's own premises, or elsewhere such as in a national archive. For example, in Thailand, the Department of Treaties and Legal Affairs of the MFA has an archive for

[23] See the full text of disclaimers on CoE Treaty Office, 'Important legal notice' www.coe.int/en/web/conventions/disclaimer accessed 21 September 2018.

original treaty documents, while very old treaties will be transferred to the National Archive for storage.[24] In the Philippines, the Foreign Service Institute Library (within the Department of Foreign Affairs) maintains a centralised archive.[25] In Vietnam, by law, the MFA is responsible for keeping custody of Vietnam's treaty original texts and official documents related to treaties (Article 58 Treaty Law 2016). In Indonesia, treaties are stored in the Treaty Room administered by the Directorate General of Law and International Treaties of the MFA. The Treaty Room is a physical room within the MFA premises, specifically designated to store treaties and designed in accordance with the Indonesian National Archives standards.[26] The Room has the capacity to archive more than 13,000 treaties. A treaty safe, fumigation room, a film and photography archive room and a treaty preservation room are among the facilities provided at the Treaty Room. The Treaty Room archive has almost 6,000 treaties to which Indonesia is a party.[27]

National archives may be located outside the centre of the capital city, where space is available at more economic cost and where there may be facility to expand in the future. For example, in the UK, the Treaty Section of the FCO initially stores treaty documents in its own archives on FCO premises; older documents for which rapid access is no longer needed are sent to the National Archives at Kew, Surrey (an outer-London suburb). The CoE stores all treaty documents permanently within their own premises. All documents are filed with the treaty to which they relate, by treaty number order. When required they are retrieved by Treaty Office staff in person. This can be done immediately.

Wherever treaties are stored, an effective system for recording and managing their storage will be required so that documents can easily be recalled if needed, and to ensure that nothing is lost or misplaced. Longer-term preservation of documents will require the services of professional archivists to ensure that the documents are held in the correct manner. They will be able to provide advice on storage at the appropriate temperature and humidity, and also how to keep documents safe from possible damage from natural causes, such as fire and flood, or from attack by insect infestations. A further source of damage to guard against is from human interference, whether deliberate or accidental.

Is it necessary to keep all treaty texts for ever? If there is pressure on storage space, the possibility may be raised of disposing of them after a certain number

[24] Interview with a Treaty Officer from Thailand's Department of Treaties and Legal Affairs in 2012, CIL archive.

[25] Interview with a Treaty Officer from the Philippines' Department of Foreign Affairs in 2012, CIL Archive.

[26] MFA of Indonesia, 'Inauguration of the Treaty Room by the Minister of Foreign Affairs' (16 October 2009) (in Indonesian) www.kemlu.go.id/id/berita/siaran-pers/Pages/Peresmian-Treaty-Room-oleh-Menlu-RI.aspx accessed 21 September 2018.

[27] Directorate General of Legal Affairs and International Treaties, 'About Treaty Room' (Ministry of Foreign Affairs of Indonesia) http://treaty.kemlu.go.id/aboutus/info/about_treaty_room accessed 21 September 2018.

of years, or if the treaty ceases to be in force. However, it *is* important to preserve all of the original texts indefinitely, or at least for several decades after the treaty has ceased to be in force. This applies both to the treaty itself and the related instruments such as ratification, reservations and amendments. They may be needed for a variety of reasons, as listed here:

- If a bilateral treaty is amended, the original may be required for executing the amendment.
- The depositary will need to produce the original of a multilateral treaty every time a new signature is added. If according to the final clauses of the treaty it is open to new signatures indefinitely, a new State may decide to sign it many years or decades after the last signature.
- If a dispute arises with another party over the application of the treaty, and there is a difference of view over the wording or whether certain texts formed part of it, the originals will need to be consulted.
- If a treaty dispute is referred to an international litigation, it might be necessary to produce the original treaty text to the court or tribunal.
- Even after the treaty has been terminated there may be continuing obligations, and disputes may arise over past obligations under the treaty.

The importance of archiving all treaties – no matter how old – can be seen in the practice of the CoE. The Treaty Office staff occasionally need to retrieve a very old treaty from its archives for a public anniversary event. For example, at a ceremony to commemorate the 60th anniversary of the European Social Charter, the original signed treaty document was displayed at the ceremony (accompanied at all times by a member of the Treaty Office).

Handling 'Treaty-Like' Instruments

Chapter 3 provides guidance on what is, and is not, a treaty. There are various kinds of international instruments that are not treaties but bear some similarity to them, and we refer to these as 'treaty-like' instruments. It is important to consider whether any of these should be stored by the Treaty Office and if so, how.

If such instruments are to be included on a treaty database, they must be suitably identified to make sure that it is clear to all users that they are not treaties. To do this, it is important to know the status of the instrument, and this can sometimes create considerable difficulties. In some cases, the negotiators themselves may not be entirely clear on the precise legal status of the instrument they are discussing, and it can be only at a very late stage in the negotiations that this is made clear, if at all.

The Treaty Database of Vietnam, for example, has a separate section to allow users to search for details of treaty-like instruments (which are not treaties) signed by different agencies and local authorities. In the past, the ASEAN Resource Centre (ARC) archived both treaties and treaty-like instruments together, and the LSAD tracked the status of both types of instruments in its 'Table of ASEAN Treaties/Agreements and Ratification'.[28] The ASEAN treaty practice changed in 2013 with the inauguration of the 'ASEAN Legal Instruments' database under the auspices of the LSAD;[29] and in 2016, ASEAN established a dedicated Treaty Division within the LSAD to deal with depositary functions and treaty archiving, presumably together with the ARC.[30]

Some IOs, such as the CoE, and some States, such as the Netherlands and the UK, do not include treaty-like instruments on their database at all. Since they are not treaties, their official treaty management functions such as publication, registration, archiving, etc., do not apply to them. The CoE makes a clear distinction between treaties and non-binding instruments. The CoE Legal Directorate gives legal advice on the full range of instruments, but the Treaty Office only handles treaties.

The UK Treaty Section does, in fact, maintain a list of treaty-like instruments that come to their attention, although this is not part of their official functions. This is of course another issue for Treaty Offices: many treaty-like instruments will be negotiated and signed by officials and ministers in government departments or in embassies without ever coming to the attention of anyone in a Treaty Office. This could be because they are regarded by the officials concerned as purely policy documents, or less important than a treaty, or simply through a lack of knowledge of procedures and processes. One reason that the UK Treaty Section keeps their list of treaty-like instruments for internal use only is that it is not possible for the list to be comprehensive, as there is no legal or official requirement for such documents to be filed with the Treaty Section or any other central government authority.

Given the different nature of treaty-like instruments, they may not always be preserved and archived in the same way as treaties. They may for example be held on the files of policy departments, which can be subject to destruction requirements after certain periods of time. But if a copy of the original is held in a Treaty Office, this may help to preserve the text for longer periods of time. As the record-keeping skills of a Treaty Office are (and should be) above the average for the rest of the organisation, their files and lists can be a useful back-up source of information.

[28] ASEAN, 'Table of ASEAN Treaties/Agreements and Ratification' (October 2012) http://asean.org/wpcontent/uploads/images/2012/resources/TABLE%20OF%20AGREEMENT%20%20RATIFICATION-SORT%20BY%20DATE-Web-October2012.pdf accessed 21 September 2018.

[29] ASEAN Treaty Division, 'ASEAN Legal Instruments' http://agreement.asean.org accessed 21 September 2018.

[30] See ASEAN, 'Organisational Structure' (January 2016) http://asean.org/asean/asean-structure/organisational-structure-2/ accessed 21 September 2018, and ASEAN, 'ASEAN Secretariat Resource Centre (ARC)' http://asean.org/asean/asean-secretariat/asean-secretariat-resource-centre-arc/ accessed 21 September 2018.

If the Treaty Office does not maintain copies of treaty-like instruments for the whole of the government or IO, and if there is no other central agency that does so, it may be advisable to consider whether there should be a central repository or list. Alternatively, guidelines might be issued to each department or agency on the types of 'treaty-like instruments' that should be filed and recorded, and how the information might be made available across the administration. This issue may be especially important for ASEAN countries because many of the most important ASEAN documents are non-binding treaty-like instruments with names such as declarations, accords, concords, blueprints, etc.

As indicated in Chapter 3, it is important that a Treaty Office sees all such instruments before negotiations are concluded, since it is only in this way that advice can be given on whether what has been negotiated is a treaty or not, and the way in which the document should be handled. Policy-makers can sometimes react with shock when advised that the document they have carefully negotiated as a non-binding instrument is in fact a treaty, especially if they have neglected to let the Treaty Office see it until the day before it is due to be signed!

Depositary Functions

Becoming a depositary for a new treaty is not a matter to be entered into lightly. The functions of a depositary may on the surface appear to be entirely routine and administrative, capable of being delegated to comparatively junior staff. But in fact they lie at the heart of the operation of the multilateral treaty system, and require the closest attention to detail and absolute accuracy of record-keeping and communication. Depositary staff who cannot manage their treaty information will very quickly find themselves in terrible difficulties.

A depositary's chief responsibilities are owed to the States which are parties to the treaty concerned, and to those States which are in the process of becoming a party. The depositary government or IO for a particular multilateral treaty is normally identified in the final provisions of that treaty. The obligations of the depositary may also be set out in detail in the final provisions. Not all treaties contain such detail. The core functions of a depositary are well established in practice, and are very clearly set out in Articles 76 and 77 VCLT 1969; these provisions serve as default provisions for all treaties. In other words, each depositary should follow any specific requirements set out in the particular treaty, which prevail over Articles 76 and 77 VCLT 1969 to the extent of any inconsistency. Otherwise, depositaries should follow the pathway set out in Articles 76 and 77, as well as the relevant provisions of Articles 78–80.

Article 77 in particular demonstrates the need for clear treaty management procedures; under the terms of this Article, depositaries must:

- keep custody of the original text and any Full Powers;
- prepare certified copies of the original text (in all its languages) and send them to the parties to the treaty and to States entitled to become parties;
- receive signatures to the treaty and keep custody of any instruments, notifications and communications;
- examine the signatures of any instrument, notification or communication in relation to the treaty to ensure that it is in due and proper form;
- inform all States Parties to the treaty, and States entitled to become parties, of all acts, notifications and communications in relation to the treaty;
- inform States entitled to become parties to the treaty when the number of instruments required to bring the treaty into force has been reached; and
- register the treaty with the UN.

It is clear that a depositary needs to be highly organised to make sure that all of these requirements are fulfilled. Treaty officials need to know where the signed originals of each treaty are, and have certified true copies ready to hand to States as they become a party to the treaty. Every communication received from a State about the treaty will have to be recorded and stored, and the information in it must be circulated to all the other States involved.

Article 76 VCLT 1969 specifies that the functions of a depositary are 'international in character', and sets out the requirement to act impartially. This means that a State may not act in furtherance of its national position or policy when performing its depositary functions. A State does not have to be a party to a treaty to act as a depositary for it – the UK is the depositary for the Constitution of the United Nations Educational, Scientific and Cultural Organisation (UNESCO), but in 1985 the UK withdrew from UNESCO. It remained as depositary however, and continued to fulfil all the obligations required by that role before returning to UNESCO in 1997.

The need to separate the functions and obligations of the depositary from the views of the State can sometimes cause problems, especially when a depositary in a State receives an instrument from another State that its government does not recognise. Questions of recognition are not for the depositary to decide however – if treaty officials are in this position, it is best to circulate the instrument with a note to the States involved with the treaty, so that they can if necessary reach a view on its validity or otherwise. The depositary should not state its national position on the matter in question. Occasionally, treaty officials may come under pressure from their policy colleagues to act in accordance with national policy; this pressure must be resisted. The national position on the particular issue may be circulated to other States by means of a separate communication, from the part of government responsible for the policy. This may be done in parallel with the Treaty Office circulating a depositary notice that is neutral on the issue in question, inviting States Parties to express their views.

Circulating information to all the parties involved in a treaty can be a laborious and sometimes costly business. If there are many parties to the treaty, a copy of the instrument received or a statement of its contents will have to be sent to each of them.[31] For some IOs with representation from Member States at their headquarters such as the UN or the CoE, this may simply be a matter of sending a notification to those representatives for onward transmission to their own State. But for governmental depositaries, the solution may not be so straightforward. They may choose to send such notifications to the embassy of the States concerned, again for onward transmission. The effectiveness of this method depends on the person receiving the notification understanding its significance and the need to forward it promptly to the Treaty Office of their government. As some embassies receive treaty notifications only very occasionally, this underlines the necessity for training in treaty procedures to be provided to all diplomats before being posted overseas.

Electronic transmission of documents has of course made all of this much easier. It has, however, created new problems, such as the need to ensure that electronic communications reach the correct recipient. This may require maintenance of an up-to-date list of email addresses and/or a system that requires a positive acknowledgement of receipt to be sent, or which uses paper communications in addition. For individual notifications, while copies of notes and instruments can be scanned and sent via email, there are some documents that necessarily remain in paper form, such as certified true copies.

An example of depositary transition to electronic communications can be seen from the CoE practice. The CoE now uses electronic means for sending notifications addressed to all Member States to inform them of the various legal acts in relation to treaties, namely signatures, ratifications, declarations, reservations and denunciations. This procedure was introduced in 2006, in place of the former practice of sending a paper note verbale to all Member States, following extensive consultation with the missions about the change. A 'notification' is now sent by email every Friday to the official email address of each mission, or immediately in the (rare) event of a derogation from the European Convention on Human Rights. The email contains a link to the notification which is posted on a website. This enables missions to access the notification even if they have deleted the email. Using the official email of the mission avoids the need to change the address every time an individual official moves on. The CoE also sends a monthly paper note verbale to each mission, listing all notifications for the month. The notifications posted on

[31] For examples of such circulation, see Annex XIV 'Examples of a Depositary Notification of Ratification and Entry into Force' at 454–56.

the CoE website are accessible to the public. For notifications to and from an individual Member State, for example about its ratification, a more formal means of paper communication is used.[32, 33]

Top Tips: Addressing Certain Issues on Managing and Using Treaty Collections

The top tips in Box 4.1 summarise some factors that have been discussed in this chapter to be considered when managing and using treaty collections, especially on designing a treaty database (what can go wrong) and archiving treaties.

Box 4.1 Top tips: Addressing certain issues on managing and using treaty collections

TOP TIPS 1
DESIGNING A TREATY DATABASE – WHAT CAN GO WRONG

Scenario: You are designing a new treaty database (or commissioning experts to do so). What are the most common pitfalls to avoid?

One of the key factors to consider when designing your database is the way in which the information will be presented to users. Bear these factors in mind:

1. If the information is not shown in a logical and clear way, users will be forced to look for other sources of information.
2. The way in which the treaty title is shown is a vital part of this, as it is all too easy to have a list of treaties from the database which looks like this:
   - Treaty between the Government of . . . and . . .
   - Agreement on Mutual Legal Assistance between . . . and . . .
   - 1994 Convention on . . .

   So, when you are designing your database, make sure that users will be able to see the whole title of each treaty result obtained from a search – and remember that treaty titles can sometimes be very long!
3. If you are having a bespoke system designed, you will need to make this clear to the designers at the start of the project.
4. If you are buying an off-the-shelf system, ensure that this feature is included in the package.

[32] The information in this paragraph was kindly provided by the CoE Treaty Office to Jill Barrett in 2012, and updated in 2018. See Acknowledgements at xxiii.

[33] For more detailed discussion of the depositary's functions in relation to ratifications, see the section on 'Duties of the Depositary' in Chapter 7 at 276–80.

Box 4.1 (cont.)

TOP TIPS 2
ARCHIVING TREATIES

Scenario: You are responsible for the treaty collection and are reviewing how original texts are stored. Space and resources are limited and you are under pressure to dispose of some of them. These questions are raised:

1. Which treaties have to be kept?
   It is essential to keep the signed original of every bilateral treaty and the certified copy of every multilateral treaty to which your State or IO is party.
2. Which other documents?
   It is also essential to keep, together with each treaty, the originals of all the associated documents received and copies of all documents sent: for example, Full Powers, instruments of ratification, reservations, etc., and copies of any side letters or EMs will also have to be kept.
3. Do we really need to keep the originals of *every* treaty we are party to?
   Yes.
4. How long for?
   Each treaty must always be kept for so long as it is in force, and thereafter for several decades at least; permanently if possible.
5. Why so long?
   While the treaty is in force, the original may be needed for executing amendments, adding new signatures, etc. After it ceases to be in force, there may still be continuing obligations, and disputes about past obligations may arise. The originals may have to be produced in court.
6. Where should they be stored?
   Until entry into force, and for some time after, treaties need to be kept close at hand. The Treaty Office needs its own storage facility for this purpose. Later they may be transferred to a more distant archive, provided they are carefully catalogued and retrieval is possible.
7. What kind of facility is needed?
   Documents must be kept secure and safe from physical harm, including damp, sunlight, heat, pests and unauthorised access.
8. Who should be allowed access?
   Access should be limited to those who need it – normally only treaty officials and archive staff. If an original treaty is required by others, such as for ceremonial purposes, it should be accompanied by a treaty or archive official.

5

Making a New Treaty: Negotiation, Drafting and Production

***

'The word 'treaty' is derived from the French word traiter, which means to negotiate.'[1]

Introduction: Applying the PLATO Principles to Making a New Treaty

Treaties are international agreements between States, or between IOs, or between any combinations thereof, which are governed by international law.[2] All aspects of treaty-making are governed by the international law of treaties. This brings the PLATO principle 'Legal' into the foreground.[3]

[1] I Roberts (ed), *Satow's Diplomatic Practice* (6th edn, OUP 2017) 541.
[2] See the section on 'Definition of a Treaty in International Law' in Chapter 3 at 93–6.
[3] For a complete explanation of the PLATO principles, see the section on 'The PLATO Principles for Good Treaty Practice' in Chapter 1 at 14.

The 'Legal' aspect of PLATO means that legal requirements must be met and legal advisers should be fully engaged. In the context of creating a new treaty, there are some key points to remember:

- The rules set out in the VCLT 1969 and the VCLT 1986 provide the international law framework for creating treaties.[4]
- The rules set out in the VCLT 1969 and VCLT 1986 are generally recognised as reflecting rules of customary international law, applicable to all States, whether or not they are party to those conventions.[5]
- Those rules are mostly residual in nature, which means they may be modified or displaced by express provisions in the new treaty.
- Those rules are flexible as to the form and name of a treaty; a document may be a treaty even if it is not called 'treaty' and does not look like one on the surface.
- International law advisers and treaty officials should be involved and consulted at all stages of treaty-making; in some governments and IOs, these are two distinct groups of personnel.
- Since a new treaty may have domestic law implications, a government negotiating team should always consult lawyers with the relevant domestic law expertise at the drafting stage (as well as international lawyers).

These principles of legality interact strongly with particular elements of two other PLATO principles: 'Assured' and 'Organised'. 'Assured' means reliable, dependable, trustworthy and guaranteed. It is especially important to make sure this applies to:

- the accuracy of all new treaty texts and related instruments; and
- the authority of each person involved in procedures relating to the creation of the treaty.

For the 'Organised' aspect, treaty management practice should be systematic, efficient and regular. When a new treaty is negotiated and produced, particular attention is needed to ensure:

- centrality, in that there should be one point of contact and a central authority responsible for treaty procedures; and
- co-ordination across government departments and agencies (or all parts of an IO) on all aspects of treaty negotiation and drafting.

[4] VCLT 1969 (adopted 23 May 1969, entered into force 27 January 1980) 1155 UNTS 331 and VCLT 1986 (adopted 21 March 1986, not in force) 25 ILM 543 http://legal.un.org/ilc/texts/instruments/english/conventions/1_2_1986.pdf accessed 9 September 2018.

[5] 'Generally recognised' means that there are some exceptions. There are a few provisions in VCLT 1969 and VCLT 1986 that are not universally accepted as reflecting customary international law, such as Article 53 on the invalidity of treaties that conflict with a peremptory norm of international law (*jus cogens*). But these exceptions rarely arise in practice.

Differences in the Making of Multilateral and Bilateral Treaties

The rules set out in the VCLT 1969 and VCLT 1986 provide a single international law framework for creating treaties of all kinds. Most of the rules apply to all treaties, while a few apply specifically to a 'multilateral treaty'[6] and one rule applies specifically to a 'bilateral treaty'.[7] The Vienna Conventions do not define the terms 'bilateral' or 'multilateral'; in practice, it is clear that 'bilateral' refers to a treaty with two parties while 'multilateral' covers all other treaties with three or more parties. However, although the law of treaties treats bilateral and multilateral treaties in much the same way, there are important differences in the treaty procedures and practices relating to each of these categories, which we will explore in this chapter.

'Multilateral' treaties vary enormously in type, and fall broadly into these categories:

- 'Global treaties': those open to all States (and sometimes IOs as well).
- 'Limited membership multilateral treaties': those open to a defined category of States and/or IOs, such as those within a particular geographical region or which are members of a particular IO, or those which meet any other criteria such as engaging in a particular industry or activity.
- 'Closed membership multilateral treaties': those open only to the negotiating States or IOs named in the treaty. These are sometimes called 'plurilateral' treaties, and they may have several parties or as few as three. This category is relatively unusual, and the procedures used for each tend to be a kind of customised hybrid mix of multilateral and bilateral procedures.

'Bilateral' treaties always have two parties, normally two States, or, less commonly, one State and one IO, or two IOs. Exceptionally, a party to a bilateral treaty may consist of more than one State or IO acting together as a single party; for example, the EU and its Member States (one party) enter into bilateral treaties with a third State (the other party). The fact that one party or even both parties to a bilateral treaty are composites does not convert it into a multilateral treaty.

Negotiating and Drafting a New Treaty: Who Is Involved?

Treaties may be negotiated by diplomats at embassies or from capital cities, policy and legal officials from home ministries and agencies, ministers or even Heads of Government or State. Treaty Office officials do not normally take the lead in negotiating a treaty, unless they combine their treaty procedures work with a legal or policy role, and are acting in the latter capacity. Treaty officials do not normally need to attend the negotiations, but occasionally it may be wise to

[6] VCLT 1969 arts 41, 55, 58, 60(2), 69(4) and 70(2) and VCLT 1986 arts 41, 55, 58, 60(2), 69(4) and 70(2).

[7] VCLT 1969 art 60(1) and VCLT 1986 art 60(1).

do so if aspects of the procedure are of particular sensitivity, such as the signing arrangements, the final clauses or the depositary responsibilities. The Treaty Office should always be kept closely informed of impending negotiations and the drafts under discussion, and it may need to play a co-ordinating role, ensuring that all parts of government or the IO are consulted on treaty processes.

Negotiating a Treaty

Preparation: Briefing, Consultation, Co-Ordinating a Position

Any negotiator needs a carefully prepared negotiating brief. Even if the lead negotiator is the most seasoned expert on the subject, he or she should have papers, whether prepared by him or herself or by others, setting out general policy objectives and bottom lines, and specific objectives on each point to be covered. Background information such as the government's existing treaty obligations in that field, legislation, policies, statistics should be clearly arranged – for example, indexed and tabbed (either colour-coded or using key words or numbers as reference) – so that the person at the microphone can quickly find the facts they need in a fast-moving negotiation.

If the person at the microphone is or might not be the subject expert, the brief should clearly separate the negotiating 'lines' (what to say and additional talking points if required) from background explanations.

The negotiating brief should be cleared in advance with all members of the delegation, and all parts of the government (or secretariat) that have a substantial policy or legal interest in the subject. When an official speaks at an international negotiation, others are entitled to assume that that person represents and speaks for the whole government (or IO), not just his or her own ministry or department.

During the process of consultation on the draft briefing, the negotiators should consider whether the envisaged treaty might require new domestic legislation and if so, which ministry is responsible. It might be wise to consult that ministry, not least to find out their attitude to this matter and seek their co-operation. The brief should include contact details for any key officials and legal advisers with responsibility for the subject who are not in the delegation, so that they can be consulted urgently if necessary. Failure to consult in advance those who will be key to implementation may result in the delegation being unable to vote for adoption of the treaty, and might delay/prevent signature or ratification.

Research: Obtaining Treaty Information

The negotiators (or their legal advisers) need to find out what treaties already exist on this subject, and whether their government/IO is party to them; if so, are they working well and if not, what is the problem? Is the aim to replace or to supplement existing treaties? If preserving obligations under an existing treaty is a priority, the negotiator may need to ensure that the new treaty has a savings clause (and there may need to be clear instructions in the negotiating brief, perhaps with a draft clause to propose). If it is a bilateral negotiation, the delegation needs to know which multilateral treaties on this subject their State/IO and the other State/IO are parties to, and any relevant reservations. If it is a multilateral negotiation, they need to be aware of whether their State/IO has existing bilateral treaty obligations that could be affected and if so, take account of them. The best prepared negotiators will have those treaty texts with them at the negotiations, as well as the VCLT 1969.

Working behind the Scenes: Importance of Drafting Committees, Working Groups and the Secretariat

In a multilateral negotiation, it is important to identify the key players: who are the proponents and supporters of the new treaty? Who are the experts? Has anyone prepared a draft text? Find out what role is played by the secretariat; are they recording oral proposals and producing negotiating text? Or is the drafting initiative with the Chair or delegations?

It is always useful to get to know the secretariat and, if the talks are fast-moving or confusing (as they often are), keep checking with the secretariat member who knows what is going on, whether you should be aware of any new texts or informal consultations. Experienced negotiators will often feed their drafting proposals in writing to the Chair, secretariat or whoever is in charge of the drafting. If the proposal is important to that delegation, but not likely to be controversial, the drafter may be willing to include it in the negotiating text. That relieves the negotiator of the need to propose it from the floor, and unless someone objects or questions it, they may not even need to speak on that issue. This is useful for a delegate who has other, more substantive, points to negotiate.

Making an early intervention from the floor on any issue of importance to you is advisable. Even if you make no concrete proposal, it will establish your delegation as one of the key players on that issue and increase your chances of being invited by the Chair to lead or join an informal consultation or drafting group.

Join in any small drafting groups on issues of importance to you; if one is set up and you are not invited, ask its convenor or the overall Chair of the negotiations whether you may participate and invariably you will be welcomed. However, this may involve working through lunch breaks, evenings and occasionally very late nights.

Drafting a Treaty Text

The Structure of a Treaty

If it is your task to draft the negotiating text, prepare a 'neutral' outline of it at an early stage. In a multilateral negotiation, if the text is tabled by the

Box 5.1 Structure of a treaty

The usual structure of a treaty is:

- Title
- Identification of the Parties
- Preamble
- Record of agreement
- Main text
- Final clauses
- Testimonium
- Signature block
- Annexes (if any)

secretariat or Chair, or by any party on behalf of the conference, it is important that it sets out a neutral framework of provisions that does not prejudge the outcome of negotiations on contested issues.

Box 5.1 shows the standard structure of a single-instrument bilateral or multilateral treaty. When a bilateral treaty is formed by an exchange of notes, the elements contained within them are essentially the same, with certain variations in sequence and style, as explained below.

The Title

The treaty title should normally indicate the subject matter of the treaty. Occasionally this is omitted for a specific reason (such as the parties being unable to agree how to characterise the subject), but it tends to cause problems later as the treaty may be more difficult to find or may be confused with other treaties. The title should be informative.

The title of a bilateral treaty should specify the parties by including the full and official name of the States or governments, for example: the Agreement between the Government of the Socialist Republic of Vietnam and the Government of the Republic of Indonesia concerning the Delimitation of the Continental Shelf Boundary, 2003.[8]

Multilateral treaties usually do not refer to the parties in the title, but limited membership treaties may indicate the nature of the limitation, especially if it is regional (for example, 'European Convention on . . .' or 'African Agreement on . . .').

Plurilateral treaty titles may state the names of the parties if there are not many, but need not. An example of a plurilateral treaty that names the parties in

[8] Agreement between the Government of the Socialist Republic of Vietnam and the Government of the Republic of Indonesia concerning the Delimitation of the Continental Shelf Boundary (signed 26 June 2003, entered into force 29 May 2007) 2457 UNTS 155.

its title: the Agreement between the United Kingdom of Great Britain and Northern Ireland, the Federal Republic of Germany and the Kingdom of the Netherlands on Collaboration in the Development and Exploitation of the Gas Centrifuge Process for Producing Enriched Uranium, 1970 (Treaty of Almelo).[9]

A few multilateral treaties refer to the place of adoption in the title, for example: the Kyoto Protocol to the United Nations Framework Convention on Climate Change, 1997 (known as the Kyoto Protocol).[10] More commonly, the formal title does not include the place name, but the treaty may be referred to by the place name for short. For example, the Convention on the Prevention of Marine Pollution by Dumping of Wastes and Other Matter, 1972 is known informally as the London Convention.[11] The insertion of the place name into the title is usually part of the bargaining process; typically, it is proposed by the State hosting the conference, and other States' agreement to this may be contingent on the outcome of negotiations on other matters. So, if you are preparing a neutral negotiating text, it may be best to start without the place name in it.

Does the Word 'Treaty' Have to Be in the Title?

No. If the parties prefer not to use the word 'treaty' in the title, there are a number of alternatives. 'Convention' or 'Agreement' are commonly used. Less common are: 'Charter' or 'Statute' (usually used for treaties that set up an institution); 'Memorandum of Understanding', 'Declaration' or 'Compact' (more commonly used for non-binding instruments and so are best avoided for treaties, unless there is a specific reason to use them in a particular case); 'Protocol' (normally used to denote a treaty which is supplementary to an existing one).

The chosen name will not affect the legal status of the instrument as a treaty (if it is one) or not a treaty (if it is not one). Its status is determined by its content and whether the parties intend it to be governed by international law.[12] Names are generally chosen for descriptive and presentational reasons.

The Opening Words: Identification of the Parties

The opening line of a treaty should identify the parties to the agreement, in much the same way that a contract does.

[9] Agreement between the United Kingdom of Great Britain and Northern Ireland, the Federal Republic of Germany and the Kingdom of the Netherlands on Collaboration in the Development and Exploitation of the Gas Centrifuge Process for producing Enriched Uranium (adopted 4 March 1970, entered into force 19 July 1971) 795 UNTS 275 (Treaty of Almelo).

[10] Kyoto Protocol on the United Nations Framework Convention on Climate Change (adopted 11 December 1997, entered into force 16 February 2005) 2303 UNTS 162 (Kyoto Protocol).

[11] Convention on the Prevention of Marine Pollution by Dumping of Wastes and Other Matter (adopted 29 December 1972, entered into force 30 August 1975) 1046 UNTS 120.

[12] For further discussion on the status of international instruments, see Chapter 3.

- *Bilateral treaties:* the names of the parties are stated. For example: the Agreement between the Government of New Zealand and the Government of the Republic of Turkey Relating to Air Services, 2010 begins:

  > The Government of New Zealand and the Government of the Republic of Turkey (hereinafter 'the Parties'):[13]

- *Multilateral treaties:* the opening words normally use a term such as 'Parties', 'Contracting Parties' or 'States Parties'. That term may be expressly defined in the main body of the treaty. If it is not, these definitions in Article 2 VCLT 1969 apply by implication:

  > (f) 'contracting State' means a State which has consented to be bound by the treaty, whether or not the treaty has entered into force;
  > (g) 'party' means a State which has consented to be bound by the treaty and for which the treaty is in force;

The final clauses of a multilateral treaty normally set out how States (or IOs) may give their consent to be bound and become party to it. For example, the United Nations Framework Convention on Climate Change, 1992 (UNFCCC) begins with 'The Parties to this Convention:'.[14] 'The Parties' are not defined expressly, so by implication this term has the meaning set out in Article 2(1)(g) VCLT 1969, and Articles 22 and 23 of that Convention specify how States consent to be bound and when it comes into force for them.

- *Plurilateral treaties:* drafters may use either the bilateral or the multilateral style. An example of a plurilateral treaty that uses the bilateral style is the Treaty of Almelo, which begins: "The United Kingdom of Great Britain and Northern Ireland, the Federal Republic of Germany and the Kingdom of the Netherlands;".

In relation to grammar, do note that, for any treaty, the opening line that identifies the parties is the first part of a long partial sentence that ends at the foot of the preamble with a verb such as 'Have agreed as follows:' (see below). Grammatically, the parties are the subject of the verb that comes at the foot of the preamble. Therefore, the opening line that refers to the parties can end with a semi-colon (;) a comma (,) or a colon (:), but never with a full stop (.).

The Preamble: An Optional Element of a Treaty

A treaty does not have to have a preamble at all. The preamble consists of statements which are not binding, and not part of the operative treaty text, but

[13] Agreement between the Government of New Zealand and the Government of the Republic of Turkey relating to Air Services (adopted 4 March 2010, entered into force 9 May 2010) UNTS Registration No. 50543, NZTS 2012 No. 06 B2010/03.

[14] United Nations Framework Convention on Climate Change (adopted 9 May 1992, entered into force 21 March 1994) 1771 UNTS 107 (UNFCCC).

are considered useful to provide some concise background. If there is nothing that needs to be said here, it is acceptable not to have a preamble. Many bilateral treaties have a very short preamble while some have none at all.

An example of a short, but sufficient, preamble is this one provided in a treaty between the Netherlands in respect of Aruba and the Cayman Islands:

> The Kingdom of the Netherlands, in respect of Aruba,
>
> and
>
> the Government of the Cayman Islands,
>
> Desiring to strengthen the relationship between them through cooperation in taxation matters,
>
> Have agreed as follows:[15]

Even if they had omitted the line beginning 'Desiring', it would have been legally sufficient.[16]

For multilateral treaties, it is usually considered useful to have some preambular paragraphs to provide some concise background, for example to:

- state the overarching aim, principle, vision or motivation for the treaty;
- state any specific real-world problem that it is intended to remedy;
- refer to any previous treaty on the subject, especially if the new treaty is intended to supplement or replace it;
- refer to any resolution that mandated or inspired the negotiations; and/or
- acknowledge the existence of existing rules of customary international law on the same subject.

The preamble, though not binding, forms part of the context which will be taken into account in the interpretation of any provision of the treaty (Article 31(2) VCLT 1969). So, it is very important to draft it carefully. It should not include:

- text which is inconsistent with the operative provisions in the main body;
- text which is unrelated to the main body; or
- substantive obligations which are intended to be binding.

In a multilateral negotiation, there is often a tendency for the preamble to become overloaded with text of a kind that does not belong there. For example, early in the negotiations, delegations may try to secure their negotiating positions by inserting their substantive proposals into the preamble. Later in

[15] The Kingdom of the Netherlands, in respect of Aruba, and the Government of the Cayman Islands as authorised under the letter of entrustment dated 1 September 2009 from the United Kingdom of Great Britain and Northern Ireland for the exchange of information with respect to taxes (with Protocol) (signed 9 and 20 April 2010, entered into force 1 December 2011) 2856 UNTS 153.

[16] An example of an exchange of notes with no preamble or introductory words is: Arrangement between the Government of the Federal Republic of Germany and the Government of the Islamic Republic of Afghanistan concerning the protection of the person and property of the experts and the members of their families belonging to their household seconded to the Islamic Republic of Afghanistan within the scope of German development cooperation (adopted 15 March 2005 and 12 July 2005, entered into force 12 July 2005) 2855 UNTS 301.

the negotiations, delegations that failed to secure agreement on their proposal in the main text may try to reintroduce it in the preamble; or other delegations may move it there in order to placate the delegation whose substantive proposal was defeated. If the Chair or those responsible for drafting the text do not keep a firm control over the preamble, it can easily end up longer than the main body, might be confusing and contradictory, and may even undermine crucial provisions in the main body.

Bearing this in mind, if you are drafting the text or leading the negotiations, a good strategy is to:

- keep the first draft of the preamble as short, simple and uncontentious as possible; and
- negotiate the preamble *last*.

Drafting a preamble is like writing the introduction to a book; it is easier to do once you know what is in the treaty. You can then ensure that it accurately reflects the contents of the body.

In relation to grammar, note that each preambular paragraph is composed as a subordinate clause, within the partial sentence that starts with the opening words identifying the parties and ends with the verb that records their agreement. Each preambular paragraph starts with the present participle of a verb, typically one of the following (although but these are just examples):

- Considering
- Noting
- Recalling
- Acknowledging
- Affirming
- Believing
- Bearing in mind
- Desiring to.

The preamble is thus the (optional) filling in the sandwich, where the top layer of bread is the opening line referring to the parties and the bottom layer is the verb that states their agreement. Therefore, each preambular paragraph should end with a comma or a semi-colon, but never a full stop.

The Record of Agreement

It needs to be made clear that the parties have *agreed* on the contents of the main body (operative part) of the treaty. The expression of agreement is the hallmark of a treaty, as opposed to a non-binding instrument that expresses mutual aspirations, or a unilateral undertaking. This is normally done by stating it at the end of the preamble, as an introduction to the rest of the text. The usual wording is: 'Have agreed as follows:'. There are other variations in use, such as 'Undertake as follows:'.

The whole of the introductory part of the treaty thus flows as a single partial sentence, which reads along the following lines: 'The parties, believing this, considering that, affirming the other, have agreed as follows: [body of treaty].'

The Final Clauses

The 'final clauses' are the provisions, normally placed at the end of a treaty, which set out how the treaty is to operate. At the minimum, they need to specify how States (and IOs, if applicable) may express their consent to be bound (for example by signature, ratification, accession) and how the treaty will enter into force. A multilateral treaty should also designate a depositary and specify which States or IOs are eligible to be party, unless they are named in the title or opening words.

In addition, it is usually desirable to have provisions on some or all of the following matters: relationship of the treaty to other treaties, settlement of disputes, amendment and review, status of annexes, duration, termination or denunciation, provisional application, territorial application, reservations, obligations of the depositary, registration and authentic texts. Specific types of final clauses and how they work in practice are considered in more detail in the remaining chapters of this Handbook.[17]

Where these matters are not covered by express provisions in the treaty, agreement on them may be expressed in related documents such as the Final Act or meeting record, or, in the case of a protocol or supplementary treaty, there may be applicable final clauses in the parent treaty. In case of ambiguity, interpretation will be guided by the VCLT 1969 and the VCLT 1986. Drafters should consider which of those matters is important to the treaty and if possible include those matters within the treaty text, to avoid ambiguity and confusion later. If it is not possible to include all the final clauses in the treaty itself, it is vital that the document they are set out in states clearly that it is related to the treaty. Final clauses should always be drafted by, or checked with, legal advisers and referred to the Treaty Office.

Drafting or Checking the Final Clauses: The Role of the Treaty Office

The final clauses in a treaty[18] may not attract much attention from the policy officials involved in drafting, as they are often viewed as merely procedural and therefore not very exciting or interesting. This is entirely the wrong impression

[17] On provisions concerning giving consent to be bound, see the section on 'Understanding Modes for Expressing Consent to Be Bound' in Chapter 6 at 220–27; and the section on 'Expressing Consent to be Bound by the Treaty' in Chapter 7 at 247–68. On provisions concerning entry into force, see the section on 'How to Draft Entry into Force Clauses in a Treaty Constituted by Exchange of Instruments' in Chapter 7 at 261–62. On provisions concerning amendment, see the section on 'Handling of Treaty Amendments' in Chapter 8 at 319–27. On provisions concerning withdrawal and termination, see Chapter 9 on 'Ending treaty relations' at 334–86.

[18] See Annex II, 'Examples of Final Clauses in a Multilateral Treaty' at 420–23.

however, since they are among the most important parts of the treaty, setting out the way in which it will operate, such as: its entry into force and means to enter into force; amendments; withdrawal from the treaty; reservations; termination of the treaty; depositary authority; and dispute settlement. They do therefore merit very close attention, as if these clauses are not properly drafted – or even omitted altogether – this will undoubtedly cause difficulties further down the line.

For instance, Article 25(1) of the Protocol on the Legal Framework to Implement the ASEAN Single Window, 2015 stipulates:

> This Protocol shall enter into force, after all Member States have notified or, where necessary, deposited instruments of ratifications with the Secretary General of ASEAN upon completion of their internal procedures, which shall not take more than one hundred and eighty (180) days after the signing of this Protocol.[19]

The provision raises several operational issues, such as: what will be the status of the Protocol if not all Member States complete their internal procedures within 180 days as required? In what situation should a Member State file a notification instead of an instrument of ratification to the Secretary General (and vice versa)? Ambiguities of this kind may easily be overlooked by policy negotiators, but they are likely to cause practical difficulties later.

Treaty officials may not necessarily be directly involved in the drafting or negotiation of these provisions. But as they can have significant implications for the operation of the treaty, treaty officials should at least have the opportunity to check that the provisions as drafted and negotiated actually make sense and are clearly set out, so that they can be readily understood at a later date. If they do not make sense, or are unclear, treaty officials may need to refer this back to the policy officials or the negotiating team.

The real interest for treaty officials often comes in the very last clauses of the treaty, since these are the ones they will frequently look at to discover what needs to be done and whether a particular course of action can or must be taken. These clauses relate to the means of signature and entry into force; whether the treaty is subject to ratification and/or accession and if so, how States can accede; whether any reservations can be made (if the treaty is a multilateral) and if so, how; who the depositary is and, occasionally, that the treaty should be registered with the UN. This latter action is in any event an obligation under Article 102 UN Charter but it can serve as a useful reminder of the responsibility for one State (if it is a bilateral treaty), or for the depositary (if a multilateral) to do so. Each of these issues are dealt with in much more detail in this chapter or in the remaining chapters of this Handbook.

[19] Protocol on the Legal Framework to Implement the ASEAN Single Window (adopted 4 December 2015, entered into force 1 August 2017) http://agreement.asean.org/media/download/20150915020056.pdf accessed 22 October 2018.

The Testimonium

The testimonium is the last formal part of the treaty text, and usually forms the lines below which the signatories actually sign. Some treaties omit the testimonium altogether, and this is not necessarily a problem as long as it is clear who has signed, where and when. The advantage of following a traditional format is that it reduces the risk of omitting something important or using words that fail to achieve the parties' purpose.

A traditional testimonium will typically state, or include, the following words:

> In witness whereof the undersigned, being duly authorised thereto, have signed this [Agreement].
>
> Done at [place], this [x] day of [month], two thousand and [year].

The order of these two paragraphs is sometimes the other way round. These elements are essentially the same for (single-instrument) bilateral treaties and for multilateral treaties. Sometimes, instead of 'Done at', a multilateral treaty may say 'Opened for signature at', if it is to be open for signature for a specified period.

There are two other important elements that may also need to be built in to the testimonium, if they are not already provided for in the final clauses: authentic languages and the number of originals.

Authentic Languages

If a treaty is concluded in more than one official language, it is essential to specify this within the treaty text and to set out which are the official languages of the treaty. It is also important to make clear the relative status of each language text: whether they are both, or all, of equal authority (sometimes expressed as 'equal authenticity'), or whether one language prevails over another in the event of inconsistency. This should be specified in the treaty text, usually in the testimonium, although some treaties do so in one of the final clauses (usually the last).

At some point in the future a question may arise over whether a language in which the treaty has been published is one of the official languages. If this is clearly set out in the treaty itself, disputes of this kind are easier to resolve. It is common for the parties or one party to decide to translate the treaty into another language for information purposes only and not to make it part of the treaty text. It is important to know the status of each language text at the outset; negotiating parties are responsible for satisfying themselves that all official language versions are consistent. No such responsibility need be taken for non-official translations.

Multilateral treaties are often concluded in several equally authentic languages. Some are concluded in only one language, usually but not necessarily English. Bilateral treaties are very often in two languages, these being the official language of each State involved. They are sometimes done in three or more languages; for example, where a State has more than one official language, or where the two States wish to add another language that is not the official language of either of them. Some treaties specify that they are concluded in one language only. This may be dispensed with if it is obvious; for example, if the UK and New Zealand conclude a bilateral agreement, they may not consider it necessary to state that it is done in English only. If there is any possible room for doubt later, it should be stated.

The statement about official languages is typically placed within the testimonium, though it could be done within the final clauses instead. Below are examples of testimoniums with languages specified:

- Multilateral – example of languages specified in the testimonium:

  Done at Warsaw, this 16th day of May 2005, in English and in French, both texts being equally authentic, in a single copy which shall be deposited in the archives of the Council of Europe.[20]

- Multilateral – example of languages specified in a final clause:

  Article 85
  Authentic Texts
  The original of the present Convention, of which the Chinese, English, French, Russian and Spanish texts are equally authentic, shall be deposited with the Secretary General of the United Nations.[21]

- Bilateral – two examples of languages specified in the testimonium:

  DONE at Ankara, this fourth day of March, 2010, in the English and Turkish languages. In the event of any inconsistencies, the English version shall prevail.[22]
  DONE in two originals at London this 26th day of June 2006 in the English language only.[23]

- Trilateral (in bilateral format) – example of languages specified in the testimonium:

  DONE in triplicate at Almelo this 4th day of March 1970, in the English, German and Netherlands languages, each text being equally authoritative.[24]

Note that when a treaty text is done in more than one language, the treaty text comprises all the authentic languages. That is to say, it is one treaty text containing several languages, not several different treaty texts.

[20] Council of Europe Convention on Action against Trafficking in Human Beings (adopted 16 May 2005, entered into force 1 February 2008) 2569 UNTS 33, ETS 197.

[21] VCLT 1969 art 85.

[22] Agreement between the Government of New Zealand and the Government of the Republic of Turkey Relating to Air Services. See n 13.

[23] Agreement between the Government of the Kingdom of The Netherlands and the Government of the United Kingdom of Great Britain and Northern Ireland on the Reciprocal Holding of Stocks of Crude Oil and/or Petroleum Products (signed 26 June 2006, entered into force 1 June 2008) 2579 UNTS 201.

[24] Treaty of Almelo, (n 9).

Number of Originals

It is also essential to make clear how many original texts there are. Each original must of course be identical to any other (except for precedence; see below) and each must be signed by both/all parties. This information is normally incorporated into the testimonium, for example:

> Done in duplicate [or Done in two originals] [in the x, y and z languages, each being equally authentic] at [place] on this [day] of [month][year].[25]

A bilateral treaty will normally be done in duplicate, as each side will keep a signed original (see below). This is the case whether it is done in one language, two or more. Each original will consist of both/all languages.

Some treaties expressly state in the testimonium that they are done 'in a single original', or that 'The original of the present Convention . . . shall be deposited with . . .', in which case it is clear that there is only one. Where it is not stated how many originals there are, the natural presumption is that a multilateral treaty has only one original with all the signatures on it, which is kept by the depositary, and a bilateral treaty normally has two originals with both signatures on both, with each side keeping one each.

Inserting the Place and Date into the Testimonium by Hand

For bilateral treaties due to be signed at a meeting, it is better not to type the date, or even place, of signature on the original document. These should instead be written in by hand at the signing ceremony, as it cannot always be guaranteed that the signature ceremony that has been so carefully planned will actually go ahead at the time and place arranged. If the date and place are typed in, and the treaty has been bound and sealed (see below) before the change occurs, this then creates problems since treaty officials will need to break the seal, unbind the treaty and amend the signature pages, or, worse still, produce the whole document again. Either way it would have to be rebound and resealed in the presence of the other party. Another option would be to amend the date and/or place by hand and have the signatories sign or initial and date the amendment as well as sign in the signature block; but most treaty parties would consider that undesirable for presentational purposes, and prefer to remake the treaty. It is far safer to avoid this issue completely by simply writing in the date and place of signature on the day, just before it takes place.

This also raises an issue for formatting and production of the treaty prior to signature, which is examined below. Unlike bilateral treaties, the place and date that a multilateral treaty was opened for signature can be typed in, since these are unlikely to change in view of the advance preparations needed for a signing ceremony involving multiple parties.

[25] See also the examples above at 172.

Signature Blocks

Beneath the testimonium are the signature blocks. This is simply a space in which the signatories sign, usually above the name of their State or IO, or sometimes to the right. The names of the States (and/or IOs) that are going to sign the treaty should be typed into the signature block. Below (or to the left of) each space for signature should be written 'For the Government of [State]' or 'For [IO]'. On a bilateral treaty, the two States' names will be positioned according to the custom of precedence with one on the left and one on the right, or one above the other, alternating on each of the two originals (see page 180 on 'precedence'). On a multilateral treaty, the names of the States (and IOs if any) signing the treaty will usually be listed in alphabetical order. It is important for treaty officials to make sure that they have the correct title of the State(s) concerned typed into the signature blocks, as a mistake here could possibly cause grave offence! Any States or IOs who sign the treaty after it has been opened for signature, and whose names cannot therefore be added alphabetically, will add their signatures at the end. Multilateral treaties that remain open for signature should be produced with blank pages at the end for additional signatures.

It is not advisable or necessary to type the name of the individual who is going to sign. Signatories can and sometimes do change just before the treaty is signed; for example, with a change of minister or government, or just non-availability on the day of signature. It is important for treaty officials to make sure on the day of signature that they have the correct names of the signatories. Officials should also record the names of the individual who signed for each State or IO in their treaty database for future reference. For example, if the treaty is retyped for publication, the names of the individuals will need to be typed in place of the signatures.

Annexes (if any)

Annexes are sometimes used, for a variety of reasons. For example, it may be useful to move a mass of technical detail or a long list of items out of the main text, to avoid cluttering it and making it difficult to read. Another reason is that the negotiators may decide that there should be an easier amendment procedure for technical provisions that may need frequent updating, such as a list of banned chemicals. It is also possible to have annexes associated with a treaty that do not form part of the treaty text, and are not intended to be binding, such as a programme of action.

If annexes are intended to be part of the treaty, they must always be linked to wording in an operative provision in the main body. Such annexes must never be left 'floating'. There must be an operative provision that states the function of the annex, that it forms part of the treaty text, and whether there are any special amendment procedures. For example, the UNCLOS contains the following provision headed 'Status of Annexes':

> The Annexes form an integral part of this Convention and, unless expressly provided otherwise, a reference to this Convention or to one of its Parts includes a reference to the Annexes relating thereto.[26]

Each annex also should be given effect in an operative provision that explains the function of that annex. For example, the UNCLOS has eleven annexes, each of which is connected to an operative provision in the relevant part of the treaty. Annex I on 'Highly Migratory Species' is given effect by Article 64, which reads:

> **Article 64 Highly migratory species**
> The coastal State and other States whose nationals fish in the region for the highly migratory species listed in Annex I shall co-operate directly or through appropriate international organizations with a view to[27]

Annexes are normally placed after the testimonium and signature block.

If annexes related to the treaty are not intended to be part of it, it is preferable to state this explicitly in the treaty or in the annexes. If however this is not made clear, the default presumption will be that they are not part of it.

Translations

Translation can be a difficult issue for treaty officials and negotiators. They might be presented with a draft treaty text in a foreign language, with no way of knowing whether it accurately represents the text in the language(s) they are able to read. As well as being in a different language, it may even be in a different script. This is where the importance of good translators is vital.

Some larger foreign ministries will have access to a specific translation service who should be able to check the text to ensure that it is accurate. They should also be able to provide a written list of any discrepancies, explained in the treaty officials' own language (and if necessary also in one of the treaty's other official languages, so that it can be shared directly with other negotiating parties and/or the secretariat). Others may have to buy in specialist translators to do this, but in this case it is important to bear in mind that treaty language is often very subject-specific and translators might need to be specialised not only in international legal language but also in the technical language of the particular subject. In addition, any outside translators bought in may have to be cleared for security if any aspects of the treaty are confidential, or at least sensitive, before it is signed or published.

In any case, however it is done, each State or IO party is responsible for checking the final text of all language parts of a treaty and satisfying itself that they all mean exactly the same, *before* proceeding to adoption and signature.

[26] UNCLOS (adopted 10 December 1982, entered into force 16 November 1994) 1833 UNTS 3 art 318.

[27] ibid art 64(1).

Even though the treaty may have been negotiated in one language, and the other language version(s) may have been translated from the negotiated text, once the treaty is adopted and signed then all 'equally authoritative' or 'equally authentic' versions are just that – equal. This is crucial because if any dispute as to the meaning of the treaty later arises, both or all official language texts will be used to interpret the treaty.[28]

Production of Treaty Texts

Once a treaty text has been agreed, it must be formatted and prepared for signature. This is usually done by treaty officials, and consists of going carefully through an electronic copy of the text and putting it all into a consistent format and layout; for example, ensuring that all the Article headings and paragraph numberings are in the same font throughout. The formatting of a multilateral treaty will be done by the secretariat, where the negotiation was hosted by an IO or treaty body, or by the Treaty Office of the government that is going to host the signing event (usually the government appointed as depositary for the treaty). Where a bilateral single-instrument treaty is in a single language, the formatting is normally done by the Treaty Office of the party that is going to host the signing event. Where there is more than one language, each side will normally take responsibility for formatting the text(s) in their own language(s).

Bilateral treaties formed by exchanges of notes do not need to be formatted and produced in any special way. Each side will format its own diplomatic note in its own usual style. The layout of the contents will effectively be determined by the party that sends the initiating note, as the reply note normally sets out the contents of the first note verbatim, with a short statement of agreement.[29]

Practicalities of Formatting and Printing

Formatting

Very often the draft that has been negotiated will have had many insertions, amendments and deletions, so the text can easily become inconsistent. The task of treaty officials is to ensure that the whole text is consistent in such matters as:

- style and position of article numbers (such as Arabic or Roman numerals);
- article and paragraph numbers running consecutively; any numbered 'bis', 'ter' etc. during negotiations must be given correct sequential numbers;
- all articles have headings that are consistent in style and position – or no article headings are used;

[28] See VCLT 1969 art 33.

[29] See the section on 'Preparing a Treaty Formed by Exchange of Instruments' below at 183–84 and the section on 'Conducting an 'Exchange of Instruments Constituting a Treaty'' in Chapter 7 at 256–68.

- style and position of paragraph and subparagraph numberings (such as numbers or letters; with or without brackets; consecutive numbering);
- font style and size;
- correct and consistent spellings and punctuation (for example, 'seabed' or 'sea-bed');
- capitalisation (for example, 'States Parties' or 'states parties');
- text justification (right, centre or left).

Treaty officials need to be very careful not to make any changes in substance to the text: sometimes individual words and punctuation have been the subject of prolonged negotiation, and an error in formatting could inadvertently undo months or sometimes years of work. One particular comma (or the absence of it) may have been vital to one delegation or group of delegations. So it is dangerous for treaty officials to try to 'improve' the text grammatically on their own initiative! If the text appears to contain grammatical or punctuation errors, these should be pointed out to the negotiators, or in a multilateral context, to the Chair or secretariat in charge of the negotiations. For example, if a paragraph of an article contains several sub-paragraphs numbered (a), (b), (c) and there is another line of text with no number, it should not automatically be numbered (d); treaty officials should ask the head of negotiations whether it should be numbered subparagraph (d) or whether that line belongs to the main paragraph.

Rechecking Translations

In addition to formatting, there is the question of language. Most bilateral treaties will be in the language of both parties, although some may be in more than one language for a party where that State has two or more official languages. Multilaterals will often be in several languages, as mentioned above. It is during formatting that the text in each language should be checked (or rechecked) by an accredited translator, and any queries or errors in language resolved.

Proofreading

Once all the formatting has been done, treaty officials should carefully check and proofread the text against the final draft. At the same time, treaty officials should be checking it to ensure that all formatting has been done correctly. It is advisable at this stage for a senior official with policy responsibility for the treaty concerned to proofread it as well, in advance of attending the meeting with the other party for 'authenticating and sealing the text'.[30] It is also useful to send the formatted text to the other party or parties to give them an opportunity for checking and raising any queries informally, in advance of printing and preparing for the formal authentication procedure.

[30] See the sections on 'Authenticating and Sealing a Single-Instrument Bilateral Treaty' below at 184–85 and 'Preparing a Multilateral Treaty Text for Its Adoption and Signature' below at 185–88.

Binders

Bilateral single-instrument treaties are produced in two originals with one retained by each party. Each party normally wants its original to be bound in its own style of hard binder, for example, in a particular colour and with a national crest (see Figure 5.1 for two examples: the UK binder is red with gold crest and the Moroccan binder is green with gold crest). If the visiting party wishes to use its own style of binder, it should bring it to the sealing ceremony, together with its own style of ribbon (if any). If the visiting party does not have its own style of binder, the hosting party would naturally offer to prepare one of its own binders for them.

Figure 5.1 Front covers of the UK (left) and Morocco (right) treaty binders

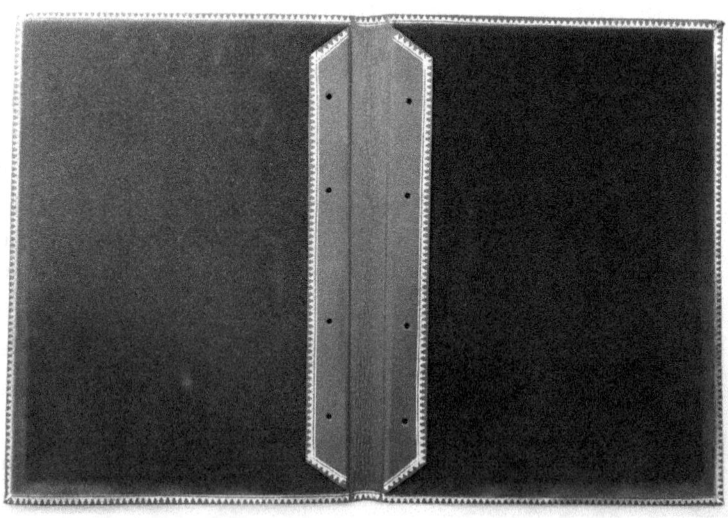

Figure 5.2 Inside the Moroccan treaty binder

Paper

Some States have a specific type of treaty paper onto which the text of the treaty to be signed and retained by their side has to be printed. Even if one State does not, the other State or IO (in a bilateral) may well have specific treaty paper and want it to be used to print the original that they will retain. For a multilateral, the treaty paper will be that used by the depositary or the IO hosting the signature ceremony. Treaty paper can differ in size and style but it is useful if the paper is A4 size, as this means it can be easily printed by any printer. If it is an unusual size, specific printing equipment will be required. It is important to clarify any specific requirements relating to paper at an early stage when formatting a treaty; if this is left too late, it may be difficult or impossible to get the treaty printed in time for the signature ceremony. The quality of treaty paper is not only a matter of aesthetics or prestige; its function is to facilitate the permanent preservation of treaty texts in archives.[31]

Printing

For a bilateral treaty in two languages, each State will usually print the text in their own language. Where the treaty is formatted such that each language text has its own testimonium and signature block, each State will print two texts in its language; one with precedence for its State and the other giving precedence to the other State. The visiting State would normally print their language texts in their embassy and bring them over to the offices of the hosting State for the sealing. If either side requires their retained treaty original to be printed on their special paper, they will need to provide the paper to the other side for printing, *in advance of the sealing ceremony*. This is because each State needs to print their language text that gives precedence to the other State *on the other State's paper*. Treaty officials of the hosting State should discuss this with the other State's embassy staff, as the latter are unlikely to have a detailed knowledge of treaty procedures. They will often simply have been sent a supply of their State's treaty paper and any seals used, but sometimes not even that.

Precedence of the Two States in a Single-Instrument Bilateral Treaty

It is in the production of the text that precedence becomes important, as the hosting State should retain a treaty original with its precedence in both (or all) languages, with its language being placed first. The visiting State will retain an original with the opposite – with its precedence in all the languages and its language text positioned first.[32]

[31] See the section on 'Archiving Treaties: Permanent Storage, Preservation and Retrieval' in Chapter 4 at 149–53.

[32] A Aust, *Modern Treaty Law and Practice* (3rd edn, CUP 2013) 383.

Precedence comes at the beginning and end of a bilateral treaty text. It means the order in which the States are named in the title, the order in which the languages are listed in the testimonium, the position of the signature blocks and the order in which the language texts are placed. None of this has the slightest effect on the substance; this custom is observed only for reasons of diplomacy, to ensure that both States are treated equally in presentational terms.

So, for example, a treaty between State X and State Y would have, in State X's original, the title 'Agreement between the Government of State X and the Government of State Y on [xxx]'; the X language text is placed before the Y language text; the testimonium states that the treaty is in the X and Y languages, with each language having equal authority; and the signature block for State X's representative is on the left of the document, while the signature block for State Y's representative is on the right. By contrast, in State Y's original, the title would be 'Agreement between the Government of State Y and the Government of State X on [xxx]', and so on.

Precedence only appears in these places in the treaty. Elsewhere in the treaty, the order in which the two States are referred to remains unchanged in each language version. The same principles apply to a treaty between a State and an IO or between two IOs, or even between a State and a non-State entity. However this is only a custom and is not mandated by international law; if any two parties decided to adapt the presentation of their treaty to suit their circumstances, they are free to do so.

In multilateral treaties, precedence is not an issue as there is normally only one original. The parties' names are usually listed in alphabetical order in the signature block. Of course, where the treaty has more than one official language, the alphabetical order of the parties' names has to be determined according to their names in one language (which will usually be chosen by the secretariat or host government that prepares the treaty, in accordance with the working custom of that organisation or group of States).

Production of the Testimonium and Signature Block in more than One Language

When the treaty is in more than one authentic language, there are two alternative ways of producing the testimonium and signature block:

- Method (a) Single testimonium and signature block in both/all languages. The complete text of the treaty (except for the testimonium and signature block) is set out in each language. At the end there is one testimonium in each language, followed by one signature block in each language.

- Method (b) Separate testimonium and signature block for each language text. The complete text of the treaty *including* the testimonium and signature block is set out in the first language, then the complete text *including* the testimonium and signature block in the second language, and then in any others in turn in the same way. Each signatory must sign on the signature block of each language version.

Method (a): Single Testimonium and Signature Block in both/all Languages

Multilateral treaties are usually formatted according to method (a). It has several advantages: it simplifies the signing ceremony as each signatory only has to sign the treaty once; it produces a much neater original, with all the signatures at the end; it produces a more compact original on fewer sheets of paper. However, it requires more advance preparation to produce the document, as the testimonium can only be put together once all the translations are final. Then there is the intricate task of cutting the testimonium off each language text and placing it in the correct sequence with the other language versions of the testimonium, and then each signatory's name has to be inserted in each of the languages in the correct sequence. This is the way the UN produces treaty texts, with every treaty in six official languages and a single testimonium at the end in the six languages, followed by a signature block with each signing State's name in the six languages.

Multilateral treaties concluded within the CoE are always done in English and French, both texts being equally authentic, in a single copy. The English text is placed on each left-hand page and the same provisions in French are placed on the facing right-hand page, all the way through. The testimonium is on one page at the end (before any annexes or appendices) in two columns, with the English on the left-hand side and the French on the right-hand side. A single signature block in both languages is placed below the testimonium.

Method (a) works very well in IOs and treaty bodies where the official languages are always the same, and the secretariat is therefore well equipped to deal with the translation and printing of all of them. Moreover, the secretariat is usually able to arrange the timing of a signing ceremony so as to allow enough time for translating, formatting and production.

An example of a multilateral treaty produced in a single testimonium format is the Antarctic Treaty 1959, which has four equally authentic language texts: English, French, Russian and Spanish. The single testimonium is placed after the Spanish text, in the four languages, and then in the signature block each State's name is typed in those four languages with the signature beside it.[33] Each signatory would have signed once only.

[33] A scanned copy of what appears to be the signed original Antarctic Treaty is on the website of the Antarctic Treaty Secretariat at: www.ats.aq/documents/ats/treaty_original.pdf accessed 25 September 2018. The testimonium and signature pages are at the end. It is an unsigned certified copy.

An example of a trilateral treaty arranged in this way is the Treaty of Almelo between the UK, Germany and the Netherlands, done in English, German and Dutch. Its single testimonium in all three languages is positioned after the third language text of the main body of the treaty, but before the annexes. The single signature block sets out the names of the three signatory States in the three languages. The signatories signed once on each of the three treaty originals (it was done in triplicate so that, in accordance with the customary precedence, each State would take away one original with its name and language placed first).[34]

Method (a) also has much to commend it for bilateral treaties, where it is feasible. This is likely to be where there is ample time between adoption and signature and where the languages are similar. Where a bilateral treaty is done in two languages in this format, each signatory would sign twice; once only on each of the two bound originals.

Method (b): Separate Testimonium and Signature Block for each Language Text

Bilateral treaties are usually formatted according to method (b). It has the advantage that the document for signing is easier to produce, especially where time is short and/or the hosting State is not equipped to print in the script of the other State's language. Where the treaty is in two or more languages, typically each side takes responsibility for providing the text in its own language(s), translating from the negotiating text if required. Each side will print two texts in its own language(s), one in each precedence version.

So, for a bilateral treaty in two languages, there will be four texts, each with its own testimonium and signature block. The visiting State will print two in its language and bring them to the sealing ceremony, where both sides will check all four texts before binding and sealing them together, making two originals. Each signatory will sign four times; twice on each of the two originals. If there are three official languages, each signatory will have to sign six times. For example, the UK/Norway Double Taxation Treaty is formatted in this way and has two testimoniums and signature blocks, one at the end of each language.[35] Another example is a UK/China amending treaty which has a testimonium and signature block in English at the end of the English text and then another in Chinese at the end of the Chinese text.[36]

[34] Treaty of Almelo. See FCO (n 9) and FCO, 'Treaty Series No. 69 (1971)' 27 http://treaties.fco.gov.uk/docs/pdf/1971/TS0069.pdf accessed 21 September 2018.

[35] Convention between the Government of the United Kingdom of Great Britain and Northern Ireland and the Government of the Kingdom of Norway for the Avoidance of Double Taxation and the Prevention of Fiscal Evasion with respect to Taxes on Income and Capital (signed 12 October 2000, entered into force 21 December 2000) 2431 UNTS 133. The testimonium in English is at p 22 and in Norwegian at p 50 of the Convention. In the Norwegians' original, the sequence would be Norwegian first.

[36] Amendment to the Protocol on Scientific and Technological Co-operation between the Government of the United Kingdom of Great Britain and Northern Ireland and the

Method (b) can also be used for multilateral treaties. Although method (a) is to be preferred when it is feasible, it can be difficult to organise in certain circumstances, such as for a government appointed as depositary to a one-off treaty in languages with unfamiliar scripts.

The main disadvantage with method (b) is the need for multiple signatures by each signatory. A bilateral treaty in two languages needs to be signed four times by each signatory, a total of eight signings. A multilateral treaty in six languages must be signed six times by each signatory. If, say, 40 signatories attend the ceremony, 240 signatures are needed. It will take a lot of organising of paperwork and a lengthy ceremony. The worst risk is that signatures will be missed out in error, as dignitaries may miss signature pages or stop signing before they reach the end. If a prime minister signs once then stands up and starts shaking hands, it can be awkward for a treaty official to intervene! The key is meticulous advance preparation, briefing, rehearsal and a treaty official keeping a careful watch over the shoulder of each signatory, pointing at the next place to sign when necessary.

Preparing a Treaty Formed by Exchange of Instruments

Treaties can sometimes be in the form of an exchange of notes between two governments or two IOs, or between a government and an IO. Occasionally, a treaty between three or more parties can consist of parallel exchanges between all of them. The point is that a treaty does not have to consist of a single document; it can consist of a pair or a series of linked documents. Diplomatic notes are the form most commonly used for this purpose, but other forms are possible such as letters.

Not every exchange of notes is a treaty. Notes, like letters, emails or any other means of communication, may have any content. The question is whether the contents establish an international agreement concluded between States and/or IOs, governed by international law.[37]

A bilateral exchange of notes is usually initiated by one State sending a note containing a proposal, and completed by the State receiving that note confirming their acceptance of that proposal in their note in reply. This reply note should set out the text of the initiating note in full. How to draft the formal parts of the initiating and reply notes is explained in more detail in Chapter 7.[38]

Government of the People's Republic of China (signed 17 September 1998, entered into force 17 September 1998) UKTS 75 (1999).

[37] This is explained in the section on 'Definition of a Treaty in International Law' in Chapter 3 at 93–6.

[38] See the section on 'Conducting an "Exchange of Instruments Constituting a Treaty"' in Chapter 7 at 256–68. See Annex III, 'Example of Exchange of Notes Constituting a Treaty' at 424–25.

Exchanges of notes can potentially be the source of endless confusion, delay and difficulty for treaty officials. It is important to have good communications with the other State or IO with whom the notes are to be exchanged, and of course also with the relevant policy officials. To make sure that things proceed smoothly, it is a good idea, in advance of the exchange, to agree informally on the wording of both the initiating note and the reply in draft with the other party, so that both parties know what is intended. It is not unusual, however, for the draft to be taken by the other party as the actual note and for confusion to arise.

It is also important that treaty officials keep effective and detailed records of action taken. It could be some time, perhaps months or sometimes years, between sending an initiating note and receiving a substantive reply note, and responsibility for conducting negotiations or enquiring about progress on the other side will be in the hands of policy or embassy officials. It is vital that the Treaty Office is aware of the exact status of the exchange at all times. Treaty officials should also ensure that the relevant policy officials (and their successors) are aware of the action taken and what to do with a note should they receive one – which is to send it to the Treaty Office as soon as possible.

Exchanges of notes can also be used to bring a bilateral treaty into force by confirming the completion of each State's constitutional procedures; this is explained in more detail in Chapter 7.[39]

Authenticating and Sealing a Single-Instrument Bilateral Treaty

When a treaty consists of a single document to be signed by both parties, it is important to make certain that both parties are in possession of the *exact same* final text of the treaty. It is surprisingly easy for misunderstandings to occur, especially when there have been multiple meetings and/or exchanges of correspondence over different aspects of the text, and also when communications between the two sides have involved various individuals.

Once the treaty text has been formatted, in all its language versions, it should be authenticated. For bilateral treaties, this would usually be done by each side initialling the text. For a bilateral treaty, representatives for each party should meet a few days before signature to carefully go through the text line by line and ensure that each version conforms exactly to the other and to the final formatted draft. Treaty officials from the State which is going to host the treaty-signing event ('the hosting State') should organise and lead this meeting, which can be attended by senior representatives (and sometimes even the ambassador) from the other State ('the visiting State'), and if

[39] See the section on 'How to Write a Note to Confirm Completion of Domestic Procedures' in Chapter 7 at 266–67. See also Annex XIII, 'Example of a Note Confirming the Completion of Domestic Procedures' at 453.

possible should be joined by policy officials in case issues of substance arise while checking the text.

If the treaty is in more than one official language, it is also extremely valuable if you have a translator on hand in case issues of the correct use of language come up. Even though the contents should already have been checked by translators, treaty officials should recheck all printed texts that they are handling; even if they cannot read the other languages, they should at least compare the features they can see, for example that all texts have the same number of articles and paragraphs, and there is not a page missing.

When the representatives of both States are content that the text is accurate in all languages, it can be bound and sealed into the two treaty binders. Binding can be a delicate process of its own (see Figure 5.2 for an example of the inside of a treaty binder), and another area where pitfalls await the unwary. Many States, but by no means all, have their own treaty ribbon – sometimes in their national colours, as well as their own binder, and will need to bring this with them. The hosting State's treaty officials should check all of this with the other State (or IO) well before the sealing takes place to avoid any last-minute delays.

Once bound, the ends of the ribbon are physically sealed onto the inside back leaf of the binder, thus permanently maintaining the integrity of the text and preventing any pages from being added or removed. In some States, the sealing is still done with metal seals and hot melted wax, but in many others an imprinted paper seal is taking over from the more traditional methods; each is equally acceptable. There is, however, no absolute requirement to seal the ribbon; while omitting this does not affect the validity of the treaty, sealing does provide an element of confidence in the integrity of the text and for this reason is to be recommended.

A cautionary tale: when the UK's Treaty Office hosts a bilateral treaty-signing, they normally seal the treaty, in the presence of the other party, before the signing. However, on one occasion this was not done as the other party's officials did not turn up for the sealing ceremony, which had been arranged for the day before the signing ceremony. After the ministers had signed, the other State's officials asked to substitute a new 'corrected' page for one of the pages of the treaty in their language. It was in a script the UK treaty officials could not read. The UK treaty officials declined, and quickly sealed the treaty. This was the correct response, as the request was not in accordance with Article 79 VCLT 1969. This incident reinforced the importance of always sealing the treaty text before it is signed.

Preparing a Multilateral Treaty Text for Its Adoption and Signature

When the negotiations are successfully concluded, it is essential to make certain that all negotiating parties are in possession of the *exact same* final text of the treaty. A surprising number of draft treaties (even successive drafts of the same treaty) are labelled 'final' by optimistic negotiators and Chairs of meetings! It is not uncommon for confusion to arise later as to which is the agreed text, especially when the end of negotiations move rapidly, with the text still in several pieces, amendments being adopted at the last minute, and the Chair bringing down the gavel quickly as soon as there is consensus in the room. Parties need the definitive text, properly cleaned up and formatted, to circulate around their government or IO for consideration before they proceed to signature.

If the convenor of the negotiations – whether secretariat, host government or Chair of the meeting – allows delegations to go home, and then cleans up the text and circulates it, the risk is clear. Almost certainly errors will be found: one delegation or another will dispute that an amendment was agreed or that a particular comma was there, or that this version is the final draft of that article. The whole agreement might then unravel, or require a further meeting (or protracted correspondence) to resolve.

Therefore, a procedure should ideally be undertaken *at the meeting* to ensure that all delegations have agreed to adopt the exact same text. Typically, a representative of each negotiating party may be asked to initial the text, or sign the Final Act (record of the meeting) containing the text. If the negotiation was concluded by correspondence or video-conference, some equivalent formal procedure to confirm the agreed text should be chosen. This procedure is known as 'authentication' of the text.[40]

The secretariat (or officials servicing the negotiation, whether from a government or IO) will naturally require time between the end of the negotiation and the authentication of the text, in order to produce the cleaned-up version. This means putting together any pieces; for example, where different provisions were contained in different negotiating documents, or where amendments were agreed and need to be incorporated. If amendments were made and/or accepted orally, the secretariat will need to check their meeting records very carefully to ensure that nothing is left out. Once the pieces are united into a single text, the formatting must be made consistent, such as article numberings and headings.[41] (If headings have not been agreed in the negotiating text, it is safer to omit them since the addition of any heading at this stage could be controversial.) Spellings must be consistent. This process is known among diplomats (not only the French speakers) as 'toilettage', which means cleaning or tidying up the text. It will normally take several hours and should be done in the peace and quiet of a back office, not in the conference room. Ideally, the treaty negotiations should conclude with some time to spare for other business, but if this is not practical then the secretariat will usually

[40] VCLT 1969 art 10.

[41] For further examples of formatting tasks, see the sections above on 'Practicalities of Formatting and Printing' at 176 and 'Formatting' at 176.

work through the evening as required. Legal advisers from delegations may then wish to check the toilettage before the text is formally adopted, and are well used to having to grind through this task and even convening a meeting at all hours of the night, long after their heads of delegation have gone out to dinner to celebrate their negotiating success.

When the treaty is going to have more than one official language text, an important question is whether those texts need to be ready for the formal adoption. Sometimes it is an absolute necessity, such as when the negotiations are conducted through interpreters and some delegates are not comfortable adopting a text in only one language (usually English). Some delegations whose national language is one of the official treaty languages might insist on adopting it in their language as a matter of principle. In a large IO, this is not normally a problem as the IO's translators will already have translated the negotiating text into the other languages, and will update their translation whenever a new draft is issued. So, the final text in all the official languages will normally be ready for adoption within a day or so, or even overnight if necessary. When a treaty is negotiated among States outside an organisation, the production of instant translations might be more difficult or impossible. In such circumstances, delegations will usually be prepared to adopt it in English only (or whatever language the negotiating text was in) on the basis that translations will be prepared promptly, and they will have ample opportunity to check their accuracy and request corrections before the treaty is opened for signature. If the treaty provides that all language texts are equally authoritative, all negotiating parties are entitled to check all of them to ensure that they are consistent, and should do so.

The cleaned-up text (in all official languages unless it has been agreed that translation may follow) is then presented to the meeting for formal adoption and authentication. Procedures vary; when a treaty is negotiated in an IO this may be done by tabling a resolution with the text of the treaty annexed to it. The representatives then vote, and the voting majorities of the IO's rules of procedure apply. When the negotiation takes place at a diplomatic conference, the treaty text is normally adopted by consensus, or, in default of consensus, by a vote according to the rules of procedure for the conference. After toilettage, the treaty text is annexed to the Final Act, which is a record of the proceedings of the meeting. The delegates may be asked to sign or initial the Final Act, which is to certify that it is a correct record of the meeting and the treaty text. Signing the Final Act does not amount to signing the treaty, and does not create any obligation to become party.

There is usually a gap between adoption of the text and its opening for signature, of several days or two or three weeks, to allow the secretariat time to finalise translations, format and produce the text for signature, etc. However, if political or practical considerations dictate, such as concern that any delay may result in some States regretting the deal, the treaty may be opened for signature immediately after adoption. Although far from ideal from a treaty procedure perspective, it can be accommodated if the treaty officials concerned have anticipated the need and made advance preparations.

Full Powers

Any person who adopts, initials or signs a treaty must have authority to do so, as laid down by international law.[42] The international law requirements are set out in Article 7 VCLT 1969, which provides:

1. A person is considered as representing a State for the purpose of adopting or authenticating the text of a treaty or for the purpose of expressing the consent of the State to be bound by a treaty if:
   (a) he produces appropriate full powers; or
   (b) it appears from the practice of the States concerned or from other circumstances that their intention was to consider that person as representing the State for such purposes and to dispense with full powers.
2. In virtue of their functions and without having to produce full powers, the following are considered as representing their State:
   (a) Heads of State, Heads of Government and Ministers for Foreign Affairs, for the purpose of performing all acts relating to the conclusion of a treaty;
   (b) heads of diplomatic missions, for the purpose of adopting the text of a treaty between the accrediting State and the State to which they are accredited;
   (c) representatives accredited by States to an international conference or to an international organization or one of its organs, for the purpose of adopting the text of a treaty in that conference, organization or organ.

The reason for requiring a Full Powers document is to provide irrefutable evidence that the person named in it is authorised to represent the State concerned for the stated purpose. Under Article 7 VCLT 1969, only three State representatives can sign a treaty without the need to produce Full Powers: the Head of State, the Head of Government and the Foreign Minister. This is because the very nature and function of the position they hold means they can be regarded internationally as representing their State for such purposes. Every other person signing a treaty has to produce Full Powers from one of these three authorities of State – although there are some exceptions.

There are several different means of expressing Full Powers. In order to be regarded as valid, a Full Powers instrument must contain a number of elements. First and foremost, it must be clearly signed by one of the three

[42] Additionally, there may also be domestic law requirements to satisfy as well. Such requirements are considered in the section on 'Internal Preparations to Give Consent to Be Bound' in Chapter 6 at 227–43.

authorities, and must clearly and unambiguously empower a named individual to sign the treaty concerned. Simply stating their *position*, such as Ambassador to State X, is not sufficient – the person must be named in full. Usually, Full Powers are limited to one person, but there could be an occasion when they would need to provide for more than one person to be named – for example, if it is not certain which representative will attend a particular conference where a treaty is to be signed.

The instrument must give the full formal name of the treaty to be signed. It must be complete and accurate. Full Powers are almost always for the signature of one specific treaty only. A few States such as the UK grant General Full Powers to their representatives at certain IOs such as the UN and the EU, but this is the exception rather than the rule.

The instrument may specify the date and place of signature, if the meeting or ceremony is already arranged, or if it is a multilateral treaty that has already been opened for signature. Practices differ on this point. When the UN Secretary General is the depositary, UN guidelines provide that the date and place of signature *must* be indicated.[43] Specifying the date and place of signature is advantageous as it ensures that there is no doubt about the treaty that the representative is authorised to sign; there may be more than one treaty with the same or a similar title. Treaty signings at the UN are normally arranged well in advance and are unlikely to be rescheduled. However, for a bilateral treaty it may be more practical not to specify the date, so as to leave more flexibility in case of diary changes, which are not uncommon events.[44] In the case of other multilateral treaties, where the treaty has already been opened for signature, it is desirable to refer to this date in the Full Powers instrument.[45] When it has not, the depositary should consider whether it is more important to have the treaty defined with maximum precision in the Full Powers instruments, or to leave flexibility in case the planned date or place of signature is changed and advise the States that are going to sign accordingly.[46]

In the case of a multilateral treaty which is open to either definitive signature or signature subject to ratification, the Full Powers document should specify which type of signature is authorised. If it does not, the depositary should accept it only as authorisation to sign subject to ratification.[47]

[43] Treaty Section of the Office of Legal Affairs, *Treaty Handbook* (2nd edn, UN 2012) 7 para 3.2.3. See also Annex V, 'United Nations Model Instrument of Full Powers' at 437.

[44] See an example of a Full Powers instrument for signing a bilateral treaty in Annex VI.A, 'Full Powers for Signing a Bilateral Treaty' at 438.

[45] See example of a Full Powers instrument for signing a multilateral treaty in Annex VI.B 'Full Powers for Signing a Multilateral Treaty' at 439.

[46] See an example of a Full Powers instrument for signing a multilateral treaty for which ASEAN is the depositary in Annex VIII, 'Example of an Instrument of Ratification' at 441.

[47] VCLT 1969 art 12(1)(c).

Adding an official seal is common practice but optional. It cannot replace the signature of one of the three authorities of State.

The Full Powers instrument should be prepared by treaty officials, and then submitted to the Foreign Minister, the Head of Government or in some circumstances the Head of State for their signature. It is important for treaty officials to make sure that all details in the instrument are correct. It is also important that this is done in good time before the treaty is to be signed, especially if that signature is to take place overseas. This is where close liaison in good time between the policy officials who may be arranging the signature ceremony and officials dealing with the treaty is vitally important, as leaving such things to the last minute can have adverse consequences.

When an IO is involved in making a new treaty *as a potential party* (that is, not when its role is merely hosting the negotiations), its representative must likewise have Full Powers to adopt, initial or sign it. The requirement for Full Powers, as it applies to the representative of an IO, is set out in Article 7(3) VCLT 1986, which reads:

> 3. A person is considered as representing an international organization for the purpose of adopting or authenticating the text of a treaty, or expressing the consent of that organization to be bound by a treaty, if:
>   (a) that person produces appropriate full powers; or
>   (b) it appears from the circumstances that it was the intention of the States and international organizations concerned to consider that person as representing the organization for such purposes, in accordance with the rules of the organization, without having to produce full powers.

The VCLT does not specify at what level of an IO the Full Powers must be signed, but sets a more general requirement that the Full Powers be 'appropriate'. They are normally signed by the head of the IO or person deputising for the head. Whether any other high-ranking official of the IO could be considered 'appropriate' to sign Full Powers is a question of judgement for each IO, in consultation with the other party or parties to the treaty in question. The possibility of dispensing with Full Powers is considered below.

Full Powers: What Can (and often Does) Go Wrong

Without sight of an actual instrument, there can be a great deal of confusion and uncertainty over who has Full Powers and who does not. For example, some Ambassadors may state very assertively that they have Full Powers to sign a treaty simply by virtue of their appointment. Unless they have a Full Powers document signed by one of the three qualified authorities of State giving them such a Power, they do not! This misunderstanding sometimes arises from a misreading of Article 7(2)(b) VCLT 1969, which states that Full Powers are not required for 'heads of diplomatic missions, for the purpose of adopting the text of a treaty between the accrediting State and the State to which they are accredited'. Note that this relates to 'adopting the text' – which does not equate with 'signing' it. Nor does it relate to a treaty with any other parties.

There can of course be last-minute difficulties, for example if the named individual who is authorised to sign a treaty is a government minister who resigns or is removed from office, very shortly before the treaty is to be signed. In such circumstances, treaty officials will have to ensure that new Full Powers for his or her successor can be produced very quickly. If this is not possible then the signature ceremony may have to be postponed.

If the Foreign Minister is away, whether travelling on official business or on leave, the question of who should sign the Full Powers can arise. Could it be submitted to his or her deputy to sign? Article 7 VCLT 1969 is quite clear that only one of the three authorities can sign. This means that signature by a deputy would not suffice, unless he or she is the acting Foreign Minister or formally in charge of the ministry ad interim.[48] Even then the other State may not be prepared to accept Full Powers signed by someone other than one of the three authorities. In these circumstances, treaty officials may have to see if one of the other two authorities, either the Head of Government or the Head of State, would be able to sign the Full Powers.

But if things do go wrong, or arise at the last minute when there is insufficient time for Full Powers to be prepared, signed, dispatched and delivered, there may be alternatives. It may be possible for a photocopy of the *signed* Full Powers to be faxed or scanned and emailed to the other State or to the depositary organising the signature ceremony. This will need to be confirmed in advance however, and their willingness to accept this cannot just be assumed; this is especially true if the treaty is to enter into force on signature, when it is unlikely that this alternative would be accepted. In any event, if it is accepted at all, it will be on condition that the signed original Full Powers is sent very soon afterwards.

Dispensing with Full Powers

With some treaties, usually bilateral, it may be possible to dispense with Full Powers altogether, as indicated in Article 7(1)(b) VCLT 1969.[49] Dispensing with Full Powers is not a step to be taken lightly however, and it needs to be agreed well in advance either with the other party for a bilateral or with the depositary for a multilateral. An agreement to dispense with Full Powers is the exception rather than the rule and is normally made in relation to one specified treaty only. It can produce problems further down the line if any doubt or dispute should arise about the validity of the signature, and therefore any agreement to dispense with Full Powers must be fully and clearly recorded in writing. An exchange of diplomatic notes is usually the best way to record such an agreement.

[48] *Aust* (n 32) 76.

[49] VCLT 1969 art 7(1)(b). See the first paragraph in the section on 'Full Powers' above at 188–92.

Occasionally, an agreement to dispense with Full Powers might be established on the basis of a consistent practice. For example, certain pairs of States may routinely conclude bilateral treaties by exchange of notes without requiring the other side's signatory to produce a Full Powers document to prove authority to sign the note. If one side believes this to be the case, they should raise it in good time, and the other side should check that there are precedents or a past agreement to this effect on their files. If there is any doubt, a new record should be made of the agreement to dispense with Full Powers, ensuring that it is clear whether it is for one treaty only or a category of treaties, who the permitted signatories are and any other conditions that apply.[50]

When an IO is a negotiating party or signatory to a treaty, there is a similar exception to the requirement for its representative to produce Full Powers when 'it appears from the circumstances that it was the intention of the States and international organizations concerned to consider that person as representing the organization for such purposes, in accordance with the rules of the organization, without having to produce full powers'.[51]

If an IO asserts that its representative is entitled to adopt, initial or sign a treaty without Full Powers, it should be able to demonstrate this by reference to the IO's rules and/or a decision of an organ of the IO, or some other documentary evidence such as a set of precedents. In any case, if an IO is going to conclude a treaty with another IO or with a non-Member State, the other party is not obliged to follow a practice established within the IO and may, if it so wishes, insist upon the production of Full Powers.

It is worth emphasising that, except when treaties are formed by exchange of notes, it is unusual for parties to dispense with Full Powers for signing a treaty. Using Full Powers is good treaty practice, reflecting the PLATO 'Assured' principle, in particular the importance of making clear who is authorised to perform treaty acts and of using procedures to ensure that unauthorised acts do not occur.

Signing Ceremonies

Preparing and Hosting a Bilateral Signature Ceremony

For bilateral treaties in particular, the signature ceremony is an important point on the treaty's journey from draft to entry into force. If the treaty is to enter into force on signature, as some bilateral treaties do, this is its most significant moment.

[50] See the section on 'Who Needs to Sign the Note (or Letter) on Each Side (where the Notes Form the Treaty)?' in Chapter 7 at 262–63.

[51] VCLT 1986 art 7(3)(b). See the section on 'Full Powers' above at 188–92 and the section on 'Who Needs to Sign the Note (or Letter) on each Side (where the Notes Form the Treaty)?' in Chapter 7 at 262–63.

Having bound and sealed the treaty, the next step for the Treaty Office is to arrange the ceremony – in fact, this should have been arranged before the sealing took place as the diaries of ministers and senior officials can become booked up a long way in advance. The decision on who (on its own side) is to sign the treaty can be influenced by a number of factors such as the subject matter, timing of an official or State visit, the need to sign the treaty in conjunction with another event or significant anniversary, and so on. Policy officials will normally have a view on who should sign, and must be fully involved and consulted in this decision-making process. Once it has been agreed who should sign, the Treaty Office needs to ensure that Full Powers are obtained (unless of course they are not required because the signatory is one of the three authorities). Signatories on each side do not necessarily have to be of equal ministerial or diplomatic rank, but should always be at least a government minister or a senior official.

Once a date, time and venue have been agreed, the Treaty Office should liaise with the various stakeholders to ensure that everyone who needs to know about the event has been informed. If there is to be media coverage of the signature, this will have to be arranged beforehand and any appropriate passes issued. The media are not routinely invited to attend treaty-signing ceremonies, but they may be invited where the importance and profile of the treaty is considered to warrant it. This decision would normally be made by the lead policy department rather than treaty officials, but those organising the venue, seating and timetable will need to take account of it. Policy officials will also want to prepare relevant press briefing. The minister or senior official who is to sign the treaty will probably ask for briefing, and treaty officials may be required to brief on the procedures to be followed. They should also (re)confirm who is signing the treaty for the other party and, if that person is not known, locate a photograph if possible – sometimes a large group can arrive, and it is useful to be able to identify the signatory easily.

On the day of the signing, treaty officials should be at the venue in good time to ensure that all is in order. There should be a table large enough for the two signatories to sit side by side, and with sufficient room for the treaties and any other documentation. There should also be enough room for an assistant to stand each side of the signatories to allow for the treaties to be exchanged (see below). Space in the room may also be required for high-level officials wishing to witness the ceremony.

Flags can be a problem. They certainly add to the colour of a signature ceremony and provide an excellent photo opportunity, but care is needed to ensure that the right flag is in position and that it is the right way up. This does not only apply to the flag for the other State; it is not unknown for a host State's own flag to be displayed the wrong way up.[52] Another hazard to avoid is placing

[52] For example, BBC News, 'Flag mistake at UK–China ceremony' (3 February 2009) http://news.bbc.co.uk/1/hi/uk_politics/7866938.stm accessed 25 September 2018. Comment: the error was not made by treaty officials.

the flags too close to the signature table, as this could result in one of them being knocked over during the ceremony with potentially embarrassing results.

Pens can also be a contentious issue. Treaties should be signed in ink, ideally with a fountain pen. Some States have their own special treaty-signing pens and will wish to use them, but others will expect the host government to supply them, so this is another point to clarify with the other party beforehand, for example when sealing the treaty. Sometimes pens might run out of ink or not work after several weeks of non-use, so the pens to be used for signature should be tested before the ceremony. There was at one time a tradition that the signatories of a treaty kept the pens they had signed it with, but this is not often followed now as a regular supply of good quality pens can become a drain on departmental finances!

Each signatory will require an assistant, who will exchange originals of the treaty with the other signatory's assistant as they are signed. Ideally, this should be a treaty official for the host State and an official from the other State, usually one of the senior staff from the relevant embassy or mission. Just before the treaty is signed, the two assistants should write in the date and place of signature in the testimonium blocks, in the relevant languages.

Beneath the testimonium will be two signature blocks, which should say 'For the Government of State X' and 'For the Government of State Y'. The signatories will sign above these blocks. If the treaty is in more than one language and is formatted such that each language text has its own signature block, treaty officials should check before the ceremony takes place where exactly their signatory should sign in any unfamiliar language(s).

The ceremony process itself is quite straightforward. Each signatory sits at the table with the original of the treaty in his or her State's precedence, and with his or her assistant standing to the side (see photograph on front cover of this Handbook). They each sign. If the testimonium and signature block is repeated at the end of two language texts, each will sign twice (if there are three, each will sign three times, etc.). The assistants then exchange the treaties behind the seated signatories. Each signatory then signs the other original (twice or more again, for each language text), Then, typically, they will stand up, shake hands and exchange originals so that each State takes away their own original of the treaty, with their State's precedence and in their State's binder. This is the moment for photographs if required, and the signing ceremony is then concluded. If the media are present, the signatories may wish to make speeches. This may be done at any stage of the proceedings; before the signing is the usual preference.

Arranging and Hosting Signature Ceremonies for Multilateral Treaties

When a multilateral treaty is opened for signature, it is customary to hold a ceremony for those States (and IOs if applicable) wishing to sign on the first day. The purpose of the ceremony is primarily to celebrate the birth of the treaty and the success of the negotiations, and to promote the treaty to other eligible States. The media may be invited if there is high public interest in the treaty and/or the aim is also to raise public awareness of its importance. It is also a convenient way for the Treaty Office to manage a large number of dignitaries wishing to sign at the same time. A ceremony is not, however, a legal requirement. All that is needed is for the treaty to be available for signature at the depositary's office and for a State/IO wishing to sign to make an appointment with the depositary to do so, and produce the requisite Full Powers. Treaties usually remain open for signature for a period of time or indefinitely (as stipulated in the final provisions of the treaty), so even when a ceremony is held on the opening day, any eligible State/IO wishing to sign later will normally do it by individual appointment.

The CoE practice is that the Treaty Office always arranges a ceremony for the signing of treaties, with the Secretary General or Deputy Secretary General in attendance. The Treaty Office informs the Press Department of Communications Directorate that a signing ceremony is going to take place and the latter decides whether to put out a press release. Very few occasions are attended by the media; this is only likely if a minister is attending and the treaty is high profile.

Signing Subject to Ratification or other further Procedures

Signature of a treaty can be subject to a number of different further procedures to confirm consent to be bound. Some bilateral treaties specify that they enter into force on signature, and so once each side has signed, the treaty is in force immediately or after a specified period of time. This type of signature ('definitive signature'), however, is not frequently used, and it is more usual for the treaty to be subjected to an additional procedure.

For bilateral treaties, the required further procedure could be an exchange of instruments of ratification, or an exchange of notes confirming that the relevant domestic procedures necessary for each side have been completed. Ratification and accession are the most frequent means of expressing consent to be bound for multilateral treaties, and this is discussed in much more detail in Chapter 6.[53] Bilateral treaties do not normally offer a choice of signing definitively or subject to a further procedure; both parties normally agree upon the same method as part of the negotiations, and this should be clearly set out in the final clauses.

Some multilateral treaties provide a choice of a one-step or a two-step procedure, from which each signatory State or IO may choose. If the choices include both a definitive signature and a signature subject to ratification, a signatory choosing the latter must make this abundantly clear. This may be done in one of two ways:

- On the treaty text itself, with the signature. This means that the person who signs (usually a minister, sometimes a Head of Government or Head of

[53] See the section on 'Understanding Modes for Expressing Consent to Be Bound' in Chapter 6 at 220–27. See also the section on 'Expressing Consent to be Bound by the Treaty' in Chapter 7 at 247–68.

State) has to be advised by officials to write '(subject to ratification)' after or below their signature; or

- By delivery of a note verbale to the depositary at the time of signature, stating that the signature is subject to ratification. The note can be prepared, signed in advance and handed over by an official accompanying the dignitary who signs.

The advantage of the signer writing the words onto the treaty text is that they cannot be later lost or detached. However, this method should only be used when officials are very confident that the signer will remember to write in the words, and do so accurately and legibly. If there is any doubt, the note verbale method should be used. At a treaty-signing ceremony, the accompanying official (the 'assistant') may not be close enough to check what the signer has written, and, once the dignitaries have stood up and shaken hands it will not be possible to ask one of them to sit down again to write in the forgotten words!

If the status of the signature is not specified, the depositary should not simply assume that definitive signature was intended, but should contact the State or IO concerned to clarify the matter. In fact, a well-organised depositary will have asked each signatory State or IO in advance which method they intend to choose, and will have advised on appropriate wording to be included in the Full Powers. The signatory however would be well advised not to take this for granted. It is too risky to leave any scope for doubt.

Certified True Copies

There will be only one original of a multilateral treaty, which is the document that everyone signs. When a State or IO signs a multilateral treaty, the depositary of that treaty should provide them with a certified true copy of the treaty concerned.

This must be an exact copy of the treaty that has been signed, except that it will not usually be possible to photocopy the signed original (as it will be bound and should never be unbound). To be precise then, it will be an exact copy of the treaty that has been signed, as it was before the first signing. Great care must be taken when proofreading the copies to *ensure* that the text provided exactly matches the text that has been signed, and each copy should be signed by a senior treaty official to certify that it is accurate. The pages should be bound together and sealed. Binding them into a formal hard binder is optional and not usually done nowadays, as binders are expensive.

Ideally, the certified true copies should be prepared before the signature ceremony and sent in advance to the signing State(s) or presented to them at the ceremony. Failing that, they should be sent to all signatory States as soon as possible after the ceremony. Certified true copies are also provided to States on ratification or accession, and to the UN when registering a copy of the treaty.

Top Tips and Checklists: From Negotiating to Signing a Treaty

Top Tips on Preparing for the Process of Negotiating, Drafting and Signing a Treaty

The top tips in Box 5.2 highlight selected key points in this chapter. The top tips provide pointers for treaty negotiators and treaty officials on the following particular issues: treaty negotiating; treaty drafting; official language(s) of the text; production of a treaty text; and hosting a treaty-signing ceremony.

Box 5.2 Top tips on preparing for the process of negotiating, drafting and signing a treaty

TOP TIPS 1
TREATY NEGOTIATING

- Prepare a full written brief in advance, even if you are the sole negotiator, and consult others in your government/IO with a policy interest or responsibility for implementation.
- Find out at the meeting who is the keeper of the negotiating text, e.g. secretariat, member of the Chair's delegation, and ask them regularly for updates on new text.

TOP TIPS 2
TREATY DRAFTING

- Make life easy: prepare a table of contents, especially if the text is long, and use headings (e.g. for each part of the treaty).
- Keep it simple. The more difficult a treaty is to understand, the more cautious delegates will be about agreeing to it, and the less likely that it will be implemented.

TOP TIPS 3
TREATY NEGOTIATORS – CHECK ALL OFFICIAL LANGUAGE TEXTS

- Just because you negotiated the text in English, and English is your mother tongue or preferred negotiating language, does not mean that you can safely ignore the translations of the treaty into other languages! If the treaty languages are all equally authentic, the accuracy of translations matters to all parties. If your ministry does not have a translation service, you could consult with other delegations from your language group and perhaps arrange to share the burden.
- If the treaty is bilateral, have the other side's language text checked by your own translators. Buy in a freelance service if necessary. Or

Box 5.2 (cont.)

propose that the treaty shall be done in only one language that your State can work in.

TOP TIPS 4
PRODUCTION OF A TREATY TEXT

- Make sure all the pages of the treaty text, in all its official languages, are bound together and sealed, before the signature ceremony.
- If textual errors are discovered at or after signing, they can only be corrected by agreement of both/all parties, in accordance with the procedures set out in Article 79 VCLT 1969.
- Do not unbind a treaty after it has been sealed and signed, in any circumstances.

TOP TIPS 5
HOSTING A TREATY-SIGNING CEREMONY

- Ask all States/IOs intending to sign to notify their intention in good time, and to stipulate choice of any available options (e.g. signature subject to ratification or definitive signature).
- Ask all States/IOs intending to sign to send a copy of their representative's Full Powers in advance for checking.

Checklists for Hosting State and Depositary: Making a New Bilateral and Multilateral Treaty

Making a New Bilateral Treaty: Checklist for State Hosting the Signing

The checklist in Box 5.3 provides practical pointers for the Treaty Office of a State that is preparing to host a signing ceremony for a bilateral treaty. Some of the points on preparation of the text (such as checking or rechecking final clauses and translations) may also be relevant for the other party.

Box 5.3 Making a new bilateral treaty: checklist for State hosting the signing

PREPARATION

- Do the final clauses make sense and are they clear?
- Do you know which official languages the treaty will be in and are they equal?
- Does the testimonium state this?

Box 5.3 (cont.)

PRODUCTION

- Have you had the other State's language text checked by translators?
- Do not type date and place of signature in the testimonium – write it in by hand at the last minute. Check that the other State also know to do this. Do not type names of individuals who are going to sign.
- Check in advance with the other State about the paper they will use. Is it a standard A4 size or does it require specific printing equipment? If so, is that available?
- Check the ribbon and binders, and if the other State has a paper seal or will use wax.
- Proofread the final text very carefully.

SIGNATURE

- Who is going to sign the treaty? Do they need Full Powers?
- Consult with stakeholders on arranging date/venue of signature ceremony.
- Once arranged, make sure everyone who needs to know has been told and any passes issued.
- Does your signatory wish to have a briefing about the procedure?
- Flags – do you need them? If so, make sure you have the correct flags and that they are both the right way up. Keep them away from the signature table so you have space to move.
- Where does your signatory sign in the other language(s)? Check that you know this before the ceremony starts.
- Check that you know who the other signatory is. Source a photo if possible so that you will recognise him or her.
- Make sure that you end up with the right copy of the treaty at the end of the ceremony (the one that gives precedence to your State).

Making a New Multilateral Treaty: Checklist for Depositary

The checklist in Box 5.4 provides practical pointers for a depositary on the making of a multilateral treaty, after adoption of the text. It suggests ways to produce the treaty text, and prepare for and conduct a signing ceremony, including steps to be taken after the ceremony.

Box 5.4 Making a new multilateral treaty: checklist for the depositary

PRODUCTION OF TREATY TEXT

- When the treaty text has been adopted and the decision is made to open it for signature, prepare a provisional edition of the treaty text. Ensure that it is correctly formatted and has been carefully proofread.
- Send the text to translators to prepare all of the official language versions (if this has not already been done during negotiations).
- Ensure that all language versions are checked for consistency with each other, including the version used in the negotiations.
- Provide electronic copies of the provisional edition to negotiating States and any others eligible to become party (place on a website if that is the practice of the IO).
- Invite negotiating States to submit any comments on the accuracy of translations to the depositary.
- Ask eligible States (and IOs if any) to indicate whether they intend to sign.
- Finalise and proofread all language texts.
- Type the names of signatory States (and IOs if applicable) in alphabetical order in the appropriate language (working language of the treaty or IO) into the signature block of the treaty. DO NOT type the names of the representatives.
- Produce the final text of the treaty with the list of signatories on the signature block for binding and sealing.
- Produce certified true copies (without the list of signatories) and send them to the embassies/missions of all eligible States, or have them ready to hand to signatories when they sign.

PREPARATION FOR OPENING SIGNATURE CEREMONY

- Invite the negotiating States (or the member of States of the IO concerned) to the treaty-signing ceremony, and provide each with a copy of the provisional edition of the treaty.
- List the States wishing to sign, with names and titles of representatives.
- Check that each State wishing to sign is entitled to do so (check final clauses and any other conditions, such as adherence to a parent treaty).
- Advise signatory States of the need for Full Powers (except for a representative with General Full Powers lodged with the depositary beforehand).
- Receive and verify the Full Powers of each signatory. Request a copy in advance and check that it:

Box 5.4 (cont.)

- Is signed by the Head of State or Government or Foreign Minister, or a person officially appointed to discharge one of those offices ad interim;
- Sets out the exact and complete title of the treaty in question;
- Expressly authorises the named person to *sign* the treaty in question (not just adopt and initial it);
- Sets out the name, forename and title of the person duly authorised to sign; and
- Is in the official language(s) of the IO or treaty, as appropriate.

- Confirm details of date, place, timing and other practical arrangements to representatives coming to sign.
- Inform other relevant parts of the ministry/secretariat of the arrangements and the list of signatories and names of representatives coming, e.g. press office, protocol department, policy/geographical departments.
- Have the room prepared with the following layout:
  - Chair and desk/table with desk pad, table flag and flowers, for the signatory;
  - Host IO or Government flag at the back;
  - Table for treaty officials or space for them to stand close to the signing table;
  - Desk with microphone for the official conducting the ceremony (if required) and lectern with microphone for signatories to speak (if speeches are to be made);
  - Labelled chairs for signatories;
  - Marked-off press area (if media representatives are invited); and
  - Designated chairs or standing space for any additional Host government/IO officials.
- Rehearsal by officials to practise positioning of host (e.g. Secretary General or Minister), signatory and his/her assistant, treaty officials, Head of Protocol, etc.
- Prepare treaty: either indicate (in soft pencil) for each State where to sign, with any other *aide memoire* for words that the signatory must write, such as 'with [or without] reservation as to ratification', OR prepare this information for the treaty official who is going to stand beside the signatory and point to the exact place on the text;
- Arrange official photographer.

CONDUCTING THE SIGNATURE CEREMONY

- Each signatory's name is called by the Head of Protocol or other official conducting the proceedings.

Box 5.4 (cont.)

- Each signatory delivers the original signed Full Powers to the Director General, Minister or dignitary representing the depositary IO/State.
- Dignitaries shake hands in front of photographers (the depositary's photographer, plus any media if present).
- The Head of Treaty Office (or Principal Legal Adviser or Director responsible for treaties) presents the treaty to be signed.
- The treaty is signed by each representative (once only if there is a single testimonium and signature block in all the treaty languages, or once on each signature block at the end of each language text of the treaty).
- Hand each signatory a certified true copy of the treaty (if you have not sent it beforehand).

IMMEDIATELY AFTER THE CEREMONY

- Update the Treaty Office or depositary website to list the States (and IOs if applicable) that have signed and the date.
- Archive the signed treaty and the Full Powers documents (unless the treaty is to be signed by another State/IO in the near future).
- Inform all negotiating parties or Member States of the names of the signatory States (and IOs), together with the text of any declarations or reservations made on signature.

6

Preparing to Become Party to a Treaty

***

'When considering taking a treaty action . . . the process and timeframe should be carefully considered at the outset . . .[I]t is important to be aware that most treaty actions do take a considerable time to conclude, and this needs to be factored into your work plan.'[1]

Introduction

Chapter 5 covered how a new treaty is made. This chapter, and Chapter 7, concern the next steps: how to become party to a treaty, and how to bring a treaty into force.

[1] New Zealand Ministry of Foreign Affairs and Trade, 'International Treaty Making: Guidance for government agencies on practice and procedures for concluding international treaties and arrangements' (August 2018) pp 7–8 www.mfat.govt.nz/assets/Treaties/International-Treaty-Making-Guide-2017.pdf accessed 22 October 2018.

Use of Terms in this Chapter

Effective treaty-making involves three stages: (1) a treaty is made; (2) States and/or IOs express consent to be bound by it; and (3) the treaty enters into force. As an understanding of the differences between these stages is fundamental, this chapter begins by explaining how these terms are used:

1. A treaty is 'made'. The making of a treaty, as explained in Chapter 5, is a collaborative act. The making of a bilateral treaty is the *joint* act of two sides (usually two States, sometimes two IO, one State and one IO, or occasionally other combinations). The making of a multilateral treaty is a *collective* act of all negotiating parties. The treaty is 'made' when the text is agreed, in the sense that it is final and definitive. Agreement is recorded by the negotiators in a formal way, such as initialling the text or 'adopting' it by vote at a meeting.
   This does not make the obligations in it binding; States and IOs that wish to become party have to consent to be bound and bring it into force, according to the procedures applicable to that treaty. It is normal for authorities to need time to consider whether they can bind themselves to the deal that their negotiators have struck with the compromises that this usually entails.
2. States and/or IOs 'express their consent to be bound' by the treaty. 'Expressing consent to be bound' is a *unilateral* act by which an individual State or IO formally commits itself to performing all the obligations in the treaty. The act is irreversible – once a party has expressed its consent to be bound, it is legally committed to the treaty and has the status of a Contracting Party. But this act does not by itself bring the treaty into force; it depends also upon the unilateral acts of others. Until this happens, the treaty is still not binding on any State or IO that has expressed its consent to be bound.
3. The treaty 'enters into force'. The entry into force of a treaty occurs when the conditions specified in the treaty are met. It requires the specified number of consents to be bound (two for a bilateral treaty; for a multilateral it could be all or a minimum number of negotiating parties) plus any other conditions specified in the treaty such as elapse of a specified time.
   Bringing a bilateral treaty into force is a *joint* act, consisting of two unilateral acts. A bilateral treaty is either in force for both parties or neither. Bringing a multilateral treaty into force is a *collective* act, resulting from a number of unilateral acts. It enters into force for all who have consented to be bound when its threshold is met. They thereby *become party* to the treaty. Thereafter, it will enter into force for any new party when it consents to be bound and the conditions are met.

The three stages outlined above may or may not involve the same parties throughout. For bilateral treaties, all stages will involve the same two parties. For multilateral treaties they may do, if eligibility is limited to negotiating parties, but some treaties allow other States and/or IOs to become party without having been involved in the making of the treaty, as explained below.

The term 'conclusion' of a treaty is in frequent use, both generally (such as in the VCLT 1969 and the VCLT 1986) and in this Handbook.[2] However, it is not defined and its meaning is flexible. Sometimes the term refers to just the 'making' of the treaty (the adoption of the text), while in other contexts it may refer to the entire process of making, consenting to be bound and bringing it into force, or any part of it.[3] For this reason, we have used the terms as defined above to indicate each part of the process.

Becoming Party to a Treaty: Why It Does Not Always Happen

Making a treaty does not normally, in itself, create new international obligations. It means that those who participated in the negotiations (States and/or IOs) have agreed in principle on the text. Those participants normally need to take further steps to become party to the treaty and to bring it into force. If any of those steps is not completed, the treaty remains in existence but not in force. This state of 'limbo' may last for a short or a long time, or indefinitely. For example, the UNCLOS was 'in limbo' for twelve years, while the VCLT 1986 is still not in force.[4]

A bilateral treaty will only enter into force when both parties have consented to be bound. Multilateral treaties only enter into force when all the negotiating parties, or a specified number of them, have consented to be bound. If this threshold is not reached, it does not enter into force, and will remain in limbo for all participants.

There are many reasons why a State or IO might participate in adopting and even signing a treaty, but not complete the steps needed to bring it into force for a long time, or at all. Possible reasons include the following:

- Negotiators may agree on a text, but its ratification may then be blocked by some part of the government or legislature, or, in the case of an IO, its Member States.

[2] VCLT 1969 (adopted 23 May 1969, entered into force 27 January 1980) 1155 UNTS 331 (1969) and VCLT 1986 (adopted 21 March 1986, not in force) 25 ILM 543 http://legal.un.org/ilc/texts/instruments/english/conventions/1_2_1986.pdf accessed 9 September 2018.

[3] See for example VCLT 1969 art 1(a). It is clear that in this article, 'concluded' means 'made' or 'adopted' only, compared with art 8 where 'an act relating to the conclusion' refers to adoption, authentication or expressing consent to be bound. Authors use the term in varying ways; for example, 'The conclusion of the treaty has various stages, beginning with the establishment of the text and usually ending with its signature': G Korontzis, 'Making the Treaty' in D Hollis (ed), *The Oxford Guide to Treaties* (OUP 2012) 184; Aust regards a treaty as 'concluded' when it has been signed by both States (bilateral) or when the final act has been signed or the treaty opened for signature (multilateral): A Aust, *Modern Treaty Law and Practice* (3rd edn, CUP 2013) 86.

[4] UNCLOS (adopted 10 December 1982, entered into force 16 November 1994) 1833 UNTS 3.

- Government policy may change due to a change of administration or change in domestic or international circumstances.
- The work involved in preparing for ratification may take a long time due to its complexity, or be stalled due to bureaucratic inertia, lack of expertise or resources, higher priorities or national crisis such as natural disaster or civil war.
- The further steps needed to bring the treaty into force might be misunderstood or overlooked.

There are many other reasons, good and bad, avoidable and unavoidable. There is no obligation on a State or IO to ratify a treaty. Signing a treaty subject to ratification entails only a general obligation 'to refrain from acts which would defeat the object and purpose of the treaty'.[5]

For example, New Zealand has signed but not ratified twenty multilateral treaties, of which six are dormant and never likely to be ratified for various reasons: the treaty is unlikely to enter into force at the international level, or it has been superseded by a more recent treaty or a separate agreement to which New Zealand is party. The Netherlands has likewise signed but not ratified about twenty treaties. In 2009 the UK Government informed Parliament that it had signed but not ratified twenty-six treaties for which the UN was depositary.[6] The practice of the UK is not to sign a treaty subject to ratification unless it has a firm intention of ratifying, and so it could be inferred that the UK was still working towards ratification of most of these treaties, but that possibly in a few cases ratification was no longer intended due to a change of government policy or circumstances of the kind cited by New Zealand. The position of Indonesia in relation to the International Convention for the Protection of All Persons from Enforced Disappearance, 2006[7] provides another illustration. After a long history of enforced disappearance of human rights activists and political dissidents, Indonesia signed the Convention on 27 September 2010. However, the Government of Indonesia has still not ratified the Convention as it is still awaiting the approval of the House of Representatives.[8] The delay appears to be due to waning enthusiasm

[5] VCLT 1969 art 18.

[6] Information about New Zealand and Netherlands treaties provided to Jill Barrett by New Zealand Department of Foreign Affairs and Trade treaty officer and Netherlands former treaty officer, respectively, in 2012. In 2009 the UK Government informed Parliament that it had signed but not ratified twenty-six treaties for which the UN was depositary. See Written Answer by Lord Malloch-Brown, Minister of State, FCO, to Lord Roberts of Llandudno in 'United Nations: Conventions – House of Lords written question – answered on 5 May 2009' (HL Deb, 5 May 2009) c114W www.theyworkforyou.com/wrans/?id=2009–05-05a.113.0 accessed 25 September 2018.

[7] International Convention for the Protection of All Persons from Enforced Disappearance (adopted 20 December 2006, entered into force 23 December 2010) 2716 UNTS 3.

[8] Directorate General of Human Rights, 'Ratification of the Convention on Enforced Disappearance' (Ministry of Law and Human Rights, 15 January 2014) (in Indonesian) http://ham.go.id/ratifikasi-konvensi-orang-hilang/ accessed 25 September 2018.

for the 'reform' era and the House's lack of interest in debating and enacting a domestic law to ratify the Convention.[9]

Looking at the practice of IOs as parties to treaties, it is evident that they too may participate in negotiating a treaty and even sign it, yet for various reasons not complete all the steps to becoming party. For example, the CoE is not party to any multilateral treaty. It has signed one multilateral treaty, namely the VCLT 1986. The CoE signed it in 1987 but has still not ratified it.[10] In its decision of 1987 (adopted by vote) the Committee of Ministers authorised the Secretary General to deposit an instrument of ratification, but he has not yet done so, due to the objections of one Member State (France) which happens to be the host State of the CoE. Even when authorisation is granted, the Secretary General retains discretion as to *when* to act upon the mandate and may take into account the views of a Member State when considering discretion even when, as in this case, that State has been outvoted in the Council of Ministers.[11]

The effects of a particular treaty not entering into force (for one participant, or at all) vary from one case to another; the impact on international relations and international law may be considered negative by some and positive by others. One thing is clear however; the work and resources involved in negotiating the treaty, and the goodwill generated by reaching agreement on a text, will be lost. The failure of a treaty to enter into force is not necessarily due to any deficiency in the treaty procedures of individual States or IOs. It may reflect a *collective* misjudgement on the part of all negotiating parties in adopting a text that was not capable of attracting sufficient ratifications, or it may simply be that the treaty has been overtaken by unforeseen events. The aim of this chapter is to help avoid those cases that occur due to an oversight, misunderstanding or error in treaty procedures.

[9] D H Widhana, 'Long Road for Justice for the Disappearance of Three "98" Activists' *Harian Merdeka* (Jakarta, 8 May 2016) (in Indonesian) www.merdeka.com/peristiwa/jalan-panjang-mencari-keadilan-hilang-13-aktivis-98.html accessed 25 September 2018; and Y Linggasari, 'International Human Rights Award Recipient is not Being Supported by the Government' CNN Indonesia (Jakarta, 16 December 2015) (in Indonesian) www.cnnindonesia.com/nasional/20151215212842-20-98487/peraih-penghargaan-haminternasional-tak-disokong-pemerintah/ accessed 25 September 2018. See also, KontraS, '20 years on KontraS advocates for courage and humanity to the people' *Requisitoire Magazine* (Jakarta, 20 March 2018) (in Indonesian) http://requisitoire-magazine.com/2018/03/20/20-tahun-kontras-ajak-masyarakat-bersama-menyebarkan-keberanian-dan-merawat-kemanusiaan/ accessed 25 September 2018.

[10] UNTC, 'Vienna Convention on the Law of Treaties between States and International Organisations or between International Organisations' (status as at 14 October 2019) https://treaties.un.org/Pages/ViewDetails.aspx?src=TREATY&mtdsg_no=XXIII-3&chapter=23&clang=_en accessed 22 October 2018.

[11] Committee of Ministers, 'Conclusions of the 405th Meeting of the Ministers' Deputies' CM/Del/Concl (87) 405 (12 February 1987) Item 24 – Vienna Convention on the Law of Treaties between States and International Organisations or between International Organisations.

Why Good Preparation for Treaty Ratification Matters: What Can Go Wrong

Treaties can be left unratified due to administrative oversight, misunderstanding or an error in treaty procedures within one or more of the negotiating parties. This situation may go undetected for a long time, especially if there is no effective oversight by a depositary and no regular review by each Treaty Office of the status of the treaties its State/IO has been involved in making.

The following scenario illustrates an example of a type of error – accidental failure to ratify a treaty – that appears to have occurred in a number of cases.

Scenario: Accidental Failure to Ratify a Treaty

A newly independent State signed a BIT with another State in 1992. In 2011, a foreign investor with a substantial stake in the oil industry of the newly independent State brought a very large claim against that State before an international tribunal, under the BIT. The entry into force provision of the BIT provided: 'This Agreement shall enter into force on the date on which the exchange of instruments of ratification has been completed.' Both sides asserted that the treaty had entered into force in 1995.

However, neither side was able to provide any evidence that instruments of ratification had been exchanged in 1995, or at all. It appeared (with hindsight) that this procedure had been overlooked, and in fact the treaty was not in force. Both governments had published the treaty in their official gazette and obtained the approval of their respective legislatures to ratify it, and it appeared that officials of both States had confused the national 'ratification' procedures with the international law requirement for the two governments to exchange instruments of ratification.[12]

Applying the PLATO Principles to Preparation for Becoming Party to a Treaty

Becoming party to a treaty and its entry into force are governed by the international law of treaties. The PLATO principle 'Legal' guides all stages of the process, for the reasons set out in Chapter 5 in relation to making a treaty.[13] In addition, the need to co-ordinate the international law processes with those in the domestic legal system is paramount.

The PLATO principle 'Transparency' comes prominently into play when considering whether and how to become party to a treaty, important elements

[12] This example is based on the facts of an ICSID investment treaty arbitration on which one of the authors (Jill Barrett) advised. In that case, a settlement was reached, and the pleadings are not published. The Respondent Government chose not to advance the argument that the treaty was not in force. Had it done so, and succeeded, the implications for both Governments and the investors of both States would have been considerable. Both Governments have continued to act on the basis that the treaty is in force.

[13] See the section on 'Introduction: Applying the PLATO Principles to Making a New Treaty' in Chapter 5 at 159–62. For a complete explanation of the PLATO principles, please refer to the section on 'The PLATO Principles for Good Treaty Practice' in Chapter 1 at 14.

of which are 'Accountability' and 'Accessibility'. A government's accountability to its national legislature, an IO's accountability to its Member States, and democratic principles of accountability to the public need to be factored into the process of becoming party to treaties:

- 'Accountability' means that sufficient information must be published to enable democratic oversight of the exercise of treaty-making powers and other treaty acts. Furthermore, there needs to be a meaningful opportunity for elected representatives/Member States to scrutinise treaties before obligations are incurred.
- 'Accessibility' means that publications of treaty texts should be widely and publicly accessible and user-friendly. The same applies to information about the acts of the State or IO in relation to the treaty and its status (such as whether it is in force).

These principles of 'Legality' and 'Transparency' interact strongly with particular elements of two other PLATO principles: 'Assured' and 'Organised'. These are even more crucial for the Treaty Office at the stage of becoming party and immediately afterwards, and will be looked at in more detail in Chapter 7.

Eligibility to Join a Treaty

Before the issue of *how* a State or IO can consent to be bound to a particular treaty arises, it may be necessary to consider the prior question of *whether* it is eligible to do so. For bilateral treaties, or treaties which are negotiated among a closed group of States and/or IOs, any issue of this kind would be addressed during negotiations. Once a treaty has been made, questions of eligibility could be an issue for any other State or IO wishing to participate, or for entities whose status as a State or IO is unclear. These issues need to be clarified before the Treaty Office of the State or IO concerned starts to prepare formalities for giving consent to be bound. If you are the depositary for a treaty, the issue may arise when a State or IO consults you about its eligibility to join it, or when you receive its formal instrument.

There are two sets of eligibility questions that need to be considered. One concerns international law: is this State or IO eligible to become party to this particular treaty, as a matter of international law? The other concerns domestic or internal law: does this State or IO have internal competence to join this treaty, under its domestic law or constitution? Both questions need to be considered but not necessarily in this order or by the same personnel. This section concerns the question of eligibility in international law; questions of internal capacity are considered below.

The first place to look is the treaty text itself. A treaty text normally contains provisions that specify who may become party to it, and how. These are normally at the end, in the section called 'Final Clauses' or 'Final

Provisions'.[14] These provisions must be consulted carefully, as each treaty is governed by its own final clauses, which may not necessarily be the same as any other. It is also important to read the opening provisions of the treaty including any definitions, which may explain terms used in the final clauses, such as 'State Party' or 'Contracting Party'.

Treaties are normally open only to States, or to States and IOs. Every State possesses capacity to enter into treaties.[15] By contrast, the capacity of an IO to enter into a treaty is not so straightforward; it is governed by its organisational rules.[16] The number of treaties open to IOs is comparatively small; they tend to be the exception rather than the rule.

Eligibility of States to Participate in Multilateral Treaties

Bilateral treaties typically name the two parties in the title and in the opening and final provisions of the text. Some closed multilateral treaties do likewise; the negotiating States are named in a list at the beginning and/or end of the treaty, for example in the preamble or signature block, and there is no provision for any other State to join. For the named States, there should not then be any problem.

Problems can arise for States when they are not named in the treaty. Some multilateral treaties specify that they are open to all States,[17] whereas others provide that only States that meet specified criteria may become party.[18] Some closed membership treaties allow existing parties to agree to invite others to participate or consider applications to join.[19] Such treaties typically contain only an outline (at best) of the procedures to be followed in such cases, and so the depositary may need to devise some. The following examples show how this may be done.

Example of a Treaty which Provides for Accession by States that Meet Certain Criteria

The Convention on the Conservation of Antarctic Marine Living Resources, 1980 (CCAMLR) provides that:

> This Convention shall be open for accession by any State interested in research or harvesting activities in relation to the marine living resources to which this Convention applies.[20]

[14] See the section on 'The Final Clauses' in Chapter 5 at 169–71. [15] VCLT 1969 art 6.

[16] ibid.

[17] For example, Convention on the Rights of the Child (adopted 20 November 1989, entered into force 2 September 1990) 1577 UNTS 3, arts 46–48. The final clauses are reproduced in Annex II.

[18] For example, Council of Europe Convention on Action against Trafficking in Human Beings (adopted 16 May 2005, entered into force 10 February 2008) CETS 197, art 42. The final clauses are reproduced in Annex II.

[19] For example, ibid art 43.

[20] Convention on the Conservation of Antarctic Marine Living Resources (adopted 20 May 1980, entered into force 7 April 1982) 1329 UNTS 47 art XXIX(1) (CCAMLR).

The procedure for demonstrating that the criteria are met is not set out in the Convention itself, but on the website maintained by the CCAMLR Secretariat (which provides treaty administration, but is not the depositary). The interested State must submit a note verbale to the Depositary Government (Australia) stating that State's interest in research or harvesting, and

> The note, to the extent possible, should outline the Acceding State's scientific research interests and include any details of research being undertaken, or being planned for, in the Convention Area. On request, the Secretariat will provide an example of an Instrument of Accession.[21]

The Instrument of Accession must, as usual, be deposited with the Depositary.

These CCAMLR procedures illustrate clearly the normal division of function between a treaty depositary, on the one hand, and an operational treaty secretariat, on the other (for treaties which have a secretariat). The depositary handles all formal treaty instruments, whereas the secretariat provides factual information.

Example of Procedures for Deciding on Discretionary Invitations to Accede to Treaties

Participation in most CoE treaties is not limited to the CoE Member States. Most treaties are open to accession by non-Member States, provided that they have been invited to accede by the Committee of Ministers of the CoE. The outline of the procedure is set out in each treaty. The Secretariat and Member States have developed further procedures to make it work in a transparent way.[22]

A typical example of such a provision is Article 37(1) of the Convention on Cybercrime, 2001,[23] which provides:

> After the entry into force of this Convention, the Committee of Ministers of the Council of Europe, after consulting with and obtaining the unanimous consent of the Contracting States to the Convention, may invite any State which is not a member of the Council and which has not participated in its elaboration to accede to this Convention. The decision shall be taken by the majority provided for in Article 20.d. of the Statute of the Council of Europe and by the unanimous vote of the representatives of the Contracting States entitled to sit on the Committee of Ministers.

The procedure used by the Secretariat to facilitate this decision (and those provided for in similar treaty provisions) is as follows:

[21] Commission for the Conservation of Antarctic Marine Living Resources, 'Acceding to the Convention' (last modified 19 April 2013) www.ccamlr.org/en/organisation/acceding-convention accessed 25 September 2018.

[22] Treaty Office, 'Practical Guide' (CoE, October 2013). This is a restricted document produced for internal purposes.

[23] Convention on Cybercrime (adopted 23 November 2001, entered into force 1 July 2004) ETS 185.

- The non-Member State writes a letter to the CoE Secretary General to express interest in an invitation to accede to a specified Convention.
- The Secretariat informally ascertains the opinion among CoE Member States' delegations.
- The request is examined by the Committee of Ministers. If there is agreement in principle, non-Member States which are party to that convention are consulted, with a time limit to express any objection, usually two months.
- Provided there is no objection, the Council of Ministers decides formally to invite that State to accede, and the Secretariat writes to inform the requesting State of the invitation, which is valid for five years.[24]
- The requesting State may then deposit its instrument of accession.[25]

Eligibility of IOs to Participate in Multilateral Treaties

Where a treaty provides for one or more IOs to become party, there will always be specific criteria that define which IOs may qualify. Even a treaty as general as the VCLT 1986 is not open to all IOs; its final clauses specify that it is open to IOs which were invited to participate in the conference that negotiated that treaty, and to any IO 'which has the capacity to conclude treaties'.[26] So far, only thirteen IOs are party.[27]

More typically, a treaty which is open to IOs will concern a specific substantive subject and limit participation to one or more named IOs, or to IOs with competence in that subject. Moreover, it is common for such provisions to specify that the IO must have competence in that subject transferred to it by its Member States. A typical example is UNCLOS, which is open only to an IO 'constituted by States to which its Member States have transferred competence over matters governed by the Convention, including the competence to enter into treaties in respect of those matters'.[28] The EU is the only IO to have become a party to UNCLOS, and is probably the only one currently qualified to do so.[29]

Some treaties specify additional substantive criteria that involve the exercise of discretion. In such cases, the depositary should not exercise that discretion without consulting the existing treaty parties; and it is usually wise to place the

[24] An example of a decision taken on a request to accede to this convention is 'Ministers' Deputies Decisions at the 1171 meeting' CM/Del/Dec (2013)1171 (31 May 2013) Item 10.3 Council of Europe Convention on Cybercrime (ETS No. 185) – Request by the Republic of Colombia to be invited to accede (GR-J(2013)10) p 15 https://rm.coe.int/16805c8260 accessed 25 September 2018.

[25] *Treaty Office* (n 22) 65. [26] VCLT 1986 arts 82–84. [27] *UNTC* (n 10).

[28] UNCLOS Annex IX Participation by International Organizations art 1.

[29] UNTC, 'United Nations Convention on the Law of the Sea' (status as at 22 October 2018) https://treaties.un.org/pages/ViewDetailsIII.aspx?src=TREATY&mtdsg_no=XXI-6&chapter=21&Temp=mtdsg3&clang=_en accessed 22 October 2018.

decision entirely in their hands, in view of the controversies which can arise over the competence of an IO.

An example of a treaty which expressly requires consultations before the accession of an IO can be accepted is CCAMLR. It provides:

> This Convention shall be open for accession by regional economic integration organisations constituted by sovereign States which include among their members one or more States Members of the Commission and to which the States members of the organisation have transferred, in whole or in part, competences with regard to the matters covered by this Convention. The accession of such regional economic integration organisations shall be the subject of consultations among Members of the Commission.[30]

These consultations are normally conducted at a meeting of the CCAMLR Commission, in accordance with its decision-making procedures. The Depositary Government will then accept the IO's Instrument of Accession, or not, as decided by the Commission Members.

Case Study: Is the CoE Eligible to Become Party to CoE Treaties?

Could the CoE become party to any of the over 220 multilateral treaties that its Member States have concluded under its auspices? Some are open to accession by non-Member States and organisations by invitation. The CoE is not party to any of these treaties.

Normally the question does not arise as the subject matter of the treaties is wholly within the competence of the Member States, and could not be fulfilled by the organisation itself. One possible exception is the Council of Europe Convention on Access to Official Documents, 2009,[31] as the obligations of the Convention could in principle be applied by the Secretariat to the organisation's own documents (as well as by the Member States to their official documents). However, the question has not yet arisen as that Convention is not yet in force. After its entry into force, the Convention parties could decide (by unanimous vote) to invite the CoE to accede.[32]

Eligibility of Other Entities to Participate in Multilateral Treaties

A few treaties make provision for entities that are neither States nor IOs to become party. In special circumstances this might be done to accommodate a specific territory or a category of territories, such as non-independent internally self-governing territories, where their participation as a party is deemed to be important to the success of the treaty. For example, UNCLOS is open for signature and ratification, or accession, by several specified

[30] UNCLOS art XXIX (2).

[31] Council of Europe Convention on Access to Official Documents (adopted 18 June 2009, not in force) CETS 205 www.coe.int/en/web/conventions/full-list/-/conventions/treaty/205/signatures?p_auth=MeRqRDwR accessed 22 October 2018.

[32] ibid art 17.

categories of 'other entities'.[33] The same provision is made in the United Nations Agreement for the Implementation of the Provisions of the United Nations Convention on the Law of the Sea of 10 December 1982 relating to the Conservation and Management of Straddling Fish Stocks and Highly Migratory Fish Stocks, 1995.[34]

Even more unusually, a treaty may provide for a specified type of entity to exercise rights and obligations under the treaty without formally becoming a party. An example of this is the provision in the Fish Stocks Agreement, Article 1(3) that 'This Agreement applies *mutatis mutandis* to other fishing entities whose vessels fish on the high seas'.[35]

Such provisions are very unusual and any proposal to make use of them is liable to be controversial, at least from the perspective of one or more existing parties to the treaty. There may be no precedent and no established procedures for handling such cases as they may not have arisen before in that treaty. Any treaty official who is dealing with any such proposal would be well advised to act cautiously and only on the basis of legal advice, policy advice and/or consultations, as appropriate.

What if the Treaty Text Does Not Specify which States and/or IOs May Become Party?

Occasionally, a treaty text may not specify which States and/or IOs may become party. There are two other places to look for this:

- The Final Act: this is the record of the meeting at which the treaty text was agreed and formally adopted. It may contain statements concerning eligibility to become party and the procedure for doing so. In effect, the final clauses of a treaty may be found in the Final Act, rather than in the treaty itself. This is less than ideal drafting practice, but provided that there is a clear record that the Final Act was agreed by all negotiating parties, final clauses contained within it are valid.[36]
- The parent treaty or any related treaty: when a treaty amends or adds to another treaty (the 'parent treaty'), or its conclusion was foreseen in the provisions of another treaty (a 'related treaty'), the parent treaty or related

[33] UNCLOS arts 305–07. The specified categories of 'other entities' are listed in art 305.

[34] United Nations Agreement for the Implementation of the Provisions of the United Nations Convention on the Law of the Sea of 10 December 1982 relating to the Conservation and Management of Straddling Fish Stocks and Highly Migratory Fish Stocks 1995 (adopted 4 August 1995, entered into force 11 December 2001) 2167 UNTS 3 arts 37–39. The Articles should be read together with UNCLOS art 1(2)(b).

[35] ibid. The inclusion of 'other fishing entities' in the Agreement is generally understood to be intended to allow the Republic of China (Taiwan) to participate. Article 1(3), read together with art 17(3), provides a mechanism for 'fishing entities' to participate as a de facto party without formally being listed as a party.

[36] VCLT 1969 arts 10–17. See the discussion on 'Final Act' in Chapter 5 at 186–87.

treaty may contain final clauses that govern eligibility to become party to the new treaty.

An example of a treaty whose final clauses on participation and entry into force are located outside the text is Annex VI to the Protocol on Environmental Protection to the Antarctic Treaty on Liability Arising from Environmental Emergencies, 2005.[37] The clue to its status as a supplementary treaty is in its title. Its 'parent treaty', the Protocol on Environmental Protection, 1991,[38] contains a provision about annexes, which specifies how a new annex may be adopted and enter into force, and cross-refers to a provision in the Antarctic Treaty, the 'parent treaty' to the Protocol, the Antarctic Treaty, 1959.[39]

What if There Is Nothing in any Related Treaty Document that Provides which States and/or IOs May Become Party?

If the text does not contain a clause concerning participation, the implication is that only the negotiating States and/or negotiating IOs, as the case may be, can become party. This means the States, and the IOs if any, which took part in the drawing up and adoption of the text of the treaty.[40] The negotiating States and IOs may be listed by name in the treaty text, in the title, the preamble and/or the signature block, or defined elsewhere in the text. If not, you should consult the Final Act or the record of the meeting which adopted the text (whatever it is called) to see which States and/or IOs took part in the vote on adoption, or were present if it was adopted by consensus.

Can other States or IOs Become Party, even if the Treaty Does Not Provide for This?

If the treaty provides for only specified States or IOs to become party, or makes no provision for new parties at all, it is not possible for others to join without a new agreement. The parties to the treaty would need to amend it to allow additional States or IOs to become party; or adopt a new treaty between themselves and the third State or IO, setting out the terms of its membership of the main treaty. This is typically called an 'Accession Treaty' or 'Protocol of Accession'. Such an amendment or accession treaty would need the agreement of all existing parties to the main treaty.

[37] Annex VI to the Protocol on Environmental Protection to the Antarctic Treaty on Liability Arising from Environmental Emergencies (adopted 14 June 2005, not yet in force) www.ats.aq/e/ep.htm accessed 25 September 2018.

[38] Protocol on Environmental Protection to the Antarctic Treaty (adopted 4 October 1991, entered into force 14 January 1998) 2941 UNTS Registration No. 5778.

[39] Antarctic Treaty (adopted 1 December 1959, entered into force 23 June 1961) 402 UNTS 71. Thus, the final clauses of Annex VI on Liability Arising From Environmental Emergencies, 2005 on participation and entry into force are art 9 of the Protocol on Environmental Protection to the Antarctic Treaty and art IX of the Antarctic Treaty.

[40] VCLT 1969 art 2(e) and VCLT 1986 art 2(e).

For example, the Treaty establishing the European Economic Community, 1957 provided for ratification only by the original six signatory States: Belgium, France, Germany, Italy, Luxembourg and the Netherlands.[41] Article 237 of the Treaty provided that any other European State may apply to join the European Economic Community (EEC), and, if all existing Member States agree, a new agreement shall be negotiated to set out the terms of accession.[42] In 1961, Denmark, Ireland, Norway and the UK applied to join. France vetoed the UK membership for some years; eventually, after the French veto was lifted, negotiations began in 1970 and the EEC Member States signed an accession treaty with those four States in 1973.[43] It was subject to ratification by all ten States. The six EEC States, Denmark, Ireland and the UK ratified the treaty but Norway did not. Accordingly, Denmark, Ireland and the UK (but not Norway) became Member States of the EEC on 1 January 1973 when the treaty entered into force.

If there is no provision at all for non-signatory States (or IOs) to accede to the treaty in question, the position is essentially the same as that set out expressly in Article 237 of the Treaty establishing the EEC. It is always within the power of the existing parties to agree to accept a new participant and to amend the treaty to enable this, or to conclude a new treaty of accession. Equally, it is within their power to say no; the decision is a matter for politics and negotiations.

In another example, the Treaty of Amity and Cooperation in Southeast Asia, 1976 originally provided for ratification and accession only by States in Southeast Asia.[44] In 1987 a protocol was concluded to allow States outside Southeast Asia to accede with the consent of the original Southeast Asian signatory States.[45] In 2010 another protocol was concluded to allow regional organisations to accede.[46] Prior to the accession of a non-ASEAN State or an IO to the Treaty of Amity and Cooperation, ASEAN Member States will first need to issue a declaration of consent regarding such accession. Similarly, several ASEAN treaties provided for ratification only by ASEAN Member

[41] Treaty establishing the European Economic Community (adopted 25 March 1957, entered into force 1 January 1958) 298 UNTS 3, art 247.

[42] ibid art 237.

[43] Treaty between the Kingdom of Belgium, the Federal Republic of Germany, the French Republic, the Italian Republic, the Grand Duchy of Luxembourg, the Kingdom of the Netherlands (Member States of the European Communities), the Kingdom of Denmark, Ireland, the Kingdom of Norway and the United Kingdom of Great Britain and Northern Ireland concerning the accession of the Kingdom of Denmark, Ireland, the Kingdom of Norway and the United Kingdom of Great Britain and Northern Ireland to the European Economic Community and to the European Atomic Energy Community (adopted 22 January 1972, entered into force 1 January 1973) 1374 UNTS 40.

[44] Treaty of Amity and Cooperation (adopted 24 February 1976, entered into force 21 June 1976) 1025 UNTS 297, art 18.

[45] Protocol Amending the Treaty of Amity and Cooperation in Southeast Asia (adopted 15 December 1987, entered into force 2 July 1988) ADS (1967–1988), art 1 http://agreement.asean.org/media/download/20131231005052.pdf accessed 22 October 2018.

[46] Third Protocol Amending the Treaty of Amity and Cooperation in Southeast Asia (adopted 23 July 2010, entered into force 8 June 2012), art 1 http://agreement.asean.org/media/download/20140117144104.pdf accessed 22 October 2018.

States. When a new Member State is admitted to ASEAN, the existing Member States usually sign a declaration agreeing that the new Member State shall accede to all existing ASEAN treaties.[47] The new Member State is then required to submit a 'Protocol of Accession' which lists the ASEAN agreements that the new Member State will accede to upon its admission to ASEAN.[48]

What Procedure Applies where There Is Doubt about Who May Become Party to a Particular Treaty?

If a State or IO is still unsure whether it can accede to a particular treaty, even after consulting its international law advisers (whether because the treaty contains no provision or because it is not clear how the specified criteria or procedures apply to that State or IO), the next step is to consult the depositary. Alternatively, if the treaty concerned has a secretariat, its staff may be able to help in the first instance, for example by providing information about how similar cases in the past have been dealt with. If the secretariat and depositary are separate organisations, it is likely that the latter will have more direct responsibility for handling applications, and so its advice may be more authoritative.

If the treaty's depositary or secretariat receives an instrument of accession or an enquiry about accession from a State or IO, but are unsure how to proceed, they should take great care not to exceed their authority or act inconsistently with their duty of impartiality. If more than one legal interpretation is tenable,

[47] See Declaration on the Admission of the Socialist Republic of Vietnam into the Association of Southeast Asian Nations (adopted 28 July 1995) http://arc-agreement.asean.org/file/doc/2015/01/declaration-on-the-admission-of-the-socialist-republic-of-vietnam-into-the-association-of-southeast-asian-nations.pdf accessed 22 October 2018; Declaration on the Admission of the Lao People's Democratic Republic into the Association of Southeast Asian Nations (adopted 23 July 1997) http://arc-agreement.asean.org/file/doc/2015/01/declaration-on-the-admission-of-the-lao-people-s-democratic-republic-into-the-asean.pdf accessed 22 October 2018; Declaration on the Admission of the Union of Myanmar into the Association of Southeast Asian Nations (adopted 23 July 1997) http://arc-agreement.asean.org/file/doc/2015/01/declaration-on-the-admission-of-the-union-of-myanmar-into-asean.pdf accessed 22 October 2018.

[48] See Protocol for the Accession of the Socialist Republic of Vietnam to the Agreement on the Common Preferential Tariff Scheme for the ASEAN Free Trade 1995 (adopted 15 December 1995, entered into force 1 January 1996) ADS (1994–1995) http://arc-agreement.asean.org/file/doc/2015/01/protocol-for-the-accession-of-the-socialist-republic-of-vietnam-to-the-agreement-on-the-common-effective-preferential-tariff-scheme-(cept)-for-the-asean-free-trade-area-(afta).pdf accessed 22 October 2018; Protocol for the Accession of the Union of Myanmar to ASEAN Agreements 1997 (adopted 23 July 1997, entered into force 23 July 1997) ADS (1996–1997) http://arc-agreement.asean.org/file/doc/2015/01/1997-protocol-for-the-accession-of-the-union-of-myanmar-to-asean-agreements.pdf accessed 22 October 2018; Protocol for the Accession of the Lao People's Democratic Republic to ASEAN Agreements (adopted 23 July 1997, entered into force 23 July 1997) ADS (1996–1997) http://arc-agreement.asean.org/file/doc/2015/01/second-protocol-for-the-accession-of-the-lao-people-s-democratic-republic-to-asean-agreements.pdf accessed 22 October 2018; and Protocol for the Accession of the Kingdom of Cambodia to ASEAN Agreements 1999 (adopted 30 April 1999, entered into force 30 April 1999) ADS (1998–1999) https://asean.org/?static_post=table-of-contents-asean-documents-series-1998-1999 accessed 22 October 2018.

or there is more than one view among the parties whether reasonable or not, the depositary should not attempt to 'adjudicate'. The safest course of action is to refer the matter to the treaty parties and request them to make a decision. The depositary should normally take the lead on initiating this process (rather than the secretariat which administers the treaty, if there is one).

The depositary may be in doubt for various reasons; for example, as to whether the applicant entity is a State or otherwise eligible to join the treaty (Palestine, Cook Islands, Taiwan and Hong Kong are examples of cases that need very careful handling); or as to whether it is an IO, or whether it meets any substantive criteria in the treaty.

Possible Procedure when There Is a Meeting of Parties

If a meeting of treaty parties is planned, the question of the proposed accession can be placed on the agenda. This gives the depositary an opportunity to circulate the communication received from the applicant State or IO, and to ask the meeting to provide guidance to the depositary on how to respond. The Chair of the meeting will be responsible for ensuring that the meeting arrives at a decision in the appropriate manner. The depositary or secretariat should brief the Chair in advance on the treaty provisions and decision-making rules.

The depositary or secretariat can usefully provide background information to the meeting, such as setting out the relevant treaty provisions (if any), and any similar decisions taken in the past. It may also be useful to set out the range of possible responses (if there are any options between accepting the accession or refusing it). They should not normally express an opinion on which way the decision should go, although if pressed to do so by the Chair of the meeting on behalf of all the parties, they may decide to offer an opinion if they are able to formulate one on the basis of past precedents.

Possible Procedures when There Is No Meeting of Parties

If no meeting of parties is planned, the depositary will have no choice but to resolve the issue by correspondence with the treaty parties. The same principles apply; the depositary should take a neutral position, setting out (or attaching) the communication received from the State or IO wishing to join the treaty, with any relevant background information and a clear request for guidance. The depositary may need to be proactive in proposing a procedure that will lead to a clear decision within a reasonable timeframe. For example, the depositary may request all parties to submit their view by a certain date. If the issue is very sensitive, or concerns a treaty which provides no provision on accession, the safest way to proceed may be to take the decision in two steps. For example, the first step could be to consult on a proposed procedure, such as acceptance of the accession on a majority vote, or, alternatively, on a unanimous vote, or on no objection. The second stage would then be to request views on the substance of the accession by a deadline.

For treaties with a large number of parties and no meeting, a non-objection procedure may be more convenient. The depositary could consider combining the two steps mentioned above into one, by circulating a notice to the parties: this would set out the facts of the communication received from the State or IO wishing to accede, and propose that the depositary accepts the accession, provided that no existing treaty party objects, either to the accession or to the procedure proposed, within a specified period (which should be a reasonably lengthy one of several months).

The effect of such a procedure is that if a single party objects, the accession is blocked. The onus will then be on any parties wishing to support the accession to consult on another procedure; meanwhile the depositary will have discharged its duty and should take no further action unless and until there is consensus among the parties.

Understanding Modes for Expressing Consent to Be Bound

What Are 'Modes of Expressing Consent to Be Bound'?

The range of possible modes are, in general, those set out in Article 11 VCLT 1969 (and there is an equivalent provision in Article 11 VCLT 1986):

> The consent of a State to be bound by a treaty may be expressed by signature, exchange of instruments constituting a treaty, ratification, acceptance, approval or accession, or by any other means if so agreed.

Each of the four modes identified, namely, 'signature', 'exchange of instruments constituting a treaty', 'ratification, acceptance, approval or accession', or 'by any other means if so agreed' are explained more fully in this section.

Some treaties that are open to IOs to become party use the term 'act of formal confirmation' instead of 'ratification' for IOs. An 'act of formal confirmation' is equivalent to 'ratification'.[49] The use of different terminology for IOs is not mandatory however; some treaties provide for 'ratification' to be available to both States and IOs. In this chapter, references to 'ratification' should be understood to include 'act of formal confirmation', for treaties that use this term.

How Early Do Modes of Expressing Consent to Be Bound Need to Be Considered?

The mode that is going to be used for expressing consent to be bound to a particular treaty needs to be considered at the first stage of preparations. If the treaty provides a choice, it is wise to make it early. The domestic procedures that need to be planned – not only the work plan for officials but the consultations and, if applicable, legislative timetable – may be very different according to the international procedures required.

[49] VCLT 1986 arts 2(1)(b bis), 11(2) and 14(2).

Typically, a bilateral treaty will stipulate one mode only, as it will have been agreed by both parties during the negotiation of the text. Multilateral treaties more commonly provide a choice of mode, to suit the varying circumstances of different potential parties.[50]

If you are the depositary and you are approached by a State or IO wishing to become party and asking for guidance on procedures, the mode for expressing consent to be bound will be one of the first issues for you to look at. Moreover, if a question of eligibility has arisen, it will be intertwined with the provisions on expressing consent to be bound.

The procedure for consenting to be bound is governed by both international law and domestic law. Which mode is required for a particular treaty is governed by the international law of treaties, which will determine whether a particular State or IO has validly become a party. The procedure is also governed by domestic law. In the case of a State, it is likely that there are provisions in the constitution, statutes or regulations that govern who has the authority to give the consent of the State to be bound by a treaty, alongside how and whether the legislature must be consulted. An IO will have internal rules that govern these matters, and with which its officers need to comply. Failure to comply with domestic law requirements does not normally have any effect on the validity of treaty obligations incurred in international law; but it may affect the ability of the State to implement those obligations.

The PLATO principle of 'Legality' is of paramount importance in this context: both international and domestic law must be complied with, and legal advisers versed in both must be fully engaged.

Box 6.1 International law on expressing consent to be bound by a treaty

KEY PRINCIPLES OF THE INTERNATIONAL LAW OF TREATIES

- The VCLT 1969 and the VCLT 1986 provide the international law framework for expressing consent to be bound by a treaty.
- The most important provisions are in Part II on 'Conclusion and Entry into Force of Treaties' (Articles 6–18 of both VCLTs).
- The Vienna Conventions' rules are generally recognised as reflecting rules of customary international law, applicable to all States, whether or not they are party to those conventions.
- Those rules are mostly residual in nature, which means they may be modified or displaced by express provisions in the treaty in question.

[50] For example, Council of Europe Convention on Action against Trafficking in Human Beings art 42(2). The final clauses are reproduced in Annex II, 'Examples of Final Clauses in a Multilateral Treaty' at 420–23.

Signature

There are two types of signature: 'definitive signature' and 'signature subject to ratification'. A definitive signature means that the signature is effective, by itself, to bind that State or IO. A signature subject to ratification means that it is not sufficient by itself to bind the State or IO to the treaty, but is rather the first step of a two-step procedure, the second part of which is to be completed at a later date. A signature is normally written by hand, by an authorised representative of the State or IO, onto the original treaty document.

Definitive signature is a fairly common procedure in bilateral treaties, less so in multilaterals. Negotiating parties normally only agree upon this one-step procedure when they do not need to take any domestic action to implement the treaty, such as enacting new legislation. If they do anticipate that domestic action is required, they will insist upon a two-step process such as signature followed by ratification, or a choice of procedures.

Examples of Definitive Signature and Signature Subject to Ratification

An example of a definitive signature procedure in a *bilateral treaty* can be found in the Agreement between the Government of the United Kingdom of Great Britain and Northern Ireland and the Government of the Russian Federation on Co-operation in the Peaceful Uses of Nuclear Energy, London, 1996.[51] Article 9(1) reads '[t]his Agreement shall enter into force on the ninetieth day following the day of signature'. This provision makes clear that signature is the only procedure required for giving consent to be bound.

An example of a definitive signature procedure in a *multilateral treaty* can be found in the Agreement for the Establishment of an ASEAN Development Fund, 2005. Article II(1) provides: 'This Agreement shall enter into force on the date of signature of all the ASEAN Member Countries.'[52]

Lastly, an example of a 'signature subject to ratification' procedure in a *multilateral treaty* can be found in the UNFCCC, 1992.[53] The effect of signature is clear when Articles 20, 22 and 23 are read together:

[51] Agreement between the Government of the United Kingdom of Great Britain and Northern Ireland and the Government of the Russian Federation on Co-operation in the Peaceful Uses of Nuclear Energy (signed 3 September 1996, entered into force 3 December 1996) 1957 UNTS 253.

[52] Agreement for the Establishment of an ASEAN Development Fund (adopted 26 July 2005, entered into force 26 July 2005) ADS (2005) 33.

[53] UNFCCC (adopted 9 May 1992, entered into force 21 March 1994) 1771 UNTS 107. See also Convention on the Rights of the Child, arts 46–47 and Council of Europe Convention on Action against Trafficking in Human Beings art 42(1)–(2). The text of the final clauses is reproduced in Annex II, 'Examples of Final Clauses in a Multilateral Treaty' at 420–23.

Article 20

This Convention shall be open for signature by States Members of the United Nations or of any of its specialized agencies or that are Parties to the Statute of the International Court of Justice and by regional economic integration organizations at Rio de Janeiro, during the United Nations Conference on Environment and Development, and thereafter at United Nations Headquarters in New York from 20 June 1992 to 19 June 1993.

Article 22(1)

The Convention shall be subject to ratification, acceptance, approval or accession by States and by regional economic integration organizations.

Article 23(1)

The Convention shall enter into force on the ninetieth day after the date of deposit of the fiftieth instrument of ratification, acceptance, approval or accession.

The combined effect of these provisions is to make clear that signature has to be followed by ratification, and it is ratification not signature that counts for bringing the treaty into force.

Exchange of Instruments Constituting a Treaty

A treaty does not have to consist of a single text; it can consist of two or more linked documents.[54] An 'exchange of instruments' is a commonly used form for bilateral treaties between States. One side sets out the terms of the (already negotiated) agreement in a diplomatic note or letter, and presents it to the other side as a proposal. The other side responds by accepting the proposal, usually reiterating it in full. If both notes (or letters) specify that together they shall constitute an agreement, which shall enter into force on the date of delivery of the second note (or automatically after a stipulated period of time), it means that each delivery *is* the expression of consent to be bound. Note that the effective date of consent is the date of *delivery*, not the date on which the note was signed, although these dates are often the same.

Alternatively, the agreement set out in the notes may specify that a further procedure is required to bring it into force. For example, it may stipulate that following the exchange of notes, each side shall deposit an instrument of ratification or notify the other of the completion of its domestic procedures. If that deposit or notification is not made by either side, it has not consented to be bound. In this case, the 'exchange of instruments constituting a treaty' does not express the consent of each side to be bound. Rather, the delivery of the instrument setting out the agreement by each side to the other is the first step only of a two-step procedure; the treaty is made but consent to be bound has not yet been expressed.

[54] See the section on 'Definition of a Treaty in International Law' in Chapter 3 at 93–6.

A treaty may also be formed by an exchange of letters, in exactly the same way (both notes verbales and letters are types of 'instruments').[55]

Example of a Treaty Constituted by an Exchange of Notes, where Delivery of Each Note to the other Side Expresses Consent to Be Bound

An example of this type is the 2014 Exchange of Notes constituting an agreement between the UK and China on the establishment of Consulates-General at Wuhan and Belfast.[56] The first note provides:

> If the above agreement is confirmed by the Ministry of Foreign Affairs of the People's Republic of China on behalf of the Government of the People's Republic of China, this note together with the reply from the Ministry of Foreign Affairs shall constitute an Agreement between the Government of Great Britain and Northern Ireland and the Government of the People's Republic of China which shall enter into force on the date of the latter's reply.

The delivery of this note expressed the consent of the UK to be bound by the agreement set out within it. The delivery of a reply note in the same terms expressed the consent of China to be bound, and accordingly the treaty entered into force on the date of that second delivery.

Example of a Treaty Constituted by an Exchange of Notes, where Consent to Be Bound Has to Be Expressed by a Further Procedure

An example of this type is the 2017 Exchange of Notes constituting an agreement between Canada and the UK to amend an earlier Canada–UK double taxation treaty.[57] The first note includes this paragraph:

> If the above proposal is acceptable to your Government, I further propose that this Note, which is authentic in English and French, and your reply Note reflecting such acceptance shall constitute an agreement between our two Governments which shall enter into force and have effect on the date of the second note by which our two Governments notify each other that they have completed their internal procedure required to bring into force this Note.

[55] See examples of an exchange of letters constituting a treaty in Annex IV, 'Examples of an Exchange of Letters Constituting a Treaty' at 426–36.

[56] Exchange of Notes constituting an Agreement between the Government of the United Kingdom of Great Britain and Northern Ireland and the Government of the People's Republic of China Concerning the Establishment of a Consulate-General of each Country in the other at Wuhan and Belfast (signed 20 February and 21 February 2014, entered into force 21 February 2014) UKTS 23 (2016). The full text of the Notes is reproduced in Annex III, 'Example of an Exchange of Notes Constituting a Treaty' at 424–25.

[57] Exchange of Notes to amend the Convention between the Government of the United Kingdom of Great Britain and Northern Ireland and the Government of Canada for the Avoidance of Double Taxation and the Prevention of Fiscal Evasion with respect to Taxes on Income and on Capital Gains signed at London on 8 September 1978, as amended by the Protocol signed at Ottawa on 15 April 1980, by the Protocol signed at London on 16 October 1985, by the Protocol signed at London on 7 May 2003 and by the Protocol signed at London on 21 July 2014 (signed 27 July 2015 and 11 August 2015, entered into force 21 December 2016) UKTS 10 (2017).

The Reply Note accepted the proposal. The Exchange of Notes was thus concluded on the date of delivery of the Reply Note, meaning that the treaty was adopted, but consent to be bound had not yet been given. It was this *later* exchange (which occurred four months later) that expressed the consent of each party to be bound. This treaty is not therefore an example of consent to be bound being expressed by 'exchange of instruments constituting a treaty' but rather 'by any other means if so agreed'. It is presented in this section to illustrate the importance of looking beyond the title 'Exchange of Notes' to notice these variations in modes of consenting to be bound. It is also important to recognise the difference between an 'exchange of notes constituting a treaty' and an 'exchange of notes notifying completion of domestic procedures'; each has a different legal function.

Ratification, Acceptance, Approval or Accession

These are the most common modes for multilateral treaties. They are also sometimes used for bilateral treaties. The State or IO draws up a formal document, called an 'instrument of ratification' or of 'acceptance', 'approval' or 'accession' (hereafter expressed as 'ratification etc.'), which must be signed by its authorised representative. Normally, it is signed by the Foreign Minister or Head of Government, or, occasionally, the Head of State (in the case of States) or the Head of the IO. It could also be signed by a person with Full Powers to do so, but as the instrument of ratification etc. is normally prepared within the foreign ministry (or IO headquarters), it makes sense to obtain one signature on the instrument itself, rather than one on the Full Powers and then another on the instrument.[58]

The instrument must be deposited directly with the other party to the treaty (if it is bilateral) or with the depositary (if it is multilateral). When the instrument is received, consent to be bound has been given by the depositing party.

Some treaties offer a choice of 'ratification, acceptance, approval or accession', while others offer only one or fewer choices. The treaty may define which mode is open to which types of parties, or leave it open to States and IOs to choose the one that they prefer, or which their constitution dictates.

Typically 'ratification' is for signatories, and so it is the second step of a two-step procedure. Similar modes equivalent to ratification but with different names such as 'acceptance' or 'approval', or 'formal confirmation' are typically offered for IOs instead of 'ratification'. 'Accession' is a one-step procedure, available for States and IOs that have not signed. In some treaties, accession is provided as an option only after the treaty is closed for signatures, typically one year. It is not important which terms are used, as long as any stipulations in the treaty are followed. In each case, a formal instrument is expected,

[58] VCLT 1969 art 7 and VCLT 1986 art 7.

prepared in the customary manner (with pages bound and sealed into a hard folder – see below).

It should be noted, however, that ratification of a treaty under the international law of treaties is not to be confused with national procedures referred to as 'ratification' of a treaty in certain domestic legal systems. The latter may consist of a constitutional requirement for the consent of the legislative body as a precondition for the government ratifying a treaty on the international plane.[59] For example, in Thailand, the legislature must give its consent before certain categories of treaty can be ratified on the international plane; this kind of domestic law procedure may be referred to as 'ratification'. In some other domestic legal systems there is a national procedure for implementing treaty obligations which may be called 'ratification' in that country. For example, in Indonesia, the Parliament will adopt a 'Ratification Law', which stipulates that Indonesia has ratified the treaty and relevant implementing laws or amendments of existing laws to implement the treaty.[60]

Any other Means if so Agreed

The words 'or by any other means if so agreed' show that the parties to a treaty have contractual freedom to agree upon any procedure they wish, and if their chosen procedure is specified clearly in the treaty, that is what will apply. The VCLT procedures are residual – they apply in the absence of any contrary agreement expressed in the treaty provisions.

'Other means' of a less formal nature than ratification are sometimes used when the States or IOs concerned are already in a treaty relationship, and the new treaty is an amendment or supplement to the existing one. In such cases the procedure may be to submit a letter expressing approval or acceptance, usually to the depositary but sometimes to the head of the treaty secretariat. Its function is equivalent to ratification. However, a letter is a less formal document than an instrument of ratification, and, being an ordinary type of business communication, may (if the treaty so provides) be sent by a ministry other than the foreign ministry.

An example of establishing consent by 'other means' in a multilateral treaty is the procedure in the Protocol on Environmental Protection to the Antarctic Treaty, 1991 for consenting to be bound to new Protocol Annexes.[61] A new Annex has to be 'approved' by all Antarctic Treaty Consultative Parties, and

59 For more details, see the section on 'The Law of Treaties: International Law versus Domestic Law' in Chapter 1 at 8–9.

60 Law 24 of 2000 on International Agreements, 23 October 2000, State Gazette 2000 No. 185. An unofficial translation of the Law is provided by the MFA of Indonesia and is on file with the authors.

61 See the example 'Annex VI to the Protocol on Environmental Protection to the Antarctic Treaty on Liability Arising from Environmental Emergencies' discussed in the section on 'What if the Treaty Text Does not Specify which States and/or IOs may become party?' above at 215–16.

this is done by sending a diplomatic note to the depositary (not a formal instrument).[62]

In a bilateral treaty, one of the commonly used 'other means' of establishing consent to be bound is the 'mutual notification of the completion of domestic procedures'. This is typically the second step of a two-stage procedure for consenting to be bound, where the first step consists of signing the treaty or exchanging instruments constituting the treaty.

An example of this type is the Agreement between the Government of the United Kingdom of Great Britain and Northern Ireland and the Government of India for Co-operation in the Peaceful Uses of Nuclear Energy, 2015.[63] Article XV(1) provides:

> This Agreement shall come into force on the last date upon which the Parties notify each other in writing of the completion of their internal procedures necessary for the entry into force of this Agreement.

The Agreement was a single-instrument bilateral treaty which was signed, but the parties had not consented to be bound by it until they each delivered the further notification to the other. This further procedure is an example of expressing consent to be bound 'by any other means if so agreed'.

An example of this type of 'other means' procedure in a bilateral treaty constituted by exchange of notes is the 2017 Exchange of Notes constituting an agreement between Canada and the UK to amend an earlier Canada–UK double taxation treaty, discussed above.[64]

These procedures are explained more fully in Chapter 7.[65]

Internal Preparations to Give Consent to Be Bound

Before a government takes the formal step of expressing its consent (internationally) to be bound by a treaty, there are many actions that need to be taken on the domestic plane to prepare for this. The extent of internal preparations required will depend to a large extent on domestic law, especially constitution provisions on the power to conclude treaties and any requirements to consult the legislative body and the general public. The amount of work involved will also vary greatly, according to the complexity and sensitivity of each treaty.

62 Protocol on Environmental Protection to the Antarctic Treaty, art 9(2) and Antarctic Treaty, art IX(4). See (n 38 and 39) above.

63 Agreement between the Government of the United Kingdom of Great Britain and Northern Ireland and the Government of India for Co-operation in the Peaceful Uses of Nuclear Energy (adopted 13 November 2015, entered into force 16 December 2016) UKTS 1 (2017).

64 See the section on 'Example of a Treaty Constituted by an Exchange of Notes, where Consent to Be Bound Has to Be Expressed by a Further Procedure' above at 224–25 and n 52.

65 At 265–8 below. For an example of a note confirming the completion of domestic procedures, see Annex XIII, 'Example of a Note Confirming the Completion of Domestic Procedures' at 453.

The legal and political processes that need to take place at the domestic level before joining a treaty are considerable and can take some time – several months is normal, and several years not uncommon. This is why most treaties provide for a two-step procedure to express consent to be bound, as it allows a government to express its support in principle for the treaty at an early stage, while allowing adequate time for the democratic process including the risk that the treaty is rejected.

An IO must also conduct internal preparations before expressing consent to be bound by any treaty. Consultations with other branches of the secretariat ought normally to be more straightforward than consulting across a government. However, consultations with representative organs and/or with Member States of the IO might be complex and lengthy, and in some cases obtaining the necessary mandate might be sensitive or controversial.

Before taking action on the international plane to ratify the treaty (or give consent to be bound by any other mode), it is crucial to ensure that all requirements of domestic law have been met. By 'domestic law' we mean, for States, the national constitution and legal system, and for IOs, the constitution and internal rules of the particular IO. As 'domestic law' for States and IOs is very different, this aspect of preparations will be treated separately below.

Internal Consultations on the Requirements of the Treaty

The following are the first actions that need to be taken within the government or, where an IO proposes to become party to a treaty, within the IO's secretariat:

- Consult all ministries and agencies across government (or all departments within an IO, as well as the Member States) that might be affected by the treaty. Any ministry or unit that might have responsibilities to implement the treaty in domestic law, or by its own officials, needs to plan how it is going to do so, and confirm that it is willing and able to perform its responsibilities.
- Resolve any disagreement among ministries or administrative units about whether the treaty should be ratified, or how it will be implemented. Every government and IO needs to have a mechanism for resolving such internal disputes, whether through a regular mechanism such as the Cabinet or Board of Directors, or through a specific treaty committee.
- Obtain advice from the government (or IO)'s international lawyers on the requirements of the treaty, and whether new legislation or administrative measures will be needed to implement it. International lawyers may need to liaise with lawyers with expertise in the area of domestic law concerned. For example, if the treaty concerns safety of navigation, the treaty lawyers will

need to work with those who have responsibility for shipping legislation (for example, in the transport ministry).

- (States) Draw up an action plan for drafting any new legislation required to implement the treaty in the national legal system, and prepare all documentation required for introducing it to the legislature. Plan the timetable to ensure that it will be enacted before ratification.
- (IOs) Equivalent planning in respect of any new regulations or administrative action that will be needed to carry out the IO's obligations under the treaty.

For multilateral treaties, the following additional matters need to be considered:[66]

- *Reservations*: advice is needed from international lawyers as to whether the treaty permits reservations to be made, and if so under what conditions. Whether the government (or IO) should avail itself of any option to make a reservation is partly a legal question and partly a policy decision. A decision needs to be made by the administrators and lawyers together, and agreed across the government (or IO), not only on the principle of whether to make a reservation but also on its drafting. The final decision may be taken elsewhere, such as by the legislature or the Member States, but the executive branch needs to be able to put forward a recommendation.
- *Other parties' reservations*: all reservations already tabled by other parties should be studied, to see if there are any to which the government or IO may wish to object, on legal or policy grounds. Internal consultations with legal advisers and policy officials will be necessary before making a decision. If any objections are to be made, this should be done at the same time as ratifying.
- *Interpretative and other declarations*: consideration needs to be given to whether the government (or IO) needs to table an interpretative declaration to set out its view on any particular provisions of the treaty, or to explain how it intends to apply it, or any other kind of declaration. In the same way as for reservations, the question is one for policy and legal officials to consider together.
- *Other parties' interpretative and other declarations*: before ratifying, it is wise to look through all declarations tabled by existing parties, to see if there are any that might cause difficulties. For example, if another party has stated an interpretation of a treaty provision that the government or IO considers incorrect and which concerns a matter of importance, it may wish to consider setting out a different interpretation.

[66] All of these points are covered in more detail in Chapter 7. See also Annex XI, 'United Nations Model Instrument of Reservation/Declaration' at 446 and Annex XII, 'Examples of an Instrument of Reservation' at 447–52.

- *Exercising options to opt in, opt out or make a choice*: the treaty should be studied carefully to see if it provides for any such option. If so, look to see if it needs to be exercised at the time of ratification or if it could be done at a later date. Provisions on settlement of disputes commonly allow for States to opt in to mandatory recourse to an international court or tribunal, or opt out, or to make a choice among several procedures. If it is mandatory to make a choice at the time of ratification, depositing an instrument of ratification without doing so is likely to be rejected by the depositary. The decision on whether to exercise an option or which choice to make has both legal and policy elements.
- *Any mandatory notifications*: some treaties require certain information to be notified to the secretariat or depositary on ratification, such as a designated national authority for dealing with matters under the treaty. This may be a matter of sensitivity in the domestic sphere, for example where ministries are competing for the lead, or where authorities at national and federal or devolved level disagree as to where responsibility lies. Any such issue will need to be resolved as part of the domestic preparations before the treaty is ratified.

States: Constitutional and Legal Requirements

In a State, the national constitution or legislation usually contain provisions that set out requirements ranging from publishing the text of the treaty in an official form (such as a gazette or treaty series) to informing or consulting the legislature about the treaty. In some States, it is relatively easy to find the domestic legal framework, as it is set out in the constitution and/or a statute on the ratification of treaties. In other States, the relevant legal rules may be difficult to identify, and the most important rules may be of an administrative or customary nature. Some Treaty Offices set these out in a guidance document for staff; others have not yet done so, and so newcomers to the job may have to work it out.

The case studies below illustrate the types of domestic law provisions concerning the conclusion of treaties that are commonly found in States, as well as their complexity and the difficulty in locating and identifying them. This underscores the importance of both aspects of the PLATO principle of 'Legality': the necessity for compliance with international and domestic law requirements, and for the government's legal advisers to be engaged in all aspects of the work.

The full texts of the provisions on treaty ratification referred to in the case studies below, and the equivalent provisions from selected other States and IOs, may be found in the 'Compilation of Constitutional and Legislative Provisions on Treaty Practice of Selected States and International Organisations' which was compiled by the authors of this Handbook.[67]

[67] CIL, 'International Workshop on Treaty Law and Practice' https://cil.nus.edu.sg/event/international-workshop-on-treaty-law-and-practice/; and BIICL, 'Compilation of Constitutional and Legislative Provisions on Treaty Practice of Selected States and International Organisations' www.biicl.org/research-treaty-online-resource accessed 25 September 2018.

Identifying a State's Domestic Law Requirements: Case Studies of Vietnam and Australia

Vietnam is an example of a State where the relevant national provisions are relatively easy to locate. The Vietnamese Constitution provides that the legislature (National Assembly) has the power to ratify treaties related to war, peace and national sovereignty, treaties on Vietnam's membership in important international and regional organisations, treaties on human rights or fundamental rights and obligations of citizens, and other treaties that are not consistent with the laws or resolutions of the National Assembly.[68] The President has the authority to decide on the ratification of other treaties in the name of the State.[69] The Government has the authority to decide on the conclusion and approval of treaties in the name of the Government.[70] The 2016 Treaty Law sets out the detailed requirements for all aspects of the ratification of treaties.[71]

Australia is an example of a State where the relevant national provisions are relatively difficult to locate. The Australian Constitution (Commonwealth of Australia Constitution Act, 1900) contains no provisions concerning the ratification of treaties, nor are there any statutory provisions on this subject. This does not mean however that there is no relevant law. The Constitution contains general provisions vesting legislative, executive and judicial power, which apply to treaty-making functions.[72]

To find the specific rules relating to treaty ratification, it is necessary to look at the *Australian Government Cabinet Handbook*[73] and the *Federal Executive Council Handbook*'[74] as well as information on the website of the DFAT.[75] These documents are available on the internet, when you know what to look for;

68 2013 Constitution of the Socialist Republic of Vietnam, 28 November 2013, entered into force 1 January 2014 art 70(14).

69 ibid art 88(6). 70 ibid art 96(7).

71 Law on Treaties, 9 April 2016, 108/2016/QH13. This Law was passed by the XIIIth National Assembly of the Socialist Republic of Vietnam at its 11th session. The full text in its original language (Vietnamese) can be accessed on the official website of Vietnam's National Legal Normative Documents Database http://vbpl.vn/TW/Pages/vbpq-van-ban-goc.aspx?ItemID=101899 accessed 25 September 2018. An unofficial English translation version is available on National Legal Normative Documents Database, 'Law on Treaties' http://vbpl.vn/TW/Pages/vbpqen-toanvan.aspx?ItemID=11039 accessed 25 September 2018.

72 Commonwealth of Australia Constitution Act, 9 July 1900 (as amended in September 2013), ss 1, 51, 61 and 75(i). See Parliament of Australia, 'The Australian Constitution' www.aph.gov.au/About_Parliament/Senate/Powers_practice_n_procedures/Constitution accessed 25 September 2018.

73 Commonwealth of Australia, *Cabinet Handbook* (11th edn, Department of the Prime Minister and Cabinet, Canberra 2018) www.pmc.gov.au/sites/default/files/publications/cabinet-handbook-11th-edition.pdf accessed 22 October 2018.

74 Commonwealth of Australia, *Federal Executive Council Handbook 2017* (Department of the Prime Minister and Cabinet, Canberra 2017) www.pmc.gov.au/sites/default/files/publications/federal-executive-council-handbook-2017.pdf accessed 22 October 2018.

75 Australian Government DFAT, 'Treaty making process' http://dfat.gov.au/international-relations/treaties/treaty-making-process/pages/treaty-making-process.aspx accessed 22 October 2018.

the challenge lies in understanding the constitutional importance of these non-statutory materials.

The *Cabinet Office Handbook* provides guidance on when treaty ratification requires consideration by the Cabinet. The *Federal Executive Council Handbook* sets out the powers of the Federal Executive Council, the Governor in Council and the Prime Minister in relation to Australia's ratification of treaties.

The Minister for Foreign Affairs is responsible for seeking Executive Council approval for Australia to enter into treaties. All recommendations relating to the signature, the issuing of Full Powers, ratification, acceptance, approval, accession, amendment or termination are prepared by the DFAT and are submitted through the Minister for Foreign Affairs to the Executive Council. The process of tabling treaties for Parliament and parliamentary scrutiny of treaties is governed by parliamentary rules and practices, on which a convenient source of information is to be found on Government and Parliament websites.[76]

Publication of the Treaty Text for Consultation

Some States, such as the UK, have a statutory requirement for the treaty to be published and laid before Parliament for a specified number of days before ratification (or its equivalent) can proceed,[77] and States such as Australia and New Zealand also apply a similar constitutional practice on a non-statutory basis. Whatever form the consultation with the legislature takes, it will be necessary for the text of the treaty to be published to facilitate it. Publication may be in a number of forms, but what matters most is that the text is an accurate version of the treaty that has been signed, and if it is retyped for publication then very careful proofreading will be an absolute necessity.

Need for Implementing Legislation

Two types of domestic legal action may be required, one concerning the treaty and the other concerning legislation:

- Consult or inform the legislature about the *treaty*, and/or obtain legislative approval for ratification of the treaty (step 1).
- Secure the enactment of any domestic *legislation* needed to implement the treaty (step 2).

In some legal systems (sometimes referred to as 'monist'), when the legislature approves the treaty or when the government publishes it in a gazette, it automatically takes effect in domestic law. In such cases, step 1 may fulfil

[76] Australian Government DFAT, 'Tabling of Treaty Actions in Parliament' http://dfat.gov.au/international-relations/treaties/treaty-making-process/Pages/tabling-of-treaty-actions-in-parliament.aspx accessed 22 October 2018. See also Parliament of Australia, 'Joint Standing Committee on Treaties' www.aph.gov.au/Parliamentary_Business/Committees/Joint/Treaties accessed 25 September 2018.

[77] Constitutional Reform and Governance Act 2010, s 20. See J Barrett, 'The United Kingdom and Parliamentary Scrutiny of Treaties: Recent Reforms', ICLQ, Vol 60 (2011) 225–45.

step 2. However, it will not necessarily suffice; there may be a need for more detailed implementing legislation to make it work and define powers, sanctions, penalties, etc.

In some legal systems (sometimes referred to as 'dualist'), a ratified treaty is not part of the domestic legal system unless it is incorporated by legislation. Step 1 does not fulfil step 2.

Whatever the type of legal system, it will be important to consider whether, for this particular treaty, any new domestic legislation is needed. If it is needed to implement mandatory provisions in the treaty, its enactment should be taken care of before the treaty is ratified. If it is not, the government will put the State at risk of violating its treaty obligations. It may be appropriate to postpone entry into force of the legislation until entry into force of the treaty, but the important thing is not to leave legislative action until later, in case it fails to go to plan.

It is also important to consider not only legal requirements for consultation, but also the political or practical imperatives of engaging the public, or the sectors affected by a treaty, in decisions about ratification. Both of these involve a number of challenges, which the following sections will explain with illustrative examples.

IOs: Internal Capacity and Mandate

Unlike States, IOs do not have full capacity in international law to enter into treaties. An IO's actions are constrained by the provisions of its constitution and other governing instruments. Whether a particular IO has the capacity to enter into a particular treaty, and if so, whether it needs a specific mandate from its Member States or governing organ, depends on the rules and established practices of each organisation.

The rules that govern an IO's capacity to enter into treaties in its own name are not always in its founding constitution. To find the relevant rules of a particular IO, it may be necessary to look at a range of internal rules and instruments adopted by its governing organs. They may be scattered around in several documents. Even then, its powers may be implicit rather than express, and there may be room for argument as to their scope. As most IOs do not enter into treaty relations very often, any decision to do so might raise questions or sensitivities. It follows that an IO's secretariat should always consult its international law advisers before considering the possibility of the IO becoming party to any treaty. It would be wise to apply the same caution even when the proposed instrument is of a non-binding nature. An internal mandate may still be required to conduct any kind of external relationships, even at a purely administrative level with other secretariats.

Identifying an IO's Internal Law Requirements: Case Study of the CoE

This case study illustrates the importance of identifying an IO's internal law and procedures relating to its authority to become party to a treaty; where one might need to look to find them; and how complex a task it may sometimes be.

The Constitution of the CoE is the Statute of the Council of Europe, 1949.[78] Article 15a of the Statute sets out the following provision with regard to the conclusion of treaties:

> On the recommendation of the Consultative Assembly or on its own initiative, the Committee of Ministers shall consider the action required to further the aim of the Council of Europe, including the conclusion of conventions or agreements and the adoption by governments of a common policy with regard to particular matters.

However, this provision does not make clear whether it is referring to treaties entered into by the CoE itself. It has been interpreted as referring only to the conclusion of treaties by the Member States under the auspices of the CoE, which is the main treaty-making activity of the organisation.

There is no express provision in the Statute concerning the conclusion of treaties by the CoE itself. Rather, the power to negotiate, conclude, sign and give consent to be bound by treaties is considered to be inherent in the international legal capacity of the CoE as an IO, and is confirmed by Article 1 of the General Agreement on Privileges and Immunities of the Council of Europe 1949.[79] The General Agreement is a treaty concluded among the Member States of the CoE to provide for privileges and immunities for the organisation throughout the territories of all Member States.[80] To understand fully how this inherent power has been interpreted, it is necessary to consider the practice of the CoE since its founding, to see what kinds of treaty the CoE has concluded and what powers and procedures were used.

The CoE has concluded three types of treaties (and other treaty-like instruments): (1) multilateral treaties; (2) bilateral seat agreements; and (3) bilateral and multilateral inter-organisational 'co-operation agreements'. The CoE is not party to any multilateral treaty, but it has signed one: the VCLT 1986. The procedure followed in that case is instructive: the CoE's Council of Ministers authorised the Secretary General to sign and ratify the VCLT 1986, in a decision adopted by vote in 1987. The Secretary General signed it but has postponed depositing the instrument of ratification due to the stated objection

[78] Statute of the Council of Europe 1949 (adopted 5 May 1949, entered into force 3 August 1949) 87 UNTS 103, ETS No. 001.

[79] This view of the source of the legal power of the CoE to enter into treaties was expressed informally by the Head of the Legal Directorate of the Council of Europe, in a meeting with Jill Barrett during her visit to the Council CoE in December 2011.

[80] General Agreement on Privileges and Immunities of the Council of Europe (adopted 2 September 1949, entered into force 10 September 1952) 250 UNTS 12, ETS 002 art 1, which provides:

> The Council of Europe shall possess juridical personality. It shall have the capacity to conclude contracts, to acquire and dispose of movable and immovable property and to institute legal proceedings. In these matters the Secretary General shall act on behalf of the Council of Europe.

of France.[81] If in future the CoE Member States wished the CoE to become party to any other multilateral treaty, this precedent would no doubt be a starting point for considering the process.

The CoE has concluded only two bilateral treaties.[82] These are both with France, the host State of the organisation. The first treaty provides for the CoE's headquarters at Strasbourg, France,[83] and the other provides for privileges and immunities in France.[84] Each treaty sets out, in its preamble, the provisions of the Statute of the CoE and/or the General Agreement as the source of authority for the Council of Europe to conclude that treaty.

The CoE has concluded a considerable number of bilateral and multilateral 'co-operation agreements' with other IOs and some NGOs.[85]An express mandate for the conclusion of agreements and arrangements of this kind was set out in a Resolution Adopted by the Committee of Ministers 1951.[86] It seems that those so far concluded are not treaties, but rather non-binding instruments of an administrative nature.[87]

Other Entities: Capacity and Mandate

States may occasionally wish to enter into a bilateral treaty with an entity that is not generally recognised as a State or IO, such as a non-independent territory

[81] *Committee of Ministers* (n 11).

[82] Treaty Office, 'Glossary' (Council of Europe) www.coe.int/en/web/conventions/glossary accessed 25 September 2018.

[83] Special Agreement Relating to the Seat of the Council of Europe (adopted 2 September 1949, entered into force 2 September 1949) ETS 003.

[84] Supplementary Agreement to the General Agreement on Privileges and Immunities of the Council of Europe (adopted 18 March 1950, entered into force 18 March 1950) ETS 004.

[85] Council of Europe, 'Agreements concluded by the Council of Europe with other international intergovernmental organisations or public international institutions' (5 October 2018) https://rm.coe.int/16806bdf0b accessed 22 October 2018.

[86] See 'Text of statutory character' (adopted May 1951) ETS 008 I – Resolution adopted by the Committee of Ministers at its 8th Session, May 1951 p 3 https://rm.coe.int./CoERMPublicCommonSearchServices/DisplayDCTMContent?documentId=0900001680063779 accessed 22 October 2018. The Resolution provides:

Relations with intergovernmental and non-governmental international organisations

(i) The Committee of Ministers may, on behalf of the Council of Europe, conclude with any intergovernmental organisation agreements on matters which are within the competence of the Council. These agreements shall, in particular, define the terms on which such an organisation shall be brought into relationship with the Council of Europe ...

(iv) The Committee of Ministers may, on behalf of the Council of Europe, make suitable arrangements for consultation with international non-governmental organisations which deal with matters that are within the competence of the Council of Europe.

The texts are of statutory character and adopted by the Committee of Ministers in the course of its 8th and 9th Sessions with a view to their ultimate inclusion in a revised Statute of the Council of Europe.

[87] See the section on 'Written Guidance on Distinguishing between Treaties and Non-Binding International Instruments' in Chapter 3 at 84–8.

or an organisation that is not an IO. Occasionally a group of States may agree to allow such an entity to participate in a multilateral treaty.[88] When States wish to facilitate this, the question of the eligibility of that entity to join the treaty has to be dealt with in the text of the treaty. In particular, the final clauses will need customised drafting to provide for that entity to become party or participate in some other way. The question of the internal capacity of that entity to undertake treaty obligations will need to be considered at the same time, and those internal law issues inevitably will be intertwined with the international law questions and the treaty drafting.

These issues have arisen in a few cases where States wished to conclude a treaty with an organisational entity, such as a secretariat, programme or CoP, without recognising it as an IO (for political, resource or other reasons). For example, a headquarters agreement may have been considered necessary for the effective functioning of that organisational entity. The question of how that entity may be authorised to enter into a treaty has to be addressed in each case. In some cases, the entity may be given delegated authority to enter into that treaty by an IO acting as its parent body (for example, a UN programme may be authorised by the UN); while in others, the States concerned may agree to confer authority on that entity to enter into that specific treaty in some other way. In every case, the treaty form and procedures have to be customised to reflect the specific agreement, and require exceptionally careful handling in accordance with legal advice.

An example of this is the Headquarters Agreement for the Secretariat of the Antarctic Treaty, 2010.[89] Although it was negotiated in a multilateral forum, it is a bilateral treaty between the Argentine Republic and the Antarctic Treaty Consultative Meeting (ATCM). The latter has not been recognised as an IO but the States concerned authorised it to conclude that treaty (only). The procedures for concluding this treaty, signing it and bringing it into force had to be carefully devised to reflect the unusual status of the ATCM as party.

This example, like any others involving 'other entities', may be idiosyncratic and not necessarily useful as a precedent for any other treaties. They do however serve to illustrate that whenever treaty officials are dealing with any non-State entity becoming party to a treaty, routine treaty procedures cannot simply be applied automatically. Every aspect of the treaty process needs to be reviewed and adapted to ensure that its wording and functioning are appropriate to the status of the entity concerned. It also illustrates the importance of

[88] See the section on 'Eligibility of other Entities to Participate in Multilateral Treaties' above at 214–15.

[89] Headquarters Agreement for the Secretariat of the Antarctic Treaty (signed 10 May 2010, entered into force 10 May 2010) 2775 UNTS 321. The Chair of the Antarctic Treaty Consultative Meeting was authorised to sign the Agreement on behalf of the ATCM by Measure 1 (2003). See Measure 1(2003): Secretariat of the Antarctic Treaty (adopted 20 June 2003) art V(2). Texts of both instruments can be viewed on Secretariat of the Antarctic Treaty, 'Key Documents of the Antarctic Treaty System' https://www.ats.aq/e/ats_keydocs.htm accessed 25 September 2018.

the PLATO principles 'Legal' and 'Professional', in particular that: treaty procedures allow flexibility and are adaptable to new situations; treaty staff are trained to understand the reasons for procedures and are able to make sensible judgments about when to be flexible, balancing legal and other requirements.

States: Transparency and other Reasons for Wider Consultation

As well as meeting *legal* requirements, any government needs to consider whether there are *other* reasons for conducting consultations or publishing information about the treaty, before it commits irrevocably to becoming a party. This is one of the most important applications of the PLATO principle of 'Transparency'.

Within a State, there may be constitutional conventions or practices with regard to consulting other levels of authority, such as provincial, devolved or local governments or legislatures, if the treaty concerns matters within their competences. The legislature may expect to be informed or consulted beyond any legal requirements and there may be political pressure from parliamentary committees. There may be public expectations about wider consultation on treaties, or certain types of treaty of major political importance. It may also be in a government's own self-interest to consult those sections of society who will be affected by the treaty. This is especially so where the treaty will require new obligations to be imposed on and enforced against private persons.

The aims of such consultation may be to seek the support of the affected constituencies, to find out if there is any strong opposition and/or to survey opinion on how the implementation of the treaty may best be carried out, and the effects it might have on the sectors concerned. For example, if the treaty will affect a particular section of industry, the government may need to find out whether and how willing it is to adapt, how much it will cost and what kinds of new legislation, support, incentives or penalties may be needed. Public or parliamentary consultations may also assist the government to decide whether any reservations are needed, or which option to choose if the treaty offers any options.

There are a variety of ways in which a government may carry out pre-ratification consultations on a treaty. It may achieve this through mechanisms for public involvement in the legislature, or it may seek to engage the public directly. Where a government chooses to go beyond legal requirements, it can do so on a regular basis or ad hoc for a particularly important treaty. The following is only a small selection of the possible methods of consultation used by governments around the world.

Publishing a White Paper (or Official Proposal Document)

A White Paper or other kind of consultation document might be used at the policy stage, before the government has decided whether to ratify a particular treaty, or how it intends to implement it. It may invite public comments on the merits of ratifying the treaty and on the proposed manner of domestic implementation, and on any options that the government may wish to consider such as the terms of reservations or whether to opt in to or out of a settlement of disputes mechanism (if appropriate to the treaty in question).

Public Inquiry in Parliament

A good example of this kind of procedure is the Australian Parliament's Joint Standing Committee on Treaties (JSCOT), which is mandated to review and report on all treaty actions proposed by the Government before any binding action is taken. The Committee was first established in 1996 as part of a package of reforms to improve the openness and transparency of the treaty-making process in Australia. All treaties other than minor ones are subject to a public inquiry. The Committee advertises its reviews in the national press and on its website, inviting comments from anyone with an interest in the subject matter of the proposed treaty action. The Committee routinely takes evidence at public hearings from government agencies and may also invite people who have made written submissions to appear. At the completion of its inquiries, the Committee presents a report to Parliament containing advice on whether Australia should take binding treaty action and on other related issues that have emerged during the review.[90]

According to an Australian treaty expert: '[t]he role of JSCOT is critical in ensuring that our domestic constituency's views and concerns are listened to when determining Australia's treaty policy outlook on any given subject'.[91] A Canadian expert has suggested that JSCOT serves as a model for reforming the Canadian treaty-making process, particularly given Canada and Australia's shared legal heritage and similar political structure.[92] It could be a useful model for the UK Parliament to consider, and perhaps also for other parliaments in Commonwealth countries with similar constitutions. Even where there is no legal requirement, a government or legislature could choose to consult the public in this way in relation to a particular treaty where the need for public input is greater than usual.

Publishing an Information Document with the Treaty

When a government transmits a treaty to the legislature with a proposal to ratify it, the effectiveness of the scrutiny it receives will depend largely on the quality of information accompanying it. It is good government practice to

[90] *Parliament of Australia* (n 76).

[91] D Mason, 'The Constitutional Evolution of Deliberative Democracy in Treaty Making', paper presented at the Australian and New Zealand Society of International Law Conference in Canberra, 30 June 2007, p 26. See also D Mason, '"Deliberative democratising" of Australian treaty making: Putting into context the significance of online access to the treaty process' (2016) 24 *Journal of Law, Information & Science* 1.

[92] J Harrington, 'Redressing the Democratic Deficit in Treaty Law Making: (Re)Establishing a Role for Parliament' (2005) 50 *McGill Law Journal* 465, 491.

publish an information document such as a National Interest Analysis (NIA) that includes the following types of information:

- summary of the aims and effects of the treaty;
- reasons why the government considers it appropriate to enter into the treaty;
- any financial implications for the public purse or the private sector;
- how the government proposes to implement the treaty, including whether any new legislation will be needed; and
- whether the government proposes to enter any reservations or declarations, use any opt-in or opt-out options.

Examples of Treaty Information Documents Presented to the Legislature

The following are examples of treaty information documents presented to the legislature in several States:

- *Australia*: when the Government of Australia tables a treaty in Parliament, it provides an NIA for all treaties other than minor ones.[93] For major treaties, these can be substantial documents. For example, when the Trans-Pacific Partnership, 2016 (TPP)[94] was tabled on 9 February 2016, it was accompanied by a nineteen-page document with four attachments and twenty-seven side letters.[95]
- *New Zealand*: the Government is required by Standing Orders of the House of Representatives to present an NIA for all treaties tabled before Parliament, which must cover certain matters specified by Parliament.[96] When it published the TPP on 26 January 2016, it published a 277-page NIA, as well as several more concise 'Fact sheets' and other information materials.[97]
- *The UK*: Since 1997, when a treaty is laid before Parliament it is accompanied by an EM which explains the provisions of the treaty and the reason for ratification. This practice was made obligatory by statute in 2010, but

[93] See JSCOT, 'Role of the Committee' (Parliament of Australia) www.aph.gov.au/Parliamentary_Business/Committees/Joint/Treaties/Role_of_the_Committee accessed 25 September 2018 for an explanation of the content of Australia's NIA documents.

[94] Trans-Pacific Partnership (adopted 4 February 2016, not in force) www.mfat.govt.nz/en/about-us/who-we-are/treaties/trans-pacific-partnership-agreement-tpp/text-of-the-trans-pacific-partnership/ accessed 22 October 2018.

[95] JSCOT, 'Treaty tabled on 9 February 2016 – Treaty under consideration' (Parliament of Australia) National Interest Analysis (2016) with attachments www.aph.gov.au/Parliamentary_Business/Committees/Joint/Treaties/9_February_2016/Treaty_under_consideration#nia accessed 25 September 2018.

[96] Standing Orders of the House of Representatives (last amended 30 July 2014, with effect 15 August 2014) SO 397-400 (International treaties) www.parliament.nz/resource//uenNZ/00HOHPBReferenceStOrders4/eb7c8b9e4a6c7aa88a47d14dc4100513b2557e60 accessed 25 September 2018. See in particular SO 398 – National Interest Analysis.

[97] New Zealand Ministry of Foreign Affairs and Trade, 'Trans-Pacific Partnership – Resources' National Interest Analysis' www.tpp.mfat.govt.nz/resources accessed 25 September 2018. See also New Zealand Ministry of Foreign Affairs and Trade, 'Trans-Pacific Partnership National Interest Analysis' (25 January 2016) /www.tpp.mfat.govt.nz/assets/docs/TPP%20National%20Interest%20Analysis.pdf accessed 22 October 2018.

Parliament has not specified what it should contain. The FCO has issued guidelines to government officials on EMs to Treaties.[98] The contents of EMs are generally much less informative than the New Zealand and Australian NIA documents. See for example, the 3-page Memorandum tabled on 7 October 2016 with the Paris Agreement, 2015 (on climate change).[99] The more active approach of the Australian and New Zealand parliaments, in stipulating the information the government should provide with a treaty, is to be commended.

Publishing Draft Legislation to Implement a Treaty

In recent years, the UK Government has instituted a practice of publishing some legislation in draft before formally introducing it to Parliament. This enables it to receive scrutiny by parliamentary committees and the public at an earlier stage. The Government considers the responses, revises the draft legislation in light of them and then introduces the Bill formally to Parliament, for parliamentary scrutiny in the normal way.[100] This method has been used several times for legislation designed to implement a treaty that the Government proposes to ratify, thus enabling in-depth parliamentary and public discussion of the treaty and the proposed terms of ratification, alongside consideration of the legislative proposals.

An example is the Draft Antarctic Bill which was designed to implement a new annex to the Environmental Protocol to the Antarctic Treaty. The UK Government published it and laid it before Parliament in 2009, together with a consultation paper and the text of the new treaty (the Liability Annex).[101] The public were invited to submit comments. The Government published a report summarising the results of the consultation process and its response in 2010.[102] The Antarctic Bill was introduced to Parliament in 2012 and was enacted as the

[98] Treaty Section, *Treaties and Memoranda of Understanding (MOUs): Guidance on Practice and Procedures* (2nd edn, Foreign and Commonwealth Office, updated March 2014) 9–14 https://assets.publishing.service.gov.uk/government/uploads/system/uploads/attachmen/ut_data/file/293976/Treaties_and_MoU_Guidance.pdf accessed 25 September 2018. Paris Agreement (adopted 12 December 2015, entered into force 4 November 2016) UNTS Registration No. 54113, 55 ILM 740.

[99] FCO, 'Explanatory Memorandum for the Paris Agreement' (published 7 October 2016) Command Paper No. 9338 https://assets.publishing.service.gov.uk/government/uploads/system/uploads/attachment_data/file/558185/EM_Paris_Ag.pdf accessed 22 October 2018. For other examples of EMs, see FCO, 'Multilateral Treaties Published in the Miscellaneous Series' (last updated 28 September 2016) www.gov.uk/government/collections/miscellaneous-treaties-2013#2017 accessed 25 September 2018.

[100] UK Parliament, 'Draft Bills before Parliament' www.parliament.uk/business/bills-and-legislation/draft-bills/ accessed 25 September 2018.

[101] FCO, 'Draft Antarctic Bill – Presented to Parliament by the Secretary of State for Foreign and Commonwealth Affairs', (November 2009) Annex B, Appendix 1, 57–65 https://assets.publishing.service.gov.uk/government/uploads/system/uploads/attachment_data/file/238587/7635.pdf accessed 25 September 2018.

[102] FCO, 'Government Response to the Consultation on the Draft Antarctic Bill', (April 2010) available on the website of The National Archives, https://webarchive.nationalarchives.gov.uk

Antarctic Act 2013 on 26 March 2013. This enabled the Government to implement the Liability Annex, and the UK's ratification was delivered to the depositary on 18 April 2013.

Private Consultations with Sectors of Civil Society or Affected Groups ('Stakeholders')

Governments commonly decide to hold private consultations with interested organisations and experts, for example, trade or professional associations, academic specialists, NGOs, chambers of commerce, community organisations, religious bodies, etc. This may be done in addition to, or in the absence of, parliamentary procedures and public consultation.

For example, when publishing its Draft Antarctic Bill, the UK Government also sent a more detailed 'consultation package' to a range of interested organisations ('stakeholders')[103] and invited them to request a meeting to receive further briefing on the proposals. Several such meetings between government officials and Antarctic Treaty stakeholders were held.

IOs: Transparency and other Reasons for Wider Consultation

An IO secretariat needs to consider whether, even if it already has *legal* authority to conclude a new treaty, it would be *politically* wise to consult the Member States further on the details, directly or through the representative organ of the organisation. There may also be a case for an IO conducting a public consultation, if its implementation of the convention will directly affect the public.

For example, in 2014, the European Commission (the EU's executive branch) conducted an online public consultation on issues related to the ratification and implementation by the EU of the Minamata Convention on Mercury, 2013.[104] The EU had signed the Convention in October 2013. This was in addition to consulting the Member States directly. The aim of the public consultation was to solicit stakeholders' input on specific issues related to the implementation of the Convention, including new EU legislation. The public consultation received 3,702 responses from individuals and organisations, including 6,405 comments. Individuals from twenty-eight Member States and organisations from eighteen Member States, as well as respondents from fourteen non-EU countries participated in this survey. The results of the survey were published and the Commission concluded thus:

> As the comments represent a wide range of interests and stakeholder groups and additionally provide specific and expert recommendations and ideas for improvement concerning the implementation of the Minamata Convention by

/20110703135523/http://www.fco.gov.uk/en/publications-and-documents/publications1/antarctic-bill/ accessed 22 October 2018.

103 See *Foreign and Commonwealth Office* (n 101) 2 and Annex D 93–94 for the list of consultees.

104 Minamata Convention on Mercury (adopted 10 October 2013, entered into force 16 August 2017) UNTS registration No. 54669.

the EU these contributions by the European public are an excellent input basis for the EC regarding the implementation process of the Convention and the needed amendments to EU legal framework.[105]

Top Tips for States or IOs Preparing to Become Party to a Treaty and What To Do When Acting as Depositary

The top tips in Box 6.2 provide pointers, based on the discussion in this chapter, on what treaty officers need to consider and do in preparing their State or IO to become party to a treaty, or in handling new parties when acting as depositary to a treaty.

Box 6.2 Top tips for States or IOs preparing to become party to a treaty and what to do when acting as depositary

TOP TIPS 1
STATES OR IOs PREPARING TO BECOME PARTY TO A TREATY

1. Engage legal advisers in the process right from the start, including the deliberations on whether and how to join the treaty. Legal expertise is needed on international law of treaties and on constitutional law (national law or the internal law of the IO).
2. Ensure that your work plan factors in realistic time periods for internal consultations, and, as required, legislative scrutiny, public consultations, drafting legislation and securing its enactment, preparing reservations and declarations, preparing formal instruments and getting them signed [sealed] and delivered to the other party/parties or depositary.
3. Check that your State/IO is eligible to join the treaty, and take care to choose the correct procedure for consenting to be bound. Consult the other side or the depositary if in doubt.
4. Check internal competences: the constitutional rules and practices (of the State or IO) regarding treaty-making powers and decision-making procedures. For IOs, it is particularly important to look at the past treaty-making practice of the organisation.

[105] European Commission, 'Public Consultation on the Ratification by the EU of the Minamata Convention on Mercury' (14 August to 14 November 2014) http://ec.europa.eu/environment/consultations/mercury_en.htm accessed 25 September 2018. The results are published in European Commission, 'Commission Staff Working Document Impact Assessment Ratification and Implementation by the EU of the Minamata Convention on Mercury' (2 February 2016) SWD(2016) 17 final http://eur-lex.europa.eu/legal-content/EN/TXT/?uri=CELEX:52016SC0017 accessed 25 September 2018.

Box 6.2 (cont.)

5. Consider whether, beyond legal requirements, additional transparency and parliamentary, stakeholder or public consultation is necessary or desirable, for example to satisfy expectations of accountability and to facilitate implementation of treaty obligations.

TOP TIPS 2
DUTIES OF A TREATY DEPOSITARY WHEN A STATE OR IO WISHES TO JOIN THE TREATY

1. If you receive an enquiry or request to join the treaty from a State or IO which is not automatically entitled to do so, or from an entity which might not be a State or IO, inform the treaty parties and seek their guidance.
2. If it is not possible to consult the States Parties at a meeting, use a procedure that facilitates decision-making by correspondence in a manner consistent with the treaty. Design a procedure that is capable of producing a decision within a specific timeframe.
3. Take great care not to exceed your authority or act inconsistently with your duty of impartiality. In any cases of doubt about the validity of a treaty instrument, consult the treaty parties.
4. Encourage any State or IO preparing to become party to send you a copy of their instrument of ratification (or other formal document) in draft for checking in advance. That way, any issue regarding eligibility or procedure can be addressed at any early stage.

7

Becoming Party to a Treaty: Consent to Be Bound and Entry into Force

***

'There's many a slip twixt cup and lip.'[1]

Introduction

As explained in Chapter 6, there is a crucial difference between creating a treaty, expressing consent to be bound by it and bringing it into force. Chapter 6 dealt with the preparatory stages of considering whether and how to become party to a treaty, and the institutional consultations and approvals that may be needed in advance. The focus of this chapter is on what is needed to complete the process, once the decision to become a party has been finally taken and treaty officials are asked to prepare the documentation and take care of procedures, at both the international and domestic levels.

Applying the PLATO Principles to Becoming Party to a Treaty

The PLATO principle 'Legal' guides all stages of the process, from preparation to execution. Chapter 6 looked at the importance of the 'Transparency' principle, especially 'Accountability' and 'Accessibility', during the stage of national or internal consultations. Once the political decisions are made, and it is up to treaty officials to organise the documentation, two other PLATO principles come to the fore: 'Assured' and 'Organised'.

- 'Assured' means reliable, dependable, trustworthy, and guaranteed. It is especially important to make sure this applies to:
    - the accuracy of published treaty texts and treaty information; and
    - the authority of the person who signs the treaty and instruments to express consent to be bound.
- 'Organised' means that treaty management should be systematic, efficient and regular. When a State or an IO becomes party to a treaty, or is involved as depositary in its entry into force, particular attention is needed to ensure that there is:

[1] Traditional English proverb (similar versions exist in other languages), meaning that even the most carefully laid plan can go wrong in the execution.

- a central authority responsible for treaty procedures; and
- 'co-ordination' across the administration with regard to the domestic implementation of the treaty, and the monitoring of its entry into force.

Why Good Management of Ratification and Entry into Force Matters: Scenarios on What Can Go Wrong

Scenario 1: Accidental Delay in Depositing an Instrument of Ratification

An IO acting as Depositary for a multilateral treaty received an instrument of accession from a State. It was delivered by that State's Permanent Mission to the organisation on 1 March 2017. Upon examination of the instrument, it was found to have been signed by the Foreign Minister of that State on 10 December 2010. The Treaty Office contacted the Permanent Mission, who explained that they had received the instrument from the Foreign Ministry in 2010 with instructions to deposit it immediately, but due to staff changes this had been overlooked. The documents had just been found in a cabinet. The Mission asked the Depositary to backdate their accession to 2010, as otherwise they would face extreme difficulties given that their Ministry had assumed the deposit was carried out in 2010, and their Government had been implementing the treaty since then.

The Depositary accepted the instrument of accession as valid, but (correctly) said they could not agree to backdate it. The date of accession was published on the Depositary's website as 1 March 2017. The Permanent Mission was forced to admit its mistake to the Foreign Ministry, which then had to inform other government departments and address the consequences for its treaty relations and its domestic legal system.

Scenario 2: Instrument of Ratification Signed by an Unauthorised Person

A State deposited an Instrument of Ratification to a major new multilateral environmental treaty. The Government's environment officials had worked hard for months to prepare the necessary approvals and paperwork in order to ratify in time for the treaty to enter into force for that State before the first COP. The timing was critical as the Government wished not only to have a vote, but also to compete to host the treaty secretariat in their country. The instrument was rejected by the Depositary as it was signed by the Minister for the Environment, who did not have Full Powers to do so. Officials had to approach their foreign ministry to ask for a new instrument to be prepared and signed by the Foreign Minister. Consequently that State had not become party by the time of the conference, and so was not entitled to vote or offer to host the secretariat, which was duly established in another State. This important opportunity was missed due to an error that could have been avoided, had the environment ministry consulted the foreign ministry's Treaty Office at the outset.

Expressing Consent to Be Bound by the Treaty

As explained in Chapter 6,[2] there are four modes of expressing consent to be bound by a treaty, as defined in Article 11 of both the VCLT 1969 and the VCLT 1986:[3]

- definitive signature;
- ratification, acceptance, approval or accession;
- exchange of instruments constituting a treaty; and
- 'By any other means if so agreed'.

Chapter 6 explains what each mode means, and that each treaty specifies which mode is required or sets out the permitted options from which those wishing to participate may choose. In this chapter we consider, in relation to each of these modes, what officials need to do to complete this step.

The term 'act of formal confirmation' is equivalent to 'ratification'.[4] It is occasionally provided for in treaties that are open to IOs to become party. The procedures set out in this chapter for 'ratification' apply in the same way to an 'act of formal confirmation'. This use of terminology for IOs is not mandatory however; some treaties use the term 'ratification' for a mode available to both States and IOs. In this chapter, references to 'ratification' should be understood to include 'act of formal confirmation', for treaties that use this term; and references to 'ratification etc' also include acceptance, approval or accession.

Definitive Signature

Some treaties enter into force on signature, either instantly or after the expiry of a specified number of days. This mode of giving consent to be bound is known as 'definitive signature' and is a one-step procedure.[5] It can be used in both bilateral and multilateral treaties. It means that once it has signed, the signing party has given final consent to be bound by the treaty. It may enter into force for that party immediately upon signature (or the later of the two signatures, if the treaty is bilateral) or it may do so after a specified number of days, but the point is that it will do so automatically. Whenever definitive signature is the specified mode for a particular treaty, or has been chosen by a particular signing party, the process must be handled with great care and attention. The signing party needs to ensure that all the necessary domestic steps have been taken – if any are required – before the treaty is signed.

[2] See the section on 'Understanding Modes for Expressing Consent to Be Bound' in Chapter 6 at 220–27.

[3] VCLT 1969 (adopted 23 May 1969, entered into force 27 January 1980) 1155 UNTS 331 and VCLT 1986 (adopted 21 March 1986, not in force) http://legal.un.org/ilc/texts/instruments/english/conventions/1_2_1986.pdf accessed 9 September 2018.

[4] VCLT 1986, art 2(1)(b bis), art 11(2) and art 14(2).

[5] See the section on 'Understanding Modes for Expressing Consent to Be Bound' in Chapter 6 at 220–27.

Definitive signature is less commonly chosen today than it used to be, due to the increasing tendency for treaties to be submitted to scrutiny by the legislature before the government commits itself. It is sometimes agreed as the mode of expressing consent in a bilateral treaty, where neither side needs time after signature for any further consultations or parliamentary process. Multilateral treaties that provide for definitive signature commonly offer it as one of several options, but it is not usually chosen by many States. For example, multilateral treaties concluded within the CoE usually offer this choice. Occasionally a multilateral treaty may stipulate that it will enter into force on signature for all parties, where that has been agreed in advance by the negotiating parties. For example, the ASEAN used this mode of entry into force in, among others, the Agreement for the Establishment of an ASEAN Development Fund, 2005 and in several instruments of incorporation of certain rules to the Protocol to the ASEAN Charter on Dispute Settlement Mechanisms.[6]

What To Do when Definitive Signature in a Draft Treaty Turns Out to Be Difficult?

Scenario: your government is preparing to sign a bilateral treaty that provides that it will enter into force on signature. A date has been set for the treaty-signing ceremony to coincide with a ministerial visit. But you now realise that your government needs to secure the enactment of new legislation to implement the treaty, and this cannot be done before the ceremony. You consider the option of postponing the signing, but ministers wish to proceed on the agreed date.

Suggestion: if the treaty text has not yet been bound and sealed, it may be possible to agree to redraft the final clauses, to accommodate your government's need for time to complete domestic procedures. Explain the problem to the other party. Ask if they could agree to change the definitive signature provision to signature subject to a further step, such as each side notifying the other of the completion of their domestic procedures. And then postpone entry into force until both sides have notified. If this is agreed, it would allow the signing ceremony to proceed as planned, while each side's respective domestic procedures take their course at different speeds thereafter.

What To Do when a Signature Is Unclear as to whether It Is Definitive?

Scenario: your government or IO is depositary for a multilateral treaty that provides for signature with or without reservation as to ratification, at the option of each signatory. After the signature ceremony, you find that one

[6] Agreement for the Establishment of an ASEAN Development Fund (adopted 26 July 2005, entered into force 26 July 2005) ADS (2005) 33 art II(1); Instrument of Incorporation of the Rules for Reference of Non-Compliance to the ASEAN Summit to the Protocol to the ASEAN Charter on Dispute Settlement Mechanisms (adopted 2 April 2012, entered into force 2 April 2012) ADS (2012) 59 art 2(1); and Instrument of Incorporation of the Rules for Reference of Unresolved Disputes to the ASEAN Summit to the Protocol to the ASEAN Charter on Dispute Settlement Mechanisms (adopted 27 October 2010, entered into force 27 October 2010) ADS (2010) 31 art 2(1).

signatory did not specify against their signature which type of signature was intended.

Suggestion: a definitive signature needs to be clearly expressed. If it is not made clear, it should be presumed that signature subject to ratification was intended. If that signatory did wish to express consent to be bound, this could be remedied by submitting an instrument of ratification. But if they were wrongly presumed to have signed definitively, it would have serious consequences for that party.

This kind of problem can usually be avoided by asking signatories to indicate in advance whether they intend to sign with or without reservation as to ratification. This makes sure that all signatories are aware of the difference and have made a clear choice. It should also be made clear in the wording of the Full Powers presented (see the section on Full Powers in Chapter 5 at page 188–9).

Ratification, Acceptance, Approval or Accession

When Should the Treaty Office Prepare the Instrument?

Once a State or IO deposits an instrument of ratification, acceptance, approval or accession, it has expressed its consent to be bound by the treaty. It is committed. All the obligations and requirements in that treaty apply to it, although most of them only become binding when the treaty enters into force. It is not therefore something that the Treaty Office can undertake lightly.

As explained in Chapter 6, any necessary parliamentary approval or legislative steps need to have been completed before the instrument is deposited. This can take some time. Even after that, there may be other policy or political reasons why a government or IO does not wish to ratify the treaty at this particular point in time. For example, in the case of a government, it may decide to wait for certain other States to ratify first, or it may wish or need to co-ordinate with another State or group of States. If a general election is imminent, it may need (or prefer) to wait until after the election. Or it may simply have other more urgent priorities for the moment. Likewise, the Secretary General of an IO may decide to postpone ratifying a treaty even after being authorised to do so by the governing body of the organisation, for reasons of circumstance or pragmatism.[7]

It would clearly be unwise for a treaty official to assume that, just because there is a mandate to ratify, he or she should carry it out. The Treaty Office should obtain clear written instructions from senior administrators with policy responsibility for the treaty, before proceeding to prepare the necessary documentation. Those instructions should also confirm that all the necessary

[7] For example, the Committee of Ministers of the CoE authorised the Secretary General to deposit an instrument of ratification on behalf of the CoE to become party to the VCLT 1986, but he has not yet done so due to the views of one Member State, which happens to be the Host State. This example was mentioned in the section on 'Becoming Party to a Treaty – Why It Does not Always Happen' in Chapter 6 at 206–08.

domestic legislative steps have been taken, and any necessary consents have been obtained (from other ministries, the legislature, etc.). The Treaty Office would be well advised to issue internal guidance that specifies what information these written instructions should contain, and at what level of seniority they should be signed off. This is particularly useful where the request comes from a domestic ministry that does not deal regularly with treaties. For example, in the UK's practice, when a ministry with the policy lead for a particular treaty requests the FCO to prepare a ratification instrument, the FCO requires a written request at director level. The letter has to include a statement that all government departments, agencies and devolved or other authorities with an interest have been consulted; and an assurance that all necessary domestic legislation or other implementing measures are in place (with details).[8]

Producing an Instrument of Ratification, Acceptance, Approval or Accession

An instrument of ratification is a very formal document, which governments customarily produce in a special format that normally only a Treaty Office is equipped to prepare. Governments normally print the text on special high quality paper, bind it with ribbon and seal it into a special hard folder in its national colour with its national crest on the cover. For this reason, such instruments are almost always prepared by the government's Treaty Office or in the headquarters of an IO, not in embassies or other places.

When the treaty is bilateral, the two States usually exchange instruments of ratification, so that each State keeps the other State's original instrument. When the treaty is multilateral, each State (or IO) normally deposits its instrument with the depositary, who is then responsible for the safekeeping of all instruments on behalf of all parties. For plurilateral treaties, if there is a small number of parties and they do not wish to appoint a depositary, the method usually chosen would be exchanges of notes rather than exchanges of instruments of ratification, as notes can more easily be issued in multiple originals.

An instrument of ratification does not have to contain a set form of words. However it must contain the essentials: the full title of the treaty being ratified, and the place and date of its signature. As a rather obvious point, but sometimes missed, the instrument should also unequivocally set out the intention of the State or IO to ratify the treaty in question.[9] There may also be a question on whether any declarations or reservations should be included in the instrument, and this is dealt with in more detail below. If they are not included, the instrument should contain a reference to the accompanying document. It is

[8] Treaty Section, *Treaties and Memoranda of Understanding (MOUs): Guidance on Practice and Procedures* (2nd edn, FCO, updated March 2014) 6 https://assets.publishing.service.gov.uk/government/uploads/system/uploads/attachmen/ut_data/file/293976/Treaties_and_MoU_Guidance.pdf accessed 25 September 2018.

[9] For an example of a ratification instrument, see Annex VIII, 'Example of an Instrument of Ratification' at 441.

wise to use a template so as to ensure that essential elements are not left out in error and to maintain consistency in style. Each government or IO is best advised to develop its own template, based on its own practice. Useful guidance can be found in the model instruments provided in the UN Treaty Handbook, which may be used for multilateral treaties.[10]

An instrument of ratification can only be signed by one of the three authorities: Head of State, Head of Government or Foreign Minister (as for Full Powers). If desired, the instrument may also be signed by a minister, perhaps the one with policy responsibility for the subject of the treaty concerned, but it is still necessary for the instrument to be signed by one of the three authorities. In the UK, instruments of ratification are usually signed by the Foreign Secretary but there are some instruments, mainly relating to EU treaties, which are signed by Her Majesty the Queen. Obtaining the signature of the Head of State in the UK involves a much longer procedure than other signatories, since after signature the instrument must be sent to the Crown Office in the House of Lords for the Royal Seal to be attached. For most instruments, however, once signature has been obtained then a seal can be attached, in much the same way as a treaty would be sealed, and the instrument is then ready for exchange or deposit.

Instruments of accession[11] are handled in exactly the same way as instruments of ratification, and must be prepared by the Treaty Office and signed by one of the three authorities. It is important to use the correct term in the instrument, as ratification is normally only available to States that have already signed the treaty, whereas accession is a one-step procedure. The first step for treaty officials should be to look at the provisions of the treaty itself and determine whether their State or IO needs to ratify or accede, and check treaty records to see if their State or IO signed the treaty when it was open for signature. If in doubt, the depositary should be contacted as they will be able to provide definitive status information and advice on the required type of instrument. The essential content of the instrument is the same as for ratification, and it is likewise advisable for the Treaty Office to use a template.[12]

Instruments of acceptance or approval are less commonly used. Whether they are equivalent to ratification (following signature) or accession (a one-step procedure) depends on how they are defined in the treaty in question. They are prepared and deposited in the same way as instruments of ratification and accession.

Exchanging Instruments of Ratification of a Bilateral Treaty

When a bilateral treaty is subject to ratification, each instrument has to be deposited with the other side. 'Deposit' refers to its actual receipt by the other

[10] See Annex VII, 'United Nations Model Instrument of Ratification/Acceptance/Approval' at 440.

[11] On the meaning of accession, see the section on 'Understanding Modes for Expressing Consent to Be Bound' in Chapter 6 at 220–27.

[12] See Annex X, 'Example of an Instrument of Accession' at 443–45.

side, not mere delivery. Actual receipt means that a responsible official (usually in the Treaty Office) has opened the envelope and acknowledged receipt of the contents. So if, for example, someone posts an envelope containing the instrument through the recipient organisation's letterbox when it is closed over the weekend, that is not a 'deposit'; the date of the deposit will be when the document has arrived through the internal system on the desk of a treaty official and been stamped with that day's date (which should happen on the next working day).

Unless the treaty provides otherwise, it enters into force when the instruments of ratification are exchanged.[13] An 'exchange of instruments' means that each side has received the other's instrument. Unless the treaty requires the two deliveries to take place simultaneously, the two deposits could be done at different times and places, for example, by an ambassador or representative of each side delivering it to the foreign ministry or headquarters of the other. Normally, each delivery would take place at a formal meeting arranged by appointment, but not necessarily on the same date as the other. A permanent record must be made of the date of delivery of each instrument, as this will be critical in determining the date of entry into force of the treaty. Where the deliveries take place on different dates, the later one will be the critical date as that is when the exchange is complete. It is therefore essential for each side to provide the other with an acknowledgement of receipt to confirm the date on which their instrument was received.

A ceremony of exchange, in which both instruments are deposited with the other side at the same time and place, is usually the preferred arrangement. Not only does this provide an occasion for celebration, photographs and other diplomatic niceties, it is also the simplest way to ensure that there is clarity about the date of the exchange. In such cases, although not mandatory, it is often good protocol for the exchange ceremony to take place in the *other* State to where the treaty was signed. So, if State A hosts the signing of the treaty, State B hosts the exchange of ratification instruments. Prior to the exchange ceremony, a 'certificate of exchange' should be drawn up which confirms the date and place of exchange. In the same way as the bilateral treaty, these certificates should be in both or all of the official languages of the treaty, and should be agreed in advance with the other State. Ceremonies of exchange are similar to treaty-signing ceremonies and so the involvement of policy colleagues in arranging the ceremony is vital, although they are not necessarily held at ministerial level. It could for example be that the Ambassador or Head of Mission of a State calls on a senior official – usually at director level or above – in the hosting State to conduct the ceremony. At the ceremony the two instruments of ratification are exchanged and the certificates of exchange are signed by the two participants.

Obviously, the State (or IO) that is not hosting the ceremony will need to ensure that its instrument of ratification has been sent to its embassy or representative office in good time (normally through the diplomatic bag or by official courier).

[13] VCLT 1969 art 16.

Arranging the Deposit of an Instrument of Ratification of a Multilateral Treaty

If a multilateral treaty is being ratified, the normal procedure is to deposit the instrument with the depositary of the treaty concerned. The instructions set out in the final clauses of the treaty must be followed carefully. It will normally state in the treaty who the depositary is, and it is of course vitally important that the instrument is sent to the correct place. Once the instrument has been signed and sealed, the Treaty Office should forward it to their embassy or mission in the State concerned, or to their representative at the relevant IO, with a covering note asking them to deposit it. The instrument should if possible be physically deposited by a member of staff from the embassy or mission. It is permissible to send it by courier or post, but this naturally carries a degree of risk. It is important that a receipt for deposit is obtained from the depositary, stating the date of deposit, as this will be crucial information for treaty records.

Box 7.1 Depositing an instrument of ratification at the United Nations or any other IO

- It is worth the trouble of taking the instrument in person during office hours.
- If you go directly to the Treaty Office, you can ask to stand there and watch while the responsible officer opens the envelope, and then you can ask for a written and dated confirmation of receipt to take away with you.
- To make sure of this opportunity, you could contact the Treaty Office in advance to arrange a time to visit. That way, you will know not only that it has been safely received, but also the definitive date of deposit.
- You can then inform your own authorities straight away of the date of deposit, which may then determine the date of entry into force.
- Otherwise, if you simply send it by courier, or leave it with a reception desk, you will not know when it will be received in the Treaty Office, and you may have to wait some time to receive written notification of the date of deposit. That may leave your authorities waiting to find out when the date of entry into force will be – or was.

What Can Go Wrong?

Scenario 1: The Wrong Type of Instrument is Deposited

You have submitted an instrument of accession to the depositary of a treaty without first checking whether this was the correct instrument to send. You then find that in fact your State had signed the treaty, and should therefore have ratified and not acceded. What might the depositary do?

In such circumstances, the depositary should recognise that your State should have ratified and not acceded, and point this out when acknowledging receipt of the instrument. In this case, you will need to prepare a new instrument in the correct form, have it signed by the Minister, and then deposit it afresh. (This may cause considerable internal embarrassment, and will also result in the date of deposit being delayed.) However, the depositary may be prepared to accept the instrument as (in effect) an instrument of ratification and not accession, and make this clear when it informs other States and IOs of the deposit of your instrument. If the depositary is willing to take the second course of action, they would effectively be correcting the error for you. It would be reasonable for a depositary to treat an instrument of accession as in effect a ratification, or vice versa, provided that the sender confirms that that was their intention, as the difference between such documents is one of form only.

Scenario 2: National Process in the Legislature Is Confused with 'Ratification'

You are the depositary for a multilateral treaty and a State sends you a photocopy of their official gazette, confirming that the treaty has been ratified by the national legislature of their State, with a covering letter from their embassy stating that this is their instrument of ratification. Do you accept this?

As a valid instrument of ratification or accession (as appropriate) signed by one of the three authorities has not been submitted, as a depositary you could not accept this as a valid expression of consent to be bound, even if the embassy says it is. It is common for people, even diplomats, to confuse approval by the national legislature with the international act of ratification of a treaty. This is especially likely to happen in States that refer to the national process of legislative approval of a treaty as 'ratification'.

A depositary should not accept an instrument of ratification without a properly authorised signature, as it leaves doubt as to whether the State actually consents to be bound.

Scenario 3: Conflict between a State's National Policy and Its Duty of Impartiality as Depositary

When acting as a government depositary for a multilateral treaty, you receive an instrument of ratification or accession from an entity claiming to be a State but not a member of the UN. It is not recognised as a State by your government. How should you act?

Simply because your State does not recognise the entity concerned as a State does not mean that as a depositary you should necessarily refuse the instrument. However, if it is not a member of the UN, its status as a State may be problematic for the treaty parties generally. The depositary must act impartially and should not take decisions on the basis of any national position. You could circulate a copy of the instrument to all the States Parties to the treaty without comment, or with a request for their views as to whether it should be accepted. Meanwhile, it would be wise not to include that entity on your published list of ratifications of that treaty.

Conducting an 'Exchange of Instruments Constituting a Treaty'

When a bilateral treaty is created by an exchange of instruments (usually diplomatic notes, often referred to as notes verbales), one side sends a note verbale setting out the terms of the (already negotiated) agreement in the form of a proposal, and the other side sends a reply note accepting the proposal. The two documents *together* constitute the treaty.[14]

The exchange can be carried out by correspondence or in person. The notes do not need to be exchanged simultaneously at a single meeting; it is common for the first note to be delivered by the embassy of State A to the foreign ministry of State B; and then for the reply note to be delivered at a later date by the embassy of State B to the foreign ministry of State A. The person who signs the note needs to have Full Powers (unless there is an agreement to dispense with this) but the delivery can be carried out by any embassy official, not necessarily the person who signed.

Exchanging notes is therefore a convenient and flexible procedure, especially useful for less formal agreements or when ministers are not available to attend or see no need for a signing ceremony.

The 'instruments' do not have to be in the form of notes; they can be in the form of an ordinary business letter or any other kind of document. The formality of a diplomatic note is usually preferred for a treaty. A useful feature of a diplomatic note is that it is usually assigned a registration number by the issuing institution, by which the note can be unambiguously referenced in the reply note, and a permanent record can be easily located. However, a letter will do the job just as well provided that it is clear that it is intended, together with the reply letter, to constitute a binding agreement. A note is typically expressed in the third person, either as from the institution (such as ministry, embassy or IO) or from the head of it (such as minister, ambassador or director), with customary diplomatic salutations at the beginning and end, stamped by the ministry or embassy, with the signature or initials written across the stamp. However, a note from the head can also be expressed in the first person ('I') and address the recipient as 'Your Excellency' and then 'you'. The difference in form between a first-person note and a letter can be hard to discern when the text is published without the formal 'top' and 'tail', and is of little importance except to those who need to prepare the documents. The reply should follow the same format as the first instrument.[15]

[14] See the section on 'Preparing a Treaty Formed by Exchange of Instruments' in Chapter 5 at 183–84 and the section on 'Exchange of Instruments Constituting a Treaty' in Chapter 6 at 223–25.

[15] The following examples are useful for comparison:

How to Prepare an Initiating Note

The initiating note sets out the already negotiated agreement in the form of a proposal addressed to the other party. It will then propose that, if this proposal is acceptable to the other side, this note and the reply note shall together constitute a treaty (or agreement), and it will also specify the entry into force date or further procedure.

To show how an initiating note is normally structured, we will look at each element of the following example, the Exchange of Notes constituting an Agreement between the Government of the United Kingdom of Great Britain and Northern Ireland and the Government of the People's Republic of China Concerning the Establishment of a Consulate-General of each Country in the other at Wuhan and Belfast, 2014.[16]

The initiating Note from the UK to China begins with:

> Her Majesty's Embassy at Beijing to the Ministry of Foreign Affairs for the Government of the People's Republic of China
> 20 February 2014
> Note No. 021/14

The registration number would have been assigned by the UK embassy for its internal records.

The body of the Note begins with the customary diplomatic greeting that is used in all notes (whether treaty-related or not), expressed in the third person (equivalent to 'Dear X' in a letter):

- Exchange of notes expressed in the third person: Exchange of Notes between the Government of the United States of America and the Government of the United Kingdom of Great Britain and Northern Ireland Concerning the Use of Wideawake Airfield on Ascension Island by Civil Aircraft (signed 6 June 2016, entered into force 6 June 2016) UKTS 31 (2016) https://assets.publishing.service.gov.uk/government/uploads/system/uploads/attachment_data/file/537884/TS_31_2016_Cm_9318_Wideawake_PRINT.pdf accessed 26 September 2018.
- Exchange of notes expressed in the first person: Exchange of Notes between the Government of the United Kingdom of Great Britain and Northern Ireland and the Government of the State of Qatar amending the Air Services Agreement done at London on 24 June 1998 (signed 26 and 27 August 2007, entered into force 27 August 2007) UKTS 03 (2009) https://assets.publishing.service.gov.uk/government/uploads/system/uploads/attachment_data/file/238646/7554.pdf accessed 26 September 2018.
- Exchange of letters: Agreement in the form of an Exchange of Letters between the European Community and the Kingdom of Norway concerning a Cooperation Programme for Economic Growth and Sustainable Development in Bulgaria (signed 25 July 2007) OJ L 221 25/08/2007 https://eur-lex.europa.eu/legal-content/EN/TXT/PDF/?uri=CELEX:22007A0825(06)&from=EN accessed 26 September 2018.

[16] Exchange of Notes constituting an Agreement between the Government of the United Kingdom of Great Britain and Northern Ireland and the Government of the People's Republic of China Concerning the Establishment of a Consulate-General of each Country in the other at Wuhan and Belfast (signed 20 and 21 February 2014, entered into force 21 February 2014) UKTS 23 (2016). See the section on 'Exchange of Instruments Constituting a Treaty' in Chapter 6 at 223–25 where this UK/China Exchange of Notes is discussed. The Exchange of Notes is reproduced in Annex III, 'Example of an Exchange of Notes Constituting a Treaty' at 424–25.

> The Embassy of the United Kingdom of Great Britain and Northern Ireland in China presents its compliments to the Ministry of Foreign Affairs of the People's Republic of China . . .

It continues with the opening commonly used in a treaty note to make clear that it is intended to bind the governments:

> and, on behalf of the Government of the United Kingdom of Great Britain and Northern Ireland, has the honour to propose that . . . the Government of the United Kingdom of Great Britain and Northern Ireland and the Government of the People's Republic of China hereby agree to [. . .]

It then sets out the text of the agreement (which would have been pre-negotiated at official level).

It concludes with a clear statement that the two Notes 'shall constitute an Agreement'. This is crucial, to make it clear that it is intended to be binding under international law, and to distinguish it from other exchanges of notes which record understandings which are not intended to be binding. It also sets out how consent to be bound is to be expressed by the other side and how the agreement is to enter into force (there are various options that could be used here – see below):

> If the above agreement is confirmed by the Ministry of Foreign Affairs of the People's Republic of China on behalf of the Government of the People's Republic of China, this note together with the reply from the Ministry of Foreign Affairs shall constitute an Agreement between the Government of the United Kingdom of Great Britain and Northern Ireland and the Government of the People's Republic of China which shall enter into force on the date of the latter's reply.

The note ends with the traditional diplomatic courtesy greeting used on all third-person notes (which serves the same function as 'Yours sincerely, Y' on a letter):

> The Embassy of the United Kingdom of Great Britain and Northern Ireland in China avails itself of this opportunity to renew to the Ministry of Foreign Affairs of the People's Republic of China the assurances of its highest consideration.[17]

How to Prepare a Reply Note

The reply note needs to state that the proposal is accepted and that the two notes together constitute an agreement. It is essential to refer to the initiating note by its date and any official reference number, so that there can be no doubt which note is being replied to. It is also good practice to repeat the full text of the first note verbatim, so that there can be no doubt of the terms of the agreement.

It is not acceptable to add any additional text or to paraphrase the terms of the agreement in your reply note, as then the notes will not record an

[17] ibid.

agreement. If the proposal is not acceptable or not complete, negotiations need to be reopened until there is agreement on the exact text. If a revised text is then agreed, the process should be started again (by either party) with a new initiating note. To show how a reply note is normally structured, we will look at the Reply Note from China to the UK, in the Exchange of Notes concerning the Establishment of a Consulate-General of each Country in the other at Wuhan and Belfast, which begins:

> Ministry of Foreign Affairs of the People's Republic of China to the Embassy of the United Kingdom of Great Britain and Northern Ireland in China
> 21 February 2014
> Note No. (2014) 70

The registration number would have been assigned by the Chinese Ministry, according to its internal system.

The Note begins with the customary greeting:

> The Ministry of Foreign Affairs of the People's Republic of China presents its compliments to the Embassy of the United Kingdom of Great Britain and Northern Ireland in China

It continues by referencing the Initiating Note:

> [. . .] and has the honour to acknowledge receipt of the latter's Note No.021/14 of 20 February 2014 which reads as follows:

It sets out the full text of the Initiating Note.[18]

It then confirms the Agreement:

> On behalf of the Government of the People's Republic of China, the Ministry of Foreign Affairs of the People's Republic of China has the honour to confirm its agreement to the content of the above note.

The Reply Note ends with the customary greeting (as is universally used in diplomatic notes):

> The Ministry of Foreign Affairs of the People's Republic of China avails itself of this opportunity to renew to the Embassy of the United Kingdom of Great Britain and Northern Ireland in China the assurances of its highest consideration.

The Agreement duly entered into force, in accordance with its terms, on 21 February 2014.

Exchange of Letters

A bilateral treaty may also consist of an exchange of letters.[19] A letter differs from a note only in matters of style. A letter is usually expressed in the first

[18] The full text of the Initiating Note is set out verbatim in the original Reply Note, but is omitted in the UK published version of the Notes. The fact that the full text is in the original is indicated as follows: '[As in Note no. 1]'.

[19] See Annex IV, 'Examples of an Exchange of Letters Constituting a Treaty' at 426–36.

person ('I'), addressed to a named individual and signed by a named individual. In all other respects, a letter performs the same function as a note provided that it contains the necessary substance, and is signed by a properly authorised person. To show how such a letter is normally structured, we will look at each element of the following example: Exchange of Letters amending the Agreement on a Working Holiday Scheme between the Government of New Zealand and the Government of the Argentine Republic, 2010, signed on 5 November and 13 December 2010.[20]

The Initiating Letter from Argentina to New Zealand is on paper headed with the name of the Argentine Foreign Ministry at the top. It is addressed personally to the Foreign Minister of New Zealand by name, and begins (in translation):

> Buenos Aires, November 5, 2010
>
> Your Excellency,
>
> I have the honour to refer to [the subject of the proposal].
>
> In this regard [. . .], I would like to propose, on behalf of the Argentine Government, the following [. . .]:

It then sets out the text of the agreement (which would have been pre-negotiated at official level) in numbered paragraphs.

It concludes with a clear proposal to enter into a binding agreement:

> Should the foregoing be agreeable to the Government of New Zealand, I have the honour to propose that this Note and the Note from Your Excellency giving consent shall constitute an agreement between our two Governments . . ., which shall enter into force on the date of receipt of the last notice by which the Parties inform each other of the fulfilment of their internal procedural requirements for entry into force.

The signature is preceded by a customary greeting (a formal diplomatic equivalent of 'Yours sincerely', written in the first person): 'Please accept, Your Excellency, the assurances of my highest consideration.' It ends with the signature of the Argentine Foreign Minister, with his name and official title printed underneath.

The Reply Letter from New Zealand is addressed to the Argentine Foreign Minister by name, and begins:

> Your Excellency,
>
> I have the honour to refer to your Note of 5 November 2010 regarding the [subject] which reads as follows:
>
> [the whole of the Argentine letter is set out in full].

[20] Exchange of Letters amending the Agreement on a Working Holiday Scheme between the Government of New Zealand and the Government of the Argentine Republic (signed 13 December 2010, entered into force 28 July 2011) 2833 UNTS Registration No. 43824, NZTS 2011 No. 8 B2010/28. It is interesting that, although in the form of a letter, there is a reference in the letter to 'this Note'. However, the subsequent New Zealand note on completion of procedures refers to it as the 'Exchange of Letters'. In the opinion of the authors, the latter is the more apt description, but we would comment that the fact that the New Zealand Ministry initially called it a 'Note' illustrates that the difference is not significant. The text of the Exchange is reproduced in Annex IV.B, 'Example of Exchange of Letters B' at 429–36.

It concludes with a clear statement of agreement:

> I am pleased to confirm that the proposed changes are acceptable to the Government of New Zealand and that your Note, together with this Note in reply, shall constitute, between our two Governments, an agreement . . . which shall enter into force on the date of receipt of the last notice by which the Parties inform each other of the fulfilment of their internal procedural requirements for entry into force.

How to Draft Entry into Force Clauses in a Treaty Constituted by Exchange of Instruments

The timing and procedure for entry into force should have been discussed during the negotiations on the substance. Moreover, whether or not time is required after the exchange to carry out consultations and/or parliamentary procedures should have been considered by each side as part of their internal preparations for the exchange. The task of the Treaty Office will normally be to arrange the exchange and entry into force in accordance with the already agreed text. However, if this has not been done, administrators may request the Treaty Office to add some suitable final clauses at the same time as preparing the notes (or letters).

The entry into force provisions should be included in the initiating note as part of the proposal. There are several options. It could propose that the agreement shall enter into force:

1. On the date of receipt of the later of the two notes constituting the agreement. This is only suitable if neither side will need time for domestic procedures such as enacting implementing legislation. A record will need to be made of the date of receipt of the later note.
2. On a specified date (after the exchange). This has the advantage of clarity; the date of entry into force is stated on the face of the agreement itself. This may be the best approach if there is a specific date on which both sides are agreed, and if it is certain that the exchange will take place before that, for example at a pre-arranged meeting. Otherwise, if it is uncertain when the reply note will arrive, this method will not suit.
3. A specified length of time after the date of receipt of the later of the two notes constituting the agreement, for example, x days. This is suitable if one or both sides will need a known length of time for domestic procedures of a formal nature, such as publishing the agreement or notifying internal authorities, between the exchange of notes and entry into force of the agreement.
4. After both parties have notified the other of the completion of their respective domestic procedures, that is, on the date of receipt of the later of the two notifications (for examples of this kind of wording, see below). This is suitable if one or both sides will need an uncertain length of time for domestic procedures such as consulting the legislature, securing the

enactment of legislation or putting in place new administrative measures, between the exchange of notes and entry into force of the agreement. It can also accommodate a case where one or both parties are uncertain whether they will be able to complete domestic procedures at all.

5. A specified length of time after both parties have notified the other of the completion of their respective domestic procedures, for example, x days.

Method 5 is suitable where one or both parties need an uncertain length of time for domestic procedures to implement the agreement, and so both sides wish to have a fixed period of notice of the entry into force date. This is to avoid a situation which could arise with method 4, where the first party to notify completion waits a long time to receive notification from the other party, and is then taken by surprise by a sudden entry into force when the second note arrives without warning.

Who Needs to Sign the Note (or Letter) on Each Side (where the Notes Form the Treaty)?

As for all treaties, the person who signs the note verbale on each side must have authority to do so as a matter of international law, and there may also be domestic law requirements.[21] Typically, each diplomatic note forming part of a treaty between two States is signed in the capital city by the Foreign Minister, or in the embassy to other State by the ambassador. When it is signed by anyone other than the Foreign Minister, the question of Full Powers must be considered.

It will be recalled that Article 7 VCLT 1969 provides that a person is considered as representing a State for the purpose of expressing the consent of the State to be bound by a treaty if he or she produces Full Powers. Heads of State, Heads of Government and Foreign Ministers do not need to produce Full Powers for this, but all other persons do. When an IO is party to an exchange of notes, its representative must likewise have Full Powers, but there is no automatic exception for any senior officials, even the Head of the IO. The provisions concerning Full Powers for an IO representative are in Article 7(3) VCLT 1986.

There is an option to 'dispense with Full Powers' if both parties to the treaty agree to do so. Article 7(1)(b) VCLT 1969 provides for the exception to apply to a representative of a State if 'it appears from the practice of the States concerned or from other circumstances that their intention was to consider that person as representing the State for such purpose and to dispense with full powers'. Similarly, for a bilateral exchange of notes between a State and an IO, or two IOs, the parties may opt to dispense with Full Powers if:

21 See the section on 'Full Powers' in Chapter 5 at 188–92 which sets out the text of VCLT 1969 art 7 and VCLT 1986 art 7(3). See also Annex V, 'United Nations Model Instrument of Full Powers' at 437. See also Annex VI, 'Examples of Full Powers' at 438–39.

it appears from the circumstances that it was the intention of the States and international organizations concerned to consider that person as representing the organization for such purposes, in accordance with the rules of the organization, without having to produce full powers.[22]

Dispensing with Full Powers for an Exchange of Instruments

Although it is unusual to dispense with Full Powers for most kinds of treaties, it is fairly common for States to do so for a bilateral treaty with another State formed by an exchange of diplomatic notes. It should be emphasised that it is never an option that can be exercised by unilateral decision; this can only be chosen if it is acceptable to both sides. The two States concerned may agree to dispense with Full Powers for the purposes of this particular exchange. For example, they may agree that they will each accept a note signed by the other State's ambassador without Full Powers, or even, in the case of a very minor treaty, a note stamped by the embassy and signed by a lower ranking official. Any such agreement made for the purposes of a specific treaty exchange should be recorded in writing, usually by diplomatic note.

In the case of some pairs of States with many bilateral treaties, there may be a long-standing practice established between them of dispensing with Full Powers for all treaties formed by exchange of notes. Where the practice is well known to the Treaty Office on both sides, there may be no need to confirm it in writing on every occasion. However, the onus lies on the State that asserts that there is such a practice to demonstrate it, if the other side's officials are uncertain. It is not uncommon for officials to be mistaken about this. In particular, it should be noted that the power of an ambassador to act without Full Powers (set out in Article 2(b) VCLT 1969) is limited to *adopting the text of a treaty* which does not include signing it. It is also limited to *bilateral treaties with the host State*, and so does not include adopting the text of a treaty with any other State.

As IOs conclude far fewer bilateral treaties than States, there is much less established practice with regard to IOs dispensing with Full Powers for exchanges of notes. If an IO asserts that its representative is authorised to sign a treaty note without Full Powers, it should demonstrate this by showing that it has been expressly granted such authority in its internal rules or by a decision of an organ of the IO. In any case, if an IO concludes a treaty with a non-Member State by exchange of notes, that non-Member State is not obliged to follow a practice established within the IO. Either party may insist that Full Powers documents are exchanged. The same principles apply to a treaty consisting of an exchange of letters or any other form of instrument.

[22] VCLT 1986 art 7(3)(b).

Scenario: When only One Party Expects to Dispense with Full Powers for an Exchange of Notes

Scenario: you are an official in a foreign ministry or embassy and you are arranging an exchange of notes that will create a treaty. An official on the other side asserts that there is already an agreement to dispense with Full Powers, or an established bilateral practice of doing so, but you were not aware of this. You should check with the Treaty Office in your own foreign ministry that this is indeed the case. The official on the other side may be mistaken; for example, it is not uncommon for misunderstandings to arise about the scope of an Ambassador's authority to act without Full Powers.

If it is not the case, you could (with approval from the appropriate level of your authorities) agree with the other side to dispense with Full Powers for this exchange. You should make clear that this dispensation is for this exchange only, record it in writing, and send the record to the Treaty Office. Or you could insist upon Full Powers. Be aware that if you dispense with Full Powers, the other side's note may come with an illegible signature or initials scrawled across the stamp of the ministry, embassy or IO. It is common practice for routine (non-treaty) diplomatic notes to be expressed as from the institution only, with no named signatory, in which case you may have no idea of the identity or even level of the official who signed it. It is preferable, when the note is to form part of a treaty, to express it as from a named individual, such as a minister, ambassador or other senior official, and for that person to be the signatory. If you agree with the other side to dispense with Full Powers, it would be wise to clarify the form of address and the signatory on each side at the same time.

If the exchange is by letter, it will be clear who has signed it.

How to Deliver a Note or Letter which Forms Part of the Treaty

The initiating note and the reply note (that together will constitute the treaty) may be delivered to the other side by any person. The requirements of Article 7 VCLT 1969 regarding Full Powers concern the signature of the note, not its delivery. However, since delivery is not effective until the note is received by the other side, it is important to be sure that it has been received and to know the date of receipt. This is especially important when the date of receipt of the second note determines the date of entry into force of the agreement. Therefore, it is advisable for the note to be delivered in person by a responsible official and for that official to take away a written certificate of receipt from the other side. If the agreement is important, the ambassador may wish to arrange a meeting to hand it over in person to a minister or senior official on the other side. If feasible, both sides may arrange appointments on the same date so that the exchange occurs simultaneously, albeit in two locations.

However the deliveries are carried out, it is important that both sides confirm to each other in writing the date on which they were effective. If this is not done, confusion may arise later over the date of entry into force, especially after the diplomats who delivered the notes have moved on. In addition, if the agreement states that it is to enter into force x days after the exchange is complete, officials of each side will need to confer to ensure that they are of the same understanding regarding calculation of the date. It is all too easy for misunderstandings to occur about technicalities, such as whether to count the actual date of deposit as the first day of the x-day period.

Requirement for Notification of Completion of Domestic Procedures

Bilateral treaties, whether constituted by an exchange of instruments or a single document, may specify that the agreement shall enter into force after 'mutual notification of the completion of domestic procedures'.[23] This means that a further communication from each side to the other is needed. The notification is equivalent to depositing an instrument of ratification but is a less elaborate procedure. The rather general reference to 'domestic procedures' is used to accommodate any possibility on either side, ranging from a requirement for parliamentary approval, to a reporting or publishing requirement, or no procedure at all.

Below are examples of how this kind of consent to be bound and entry into force provisions may be used in a bilateral treaty.

> **Example 1**
> This Agreement shall come into force on the last date upon which the Parties notify each other in writing of the completion of their internal procedures necessary for the entry into force of this Agreement.[24]

> **Example 2**
> Each of the Contracting States shall notify the other, through diplomatic channels, of the completion of the procedures required by its law for the bringing into force of this Convention. The Convention shall enter into force on the date of the later of these notifications [. . .][25]

Examples 1 and 2 are essentially the same, except that example 2 specifies use of diplomatic channels, whereas example 1 requires only that notice shall be 'in writing'. For an example of this type of entry into force provision in an exchange of letters, see the final paragraph in Exchange of Letters amending the Agreement on a Working Holiday Scheme between the Government of New Zealand and the Government of the Argentine Republic, 2010.[26] It is

23 See the section on 'Understanding Modes for Expressing Consent to be Bound', especially on 'Any other Means if so Agreed' in Chapter 6 at 226–27.

24 Agreement between the Government of the United Kingdom of Great Britain and Northern Ireland and the Government of India for Co-operation in the Peaceful Uses of Nuclear Energy (done at London, 13 November 2015) UKTS 1 (2017) art XV(1).

25 Agreement between the Government of the United Kingdom of Great Britain and Northern Ireland and the Oriental Republic of Uruguay for the Avoidance of Double Taxation (done at Montevideo, 24 February 2016) UKTS 8 (2017) art 28(1).

26 See Annex IV.B, 'Example of Exchange of Letters B' at 429–36. See also the discussion in the section on 'Exchange of Letters' above at 259–261.

similar to Example 1 in that it only requires parties to 'inform each other' of the fulfilment of their internal procedures, but it was in fact carried out by exchange of notes (see below). Some treaties enter into force a specified time after the notifications:

> **Example 3**
> This Convention shall enter into force 30 days after [the] date on which the parties inform each other through an exchange of notes that their domestic constitutional procedures for the entry into force have been completed.[27]

> **Example 4**
> This Agreement shall enter into force on the first day of the second month after each Government has notified the other Government through the diplomatic channel of the completion of their respective procedures necessary for the entry into force of the Agreement.[28]

The purpose of requiring a further exchange, after signature or exchange of notes, is the same as ratification, that is, to allow each side the time it needs to carry out domestic procedures, of the kind detailed in Chapter 6. The procedures may be very different on each side; sometimes one side has no procedures at all, while the other side requires a very lengthy legislative process. Although this further exchange of communications need not be done by note verbale unless the treaty requires it, this is in fact the most common form used.

How to Write a Note to Confirm Completion of Domestic Procedures

The note should be prepared by the Treaty Office. It does not need to be long or elaborate. It should refer to the treaty by its full title (the title of the exchange of notes or single-instrument agreement) and its date(s) of signature. It should confirm that your State (or IO) has completed its domestic procedures and is therefore in a position to express its consent to be bound in accordance with the provisions of the exchange of notes (or Article x of the agreement). It is best to express this in words which match the words of the treaty provision. It is not necessary for the note to state what the domestic procedures were. The note must be dated. It does not need to be signed by a person with Full Powers (unless the treaty specifies this).

The side that sends the second note should do exactly the same. In addition, it is useful to refer to the first side's note in which they confirmed completion of their procedures. It is especially important to ensure that the second note is

[27] Agreement between the Republic of Finland and the Kingdom of Norway on the construction and maintenance of reindeer fences and on other measures to prevent reindeer from entering the territory of the other country (adopted 9 December 2014, entered into force 1 January 2017) UNTS Registration No. 54172 art 27.

[28] Agreement between the Government of the Kingdom of The Netherlands and the Government of the United Kingdom of Great Britain and Northern Ireland on the Reciprocal Holding of Stocks of Crude Oil and/or Petroleum Products (adopted 26 June 2006, entered into force 1 June 2008) 2579 UNTS 201 art 8. The final clauses of this Agreement are reproduced in Annex I, 'Example of Final Clauses in a Single-Instrument Bilateral Treaty' at 418–19.

dated – receipt of an undated note will cause endless confusion about the exact date of entry into force. If the delivery of the second note brings the agreement into force, it may be useful to state this in the note, in the way that the New Zealand note does in the example below.

Example of a note confirming completion of domestic procedures (which is the second of the two):

> The Ministry of Foreign Affairs and Trade presents its compliments to the Embassy of Argentina and has the honour to refer to the Exchange of Letters amending the Agreement of a Working Holiday Scheme between the Government of New Zealand and the Government of the Argentine Republic signed on 5 November and 18 December 2010 and the Argentine Ministry of Foreign Affairs note no 27/11 dated 24 January 2011 advising, that the Argentine Republic has completed its internal requirements for the modification of the Agreement to enter into effect.
>
> The Ministry of Foreign Affairs and Trade has the further honour to notify the Embassy of Argentina that New Zealand has completed its internal requirements for the modification of the Agreement to enter into effect. In accordance with the Exchange of Letters, the modifications to the Agreement will enter into force on the date of receipt of this Note.[29]

How to Deliver a Note to Notify Completion of Domestic Procedures

Unless the treaty specifies a particular mode of delivery, this notification may be delivered by any effective means, that is, effective to ensure that it arrives in the requisite form. If the agreement requires notification to be made by diplomatic note, this is normally stamped and signed or initialled, so the paper original must be delivered. However, if the agreement merely requires notification 'in writing', it may be acceptable to the other side to receive it electronically.

For the side which is second to notify, it is best to deliver a note in person, ideally on the date on which it was issued, and to schedule an appointment in the receiving ministry, embassy or office, for this purpose. The point is that the notification is only effective when it is received. If it is sent by post or courier, the sending party will have to wait to find out when it was received. If it is handed over at a meeting, both parties will know the date of receipt immediately. This way, there will be no confusion about the date that the treaty enters into force.

As with all exchanges of notes, the time gap between them can be variable. One State or IO may have completed its domestic procedures and sent notification, but if the other side has not, it could be some time before they are in a position to do so; or they may never do so at all. The side that has

[29] New Zealand Ministry of Foreign Affairs and Trade Note No. ARG/NZ/2/3/1 (27 July 2011) to the Embassy of Argentina notifying its completion of internal procedures to bring the Exchange of Letters amending the Agreement of a Working Holiday Scheme. A full copy of New Zealand Note is reproduced in Annex XIII, 'Example of a Note Confirming the Completion of Domestic Procedures' at 453.

already notified must have accurate records in its Treaty Office, so that when notification is received from the other party, it is immediately recorded, along with the record of the first note. This is vital to ensure that the entry into force date for the treaty is accurately determined.

Good communications between the two sides may make it possible for the exchange of notification notes to be co-ordinated and sent almost at the same time, but this may not always be feasible.

Procedures for Reservations and Declarations

When treaty officials prepare an instrument of ratification or accession, they need to know whether any reservations, interpretative declarations or any other sort of declarations are to be made. This should be considered by the relevant policy officials and legal advisers during the preparatory stages, and may have been debated during parliamentary or public consultations.[30] If a final decision has not yet been made, or if an intended reservation or declaration has not yet been drafted, treaty officials will need to prompt the necessary action, and ensure that any drafts have been checked by international law advisers.

Reservations

What Are Reservations?

A reservation is a condition which a State or IO decides to attach to its consent to be bound by a treaty. It says, in effect, that 'We agree to be bound by the obligations in this treaty, except for [X]'. The exception X may concern a specific provision of the treaty; for example, 'We reserve the right not to comply with the obligation in Article y, paragraph z'. It may concern the application of the whole treaty to a specific sector or item; for example, 'We reserve the right not to apply the treaty on fruit to blackberries'; or it may carve out an exception by reference to its own law; for example, 'We reserve the right to apply a specific national law' even if it diverges (in some minor respect) from the treaty requirements.

The legal definition of a reservation is as follows:

> 'Reservation' means a unilateral statement, however phrased or named, made by a State or an international organization when signing, ratifying, formally confirming, accepting, approving or acceding to a treaty, or by a State when making a notification of succession to a treaty, whereby the State or organization purports to exclude or to modify the legal effect of certain provisions of the treaty in their application to that State or to that international organization.[31]

30 See the section on 'Internal Consultations on the Requirements of the Treaty' in Chapter 6 at 228–230.

31 ILC, 'Guide to Practice on Reservations to Treaties 2011' reproduced in ILC, *Yearbook of the International Law Commission* (vol II, 2011 (Part 2)) (ILC Guide) para 1.1 http://legal.un.org

Not all purported reservations are permissible however. International law governs the permissibility and the effect of reservations. It is very important to apply these rules correctly, otherwise the reservation you make may not have the intended legal effect, and it may attract objections from other treaty parties.

How to Determine whether a Particular Reservation Is Permissible

First, it is necessary to read through the treaty that is to be ratified, to see if there are any provisions that mention reservations. If there are any, they are usually found near the end, in or close to the section which is often called 'final clauses'.[32] However, they may exceptionally be elsewhere in the treaty; for example, near the beginning in a section that defines scope and terms, or at the end of a particular part, or even in an annex.

Some treaties expressly prohibit all reservations. If so, that is the end of the matter. An example of such a provision is Article 24 UNFCCC, which reads: 'No reservations may be made to the Convention.'[33]

Some treaties prohibit all reservations except those that are expressly permitted. An example is Article 309 UNCLOS, which reads: 'No reservations or exceptions may be made to this Convention unless expressly permitted by other articles of this Convention.'[34] In such cases, the permitted reservations are limited to those that are expressly provided for, and those may be limited to particular obligations only.

Some treaties contain no provision on reservations. Other treaties contain a provision on reservations that is only about procedure. In such cases, the general rules on reservations in the international law of treaties apply. These are set out in the Articles 19–23 of the VCLT 1969 and VCLT 1986. In essence, a reservation may not be made if it is 'incompatible with the object and purpose of the treaty'.[35] These rules are difficult to apply. Reservations should therefore be drafted by, or in consultation with, international law advisers.

A useful resource containing guidance is the ILC Guide.[36] It is particularly useful on procedures; whereas the Conventions contain only one article on the procedure regarding reservations (Article 23), the ILC Guide contains a whole

/docs/?path=../ilc/texts/instruments/english/draft_articles/1_8_2011.pdf&lang=EF accessed 22 October 2018. This definition is a merger of the two definitions in VCLT 1969 and VCLT 1986, art 2(1)(d). The Commentary to the ILC Guide is included in: UNGA Res 66/10/Add.1 'Report of the International Law Commission' (2 April–3 June and 4 July–12 August 2011) (ILC Guide Commentary) http://legal.un.org/docs/?symbol=A/66/10/Add.1 accessed 22 October 2018.

32 See Annex II, 'Examples of Final Clauses in a Multilateral Treaty' at 420–23.

33 UNFCCC (adopted 9 May 1992, entered into force 21 March 1994) 1771 UNTS 107.

34 UNCLOS (adopted 10 December 1982, entered into force 16 November 1994) 1833 UNTS 396. Another example is the Council of Europe Convention on Action against Trafficking in Human Beings Beings (adopted 16 May 2005, entered into force 10 February 2008) CETS 197 art 45. The text of Article 45 is reproduced in Annex II, 'Examples of Final Clauses in a Multilateral Treaty' at 420–23.

35 VCLT 1969 art 19(3). 36 *ILC Guide* (n 31).

section on procedure.[37] If you have a specific question as to procedure, it is also worth referring to the relevant part of the commentaries to the ILC Guide.

At what Time Can a Reservation Be Made?

The general rule is that a reservation can be made when signing, ratifying, accepting, approving or acceding to a treaty; but if the treaty in question specifies otherwise, those terms prevail. If a reservation is made when signing a treaty subject to ratification (or any similar step), it must be confirmed on ratification (or further step), that is, when consent to be bound is expressed.[38] A reservation expressed at the time of adoption of a treaty, for example, in a statement at a conference, is not effective.

Reservations should not be made after ratification (or whatever procedure is used to express consent to be bound), unless the treaty expressly permits later reservations. If a late reservation is submitted, the other parties are entitled to reject it.

What Happens if a Reservation Is Submitted Late?

If, as a depositary, you receive a late reservation, you could simply reject it if that is the practice of your organisation or among those treaty parties. If however there is no clear practice, the safest course is to circulate it to the treaty parties, stating clearly that it is a late reservation. Your note should specify the date on which the reservation was received, and the date on which that party had previously expressed its consent to be bound by the treaty. It should invite any party which objects to the late reservation – whether the objection relates to the substance or to the lateness – to inform the depositary within a specified time (usually twelve months) of the date of the circular. If you receive no opposition within that time period, you may then notify the party that submitted the late reservation that it has been accepted. If you receive any objections – even only one – then you should inform the party concerned that its reservation has not been accepted. That State or IO will remain party to the treaty without the benefit of the rejected late reservation.[39]

What Format Should Be Used for Making a Reservation?

The only legal requirement as to format is that a reservation must be formulated in writing and communicated to the treaty parties and other States and IOs entitled to become parties.[40] Where there is a depositary, it should be sent to the depositary, who has an obligation to circulate it to all concerned.[41] If there is no depositary, the reservation must be sent individually to all those States and IOs concerned.

[37] ibid para 2 – *Procedure*. See also *ILC Guide Commentary* (n 31) 132–328.

[38] VCLT 1969 arts 19 and 23; VCLT 1986 arts 19 and 23.

[39] *ILC Guide* (n 31).

[40] VCLT 1969 art 23; VCLT 1986 art 23.

[41] This is one of the duties of a depositary set out in VCLT 1969 art 77(1)(e).

As a reservation is a condition attached to ratification (or consent to be bound), it is vital that it does not become separated from the consent instrument. To avoid this, the following steps are recommended:

- If the text of the reservation is short, it can be included in the instrument of ratification (or accession) itself. This has the advantage that it cannot be overlooked by the recipient, or become detached from the instrument at any later date. It also has the advantage that no extra signature is required; it will be authorised by the signature on the ratification instrument.
- If the reservation is long, it may not be practical to include it in the ratification instrument. It should then be sent in the form of a diplomatic note or other formal note to the depositary, which should accompany the instrument of ratification.
- If the reservation is placed in a separate note, it is essential that both documents clearly refer to each other. It should be made clear in the instrument of ratification that it is subject to a reservation which is contained in a note accompanying it. The note containing the reservation must then be delivered to the depositary at the same time as the instrument is deposited. The text of the note containing the reservation should set out the full title of the treaty, clearly and fully state the provisions which are being reserved, and state that the reservation (or reservations) are appended to the instrument of ratification.[42]

Signature of a Reservation Contained in a Separate Note

If the reservation is in a separate document from the ratification instrument, it must be signed by a person who has authority to sign the instrument of ratification. Normally, the instrument of ratification is signed by the Foreign Minister or Head of Government, or, occasionally, the Head of State (in the case of States) or the Head of the IO.[43] It makes practical sense to present the reservation note to the same person for signature together with the instrument, if at all possible. Both will then bear the same date of signature, and this also helps to make clear that both documents are linked.

However, if that is not practical, there are other options. Provided that the instrument of ratification expressly states that it is subject to a reservation that is contained in a note or letter from its diplomatic representative, the depositary may accept that note or letter with the ambassador or representative's signature. If the instrument does not refer to the reservation, the representative may only sign it if he or she already has General Full Powers (most do not). Otherwise it will be necessary to obtain Full Powers to sign it. The depositary might be prepared to accept a faxed or scanned copy of the signed Full Powers,

[42] See Annex XII, 'Examples of an Instrument of Reservation', 447–52.

[43] See the section on 'Producing an Instrument of Ratification, Acceptance, Approval or Accession' above at 251–52.

pending receipt of the original. These options might be useful in circumstances where a State urgently needs to deposit its ratification within a tight timeframe. The ratification instrument normally has to be made in a Treaty Office and physically sent (bound into its hard cover). If, at the time of signing the instrument, the wording of the reservation is not yet final, the instrument can be dispatched by courier or bag to the embassy or representative office. When the reservation text is ready, it can be sent electronically to the ambassador (representative) with a request to print, sign and deposit it, together with the ratification instrument.

An example of a reservation is Japan's reservation to the Convention on the Rights of the Child, 1989:[44]

> In applying paragraph (c) of article 37 of the Convention on the Rights of the Child, Japan reserves the right not to be bound by the provision in its second sentence, that is, 'every child deprived of liberty shall be separated from adults unless it is considered in the child's best interest not to do so', considering the fact that in Japan as regards persons deprived of liberty, those who are below twenty years of age are to be generally separated from those who are of twenty years of age and over under its national law.[45]

This is a good example of a reservation that is clear in scope, specifies very precisely the treaty provision that is being reserved, and states the reason succinctly.

Responding to Other Parties' Reservations

Parties are entitled to object to any reservations made by another party, or respond in other ways. The legal effects of reservations, and of other parties' objections and other responses to them, is a complex area of the law of treaties (even for international law experts). The legal framework is set out in Articles 20–23 VCLT 1969 and VCLT 1986. Section 2.8 of the ILC Guide provides useful guidance.

Treaty Office officials need to be aware, above all else, of the legal deadline for objecting to reservations made by other States or IO parties to a treaty: twelve months after receiving notification of the reservation or the date of its own ratification (or accession, etc.), whichever is the later.[46] That means that within a year of ratifying a treaty, it is necessary to review all existing reservations and make any objections deemed necessary.

It makes sense to do this, if possible, while preparing for ratification, and to submit any objections to the depositary along with the instrument of ratification. This is desirable practice because (a) it will be easier to reach agreement at

[44] Convention on the Rights of the Child (adopted 20 November 1989, entered into force 2 September 1990) 1577 UNTS 3.

[45] UNTC, 'Convention on the Rights of the Child – Declarations and Reservations' (status as at 26 October 2018) United Nations Treaty Series Online https://treaties.un.org/ (Use search function).

[46] VCLT 1969 art 20(5) and VCLT 1986 art 20(5). See also *ILC Guide* (n 31) paras 2.6.12–13.

the domestic level on this while attention is focused on the ratification, than to raise it a few months later as a separate issue; and (b) studying reservations by other parties may help to inform domestic consideration of your own. Of course, if ratification has to be prepared within a tight timeframe, the question of objecting to other parties' reservations can be put to one side, but the Treaty Office should then set up reminders to ensure that the review is completed within the twelve-month deadline.

Declarations

Interpretative Declarations

At the time of expressing consent to be bound, it is important to consider whether any interpretative declaration should be made. An interpretative declaration (also sometimes called an 'interpretative statement' or 'declaration of understanding') is a statement that a party chooses to make to all other parties, setting out its interpretation of a particular provision of a treaty, or a particular matter governed by the treaty. It is provided for information, not as a condition of consenting to be bound. It is commonly done where that State (or IO) considers that a specific provision is ambiguous, and it wishes to assert that a particular interpretation is the correct one.

There is no definition of an interpretative declaration in the VCLT 1969, nor in the VCLT 1986, but international practice in relation to them is well established. The ILC Guide offers this definition:

> 'Interpretative declaration' means a unilateral statement, however phrased or named, made by a State or an international organization, whereby that State or that organization purports to specify or clarify the meaning or scope of a treaty or of certain of its provisions.[47]

An interpretative declaration differs from a reservation in that consent to be bound is not conditional on it. It is an attempt to influence, which may or may not succeed. If other parties express agreement, and/or if no party expresses disagreement within twelve months, it will strengthen the evidence in favour of that interpretation. But if it turns out that other parties do not agree with it, and/or if the matter is finally decided by a court or tribunal which does not agree with it, the declaration may be without any effect. The party making it has to accept that risk.

The reason this definition contains the phrase 'however phrased or named' is that States sometimes submit a text entitled 'interpretative declaration', even though it is expressed as a limitation on the treaty obligations it is accepting. This makes it in substance a reservation. The definition of 'reservation' also contains this phrase, indicating that it is the content that matters, not the label. If the treaty concerned prohibits reservations, a reservation disguised as an

[47] *ILC Guide* (n 31), para 1.2.

interpretative statement will not be effective. It is therefore just as essential to consult international lawyers on the drafting of an interpretative statement as for a reservation.

Making an interpretative declaration is always optional, and should be done sparingly. There are several factors that need to be weighed up in deciding whether it is on balance safer to do it or not, including: how legally credible is our preferred interpretation? How great is the risk of an adverse interpretation? Have any other parties expressed any views? If we put our view publicly on the table, might we raise doubt where there were none before, or risk provoking opposing statements? If our view is not shared by others, can we live with an adverse interpretation? (If the answer to that is 'No', you should consider whether a reservation is permissible, and if not whether becoming party to this treaty is the right thing to do.) These are mixed legal and policy judgements.

What Format Should Be Used for Making an Interpretative Declaration?

The procedure and form for making an interpretative declaration is the same as for reservations, except that it may be done at any time (unless the treaty concerned specifies otherwise, which is unusual).[48]

Examples of interpretative declarations can be seen in the declarations made by Argentina and the UK, respectively, under the Convention on the Rights of the Child:[49]

> Declaration of Argentina:
>
> Concerning article 1 of the Convention, the Argentine Republic declares that the article must be interpreted to the effect that a child means every human being from the moment of conception up to the age of eighteen.
>
> Declaration of the United Kingdom:
>
> The United Kingdom interprets the Convention as applicable only following a live birth.

Other Kinds of Declarations: Mandatory and Optional

Some treaties *require* parties to make a certain type of declaration at the time of consenting to be bound; for example, to express a choice between specified options or to provide required information, such as the name and address of a national contact point, or details of implementing legislation. When such a requirement is obligatory, the depositary is likely to, and should, decline to accept an instrument of ratification or accession unless it is accompanied by the requisite declaration.

An example of an obligatory declaration is Article 3(2) of the Optional Protocol to the Convention on the Rights of the Child on the Involvement of Children in Armed Conflict, 2000, which provides:

[48] *ILC Guide* (n 31) para 2.4. See also Annex XI, 'United Nations Model Instrument of Reservation/Declaration', 446.

[49] *UNTC* (n 45).

> Each State Party shall deposit a binding declaration upon ratification of or accession to this Protocol that sets forth the minimum age at which it will permit voluntary recruitment into its national armed forces and a description of the safeguards that it has adopted to ensure that such recruitment is not forced or coerced.[50]

Some treaties specify options that *may* be chosen by declaration on ratification or accession. For example, there may be a provision that permits parties to opt out of or in to certain substantive obligations, or certain settlement of dispute mechanisms. In some cases, it may be a genuine option which parties are free to exercise or not, at any time. In other cases, there may be an option with a specified default.

An example of a treaty which provides for an optional declaration with a specified default is Article 287 on Choice of Procedure of the UNCLOS, which provides:

> 1. When signing, ratifying or acceding to this Convention or at any time thereafter, a State shall be free to choose, by means of a written declaration, one or more of the following means for the settlement of disputes concerning the interpretation or application of this Convention:
>   (a) the International Tribunal for the Law of the Sea established in accordance with Annex VI;
>   (b) the International Court of Justice;
>   (c) an arbitral tribunal constituted in accordance with Annex VII;
>   (d) a special arbitral tribunal constituted in accordance with Annex VIII for one or more of the categories of disputes specified therein
>
> . . .
>
> 3. A State Party, which is a party to a dispute not covered by a declaration in force, shall be deemed to have accepted arbitration in accordance with Annex VII.

Role of the Treaty Office

The Treaty Office has an important role to play; during preparation for 'ratification, etc.', treaty officials should check the treaty carefully for any provisions on declarations. They are usually in the final clauses section near the end of the treaty, but not always; for example, Article 287 UNCLOS is in Part XV, Settlement of Disputes. It is especially important to note any

[50] Optional Protocol to the Convention on the Rights of the Child on the Involvement of Children in Armed Conflict (adopted 25 May 2000, entered into force 12 February 2002) 2173 UNTS 222. The declarations made by the parties (168 parties as at 26 October 2018) may be viewed on UNTC, Multilateral Treaties Deposited with the Secretary-General, Status of Treaties, 'Chapter IV Human Rights – 11b Optional Protocol to the Convention on the Rights of the Child on the Involvement of Children in Armed Conflict' (status as at 26 October 2018) https://treaties.un.org accessed 26 October 2018.

provision which makes it mandatory to make a declaration at the time of becoming party, or if failure to do so will result in a mandatory default. The Treaty Office should draw this to the attention of policy and legal officials concerned, and make sure that the declaration is ready to be deposited with the instrument. It may also be helpful to provide the officials concerned with information about any declarations that have already been deposited by other parties to the treaty.

Responding to other Parties' Declarations

Each party is entitled to respond to other parties' interpretative declarations. The response may express agreement or disagreement with the interpretation, or express an alternative interpretation. It may also express the view that the declaration is in substance a reservation, and in that case it may express its objection to it on the basis of its view that it is a reservation.[51] There is no deadline for responding to a declaration; it may be done at any time.[52] Nonetheless, it makes sense, if possible, to review existing parties' declarations during the preparatory work to ratification (or accession, etc.), and to make any response deemed necessary at the same time as ratifying.

The same procedures apply as for making reservations and interpretative declarations, with respect to form, signature and depositing.

Duties of the Depositary

Check that the Instrument Is in Order

Whenever the depositary receives a treaty instrument, it is expected to check that it is in order. This fundamental duty is set out in Article 77(1)(d) VCLT 1969, and is assumed to be part of the depositary's functions for any treaty, whether or not stated in that treaty explicitly. Article 77(1)(d) sets out this duty as follows:

> Examining whether the signature or any instrument, notification or communication relating to the treaty is in due or proper form and, if need be, bringing the matter to the attention of the State in question;

It is important to bear in mind the key points to be verified, complied with or performed for each stage of the management of treaties. When the depositary receives an instrument of ratification, accession, approval or acceptance, or any equivalent act such as a notification of the completion of domestic procedures, it must ascertain, in particular whether:

- the submitting State or IO is entitled to ratify (or accede to, etc.) the treaty in question;[53]

[51] See *ILC Guide* (n 31) para 2.9. [52] See ibid para 2.9.4.

[53] See the section on 'Eligibility to Join a Treaty' in Chapter 6 at 210–20.

- the instrument of ratification (or accession, etc.) contains the mandatory elements: full title of treaty, explicit statement of the government's ratification/accession, date of signature of the treaty (in the case of a ratification);[54]
- the instrument is signed by a person who is authorised to sign;[55]
- any mandatory declarations are made;[56]
- any reservations accompanying it are authorised;[57]
- the instrument is in one of the official languages of the treaty, or, if not, is accompanied by a translation.[58]

What Should the Depositary Do if the Instrument Is Not in Order?

The depositary should contact the State or IO concerned immediately to draw their attention to the problem. If possible, alert a senior official in the embassy or representative office personally to explain the problem. Follow this up with a note verbale. In most cases, the State or IO concerned will accept the advice and take the necessary corrective action. In some cases, a formal clarification might suffice, but in others it will be necessary for the depositing State or IO to prepare a new instrument, have it signed afresh, and deposit it again. Clearly, this will not be welcome, as it will result in embarrassment (not least when explaining to the minister why he or she is being asked to sign the same instrument again) and a delay in the date of ratification. This situation can always be avoided if the depositing State or IO sends their instrument in draft to the Depositary for checking in advance.

If the depositing State or IO is unwilling to accept the depositary's advice, the depositary should refer the matter to the treaty parties for their guidance. This circular should set out the information concerning the instrument received, attach a copy, and explain the depositary's concern as to why it is not in order. With the agreement of the State or IO concerned, its note or letter stating its response may also be circulated. The depositary should request guidance from the treaty parties as to whether this instrument should be accepted.

Duties of the Depositary on Receipt of an Instrument of 'Ratification etc.'

It is part of the core responsibilities of the depositary to acknowledge receipt of the instrument as soon as possible, informing the State or IO concerned of the date of deposit. If the treaty is already in force internationally, the notification should also inform the depositing State or IO of the date of entry into force of the treaty for it.[59]

54 See the section on 'Producing an Instrument of Ratification, Acceptance, Approval or Accession' above at 251–52.
55 ibid.
56 See the section on 'Other Kinds of Declarations: Mandatory and Optional' above at 274–75.
57 See the section on 'Procedures for Reservations and Declarations' above at 268–76.
58 See the section on 'Authentic Languages' in Chapter 5 at 171–72.
59 VCLT 1969 art 77. Article 77 applies unless the treaty in question provides otherwise.

The depositary should also inform all other parties, and those entitled to become parties, of the deposit of each new instrument of 'ratification etc.'.

When the number of ratifications reaches that required to bring the treaty into force, the depositary should promptly inform all Contracting Parties, and those entitled to become parties, of the date of entry into force.

Examples of Good Depositary Practices Regarding Notification of Ratification and Entry into Force (States)

The following is an example of depositary notification of ratification and entry into force, issued to a State Party. The notification concerns the Convention on the Conservation and Management of High Seas Fishery Resources in the South Pacific Ocean, 2009[60] and was issued by New Zealand acting as Depositary:

> Government of New Zealand acting as Depositary for the Convention on the Conservation and Management of High Seas Fishery Resources in the South Pacific Ocean 2009, Note to Chile dated 25 July 2012.[61]

This Note informs Chile of the effective date of deposit of its instrument; and the date of entry into force of the treaty for all parties, as it was triggered by the deposit of the Chilean instrument.

Another example of a depositary notification of ratification and entry into force is given here. This Note concerns the Trans-Pacific Strategic Economic Partnership, 2005[62] issued by New Zealand as Depositary:

> Government of New Zealand acting as Depositary for the Trans-Pacific Strategic Economic Partnership 2005, Note to Singapore dated 28 April 2006.[63]

This Note advised Singapore of the effective date of deposit of its instrument of ratification. It also informed Singapore of the date of entry into force of the Agreement for Singapore.

It is noteworthy that in both of these examples, the depositary notice was sent out to the ratifying State on the same day as its instrument of ratification was received. Moreover, the Note to Chile stated that the other Contracting

[60] Convention on the Conservation and Management of High Seas Fishery Resources in the South Pacific Ocean (done at Auckland, 14 November 2009, entered into force 25 July 2012) 2899 UNTS Registration No. 50553.

[61] New Zealand Ministry of Foreign Affairs and Trade, 'Depositary Notification on the Entry into Force of the Convention on the Conservation and Management of High Seas Fishery Resources in the South Pacific Ocean to the Republic of Chile' (signed 25 July 2002) LGL/FISH/SPFO. The text is reproduced in Annex XIV.A. 'Depositary Notification to a State of the Date of its Ratification and Entry into Force of the Treaty' at 454.

[62] Trans-Pacific Strategic Economic Partnership (adopted 18 July 2005, entered into force 1 May 2006) 2592 UNTS 225.

[63] New Zealand Ministry of Foreign Affairs and Trade, 'Depositary Notification on the Entry into Force of the Trans-Pacific Strategic Economic Partnership to Singapore' (dated 28 April 2006), LGL/BTE/FTA/TRI. The full text of the notification is reproduced in Annex XIV.B. 'Depositary Notification to a State of the Date of its Ratification of the Treaty' at 455–56.

Parties had been duly notified.[64] This illustrates best depositary practice; no delay at all between receiving an instrument and notifying all concerned.

It is also worth noting that New Zealand, in its notice to Singapore, advised that 'in its capacity as Depositary for the Agreement, it received an Instrument of Ratification to the Agreement from the Government of New Zealand on 20 April 2006'.[65] This illustrates best practice where a government serves as depositary, in that it acts in two distinct capacities, ensuring that as depositary it maintains neutrality whereas in its national capacity it is free to act in its national interest.

Examples of Good Depositary Practices Regarding Notification of Ratification and Entry into Force (IOs)

The duties of an IO when receiving a treaty document is similar to that of States that serve as a depository. This is illustrated by the following summary of the practice of the CoE.

The CoE Treaty Office processes each treaty act as soon as it is received. When an instrument of ratification (or accession, etc.) is received, the status list on the website is updated to show the date of the deposit of the instrument, so that information is available to the public immediately (usually the same day). The Treaty Office sends out an official notification to the depositing State, to acknowledge the date of deposit, the date of entry into force (if known) and any reservations or declarations. Each notification is copied to all Member States and other parties to the convention, and posted on the website in a secured and printable pdf format. These are posted by the end of the week of receipt, and a weekly email is sent to Member States and other States concerned, listing the treaty acts deposited that week and containing a link to the pdf copy of each notification. Each new deposit is highlighted in a 'news' section on the home page of the Treaty Office website, so that the public can easily identify changes.[66]

At the end of each month, the Treaty Office sends a paper note verbale to the Permanent Representatives of all Member States listing all actions that month. When a treaty already in force is ratified or acceded to, the Treaty Office also sends a paper letter to the UN with paper copies of the notification, in the two official languages of the CoE (English and French) and in two copies each.

An example of a CoE Depositary notification of ratification and entry into force is the following: Council of Europe Notification of Ratification by the

[64] *New Zealand Ministry of Foreign Affairs* (n 61).

[65] *New Zealand Ministry of Foreign Affairs* (n 63).

[66] The home page of the Treaty Office website is: Treaty Office 'Treaty Office' (Council of Europe) www.coe.int/en/web/conventions/home accessed 24 June 2017. As an example of the promptness of updating, when this page was viewed on 24 June 2017, the highlighted recent treaty actions were dated 13, 19, 20 and 21 June 2017. The complete list of CoE treaties showing the up-to-date status of each one, updated daily, is at: www.coe.int/en/web/conventions/full-list accessed 24 June 2017.

Republic of Moldova to the 'Council of Europe Convention against Trafficking in Human Organs, 2015':

Date of Ratification: 21 June 2017
Date of Notification: 23 June 2017 (to Republic of Moldova, copied to all member states and states parties concerned in the treaty)
Date of posting of notification on Council of Europe website: 23 June 2017.[67]

Difficult Issues for Depositaries: When the Signatory Is No Longer in Office

It sometimes happens that between the signing of the instrument of ratification (or accession) and the date of its receipt in the Treaty Office, the person who signed it dies, resigns, is dismissed from office, or the whole government changes following an election or a coup. What should the Treaty Office do?

The instrument is valid provided that it was signed by a person who was duly authorised to sign it on the date they did so. Whatever happens to that person after their signature does not invalidate the instrument. The Treaty Office should check that the person who signed it was the holder of one of the three offices (Head of State, Head of Government or Foreign Minister) on the date of signature. If there is doubt, it is wise to check the facts and the signature as far as possible with geographical experts or published information.

An example of this kind of problem, and the correct depositary response, is the ratification by France of the European Convention on Human Rights. The sequence of events was as follows: on 8 March 1974 Georges Pompidou, President of the French Republic, signed the instrument of ratification. On 2 April 1974 President Pompidou died. On 3 May 1974 the instrument was deposited at the CoE. It was accepted.

Action Necessary between Ratification and Entry into Force

Just because an instrument of ratification or accession has been deposited or exchanged does not necessarily mean that the treaty concerned is in force for that State or IO. Many multilateral treaties provide that the treaty will enter into force only after a specified number of States have deposited their instrument of ratification or accession. This could take months or years. Even a bilateral treaty may take years to enter into force for a State that has ratified it, if the other side's ratification is delayed.

Some treaties never enter into force despite a number of States ratifying or acceding to it. For example, the VCLT 1986 has not yet entered into force,

[67] Council of Europe Convention against Trafficking in Human Organs 2015 (adopted 25 March 2015, entered into force 1 March 2018) UNTS Registration No. 68363, CETS 216. Treaty Office, 'Notification of Ratification – Moldova: Council of Europe Convention against Trafficking in Human Organs' JJ8432C Tr./216-8 (Council of Europe, 23 June 2017) https://wcd.coe.int/com.instranet.InstraServlet?command=com.instranet.CmdBlobGet&InstranetImage=2973073&Sec Mode=1&DocId=2404200&Usage=2 accessed 23 June 2017.

despite having forty-three parties. Article 85 of the Convention requires thirty-five ratifications or accessions by States to bring it into force; instruments deposited by IOs are not counted for this purpose. Over thirty years on, it is still four States short of the threshold, with entry into force in the near future looking unlikely, although not impossible.[68] It can also happen that a bilateral treaty never enters into force, because one or both parties change their mind, it is overtaken by events or it is simply forgotten.

It is important for any Treaty Office to monitor multilateral treaties that its State or IO has ratified or acceded to but which have not yet entered into force. Another ratification may suddenly bring a treaty into force for its State or IO. The depositary of the treaty concerned will – or certainly should – notify all States who have ratified or acceded that the treaty is now in force for their State or IO, and this will be the definitive notification. But it is worthwhile carefully monitoring the websites of depositaries, to be aware of when a treaty is nearing the threshold for entry into force. Failure to monitor the progress of a treaty towards entry into force could result in a Treaty Office being taken by surprise by a notification that it has already happened. Take for example the case mentioned above of the VCLT 1986, which does not appear likely to enter into force any time soon. Yet, if four States happen to ratify or accede in a short space of time, or do so as a result of co-ordinated action, a notice from the Depositary announcing that it entered into force last week (or last month, if the Depositary is less efficient) could suddenly arrive. For some treaties and some parties, this could be a problem, if implementing legislation or other measures need to be brought into force domestically at the same time as the treaty enters into force (see below). Therefore, if treaty officials notice that a treaty is close to receiving the number of ratifications necessary to bring it into force, it is wise to alert those in their government or IO who are responsible for its implementation.

The Treaty Office should also keep the status of a bilateral treaty under regular review after ratifying or notifying the other party that it has completed its necessary domestic procedures, where no reply has yet been received. If the period without a response becomes protracted, for example more than a year, it may be necessary to send a further note politely enquiring about the position.

Action on the Domestic Plane: Publication of the Treaty

Most States and IOs have a legislative or constitutional requirement to publish a treaty after it has entered into force. Sometimes this will be accomplished by publishing the treaty text in an official Treaty Series, as for example, in New Zealand, the UK and Australia; or in an official gazette, as for example in Brunei, Cambodia, Indonesia, Laos, the Philippines and Vietnam; or in other States, such as Myanmar, the treaty is published as

68 See the section on 'Becoming Party to a Treaty: Why It Does not Always Happen' in Chapter 6 at 206–08.

part of the implementing legislation. In some States, such as the Netherlands, the official publication of the treaty gives it the force of law at the domestic level.

In some States, such as the UK, a treaty which is signed subject to ratification has to be published twice; it is published and laid before Parliament for scrutiny before ratification, along with an EM,[69] and when it enters into force for the UK, it is published again and presented to Parliament for information. This latter publication, in what is known as the Treaty Series, specifies the date the treaty entered into force for the UK.[70] It also includes the text of any reservations, declarations or objections made by the UK at the time of ratification. It used to be the practice to include other useful information such as a status list of States (and any IOs) that have signed or ratified the treaty up to the date of publication and the full texts of any reservations, declarations or objections that have been deposited with the depositary (not only by the UK). These documents can therefore be very useful as a research tool, but of course only the depositary can provide the definitive versions.[71]

Treaties are often published electronically as a part of an online gazette or database.[72] This has the advantage of making the treaty text easier to locate for those searching online, and therefore more accessible. But again treaty officials will need to be certain that the text that is being published online is absolutely accurate and cannot easily be changed or amended, so publication in a pdf format is highly recommended.

If the treaty is published both in print and online, it is important to specify which is the authoritative version in case of any discrepancy.[73] This is especially the case if the online publication is not a scan of the printed one.

[69] See for example, Paris Agreement (adopted 12 December 2015, entered into force 4 November 2016) UNTS Registration No. 54113 55 ILM 740 (published in the UK prior to ratification as Miscellaneous Series No. 7 (2016)), together with FCO, 'Explanatory Memorandum for the Paris Agreement', (published 7 October 2016) Command Paper No. 9338 https://assets.publishing.service.gov.uk/government/uploads/system/uploads/attachment_data/file/558185/EM_Paris_Ag.pdf accessed 22 October 2018.

[70] See for example, Paris Agreement ibid, published after entry into force for the UK as UK Treaty Series No. 4 (2017).

[71] See FCO, 'Guidance to the Work of the Foreign and Commonwealth Office (FCO) Treaty Section' (2 July 2013), 'Publication of Treaties' www.gov.uk/guidance/uk-treaties#publication-of-treaties accessed 25 September 2018.

[72] For an example of an official publication of a treaty, see Annex XVI, 'Example of an Official Publication of a Treaty', 458–59.

[73] For example, the CoE Treaty Office website displays the following disclaimer:

> Please note that it can't be guaranteed that a document available on-line exactly reproduces an officially adopted text. Only the treaties published by the Secretary General of the Council of Europe, each in a separate booklet of the 'Council of Europe Treaty Series' (CETS), are deemed authentic.

Treaty Office, 'Important legal notice – Disclaimer' (CoE, 2018) www.coe.int/en/web/conventions/disclaimer accessed 29 October 2018.

Co-Ordinating Entry into Force of the Treaty and Implementing Legislation

As soon as the Treaty Office is aware of the date that the treaty will enter into force, or has entered into force, it should actively notify all those across government (or the IO), and any other public authorities that are responsible for implementation. It may also be advisable to inform any directly affected stakeholders or representative organisations in the private sector. Those authorities then need to ensure that any implementing legislation is brought into force, and any new administrative arrangements have been activated.

For some treaties, implementing legislation may already be in force before the treaty. This may be the case, for example, where the treaty sets standards in a field in which that State is already leading. However, in other contexts, a State may wish to implement the treaty obligations only on a reciprocal basis with other parties. It may then enact implementing legislation but postpone bringing it into force until the date of entry into force of the treaty. In such cases, advance notice of the date of entry into force of the treaty is needed, in order to synchronise the entry into force of the legislation. Ensuring that this information is obtained and provided to those who need it is one of the most critical roles of the Treaty Office.

Registering the Treaty at the UN

Once a treaty has entered into force, it should be registered with the UN Secretariat. Article 102 of the UN Charter requires that:

> Every treaty and every international agreement entered into by any Member of the United Nations after the present Charter comes into force shall as soon as possible be registered with the Secretariat and published by it.

But this is not the only requirement to register. Article 80 VCLT 1969 also says that:

> treaties shall, after their entry into force, be transmitted to the Secretariat of the United Nations for registration or filing and recording, as the case may be, and for publication.

So there is a double requirement to register treaties when they have entered into force.[74]

However, just registering an international instrument does not automatically confer the status of a treaty onto it. The UN Secretariat will examine any instrument that is submitted to it for registration to see if that instrument is capable of being registered. If it is patently clear on its face that the document is not a treaty, the UN will reject the registration. However, the UN Secretariat generally take the (diplomatic) approach that they respect the view of the party submitting the instrument so that, in so far as that party is concerned, the

[74] There is no distinction in international law between 'treaty' and 'international agreement' as referred to in art 102. Note that in the VCLT 1969, only one term is used: 'treaty'.

instrument is a treaty or an international agreement within the meaning of Article 102. In other words, if the instrument appears on its face to be a treaty, and to qualify for registration, the UN will register it without passing any authoritative judgement on its status. So if a non-binding instrument is submitted and registered, it is still non-binding.

Requirements for Registration with the UN Secretariat

In order to be accepted for registration, a treaty where at least one party is a member of the UN must have entered into force for at least two parties. When being submitted for registration, the copies of the treaty – which must be submitted in all its authentic languages – must be accompanied by a certifying statement.[75]

This statement must certify that the attached text is a 'true and complete copy' of the treaty and that it includes all reservations made by parties thereto. The certifying statement must include:

- the title of the treaty;
- the place and date of conclusion;
- the names of the parties;
- the date and method of entry into force for each party; and
- the authentic languages in which the treaty was drawn up.

When reviewing the certifying statement, the UN Treaty Office will check that all the enclosures such as protocols, exchanges of notes, authentic texts, annexes and so on that are mentioned in the text of the treaty as forming a part of it are attached to the copy sent for registration. If any enclosures are omitted, the Secretariat will bring the omission to the attention of the registering party and defer action on registration until the material is complete.

Once the treaty has been accepted for registration by the Secretariat, a certificate of registration is sent out to the registering party confirming the date of registration. Each month the Secretariat publishes a statement of the treaties that have been registered during the preceding month. This statement does not contain the texts of treaties, although it does provide some information about them. After registration, the text of a treaty is published in the UN Treaty Series and is available online on the UN Treaty Database. This can take some time however – there is no obligation on a State to register a treaty within any given time frame, and once registered with the UN it can take some time before the treaty appears on their website.

It is not just the treaty itself and its accompanying documents that should be registered. All subsequent actions effecting a change in the parties to, or the terms, scope or application of, a treaty previously registered should also be registered with the Secretariat. So for example such actions may involve ratifications, accessions,

[75] See Annex XV, 'United Nations Model Certifying Statement for Registration or Filing and Recording' at 457.

extensions to territories, or denunciations. For bilateral treaties, it would usually be the party responsible for the subsequent action that registers it, but the other party to the agreement can also do this. For a multilateral treaty, the depositary usually registers such actions. Where a new instrument modifies the scope or application of a parent agreement, this instrument must also be registered with the Secretariat. However in order for such an instrument to be registered, the original treaty to which it relates must first have been registered.

Who Should Register a Treaty?

Any Member State of the UN may register a treaty. If it is a multilateral treaty with a depositary, it is the function of the depositary State or organisation to register the treaty.[76] For bilateral treaties, either party may register the treaty – if they wish, both may register but registration only needs to be undertaken by one State to be effective. Registering bilateral treaties with the UN is one of the core functions of the Treaty Office of any government. As soon as the treaty enters into force, the Treaty Office should put the registration in motion, or liaise with the Treaty Office of the other State to agree which of them will do it.

What Are the Effects of Registering or not Registering?

The act of registration will not confer the status of 'treaty' on a document, if it is not a treaty. It does, however, provide evidence that the party which registered it considers it to be a treaty, and that it took that view at the outset. This may be useful if there is later any doubt about whether it is a treaty or a non-binding instrument. That is in itself a good reason for States always to undertake the registration of their bilateral treaties.

What might the effect of not registering a treaty be? The main effect of failing to register may only surface if and when a dispute about the treaty arises. Article 102 of the UN Charter does not specify an obligation on any particular party to register, nor does it impose any immediate sanction for failure to register. But Article 102 does go on to say, in the second paragraph, that:

> No party to any such treaty or international agreement which has not been registered in accordance with the provisions of paragraph 1 of this Article may invoke that treaty or agreement before any organ of the United Nations.

The ICJ has not as yet ever refused to consider an unregistered treaty in the few cases where one was invoked; but there is no guarantee that this provision might not be invoked in the future. A further disadvantage of not registering a treaty might be that if the other party argues later that it was not intended to be binding, it might be difficult to counter that argument if your government did not register it either.

[76] VCLT 1969 art 77(1)(g) and VCLT 1986 art 78(1)(g).

Role of the Treaty Office of each Party After Entry into Force of the Treaty

The role of the Treaty Office of each party does not end as soon as the treaty has entered into force for its State or IO. If it is a multilateral treaty, there will be numerous communications about the treaty from the depositary and possibly from other States too. These may be sent as paper notifications and/or circulated in electronic form or as amendments to web pages. Notifications may relate to other States (and IOs) becoming parties to the treaty and submitting declarations, reservations, objections to reservations and responses, and counter-responses to objections. There is also a time limit to consider, since Article 20(5) VCLT 1969 provides that, except if the treaty provides otherwise, a reservation is considered to be accepted by a State if it has not objected within twelve months of the date it was notified of the reservation, or by the date it expressed its consent to be bound by the treaty, whichever is the later. It may be important to object to another party's reservation if it is legally impermissible, or for other reasons.[77] Each party that has made a reservation or declaration needs to keep monitoring other parties' responses to it, especially during the first twelve months.

It is therefore vitally important that treaty officials regularly monitor all notifications received from the depositary, and other sources such as depositary web pages, to see if they contain a declaration, reservation or objection, since there will only be twelve months in which to respond. Treaty officials should consider this in conjunction with advice from policy and legal colleagues dealing with the subject concerned, who will make the final decision on whether to object to a declaration, reservation or objection.

There is also a wider need to be aware of events taking place across the world. New States may evolve, and other States and IOs may need to decide how to react. Treaty officials need to be aware of any controversy surrounding the status of such entities and not take action in relation to them without first seeking advice from policy and legal colleagues. A new State may wish to succeed to the treaties, or some of the treaties, to which the former State was a party, and the Treaty Office may be the first in their government to become aware of it. Treaty officials should always ensure that all other relevant officials in their administration are fully informed of such developments and that advice is sought before acting, since their State may wish to accept such succession or object to it.

Role of the Depositary after Entry into Force of the Treaty

Notifying all concerned of the entry into force of a treaty is one of the most important duties of any depositary. This duty is defined in the Article 77(1)(f) VCLT 1969 as:

[77] See the section on 'How to Determine whether a Particular Reservation is Permissible' above at 269–70. See also the section on 'Responding to other Parties' Reservations' above at 272–73.

Informing the States entitled to become parties to the treaty when the number of signatures or of instruments of ratification, acceptance, approval or accession required for the entry into force of the treaty has been received or deposited;

Chapter 8 covers a range of further issues that may require continuing engagement during the life of a treaty.

Top Tips for States or IOs Becoming Party to a Treaty

Based on the discussions in this chapter, Box 7.2 summarises key points that States and IOs may consider in becoming party to a treaty.

Box 7.2 Top tips for States or IOs becoming party to a treaty

- Engage legal advisers in the process right from the start, including deliberations on whether and how to join the treaty; ensure legal expertise covers international law of treaties and constitutional law (national law or the internal law of the IO).
- Treaty Office – issue standing guidance to all officials across government or IO on how your office wishes to receive instructions to prepare an instrument of ratification (or accession etc.): specify the information and assurances it must contain and the level of seniority at which it must be signed off.
- Develop a template for Treaty Office officials to use when preparing instruments of ratification, accession, approval or acceptance, and sending notifications.
- Reservations: ensure that any reservation you make (or confirm) on ratification (or accession, etc.) cannot become separated from the ratification instrument. If the reservation is placed in a separate note, it is essential that both documents clearly refer to each other.
- If it is your job to prepare an instrument of ratification (or accession etc.), send a draft in advance to the depositary for checking, especially if you (or your government or IO) are not very experienced in this matter.
- If it is your job to deposit an instrument of ratification (or other treaty instrument), it is worth the trouble of delivering it in person during office hours. Ask for a written and dated confirmation of receipt to take away with you.
- Be alert to when a treaty you have ratified (or acceded to, etc.) is about to enter into force. When it does so, promptly notify all officials throughout your government or IO who may be concerned in its implementation.

Top Tips for States or IOs Acting As Depositary to a Treaty

Based on the discussions in this chapter, Box 7.3 summarises key points that States and IOs may consider when acting as depositary to a treaty.

Box 7.3 Top tips for States or IOs acting as depositary to a treaty

- Take great care not to exceed your authority or act inconsistently with your duty of impartiality. In any cases of doubt, consult the treaty parties by circular, or at a meeting of treaty parties.
- Encourage any State or IO preparing to become party to send you a copy of their instrument of ratification (or other formal document) in draft for checking in advance.
- Send notifications promptly; as soon as you receive any instrument or notification, enter it into your database, acknowledge it to the sending party and inform all other parties straight away – on the same day if possible.

8

Continuing Engagement with the Treaty Throughout Its Life

***

'Modern treaties, in the majority of cases, are not one-off transactions in which parties exchange commitments and advantages.'[1]

Introduction

As has been discussed in previous chapters, it can be a lengthy process to negotiate and finally ratify a treaty – preparing domestic implementation legislation, obtaining cabinet and/or parliamentary approval of the treaty, preparing and depositing instruments of ratification, acceptance or accession, and the immediate follow-through such as publication and registration. It can often seem a great relief to get to the end of all of these processes, especially for the officials that have taken the lead in shepherding them to conclusion.

But the work does not stop there.

Many treaties have increasingly elaborate processes and obligations which kick in once the treaty enters into force, requiring States Parties to continue to engage with the treaty for as long as they remain party. And some of these continuing processes and obligations can be quite onerous, ranging from attending regular meetings of the COP, to participating in rigorous compliance assessments or audits by external parties.

The purpose of these various processes and obligations is generally to ensure that the treaty is not forgotten or ignored by States Parties after the hard work of ratification is complete, and to ensure that there are mechanisms in place to support the effective implementation of the treaty, and also that States Parties comply with it. For some treaties, the processes may also play an important role in reassuring States Parties that others are complying as rigorously as they are, thus ensuring a level playing field (for example, where standards are set for trade or industry).

Continuing engagement with a treaty requires action on both the domestic and international planes. On the domestic plane, the lead agency responsible for continuing engagement is likely to be the department of government that is responsible for the subject matter of the treaty. However, they will have to consult the government's international law advisers on certain issues. The Treaty Office may not have a major role unless the continuing engagement includes amendments to the treaty or its annexes or the drafting and adoption of additional protocols, or legal issues arise concerning reservations or declarations. As has been emphasised throughout this Handbook, effective co-ordination is required between the relevant officials and departments at both the domestic and international levels. This includes the officials in the government department responsible for the subject matter of the treaty, the lawyers in the office providing legal advice on issues of international law and the Treaty Office. It may also include government officials in the overseas mission who attend meetings of the COP.

[1] J Bruneé, 'Treaty Amendments' in D Hollis (ed), *The Oxford Guide to Treaties* (OUP 2012), 347.

Applying the PLATO Principles to Continuing Engagement with the Treaty Throughout Its Life

Applying the PLATO principles are important when addressing the issue of continuing engagement. Again, the PLATO principle 'Legal' should guide a State's continuing engagement with the treaty, especially on the domestic plane. It is particularly important that lawyers are fully engaged during this phase. For example, officials from the lead agency responsible for the subject matter need to be aware that they should consult the Treaty Office or international law advisers when certain types of issue arise in the course of their work.

The government must be 'Organised'; above all, the roles of the officials within the relevant agencies must be 'Co-ordinated'. Procedures should be adopted for continuing engagement that set out the roles and responsibilities of the different government agencies. These procedures must also be 'Centralised', 'Written' and 'Recorded'.

The procedures must not only be co-ordinated, they must also be 'Transparent' – clear and easy to understand, available and accessible. In continuing engagement with the treaty, several important elements of the 'Transparency' principle should be fully considered:

- 'Clear' treaty information, including related information such as amendments and reservations, should be provided to all relevant ministries and agencies responsible for continuing engagement with the treaty.
- 'Communicated' means that procedures adopted for continuing engagement with the treaty are actively disseminated to ensure that they are known and understood by relevant ministries and agencies.
- 'Accessible' means easy access to all relevant information and procedures, especially for ministries and agencies responsible for continuing engagement with the treaty.

The Key Challenge with Continuing Engagement: The Bulk of the Work Moves Away from the Treaty Office

A key challenge that arises in respect of all aspects of continuing engagement with a treaty, is that once a treaty has been ratified, responsibility for most of the action will move to the lead agency, and the involvement of the Treaty Office will probably be only occasional. The lead agency is usually a separate domestic agency or department which covers the subject matter of the treaty.

Let's look at some examples, starting with New Zealand: while the Treaty Office at the Ministry of Foreign Affairs and Trade will be heavily involved in the ratification processes for all International Maritime Organization (IMO) treaties, once these are complete, responsibility for the implementation of the treaty and ongoing engagement typically rests with Maritime New Zealand, because this is the national agency responsible for representing New Zealand's interests at the IMO.

In Vietnam, as soon as the MFA completes the diplomatic procedures for a treaty to enter into force, the relevant policy ministry takes the lead in drafting and executing the implementation plan of the treaty. For example, the lead agency for bilateral treaties between Vietnam and another country on the transfer of sentenced persons is the Ministry of Public Security and not the MFA. Even for those treaties for which the New Zealand or Vietnam Foreign Ministry remains the lead agency, once the treaty has been ratified, responsibility for action usually shifts from the Treaty Office to the relevant policy department within the Foreign Ministry. For example, for treaties dealing with Antarctica, the lead department within the New Zealand Ministry is the Environment Division and not the Legal Division or Treaty Office. For treaties dealing with the overall relationship between Vietnam and China, the lead department within the Vietnam Ministry is the Department of North Asia and not the Department of International Law and Treaties. And this makes sense because the majority of issues that will arise in respect of the treaty from this point are best dealt with by those officials who are experts in the subject matter.

However, this shift in responsibility can be challenging, as the lead agency responsible for implementing and continuing to engage in a treaty may be a domestically focused department that does not have officials with expertise in international law or treaty practice. The lead agency may not give a high priority to the continuing obligations of the treaty, or fully appreciate the importance of complying with them. As the officers in the lead agency may not be experts in international law or the law of treaties, they may not recognise when issues arise in the course of their work on which they should seek advice from the government's international law experts. Thus, a key issue for all States is how best to manage ongoing treaty obligations and processes when responsibility for the treaty has shifted away from the Treaty Office and international law experts, to the lead agency responsible for the subject matter. This issue will be even more acute for States that are developing and/or small countries with capacity constraints.

The Treaty Office will in any event retain specific responsibilities for the treaty throughout its life. The most significant responsibilities are the ongoing treaty information functions: maintaining treaty records and publishing treaty texts and treaty status information. For a bilateral treaty, the Treaty Office's work *may* be concluded once it has recorded the date of entry into force of the treaty and filed the original treaty and related instruments, published and registered it, and informed all within the organisation (government or IO) who need to be aware. For multilateral treaties, however, certain tasks will necessarily continue for the life of the treaty.[2]

For a multilateral treaty, ideally, treaty officials will need to record and retain every notification concerning the signature, ratification or accession of other States and IOs before the treaty enters into force, keep track of progress

[2] See the sections on 'Managing Treaty Collections' and 'Depositary Functions' in Chapter 4 at 132–39 and 153–56 respectively.

towards the threshold for entry into force and alert all within the organisation to the date of entry into force when it is notified by the depositary. After entry into force, the Treaty Office will need to record all new signatures, ratifications and accessions, and deal with all other notices that arrive from the depositary, such as those concerning reservations and declarations, objections and other responses. The Treaty Office will also need to record any treaty amendments that may be adopted, keep a status list for each one and fulfil national requirements for the publication of texts and information.

However, maintaining complete records of all notifications received from depositaries requires significant resources. Accordingly, Treaty Offices may need to prioritise the information that they record in their databases. For example, they might maintain records of their own State's treaty acts but decide to rely on the depositary's website for information about the treaty acts of other parties. In some cases, more restrictive criteria are applied. For example, Indonesia's Treaty Room will only record and retain detailed information for multilateral treaties to which Indonesia is the Depositary. For other multilateral treaties, the key information recorded by the Treaty Room usually consists of the date of Indonesia's signature and/or ratification, date of entry into force and information on domestic legislation that has been adopted to implement the treaty.

If its own State or IO engages in further formal acts in relation to the treaty, the Treaty Office may be responsible for the formal procedures. For example, if it is decided to respond to a new reservation entered by another party, or to a new objection to its own reservation, the Treaty Office will need to prepare and send a formal notice to the depositary. If an amendment is adopted, and is subject to signature, ratification or other formal modes of approval, the Treaty Office will need to take care of that. If an amendment is adopted, and is subject to a tacit approval procedure, the Treaty Office will need to be aware of its entry into force, or, if its authorities wish to object, will need to take care of the formal procedure for doing so. Depending on the treaty, there may be other matters on which the government needs to engage formally with the depositary, or has the option to do so; for example, where the treaty provides for an option to make or change a declaration after ratification, on such matters as the choice of settlement of dispute procedures, geographical application or optional provisions. The Treaty Office will need to be engaged, if not to draft and send the necessary formal note, at least to advise and check it before it is sent. The instrument, or note, may need to be sent to the *depositary* for the treaty, which may not be the secretariat.

When the treaty is in force, the main engagement between or among parties will be by the officials in the lead agency who have responsibility for the substance of the treaty – the implementation, and the further international policy-making, review and monitoring. If the treaty is multilateral and served by a secretariat, the lead agency will normally be the main point of contact for the parties and act as hub for further activities and communications under the treaty. Most of these communications are of a policy or substantive nature, and will not concern the Treaty Office. If the lead agency is a domestic ministry, further communications are likely to be sent directly to the policy officials in that ministry, and will not necessarily be sent through embassies or copied to foreign ministries.

The *depositary* for the treaty will continue throughout the life of the treaty to be responsible for depositary functions, such as receiving new signatures, instruments of ratification, etc., and circulating formal notices concerning the status of the treaty and acts relating to it. These dealings may be carried out through embassies or foreign ministries. The depositary may or may not be within the same organisation as the secretariat which services the meetings of the treaty. If it is, it may well be in a different part of the organisation.

Thus, there may be more than one channel of communication pertaining to the same treaty. For example:

- depositary (IO or government Treaty Office) to embassies or missions of States Parties, and on to the foreign ministry of each State Party.
- secretariat (operational department) to policy contacts in the lead domestic ministry of each State Party.

It is therefore essential that each State (or IO) Party maintains effective internal communications, with a system that ensures flow of information to those who need to act upon it. This is one of the most challenging issues for any government or IO.

As will be evident below, this is a key challenge that arises in all aspects of continuing engagement with treaties, and at the conclusion of this chapter we set out tips and suggestions for addressing this issue.

Continuing Engagement with Treaty Institutions

COPs Established by Treaties

Many modern multilateral treaties, especially environment, disarmament and counter-transnational crimes treaties, establish regular meetings of the States Parties.[3] These meetings, which are usually called COPs,[4] are a key source of States' continuing engagement obligations with many multilateral treaties. Below we explain what a COP is and what it does. Then, we look at best treaty practice in respect of COP meetings and the instruments produced by COPs.

[3] Note that attendance at such meetings is not mandatory, but usually any State Party that does not attend forfeits its right to participate in decisions, including voting where required.

[4] Some treaties use different titles: for example, Meeting of the Parties (MOP) is commonly used, and variety of other terms are used, such as the Convention on Long-range Transboundary Air Pollution, 1979 which uses the term 'Executive Body'. See Convention on Long-range Transboundary Air Pollution (adopted 13 November 1979, entered into force 16 March 1983) 1302 UNTS 2017, art 10.

What Is a COP, and What Does It Do?

COPs are designed to act as the 'principle policy-making body' for the treaty. They set the future agenda for a treaty.[5] Typically, they are tasked with meeting periodically (usually annually or at least regularly)[6] to take stock of the implementation of the treaty and to consider further action. Their functions and powers are normally set by the treaty itself. COPs invariably have a consultative function – they provide a forum for discussion of matters relating to the treaty. Some are limited to discussion, whereas others have the power, and sometimes even the duty, to adopt further instruments, such as decisions, resolutions or recommendations, measures, programmes or guidelines, for the future implementation of the agreement. If the founding treaty of an IO or a COP confers a power to adopt binding instruments, it may do so. Instruments which are adopted *in exercise of such a power* will then be considered binding by the Parties. If the treaty does not confer an express power on the IO or COP to adopt binding instruments, any instruments it adopts will normally be considered to be non-binding policy documents. All such instruments could be termed 'secondary law-making' under the treaty, in the sense that they are not treaties in their own right; rather, their legal effect is dependent upon the provisions in the treaty under which they were made.[7]

A multilateral treaty which establishes a COP may confer a role on the COP in relation to the negotiation and adoption of amendments, protocols and annexes. These texts *are* treaties in their own right, in that they amend the text of the parent treaty, or add a new supplementary treaty. The status of such

[5] UNEP, *Glossary of Terms for Negotiators of Multilateral Environmental Agreements* (UNEP, 2007) https://wedocs.unep.org/bitstream/handle/20.500.11822/7569/-Glossary%20of%20Terms%20for%20Negotiators%20of%20Multilateral%20Environmental%20Agreements-2007762.pdf?amp%3BisAllowed=&sequence=3 accessed 1 November 2018.

[6] See for example, Vienna Convention for the Protection of the Ozone Layer (adopted 22 March 1985, entered into force 22 September 1988) 1513 UNTS 293 art 6(1); and Montreal Protocol on Substances that Deplete the Ozone Layer (adopted 16 September 1987, entered into force 1 January 1989) 1522 UNTS 3 (Montreal Protocol) art 11(1) also provides for MOPs to be held at 'regular intervals'.

[7] See for example, Convention for the Protection of the Marine Environment of the North-East Atlantic (signed 22 September 1992, entered into force 25 March 1998) 2354 UNTS 67 (OSPAR), art 13, which distinguishes between binding decisions and non-binding recommendations:

1. Decisions and recommendations shall be adopted by unanimous vote of the Contracting Parties. Should unanimity not be attainable, and unless otherwise provided in the Convention, the Commission may nonetheless adopt decisions or recommendations by a three-quarters majority vote of the Contracting Parties.
2. A decision shall be binding on the expiry of a period of two hundred days after its adoption for those Contracting Parties that voted for it and have not within that period notified the Executive Secretary in writing that they are unable to accept the decision, provided that at the expiry of that period three-quarters of the Contracting Parties have either voted for the decision and not withdrawn their acceptance or notified the Executive Secretary in writing that they are able to accept the decision. Such a decision shall become binding on any other Contracting Party which has notified the Executive Secretary in writing that it is able to accept the decision from the moment of that notification or after the expiry of a period of two hundred days after the adoption of the decision, whichever is later . . .

5. Recommendations shall have no binding force.

texts, and their relationship to the parent treaty, will be governed by final clauses – which may be in the parent treaty, the new treaty or in a separate document such as the adopting resolution.[8]

The establishment of a COP and articulation of its specific functions and working methods will usually be done in the treaty. An example is Article 23 of the Convention on Biological Diversity, 1992 (CBD),[9] which provides:

1. A Conference of the Parties is hereby established. The first meeting of the Conference of the Parties shall be convened by the Executive Director of the United Nations Environment Programme not later than one year after the entry into force of this Convention. Thereafter, ordinary meetings of the Conference of the Parties shall be held at regular intervals to be determined by the Conference at its first meeting.
2. Extraordinary meetings of the Conference of the Parties shall be held at such other times as may be deemed necessary by the Conference, or at the written request of any Party, provided that, within six months of the request being communicated to them by the Secretariat, it is supported by at least one third of the Parties.
3. The Conference of the Parties shall by consensus agree upon and adopt rules of procedure for itself and for any subsidiary body it may establish, as well as financial rules governing the funding of the Secretariat. At each ordinary meeting, it shall adopt a budget for the financial period until the next ordinary meeting.
4. The Conference of the Parties shall keep under review the implementation of this Convention, and, for this purpose, shall: (a) Establish the form and the intervals for transmitting the information to be submitted in accordance with Article 26 and consider such information as well as reports submitted by any subsidiary body; (b) Review scientific, technical and technological advice on biological diversity provided in accordance with Article 25; (c) Consider and adopt, as required, protocols in accordance with Article 28; (d) Consider and adopt, as required, in accordance with Articles 29 and 30, amendments to this Convention and its annexes; (e) Consider amendments to any protocol, as well as to any annexes thereto, and, if so decided, recommend their adoption to the parties to the protocol concerned; (f) Consider and adopt, as required, in accordance with Article 30, additional annexes to this Convention; (g) Establish such subsidiary bodies, particularly to provide scientific and technical advice, as are deemed necessary for the implementation of this Convention; (h) Contact, through the Secretariat, the executive bodies of conventions dealing

[8] For a legal analysis of the status of secondary law-making under treaties, see: D Costelloe and M Fitzmaurice, 'Lawmaking by Treaty: Conclusion of a Treaty and the Evolution of a Treaty Regime in Practice' in C Brölmann and Y Radi (eds), *Research Handbook on the Theory and Practice of International Lawmaking* (Edward Elgar Publishers, Cheltenham 2016); and G Ulfstein, 'Treaty Bodies and Regimes' in *Hollis* (n 1).

[9] Convention on Biological Diversity (adopted 5 June 1992, entered into force 29 December 1993) 1760 UNTS 79 (CBD).

with matters covered by this Convention with a view to establishing appropriate forms of cooperation with them; and (i) Consider and undertake any additional action that may be required for the achievement of the purposes of this Convention in the light of experience gained in its operation.

5. The United Nations, its specialized agencies and the International Atomic Energy Agency, as well as any State not Party to this Convention, may be represented as observers at meetings of the Conference of the Parties. Any other body or agency, whether governmental or non-governmental, qualified in fields relating to conservation and sustainable use of biological diversity, which has informed the Secretariat of its wish to be represented as an observer at a meeting of the Conference of the Parties, may be admitted unless at least one third of the Parties present object. The admission and participation of observers shall be subject to the rules of procedure adopted by the Conference of the Parties.

Another example is Article 18 of the ASEAN Agreement on Transboundary Haze Pollution, 2002[10] which provides:

1. A Conference of the Parties is hereby established. The first meeting of the Conference of the Parties shall be convened by the Secretariat not later than one year after the entry into force of this Agreement. Thereafter, ordinary meetings of the Conference of the Parties shall be held at least once every year, in as far as possible in conjunction with appropriate meetings of ASEAN.
2. Extraordinary meetings shall be held at any other time upon the request of one Party provided that such request is supported by at least one other Party.
3. The Conference of the Parties shall keep under continuous review and evaluation the implementation of this Agreement and to this end shall:
   a. Take such action as is necessary to ensure the effective implementation of this Agreement;
   b. Consider reports and other information which may be submitted by a Party directly or through the Secretariat;
   c. Consider and adopt protocols in accordance with the Article 21 of this Agreement;
   d. Consider and adopt any amendment to this Agreement;
   e. Adopt, review and amend as required any Annexes to this Agreement;
   f. Establish subsidiary bodies as may be required for the implementation of this Agreement; and
   g. Consider and undertake any additional action that may be required for the achievement of the objective of this Agreement.

COPs will typically adopt their own rules of procedure which govern how such meetings are run and cover issues such as the places and dates of

[10] ASEAN Agreement on Transboundary Haze Pollution (adopted 10 June 2002, entered into force 25 November 2003) ADS (2002) 138.

meetings, rules around attendance (such as whether non-parties and NGOs can attend as observers), the agenda, voting procedures and languages/translation issues.[11] In some cases, important matters such as voting majorities, may be governed by the treaty itself.

Attendance by States Parties at COPs can be very important, particularly for States Parties that have a major stake in the issues regulated by the treaty and who want to influence, and have input into, the future direction of the treaty. States Parties attendance at COPs is not compulsory in a legal sense – there is usually no specific requirement in a treaty that States Parties must attend COPs. For example, while Article 23 CBD is clear on the obligations and responsibilities of the COP, it does not impose any obligations on individual States Parties. While Article 63 of the United Nations Convention against Corruption, 2003 requires States Parties to provide the COP with information on its programmes, plans and practices, as well as on legislative and administrative measures to implement the Convention, it does not require States Parties to attend the COP.[12] However, States Parties that do not attend COPs forfeit their right to participate in COP procedures and decision-making. For example, amendments to multilateral treaties are typically considered and adopted at COPs, and those States Parties not in attendance are not able to participate in negotiations and/or vote on amendment proposals.[13]

While COPs are generally only established by multilateral treaties, bilateral treaties can also include similar ongoing meeting requirements. An example is the Thailand–New Zealand Closer Economic Partnership Agreement, 2005 which establishes a Closer Economic Partnership Joint Commission, the mandate of which is very similar to a COP: to meet annually to ensure the proper implementation of the agreement, consider amendments, and to periodically review the economic relationship and partnership between the two Parties.[14] Similar provisions can also be found in many regional agreements, for example: the ASEAN Framework Agreement on the Facilitation of Inter-State Transport, 2009 which sets up a Transit Transport Coordinating Board;[15] and the ASEAN Agreement on Customs, 2012 which establishes the ASEAN Directors-General of Customs Meeting.[16]

[11] See for example, CBD, 'Rules of Procedure for Meetings of the Conference of the Parties to the Convention on Biological Diversity' www.cbd.int/convention/rules.shtml accessed 15 September 2018.

[12] United Nations Convention against Corruption (adopted 9 December 2003, entered into force 14 December 2005) 2349 UNTS 41.

[13] See for example ibid art 69 and CBD art 29.

[14] Thailand–New Zealand Closer Economic Partnership Agreement (signed 19 April 2005, entered into force 1 July 2005) NZTS 2005 No. 8 B2005/03, arts 16.1, 16.2 and 16.3.

[15] ASEAN Framework Agreement on the Facilitation of Inter-State Transport (adopted 10 December 2009, entered into force 30 December 2011) ADS (2009) 212, art 27(2).

[16] ASEAN Agreement on Customs (adopted 30 March 2012, entered into force 7 November 2014), art 53(1) http://agreement.asean.org/media/download/20140117163238.pdf accessed 15 September 2018.

In addition to COPs, many treaties also establish subsidiary bodies (committees, working groups etc.). See for example Article 25 CBD (note 9 above) which provides:

1. A subsidiary body for the provision of scientific, technical and technological advice is hereby established to provide the Conference of the Parties and, as appropriate, its other subsidiary bodies with timely advice relating to the implementation of this Convention. This body shall be open to participation by all Parties and shall be multidisciplinary. It shall comprise government representatives competent in the relevant field of expertise. It shall report regularly to the Conference of the Parties on all aspects of its work.
2. Under the authority of and in accordance with guidelines laid down by the Conference of the Parties, and upon its request, this body shall:
   (a) Provide scientific and technical assessments of the status of biological diversity;
   (b) Prepare scientific and technical assessments of the effects of types of measures taken in accordance with the provisions of this Convention;
   (c) Identify innovative, efficient and state-of-the-art technologies and know-how relating to the conservation and sustainable use of biological diversity and advise on the ways and means of promoting development and/or transferring such technologies;
   (d) Provide advice on scientific programmes and international cooperation in research and development related to conservation and sustainable use of biological diversity; and
   (e) Respond to scientific, technical, technological and methodological questions that the Conference of the Parties and its subsidiary bodies may put to the body.
3. The functions, terms of reference, organization and operation of this body may be further elaborated by the Conference of the Parties.

Article 63 of the United Nations Convention against Corruption likewise provides that 'the Conference of the States Parties shall establish, if it deems it necessary, any appropriate mechanism or body to assist in the effective implementation of the Convention'.

Such bodies are different from COPs as they cover only a specific subject issue, and will be subsidiary to the COP. COPs, or the treaty itself as is the case with the CBD, will usually provide such bodies with specific tasking, and the body will usually be expected to report back regularly to the COP, in the form of recommendations, for decision by the COP. While such meetings are open to all States, typically only those States with a particular interest in the subject matter will attend such meetings.[17] For example, the Protocol on

[17] ibid arts XIV–XV.

Environmental Protection to the Antarctic Treaty, 1991[18] establishes the Committee on Environmental Protection to provide advice and formulate recommendations to the Parties in connection with the implementation of the Protocol for consideration at the ATCMs.[19]

A key issue for States, particularly small and developing States, is the resource implications of regular COP and other meetings. First is the cost of sending officials to meetings in far-flung locations that can last up to four weeks.[20] Another issue is that COP sessions can often involve multiple meetings running at the same time (for example, while the COP session is happening in plenary, subject-specific committees or working groups may also be meeting separately). This can be especially tricky for States that are only able to send small delegations to COPs, as they may not be able to cover multiple meetings happening at the same time. In such situations, delegations need to be careful to stay abreast of the output of separate working groups/committees that they are not able to attend, and to clearly prioritise issues of key importance.

When Should Instruments Produced by COPs Be Handled as Treaties?

A key issue from a treaty practice perspective is determining which instruments produced by COPs should be handled as treaties. Research conducted by the United Nations Environment Programme has shown that COPs can be extremely productive and, as a result, can generate enormous amounts of paperwork. For example, the 12th COP for the CBD, held in Korea in October 2014, generated a hundred documents and thirty-five decisions on a large range of issues, from co-operation between the CBD and other conventions to access and benefit-sharing of genetic resources.[21] Bilateral treaty body meetings can also generate significant paperwork, although not usually to the same extent as COPs.[22]

Because of the volume of material and range of instruments produced by COPs and bilateral treaty bodies, this can be difficult. Sometimes the status of an instrument should be relatively clear. For example, treaty amendments

[18] Protocol on Environmental Protection to the Antarctic Treaty (adopted 4 October 1991, entered into force 14 January 1998) 2941 UNTS Registration No. 5778.

[19] ibid arts 11–12.

[20] While some COPs meet regularly at a set location, many meet at a different location each meeting (for example, the last five CBD COPs have been held in Korea, India, Japan, Germany and Brazil respectively).

[21] See CBD, 'Conference of the Parties (COP)' www.cbd.int/cop/ accessed 1 November 2018. Helpfully, most of the newer multilateral conventions now have their own website, providing access to all relevant material, including draft documents and decisions. See for example the CBD's website: www.cbd.int/ which provides access to all relevant documentation, including from previous COPs.

[22] For example, the third annual meeting of the Thailand–New Zealand Closer Economic Partnership Joint Commission held in 2011 produced a 53-page 'Joint Review Report' which reviewed the operation of the agreement for the first five years from its entry into force. See New Zealand Ministry of Foreign Affairs and Trade, 'New Zealand–Thailand Closer Economic Partnership Agreement: Joint Review 1 January 2005–31 December 2010' (2011) www.mfat.govt.nz/assets/FTAs-agreements-in-force/Thailand-FTA/thai-final-cep-joint-review.pdf accessed 1 November 2018.

adopted by COPs should generally be handled as treaties (see the section below on amendments). Normally, the depositary or secretariat which circulates the text in question will indicate the procedure which applies for its entry into force. Whenever a text is circulated by the depositary of a treaty, this is an indication that it should be treated as a treaty, or at least, it should be sent to the Treaty Office to decide.

However, what about decision documents produced by COPs? Many such documents use very formal language, including preambles, similar to those typically found in treaties. Should these types of documents be handled as treaties? How can you determine the intended status of these types of instruments? As indicated above, there is a large amount of secondary law-making made under treaties, and it is not always easy to distinguish binding from non-binding instruments. Where there is no ratification or formal approval procedure for each Party, the secretariat may not make its status clear. It will then be crucial for each Party to consult its own international law advisers.

In respect of all such instruments, it will be a matter of applying the principles set out in Chapter 3 to determine the status (or to ensure that its language is consistent with its intended status).[23] As a first step, it is always wise to consult the text of the treaty to see if it has guidance on the status of particular instruments. For example, Article 30(1) CBD provides that 'The annexes to this Convention or to any protocol *shall form an integral part of the Convention*' (emphasis added). Thus, any annex or protocol produced by the CBD COP, unless otherwise specified, will form an integral part of the CBD and will therefore have the same treaty status. In accordance with Article 30(1), parties to the CBD should make sure that any annexes or protocols adopted by the COP adopt appropriate legally binding language, and are correctly handled by the parties (each party will need to treat them as a treaty and go through their own domestic treaty approval processes before formal ratification or acceptance, see also note 9 above).

Where the treaty has no guidance on the status of the particular instrument, the language of the instrument will be the primary guide, interpreted in accordance with the rules of interpretation in the law of treaties. To illustrate the process of analysing the status of instruments adopted by COPs, we take the Kyoto Protocol[24] and the Convention for the Protection of the Marine Environment of the North-East Atlantic, 1992 (OSPAR)[25] as case studies. Box 8.1 provides a breakdown of our analysis – factors that need to be taken into account – of the status of instruments produced by the treaties' respective COP.

[23] See the sections on 'Good Practice in Distinguishing between Treaties and other Kinds of International Instruments: Applying the PLATO Principles' and 'How to Distinguish between Treaties and Non-binding International Instruments' in Chapter 3 at pp 83–93 and 106–11 respectively.

[24] Kyoto Protocol (adopted 11 December 1997, entered into force 16 February 2005) 2303 UNTS 162.

[25] See n 7.

Box 8.1 Analysing the status of instruments produced by COPs

KYOTO PROTOCOL

NAME OF INSTRUMENT:
Procedures and mechanisms relating to compliance under the Kyoto Protocol, 2005.[26]

ADOPTION AND MODE OF ADOPTION:
This instrument was adopted by Decision of the COP for the Kyoto Protocol in December 2005. It was included as an Annex to the COP decision document.[27]

GUIDANCE IN THE TREATY:
Article 18 of the Kyoto Protocol provides that COP 'shall, at its first session, approve appropriate and effective procedures and mechanisms to determine and to address cases of non-compliance with the provisions of this Protocol … Any procedures and mechanisms under this Article entailing binding consequences shall be adopted by means of an amendment to this Protocol'.

Article 20 is the amendment provision.

GUIDANCE IN INSTRUMENT OR LANGUAGE?
The preambles of the instrument notes that it has been 'approved and adopted' by the Parties to the Protocol, and references Articles 18 and 20 of the treaty.

All the obligations in the instrument are expressed in binding terms, through the use of 'shall'.

CONCLUSION:

- The instrument references Articles 18 and 20 of the treaty, which provide that non-compliance procedures should be adopted by means of an amendment.

[26] Procedures and mechanisms relating to compliance under the Kyoto Protocol (adopted 10 December 2005) Decision 27/CMP.1, FCCC/KP/CMP/2005/8/Add.3. The instrument was adopted by the COP serving as the meeting of the Parties to the Kyoto Protocol at its 9th plenary meeting.

[27] ibid. The instrument can be accessed on United Nations Climate Change, 'Compliance under the Kyoto Protocol' https://unfccc.int/process/the-kyoto-protocol/compliance-under-the-kyoto-protocol accessed 4 December 2018.

Box 8.1 (cont.)

- Article 20 makes clear that amendments to the Protocol have treaty status.
- Consistent with the above, the instrument uses binding treaty language.

OSPAR

NAME OF INSTRUMENT:
OSPAR Recommendation 2012/5 for a risk-based approach to the Management of Produced Water Discharges from Offshore Installations, 2012.[28]

ADOPTION AND MODE OF ADOPTION:
OSPAR 12/22/1, Annex 18.

GUIDANCE IN THE TREATY:
OSPAR, Articles 10 and 13:

- Article 10(3) provides: 'To these ends the Commission may, inter alia, adopt decisions and recommendations in accordance with Article 13.'
- Article 13(5) provides: 'Recommendations shall have no binding force.'

It is clear that the OSPAR Commission has the power to adopt both binding and non-binding instruments.

GUIDANCE IN INSTRUMENT OR LANGUAGE?
Title uses a term defined in Article 13:

'The Contracting Parties to the Convention for the Protection of the Marine Environment of the North-East Atlantic recommend'.

Non-mandatory language is used.

CONCLUSION:
It is not binding.

If a delegation or policy officials are in doubt as to the legal status of any documents adopted by a COP or other treaty body, they should always send it

[28] OSPAR Recommendation 2012/5 for a risk-based approach to the Management of Produced Water Discharges from Offshore Installations (adopted 2012, entered into force 29 June 2012).

to the Treaty Office of their government or IO (who should have ready access to international law advice, if they are not international lawyers themselves).[29]

A key practical issue in relation to COP instruments is that very often they are finalised at COP meetings where delegations may not have access to their legal experts. Because, as noted above, the monetary and resourcing costs of sending delegations to regular COP meetings can be high, typically State Party delegations, especially those from smaller and developing countries, may not include a legal expert. For example, for CBD COPs, the New Zealand delegation is usually made up of officials from the Environment Division of the Foreign Ministry, which is the New Zealand policy lead for CBD matters, and other relevant ministries including the Ministry for the Environment and Department of Conservation. Usually only where the COP involves the negotiation of a protocol or an amendment will a lawyer be part of the delegation. And there may be many COP-like meetings where a State Party, for cost and resourcing issues, does not send any officials from the capital. In such cases, local diplomats, often with no background in either the policy issues at stake or international law, may be required to cover the meeting.

Without an international lawyer as part of the delegation, it can be challenging for States to ensure that COP instruments and products are consistent with international and domestic treaty law and practice – especially as much of the material produced by the COP will be adopted on the ground, with limited ability for officials to consult key stakeholders back home.

To overcome this challenge, New Zealand practice has been to ensure COP delegations:

- have at least a basic understanding of how to identify treaty practice issues; and
- have ready access to a legal expert in the capital city that they can send questions and comments to via email throughout COP meetings.[30]

The former can be more difficult to achieve, but the primary method employed by New Zealand for this is the holding of regular seminars for all New Zealand Government officials involved in international treaties and the production of the *Treaty Making Handbook*.[31] In relation to the latter, New Zealand practice is to try and ensure that there is at least one lawyer in the foreign ministry allocated to each treaty who is involved in COP preparations / known to the COP delegation and who can be a contact point for the delegation (although time-differences and pressure to deal with issues quickly at COP meetings can affect the utility of this).

In summary, COPs and other treaty-related meetings are a major ongoing commitment that can have major resource implications for States, especially those

[29] See the section on 'Other International Instruments that are "Treaty-like" but not Treaties' in Chapter 3 at 96–104.

[30] That legal expert, being in the MFAT legal division, will have ready access to the Treaty Office.

[31] See the section on 'Providing Guidance on Treaty Procedures across the Government or IO', Chapter 2 at 76–8.

States with a key interest in the policy issue being regulated by the treaty. COPs can be intensive meetings, dealing with a multitude of issues and producing many different instruments. Ensuring clarity on the status of such instruments and making sure that appropriate domestic approval processes are complied with are very important, but can be difficult when many COP decisions are made on the ground, without the ability to consult with experts in the capital city. Ensuring effective communication between the COP delegation and the capital is essential; and, in the capital, between the lead agency and the Treaty Office, as necessary.

Reporting Requirements in Treaties

Reporting requirements are another major source of States' continuing engagement obligations with an international treaty. They can be found in many modern multilateral treaties, particularly human rights, environment and disarmament treaties, but are less common in bilateral treaties. Those found in multilateral treaties generally fall into two categories:

Requirements for Parties to Report on Steps They Have Taken to Implement the Obligations in the Treaty

The following are examples of treaties that require parties to submit regular reports on steps that have been taken to implement their obligations under the treaties.

- Article 26 CBD requires Contracting Parties to submit to the COP regular reports on measures they have taken to implement the Convention and the effectiveness in meeting the Convention's objectives.[32]
- Article 35 of the Convention on the Rights of Persons with Disabilities, 2007 requires States Parties to submit regular reports on the measures they have taken to give effect to the obligations in the treaty.[33]
- Article 5 of the Vienna Convention for the Protection of the Ozone Layer, 1985 requires Parties to report on measures adopted by Parties to

[32] CBD (n 9) art 26:

> Each Contracting Party shall, at intervals to be determined by the Conference of the Parties, present to the Conference of the Parties, reports on measures which it has taken for the implementation of the provisions of this Convention and their effectiveness in meeting the objectives of this Convention.

[33] Convention on the Rights of Persons with Disabilities (adopted 30 March 2007, entered into force 3 May 2008) 2515 UNTS 3, art 35:

> 1. Each State Party shall submit to the Committee, through the Secretary-General of the United Nations, a comprehensive report on measures taken to give effect to its obligations under the present Convention and on the progress made in that regard, within two years after the entry into force of the present Convention for the State Party concerned.
> 2. Thereafter, States Parties shall submit subsequent reports at least every four years and further whenever the Committee so requests.

implement the Convention and also submit regular reports on the implementation of the Convention's Protocols.[34]

- Article 18 of the Single Convention on Narcotic Drugs, 1961 requires States Parties to regularly submit reports on the working of the convention in their territory and all laws and regulations promulgated to give effect to the Convention.[35]

Requirements for Parties to Report on Their Participation in the Core Activities Controlled by the Treaty

The following are examples of treaties that require parties to submit regular reports on their participations in the core activities controlled by the treaties.

- Article 13 of the Arms Trade Treaty 2013, which provides:

> Each State Party shall submit annually to the Secretariat by 31 May a report for the preceding calendar year concerning authorised or actual exports and imports of conventional arms.[36]

- The Montreal Protocol on Substances that Deplete the Ozone Layer, 1987 similarly requires States Parties to submit annual reports on their production, import and export of substances deemed to deplete the ozone layer, and requires that parties notify the Secretariat of any allowed transfer of production between parties and of any addition to calculated production levels allowed by the Protocol.[37]
- The Basel Convention on the Control of Transboundary Movements of Hazardous Wastes and their Disposal, 1989 likewise requires parties to

[34] Vienna Convention for the Protection of the Ozone Layer art 5:

> transmit, through the secretariat, to the Conference of the Parties . . . information on the measures adopted by them in implementation of this convention and of protocols to which they are a party in such form and at such intervals as the meetings of the parties to the relevant instruments may determine.

See also CBD (n 9).

[35] Single Convention on Narcotic Drugs (adopted 30 March 1961, entered into force 8 August 1975) 520 UNTS 151, art 18:

> 1. The Parties shall furnish to the Secretary-General such information as the Commission may request as being necessary for the performance of its functions, and in particular:
>   a) An annual report on the working of the Convention within each of their territories;
>   b) The text of all laws and regulations from time to time promulgated in order to give effect to this Convention;
>   c) Such particulars as the Commission shall determine concerning cases of illicit traffic, including particulars of each case of illicit traffic discovered which may be of importance, because of the light thrown on the source from which drugs are obtained for the illicit traffic, or because of quantities involved or the method employed by illicit traffickers; and
>   d) The names and addresses of the governmental authorities empowered to issue export and import authorisations or certificates.

[36] Arms Trade Treaty (adopted 3 June 2013, entered into force 24 December 2014) UNTS Registration No. 52373, (2013) 52 ILM 988, art 13.

[37] Montreal Protocol art 7, (n 6).

submit reports on the amount and types of wastes governed by the convention which are exported and imported.[38] Information is also required on disposal operations and efforts to reduce the amount of waste subject to transboundary movements.[39]

- The Convention on International Trade in Endangered Species of Wild Fauna and Flora, 1973 (CITES) also requires parties to report annually to the Secretariat of all transactions involving protected species, including the types of permits authorised.[40] Such reports allow the Parties to ascertain the volume of trade in a given species as well as to review the propriety of permits issued.

In general, reports are prepared and submitted by parties at specified intervals and in a specified format for distribution to other parties. Such reporting requirements are generally binding (as is clear from the use of 'shall' in the examples above) and continue for as long as the State remains a party to the treaty.

The purpose of reporting requirements is to enhance State Party compliance with the treaty and increase transparency around State Party actions related to the core obligations of the treaty. It is considered that, if parties are required to collect and submit information on the measures they have taken to implement the treaty and the core activities they have been involved in, it is more likely that they will be focused on implementation and compliance. Such reporting also provides a basis for determining whether the objectives of the treaty are being met, or whether new policies need to be developed.

While such reports are submitted to fulfil a legally binding requirement in the treaty, from a treaty law and practice perspective their content will seldom be intended to create international legal obligations. Rather, their purpose is to provide factual information in accordance with a specific treaty obligation. As such, consistent with the guidance in Chapter 3, their language should reflect this.

From a State perspective, the greatest challenge in relation to such reporting requirements will be ensuring the necessary resources to comply with them. Many of the reporting requirements in multilateral treaties can be quite

[38] Basel Convention on the Control of Transboundary Movements of Hazardous Wastes and their Disposal (adopted 22 March 1989, entered into force 5 May 1992) 1673 UNTS 57, art 13(3)(b):

> The Parties, consistent with national laws and regulations, shall transmit, through the Secretariat, to the Conference of the Parties established under Article 15, before the end of each calendar year, a report on the previous calendar year, containing the following information: . . . (b) Information regarding transboundary movements of hazardous wastes or other wastes in which they have been involved, including: (i) The amount of hazardous wastes and other wastes exported, their category, characteristics, destination, any transit country and disposal method as stated on the response to notification; . . . (iv) Efforts to achieve a reduction of the amount of hazardous wastes or other wastes subject to transboundary movement.

[39] ibid.

[40] Convention on International Trade in Endangered Species of Wild Fauna and Flora (adopted 3 March 1973, entered into force 1 July 1975) 993 UNTS 243 (CITES), art VIII(6) and (7).

onerous and require co-ordination among various agencies. For example, the process of compiling information for New Zealand's first report in accordance with Article 13(3) of the Arms Trade Treaty required co-ordination between New Zealand's Ministry of Foreign Affairs and Trade, police, Ministry of Defence and Customs Office.

For Vietnam, to prepare its periodic reports on the implementation of the Convention on the Elimination of All Forms of Discrimination against Women, 1979,[41] the lead agency, which is the Ministry of Labour, Invalids and Social Affairs, has to co-ordinate with the MFA, the Ministry of Education and Training, the Ministry of Health, the Ministry of Justice, the Ministry of Culture, Sports and Tourism, the Ministry of Information and Communication and the Ministry of Public Security. Such extensive co-ordination can take significant time and effort for which States Parties need to start preparing well in advance of the treaty deadline for the report. In the case of Indonesia, the preparation of the implementation reports of the Convention on the Elimination of All Forms of Discrimination against Women may be even more complicated and extensive as the process involves not only ministries and government institutions at the national level but also regional governments, which consist of 34 provinces and more than 500 cities, and numerous NGOs. Such an extensive process of information-collecting can cause delays in submitting the report and sometimes forces Indonesia to combine implementation reports garnered over several years.

Collecting and compiling information held by multiple agencies can be costly and time-consuming and, depending on the scope of the information required, new data collection and storage processes may be required to ensure that reporting obligations are complied with. In the case of New Zealand, new procedures were needed, with a significant commitment of time and money, to ensure that required information was collected in such a way as to guarantee that Arms Trade Treaty reporting obligations could be annually complied with. Issues may also arise in relation to whether certain information should not be disclosed in reports because it is either commercially sensitive or classified. Most treaties enable States Parties to withhold such information. For example, the Arms Trade Treaty provides: 'Reports may exclude commercially sensitive or national security information.'[42] However, the process of determining what is commercially sensitive and/or national security information can be resource-intensive, especially when multiple agencies are involved, and a consistent approach must be taken across government.

Some treaties or COPs may also establish reporting templates, which provide guidance to States Parties on the specific information that should be included in reports (often the reporting requirement found in the treaty will

[41] Convention on the Elimination of All Forms of Discrimination against Women (adopted 18 December 1979, entered into force 9 September 1981) 1249 UNTS 13.

[42] Arms Trade Treaty, art 13(3).

not include any detail on presentation of data). An example is the CBD COP which has developed a detailed reporting template for States Parties to follow.[43] Under the United Nations Convention against Corruption, a Comprehensive Self-Assessment Checklist on Implementation has been created for States Parties.[44] A similar tool is currently being developed for the Arms Trade Treaty as part of the COP process. States Parties should ensure that, as much as possible, they are involved in the development of such templates, so as to ensure that the product adopted is workable, achievable and consistent with internal data collection and production processes. In the long term, it is much better to be part of template negotiations than have to struggle later to fit an unworkable template.

The last point to note on such templates is that they may or may not be legally binding. If they are prescribed in the treaty, States Parties will generally be obliged to comply with the treaty. However, if they are developed later by the COP or a specialised working group, they may offer more flexibility. States Parties should check the COP decision adopting the template to identify whether it is something they are legally bound to comply with, or whether it is something they can tailor to fit their own specific needs.

A final issue that can arise for States Parties in relation to reporting obligations is transparency. Should reports be disclosed to the public, or only circulated to the States Parties? Some treaties are not conclusive on this point. For example, the Arms Trade Treaty simply states that reports 'shall be made available, and distributed to the States Parties by the Secretariat'. There was initially no consensus among the States Parties as to whether this meant that reports should be made available to the public. The practice now followed is that States Parties can elect whether to make their reports publicly available, or available only to other States Parties, on the Arms Trade Treaty Secretariat website.

Irrespective of treaty requirements, individual States Parties are of course always entitled to make their own reports available to the public, by posting them on their own websites. In terms of the overall goal of reporting, disclosure of reports to the general public is obviously more effective in terms of ensuring robust public scrutiny. However, some parties may take the position of only disclosing reports where they are legally required to do so by the treaty.

In summary, while reporting obligations might seem a minor point in a treaty at the time of its negotiation and adoption, they can (like COPs) have major resource implications for States Parties. Care should be taken at the negotiating stage and before ratifying a treaty to ensure that the implications of these obligations are thought through, and that the resources and processes are in place to ensure State Party compliance.

[43] See CBD, 'National Reports' www.cbd.int/reports/ accessed 15 September 2018. See also CBD (n 9).

[44] See United Nations Office on Drugs and Crime, 'Comprehensive Self-Assessment Checklist on the Implementation of the United Nations Convention against Corruption' www.unodc.org /unodc/en/treaties/CAC/self-assessment.html accessed 15 September 2018.

Role of the Treaty Office

The internal responsibility for compiling periodic reports required by treaties falls naturally to the lead agency. The treaty will normally indicate to whom the report must be sent, and most commonly it is the secretariat which services the meetings, not the depositary. Each government may choose how and by whom it is sent; most commonly it will be the lead agency which takes care of this, as the report is not a document which requires any special treaty procedure. However, some governments may choose to submit their report through the Treaty Office, or via their diplomatic representation.

The Treaty Office may have a role in recording the date of submission of the report in its database, and archiving a copy. It may also publish the report in an official publication series; it may deposit it with the legislature for information; it may publish it on a treaty website. Equally, this could be done by the lead agency. These matters are governed by national laws and practices; the important thing is for there to be clear agreement between the ministries involved as to where these responsibilities lie.

Treaty Secretariats

When a treaty is created, it involves many actors such as States, the COP, subsidiary bodies and other stakeholders, for example, NGOs. To deal with this, many treaties provide for a secretariat and set out its functions and authority in the treaty text. Secretariats are established to provide the link between the treaty actors and assist their efforts to address the policy challenge in question. Secretariats do this by undertaking the administrative functions arising from the treaty, for example:

- arranging and servicing meetings of the COP and any subsidiary bodies;
- preparing and transmitting reports based on information received;
- in some cases, assisting developing country parties in compiling and transmitting requisite information;
- preparing activity reports for the COP;
- co-ordinating with secretariats of other international bodies; and
- performing residual functions as required by the treaty or COP.

Since the advent of the internet, secretariats also commonly maintain a website for the treaty, with information about activities under the treaty. The website may also contain treaty status information, but this information is not authoritative. The depositary is the only authoritative source of the authentic texts of treaties and information on status. An IO or treaty secretariat which displays treaty information on its subject pages needs to co-ordinate it directly with the Treaty Office that carries out the depositary functions.

The secretariat and the depositary may be different offices within the same IO. For example, in the CoE, the Treaty Office carries out all depositary functions for CoE treaties, whereas the Secretariat for a particular treaty is the operational department of the CoE that deals with that subject. To give an example of a particular treaty, the Secretariat for the Council of Europe Convention on Action against Trafficking in Human Beings 2005[45] consists of an Executive Secretary and six administrators,[46] who maintain web pages about the Convention and its aims and activities.[47] It contains status information (about signatures and ratifications) with a link through to the authoritative full list maintained by the Treaty Office.[48]

In other cases, the depositary and the secretariat are not in the same organisation. For example, the Depositary of the Antarctic Treaty is the Government of the United States of America, and these functions are carried out by the Treaty Office of the State Department in Washington.[49] The Secretariat of the Antarctic Treaty is located in Buenos Aires, Argentina, and it maintains a website devoted to the Treaty and related instruments, which includes a database of status information.[50] That information is however only as accurate as the information the Secretariat has received from the Depositary and entered, and so may be less up to date. It may also be less reliable for other reasons; the policy staff of a secretariat may be less meticulous in the way they present treaty information than the Treaty Office.

Secretariats are responsible for the efficient conduct of the work of the treaty, their main task being to ensure the smooth functioning of all meetings and conferences organised under the aegis of the treaty. Depositaries on the other hand are responsible for maintaining the legal records and status information. The States Parties to a treaty need to be aware of their distinctive roles and ensure that they have effective contacts with both. If a national Treaty Office requires a 100 per cent reliable authentic treaty text or treaty status information, it should obtain it directly from the depositary, not rely on a secretariat website.

Of note, the Secretariats of the UNFCCC[51] and the CBD also organise technical workshops to advance discussions in subsidiary bodies and then summarise the result. Some secretariats may also have a compliance monitoring role, if this has been agreed by the parties. For example, under the CITES,

[45] Council of Europe Convention on Action against Trafficking in Human Beings (adopted 3 May 2005, entered into force 1 February 2008) 2569 UNTS 33, CETS 197.

[46] CoE, 'Action against Trafficking in Human Beings: Contact Us' www.coe.int/en/web/anti-human-trafficking/contacts accessed 15 September 2018.

[47] CoE, 'Action against Trafficking in Human Beings: About the Convention' www.coe.int/en/web/anti-human-trafficking/about-the-convention accessed 15 September 2018.

[48] CoE, 'Chart of signatures and ratifications of Treaty 197: Council of Europe Convention on Action against Trafficking in Human Beings' www.coe.int/en/web/conventions/full-list/-/conventions/treaty/197/signatures?p_auth=C8VCXTSf accessed 15 September 2018.

[49] US State Department, 'Depository Information' www.state.gov/s/l/treaty/depositary/index.htm#ANTARCTICA accessed 15 September 2018.

[50] Secretariat of the Antarctic Treaty, 'Parties' www.ats.aq/devAS/ats_parties.aspx?lang=e and Secretariat of the Antarctic Treaty, 'Antarctic Treaty Database' www.ats.aq/devAS/info_measures_list.aspx?lang=e accessed 15 September 2018.

[51] UNFCCC (adopted 9 May 1992, entered into force 21 March 1994) 1771 UNTS 107.

the Secretariat is empowered to study reports submitted by States Parties and request any information it deems necessary to ensure the implementation of the Convention and to focus the attention of the States Parties on any pertinent matter (Article XII, 2(d) and (e)). The CITES also enables the Secretariat to notify a party directly if it believes that the Convention is not being effectively implemented, whereupon the Party in question is required to respond. (It may also request an inquiry, with information from the inquiry being furnished for the next meeting of the Parties (Article X).) The CITES example represents one of the more activist Secretariats in the environmental field. Frequently, the secretariat's authority set out in the treaty is more limited.

Secretariats are usually made up of a number of permanent staff, working in a permanent location. Secretariats of IOs can be very large – for example, the World Trade Organization (WTO) and UN Conference on Trade and Development Secretariats have about 640 and 400 employees respectively, as they do not merely serve as Secretariats for treaties under their purview but also carry out the day-to-day work of their organisations. At the other end of the scale is the secretariat for a particular treaty, such as the Arms Trade Treaty, which is likely to have, at least initially, only three to five permanent staff. A key feature of secretariats is their international character. Because secretariat staff do not owe allegiance to national governments, they may not receive instructions from any particular government but instead owe allegiance to the treaty, which leads to impartiality.

Like COPs, secretariats are usually established by the treaty. Some treaties establish their own secretariat, while others designate an existing body to take on secretariat tasks (since having their own secretariat requires more resources, the use of established secretariats may reduce these expenses). An example of the former is Article 18 of the Arms Trade Treaty, which provides:

> This Treaty hereby establishes a Secretariat to assist States Parties in the effective implementation of this Treaty. Pending the first meeting of the Conference of States Parties, a provisional Secretariat will be responsible for the administrative functions covered under this Treaty . . .
>
> The Secretariat shall be responsible to States Parties. Within a minimized structure, the Secretariat shall undertake the following responsibilities: (a) Receive, make available and distribute the reports as mandated by this Treaty; (b) Maintain and make available to States Parties the list of national points of contact; (c) Facilitate the matching of offers of and requests for assistance for Treaty implementation and promote international cooperation as requested; (d) Facilitate the work of the Conference of States Parties, including making arrangements and providing the necessary services for meetings under this Treaty; and (e) Perform other duties as decided by the Conferences of States Parties.

An example of the latter is Article 64 of the United Nations Convention against Corruption which provides: 'The Secretary-General of the United Nations shall provide the necessary secretariat services to the Conference of the States Parties to the Convention.'

Communicating with the Secretariat

Secretariats are the focal point for States Parties in relation to the submission and dissemination of documentation, providing States Parties with information on issues such as the timing, location and agenda of COPs and any proposed amendments to the treaty.

To ensure any effective information flow with secretariats, States Parties need to have a suitable national contact point to which all documentation produced by the secretariat is directed. This will usually also be the contact point used by other States Parties for any information they circulate or requests they may make. Usually it will be a requirement of the treaty to provide the secretariat with an official contact point and keep it updated. For example, Article 5(6) of the Arms Trade Treaty provides:

> Each State Party shall designate one or more national points of contact to exchange information on matters related to the implementation of this Treaty. Each State Party shall notify the Secretariat, established under Article 18, of its national point(s) of contact and keep the information updated.

If there is more than one contact point, States Parties need to make sure that information is shared internally within the government. Choosing an appropriate national contact point is very important. This can seem like a minor issue, but it is important to get it right. There have been instances where States Parties have designated an overseas embassy as their contact point, but because staff posted to the embassy rotate regularly, the information flow has stopped (for example, a new staff member who has not been properly briefed has no idea what to do with obscure documentation emanating from some unknown treaty secretariat). And so the information does not get to those who need it. This can be problematic; for example, if States Parties do not receive timely secretariat or depositary notifications of tacit acceptance amendments (see below), they may not have time to ensure that the correct domestic approval processes are complied with, and that any necessary implementing legislation is in place.

Given staff rotation issues, particularly in a foreign ministry, New Zealand practice is to establish a specific job title and generic email address as the contact point, rather than an individual official. Then, the contact point remains valid even where the individual officer rotates. If the contact point is not from the foreign ministry, care should also be taken to clarify the issues that need to be referred to the foreign ministry/Treaty Office for input/action. Likewise, the Treaty Office must pass depositary notifications to the lead agency, drawing their attention to any that might require action, such as a reservation by a new party. In the case of Vietnam and the United Nations Convention against Corruption, the Office of the Inspector-General of the Government (the contact point) works closely with the Department of

International Law and Treaties under the MFA, in communication with the COP and the Secretariat of the Convention.

Communication with a secretariat is typically done using the traditional diplomatic note format, especially when it comes to important issues such as treaty implementation or COPs (technical inquiries or logistical questions can also be done via email). Such notes should clearly state the relevant article of the treaty that the communication is being submitted in accordance with. It is always wise to verify secretariat contact points prior to sending (details are usually provided on the treaty website) and, for those communications satisfying a binding treaty obligations (for example, the submission of State Party reporting), to request confirmation of receipt from the secretariat. Unless the secretariat advises otherwise, formal notifications that affect treaty obligations should normally be addressed to the depositary.

Compliance Mechanisms

A number of multilateral treaties contain procedures that are designed to encourage States to take concrete steps to implement the treaties. The simplest procedure is a provision requiring States to report within a certain period on the measures they have taken to implement their obligations under the treaty. As discussed above in the section on reporting, this usually involves a report setting out the laws and regulations they have adopted under their national law to implement their treaty obligations. It can also include reports on the government agency responsible for implementing the treaty, the names and contact details of focal points within their government, etc.[52]

For example, the 1996 Protocol to the Convention on the Prevention of Marine Pollution by Dumping of Wastes and Other Matter of 29 December 1972 contains several provisions that are designed to encourage States to implement the Protocol.[53] Article 9 requires States Parties to make reports on the administrative and legislative measures taken to implement the Protocol. Article 11 provides that the Meeting to Contracting Parties shall establish procedures and mechanisms necessary to assess and promote compliance with the Protocol.[54] Finally, Article 26 allows Contracting Parties to give notice that for a specified transitional period, they are not able to comply with certain provisions in the Protocol.

Some modern treaties also contain provisions that permit States Parties to identify situations of non-compliance by other States Parties. These provisions

[52] See the section on 'Reporting Requirements in Treaties' above at 305–10.

[53] Protocol to the Convention on the Prevention of Marine Pollution by Dumping of Wastes and Other Matter of 29 December 1972 (adopted 7 November 1996, entered into force 24 March 2006) 36 ILM 1 (1997).

[54] For the procedures adopted in 2007, see IMO, 'Compliance Procedures and Mechanisms Pursuant to Article 11 of the 1996 Protocol to the London Convention 1972' www.imo.org /en/OurWork/Environment/LCLP/Compliance/Documents/Compliance%20Procedures.pdf accessed 15 September 2018.

are different from dispute settlement mechanisms (which apply to disputes over the interpretation and application of a treaty) in that their focus is on factual enquiry as to whether another State Party is complying with the treaty. Some treaties also provide that States Parties may refer any alleged non-compliance by another Party to the committee for consideration and recommendation to the COP; some provide for States Parties to self-refer any concerns they may have about their own compliance (often coupled with a request for technical assistance); some provide for referral by an expert body appointed by the parties; some (rarely) provide for referral by NGOs.

Procedures addressing the issue of non-compliance are most commonly found in environmental, disarmament and human rights treaties. They can take a variety of forms, and many also include a specific role for the secretariat (see the CITES example above). Other examples are given here:

The Montreal Protocol on Substances that Deplete the Ozone Layer, 1987 contains an article on non-compliance, which requires Parties at the first COP to consider and approve procedures and institutional mechanisms for establishing non-compliance and the treatment of Parties in non-compliance.[55] At the first COP, the Parties agreed to a process that led to the establishment of an 'Implementation Committee' which reports regularly to the COP with recommendations. A good example of this non-compliance procedure in operation can be seen in the case of the Russian Federation, the issue of whose record under the Montreal Protocol was raised before the Implementation Committee in 1995. By 2002, following public scrutiny and the provision of funds and assistance, the Russian Federation had achieved compliance.

The Convention on the Prohibition of the Development, Production, Stockpiling and Use of Chemical Weapons and on their Destruction, 1993 enables Parties to challenge other Parties' compliance with the convention through a compliance committee, and also incorporates a procedure for conducting 'on-site challenge inspection' of any facility or location for which compliance has been challenged by neutral inspection teams or the technical secretariat.[56] Inspection reports are prepared and circulated to all States Parties.

The International Covenant on Civil and Political Rights, 1966 (ICCPR) establishes the Human Rights Committee, which consists of independent experts that monitor the implementation and Parties' compliance to the Covenant.[57] Article 40 of the Covenant requires States Parties to submit regular reports to the Committee on the implementation of their obligations under the Covenant. The Committee then examines each report and makes

55 Montreal Protocol (n 6) art 8.

56 Convention on the Prohibition of the Development, Production, Stockpiling and Use of Chemical Weapons and on their Destruction (adopted 13 January 1993, entered into force 29 April 1997) 1974 UNTS 45, art IX.

57 International Covenant on Civil and Political Rights (adopted 16 December 1966, entered into force 23 March 1976) 999 UNTS 171, art 28.

concluding observations, a process that basically constitutes a review of a State Party's implementation and compliance to the Covenant. The country report and the Committee's concluding observations are available to the public on the website of the Office of the UN High Commissioner for Human Rights. The Committee is also empowered to receive inter-State and individual communications on alleged violations of the Covenant by States Parties.[58] However, States Parties need to ratify or accede to the Optional Protocol to the International Covenant on Civil and Political Rights, 1966 and/or make a declaration to enable these mechanisms to take effect.[59]

Unlike the COP and reporting obligations identified above, some States will never in practice need to deal with the compliance mechanisms in a treaty they are party to (because their compliance is never challenged, or they never see a need to challenge another party). However, States becoming party to a treaty with compliance mechanisms should carefully consider the implications of such mechanisms, and put in place procedures to deal with them, should the need arise. At a minimum, the lead agency that would manage a State's response should be identified; the lead agency should be clear on what the processes are and what kind of response they would be required to provide, should their compliance be challenged.

Action on reporting requirements and compliance mechanisms will normally be co-ordinated by the lead agency responsible for the subject matter of the treaty. However, if the lead agency receives any formal complaint from a body created under the treaty or from another State Party that it has failed to fulfil its reporting requirements or any responsibilities under the treaty, it should immediately consult the government's international law advisers.

Financial and Technical Assistance Available to States Parties

While the other topics in this chapter deal with continuing obligations imposed on States – attending COPs, submitting reports, engaging in compliance and dispute settlement procedures – this section is different. It deals with the assistance that developing countries can seek from States Parties, the secretariat or in some cases the COP. Recognising the challenge for many developing countries in treaty implementation, some treaties provide for assistance for developing States, ranging from financial support to technical assistance and training.

An example is the CBD which has various provisions on financial and technical assistance. Articles 20(2) and 21(1), which relate to the provision of financial resources to assist developing country participants to implement the treaty, provide:

[58] ibid, art 41 and Optional Protocol to the International Covenant on Civil and Political Rights (adopted 16 December 1966, entered into force 23 March 1976) 999 UNTS 171.

[59] ibid.

> **Article 20(2)**
> The developed country Parties shall provide new and additional financial resources to enable developing country Parties to meet the agreed full incremental costs to them of implementing measures which fulfil the obligations of this Convention and to benefit from its provisions and which costs are agreed between a developing country Party and the institutional structure referred to in Article 21, in accordance with policy, strategy, programme priorities and eligibility criteria and an indicative list of incremental costs established by the Conference of the Parties.
>
> **Article 21(1)**
> There shall be a mechanism for the provision of financial resources to developing country Parties for purposes of this Convention on a grant or concessional basis the essential elements of which are described in this Article. The mechanism shall function under the authority and guidance of, and be accountable to, the Conference of the Parties for purposes of this Convention. The operations of the mechanism shall be carried out by such institutional structure as may be decided upon by the Conference of the Parties at its first meeting. For purposes of this Convention, the Conference of the Parties shall determine the policy, strategy, programme priorities and eligibility criteria relating to the access to and utilization of such resources. The contributions shall be such as to take into account the need for predictability, adequacy and timely flow of funds referred to in Article 20 in accordance with the amount of resources needed to be decided periodically by the Conference of the Parties and the importance of burden-sharing among the contributing Parties included in the list referred to in Article 20, paragraph 2. Voluntary contributions may also be made by the developed country Parties and by other countries and sources. The mechanism shall operate within a democratic and transparent system of governance.

The CBD also contains Article 12 on the provision of research and training for the benefit of developing country participants:

> The Contracting Parties, taking into account the special needs of developing countries, shall:
>
> (a) Establish and maintain programmes for scientific and technical education and training in measures for the identification, conservation and sustainable use of biological diversity and its components and provide support for such education and training for the specific needs of developing countries;
> (b) Promote and encourage research which contributes to the conservation and sustainable use of biological diversity, particularly in developing countries, inter alia, in accordance with decisions of the Conference of the Parties taken in consequence of recommendations of the Subsidiary Body on Scientific, Technical and Technological Advice;

The CBD, like a number of other treaties, also has a voluntary trust fund to which countries and organisations can contribute. These funds are usually used to cover travel costs of developing country parties, in particular the least developed and small island developing States, and other parties with economies in transition, to enable them to attend COP and other meetings.

In Southeast Asia, ASEAN adopted the ASEAN Agreement on Transboundary Haze Pollution, 2002 that established the ASEAN Transboundary Haze Pollution Control Fund to assist States Parties in the implementation of the Agreement.[60] The Fund is administered by the ASEAN Secretariat under the guidance of the COP and is open to contributions from States Parties and other sources, subject to the agreement of or approval by the Parties. The COP, with help from the ASEAN Secretariat and the ASEAN Coordinating Council, is exploring the possibilities of increasing States Parties' contribution to the Fund.[61] Additionally, under the guidance of the COP, the existing Fund is channelled to fund activities such as the development of techniques to control burning for shifting cultivators and small farmers and the promotion of appropriate methods for disposal or use of agricultural waste.[62]

On the basis of resolution 55/7 on Oceans and the law of the sea adopted by the UNGA on 30 October 2000, a voluntary trust fund was established by the Secretary General to assist States Parties of UNCLOS[63] in connection with disputes to be settled by the International Tribunal for the Law of the Sea. In addition, the International Tribunal for the Law of the Sea also created a separate trust fund to promote human resource development in developing countries in the law of the sea and maritime affairs in general.[64] These funds have been used to provide various technical assistance and capacity-building to States. For example, funds have been used to assist developing countries prepare submissions to the Commission on the Limits of the Continental Shelf, established by UNCLOS, concerning the outer limits of their continental shelf extending beyond 200 nautical miles.

So how do States Parties find out about, and take advantage of, such funds and provisions? And what are the best ways to provide such assistance so that it has meaningful results and is in line with developing country priorities?

One example is the technical assistance provided to Pacific Island countries by New Zealand under the Arms Trade Treaty. Unlike the CBD, the Arms Trade Treaty's provisions on assistance are quite general – essentially encouraging States Parties to work together to provide necessary assistance to each

[60] ASEAN Agreement on Transboundary Haze Pollution (adopted 10 June 2002, entered into force 25 November 2003) ADS (2002) 138, art 20.

[61] Roadmap on ASEAN cooperation towards transboundary haze pollution control with means of implementation (adopted 11 August 2016) 6 https://asean.org/wp-content/uploads/2012/05/Haze-Roadmap.pdf accessed 26 September 2018.

[62] ibid 13.

[63] UNCLOS (adopted 10 December 1982, entered into force 16 November 1994) 1833 UNTS 3.

[64] See United Nations Division for Ocean Affairs and the Law of the Sea, 'International Tribunal for the Law of the Sea Trust Fund' (2011) www.un.org/Depts/los/itlos_new/itlos_trust_fund.htm accessed 1 November 2018. See also UNGA Res 55/7 'Oceans and the Law of the Sea' (27 February 2001).

other and providing examples of the types of assistance that may be provided (see Article 16). A key challenge for Pacific Island countries in implementing the Arms Trade Treaty has been understanding the legislative changes needed to implement the treaty's core obligations. Accordingly, pursuant to Article 16, the New Zealand Government has sponsored the development of model legislative provisions to assist in identifying and translating Arms Trade Treaty commitments into national legislation.[65] This model legislation has been used by Pacific countries to help with their implementation processes and has been identified as a particularly helpful tool by many countries (to such an extent that it is now being used by other regions, including the Caribbean and Southeast Asia).

Continuing Engagement with Treaty Acts

Handling of Treaty Amendments

Amendments to treaties may be proposed at any point in the life of a treaty.[66] Part IV of the VCLT 1969 and VCLT 1986, Articles 39 to 41 in both cases, deal with amendments.[67] These articles set out the general principle that a treaty may be amended by agreement between the parties, and some further rules that apply unless the treaty itself provides otherwise. The key point is that all amendments to treaties are legally binding agreements themselves – they have treaty status. So, in principle, the procedures set out in Chapters 5, 6 and 7 apply. In light of this, it is essential to involve the Treaty Office in any process to amend a treaty: the Treaty Office should review the final agreed text of the amendment to ensure that it conforms to the principles set out in Chapter 3, and will also usually play the lead role in preparing the documents to effect the amendment, on both the international and domestic planes.

Amendments to Bilateral Treaties

Bilateral treaties can be amended more easily than multilaterals. Some bilateral treaties expressly provide for amendment, and set out a procedure. Usually it is a very simple procedure such as 'an amendment may be agreed in writing'. Article 18.3 of the Thailand–New Zealand Closer Economic Partnership Agreement, 2005 is an example of a typical bilateral amendment clause: 'This Agreement may be amended by agreement in writing by the Parties, and such

[65] See Small Arms Survey, 'Arms Trade Treaty: Model Law' www.smallarmssurvey.org/fileadmin/docs/E-Co-Publications/SAS-NZ-Gov-Arms-Trade-Treaty-Model-Law.pdf accessed 15 September 2018.

[66] For example, the SOLAS 1960 was amended six times after it entered into force in 1965 – in 1966, 1967, 1968, 1969, 1971 and 1973. International Convention for the Safety of Life at Sea, (adopted 17 June 1960, entered into force 26 May 1965) 536 UNTS 27.

[67] VCLT 1969 (adopted 23 May 1969, entered into force 27 January 1980) 1155 UNTS 331 arts 39–41 and VCLT 1986 (adopted 21 March 1986, not in force) 25 ILM 543 arts 39–41 http://legal.un.org/ilc/texts/instruments/english/conventions/1_2_1986.pdf accessed 9 September 2018.

amendments shall enter into force on such date or dates as may be agreed between them.'[68]

Therefore, the first step is to check the provisions of the treaty itself to see whether amendment is provided for, and if so how.[69] However, even if the bilateral treaty does not contain an amendment provision, this does not mean that it cannot be amended. A bilateral treaty can always be amended by a later treaty between the two parties. Even if the treaty expressly states that it shall remain in force for a certain period and this has not expired, it can be amended by a new treaty. Although a bilateral treaty might provide a specific procedure for amending it, this can be disregarded if the two parties agree to amend it by a new treaty.

As for any bilateral treaty, an amending treaty may be set out in the form of a single-text agreement with final clauses, to be signed by both parties (definitively or subject to ratification), or as an exchange of notes.[70] An exchange of notes is usually more convenient to arrange than a single treaty text, as it does not require both signatures to be written onto the same document.

An exchange of notes also has advantages over less formal written methods. Although a requirement that any amendment be agreed 'in writing' could be satisfied in less formal ways such as an exchange of letters or emails, using an exchange of notes is preferable; as diplomatic notes are given official reference numbers, the amendment would be properly recorded, filed and retained on a permanent record internally within each government. The relative formality of notes also helps to make clear that both sides intend to make a legally binding amendment. It is undesirable to rely on agreement by very informal means, such as email exchanges, as there may later be doubt as to what was agreed, its intended legal effect and/or the date of entry into force.[71] Moreover, a pair of diplomatic notes would be in a suitable form for publication as a treaty document, whereas ordinary correspondence might not be.

How to Draft an Exchange of Notes Setting out Agreement to Amend a Bilateral Treaty

Typically, the initiating diplomatic note will propose the amendment and the date of entry into force or the further procedure required to bring it into force. The responding note will confirm the other party's agreement to the proposal, and will normally set out the proposal verbatim so that there can be no doubt

[68] Thailand–New Zealand Closer Economic Partnership Agreement art 18.3.

[69] For an example of a bilateral treaty with no amendment provision, see Annex I, Example of Final Clauses in a Single-instrument Bilateral Treaty, 418–19.

[70] See the section on 'Preparing a Treaty Formed by Exchange of Instruments' in Chapter 5 at 183–84 and the section on 'Exchange of Instruments Constituting a Treaty' in Chapter 6 at 223–25. For an example of an amending treaty, see Annex IV, Examples of an Exchange of Letters Constituting a Treaty, Example B, 429–36.

[71] A Aust, *Modern Treaty Law and Practice* (3rd edn, CUP 2013) 234.

what is agreed. Either party can send the initiating note. The format is the same as for any other exchange of notes constituting a treaty.[72]

The amendment or amendments may be set out in terms of the exact words to be added, deleted or replaced with new wording. For example, 'Article X shall be deleted and replaced by new Articles X1 and X2 which shall read as follows'. Alternatively, the agreement may provide that the whole of the existing treaty shall be replaced by the new treaty as amended, and set out the whole new consolidated text. The legal effect is the same, and it is a matter of convenience which form is preferred. If the whole text is replaced, it would be helpful to specify somewhere which provisions have been amended, as this may not be obvious to future readers. This could be done in a preamble, or in an accompanying explanatory note, outside the treaty text. It is best not to set out both the amendment itself and the consolidated text in the treaty; if you give both treaty status but make an error in one of them, it will not be clear which is the correct version.[73]

Prior Negotiation of the Text of the Amendment

Before concluding an exchange of notes to amend a treaty, it is highly advisable to share and agree on a draft text in advance with the other party. It is important to check that the notes are expressed in language that makes clear that the amendment is intended to be legally binding (see Chapter 3), and also that the second note incorporates the full text of the first note with 100 per cent accuracy. In other words, the exchange has to be choreographed in advance. So, although it may appear to the reader that the proposal was initiated on the date of the first note, in fact the wording will have been agreed by the negotiators of both parties before the first note is sent.

Simply initiating an exchange of notes without prior consultations with the other party on timing and content is not a good idea, as this may result in the note being misinterpreted or ignored, or a counterproposal being made in the reply note, with the outcome of the exchanges being left unclear.

Drafting an Entry into Force Provision for an Amendment to a Bilateral Treaty

If the amendment is being made pursuant to an amendment clause in the original treaty, its mode of entry into force may be set out in that clause. Otherwise, it is up to the parties to determine the date of entry into force, or how it is to be calculated, in the text of the amendment. You have several options when drafting the entry into force provisions.

If the amending agreement is in the form of an exchange of notes, you could provide for the amendment to enter into force:

[72] See the section on 'Preparing a Treaty Formed by Exchange of Instruments' in Chapter 5 at 183–84 and the section on 'Exchange of Instruments Constituting a Treaty' in Chapter 6 at 223–25.

[73] For an example of an exchange of notes to amend a treaty, see Annex IV.B 'Example of Exchange of Letters B' at 429–36.

- on a specified date;
- on the date of receipt of the later of the two notes constituting the amending agreement (although this is not a desirable option as, unless the notes are exchanged in person or further communications take place, the initiating party will not automatically know the exact date of receipt by the receiving party);
- a specified length of time after the date of receipt of the later of the two notes constituting the amending agreement (although similar problems as described above can occur if the notes are not exchanged in person), such as 'x days';
- after both parties have notified the other of the completion of their respective domestic procedures (for examples of this kind of wording, see below); or
- a specified length of time after both parties have notified the other of the completion of their respective domestic procedures, such as 'x days' (for examples of this kind of wording, see below).

The options are the same as for any other exchange of notes constituting a treaty, and the suitability of each for different circumstances is also the same.[74]

If your amending agreement is in the form of a single text to be signed by both sides at a meeting, you could provide that it will enter into force:

- on a specified future date (after the date of signature);
- on the date of signature (or the later of the two signatures if they are not done at a meeting);
- a specified length of time after the date of signature (or the later of the two signatures), such as 'x days';
- after both parties have notified the other of the completion of their respective domestic procedures (for examples of this kind of wording, see below);
- after the parties have exchanged instruments of ratification, that is, on the date of the later of the two deliveries; or
- a specified length of time after both parties have notified the other of the completion of their respective domestic procedures, or delivered their respective instruments of ratification, such as 'x days' (for examples of this kind of wording, see below).

These options are functionally the same as those for an exchange of notes.

Bringing an Amendment to a Bilateral Treaty into Force

The previous section outlines the most common types of entry into force provisions for an amending treaty. These work in exactly the same way as for any other kind of treaty.[75]

[74] See the section on 'Preparing a Treaty Formed by Exchange of Instruments' in Chapter 5 at 183–84 and the section on 'Exchange of Instruments Constituting a Treaty' in Chapter 6 at 223–25.

[75] See the section on 'Expressing Consent to Be Bound by the Treaty' in Chapter 7 at 247–68.

If the amendment is made by an exchange of notes, and the date of entry into force is specified in the notes or to be calculated by reference to the date of receipt of the later of the two notes (the first three of the options discussed above),[76] no further action is required following the exchange of notes. The two sides simply need to confirm the effective date in writing, to make sure that there is no misunderstanding with regard to the date. The best way to achieve this is to have the date specified in both notes.

Where the amendment is made by a single text agreement, and the date of entry into force is the date of signature, there is no scope for ambiguity. If the date is to be calculated by reference to the date of signature, the two sides should confer to ensure that they have made the same calculation.

If the entry into force of a treaty is to take effect after the parties have taken a further step – such as notification of the completion of the parties' respective domestic procedures or exchange of ratification instruments[77] – the specified further step needs to be taken.[78] If there is a further step of this kind, it is always wise to seek advice from the other party as to what domestic processes they will need to complete before the amendment can be brought into force and how long they are likely to take. It may be that one side will have a lengthy process while the other side may not need to complete any procedures.

Amendments to Multilateral Treaties

Multilateral treaties do of course pose more problems, simply because there are more parties to consider. Amendments to multilateral treaties are often done by means of an amending treaty which can be – but is not always – called a Protocol. The complicating issues arise when you are trying to determine which States are a party to which parts of the treaty, especially if there is more than one amending Protocol, and not all States are a party to each Protocol.

The situation may then arise that some States are a party to the original treaty only; some are a party to the original treaty and just one, or perhaps more than one Protocol; and some may even be a party to one or more of the amending Protocols only. These circumstances then require very careful consideration to determine which States are a party to which provisions within the treaty, and how those States interact with other parties. Where an amendment provision is part of a treaty, it is usually designed to meet the particular needs of that treaty; provisions therefore can and do differ from treaty to treaty, and can be quite complex.

[76] See the list of modes of entry into force provided in the section on 'Drafting an Entry into Force Provision for an Amendment to a Bilateral Treaty' at 321–22.

[77] ibid. This refers to the fourth and fifth options for exchange of notes and the fourth, fifth and sixth options for single-text agreements.

[78] See the sections on 'Requirement for Notification of Completion of Domestic Procedures' and 'Exchanging Instruments of Ratification of a Bilateral Treaty' in Chapter 7 at 265–68 and 253–54 respectively.

Such provisions will often have some similarities however, for example: stating how many parties to the treaty are required to support an amendment proposal before it can be put to all the parties; whether an amendment once adopted is subject to ratification or acceptance, and if so how many parties need to do so before the amendment enters into force; and whether the amendment also binds those parties that have not ratified or accepted it.

When considering submitting an amendment, or when you receive notification of an amendment proposal by another State from the depositary, you will need to look very carefully at the provisions of the treaty, and determine the form that the proposal should be in and the provisions required.

Usually, amendments to modern multilateral treaties with a COP will first be formally proposed and discussed at the COP. As noted above, many COPs have as a specific function the consideration of amendments, and many multilateral treaties require that any amendment proposals must be adopted by the COP.[79]

Because of the number of parties to multilateral treaties, concluding amendments can be difficult. Typically, States become parties to amendments to multilateral treaties in the same way they become party to the treaty – by depositing an instrument of ratification, acceptance or approval. For example, Article 29(3) CBD provides that amendments agreed by the COP 'shall be submitted by the Depositary to all Parties for ratification, acceptance or approval'.[80]

Typically then, amendments enter into force only once a specific number of States Parties have ratified, accepted or approved them. Because multilateral treaties have so many parties, it can take a long time for amendments to enter into force. As alluded to above, waiting for individual parties to ratify amendments can also raise complexities where some parties have ratified an amendment and others have not.

Tacit Acceptance Procedures

Some multilateral treaties have adopted alternative procedures, designed to speed up the process of technical amendments entering into force, called tacit acceptance procedures. Typically, a provision providing for tacit acceptance will set out a deadline for States Parties to express their desire not to be bound. Those that stay silent past the deadline are considered to have tacitly accepted the amendment.

A tacit acceptance procedure was developed by the IMO in the early 1970s to accelerate the entry into force of 'technical' amendments to IMO treaties. For example, the SOLAS amendments from 1966 to 1973 dealing with fire safety measures for passenger ships, arrangements for life-saving appliances, navigational equipment and routing of ships languished under the traditional explicit

79 See for example Arms Trade Treaty art 17(4)(c) and Vienna Convention for the Protection of the Ozone Layer art 6(4)(e) and (f).

80 Other examples include art 69(3) of the United Nations Convention against Corruption, which stipulates that an amendment adopted by the COPs 'is subject to ratification, acceptance or approval'.

acceptance process, but entered into force relatively quickly after the IMO adopted tacit acceptance in 1974.[81]

The modern practice of the IMO is that the main convention is a framework agreement. Technical details are set out in the Annex that is an integral part of the Convention. Almost all chapters in the Annex are amended on a regular basis in light of technological developments. The main Convention provides that a 'tacit acceptance' procedure applies to amendments of most of the chapters in the Annex.[82] Under the tacit acceptance procedure, the amendments to a chapter of the Annex will enter into force for all States Parties to the Convention and the Annex unless a certain percentage of the States Parties object to the amendments by a prescribed date.[83] This procedure ensures that all of the States Parties to the Convention are legally bound by all the technical amendments to the Annexes. Tacit acceptance has subsequently become the favoured IMO tool for safety and environmental amendments. It has also been utilised by the World Health Assembly for revisions to the International Health Regulations.

While the tacit acceptance procedure has helped amendments to enter into force quickly, it can be problematic from a domestic perspective, particularly for States whose domestic treaty processes require all treaty actions to be approved by the executive or the legislature before they enter into force. With the usual processes of ratification or acceptance of amendments to multilateral treaties, States are in control of the timing and can delay depositing their instrument of ratification/acceptance until such time as it suits them (once all domestic processes have been complied with). However, with the tacit acceptance procedure, States have no control over timing: the timeframe is pre-determined and if States Parties take no action before the deadline, they are taken to have consented to the amendment. As a result, if a State's domestic treaty process requires that all treaty actions be approved by parliament and/or the executive, this can mean that officials have to scramble to get the necessary approvals before the deadline. This is a problem for many States given the wide acceptance of IMO Conventions.[84]

This issue arose for New Zealand in 2007 in relation to the International Health Regulations (2005),[85] which was a major revision of the original International Health Regulations 1969.[86] Unusually, the Health Regulations entered into force

[81] SOLAS 1974 (adopted 1 November 1974, entered into force 25 May 1980) 1184 UNTS 277, art VIII(b)(vi)(2).

[82] ibid. This rule applies to the amendment of all chapters in the Annex, except for chapter 1; see also art VIII(b)(vi)(1).

[83] ibid art VIII(vi)(2)(bb).

[84] As an indication, for examples, the SOLAS has only 162 States Parties. See IMO, 'Status of Conventions' www.imo.org/en/About/Conventions/StatusOfConventions/Pages/Default.aspx accessed 15 September 2018.

[85] International Health Regulations (2005) (adopted 23 May 2005, entered into force 15 June 2007) 2509 UNTS 79.

[86] International Health Regulations (adopted 25 July 1969, entered into force 1 January 1971, superseded) 764 UNTS 3.

through a tacit acceptance procedure (usually the procedure is only used for technical amendments).[87] The Regulations were adopted by the World Health Assembly on 23 May 2005 and Member States had a period of 18 months, until 15 December 2006, to lodge reservations about or to reject the regulations. Any Member that stayed silent was deemed to be bound as at 15 December. However, for a variety of reasons, the Regulations were only presented to the New Zealand House of Representatives for consideration pursuant to the New Zealand treaty process on 19 December, *after* the expiry of the deadline (at the point that New Zealand was already legally bound by the Regulations).[88]

Following this incident, the New Zealand Treaty Office now ensures that where any treaty containing a tacit acceptance amendment procedure is put forward to Cabinet for approval, this issue is considered in advance and clearly highlighted in the approval documents considered by Cabinet. A procedure is in place to ensure that any governmental approval or legislation needed can be obtained within the tacit acceptance timetable.[89]

In Indonesia, the issue of tacit acceptance for 'technical amendments' is prescribed under Law No. 24 of 2000 on International Agreements. Pursuant to the Law, a 'simplified procedure' applies to any treaty amendment that is 'administrative or technical' in nature.[90] Such treaty amendment has been defined to mean 'not concerning the substance of the treaty'[91] and generally will cover an amendment subject to the tacit acceptance procedure, which largely only applies to technical amendments. In practice, the relevant lead agency will decide if a proposed amendment is administrative or technical in nature. If the lead agency considers the amendment as a technical or administrative amendment, then such amendment will not be subjected to the usual procedure for treaty actions (which consist of approval/acceptance by the President and/or House of Representatives, depending on the subject matter).[92] Vietnam has likewise established a simplified procedure for amendments of a technical nature, whereby the lead agency may be able to decide to tacitly accept the amendment without having to consult the legislature or, in some cases, without even submitting its proposal to the government or consulting other agencies.

87 International Health Regulations (2005) art 59.

88 Health Committee of the Forty-eighth Parliament of New Zealand, 'International Treaty Examination of the International Health Regulations 2005' www.parliament.nz/resource/0000024380 accessed 15 September 2018. See also New Zealand Government, 'Government Response to Report of the Health Committee on International Treaty Examination of the International Health Regulations 2005' www.parliament.nz/ennz/pb/presented/papers/48DBHOH_PAP15607_1/government-response-to-report-of-the-health-committee-on accessed 15 September 2018.

89 In the drafting instructions for New Zealand National Interest Analyses, one of the mandatory sections is 'Identify whether amendments enter into force automatically for the Parties'.

90 Law No. 24 of 2000 on International Agreements, 23 October 2000, State Gazette No. 185 art 16(4). An unofficial translation of this law is provided by the MFA of Indonesia and on file with the authors.

91 ibid art 16(4). 92 ibid. See also arts 10–11.

However, even where a simplified procedure has been put in place to ensure that approvals can be obtained quickly, the tacit acceptance process can still be problematic for States where amendments require domestic implementation. This is because, as explained in previous chapters, domestic implementation must be completed before a State becomes bound by any treaty or treaty amendment. Because States have no control over timing with tacit acceptance procedures, this can make it hard to ensure that domestic legislation is enacted prior to the expiry of the deadline – especially given that government departments often have little control over the timing of passage of legislation. It is therefore desirable when enacting legislation implementing a treaty which provides for amendment through tacit acceptance, to include a simple and quick means of amending or supplementing any relevant legislation, if possible by secondary legislation. This should be achievable as, in most cases, tacit amendment procedures apply only to technical, non-substantive issues which should be amenable to secondary legislation.

Singapore has developed a very efficient procedure for implementing IMO conventions and making the amendments to the Annexes to IMO Conventions, which are subject to the tacit acceptance procedure, part of Singapore's domestic law promptly. The Singapore Parliament amended the Prevention of the Pollution of the Sea Act in 1999 in effect to give the Maritime and Port Authority of Singapore, with the approval of the Minister for Transport, the power to issue regulations to implement any IMO Convention on marine pollution, or any amendment to an IMO Convention on marine pollution.[93] For example, the Prevention of Pollution of the Sea (Garbage) Regulations 2012 provides that Annex V of the International Convention for the Prevention of Pollution from Ships 1973 (MARPOL) 73/78 on garbage has the force of law in Singapore.[94] The subsequent amendments by the IMO to Annex V in 2013, 2015 and 2016 were implemented by the Maritime and Port Authority based on the amendments of the Regulations in 2013, 2015 and 2016.[95]

Registration of Treaty Amendments

Where a new instrument modifies the scope or application of a parent agreement, this instrument must also be registered with the UN Secretary General. However, in order for such an instrument to be registered, the original treaty to which it relates must first have been registered. In the case of bilateral treaties, either party may register the amendment. In the

[93] Prevention of the Pollution of the Sea Act 1990 (as last amended in 2017) C 243.

[94] Prevention of Pollution of the Sea (Garbage) Regulations 2012 (as last amended in 2016) C 243 S668 art 3.

[95] ibid. The regulations were amended by the enactment of amendment acts S 471/2013, S 797/2015 and S 668/2016, respectively. See Singapore Statutes Online, 'Prevention of Pollution of the Sea (Garbage) Regulations 2012 – Timeline' (Attorney General Chambers of Singapore, 1 March 2018) https://sso.agc.gov.sg/SL/PPSA1990-S663-2012?DocDate=20180228 accessed 2 November 2018.

case of a multilateral treaty, registration should normally be carried out by the depositary.[96]

Handling of Reservations and Objections to Reservations

Another aspect of continuing engagement that a State Party or IO party to a treaty has to deal with is how to handle reservations and objections to reservations. The handling of the notifications naturally falls to the Treaty Office, but the question of whether to respond to another party's reservation or response to its own reservation is a decision with both policy and legal dimensions.[97]

The Treaty Office should keep careful records of each reservation made by its own government or IO. In addition, it should maintain careful records of any objection or any other type of formal response to the reservation it receives from the depositary or direct from any other party to the treaty.

Under the general rules on reservations, other States Parties have a right to object to the reservation. In most cases the depositary would notify the reserving State of any objections to its reservation. The Treaty Office should keep a careful record of any objections and seek advice from the international law experts on whether to make an official response to any objection.

When any State (or IO) party to a treaty makes a reservation, the depositary will officially notify all other States and IO parties and signatories. Each party's Treaty Office will receive the notice that another State or IO has made a reservation. The Treaty Office should forward the information to the lead agencies for the treaty in question, and advise them of the deadline by which any objection to the reservation must be submitted, as well as the procedure for responding to a reservation. Treaty Offices may however receive a large number of notifications of this kind, especially if their State is party to many multilateral treaties. Governments will naturally focus their attention on notifications relating to treaties that are of high national interest; or where they have a specific national interest in a particular type of reservation that other parties might make (for example, relating to human rights, law of the sea or sovereignty issues). The decision on whether to respond to another party's notification will be primarily a policy decision, but it should always be informed by international law advice, and the notification to the depositary should be checked and sent by the Treaty Office.

Handling of Declarations

Another aspect of continuing engagement that a party to a treaty has to deal with is how to handle declarations made by another party. As with

[96] Treaty Section of the Office of Legal Affairs, *Treaty Handbook* (2nd edn, UN 2012) 34, para 5.5.4. See also the section on 'Registering the Treaty at the UN' in Chapter 7 at 283–85.

[97] See the section on 'Procedures for Reservations and Declarations' in Chapter 7 at 268–76.

reservations, it is the responsibility of the Treaty Office to process and record these communications, ensure that they are seen by officials across government or the IO who are responsible for the subject matter of the treaty and the international law advisers, and make sure that any response is expressed in proper form and deposited correctly. The substance of any response is a combined policy and legal decision.

There are several types of declarations. First, a treaty may contain a provision expressly providing that States Parties are required to, or have an option to, make a declaration on certain matters. Such declarations often concern the provisions on dispute settlement. For example, UNCLOS expressly provides in Article 298 that a State Party can officially declare that it does not accept the compulsory binding procedures in section 2 of Part XV of the Convention for certain categories of disputes (see page 275).

If parties make such declarations, the depositary will formally advise all parties. The Treaty Office within each party should check to determine whether the declaration is in accordance with the provisions of the treaty, and if necessary, seek advice from international law experts. Even though official records of such declarations will be maintained by the treaty secretariat, it is good practice for the Treaty Office to keep a record of such declarations.

A second type of declaration that might be made by a State Party to a treaty is a 'declaration of understanding' or interpretative declaration.[98] This is a unilateral statement by a State giving its view on how a particular provision in treaty should be interpreted. A declaration of understanding may in fact be worded in such a way that it purports to modify the legal effect of a provision. In such cases, it could be an illegal reservation. Therefore, the Treaty Office should carefully study any declaration that it receives, and if necessary, consult the international law experts in its government on the legal effect of the declaration, and on whether any response is warranted.[99]

As for responding to reservations by other parties, governments will naturally focus their attention on treaties and issues of particular national interest.

Interpretation and Application of the Treaty by Domestic Courts

A final point to bear in mind in relation to continuing engagement with a treaty is that international treaties can be, and often are, considered and interpreted by States' domestic courts. This can happen in a variety of ways, depending on how a State implements treaties in domestic law (while some States require domestic legislation to give treaties the force of law, for others treaties become part of domestic law as soon as they

[98] See the section on 'Interpretative Declarations' in Chapter 7 at 273–74. [99] ibid.

have entered into force for that State, without any need for incorporating legislation).[100]

For example, a piece of legislation implementing the obligations in a treaty may refer to the treaty and its object and purpose. A domestic court tasked with interpreting that legislation may, as part of that task, look at the treaty and its object and purpose. In some countries the text of a treaty (in whole or part) may be scheduled to its implementing Act, which will provide that the provisions of the treaty set out in the schedule shall have the force of law in the State. Again, in order to make findings, a domestic court charged with interpreting such an Act would need to look at the text of the treaty.

Different States' domestic courts take different approaches to interpreting treaties. In principle, national courts normally apply international law rules on treaty interpretation, as reflected in the VCLT 1969, Articles 31–33. Unsurprisingly, there are variations in approach, with courts in some jurisdictions tending to focus strictly on the text of the treaty, and others showing a greater willingness to look at evidence of the intention of the parties and the object and purpose of the treaty.[101] However, what is important from a treaty practice perspective is that any interpretation given by a domestic court to a treaty, and/or its implementing legislation, may affect the status of that State's domestic implementation. For example, if a domestic court interprets a treaty or implementing act in a way that is different from the way in which officials had interpreted it, this may mean that the current method of domestic implementation is no longer sufficient. In such a case, the implementing act may need to be amended or new legislation put in place to ensure full and effective implementation.

Indonesia serves as an interesting example in relation to the role of domestic courts in the application of treaties. Under its Law on International Agreements, the Indonesian Parliament or the President is required to adopt a law or a Presidential Decision affirming Indonesia's ratification of or accession to a treaty.[102] The Law is silent on whether there is any obligation to adopt legislation to implement the treaty or to harmonise existing and future legislation in accordance with treaties that Indonesia has ratified. In this regard, the judiciary plays a crucial role in relation to the application of treaties as it is authorised

[100] For details on the various approaches, see *Aust* (n 71) chapter 10, 'Treaties and Domestic Law'.

[101] R Gardiner, *Treaty Interpretation* (2nd edn, OUP 2015), 141–57.

[102] Law No. 24 of 2000 on International Agreements arts 9–11. Affirmation by the adoption of a law by the Parliament is required if the ratification or accession of the treaty concerns issues pertaining to peace, security, defence, territorial sovereignty, human rights, environment, creation of a new legal principle or foreign loans. If the treaty does not concern any of the issues mentioned, the ratification or accession of such treaty may be affirmed by means of a Presidential Decision.

to make direct reference to and implement treaties that Indonesia has ratified or acceded to.[103]

Top Tips for Continuing Engagement with the Treaty Throughout its Life

To conclude this chapter, Box 8.2 provides top tips for continuing engagement with treaties throughout their life.

Box 8.2 Top tips for continuing engagement with the treaty throughout its life

1. The Treaty Office should examine the treaty early on in order to identify any provisions requiring ongoing engagement that should be taken into account during consideration of whether to become a party.
2. The Treaty Office should make a list of the provisions in the treaty that will require continuing engagement, and a decision should be taken on which agency will be responsible for taking the lead on each of the matters. An analysis should also be undertaken of the resources that will be required for continuing engagement. This list should include provisions in the treaty on the following matters:
   - Reservations and declarations
   - Annexes and amendments to annexes by 'tacit acceptance' procedures
   - COP and its functions and responsibilities, including the frequency and location of COP meetings
   - Bodies or committees established under the treaty and their functions and responsibilities
   - Reporting requirements
   - Compliance monitoring provisions.
3. For those matters on which the lead policy department or agency will take responsibility, a list should be made of the types of issues of international law and treaty practice that could arise on which the lead agency should consult experts on international law and/or the Treaty Office.
4. For those matters under the purview of the Treaty Office, a list should be made of the type of issues on which the Treaty Office should consult experts on international law, and those matters on which the lead policy agency should be consulted or kept informed.

[103] Law No. 48 of 2009 on the Judiciary, 29 October 2009, State Gazette No. 157, art 10(1); Law No. 39 of 1999 on Human Rights, 23 September 1999, State Gazette No. 165, art 7.

9

Ending Treaty Relations

***

'Treaty exit provisions are not mere boilerplate provisions but rather a tool for States to manage the risks of international cooperation.'[1]

Introduction

The formal ending of treaty relations for one party, or for all parties, is a relatively unusual event. It is possible for a treaty official to serve for years in a Treaty Office, and to handle hundreds of treaty signings and ratifications, yet never be involved in a withdrawal or termination procedure. Consequently, there is much less practice in this area of treaty procedures, and less recorded information about how it works. Yet when a State or an IO decides to leave a treaty, or is involved in winding one up, this is a significant and sometimes sensitive event that needs to be handled correctly. Just as getting divorced is usually more difficult than getting married, ending treaty relations tends to be legally more complicated than creating them. Once the parties have locked themselves into a treaty, the availability of a way out depends upon the terms of that treaty as well as the law of treaties.

It is unwise to generalise about the procedure for ending treaty relations; and so the approach taken in this chapter is to consider various types of treaty, types of proposed exit and types of exit provisions, and look at how the procedures need to be tailored in each case. For readers with a particular treaty and exit scenario in mind, the detailed table of contents and the top tips at the end of this chapter will help signpost the most relevant pages.

Many of the difficulties commonly arising from a State or IO's wish to leave a treaty can be avoided by careful drafting of the provisions on withdrawal and/or termination ('exit provisions') at the treaty creation stage.[2] If, unfortunately, insufficient care was taken at the treaty drafting stage, the consequences may only be felt much later, for example when a party wishes or threatens to leave, or purports to do so. Badly drafted exit provisions, or an absence of provisions, leaves a situation that may be remedied only by negotiation, which may be

[1] L Helfer, 'Terminating Treaties' in D Hollis (ed), *The Oxford Guide to Treaties* (OUP 2012) 641. Helfer's observation was informed by several studies of exit clauses that reveal a wide variation in the design of these clauses and the situations in which States invoke them to end their treaty-based relationships.

[2] See section on 'The Final Clauses' in Chapter 5 at 169–171; Annex I, 'Example of Final Clauses in a Single-instrument Bilateral Treaty' at 418–19; and Annex II, 'Examples of Final Clauses in a Multilateral Treaty' at 420–23.

difficult by the time circumstances have arisen that prompt parties to try to leave – or adjudication.

Occasionally, a State's withdrawal from a treaty is high-profile and controversial. This may be because of the importance of the subject – human rights, climate change or arms control – or because of the political significance of a State leaving an organisation, such as the USA leaving UNESCO in 1984 and again in 2017, or the UK starting the process of leaving the EU in 2017. In such cases, there may be a considerable amount of work for the Treaty Office, both at the preparatory stage of working out the effect of leaving on other treaties, and in the drafting and sending of official notifications and dealing with responses. In addition to that, leaving a treaty often involves making a new one or a set of new treaties, which may have to be done at the same time.

Not all endings of treaty relations are difficult or controversial. Some are routine and can be dealt with by Treaty Offices following standard procedures. Treaty relations may also be ended by operation of a 'sunset' provision within the treaty itself or another treaty, without any procedural action. In such cases, the information functions of Treaty Offices are engaged, as they need to keep track of the changes, and record, update and publish the information.

Use of Terms: Withdrawal, Denunciation and Termination

'Withdrawal' from a treaty means that one party leaves the treaty, that is, ceases to be a party. 'Denunciation' of a treaty by one party means the same. The words 'withdrawal' and 'denunciation' are interchangeable (except that, grammatically, they are followed by different prepositions: 'withdrawal from' or 'denunciation of').

The word 'withdrawal' is usually preferred in treaty drafting (and in this Handbook), as 'denunciation' carries an implication in ordinary (non-legal) English usage of some sort of public condemnation. The legal term 'denunciation' of a treaty or 'to denounce' a treaty carries no such implication however; it simply means to withdraw from a treaty.

The 'termination' of a treaty means that the treaty ceases to be in force, for all parties.

A 'sunset clause' is a particular type of termination provision in a treaty which prescribes that the treaty shall expire after a fixed duration of time or the fulfilment of some other defined condition. In other words, the application of the clause will trigger the automatic termination of the treaty. A sunset clause may be found in both bilateral and multilateral treaties.

As a *bilateral treaty* has only two parties, if one party withdraws from it, it necessarily comes to an end. One party alone cannot stay bound by a treaty as there is no other party to owe obligations to or hold rights against. Therefore, the lawful withdrawal of one party from a bilateral treaty results in its termination. Unilateral withdrawal and termination are, in effect, the same event.

Bilateral treaties may provide for unilateral termination and/or termination by agreement. In either case, the term 'withdrawal' is not usually used in relation to bilateral treaties, as it implies an exit by one party from a treaty that continues to exist; a logical impossibility in a bilateral context. Where, occasionally, the term 'withdrawal' or 'denunciation' is used in a bilateral context, it has the same effect as termination.

As a *multilateral treaty* has three parties or more, it may be possible for one party to withdraw while the treaty continues in force for the other parties. It is also possible for the treaty to terminate for all parties at the same time. Thus, 'withdrawal' and 'termination' have distinct meanings and are usually addressed by distinct sets of provisions in multilateral treaties.

Scope of this Chapter: Role of the Treaty Office

This chapter focuses on the treaty procedures that apply to the types of withdrawal and termination that are most commonly handled in Treaty Offices, rather than the details of all the legal rules that could theoretically be invoked in a treaty dispute.

For government Treaty Offices, the unilateral termination of a bilateral treaty in accordance with its provisions is commonplace, as is termination by agreement with the other party. For example, parties routinely agree to terminate a bilateral treaty when its objectives have been achieved, or when they decide to replace it with a more up-to-date treaty. These procedures are explained below. As most bilateral treaties are governmental, the procedures are generally discussed here with reference to States, but could be applied in a similar way by an IO to its bilateral treaties.

Government Treaty Offices will occasionally need to deal with the unilateral withdrawal of one party from a multilateral treaty; whether it is itself the withdrawing party or it is responding to the withdrawal of another party. Depositary organisations and governments are likely to handle withdrawals by one party on a regular basis, and from time to time may need to take charge of the procedure for terminating a treaty, in accordance with its provisions or by agreement among the parties. These procedures are explained below.

Automatic termination in accordance with the treaty's own provisions is a different matter. It also occurs quite routinely, for example where the treaty is for a fixed duration only or provides for its own expiry when a certain condition is met (a sunset clause). This requires no procedural action on the part of the Treaty Office to make it happen. Rather, it engages the treaty information functions of the Treaty Office.[3] For depositaries of multilateral treaties, the information functions are more significant and are explained below.

[3] See Chapter 4, especially the section on 'Managing Treaty Collections' at 132–39.

By contrast, unilateral withdrawal or termination of a treaty as a result of a legal challenge on grounds, such as fraud, error or impossibility of performance, is very rare indeed. Such claims are highly unusual and would be dealt with by high-level diplomatic and legal intervention, possibly litigation, and would go well beyond the normal functions of a Treaty Office. Accordingly, this chapter does not present procedures for such cases.

Practical problems can sometimes be caused by the *non-ending* of treaty relations. The fact that relatively few treaties are formally ended, compared with the number created, means that there are numerous treaties which may have outlived their usefulness, have been forgotten or whose status may be in doubt. In other words, there are many more treaties that exist on paper than are in active operation. These 'sleeping dog' treaties may do no harm other than take up space in archives or databases. But occasionally, an apparently obsolete treaty is discovered to apply to a new situation, and a party that had forgotten about it may be 'bitten' by it.

Even when treaties are obsolete in all but name, their continued existence can cause confusion and may complicate the task of identifying the international obligations applicable to a particular situation. Obsolete treaties can become a problem for an IO that generates many treaties, particularly when new members are required to accept and implement all existing treaties. IOs sometimes carry out a 'weeding' exercise, in much the same way that States sometimes review and repeal obsolete legislation. Secretariats and Treaty Offices may play a useful role in preparing the information required for such an exercise. When (as is more often the case) obsolete treaties are *not* wound up or otherwise addressed, the role of the Treaty Offices concerned is to make sure that those treaties do not disappear from their records, and that accurate status information remains clear and accessible.

Applying the PLATO Principles to the Ending of Treaty Relations

Of all the ways in which the PLATO principles are relevant to ending treaty relations, we would highlight the following:

- 'Legal': above all, the principle of legality applies to any ending of treaty relations. Understanding and correctly applying the international law of treaties is always critical to the ending of a treaty or the withdrawal of one party. The law in this area can be highly complex, and the way it applies in each case varies enormously and may be without precedent. International lawyers need to be closely involved at all stages, especially in the drafting of treaty notices, and domestic law requirements also need to be taken into account.
- 'Organised': the management of treaty withdrawal or winding up needs to be systematic, efficient and regular. If these qualities have been lacking in the management of treaty records before this point, problems are bound to

occur now; for example, if treaty records are incomplete or inaccessible, the ending of treaty relations may have unforeseen and unwanted effects on other treaties. This is one of the many reasons why systems need to be in place to enable treaty collections and records to be organised, maintained, accessed, searched and retrieved by present and future generations of staff.
- 'Transparent': the principles of transparency need to be applied to the withdrawal from or winding up of any treaty, however routine it may seem. Clear communication of the proposal to end treaty relations to all parties is vital, as is accountability to the relevant stakeholders – be they legislatures, Member States or the public. The need for greater transparency is often a reason for terminating obsolete treaties, in order to provide clarity on current treaty obligations for the governments, secretariats or private actors concerned.

The Legal Framework: International Law and Domestic Law

Anyone dealing with a treaty withdrawal or termination will need to pay close attention to three areas of law:

- provisions in the treaty in question governing withdrawal and termination;
- general rules in the VCLT 1969 and VCLT 1986[4] on withdrawal and termination; and
- any relevant provisions in the domestic constitution or legislation (or the IO's rules in the case of an IO party) on authority or procedures for withdrawal or termination.

The international law of treaties has a number of important rules governing the termination of treaty relations. These are set out in the VCLT 1969, Part V on 'Invalidity, termination and suspension of the operation of treaties', which covers the following matters in Articles 42–72: invalidity of treaties; termination and suspension of the operation of treaties; procedure; consequences of the invalidity; termination or suspension of the operation of a treaty.

The same set of rules applies to both bilateral and multilateral treaties. A few of the provisions expressly apply only to bilateral treaties (such as Article 60(1)) or only to multilateral treaties (such as Articles 55, 58 and 60(2)), but most are worded in such a way that they can be applied to all treaties.[5] In practice, there are considerable differences in the procedures applicable to

[4] VCLT 1969 (adopted 23 May 1969, entered into force 27 January 1980) 1155 UNTS 331 Part V and VCLT 1986 (adopted 21 March 1986, not in force) 25 ILM 543 Part V http://legal.un.org/ilc/texts/instruments/english/conventions/1_2_1986.pdf accessed 9 September 2018.

[5] For a brief overview of withdrawal, denunciation and termination of multilateral treaties, see Treaty Section of the Office of Legal Affairs, *Treaty Handbook* (2nd edn, UN 2012) 27–28, paras 4.5 and 4.6.

bilateral versus multilateral treaties, but they are governed by largely the same legal rules.

It is generally accepted that most of these VCLT provisions reflect rules of customary international law, which bind all States. However, there are a few exceptions.[6] Therefore, in any dealings with a State that is not party to the VCLT 1969, it is necessary to check the status of the relevant rules and not simply assume that all of them are applicable to the State in question.

The rules applicable to treaties with IO parties are set out in the VCLT 1986, Part V on 'Invalidity, termination and suspension of the operation of treaties', Articles 42–72. These rules are very similar to those in the VCLT 1969, with modifications in the way they apply to IOs. Thus, from here on in this chapter where VCLT 1969 provisions are referred to, it may be assumed that there is an equivalent provision in the VCLT 1986.

The rules which are of most practical importance to the Treaty Office are those concerning the withdrawal from a treaty and the termination of a treaty, in Part V, section 3 (Articles 54–64) of the VCLT 1969. Underlying all of these is the fundamental principle, set out in Article 42, that:

> The termination of a treaty, its denunciation or the withdrawal of a party, may take place only as a result of the application of the provisions of the treaty or of the present Convention.

In most cases, the withdrawal or termination is carried out in accordance with the provisions of the particular treaty. Therefore, this chapter sets out a series of examples of typical provisions from a variety of treaties. Where the VCLT provisions are used, the principle one is Article 54, which provides that the termination of a treaty or the withdrawal of a party may take place in accordance with its provisions *or* by consent of all the parties.[7] Article 56 specifies the (strict) conditions under which a party is permitted to withdraw unilaterally from a treaty which contains no provision regarding its termination and which does not provide for withdrawal.[8] Article 67 sets out important

[6] For example, not all States accept that the rules in Articles 53, 64 and 71 on invalidity of treaties that conflict with a peremptory norm of general international law (*jus cogens*) are part of customary international law. Doubts have also been expressed in relation to the customary international law status of the procedural provisions in Articles 65–68. See B Simma and C J Tams, 'Reacting Against Treaty Breaches' in Hollis (n 1) 592–94.

[7] VCLT 1969 art 54, Termination of or withdrawal from a treaty under its provisions or by consent of the parties:

> The termination of a treaty or the withdrawal of a party may take place:
> (a) in conformity with the provisions of the treaty; or
> (b) at any time by consent of all the parties after consultation with the other contracting States.

[8] ibid art 56, Denunciation of or withdrawal from a treaty containing no provision regarding termination, denunciation or withdrawal:

> 1. A treaty which contains no provision regarding its termination and which does not provide for denunciation or withdrawal is not subject to denunciation or withdrawal unless:

rules regarding instruments for terminating and withdrawing from treaties, including who may sign them.

Termination of Bilateral Treaties

The main ways in which a bilateral treaty may be terminated are:

- unilateral termination in accordance with the treaty: one party exercises its right to terminate the treaty by a unilateral act, in accordance with the provisions of that treaty;
- agreed termination: both parties agree to terminate it, in accordance with the treaty's own terms or by a new agreement;
- automatic termination: the treaty terminates automatically in accordance with its own terms (a sunset clause); and
- unilateral termination on a claimed legal ground: in accordance with the VCLT (for example, implied right to withdraw, treaty defect or fault of the other party).

The first two methods are the procedures that a Treaty Office is most likely to encounter. These are explained in detail below.

Automatic termination in accordance with a sunset clause by definition requires no procedure. It does engage the treaty management responsibilities of the Treaty Office, as they need to have the termination date or possible date registered in their database with appropriate reminders, and then inform all concerned of the termination when it takes place. These procedures are similar to those for multilateral treaties, although simpler as only two parties are involved.[9]

Unilateral termination on a legal ground is rare. In some circumstances, a party could argue that there is an implied right to withdraw from the treaty, by demonstrating evidence that the parties intended to allow this, or that it is inherent in the nature of the treaty.[10] However, if the other party has already declined to negotiate an agreed termination, it is likely they would contest any use of Article 56(b) VCLT 1969. A party may also claim a right to withdraw on the basis of various legal grounds set out in the VCLT, such as error, fraud,

(a) it is established that the parties intended to admit the possibility of denunciation or withdrawal; or

(b) a right of denunciation or withdrawal may be implied by the nature of the treaty.

2. A party shall give not less than twelve months' notice of its intention to denounce or withdraw from a treaty under paragraph 1.

[9] See the section on 'Scope of this Chapter: Role of the Treaty Office' above at 336–37 and the section on 'Sunset Clause: Automatic Termination by a Provision within the Treaty Itself' below at 370–71. The procedures also form a part of treaty management; see sections on 'Managing Treaty Collections' and 'Archiving Treaties: Permanent Storage, Preservation and Retrieval' in Chapter 4 at 132–39 and 149–51 respectively.

[10] VCLT 1969 art 56(b).

corruption, coercion, material breach or fundamental change of circumstances.[11] Any of these avenues is likely to result in a dispute and possible resort to dispute settlement procedures, consideration of which is beyond the scope of this Handbook.

Unilateral Termination of a Bilateral Treaty in Accordance with the Treaty

Bilateral treaties commonly make express provision for one party to terminate the treaty by a unilateral act. Typically, a party may simply give the other formal notice of termination, which then takes effect after a specified number of days, months or years. It is rare to require more than one year's notice. Some treaties require a *minimum* period of notice, allowing the terminating party to opt to give longer notice. Some permit termination only after the treaty has been in force for a minimum period of time (usually a specified number of years). Termination provisions do not normally require any reason to be stated, leaving each party free to decide to terminate for any reason they deem to be in their national (or organisational) interest, and to explain it or not to the other party as it chooses. Such provisions normally refer to 'termination', but even if the terminology used is 'withdrawal' or 'denunciation', the effect for a bilateral treaty is the same.

Typical Example of a Bilateral Treaty Termination Provision that Permits Unilateral Termination at any time

A typical example of bilateral treaty termination provisions which permit unilateral termination at any time can be seen in the Agreement between the Government of the Republic of Latvia and the Government of the Republic of Korea on the Mutual Recognition and Exchange of Driving Licenses, 2011:[12]

> **Article 10(2)**
> Either Contracting Party may terminate this Agreement by giving the other Contracting Party written notice through diplomatic channels. In such case, termination shall take effect on the thirtieth (30th) day following receipt of the notice by the other Contracting Party.

Typical Example of a Bilateral Treaty Termination Provision that Applies only after a Specified Minimum Duration

A typical example of bilateral treaty termination provisions that apply only after a specified minimum duration and only at specified intervals can be seen

[11] ibid arts 46–53.

[12] Agreement between the Government of the Republic of Latvia and the Government of the Republic of Korea on the Mutual Recognition and Exchange of Driving Licenses (signed 8 March 2011, entered into force on 28 May 2011) 2830 UNTS 79, art 10(2). The text of this article is reproduced in Annex I, 'Examples of Final Clauses in a Single-instrument Bilateral Treaty' at 418–19. See also Annex XVII.A, 'Examples of continuing obligations provisions in bilateral treaties' at 460–61.

in the Agreement on Trade, Economic and Technical Cooperation between the Government of the Republic of Turkey and the Government of the Oriental Republic of Uruguay, 2009:[13]

Article VIII

. . .

The Present Agreement shall remain in force for a period of three years and thereafter its validity shall be automatically extended for successive periods of one year, unless a written notice of termination is given by either Contracting Party three months prior to its expiration.

Procedure for Unilaterally Terminating a Bilateral Treaty in accordance with the Treaty

A State or IO wishing to invoke its right to terminate a bilateral treaty in accordance with its provisions will need to take the following steps:

1. Identify the Applicable Treaty Provisions

All conditions for termination specified in the treaty concerned need to be complied with. Although these provisions are usually found in the 'final clauses' near the end,[14] it is important to read the whole treaty carefully as well as any documents that accompanied it at the time of signature or ratification (or consent to be bound, however expressed), such as joint or separate statements of understanding, declarations, arrangements, etc., in case there is any other relevant material. If the treaty was concluded in more than one language, you should read the termination provisions in the other language(s), if possible, especially if they are equally authentic. Even if the provision is clear in your language, it is wise to ensure that it is equally clear, in the same sense, in the other language(s). If the termination provision is not clear in your language, you should obtain professional translation of any other authentic language version of the same provision, as this is essential to the correct interpretation of the treaty.[15]

[13] Agreement on Trade, Economic and Technical Cooperation between the Government of the Republic of Turkey and the Government of the Oriental Republic of Uruguay (signed 30 April 2009, entered into force 25 October 2011) 2830 UNTS 51. See Annex XVII.A, 'Examples of Continuing Obligations Provisions in Bilateral Treaties' at 460–61. For another example of a bilateral treaty provision that permits unilateral termination only at specified times, see Agreement between the Government of the Kingdom of the Netherlands and the Government of the United Kingdom of Great Britain and Northern Ireland on the Reciprocal Holding of Stocks of Crude Oil and/or Petroleum Products (adopted 26 June 2006, entered into force 1 June 2008) 2579 UNTS 201, art 9. The text is reproduced in Annex I, 'Examples of Final Clauses in a Single-instrument Bilateral Treaty' at 418–19.

[14] See the section on 'Final Clauses' in Chapter 5 at 169–71; Annex I, 'Example of Final Clauses in a Single-instrument Bilateral Treaty' at 418–19; and Annex II, 'Examples of Final Clauses in a Multilateral Treaty' at 420–23.

[15] See VCLT 1969 art 33.

2. Check Treaty Records

Treaty records should be searched carefully for any amendments, extensions, protocols or any other subsequent agreements relating to this treaty. These may have a bearing on the conditions for termination. Moreover, it is important to know if there are related documents whose status may be affected by the proposed termination. If there is any doubt, and especially if the treaty is old, it may be wise to check the published treaty records of the other party to ensure that the documents match; and also check the UN Treaty Collection, as the treaty should have been registered by at least one party with the UN Secretary General under Article 102,[16] and will normally have been published by the UN, together with any subsequent treaty acts. If any discrepancies emerge among the three sources of published information, this should be resolved immediately. It may simply be that registration of the treaty or a subsequent act was overlooked, or that one party or the other has failed to keep its published treaty records up to date; but it is also possible that there is a difference of view as to what the treaty text consists of.

3. Consider Legal Issues

There are a number of points which the government's (or the secretariat's) international law advisers will need to consider, in particular:

- Does the treaty impose any preconditions to the right to terminate, and if so, are they satisfied in this case?
- What period of notice must be given?
- Will the date of termination automatically follow from the date of notice, or must it be specified in the notice?
- Does the treaty specify to whom and how the notice must be sent?
- Will the termination have any effect on your State's (or IO's) participation in other treaties?
- Does the treaty specify any continuing obligations after termination, for example, to protect acquired rights or ongoing co-operation? If so, how will these be implemented in domestic law? If not, do the parties need to discuss ongoing protections?
- Are there any constitutional or legislative requirements in domestic law? If so, how long might this process take?

4. Draft a Note to the other Party

Notice of termination should always be given in writing. If the treaty specifies any particular form or channel, this must of course be used. If it does not, a diplomatic note is the normal form but a letter could also be used. Its contents should include the following elements:

[16] See the section on 'Registering the Treaty at the UN' in Chapter 7 at 283–85.

- The full title of the treaty to be terminated, including the place(s) and date(s) it was signed or concluded. It is important to include the date(s) and place(s) if applicable so as to identify the treaty definitively, as there may be more than one treaty on the same subject or with a similar title. It is useful also to state the date on which your State ratified it (if applicable) and the date of its entry into force; for example:

  > The Government of X has the honour to recall the Agreement between the Government of X and the Government of Y on the subject of Z, signed at Grand City on 4 December 1967, which entered into force on 1 July 1968.

- A clear statement of termination (or denunciation or withdrawal, if that is the word used in the treaty provision you are invoking). A clear way to do this is to state something along the lines of 'the Government of X hereby gives notice of termination', or 'this Note shall constitute notice of termination' of the treaty under reference. You need to make clear that this note *is* the formal notice of termination, not simply advance warning of the State's intention to terminate at a future date.
- Reference to the applicable termination provision of the treaty. This is essential if the treaty provides for more than one ground or mode of termination. Even if only one is provided, it is useful to refer to it. It will add clarity to the termination statement, by reinforcing the message that this *is* formal notice, not just advance warning of an intention. This could be done, for example, by adding at the end of the termination statement 'in accordance with the provisions of Article x, paragraph y, of the treaty referred to above'.
- If the termination provision of the treaty specifies any preconditions, it is important to state in your note that these are fulfilled, with supporting information if appropriate. If you fail to do so, this does not mean that your note will be ineffective, but it may result in further correspondence and doubts as to whether the effective date of the notice is the date of your original note or the date of the further correspondence. For example, if the treaty provides that it shall remain in force for three years and thereafter may be terminated,[17] it is useful to refer in your note to the date on which the treaty entered into force.
- If the treaty provides for continuing obligations after termination,[18] it may be useful to refer to that provision. It is not essential, as that provision will

[17] For example, Agreement on Trade, Economic and Technical Cooperation between the Government of the Republic of Turkey and the Government of the Oriental Republic of Uruguay, art VIII. See Annex XVII.A, 'Examples of Continuing Obligations Provisions in Bilateral Treaties' at 460–61.

[18] For example, Agreement between the Government of the Republic of Latvia and the Government of the Republic of Estonia on the exchange and mutual protection of classified information (signed 6 June 2011, entered into force 1 May 2012) 2830 UNTS 11, art 17(3) and other examples in Annex XVII.A, 'Examples of Continuing Obligations Provisions in Bilateral Treaties' at 460–61.

apply anyway whether or not you refer to it, but you may wish to show that your government acknowledges these obligations and remind the other party of them. This could be done quite simply by recalling or acknowledging the provision; for example, 'the Government of X has the further honour to recall that, in accordance with the provisions of Article 17(3), Classified Information transmitted or generated within the application of this Agreement shall continue to be protected under the provisions of this Agreement'.

- Date of termination: depending on the wording of the termination provision in the treaty, it may or may not be appropriate to state the date on which termination is to take effect:
  - If it provides that termination shall take effect on an exact date measured from the date of receipt, such as 'the thirtieth (30th) day following the receipt of the notice by the other Contracting Party',[19] it is best *not* to calculate it and write it in the note. This is because you will not know, at the time your note is signed, when exactly it will be received. It would be better to add a request to the other party to kindly inform you of the date of receipt of the note and the date on which the termination shall enter into force in accordance with the provisions of Article X.
  - On the other hand, if the termination provision requires a minimum period of notice, or specifies a period of notice which may be given at any time, and you wish to give a longer period of notice, you could specify your proposed date in the note. For example: 'Each Party may terminate this Agreement through diplomatic channels at any time. In such a case, the Agreement shall expire six months after the receipt of the termination notice by the other Party.' If you wished to give notice nine months in advance, you could state (or, more politely, propose) in your note that the termination shall take effect on a specific date. Provided that it is more than six months ahead, the other party could not object, and is likely to welcome the additional notice.
- There is no need to set out reasons for terminating the treaty in the note, unless the treaty expressly requires this. It would be normal for the terminating party to have already explained its reasons before sending the note, as part of a dialogue about the treaty or routine diplomatic contacts. It would be unusual for the termination note to take the receiving party by surprise. If it is considered appropriate to set out a lengthy explanation in writing at the time of giving notice, this should normally be done in a separate document, especially if the reasons are not directly related to the treaty itself. This is because the termination note will need to

[19] For example, Agreement between the Government of the Republic of Latvia and the Government of the Republic of Korea on the Mutual Recognition and Exchange of Driving Licenses', art 10. The text is reproduced in Annex I, 'Examples of Final Clauses in a Single-instrument Bilateral Treaty' at 418–19.

be registered at the UN, and this process should not include documents of a political nature with no legal content.

5. Signature of the Note

If the termination provision of the treaty specifies who must sign the termination notice, this must of course be complied with. If it does not, Article 67(2) VCLT 1969 applies. It provides:

> If the instrument is not signed by the Head of State, Head of Government or Minister for Foreign Affairs, the representative of the State communicating it may be called upon to produce full powers.

The safest course is therefore to have the note signed by the Foreign Minister or ask that minister to sign Full Powers for the representative accredited to the other party. Alternatively, if the other party agrees to accept a note signed by the representative without production of Full Powers, that will suffice.

6. Delivery of the Note

If there are domestic constitutional, legal or political processes that need to be completed before your State (or IO) is able to commit to termination, they need to be carried out, or factored in, before the note is delivered.[20] These may include consultations across government departments and agencies, legislative action for example to repeal implementing legislation, or other procedures such as reporting to or obtaining the approval of the legislature to terminate the treaty.

If the treaty specifies that notice of termination must be given 'through diplomatic channels', as is quite common,[21] this means that the note should be sent by your diplomatic mission accredited to the other State, to the foreign ministry of the other State, or by your foreign ministry to the other State's diplomatic mission accredited to your State. If the treaty does not specify how it should be delivered, use of diplomatic channels is usually the best choice. It is much better to deliver the note directly to the other State's ministry, so that is the route used in normal circumstances. The point is that the date of the other State's receipt of the note will be the day it arrives on the appropriate desk of their foreign ministry, normally the Treaty Office. If you deliver it to their embassy, you will not know how long it might take to arrive at their ministry, and there is a risk of delay, misdirection or, in rare cases, non-delivery. If the other party is an IO, the notice should normally be delivered directly to its headquarters, rather than to a representative office elsewhere.

[20] See the section on 'Domestic Procedures for Treaty Withdrawals and Terminations' below at 375–81.

[21] For example, Agreement between the Government of the Republic of Latvia and the Government of the Republic of Korea on the Mutual Recognition and Exchange of Driving Licenses, art 10. The text is reproduced in Annex I, 'Examples of Final Clauses in a Single-instrument Bilateral Treaty' at 418–19.

It is advisable to deliver the note in person at a scheduled meeting with the appropriate official at the foreign ministry or IO's headquarters. You will then receive immediate acknowledgement of the date of receipt of the note, which will determine the effective date of termination.

Registration of the Termination and Publication by the UN

The termination of a bilateral treaty is a subsequent act affecting the status of the treaty. It should therefore be registered with the UN Secretary General. This is not expressly required by Article 102 of the UN Charter itself, but by the UNGA Regulations to give effect to Article 102 of the Charter of the United Nations, which provide as follows:

1. When a treaty or international agreement has been registered with the Secretariat, a certified statement regarding any subsequent action which effects a change in the parties thereto, or the terms, scope or application thereof, shall also be registered with the Secretariat.
2. The Secretariat shall record the certified statement so registered in the Register established under article 1 of these regulations.[22]

The UN Treaty Handbook contains the following guidance on Article 2 of the UNGA Regulations, which makes clear that 'denunciations' are a type of 'subsequent action' which must be registered. It follows that the termination of a bilateral treaty is also in this category:

> **5.5.4 Subsequent actions, modifications and agreements**
> Subsequent actions effecting a change in the parties to, or the terms, scope or application of, a treaty or international agreement previously registered must be registered with the Secretariat. For example, such actions may involve ratifications, accessions, prolongations, extensions to territories, or denunciations. In the case of bilateral treaties, it is generally the party responsible for the subsequent action that registers it with the Secretariat. However, any other party to such agreement may assume this role.[23]

According to the established practice of the UN Secretariat, the party registering a subsequent treaty action is required to indicate the date of entry into force of such an action.[24] This means that the certified statement has to specify the date on which the termination has taken effect. The statement should also state the mode by which termination was effected; for example, by

[22] UNGA Res 97(1), 'Regulations to give effect to Article 102 of the Charter of the United Nations' (14 December 1946) 1 UNTS XVI (as amended by UNGA Res 364 B (IV) (1 December 1949); UNGA Res 482 (V) (12 December 1950); UNGA Res 33/141 (9 December 1978); and UNGA Res 52/153 (15 December 1997)) https://treaties.un.org/doc/source/publications/practice/registration_and_publication.pdf accessed 18 September 2018.

[23] *Treaty Section of the Office of Legal Affairs* (n 5) 34. See also *UNGA Res 97(l)* (n 22).

[24] ibid art 8. See also: Repertory of Practice of United Nations Organs, 'Charter of the United Nations, Chapter XVI – Miscellaneous Provisions: Article 102 (Supplement No. 5 (1970–1978) vol. 5)', Annex, art 8, notes (c), 163 http://legal.un.org/repertory/art102.shtml accessed 16 November 2018.

a diplomatic note, giving the date, sender, and recipient and reference numbers. If possible, enclose a copy of the note or correspondence by which the termination was effected.

Note that the termination may only be registered if the treaty has been registered (by either party). There is no deadline for the registration of a treaty, so if both parties omitted to register it before, this may be rectified now and then the termination can be registered.[25]

The date of registration is recorded as the date of the receipt by the Secretariat of the certified statement (not the date on which it is processed and entered in the register, which may be later). However, if the documentation is incomplete, the Secretariat will inform the party concerned and postpone registration until the correct documents are received.

Terminated treaties published by the UN remain published, together with the fact of termination.

National Records and Publication of the Termination of the Treaty

The treaty text and its status for your State (the date of national signature, ratification, accession, reservations, entry into force, amendments, etc.) will normally (and should) be published in an official national publication, such as a government or parliamentary gazette, treaty series or bulletin.[26] When the treaty is terminated, the fact of termination and its effective date should also be published, together with the other status information. If an IO terminates a bilateral treaty, it should likewise publish this fact.

Should the Treaty Remain Published after It Has Ceased to Be in Force?

Yes. The treaty text and all the status information should remain published indefinitely. This is important for the reasons underlying the PLATO principles 'Assured', 'Transparent' and 'Organised':

- 'Organised' is a quality that should apply to internal treaty records; treaty officials should always be able to retrieve information about past treaty obligations as well as current ones.
- 'Transparency' refers to the importance of public access to information about the treaties that bind the State, which is an essential prerequisite for democratic accountability.
- 'Assured' requires completeness and accuracy of treaty information; if the published treaty records show that your State became party to this treaty but not that the treaty has been terminated, this may cause confusion.

Terminated treaties may contain provisions that continue to bind the parties even after termination, for a specified period or indefinitely.[27] Information

[25] See the section on 'Registering the Treaty at the UN' in Chapter 7 at 283–85.

[26] See the section on 'Action on the Domestic Plane: Publication of the Treaty' in Chapter 7 at 281–83.

[27] See the section on 'Continuing Obligations after the Ending of Treaty Relations: Bilateral and Multilateral Treaties' below at 374–75.

about past treaty obligations may also be important, both to officials and to the public, for a variety of reasons not only historical. For example, if negotiations are proposed on a new treaty, those concerned will need to know about any past ones with the same party on a similar subject. If allegations are made about past treaty breaches, this could be relevant to international relations or even litigation many years later.

Should Terminated Treaties Be Kept in Separate Records or Archives from Current Ones?

The way that records are organised and displayed, both internally and externally to the public, varies so much from one State or IO to another that it is difficult to generalise. Certainly, a terminated treaty should be clearly marked as such in official records. It is helpful if digital records can be organised and displayed in such a way that viewers can search by selected fields. It is particularly helpful for the viewer if it is possible to choose between viewing only treaties in force, or all treaties including terminated ones. Moving terminated treaties to a different database is not necessary, but might be a sensible option in some administrations if, for example, capacity is an issue. However, there would need to be a clear cross-reference from the current database to the one containing terminated treaties, bearing in mind the needs of a user who looks for a treaty in the current database without knowing that it has been terminated.

Paper archives of original treaty texts and associated documents are a different matter; once a treaty is terminated, it is less likely that access will be needed to the originals so they could be moved to historical archives in another location. They should not be destroyed however, for the reasons mentioned above.

Agreed Termination of a Bilateral Treaty

It is always possible for the parties to a bilateral treaty to agree to terminate it.[28] This can be done whether or not the treaty contains any provision for termination. If the treaty contains no provision, the parties are free to negotiate any terms. If the treaty does provide for termination, the parties may apply those provisions or agree to terminate it on different terms, or using a different procedure. The new agreement may take the form of an amendment to the treaty or a separate treaty, which does not have to be in the same form as the original treaty. The new agreement may be a standalone decision on termination, or the termination may be agreed as part of a larger new treaty on substantive matters.

28 VCLT 1969 art 54(b) and VCLT 1986 art 54(b).

Example of a Simple Agreement to Terminate a Bilateral Treaty

The following UK–Sweden Exchange of Notes concerning the cessation of responsibility for the protection of UK interests in Iran, 2014[29] serves as an example of a simple agreement to terminate a bilateral treaty where the original treaty had no provision on termination.

The UK proposed the termination of a previous UK–Sweden Exchange of Notes 2012 which did not provide for termination.[30] The 2014 Note begins:

> I have the honour to propose, on behalf of the Government of the United Kingdom of Great Britain and Northern Ireland, the termination of the agreement on protecting powers between the Government of the United Kingdom and the Government of Sweden concerning responsibility for the protection of the Diplomatic and Consular interests of the United Kingdom Government in the Islamic Republic of Iran by the Government of the Kingdom of Sweden done at Stockholm on 11 July 2012 in the following terms: [...][31]

The Swedish Reply Note accepted the proposal and agreed that the two Notes together 'shall constitute an Agreement between the two Governments in this matter which shall enter into force on the date of the present reply'.[32]

Example of an Agreement to Terminate a Bilateral Treaty Contained within a Broader Treaty

The Finland–Norway agreement on the construction and maintenance of reindeer fences 2014[33] is an example of a treaty that contains a provision to terminate an earlier bilateral treaty. The termination provision reads:

> **Article 27. Entry into force**
> This Convention shall enter into force 30 days after date on which the parties inform each other through an exchange of notes that their domestic constitutional procedures for the entry into force have been completed. On the date of

[29] Exchange of Notes between the Government of the United Kingdom of Great Britain and Northern Ireland and the Government of the Kingdom of Sweden Concerning the Cessation of Responsibility for the Protection of the Diplomatic and Consular Interests of the United Kingdom Government in the Islamic Republic of Iran by the Government of the Kingdom of Sweden (signed 3 April 2014, entered into force 3 April 2014) UKTS 22 (2016).

[30] Exchange of Notes between the Government of the United Kingdom of Great Britain and Northern Ireland and the Government of the Kingdom of Sweden concerning the Assumption of Responsibility for the Protection of the Diplomatic and Consular Interests of the United Kingdom Government in the Islamic Republic of Iran by the Government of the Kingdom of Sweden (signed 11 July 2012, entered into force 11 July 2012) UNTS Registration No. 52724, UKTS 50 (2012).

[31] *Exchange of Notes* (n 29) Note from the Government of the UK to the Government of the Kingdom of Sweden dated 3 April 2014. After the opening paragraph, there are four paragraphs in the Note setting out the terms, which confirm that there are no continuing liabilities.

[32] ibid Reply Note from the Government of the Kingdom of Sweden to the Government of the UK dated 3 April 2014.

[33] Convention between the Republic of Finland and the Kingdom of Norway on the construction and maintenance of reindeer fences and on other measures to prevent reindeer from entering the territory of the other country (adopted 9 December 2014, entered into force 1 January 2017) UNTS Registration No. 54172.

> entry into force of this Convention, the Convention of 3 June 1981 between Finland and Norway for the construction and maintenance of reindeer fences and other measures to prevent the reindeer from crossing the border between the two countries shall cease to have effect.

Note that the Convention of 1981 had provided for unilateral denunciation, in the following restrictive terms:[34]

> **Article 25 Entry into force**
> . . . The Convention shall remain in force for 10 years from the date of entry into force. Unless it is denounced two years before the expiry of the aforesaid period it shall remain in force for further successive periods of 10 years.

Clearly, the fact that the original treaty contained restrictive provisions for unilateral termination did not preclude the parties from agreeing to terminate it at a different time, by a new agreement.

Procedure for Proposing Agreement on the Termination of a Bilateral Treaty

When a party wishes to terminate a treaty that is silent on termination, or to do so on terms that are different from those provided for, a *proposal* must be made to the other side. The procedural steps are broadly similar to those for terminating a bilateral treaty in accordance with the treaty, with the essential difference that here the initiating party is making a proposal which the other party may refuse. The steps outlined above apply,[35] with the following variations:

1. Identify the Relevant Treaty Documents

Even if the treaty is silent on termination (it neither provides for termination nor prohibits it), it is still important to examine any related documents that were generated at the same time as the treaty, such as joint or separate statements of understanding, declarations, arrangements, etc., to identify any material that may be relevant to the possibility of termination.

2. Consider Legal Issues

Specific points for international law advisers to consider include the following:

- What period of notice should be given? You may propose that the termination take effect on any date you wish, and the other party may counter-propose any other date. You will need to take various factors into account, such as the expected time needed for domestic consultations and constitutional procedures on either side, if any. If you have no particular date in mind, then a reasonable starting point would be to propose an effective date

[34] Convention on the construction and maintenance of reindeer fences and other measures to prevent reindeer from entering the territory of the other country (signed 3 June 1981, entered into force 19 May 1983) 1333 UNTS 3.

[35] This section should be read together with the section on 'Procedure for Unilaterally Terminating a Bilateral Treaty in accordance with the Treaty' above at 342–47.

twelve months ahead. However, if you are already aware from informal consultations with the other party that they will not require much notice, there is no reason why you should not propose a shorter period.

- Will the termination of this treaty have any effect on your State's (or IO's) participation in other treaties with the same party? Or in any multilateral treaty? If so, your negotiations with the other party will need to address these issues, and you may wish to set out a proposed solution in your initial note.
- Will there be a need for any continuing obligations after termination to protect acquired rights or ongoing projects? It is important to think through the consequences of termination from the point of view of both governments and of any affected private parties. If so, does your government wish to propose any specific obligations as part of the termination agreement?
- Are there any constitutional or legislative requirements in domestic law? If so, how long might these matters take, and is this time factored in to the effective date of termination that you intend to propose?

3. Draft a Note to the other Party

The proposal should be made in writing and addressed to the other party. A diplomatic note is the most suitable form but a letter could also be used. It should include the same elements as a note to terminate a treaty in accordance with the treaty,[36] with the following variations:

- A clear statement of your *proposal* to terminate the treaty, and the date on which you propose that the termination take effect. Note that it should be expressed as a proposal rather than an intention.
- If there are any supplementary or related treaties or arrangements, your note should refer to them. You may wish to make clear that your proposal includes termination of these other instruments, or that it does not, or that you propose that their future be discussed between the parties.
- It may propose any continuing obligations after termination that you deem appropriate, or that the agreement state that there are no continuing obligations.[37]
- If your note sets out all the terms you consider necessary and you wish to conclude the matter straight away, you should end it by proposing that, if the foregoing is acceptable to the other party, this note and their reply to this effect shall constitute an agreement between the two parties. Omit this if the purpose of your note is to open negotiations on the terms of termination.

[36] See the section on 'Draft a Note to the Other Party' above, 343–46.

[37] See for example, *Exchange of Notes* (n 29) Note from the Government of the UK to the Government of the Kingdom of Sweden dated 3 April 2014 paras 3–4. See also the discussion on the UK Note above at 350.

4. Signature of the note

If the note setting out your government's proposal is intended simply to open negotiations, it may be signed in accordance with ordinary diplomatic practice.

If you have already negotiated the terms of termination informally, and the purpose of the note is to propose an agreement, Article 7 VCLT 1969 applies as for signing a treaty.[38]

5. Delivery of the note

As for mode of delivery, the same points apply as for termination in accordance with the treaty. There is however the difference that your proposal may specify an interval before the termination enters into force, so as to allow the time needed for any necessary domestic processes.

Registration and Publication by the UN

An agreement to terminate a bilateral treaty (not in accordance with the treaty) is itself a treaty. It should therefore be registered with the UN Secretary General in accordance with Article 102 of the UN Charter.[39] In addition, the termination of the original treaty should be registered as a subsequent act affecting the status of that treaty.[40]

National Records and Publication of the Termination of the Treaty

Similarly, the fact of termination of the original treaty and its effective date should be published in national records. In addition, the text of the new agreement should be published in the same way as any treaty.[41]

Withdrawal from a Multilateral Treaty

The main ways in which one party may leave a multilateral treaty are:

- unilateral withdrawal in accordance with the treaty;[42]
- withdrawal with the consent of all parties after consultation with all Contracting States in accordance with Article 54(b) VCLT 1969;
- unilateral withdrawal in accordance with Article 56 VCLT 1969; and
- unilateral withdrawal or ejection on a legal ground, in accordance with the VCLT.[43]

[38] See the section on 'Who Needs to Sign the Note (or Letter) on each Side (Where the Notes Form the Treaty)?' in Chapter 7 at 262–63.

[39] See the section on 'Registering the Treaty at the UN' in Chapter 7 at 283–85. See also Annex XV, 'United Nations model certifying statement for registration or filing and recording' at 457.

[40] See section on 'Registration of the Termination and Publication by the UN' above at 347–48.

[41] See the section on 'Action on the Domestic Plane: Publication of the Treaty' in Chapter 7 at 281–83.

[42] VCLT 1969 art 54(a). [43] ibid arts 46–53.

The most common method is unilateral withdrawal in accordance with the treaty.

When a treaty does not provide for withdrawal, a party wishing to withdraw will usually seek the consent of other parties in accordance with Article 54(b) VCLT 1969. These two procedures are explained in detail below.

The other methods of unilateral withdrawal are legally more problematic and rarely attempted. Unilateral withdrawal in accordance with Article 56 VCLT 1969 is a possible legal avenue for a party wishing to withdraw, where the treaty does not provide for withdrawal or that party does not meet the conditions, and where consent of all parties is not (or might not be) forthcoming. That party may argue that there is an implied right to withdraw from the treaty, by demonstrating evidence that the parties intended to allow this, or that it is inherent in the nature of the treaty.[44] The burden is on the party wishing to withdraw to present the legal arguments, and if any other party objects, the withdrawal is likely to fail. A party may also claim a right to withdraw on the basis of various legal grounds set out in the VCLT, such as error, fraud, corruption, coercion, material breach or fundamental change of circumstances. A party may also be obliged to withdraw by unanimous agreement of the other parties in the event of it being in material breach.[45] All of these avenues are likely to result in a legal dispute. The depositary, if there is one, may try to devise a consultation procedure to assist the parties to resolve the matter, failing which settlement of dispute procedures might be invoked. Beyond noting these possibilities, this Handbook does not set out procedures for dealing with them for the reasons noted above.[46]

Unilateral Withdrawal from a Multilateral Treaty in Accordance with the Treaty

Most multilateral treaties make some sort of provision for parties to withdraw from (or denounce) the treaty. Typically, this is done by giving formal notice of withdrawal to the other parties, which takes effect a specified time later. There may be other substantive or procedural restrictions on the right to withdraw, as in bilateral treaties. Some permit withdrawal only after a minimum period of time as a party, usually a specified number of years. Withdrawal provisions do not normally require any reason to be given, leaving parties free to decide to withdraw for any reason, and to explain their reason to other parties or not, as they choose.

If one party lawfully withdraws from or denounces a multilateral treaty, it does not normally have the effect of terminating the treaty; it remains in force for all other parties, provided that there is more than one party remaining. Treaties which expressly provide for a party to leave unilaterally usually refer to this procedure as 'withdrawal from' or 'denunciation of' the treaty; these two

[44] ibid art 56. [45] ibid arts 46–53.

[46] See the section on 'Scope of this Chapter: Role of the Treaty Office' above at 336–37.

terms are interchangeable. This is not the same as termination of the treaty, which is a multilateral procedure resulting in the ending of treaty relations for all parties.[47]

Examples of Common Types of Withdrawal Provisions

Multilateral treaties often permit unilateral withdrawal at any time, subject only to a requirement to give a specified period of notice. An example of this kind of provision is Article 317 UNCLOS, which permits withdrawal at any time subject to giving a minimum of one year's notice.[48]

Similarly, the CoE's 'Model Final Clauses for Conventions, Additional Protocols and Amending Protocols concluded within the Council of Europe' contains the following model clause on denunciation:

Article E Denunciation

1. Any Party may, at any time, denounce this Convention by means of a notification addressed to the Secretary General of the Council of Europe.
2. Such denunciation shall become effective on the first day of the month following the expiration of a period of [three, six, twelve, . . .] months after the date of receipt of the notification by the Secretary General.[49]

Many CoE treaties contain denunciation clauses of this type, with the notice period fixed at three, six or twelve months.

Some treaties restrict the right of unilateral withdrawal by imposing additional conditions, for example that the treaty must have been in force for the party concerned for a minimum period of time. An example of a CoE treaty with a clause of this type is the European Convention on Human Rights, 1951,[50] which provides:

Article 58 Denunciation

1. A High Contracting Party may denounce the present Convention only after the expiry of five years from the date on which it became a party to it and after six months' notice contained in a notification addressed to the Secretary General of the Council of Europe, who shall inform the other High Contracting Parties.

A required minimum period of time in the treaty is also a common precondition for withdrawal from some treaties that are open to all States. For

[47] See the section on 'Use of Terms' above at 335–36.

[48] UNCLOS (adopted 10 December 1982, entered into force 16 November 1994) 1833 UNTS 3.

[49] Ministers' Deputies of the Council of Europe, 'Model Final Clauses for Conventions, Additional Protocols and Amending Protocols concluded within the Council of Europe' (adopted 5 July 2017) 5.VII.2017 https://rm.coe.int/168072fb76 accessed 18 September 2018. Note that the same model clause on denunciation has been included in the Model Final Clauses since the first edition was adopted in 1980.

[50] Convention for the Protection of Human Rights and Fundamental Freedoms (adopted 4 November 1950, entered into force 3 September 1953, as amended), 213 UNTS 221, ETS 005.

example, Article 38 CBD provides for unilateral withdrawal by giving one year's notice, but only after the Convention has been in force for that party for two years.[51] Article 25 UNFCCC permits unilateral withdrawal by giving at least one year's notice, but only after that Convention has been in force for that party for three years.[52] The Paris Agreement, 2015 (on climate change) contains a similar provision.[53]

Procedure for Unilateral Withdrawal from a Multilateral Treaty in Accordance with the Treaty

A State or IO wishing to exercise its right to withdraw from a multilateral treaty in accordance with its provisions will need to follow broadly the same steps as those set out above for terminating a bilateral treaty.[54] The main procedural difference is that the party wishing to withdraw will need to deal with the depositary government or IO for the treaty, instead of one other party. If there is no depositary, the withdrawing party has to deal directly with all other parties. The main substantive difference is that the withdrawal of one party will not normally result in termination of the treaty. The main differences in the steps that need to be taken are as follows:

1. Identify the Applicable Treaty Provisions

Withdrawal provisions should be studied in all the authentic language versions of the treaty. If there is doubt about the meaning or any discrepancy between languages, it is best to consult the depositary as they may have a view and/or be able to access linguistic advice as necessary. The depositary may consult the treaty parties about how to apply the withdrawal clause, if they are unsure how to resolve doubts or if there is a difference of view between the party wishing to withdraw and the treaty officials in the depositary organisation.

2. Check Treaty Records

Check your treaty records regarding your State's participation in any amendments, extensions, protocols or any other subsequent agreements relating to the implementation of this treaty, and compare them to the published records of the depositary and the UN Treaty Collection status records. If you find any discrepancies, consult the depositary to resolve them. You need to be clear that you have identified all relevant treaty documents so that the full consequences of withdrawal from the treaty can be assessed.

[51] CBD art 38.

[52] UNFCCC (adopted 9 May 1992, entered into force 21 March 1994) 1771 UNTS 107, art 25.

[53] Paris Agreement (adopted 12 December 2015, entered into force 4 November 2016) UNTS Registration No. 54113, 55 ILM 740, art 28. Note that the Paris Agreement is related to the UNFCCC.

[54] Read this section together with the section on 'Procedure for Unilaterally Terminating a Bilateral Treaty in accordance with the Treaty' above at 342–47.

3. Consider Legal Issues

The legal points to consider with regard to a proposed withdrawal from a multilateral treaty in accordance with the treaty are broadly the same as those for terminating a bilateral treaty.[55] If a party is in doubt about the interpretation or application of the withdrawal provision, or any continuing obligations, the depositary may be able to advise, if the issue is procedural. If the issue is substantive, the depositary may wish to consult the other parties or may advise that party to do so, for example at a MOP if one is planned.

With regard to continuing obligations after the treaty has been terminated, if none are in the treaty, this does not preclude a withdrawing party from proposing terms of this nature (for example, to protect existing projects or investments). However as this would require a treaty amendment, or some other kind of decision by all the treaty parties, it may not be realistic to expect such a proposal to succeed.

4. Draft a Note to the Depositary or All Other Parties

Notice of termination should always be given in writing. It is not sufficient to declare it orally at a MOP even if there will be a record. Multilateral treaties usually specify that notice of termination shall be sent to the depositary, but a few multilateral treaties with a small number of parties have no depositary, and in this case notice of termination should be addressed directly to all the other parties and sent by diplomatic channels (as for bilateral treaties). If no mode is specified but there is a depositary, it may be sent to the depositary with a request to circulate it to all parties.[56]

The essential elements of the note are the same as for terminating bilateral treaties,[57] with the following variations:

- A clear statement that this note is that party's notice of denunciation or withdrawal (it is best to use the word that is used in the treaty). It is important to distinguish actual notice from an announcement about a future withdrawal. For example, the statement made by the Government of the United States in its Note to the UN of 4 August 2017 was not notice of withdrawal from the Paris Agreement, but rather advance information that the USA intended to withdraw in the future.[58]

[55] See the section on 'Procedure for Unilaterally Terminating a Bilateral Treaty in accordance with the Treaty', specifically on 'Consider Legal Issues' above at 343. In the context of multilateral treaties, for 'terminate' read 'withdraw' or 'denounce'.

[56] VCLT 1969 art 78.

[57] See the section on 'Procedure for Unilaterally Terminating a Bilateral Treaty in accordance with the Treaty', specifically on 'Draft a Note to the other Party' above at 343–46. In the context of multilateral treaties, for 'terminate' read 'withdraw' or 'denounce'.

[58] The text of the US Note of 4 June 2017 is as follows:

> This is to inform the Secretary-General, in connection with the Paris Agreement, adopted at Paris on December 12, 2015 ('the Agreement'), that the United States intends to exercise its right to withdraw from the Agreement. Unless the United States identifies suitable terms for reengagement, the United States will submit to the Secretary-General, in accordance with

- The date on which withdrawal is to take effect:
  - If the treaty provides that withdrawal shall take effect on an exact number of days, months or years measured from the date of notice (as, for example, Article 58 of the European Convention on Human Rights), the withdrawing party should not attempt to calculate it and write it in the note.[59] Rather, the note should request the depositary to confirm the date on which withdrawal shall take effect in accordance with the provisions of Article X.
  - On the other hand, if the withdrawal provision requires a minimum period of notice, and the withdrawing party wishes to give a longer period, it could specify its chosen date in the note (provided it is sufficiently longer than the minimum period to allow time for receipt and circulation). For example, if there is a provision similar to this one from the Paris Agreement Article 28, 'Any such withdrawal shall take effect upon expiry of one year from the date of receipt by the Depositary of the notification of withdrawal, or on such later date as may be specified in the notification of withdrawal', the note could, for example, specify a date eighteen months ahead.

5. Signature of the Note

As for bilateral treaties, Article 67(2) VCLT 1969 applies. The safest course is therefore to have the note signed by the Head of State, Head of Government or Minister of Foreign Affairs.[60] Alternatively, the withdrawing party could ask the depositary whether they will require Full Powers for another signatory, and if so, send the draft Full Powers document in advance to check that it will be acceptable.

Article 28, paragraph 1 of the Agreement, formal written notification of its withdrawal as soon as it is eligible to do so. Pending the submission of that notification, in the interest of transparency for parties to the Agreement, the United States requests that the Secretary-General inform the parties to the Agreement and the States entitled to become parties to the Agreement of this communication relating to the Agreement.

The text is published at Climate Home News, 'Trump letter to UN on leaving Paris climate accord – in full' (7 August 2017) www.climatechangenews.com/2017/08/07/trump-tells-un-intention-leave-paris-climate-accord-full/ accessed 19 September 2018. See UN comment on its status: UN News, 'UN officially notified of US intention to withdraw from Paris climate pact' (4 August 2017) https://news.un.org/en/story/2017/08/562872-un-officially-notified-us-intention-withdraw-paris-climate-pact accessed 19 September 2018; and comment by former US State Department legal adviser S Biniaz, in an interview on 6 August 2017 published at: S Biniaz, 'The U.S. Communication Regarding Intent to Withdraw from the Paris Agreement: What does it Mean?' (6 August 2017) http://blogs.law.columbia.edu/climatechange/2017/08/06/the-u-s-communication-regarding-intent-to-withdraw-from-the-paris-agreement-what-does-it-mean/ accessed 19 September 2018.

59 See the section on 'Examples of Common Types of Withdrawal Provisions' above for the full text of Article 58 of the European Convention on Human Rights at 355.

60 See the section on 'Full Powers' in Chapter 5 at 188–192.

6. Delivery of the Note

The note should not be delivered until any necessary domestic constitutional, legal or political processes have been completed, or the withdrawing party is certain that they will have been completed by the time that withdrawal takes effect.[61]

If the depositary is the UN Secretary General, the following guidance in the UN Treaty Handbook should be noted:

> **6.1.3 Delivery of documents**
> Most treaty actions become effective only upon deposit of the relevant instrument with the Treaty Section. States are advised to deliver instruments directly to the Treaty Section to ensure they are promptly processed. The date of deposit is normally recorded as that on which the instrument is received at Headquarters, unless the instrument is subsequently deemed unacceptable. Persons who are merely delivering instruments (rather than, for example, signing a treaty) do not require full powers.

If the depositary is another IO or a government, you should follow any guidance they have provided. The UN advice to deliver instruments directly to the Treaty Section is good advice in relation to any depositary. Personal delivery, with an immediate acknowledgement of receipt to take away, is ideal.

Registration of the Withdrawal and Publication by the UN

The withdrawal of a party from a treaty is a subsequent act affecting the status of the treaty, which should be registered with the UN Secretary General. This is required by Article 2 of the UNGA Regulations to give effect to Article 102 of the UN Charter.[62] Guidance is also provided in the UN Treaty Handbook, para 5.5.4, which indicates that in the case of multilateral treaties, registration of a withdrawal is normally the responsibility of the depositary. When the UN Secretary General is the depositary, the UN Secretariat always registers the treaty and subsequent actions such as withdrawals. The procedure for registration is the same as for bilateral treaties.[63] Note that the withdrawal may only be registered if the treaty has been registered. There is no deadline for the registration of a treaty, so if the depositary has omitted to register it before, it may rectify this now and then register the withdrawal.[64]

National Records and Publication of the Withdrawal from the Treaty

It is the depositary's responsibility to register the withdrawal with the UN, so this information will then be available to the public on the UN website. It may also be posted on a website maintained by the depositary. It is nevertheless

[61] See the section on 'Domestic Procedures for Treaty Withdrawals and Terminations' below at 375–81.
[62] *UNGA Res 97(1)* (n 22).
[63] See the section on 'Unilateral Termination of a Bilateral Treaty in accordance with the Treaty', specifically on 'Registration and Publication by the UN' above at 347–48.
[64] See the section on 'Registering the Treaty at the UN' in Chapter 7 at 283–85.

important for the withdrawing party to ensure that its internal treaty register is updated with the fact of withdrawal and its effective date. A copy of the notice of withdrawal should be retained, together with the depositary's acknowledgement and any related correspondence. If it is archived, it should be indexed and retrievable, in case any issues arise later with regard to past obligations under the treaty or the terms of withdrawal.

The fact of withdrawal and its effective date should be published in the official national treaty series of the withdrawing State. It is the depositary's responsibility to inform all other parties and States or IOs entitled to become party to the treaty of the withdrawal and its effective date.[65] Those other parties should update their own databases and, if necessary, undertake any domestic action necessary to adjust to the withdrawal, such as removing that State's name from any implementing legislation that is reciprocal in nature.

Withdrawal from a Multilateral Treaty with Consent of All Parties

It is always possible for one party to withdraw from a multilateral treaty if it has the consent of all of the other parties, in accordance with Article 54(b) VCLT.[66] This can be done whether or not the treaty contains any provision for withdrawal or termination. If the treaty contains no provision, the parties are free to agree on any terms for the withdrawal. If the treaty does provide for unilateral withdrawal, the parties may if they wish agree to a withdrawal on different terms, instead of the terms set out in the treaty. This is relatively unusual, as other parties tend to be reluctant to 'bypass' express withdrawal provisions in the treaty that form part of a previously negotiated package. The 'consent' of all other parties may be obtained through their express agreement, or by securing their tacit consent in the form of non-responses to a proposal within a specified timeframe.

A subsequent agreement on withdrawal may take the form of an amendment to the treaty or a separate treaty. It does not have to be in the same form as the original treaty. The new agreement may be a standalone decision on withdrawal or part of a larger new agreement that covers other matters.

The outcome of an attempt by a party to withdraw from a multilateral treaty with no provision for withdrawal can never be taken for granted. The success of the attempt may differ greatly from one case to another depending on the treaty, the parties and the circumstances, as the following two examples illustrate.

The Democratic People's Republic of Korea (DPRK) attempted to withdraw from the ICCPR.[67] The ICCPR's final provisions, Articles 48–53, contain no reference to withdrawal, denunciation or termination. The DPRK, which had acceded to the ICCPR in 1981, sent a notification of its withdrawal to the UN

[65] VCLT 1969, art 77(1)(e). [66] VCLT 1969 arts 54(b) and VCLT 1986 art 54(b).
[67] ICCPR (adopted 16 December 1966, entered into force 23 March 1976) 999 UNTS 171.

Secretary General as Depositary in 1997.[68] The UN Secretariat responded with an aide-mémoire to the Government of the DPRK, stating that the Secretary General was of the opinion that a withdrawal from the ICCPR would not appear possible unless all States Parties to the ICCPR agree to such a withdrawal.[69] Both the notification and the aide-mémoire were circulated to all States Parties. Fourteen States responded, of which all but one clearly stated their view that unilateral withdrawal was not permitted under the ICCPR and that they objected to the withdrawal by the DPRK.[70] The DPRK thus remains a party to the ICCPR and has participated in reporting processes under the treaty since then.[71]

Compare this with the apparently successful withdrawal of the USA from the Optional Protocol to the Vienna Convention on Consular Relations concerning the Compulsory Settlement of Disputes, 1963 which has no provision for withdrawal.[72] In March 2005, the UN Secretary General notified States Parties that he had received a communication from the Government of the USA notifying its withdrawal from that Optional Protocol.[73] No other State responded. On the UN Treaty Collection website, the USA is shown in the status list for the treaty with square brackets around its dates of signature and ratification, and is not counted in the number of parties to this treaty.[74]

Procedure for Seeking to Withdraw from a Multilateral Treaty with Consent of All other Parties

The procedural steps are broadly similar to those for a unilateral withdrawal from a multilateral treaty in accordance with the treaty. The essential difference is that the party wishing to withdraw needs to present a proposal which

[68] The Note is reproduced in UNSG, 'International Covenant on Civil and Political Rights Adopted by the General Assembly of the United Nations on 16 December 1966: Notification by the Democratic People's Republic of Korea' UN Doc C.N.467.1997.TREATIES-10 (Annex) (12 November 1997) https://treaties.un.org/doc/Publication/CN/1997/CN.467.1997-Eng.pdf accessed 19 September 2018. The Note is dated 23 August 1997.

[69] ibid Aide Mémoire (dated 23 September 1997).

[70] UN, *Final Clauses of Multilateral Treaties: Handbook* (UN 2003) 111–12, especially fn 105.

[71] The DPRK remains listed as a party to the ICCPR on the UNTC website. Aust commented that the DPRK *appears* to have accepted that it remains a party: A Aust, *Modern Treaty Law and Practice* (3rd edn, CUP 2013) 257. See also *Helfer* (n 1), 639–40.

[72] Optional Protocol to the Vienna Convention on Consular Relations concerning the Compulsory Settlement of Disputes (adopted 24 April 1963, entered into force 19 March 1967) 596 UNTS 487.

[73] UN, *Treaty Series* (vol 2308, UN 2005), Optional Protocol of the Vienna Convention on Consular Relations concerning the Compulsory Settlement of Disputes: Notification of Withdrawal United States of America (registered 7 March 2005) 71.

[74] UNTC, 'Chapter III Privileges and Immunities, Diplomatic and Consular Relations, etc – Optional Protocol to the Vienna Convention on Consular Relations concerning the Compulsory Settlement of Disputes' (status as at 5 November 2018) https://treaties.un.org/pages/ViewDetails.aspx?src=TREATY&mtdsg_no=III-8&chapter=3&clang=_en#1 accessed 5 November 2018.

the other parties are not obliged to accept. The procedural steps are as set out above,[75] with the following variations:

1. Identify the Relevant Treaty Documents

Even if the treaty has no provisions on withdrawal, it is necessary to assemble any documents that accompanied the treaty at the time of its adoption or signature, to identify any material that may indicate whether parties discussed the possibility of allowing withdrawal.

2. Consider Legal Issues

When the treaty does not expressly provide for withdrawal, the legal issues are particularly complex and include the following:

- Effective date of withdrawal: the party wishing to withdraw may make any proposal with regard to the effective date; even that it take effect immediately on the date of receipt of the note. However, unless that party knows already that other parties will accept shorter notice, it would be reasonable to propose an effective date twelve months ahead.
- If there are any related treaties such as a parent treaty or protocol, the note should make clear whether the proposed withdrawal applies to those other treaties as well as or only to the specified treaty. If the effect of the proposed withdrawal on other treaties will be complex or uncertain, the note should set out an explanation and if necessary a proposed solution.
- Will there be a need for any continuing obligations after withdrawal to protect acquired rights, budgetary commitments or ongoing projects? If the treaty has no withdrawal clause, this issue might not have been foreseen. The withdrawing party needs to think through whether there could be problems from the perspective of other parties or affected private parties. If so, it may be necessary to propose terms, or a mode for negotiating a solution.
- Are there any domestic law requirements for the withdrawing party? For example, does the legislature need to give approval or be consulted prior to withdrawing from this treaty? Does any legislation need to be repealed or amended? If withdrawal is agreed by means of a side agreement or amendment to the treaty, will this trigger domestic procedures for *ratifying* a treaty? Do continuing obligations post-withdrawal need to be given effect in domestic law? How long might these matters take, and how should they be factored in to the effective date of withdrawal?

[75] Read this section together with the section on 'Procedure for Unilateral Withdrawal from a Multilateral Treaty in accordance with the Treaty' above at 342–47.

3. Draft a Note to the Depositary or All other Parties

The note should be addressed to the depositary (if there is one), with a request to transmit it to all other parties. Otherwise, the note should be addressed to all other parties and sent directly to each one. The essential elements are broadly similar to those for a unilateral withdrawal from a multilateral treaty in accordance with the treaty,[76] with the following variations:

- A clear statement of the party's wish to withdraw from the treaty and when. If withdrawal is straightforward and opposition is not expected, this might be expressed as boldly as this notification by the USA: 'This letter constitutes notification by the United States of America that it hereby withdraws from the aforesaid Protocol.'[77] However, in cases where there are matters to be negotiated or known sensitivities, it might be wiser to phrase it in terms of a proposal, such as 'State X hereby notifies its wish to withdraw from the Y treaty and proposes that the withdrawal shall take effect on [date]'. However it may be worded, it is in fact a proposal that other parties are entitled to reject. It is good practice to give a period of notice, such as twelve months.
- If there are any supplementary or related treaties, the note should make clear whether the proposal includes withdrawal from these other instruments, or that it does not, as the case may be.
- The note should set out any proposal for continuing obligations after withdrawal, or acknowledge any issues that need to be addressed. Alternatively, the withdrawing party may wish to make it clear that there will be no continuing obligations or liabilities on its part, or towards it by others.

4. Signature of the Note

Procedure is as for unilateral withdrawal from a multilateral treaty.[78] However, if the first note is intended to set out a proposal to open negotiations, it may be signed in accordance with ordinary diplomatic practice. If and when agreement is reached, the final agreement or formal withdrawal instrument will need to be signed by an authorised person.

5. Delivery of the Note

Procedure is as for unilateral withdrawal from a multilateral treaty.[79] If the withdrawal is to be given effect by a new treaty (or treaty amendment), rather than a simple withdrawal note, it may trigger domestic processes for ratifying

[76] See the section on 'Procedure for Unilateral Withdrawal from a Multilateral Treaty in accordance with the Treaty' above at 342–47.

[77] *UN* (n 73). See the accompanying text above at 361.

[78] See section on 'Procedure for Unilateral Withdrawal from a Multilateral Treaty in accordance with the Treaty', specifically on 'Signature of the note' above at 358.

[79] See the section on 'Procedure for Unilateral Withdrawal from a Multilateral Treaty in accordance with the Treaty', specifically on 'Delivery of the note' above at 359.

a treaty, for all parties. This needs to be taken into account by each party before it gives its consent to be bound, as for any treaty.[80]

6. Wait for Responses of other Parties

In this case, there is an additional step since delivery of the note is not by itself an effective act, but rather the start of a process of consultation. If the note simply sets out the proposed withdrawal and the date of its effect, with or without any other terms, and requests the depositary to circulate it, the depositary should do so and specify a deadline for any party wishing to object or respond in any other way. The depositary should send the note not only to all other parties but also to other Contracting States (including any that have ratified but for whom the treaty is not yet in force). Article 54(b) VCLT does not specify a procedure for obtaining consent. By analogy with Article 56(2), the deadline for other parties and Contracting States to respond should not be less than twelve months. If during this period any party objects, the withdrawal will not take effect. Contracting States may express a view but have no right of veto.

Registration and Publication by the UN

The registration procedures for withdrawal from a multilateral treaty with the consent of all parties are the same as those for unilateral withdrawal from a multilateral treaty, except that the registration should not be submitted until the deadline for responses from other parties has passed, in case there is an objection and the withdrawal does not become effective.[81] Registration of any withdrawal from a multilateral treaty is normally the responsibility of the depositary.

If the withdrawal is agreed on negotiated terms, that new agreement or amendment to the treaty is itself a treaty. By analogy with a 'Protocol of Accession', such a treaty could be called a 'Protocol of Withdrawal', or any other title the parties choose. It should be registered with the UN Secretary General in accordance with Article 102 of the UN Charter.[82]At the same time, the Secretary General should be informed of the withdrawal of that party from the main treaty.

National Records and Publication of the Withdrawal

The fact of withdrawal and its effective date should be published, as for a withdrawal in accordance with the treaty.[83] If the withdrawal takes effect by means of a provision in a new treaty, that new treaty should be recorded and

[80] See the section on 'Understanding Modes for Expressing Consent to Be Bound' in Chapter 6 at 220–27.

[81] See the section on 'Procedure for Unilateral Withdrawal from a Multilateral Treaty in accordance with the Treaty', specifically on 'Registration and Publication by the UN', above at 359.

[82] See the section on 'Registering the Treaty at the UN' in Chapter 7 at 283–85.

[83] See the section on 'Unilateral Withdrawal from a Multilateral Treaty in accordance with the Treaty', specifically on 'National Records and Publication of the Withdrawal from the Treaty' above at 359–60.

published as any other treaty while the status records of the withdrawn-from treaty should also be updated.[84]

Termination of Multilateral Treaties

A multilateral treaty may be terminated in accordance with its own provisions, or by consent of all the parties after consultation with any other Contracting States (States which have ratified, but for which the treaty is not yet in force). The consent of the parties may be expressed in an instrument which is created specifically to wind up the treaty, or in a new treaty that has other content. When termination comes into effect, the treaty ceases to be in force. In other cases, termination may occur in a more gradual way as a consequence of all parties, or all but one, withdrawing. Managing these procedures is an important part of the role of the depositary.

Termination of a multilateral treaty is not an event that most government Treaty Offices will need to deal with very often. When it occurs, there may be no one in the Treaty Office who has dealt with a termination before, and those who do may never repeat the experience; so recording and handing on this knowledge is crucial.

Responsibility for most of the international procedures will normally rest with the depositary, but each State Party will have to deal with any consequences for its own domestic legal system, and ensure that the change of status of the treaty is properly recorded and published in its own systems.

The main ways in which a multilateral treaty may be terminated are:

- termination in accordance with the provisions of the treaty;
- termination by another treaty between the same parties;
- termination by consent of all parties after consultation with all Contracting States (Article 54(b) VCLT 1969);
- automatic termination: the treaty is terminated by operation of a provision within the treaty itself, such as a sunset clause or a conditions clause;
- termination as a consequence of unilateral withdrawals by all parties (or all but one) from the treaty in accordance with its provisions; and
- termination on a legal ground, in accordance with the Articles 52–68 VCLT.

The first five of these are explained below. The last, 'termination on a legal ground', refers to termination due to material breach, fundamental change of circumstances, conflict with a peremptory norm of international law, coercion, etc. and is not discussed further for the reasons referred to above.[85]

[84] See the section on 'Action on the Domestic Plane: Publication of the Treaty' in Chapter 7 at 281–82.

[85] See sections on 'Scope of this chapter: Role of the Treaty Office' at 336–37; 'Termination of Bilateral Treaties' at 340–53; and 'Withdrawal from a Multilateral Treaty' at 353–60 above.

Termination of a Multilateral Treaty in Accordance with the Treaty

Provisions for termination are not usually found in global standard-setting treaties. By contrast, they are quite common in limited membership multilateral treaties, for example those that establish co-operation for specific purposes whose end is foreseen, and in founding treaties of IOs and treaty bodies where termination would need to address the winding up of financial arrangements, property, institutions or liabilities. Such procedures do not necessarily require the consent of all parties; they may provide for a certain number of parties to be able to trigger the termination, or for termination to be decided by an organ established under the treaty. There is wide variation in the kind of procedures devised, which often need to be highly customised to the particular treaty.

Example of a Termination Provision in a Limited Membership Treaty

Article 6 of the International Agreement regarding the Maintenance of Certain Lights in the Red Sea, 1962 is an example of a termination provision in a limited membership treaty.[86] Article 6 provides:

> (1) The Government of the United Kingdom has the right to discontinue its obligation to be Managing Government by giving to the other contracting Governments written notice to this effect. Its obligation shall cease at the end of the financial year following the financial year in which notice was given.
>
> (2) In such event, the contracting Governments shall consult among themselves with a view to appointing another Government as Managing Government or making other arrangements for the management of the lights. If no such arrangements are made before the obligation of the Government of the United Kingdom ceases in accordance with paragraph (1) of the present Article, the present Agreement shall cease to be in force.

This Agreement, which had sixteen States Parties, was terminated in accordance with its Article 6, in the following way. In a note dated 17 March 1989, the Government of the UK gave notice to all contracting governments that it intended to exercise its right under Article 6(1) of the Agreement to discontinue its obligation to be Managing Government, and would cease to be Managing Government with effect from 31 March 1990. This followed an unsuccessful attempt to terminate the treaty by co-ordinated withdrawals; between 1987 and 1989, thirteen other States Parties notified their unilateral denunciations of the Agreement under Article 12(1) but two Parties did not. No other arrangements were agreed under this Agreement, and therefore it terminated in accordance with Article 6, and ceased to be in force on 31 March 1990. The UK, as Depositary Government for the Agreement, circulated a final status list to all Parties, listing the dates of each notification of denunciation and its effective date, as well as the UK's notification under Article 6 and the date on which the

[86] International Agreement regarding the Maintenance of Certain Lights in the Red Sea (signed 20 February to 19 August 1962, entered into force 28 October 1966, terminated) UKTS 08 (1967).

Agreement ceased to be in force. This information is published on the UK Government's treaty website, and remains published there, thus enabling the public to trace the history of this Agreement and its status.[87]

Example of a Termination Provision in a Treaty Establishing an IO

The International Coffee Organization was established in 1963 when the first International Coffee Agreement (ICA) entered into force in 1962 for a period of five years, and it has continued to operate under successive Agreements negotiated since then.[88] One of these was the ICA, 2000,[89] Article 52 of which stipulates the procedure for its termination:

Article 52 Duration and termination

(3) The Council may at any time, by a vote of a majority of the Members having not less than a distributed two-thirds majority of the total votes, decide to terminate this Agreement. Termination shall take effect on such date as the Council shall decide.

The ICA 2000 was terminated in accordance with its Article 52(3), to coincide with the entry into force of the treaty that replaced it: the ICA, 2007.[90] The 2007 Agreement contains a similar provision, enabling it to be terminated at any time by decision of the Council of the International Coffee Organization (Article 48(4)).

Procedure for Terminating a Multilateral Treaty in Accordance with Its Provisions

As can be seen from the sample provisions above, there is enormous variation in the type of termination provisions in multilateral treaties. Each provision is tailored to take account of the particular type of treaty and, if it establishes an organisation, the administrative and financial implications of winding it up. It is therefore difficult to generalise about the procedures for implementing such provisions. Any specific procedures mandated by the treaty must of course be followed. Responsibility for doing so will usually rest with the depositary, if there is one. As each depositary works out its own system for winding up a treaty, the PLATO principles may provide some guidance, in particular:

- 'Legal': in-house lawyers should be fully engaged at the outset to ensure that procedures follow the provisions of the treaty concerned and conform to the

[87] FCO, 'UK Depositary Status List: International Agreement regarding the Maintenance of Certain Lights in the Red Sea' www.gov.uk/government/uploads/system/uploads/attachment_data/file/603446/36._Red_Sea_Lights__1962___Status_list__NLIF_.pdf accessed 19 September 2018.

[88] See International Coffee Organization, 'History' www.ico.org/icohistory_e.asp accessed 19 September 2018.

[89] International Coffee Agreement (adopted 28 September 2000, entered into force 17 May 2005) 2161 UNTS 308 (the Agreement is addressed as 'ICA 2001' by the International Coffee Organization). Terminated on 2 February 2011.

[90] International Coffee Agreement (adopted 28 September 2007, entered into force 2 February 2011) 2734 UNTS 101.

international law of treaties as reflected in the VCLT. Each State Party concerned needs to ensure that it takes into account the requirements of its domestic law. Lastly, IO parties or depositaries need to ensure that the organisation's internal rules are observed.

- 'Transparent' means that clear information should be provided to all treaty parties regarding the proposal to terminate the treaty and the procedures to be followed, as well as adequate notice to enable them to express their views and exercise whatever rights they may have to participate in the decision. Clear information should be published about the status of the treaty after its termination, in a form which will remain accessible to the public indefinitely.
- 'Organised': record management systems have to guarantee that all actions and notifications are meticulously recorded and that the records will remain accessible to future staff. Consistency in application of treaty procedures also requires that records are kept of the way in which each treaty termination is handled, to ensure that knowledge is preserved and future depositary staff apply like procedures to like cases (adapting them as appropriate).

Termination of a Multilateral Treaty by a Later Treaty between the same Parties

Many multilateral treaties have no provision on termination, but it does not follow that the treaty cannot be terminated. The parties may, if they wish, conclude a new agreement to terminate it. Even if there is a provision on termination, the parties may agree not to use that provision but instead to terminate it on different terms set out in a later agreement.

When the parties to a treaty decide to replace it by another treaty on the same subject, they may terminate the existing treaty by means of a provision in the new treaty. For example, the Single Convention on Narcotic Drugs, 1961 provides for the termination of certain earlier treaties in the narcotics field as between parties to the Single Convention.[91] Its Article 44 reads as follows:

Termination of Previous International Treaties

1. The provisions of this Convention, upon its coming into force, shall, as between Parties hereto, terminate and replace the provisions of the following treaties: [clauses (a) to (i) list a number of treaties]

Procedure for Termination of a Multilateral Treaty by a Later Treaty between the same Parties

The depositary (or the parties themselves, if there is no depositary) will need to prepare the new treaty and organise the signing and/or ratification of it (or

[91] Single Convention on Narcotic Drugs (adopted 30 March 1961, entered into force 13 December 1964) 520 UNTS 151.

other procedure for signifying consent). The procedural steps are the same as for making any new treaty.[92]

The depositary for the new treaty is required to register it with the UN Secretary General under Article 102 of the UN Charter when it enters into force, as for any new treaty.[93] The depositary of each terminated treaty should inform the parties to that treaty that it is terminated, and register the termination as a subsequent act relating to the status of the treaty. This registration should be carried out when the termination has taken effect, that is, after entry into force of the new treaty that terminates it. Therefore, if the depositary of the new treaty is not the same as the depositary for the treaty or treaties that it terminates, the depositaries concerned need to co-operate to ensure prompt flow of information.

It should be noted that this method of termination will only be effective if *all* the parties to the existing treaty become party to the new treaty. If not, the existing treaty will remain in force, and the resulting treaty relations as between those parties which join the new treaty and those which do not will be complicated.[94] The Depositary practice of the UN Secretary General provides useful guidance to any depositary which has to handle such a situation:

> If not all the parties to the earlier treaty become parties to the later one [which terminates the earlier one], then the earlier treaty remains in effect between those that have accepted the later treaty and those which have not done so. In view of the large number and the complexity of possible situations that may result from the application of both the earlier and the later treaty by various States, the Secretary General does not specify between which States the treaties apply and, when notifying the parties of the deposit of an instrument in respect of the said treaties, restricts himself to recalling the relevant provisions of the treaties concerned.[95]

Termination of a Multilateral Treaty by Consent of all Parties

Article 54(b) VCLT sets out the principle that the termination of a treaty may take place at any time by consent of all the parties, after consultation with any other Contracting States or IOs. This applies when a treaty is silent on termination or where there is a provision on termination that the parties wish to bypass.

Termination by this method requires the consent of *all* parties, and therefore the expressed objection of a single party will be effective to block it. 'Consent' however is not the same as 'agreement'. The consent of all parties *could* be expressed in a new treaty, as shown in the examples above. However,

[92] See Chapters 5 and 6.
[93] See the section on 'Registering the Treaty at the UN' in Chapter 7 at 283–85.
[94] VCLT 1969 arts 30(4) and 41.
[95] Treaty Section of the Office of Legal Affairs, *Summary of Practice of the Secretary-General as Depositary of Multilateral Treaties* (UN 1999) para 262.

the requirement of 'consent' rather than 'agreement' allows for a more passive expression of consent by not objecting to a proposal. A proposal could be made by the depositary to terminate the treaty; the depositary could circulate it to all parties and any other Contracting States and IOs, inviting responses within a specified deadline. Although Article 54 does not set out a procedure for consultation, one would expect a period of at least twelve months to respond to such a proposal. Any party that does not respond by the specified deadline may be taken to have tacitly consented to the proposal. However, the proposal will fail if a single objection is received, even if the objection is only to the proposed procedure and not to the principle of termination. In this case, it would be open to the depositary, or any party, to make a new proposal.

Article 54(b) also requires consultation with any other Contracting States and IOs (those that have consented to be bound but for which the treaty is not yet in force). The right to be consulted is not the same as a requirement for consent, and so those Contracting Parties cannot block termination. However, if the notice period for termination is longer than the period for a ratification to take effect, they will be able to object at that point and so it is likely that the parties will take account of this.

If consent is given by all parties, expressly or tacitly, so that the termination becomes effective, it should be registered as a subsequent act relating to the status of the treaty under the UNGA Regulations on the implementation of Article 102.

If this method is used, the application of the PLATO principle of 'Transparency' to the design and execution of the consultation procedure will be especially important.[96]

Sunset Clause: Automatic Termination by a Provision within the Treaty Itself

Some treaties specify that they will remain in force for a limited period only or terminate automatically if certain conditions are satisfied. This is known informally as a sunset clause.

For example, Article 52(1) ICA 2000 provided:

> This Agreement shall remain in force for a period of six years until 30 September 2007 unless extended under the provisions of paragraph (2) of this Article or . . .

It was in fact extended, but if it had not been, it would have ceased to be in force on that date, without any further action on the part of the Depositary. The ICA 2007 contains a similar provision in Article 48:

> (1) This Agreement shall remain in force for a period of ten years after it enters into force provisionally or definitively unless extended under the

[96] See the section on 'Procedure for Terminating a Multilateral Treaty in accordance with its Provisions' above at 367–68.

provisions of paragraph (3) of this Article or terminated under the provisions of paragraph (4) of this Article.

The depositary's responsibility is to note the default expiry date, and if the date approaches without the treaty having been extended or terminated, the depositary should bring this to the attention of all parties by circulating a depositary note. Given the length of time it can take to negotiate such matters, the depositary should warn the parties at least a year before the default expiry date, if not two or more years, setting out the options available to parties and the procedures applicable to each.

If the treaty is automatically terminated by operation of a sunset clause within it, the depositary must inform the parties immediately that it has occurred. This should be done by means of an individual communication to each party. The depositary should also record the change of status in its own records and on its published status lists, and register it with the UN Secretariat.

Termination of a Multilateral Treaty by All Parties (or all but one) Unilaterally Withdrawing

Termination of a treaty may occur as a result of a series of unilateral acts of withdrawal by individual parties, provided those withdrawals are legally effective. A treaty cannot remain in force for one party only, so when the penultimate party withdraws, this terminates the treaty regardless of the wishes of the last remaining party. The withdrawals may occur due to a series of independent decisions by parties, or there may be co-ordinated withdrawals. For example, if the parties to a treaty agree that they wish to terminate it, and there is provision for withdrawal but not termination, they may decide to co-ordinate their respective withdrawals in accordance with the treaty. They may even agree to do so on the same date, if that is important. Each party then takes that action unilaterally. However, no party can be compelled to take the unilateral step of withdrawal within any specified timeframe or at all.

Example of an Unsuccessful Attempt to Co-Ordinate Withdrawals as a Means of Terminating a Treaty

The International Agreement regarding the Maintenance of Certain Lights in the Red Sea provided for unilateral denunciation under Article 12(1). Of the sixteen Parties, fourteen Parties gave notice of denunciation to take effect on 31 March 1990.[97] If one more Party had done so, this would have been effective to terminate the Agreement. However, two Parties did not denounce the Agreement, and so the Agreement was instead terminated by the action of the Managing Government under Article 6.

[97] *FCO* (n 87). See the section on 'Example of a Termination Provision in a Limited Membership Treaty' above at 366–67.

Following the termination of the Agreement, the UK as Depositary circulated an updated status list to all parties, published it and registered the termination with the UN Secretary General.

Problems Arising from Slow Pace of Withdrawals from a Treaty which Has Been Replaced by a New Treaty

When the parties to a multilateral treaty agree to replace it with a new updated treaty, if all parties are ready to move to the new treaty they may provide for the termination of the existing treaty in the new one. As noted above, this method is only suitable where *all* the parties to the existing treaty are ready to become party to the new one at the same time.[98] If the parties are likely to ratify the new treaty at very different speeds, they may decide that the old and new treaty regimes will need to remain in force, in parallel, for some time.

In that case, the new treaty should not terminate the existing one or require parties to withdraw from it; instead, the parties may decide individually when to withdraw from the old one after joining the new one. If those parties that join the new treaty become dissatisfied with the pace of ratification of the new one, it is open to them to decide to co-ordinate their withdrawals from the old, thus isolating those remaining in the old treaty in order to create pressure on them to move to the new one. Alternatively, they may decide to remain in the old treaty and run both treaty regimes in parallel until the last remaining party is ready to move, however long that may take, in order to keep treaty relations intact.

An example of the use of the gradual strategy to replace a treaty with a new one is the 1996 Protocol to the Convention on the Prevention of Marine Pollution by Dumping of Wastes and Other Matter of 29 December 1972 (the 'London Protocol').[99] The Protocol (despite its name) was intended to replace the Convention (known as the 'London Convention'), and its Article 26 provides: 'This Protocol will supersede the Convention as between Contracting Parties to this Protocol which are also Parties to the Convention.'

However, the London Protocol does not terminate the London Convention. It was left to individual Parties to decide, when becoming party to the London Protocol, whether to withdraw from the London Convention in accordance with its provisions.[100] The Protocol entered into force in 2006 and has fifty

[98] See the section on 'Termination of a Multilateral Treaty by a Later Treaty between the same Parties' above at 368–69.

[99] 1996 Protocol to the Convention on the Prevention of Marine Pollution by Dumping of Wastes and other Matter of 29 December 1972 (adopted 7 November 1996, entered into force 24 March 2006) 36 ILM 1 (1997) (London Protocol).

[100] Convention on the Prevention of Marine Pollution by Dumping of Wastes and other Matter (adopted 29 December 1972, entered into force 30 August 1975) 1046 UNTS 120 (London Convention). Article XXI of the Convention provides: 'Any Contracting Party may withdraw from this Convention by giving six months' notice in writing to a depositary, which shall promptly inform all Parties of such notice.'

Parties (as of August 2018), but there have not yet been any withdrawals from the Convention which still has eighty-seven Parties. It appears that it may be a long time before all Parties to the Convention move into the Protocol. In the meantime, the resulting treaty relations between the various groups of Parties which are in the old treaty only, or the new one only, or both, is complicated. This is the inevitable downside of the strategy chosen by the Parties to ensure that Convention Parties are not forced out of the Convention before they are ready to move into the Protocol, or left isolated.

It is difficult to achieve the termination of a multilateral treaty with many parties by means of unilateral withdrawal provisions; even if the treaty has become obsolete, there will invariably be parties that forget to withdraw, see no need or simply do not get around to it. This tendency is borne out by the experience of the CoE with respect to the over 220 treaties concluded by Member States under its auspices. CoE treaties usually have a unilateral denunciation (withdrawal) provision but no termination provision. The denunciation provisions have rarely been used, and there are only two treaties which have been denounced by all parties.[101] Denunciation of a superseded treaty by all parties is rarely achieved, even when it is a condition of becoming party to the new one.

For example, the European Convention on the Protection of the Archaeological Heritage (Revised), 1992 stipulates that Parties to the European Convention on the Protection of the Archaeological Heritage, 1969 must denounce it as a condition of joining the 1992 Convention.[102] In spite of this provision, the 1969 Convention still has three Parties and remains in force, despite one of those three having ratified the new treaty.[103] A Report issued by the CoE Secretary General in 2012 identified a long list of 'inactive' treaties, which included treaties in force but obsolete in practice as well as treaties which had served their purpose.[104] The Secretary General suggested

[101] European Convention on the International Classification of Patents for Inventions (adopted 19 December 1954, entered into force 1 August 1955) ETS 017. The denunciations of this Convention were prompted by the conclusion of a new treaty on patents in 1973. The other completely denounced treaty is the Convention relating to Stops on Bearer Securities in International Circulation (adopted 28 May 1970, entered into force 11 February 1979) ETS 072. See status lists: Treaty Office, 'Complete list of the Council of Europe's treaties' (CoE, status as of 5 November 2018) www.coe.int/en/web/conventions/full-list accessed 19 September 2018.

[102] European Convention on the Protection of the Archaeological Heritage (Revised) (adopted 16 January 1992, entered into force 25 May 1995) 1966 UNTS 305, ETS 143, art 14(2). See also European Convention on the Protection of the Archaeological Heritage (adopted 6 May 1969, entered into force 20 November 1970) 788 UNTS 227, ETS 066.

[103] Treaty Office, 'Details of Treaty No. 066 – European Convention on the Protection of the Archaeological Heritage' (CoE) www.coe.int/en/web/conventions/full-list/-/conventions/treaty/066 accessed 19 September 2018.

[104] Secretary General, 'Report by the Secretary General on the Review of Council of Europe Conventions', SG/inf(2012)12 (Council of Europe, 16 May 2012) Appendix 4 Table of classification of Group 4 Conventions: Inactive Conventions'. The Report can be accessed on Treaty Office, 'Review of the Council of Europe Conventions' www.coe.int/en/web/con

possible courses of action to resolve the status of these treaties, for consideration by Member States.[105]

Continuing Obligations after the Ending of Treaty Relations: Bilateral and Multilateral Treaties

Many treaties with withdrawal and/or termination provisions also include provisions that address the consequences of these changes of status. These may include specific obligations that continue to bind all (or both) parties even after the withdrawal or termination takes effect.

Where no specific provision is made in the treaty itself or by separate agreement, Article 70 VCLT 1969 sets out default provisions that apply to the termination of any treaty, and to withdrawals from a multilateral treaty:

Article 70 Consequences of the termination of a treaty

1. Unless the treaty otherwise provides or the parties otherwise agree, the termination of a treaty under its provisions or in accordance with the present Convention:
   (a) releases the parties from any obligation further to perform the treaty;
   (b) does not affect any right, obligation or legal situation of the parties created through the execution of the treaty prior to its termination.
2. If a State denounces or withdraws from a multilateral treaty, paragraph 1 applies in the relations between that State and each of the other parties to the treaty from the date when such denunciation or withdrawal takes effect.

The principle set out in paragraph 1(b) is especially important. Consequently, if two States Parties have a treaty-related dispute, withdrawal by one of them will not help that party evade its legal obligations because they would still apply to matters that arose prior to the withdrawal. Moreover, the treaty may provide that a withdrawal does not take effect for a time period as long as a year, in which case paragraph 2 makes clear that any treaty obligations including mandatory dispute settlement provisions will continue to apply, even to new disputes arising during the notice period.

It is fairly common for Article 70(1)(a) to be displaced by specific provisions that provide for continuing obligations after withdrawal or termination. The kinds of issues that are typically provided for are:

- completion of any project or product of co-operation under the treaty that is already in progress at the time of termination/withdrawal;

ventions/review-of-the-council-of-europe-conventionsreview-of-the-council-of-europeconventions accessed 19 September 2018.

[105] ibid para 3.4 Measures relating to inactive conventions. For the response of the CoE's Member States so far, see: Secretary General, 'Review of the Council of Europe conventions – Report by the Secretary General' (10 April 2013). The response of the CoE's Member States can be accessed on Treaty Office, 'Review of the Council of Europe Conventions' www.coe.int/en/web/conventions/review-of-the-council-of-europe-conventions accessed 19 September 2018.

- continuing protection for intellectual property rights or confidential information acquired under the treaty;
- continuing protection for investments or acquired rights of private parties;
- distributing any money remaining in a fund set up by the treaty;
- payment of any outstanding or assessed budgetary contributions;
- arrangements for any property or premises administered by the treaty;
- arrangements for any staff engaged by the treaty secretariat; and
- continuing liability for any situation arising before the termination or withdrawal.

If there are no such provisions, the parties would be well advised to consider, at the time of withdrawal or termination, whether to negotiate terms to protect their interests or acquired rights or those of private parties. It would be useful to study other treaties on similar subjects to see the kinds of continuing obligations that might usefully be negotiated. The examples set out in Annex XVII give a flavour of the possible ways in which this may be done.[106]

The negotiation of such provisions, and their application after withdrawal or termination, concerns the substance of the treaty for which policy-makers and operational branches of government (or an IO) are responsible. The Treaty Office has an important role to play in drawing these provisions (where they exist) to their attention when withdrawal or termination is under consideration and (where they do not exist) suggesting that they may wish to consider such matters. The Treaty Office might usefully compile examples of such provisions in other treaties on similar subjects, to guide this consideration.

After withdrawal or termination, the Treaty Office should make careful note of any provisions on continuing obligations in the treaty, or agreed in any separate document at the time of withdrawal/termination. These should be noted in the treaty database alongside the information about the date of termination. If the continuing obligations are of a fixed duration, this should be noted also. When the Treaty Office publishes the fact of withdrawal/termination in its gazette, treaty series or website, it should add some kind of note to draw attention to the fact that certain provisions continue to apply, and inform those concerned within its administration.

Domestic Procedures for Treaty Withdrawals and Terminations

States and IOs generally have to complete domestic constitutional or statutory procedures before they may consent to be bound by a treaty.[107] Some also have domestic procedures to complete before withdrawing from or terminating a treaty. The required procedures may be internal to

[106] See Annex XVII, 'Examples of Treaty Provisions on Continuing Obligations after Withdrawal or Termination' at 460–63.

[107] See the section on 'Internal Preparations to Give Consent to Be Bound' in Chapter 6 at 227–242.

government or may also concern the legislature. As withdrawing from or terminating a treaty is a relatively rare occurrence for a State, the procedures may not be well articulated or well known, even by the government officials who are responsible for activating them. Special care needs to be taken to research the relevant legal provisions and precedents, and expert legal advice should always be sought on the constitutional law aspects as well as international law.

In addition to treaty procedures, the termination of treaty relations may also have other implications for the domestic legal system. For example, if there is implementing legislation, it may need to be repealed or amended. Changes may also need to be made in administrative or judicial procedures. For example, if a bilateral treaty on mutual legal assistance were to be terminated, the name of the other State might need to be deleted from lists of States with which such reciprocal arrangements are in place, which may be used by government agencies and judicial administrations. The same may apply when another party withdraws from a multilateral treaty that operates reciprocal arrangements, such as a trade treaty.

States' Domestic Law Requirements for Withdrawal and Termination: National Variations and Areas of Doubt

Some States have express constitutional or legislative provisions regarding the power or procedure for termination of treaty obligations. Others have provisions on the ratification of treaties, but are silent on termination. In some States, the procedures are well established as a matter of constitutional practice or judicial decision. In others, practice is sparse and unclear.

Even where the procedures are clear, there is considerable variation in their content, ranging from those which apply the *actus contrarius* rule, which means that a treaty withdrawal or termination requires the same procedure as ratification, to those which apply a lighter procedure, or none at all. In some States, ending treaty relations is governed by legal provisions, for example laws that specify who may terminate a treaty and how, while in many other States, such action is within the discretion of the executive. In some States, the legislature has a central role in any such decision, while in other States it may have none.

For many States this is an area of considerable doubt and difficulty. The doubts are in some cases compounded by a changing political culture in which legislatures and the public tend to have higher expectations of transparency and consultation than they did in previous eras.

As the domestic legal position for every State is different, this section sets out a range of diverse examples, and a checklist of points to consider for anyone who needs to decide what legal rules to apply in a particular State where the position is not clear.

Examples of Constitutions that Clearly Require Legislative Approval for Terminating Treaties

China

The Constitution expressly allocates power to the Standing Committee of the National People's Congress 'to decide on the ratification or abrogation of treaties and important agreements concluded with foreign states' and provides that the President 'ratifies and abrogates treaties and important agreements concluded with foreign states'.[108] The Law on the Procedure for the Conclusion of Treaties provides that 'The procedures for amendment to, abrogation of and withdrawal from treaties and agreements concluded by the People's Republic of China shall follow *mutatis mutandis* the procedures for the conclusion of the treaties and agreements in question'.[109]

The Netherlands

The Constitution provides that:

> The Kingdom shall not be bound by treaties, nor shall such treaties be denounced, without the prior approval of the States General. The cases in which approval is not required shall be specified by Act of Parliament.[110]

The Kingdom Act on the Approval and Publication of Treaties provides that its provisions on approval and publication of treaties 'shall apply *mutatis mutandis* to plans to denounce treaties'.[111] In other words, if a treaty requires the approval of the legislature before it can be ratified, its denunciation also requires prior legislative approval.

Examples of Constitutions that Require Legislative Approval for Ratifying Treaties but Are Silent as to Terminating Treaties: How Silence Is Interpreted

In these cases, the procedure for terminating treaties is developed by government practice or judicial decision. Note the very different inferences drawn from the silence of the Constitution.

Austria

The Constitution specifies which treaties require the consent of the legislature prior to ratification, but is silent as to the procedure for denouncing or

[108] Constitution of the People's Republic of China (last amended in 2004), 4 December 1982, arts 67(14) and 81.

[109] The Law of the People's Republic of China on the Procedure for the Conclusion of Treaties, 28 December 1990 (promulgated by Order No. 37 of the President of the People's Republic of China, 28 December 1990) art 19.

[110] Constitution of the Kingdom of the Netherlands, 2008 (English version), art 91(1). The 'States General' is the bicameral legislature of the Netherlands.

[111] Kingdom Act on the Approval and Publication of Treaties, 20 August 1994, art 14. The Kingdom Act contains regulations concerning the approval and publication of treaties and publication of decisions of IOs.

terminating a treaty. According to experts, this is governed by the legal principle *actus contrarius*, which means that the same procedure is required for ending a treaty as for consenting to be bound.[112]

Germany

The Constitution specifies which treaties require the consent of the legislature prior to ratification, but is silent as to the procedure for denouncing or terminating a treaty.[113] Legislation sets out governmental procedures for concluding a treaty but not for terminating one.[114] According to a Federal Constitutional Court judgment, the termination or denunciation of a treaty is solely the responsibility of the executive, irrespective of whether the treaty contains an express termination clause; approval by the legislature is not required in any case. Parliament is not consulted.[115]

France

The French Constitution of 4 October 1958 devotes an entire section to treaties and international agreements. It specifies which treaties require the consent of the legislature prior to ratification, but is silent as to the procedure for denouncing or terminating a treaty. Thus, the executive is 'deemed to have discretionary power in this regard. Parliament is not involved in the termination of treaties'.[116]

Examples of States with No Constitutional or Statutory Provisions and No Parliamentary Procedures for Termination

Canada

There are no constitutional or statutory provisions on treaty-making or termination. The legal power to terminate treaties, like the power to make treaties, is an exercise of the foreign affairs power of the royal prerogative (executive power). The treaty-making power is constrained by a policy regarding the laying of treaties before parliament prior to ratification, adopted in 2008.[117] However, this policy does not apply to the termination of treaties.

[112] F Cede and G Hafner, 'National Treaty Law and Practice: Republic of Austria' in D Hollis, M Blakeslee and B Ederington (eds), *National Treaty Law and Practice: Dedicated to the Memory of Monroe Leigh* (Brill, Amsterdam 2005) 70.

[113] Basic Law for the Federal Republic of Germany, 23 May 1949 (last amended on 28 March 2019) art 59. Translation by C Tomuschat et al., Deutscher Bundestag, Basic Law for the Federal Republic of Germany (Deutscher Bundestag, Berlin 2019) www.btg-bestellservice.de/pdf/80201000.pdf accessed 9 October 2019.

[114] Rules of Procedure of the Federal Government, para 72 – International Agreements. Translation provided in *Beemelmans and Treviranus* (n 113) 335–36.

[115] German Federal Constitutional Court, Judgment, 68 BverfG 1 1984, at 85s. Cited in *Beemelmans and Treviranus* (n 114) 326.

[116] P M Eisemann and R Rivier, 'National Treaty Law and Practice: France' in *Hollis et al.* (n 112) 274.

[117] Treaty Law Division, 'Policy on Tabling of Treaties in Parliament' (Global Affairs Canada, last modified 3 March 2014) www.treaty-accord.gc.ca/procedures.aspx accessed 19 September 2018.

Examples of Constitutional or Statutory Provisions on Ratifying Treaties that Are Silent as to Terminating Treaties: Areas of Unclear Practice and Evolution

Japan

The Constitution provides that the approval of the legislature is required for ratification of treaties, but is silent as to the procedure for denouncing or terminating a treaty. According to an official of the International Legal Affairs Division of Japan's MFA, writing in 2005:

> With respect to treaties that require the Diet's approval for their conclusion, termination or withdrawal can be effected by the Government alone if the treaty in question has a termination clause. *There is no established practice yet with respect to cases where a treaty does not have a termination clause.* With respect to executive agreements, termination or withdrawal can be effected by the Government in any case.[118]

Switzerland

The Constitution specifies which treaties require the consent of the legislature prior to ratification, but is silent as to the procedure for denouncing or terminating a treaty.[119] According to experts:

> The power to terminate international agreements rests solely with the Executive. There is no requirement of parliamentary consent or approval. *Thus far, no dispute has arisen over this issue. However such a dispute might one day arise,* based on the argument that Parliament ought to give its approval to the termination or suspension of treaties. In the case of treaties conceding right to individuals directly, or where the termination amounts to a creative, political act, the unmaking of a treaty is similar to its making.[120]

United States of America

The Constitution regulates the treaty-making power but is silent as to ending treaty relations.[121] According to a legal adviser on treaty affairs at the US Department of State, writing in 2005:

> The Constitution does not address the power to terminate treaties or other international agreements. No serious question exists as to the President's authority to terminate executive agreements. *However, practice has varied with respect to*

[118] T Kawakami, 'National Treaty Law and Practice: Japan' in *Hollis et al.* (n 112), *National Treaty Law and Practice: Dedicated to the Memory of Monroe Leigh* (Brill, Amsterdam 2005) 426. Emphasis added to highlight the area of doubt.

[119] L Wildhaber et al., 'National Treaty Law and Practice: Switzerland' in *Hollis et al.* (n 112) 644–48.

[120] ibid 657–58. Wildhaber et al. gave the European Convention on Human Rights as an example of a treaty whose denunciation by the executive alone would seem inconceivable. Emphasis added to highlight the area of doubt. See ibid 658.

[121] Constitution of the United States of America, 17 September 1787 (as last amended in 1992) art II s 2(2).

treaties. The President has (a) acted on his own authority; (b) acted pursuant to a Senate resolution . . . and (c) acted pursuant to a joint resolution of Congress.[122]

United Kingdom

There is no constitutional or statutory provision concerning the procedure for termination of treaties. The practice whereby treaties are laid before Parliament prior to ratification was codified in the Constitutional Reform and Governance Act 2010, sections 20–25. The Government assumed that ending treaty relations was within the exclusive discretion of the Government, acting under the Royal Prerogative power. However, when the Government announced in 2016 that it would give notice to the EU of the UK's intention to leave it under Article 50 of the Treaty on European Union, this was challenged in UK legal proceedings. The UK Supreme Court held that the Government did not have power to do this without prior authorisation by Parliament, in view of the direct effect on the rights of individuals.[123] The Government accepted its defeat in this case, and subsequently obtained the necessary authority in the form of an Act of Parliament before giving notice to the EU under Article 50.[124] However, it is unclear to what extent this principle applies to other treaties.

This selection of examples from domestic legal systems illustrates firstly, the wide variation in procedures for the termination of treaties, and secondly, that there are often areas of uncertainty where legal rules are unclear and practice is inconsistent or in the process of evolution.

Where National Procedures Are Unclear: Factors to Consider in Relation to a Proposed Treaty Withdrawal or Termination

When a State is considering withdrawal from or termination of a particular treaty, its officials have to decide what domestic procedures to apply even when national law is unclear. These are some of the factors they may consider relevant:

- Are there any constitutional or legislative provisions, practices or administrative procedures that refer to treaty termination, withdrawal denunciation or any similar concept?
- If not, are there any provisions regarding treaty-making or ratification, and is there a legal principle that may make them applicable to the reverse process?
- Has this State withdrawn from or terminated a treaty before? If so, what procedure was followed within government and was there any parliamentary procedure?

[122] R E Dalton, 'National Treaty Law and Practice: United States' in *Hollis et al.* (n 112) 792. Emphasis added to highlight the area of doubt.

[123] *R (Miller) v Secretary of State for Exiting the European Union* [2017] UKSC 5.

[124] European Union (Notification of Withdrawal) Act 2017.

- What subjects are covered by the particular treaty in question, and which government ministries and agencies might need to be consulted?
- Will the termination or withdrawal be done in accordance with the treaty, by means of a new treaty, or in some other way?
- Is a period of notice required before termination/withdrawal takes effect?
- Does the treaty confer rights on individuals (such as human rights, investment protection) or affect individuals directly (on aspects such as trade, transport, visas)?
- Does it involve leaving or abolishing an IO?
- Will there be continuing obligations after withdrawal/termination, and if so will they need to be implemented in domestic law?
- Will a repeal or amendment of domestic legislation be necessary?
- If it is the first treaty withdrawal or termination for some time, has there been any recent increase in the expectations of the legislature and the public regarding transparency and consultation?

IOs as Party to a Treaty

The practice of IOs entering into treaties is considerably more limited than that of States, and of much more recent origin. It follows that there is even less practice with regard to IOs withdrawing from treaties. Such practice as exists is mainly in the area of bilateral treaties, such as those with the host State concerning the organisation's headquarters and those with other Member States concerning the establishment of representative offices in their territories. From time to time, such agreements may need to be replaced by a new one, in which case the termination of the old agreement may be effected by a termination provision in the new one. The organisation's procedures for becoming party to a new agreement will apply. In the rare case where the organisation wishes to terminate an agreement or withdraw from it without replacing it with a new one, the question will arise as to the correct procedures for a simple act of termination. If the organisation does not have established procedures for terminating or withdrawing from a treaty, the safest approach would be to assume that the same procedures apply as for becoming party to the treaty in question.

Top Tips on Ending Treaty Relations

To signpost the main points among the complexities addressed in this chapter, Box 9.1 contains a set of top tips on ending treaty relations:

- terminating a bilateral treaty in accordance with the treaty;
- terminating a bilateral treaty by subsequent agreement;
- withdrawing from a multilateral treaty;
- terminating a multilateral treaty; and
- responding to another party's notice of withdrawal.

Box 9.1 Top tips on ending treaty relations

TOP TIPS 1
TERMINATING A BILATERAL TREATY IN ACCORDANCE WITH THE TREATY

Scenario: You are a government treaty official. Your government wishes to terminate a bilateral treaty that has a provision about termination. 'How can you do it, and what is your role?'

1. Read the treaty provisions on termination carefully, in all the official language versions if possible.
2. Does the treaty provide for unilateral termination by one party giving notice to the other? Does it set conditions, and if so are they met? If the conditions are not met or not convenient, see Top Tips 2.
3. Consider whether terminating this treaty requires any domestic constitutional procedures, in government or the legislature, and if so how long they might take.
4. Draft a note to the other party – be clear, is it a notice of withdrawal or a proposal to discuss terms? If you are invoking a right to terminate unilaterally, and any conditions are met, the note can constitute the formal act of termination and specify the date that termination will take effect. If you wish to discuss the timing or other terms of termination with the other party, your note should set out a proposal.
5. Consider whether the treaty deals adequately with continuing obligations to protect acquired rights or ongoing projects. If not, make a proposal or raise the issue in your note.
6. Deliver the note in person if possible and ask for written acknowledgement of receipt on the spot.
7. Agree a record of the effective termination date.
8. Register the termination with the UN Secretary General.
9. Record and publish the termination in national treaty records.
10. Domestic law – complete procedures/bring legislative changes into force.

TOP TIPS 2
TERMINATING A BILATERAL TREATY BY SUBSEQUENT AGREEMENT

Scenario: You are a government treaty official. Your government wishes to terminate a bilateral treaty that has no provision about termination. Is this possible?

Box 9.1 (cont.)

1. The best approach is normally to open negotiations with the other party to agree on terms for termination. You may make any proposal for their consideration.
2. Before setting out your proposal, consider whether you wish to replace the treaty with a new one or simply terminate it.
3. Consider whether terminating this treaty will require any domestic constitutional procedures, and if so how long they might take. Factor this, and time that might be needed by the other party, into the date you propose for the termination to take effect.
4. Consider whether continuing obligations need to be negotiated to protect acquired rights or ongoing projects after termination. Look at continuation provisions in other treaties on similar subjects. Might the other side have concerns about this? If so, make a proposal or raise the issue for discussion.
5. If you agree on a new treaty to terminate, amend or replace the existing one, the formalities need to be handled in the same way as any new treaty (see Chapters 5–7).
6. The termination of the existing treaty needs to be registered with the UN Secretary General.
7. If the other party declines to negotiate termination, you may have other options to terminate the treaty by asserting a legal ground for termination (such as Articles 56(b) or 60–64 VCLT 1969). But any of these is likely to be legally difficult and contentious, with an uncertain outcome. It will usually be best to persevere with negotiation.

TOP TIPS 3
WITHDRAWING FROM A MULTILATERAL TREATY

Scenario: You are a treaty official in the depositary IO or government for a multilateral treaty. A State Party has asked if they can withdraw from the treaty, and if so how.

1. Read the treaty, and any related documents. Is there a provision for unilateral withdrawal?
2. If there is a withdrawal provision, does it set conditions, and if so are they met for this party?
3. Ask the State Party concerned to send you a copy of their withdrawal notice in draft, so you can check that it is in order before it is formally sent.
4. When you receive a formal withdrawal notice, acknowledge it without delay and inform the State Party of the date its withdrawal will take effect. Inform all other parties.

Box 9.1 (cont.)

5. If there is no provision on withdrawal in the treaty, advise the State Party wishing to withdraw to seek the consent of all other parties in accordance with Article 54 VCLT 1969. Offer to circulate their proposal to all parties and Contracting States, with a specified deadline for responses (twelve months is advisable). Advise parties that they may object to the proposed withdrawal, to the consultation procedure including the deadline, or both.
6. If any party objects to the proposed withdrawal, you should advise all parties that it will not take effect. If no party expresses objection within the specified deadline, you should inform all parties that the withdrawal is effective from the date indicated in the proposal.
7. If a proposed withdrawal fails due to an objection, and the proposing party asks you what else they can do, suggest they make a new (revised) proposal after consulting other parties directly or at a meeting of parties.
8. If/when the withdrawal becomes effective, register it with the UN Secretary General, as a subsequent act related to the treaty.

TOP TIPS 4
TERMINATING A MULTILATERAL TREATY

Scenario: You are a treaty official in the depositary IO or government for a multilateral treaty. Some parties wish to wind up the treaty and ask you how it can be done.

1. Read the treaty and any related documents. Is there a provision for termination?
2. If there is a termination provision, are conditions met? If so, advise the parties concerned to follow the procedures in the treaty.
3. If there is no termination provision, or if its conditions are not met, advise the parties concerned that they may circulate a proposal and seek the consent of all other parties in accordance with Article 54 VCLT (see Top Tips 3, point 5 above).
4. If the depositary wishes to initiate the termination process, the depositary may circulate a proposal, inviting objections within a specified deadline. It is wise to consult informally first to ensure that there is broad agreement on the proposed terms.
5. If the treaty has no termination provision, the initiator of the proposal needs to consider all the implications and set out terms for dealing with institutional winding-up, assets, liabilities, continued protection for vested rights, etc. If such provisions are complex, a new treaty may be required.

Box 9.1 (cont.)

6. When/if the termination takes effect, register it with the UN Secretary General. If it is achieved by the entry into force of a new treaty, the new treaty should also be registered.
7. Inform all parties of the effective date of termination and of any continuing obligations post-termination.

TOP TIPS 5
RESPONDING TO ANOTHER PARTY'S NOTICE OF WITHDRAWAL

Scenario: You are a government treaty official. You receive a notice from a depositary to a multilateral treaty that another State Party has given notice of its withdrawal. Should you respond?

1. Read the treaty and any related documents. Is there a provision for unilateral withdrawal?
2. If there is a withdrawal provision, are the conditions met? Does the notice state that this withdrawal is in accordance with the treaty? If the answer is yes to both, the withdrawal will be effective and there is no need to respond to the notice.
3. If point 2 applies, note the date the withdrawal will be effective in your treaty database and inform all in your government who deal with this treaty and/or this State. Note also any continuing obligations in the treaty post-withdrawal that may apply as between your State and the withdrawing party.
4. If it is unclear whether this withdrawal is in accordance with the treaty, seek clarification from the depositary or the party concerned as to the legal basis for withdrawal.
5. If the treaty has no provision for withdrawal, or if the conditions are not met, it is open to any party to object, either to the withdrawal itself or to any aspect of the procedure including any deadline specified for objections. Monitor any further communications from the depositary on this matter closely.
6. If point 4 applies, consider whether you wish to object to the withdrawal or the procedure for obtaining the consent of all parties. If the deadline is too short, inform the depositary in writing that you object to the proposal on this ground. You may wish to propose a longer deadline.
7. If point 4 applies, consider all the implications of the proposed withdrawal for your State. If you wish to object, inform the depositary in writing within the deadline. You do not have to state your reason. You

Box 9.1 (cont.)

may wish to indicate that withdrawal may be considered acceptable if certain terms are agreed, such as on finances, continuing obligations, etc.

8. If point 4 applies, if/when withdrawal is agreed, record the effective date and any terms and inform all in your government who deal with this treaty.
9. Consider whether any amendment is needed to domestic legislation or administrative arrangements that implement this treaty, such as to delete the withdrawn State's name from a list of States Parties in a reciprocal scheme.

10

The Future of Treaty Practice

***

'The Treaty is dead. Long live the Treaty!'[1]

Introduction: What Factors Might Influence Future Treaty Practice?

The importance of treaty practice in the future, and the way it is conducted, will be influenced by a range of factors. Some can already be foreseen. Trends in treaty practice are of course closely allied to the way in which treaties are used in international relations, and how international relations are conducted. The future of treaty practice is in part dependent on the future of the treaty as a legal form for conducting inter-State transactions and setting global standards. It is also a function of the way that States are structured, and the ways they interact with their stakeholders and the public, both internally and through IOs. Evolving public expectations with regard to transparency and participation in governmental decision-making are also important features

[1] Adapted from the traditional proclamation 'Le roi est mort, vive le roi!'

of the landscape that will shape the making and operation of treaties in the future. Changes in wider society such as the growth of digitisation and other technological developments will transform treaty practice as in other areas of communications. And these are just some of the predictable areas of change; there will no doubt be other new external factors that cannot yet be imagined.

Treaty practice is not merely an adjunct to the law of treaties; it is a specialisation in its own right in which treaty professionals contribute to evolutions in practice as well as react to external developments. This chapter looks at these influential factors in turn, how they are changing treaty practice now, the direction those changes might take in the future, and how Treaty Offices may best prepare themselves to handle the predictable and the unpredictable challenges.

The Importance of Treaties: Is It Increasing or Decreasing?

The importance of treaties as the main source of international obligations has been on the rise for centuries, overtaking customary international law some decades ago. The question now is whether the treaty has finally reached its high-water mark and is declining in favour of other forms of international transactions and law-making.

Are Treaties Being Replaced by other kinds of Law-Making within IOs?

The future of treaties as the dominant form of international law-making has been questioned many times. As long ago as 1970, when VCLT 1969[2] had just been concluded, the following remarks were made by two US treaty lawyers:

> It is possible to imagine a future in which the treaty will no longer be the standard device for dealing with any and all international problems – a future in which, for example, the use of regulations promulgated by international organizations in special fields of activity, such as the World Health Organization's sanitary regulations, will become the accepted international substitute for the lawmaking activity now effected through international agreement. But, in the present state of international development, this is crystal-gazing. For the foreseeable future, the treaty will remain the cement that holds the world community together.[3]

They were right to predict the growth of law-making within IOs. This has happened in numerous spheres of international relations, from the UN Security Council to the WTO, the IMO, the World Intellectual Property

[2] VCLT 1969 (adopted 23 May 1969, entered into force 27 January 1980) 1155 UNTS 331.

[3] R D Kearney and R E Dalton, 'The Treaty on Treaties' (1970) 64 *American Journal of International Law* 495, 495.

Organization and many other UN agencies, both regional and specialised organisations. In parallel with this, there has also been a rapid increase in law-making within COPs and MOPs, in a wide variety of fields such as environmental protection, climate change, marine pollution, shipping and river management.[4] But do these developments evidence a decline in the importance of treaties? While the products of this kind of law-making are not always treaties, and may consist of binding rules of a different nature, or other kinds of instruments, the legal framework for their creation is always a treaty. The constitution of an IO or a MOP is a treaty. The power of the treaty parties to adopt a new instrument is governed by that treaty; as is its legal status, how it is adopted, how it comes into force, which parties are bound. So the founding treaty of the organisation or treaty body will always play a central role in the creation of new forms of instrument within it, and in their interpretation and application. While the comments cited above make the valid point that the individual products of this kind of law-making – whether called regulations, resolutions, measures, codes or anything else – may not fit the definition of 'treaty' in the VCLT 1969, it does not follow that the parent treaty is diminished in importance – on the contrary, it remains the framework and point of reference for all law-making generated under it.

One of the practical consequences of the increase in law-making within international bodies is that it involves a far greater range of actors than traditional treaty-making did in the past. There is nothing new about a variety of government ministries and agencies being involved in treaty-making; for example, defence ministries and armed forces have been the leading actors in the making of treaties on the laws of war from as long ago as the mid-nineteenth century;[5] transport ministries and agencies have long been in the lead on air services and shipping treaties; domestic ministries and agencies responsible for fisheries have for decades led on fisheries treaties, and so on. When those treaties were negotiated, delegations would typically have included diplomats as well as the government's international lawyers. That remains a common line-up for the negotiation of a new treaty, albeit not as common as it once was. By contrast, when IOs and treaty bodies meet to adopt various kinds of regulatory policies and instruments, foreign ministry officials and international lawyers are not usually involved. The meetings are attended by officials from the lead policy or operational ministry as part of their routine

[4] See the section on 'COPs Established by Treaties' in Chapter 8 at 294–305.

[5] Starting with the Convention for the Amelioration of the Condition of the Wounded in Armies in the Field (adopted 22 August 1864, entered into force 22 June 1865, no longer in force (having been replaced)) 18 Martens Nouveau Recueil (ser. 1) 607, 129 CTS 361. The laws of war were codified at the Hague Conferences of 1899 and 1907. On the history of the development of the various Geneva and Hague Conventions on the laws of war (part of the subject nowadays called 'international humanitarian law') see Malcolm N Shaw, *International Law* (8th edn, CUP 2017) 892–94; International Committee of the Red Cross, 'War and Law' www.icrc.org/en/war-and-law accessed 25 September 2015; and International Committee of the Red Cross, 'Treaties, States Parties and Commentaries' https://ihl-databases.icrc.org/ihl accessed 25 September 2015.

administrative responsibilities. Experts meet their counterparts from other countries and make decisions, often of a highly technical nature. They may not think of it as 'foreign policy' or as a matter engaging the law of treaties. They may not have any dealings with their government's embassy nor with its Treaty Office and may not even be aware of its role. If they consult legal advisers, it may be those in their own ministry with specialised knowledge of the subject but without necessarily any training in international law or treaties.

Many governments are already facing the challenge of how to provide advice on treaty law and practice to officials in a wide range of departments and agencies with international dealings, and how to ensure that the lawyers in those agencies are aware of the role of the Treaty Office. This applies in particular to the work of lead agencies responsible for specialised treaties with secretariats and COPs, such as the numerous environmental conventions and conventions of UN agencies as the IMO, the IAEA and the International Civil Aviation Organization. One of the issues is whether to try to reverse this de facto decentralisation of treaty-related policy and legal work – or accept it and work with it. To the extent that treaties and treaty bodies deal with highly specialised subjects, it is unlikely to be feasible for central control to be re-established or maintained over the substance of the work. Much of it is too technical for generalist diplomats and international lawyers to be able to master. Not only that; the ease with which administrators in domestic agencies can nowadays contact their counterparts by email means that the days of embassies being the sole conduit for international dealings are over.

The challenge for Treaty Offices in the future is not to try to keep track of every treaty-related activity carried out by domestic ministries and agencies across government, which will become ever more impossible, but rather to raise their own profile across government, so that all officials know when they should take the initiative to engage with the Treaty Office and why. In other words, an increasing amount of the work of a treaty official may involve *getting out of* the Treaty Office, visiting other ministries and agencies, delivering training courses, promoting awareness of treaty procedures and of the services that they provide to help other officials do their jobs correctly.

Has the Era of Global Treaty-Making Come to an End?

The collapse or stalling of major multilateral treaty negotiations has sometimes been cited as a sign that the treaty has outlived its usefulness as a legal form, or even that international co-operation is fading altogether in favour of isolationism. Many of these negotiations have been on trade and related subjects. One of the first such developments was seen in the 1990s, when the OECD attempted to negotiate a Multilateral Agreement on Investment (MAI). When its draft was leaked to the public in 1997, it drew widespread criticism from civil society groups within the OECD States and developing countries, particularly over the possibility that the new agreement would make it difficult to regulate foreign investors. This was possibly the first time that non-State actors had effectively co-ordinated a campaign against a treaty by means of the internet. When France withdrew its support, consensus was effectively blocked and the negotiations were abandoned in 1998.[6] A commentator writing in 1998 concluded that 'the MAI experience has clearly demonstrated the need to create a process that is more inclusive of a broad range of State and non-State actors' while also remarking of the proposal to move negotiations to the WTO that:

> From the perspective of those who were critical of the draft MAI there is much to be said for the negotiations taking place in a venue which is much more inclusive in terms of its State membership. Whether it is a more transparent one from the perspective of those who criticized the OECD as secretive remains to be seen.[7]

It is well known that the subsequent attempts to include investment in the trade liberalization negotiations at the WTO failed. Successive rounds of negotiations were met by unprecedented protest by civil society groups and a group of developing countries. The Doha Development Round, which began in 2001, has been stalled since 2008 on a range of issues. Its future is still uncertain but the WTO continues its efforts to make progress.[8]

Trade treaty negotiations between major trading partners have all faced challenges, with varying outcomes. The unsuccessful EU–USA negotiations on a Transatlantic Trade and Investment Partnership (TTIP) encountered numerous difficulties, not least vigorous protests around Europe by non-State actors.[9] The criticisms were aimed not only at the substance of the drafts but also at lack of transparency surrounding the negotiations. Its future was already looking uncertain, even before the change of administration in the USA in 2017 and the ensuing trade disputes.

It is not only in Western countries that public protest has had an impact on the ability of governments to conclude trade treaties. A notable example from Asia is the public response in the Republic of Korea (RoK) to the Government's decision in 2011 to force the newly negotiated free trade agreement with the USA through Parliament.[10] The treaty entered into

[6] E Smythe, 'Your Place or Mine? States, International Organizations and the Negotiation of Investment Rules' (1998) 7 *Transnational Corporations* 85.

[7] ibid 115.

[8] WTO, 'The Doha Round' www.wto.org/english/tratop_e/dda_e/dda_e.htm accessed 25 September 2018.

[9] See the updates on negotiations and official draft texts on the EU and US government websites: European Commission, 'United States – Trade' http://ec.europa.eu/trade/policy/countries-and-regions/countries/united-states/accessed 25 September 2018 and Office of the US Trade Representative, 'Transatlantic Trade and Investment Partnership (T-TIP)' https://ustr.gov/ttip accessed 25 September 2018.

[10] H-J Kim, 'Tear Gas, Scuffles as S. Korea OKs U.S. Trade Deal' *The Seattle Times* (Seattle, 22 November 2011) www.seattletimes.com/nation-world/tear-gas-scuffles-as-s-korea-oks-us-trade-deal accessed 25 September 2018; H Siddique, 'South Korean MP Lets Off Teargas in Parliament' *The Guardian* (London, 22 November 2011) www.theguardian.com/world/2011/nov/22/south-korean-mp-lets-off-teargas accessed 25 September 2018.

force in 2012 despite public concerns in South Korea, but its troubles are not over. In 2017 following the Trump administration's threats to terminate the treaty, the RoK Government agreed to commence negotiations with the USA to amend it.[11]

By contrast, the Comprehensive Economic and Trade Agreement between Canada and the EU plus its Member States underwent long and difficult negotiations and public criticism, but agreement was achieved in 2014 and it is now in force.[12] Another multilateral trade agreement, the TPP originally signed on 4 February 2016, was successfully renegotiated after the USA withdrew.[13] The eleven remaining members signed the Comprehensive and Progressive Agreement for Trans-Pacific Partnership on 8 March 2018.[14]

What indications can we draw from these developments for the future of treaty relations? It would seem that trade is one area where States still see an economic imperative to seek better terms and arrangements than currently exist, and to formalise them in legally binding texts, often with mandatory dispute settlement mechanisms. The increasing demands of legislatures and the public for transparency add a new dimension to the difficulties, which is discussed below. The point here is that despite the obstacles, States persist in their efforts to negotiate trade agreements for many years, demonstrating that treaties in this field are still a very high priority.

There is no doubt that multilateral treaty-making in all fields is more difficult than it used to be decades ago, and is attempted less often. This may in part be simply that there is less need for major new treaties as there are fewer fields left uncovered. However, another obvious development is that there are more States, and therefore membership of the UN and other global bodies has increased, as has membership of most regional and specialised bodies. This

[11] H M Kang, 'US and South Korea Agree to Initiate FTA Amendment Negotiations' *The Diplomat* (Tokyo, 6 October 2017) https://thediplomat.com/2017/10/us-and-south-korea-agree-to-initiate-fta-amendment-negotiations/ accessed 25 September 2018; F Ahrens, 'Korea-U.S. Free Trade Agreement In Crosshairs As Trump Visits Asia' *Forbes* (New York, 3 November 2017) www.forbes.com/sites/frankahrens/2017/11/03/korea-u-s-free-trade-agreement-in-crosshairs-as-trump-visits-asia/#2265b0387a41 accessed 25 September 2018.

[12] Comprehensive Economic and Trade Agreement (CETA) between Canada, of the one part, and the European Union and its Member States, of the other part (signed 30 October 2016, entered into force 21 September 2017) OJ L 11 14/01/2017 0023–1079.

[13] Trans-Pacific Partnership Agreement (adopted 4 February 2016, not yet in force) www.mfat.govt.nz/en/about-us/who-we-are/treaties/trans-pacific-partnership-agreement-tpp/text-of-the-trans-pacific-partnership/ accessed 2 November 2018.

[14] Comprehensive and Progressive Agreement for Trans-Pacific Partnership (adopted 8 March 2018, entered into force 30 December 2018) https://www.treaties.mfat.govt.nz/search/details/t/3911 accessed 15 October 2019. The eleven signatories are: Australia, Brunei, Canada, Chile, Japan, Malaysia, Mexico, New Zealand, Peru, Singapore and Vietnam. The UK has announced its interest in acceding to this treaty despite its geographical distance from the region: L Fox, 'At the Crossroads: Britain and Global Trade', Speech delivered by Liam Fox, Secretary of State for International Trade (18 July 2018), www.gov.uk/government/speeches/at-the-crossroads-britain-and-global-trade accessed 25 September 2018.

inevitably makes collective decision-making more difficult and resource-intensive. This can have a number of consequences.

If consensus cannot be achieved and a treaty is adopted by vote, it may not attract sufficient ratifications or the ones that matter, and so a decision may be taken to avoid the risk of failure. Another factor is the impact of economic crises and austerity measures on national finances: committing the organisational and national resources required to negotiate a major new treaty tends to be avoided unless the need is compelling. A noticeable trend in a number of international forums is for States to respond to a proposal for a new treaty by proposing a non-binding instrument instead (this is discussed below).

Another increasing trend is to make improvements to existing treaties rather than creating new ones. Thus most of the recently concluded global human rights treaties are supplementary to existing ones, such as optional protocols to recognise a right of individual petition to a compliance committee.[15] This trend is also evident in the treaties concluded within the CoE: of the last twenty treaties adopted in the CoE, thirteen are supplementary to existing ones (a protocol or treaty revision).[16]

In many forums, there is a drive to promote wider adherence to existing treaties and better implementation of them in domestic law, in preference to negotiating new treaties. This is often accompanied by new mechanisms for international reporting and compliance monitoring by treaty bodies. Where this is the focus, the resulting work on implementation may fall to policy and operational departments of governments and IOs, rather than Treaty Offices. This however does not seem to signal any downgrading of the importance of treaties; on the contrary, it shows that governments have a strong desire to reinforce the binding nature of treaty obligations and not to devalue the currency of a treaty.

Are States Leaving Treaties at an Increasing Rate?

Among the various factors cited as possible evidence of a decline in the importance of treaties in international relations, reference is frequently made to a perceived increase in the rate of actual or threatened withdrawals from treaties by individual States.[17] High-profile examples include: the threat by the USA in 2017 to leave the Paris Agreement on climate change in 2020; the

[15] See for example: Optional Protocol to the Convention on the Rights of the Child on a Communications Procedure (adopted 19 December 2011, entered into force 14 April 2014) 2983 UNTS Registration No. 27531 and Optional Protocol to the Convention on the Elimination of All Forms of Discrimination against Women (adopted 6 October 1999, entered into force 22 December 2000) 2131 UNTS 83.

[16] Treaty Office, 'Complete List of the Council of Europe's Treaties' (Council of Europe, status as of 26 September 2018) www.coe.int/en/web/conventions/full-list accessed 26 September 2018.

[17] 'Agora: The End of Treaties?' (2014) 108 *AJIL Unbound* 30–78 www.cambridge.org/core/journals/american-journal-of-international-law/ajil-unbound-by-symposium/agora-the-end-of-treaties accessed 16 November 2018.

serving of notice by the UK in 2017 of its intention to leave the EU in 2019; and the serving of notice of withdrawal from the Statute of the International Criminal Court by Burundi, Gambia and South Africa in 2016. Gambia and South Africa subsequently withdrew their respective notices, but Burundi's notice took effect on 27 October 2017. In some cases, States leaving multilateral treaties appeared to be rejecting international co-operation on that subject altogether, while in other cases the States concerned indicated that they hoped to replace them with new bilateral treaties that would better serve their national interests.

Unilateral departures from important global treaties naturally provoke more international attention than the ending of bilateral treaties. Nevertheless, dissatisfaction with existing treaties is not confined to multilateral forums. An area in which the ending of bilateral treaty relations seems to be on the rise is that of investment protection. For example, in 2014, Indonesia gave notice to the Netherlands of its unilateral denunciation of their BIT, in accordance with the treaty.[18] It also expressed its intention to end sixty-seven BITs with other States at their renewal dates, in order to review and renegotiate new BITs with those States.[19] As at September 2018, Indonesia has unilaterally terminated twenty-nine BITs by way of notification of non-renewal of each treaty to the other party.[20] Similarly, India sent notices to fifty-seven States in July 2016 seeking termination of BITs whose initial minimum duration had expired or would expire soon.[21] This action was preceded by the Government of India's publication of a new model BIT in December 2015, which it

[18] Agreement between the Government of the Kingdom of the Netherlands and the Government of the Republic of Indonesia on Promotion and Protection of Investments (signed 6 April 1994, entered into force 1 July 1995) 2240 UNTS 323. Indonesia denounced the Agreement in accordance with art 15(1), which provides for unilateral denunciation. According to the Treaty Database of the Government of the Netherlands, the treaty was terminated on 1 July 2015. See Treaty Database, 'Agreement between the Government of the Kingdom of the Netherlands and the Government of the Republic of Indonesia on Promotion and Protection of Investment' (Government of the Netherlands) https://treatydatabase.overheid.nl/en/Verdrag/Details/005412 accessed 26 September 2018. Interestingly, although the term used in art 15(1) of the treaty is 'denunciation', Indonesian officials repeatedly denied that Indonesia's notification constituted an act of termination, preferring to characterise it as 'letting it lapse' so as to negotiate a better treaty.

[19] D Price, 'Indonesia's Bold Strategy on Bilateral Investment Treaties: Seeking an Equitable Climate for Investment?' (2017) 7 *Asian Journal of International Law* 124, 124; A H Oegroseno, 'Indonesia's Bilateral Investment Treaties: Modernising for the 21st Century' (2014) 140 *RSIS Commentary* https://www.rsis.edu.sg/wp-content/uploads/2014/07/CO14140.pdf accessed 26 September 2018.

[20] For a list of and status of Indonesia's BITs, see Investment Policy Hub 'Indonesia' (United Nations Conference on Trade and Development) http://investmentpolicyhub.unctad.org/IIA/CountryBits/97 accessed 26 September 2018.

[21] K Singh and B Ilge, 'India Overhauls its Investment Treaty Regime', *Financial Times* (London, 16 July 2016) www.ft.com/content/53bd355c-8203-34af-9c27-7bf990a447dc accessed 26 September 2018.

announced would be used for renegotiation of existing treaties and negotiation of future treaties on investment.[22]

These actual or threatened withdrawals have naturally had enormous political impact and may weaken the institutions concerned, financially and/or politically. This is especially the case where the departing State is a major financial contributor to a global organisation. Does this signal a trend away from participation in treaties generally? Let us look at each of the above examples: if the USA does withdraw from the Paris Agreement in 2020 (by serving notice of withdrawal in 2019), it may well make achievement of the treaty's objectives more challenging for the other parties. However, the fact that the USA has indicated that it intends to withdraw in accordance with the terms of the treaty, and that it will remain party to the parent treaty, the UNFCCC, makes clear the USA's continued willingness to participate in treaties in this field. If the UK proceeds to leave the EU, it will cease to be party to the EU founding treaties as well as a number of related ones. It will also fall out of a considerable number of bilateral treaties between the EU (or the EU and its Member States) on the one hand and a third State on the other, in the field of trade and other kinds of co-operation. However, it is clear that the UK Government aspires to create a complex set of new legal relationships with the EU, many of which will consist of treaties.[23] The UK Government has also stated its intention to negotiate a wide range of new bilateral treaties with third States to replace the current ones. Moreover, it intends to play a more active role in the WTO and a number of other multilateral forums following its departure from the EU.[24] While Burundi's departure from the Rome Statute of the International Criminal Court is widely regretted by other parties, it is balanced by the decision of the other two resigning African States to remain, and by several recent accessions to that Statute.[25] In announcing that it would review all existing BITs, Indonesia made it clear that it was seeking a better investment regime for the host State rather than ending investment treaty relationships indefinitely. In a similar vein,

[22] *Press Information Bureau*, 'Model Text for the Indian Bilateral Investment Treaty' (Government of India, 16 December 2015) http://pib.nic.in/newsite/PrintRelease.aspx?relid=133411 accessed 26 September 2018.

[23] Council of the European Union, 'Political Declaration setting out the framework for the future relationship between the European Union and the United Kingdom' (draft published on 22 November 2018) www.consilium.europa.eu/en/press/press-releases/2018/11/22/draft-political-declaration-setting-out-the-framework-for-the-future-relationship-between-the-eu-and-the-uk-and-article-132-of-the-draft-withdrawal-agreement/# accessed 4 December 2018.

[24] Department for International Trade, 'Preparing for our future UK trade policy', Cm 9470 (UK Government Policy Paper, October 2017) https://assets.publishing.service.gov.uk/government/uploads/system/uploads/attachment_data/file/654714/Preparing_for_our_future_UK_trade_policy_Report_Web_Accessible.pdf accessed 26 September 2018.

[25] The Rome Statute has 123 parties as at 26 September 2018. The most recent accessions are: El Salvador in 2016, State of Palestine in 2015 and Guatemala in 2012. See UNTC, 'Chapter XVIII – Penal Matters: 10. Rome Statute of the International Court' (status as at 26 September 2018) https://treaties.un.org/pages/ViewDetails.aspx?src=TREATY&mtdsg_no=XVIII-10&chapter=18&clang=_en accessed 26 September 2018.

the Indian Government indicated that by promoting a new model BIT, its aim was to adjust the balance between the rights of the host State and foreign investors, and not to terminate those bilateral treaties indefinitely.[26]

It does not seem that the decisions of individual States to repudiate particular treaties for highly publicised political reasons are influencing many other States to follow suit; still less are they indicative of any general trend away from participation in treaties. The same may be said of previous high-profile withdrawals such as the USA, UK and Singapore withdrawals from UNESCO in the 1980s; the UK rejoined in 1997, the USA in 2003 and Singapore in 2007. Indonesia left the UN in 1965 but rejoined the following year. China joined the WTO in 2001 and has been steadily resuming and increasing its participation in IOs over decades. States are still applying to join the EU, ASEAN, WTO, the UN, and many other IOs and treaties.

At the CoE, the present rate of withdrawals from treaties is far outweighed by the number of new accessions. Moreover, there has been a steady increase in the participation of non-Member States, as well as the EU and other IOs in the elaboration of treaties, as well as an increase in requests from non-member States of the CoE for accession to CoE treaties.[27] This has served to strengthen existing treaties whose participation is becoming global. This trend for broadening participation beyond the European region stands in interesting contrast to the reduction in the rate of new treaty-making. For the CoE Treaty Office, it means that while they may have a reducing workload in connection with drafting new treaties, this is balanced by increasing amounts of work generated by new participants, additional complexity in accession procedures, final clauses, more reservations, objections, etc. in relation to existing treaties.

In short, while particular organisations may form and disband or wax and wane in importance, multilateral treaty relations may be replaced by bilateral ones or vice versa, it seems that these changes usually result in the reconfiguration rather than abolition of treaty relations.

Could the Use of Non-Binding Instruments in International Relations Gradually Replace Treaties?

The rise of informal co-operation and use of non-binding instruments in international relations has also been said to herald a decline in treaty-

[26] Press Information Bureau (n 22). See also, Baker & McKenzie, 'Withdrawal from Investment Treaties: An Omen for Waning Investor Protection in AP?' (12 May 2017) www.bakermckenzie.com/en/insight/publications/2017/05/withdrawal-from-investment-treaties accessed 26 September 2018.

[27] In 2017, the CoE received twenty-two requests from eighteen non-member States for accession to a CoE treaty. There were six denunciations of treaties by individual parties in 2017. This information was kindly provided to Jill Barrett by the CoE Treaty Office on 31 May 2018.

making. It is difficult to quantify the extent to which States and other international actors use non-binding instruments (sometimes referred to as 'soft law') as there is no international law requirement to publish them, and many of them are not published.[28] Consequently, it cannot be proved that their use is on the increase. There is certainly a perception that it is,[29] but this could be due, in part at least, to an increasing willingness of governments to publish them or for their existence to become known by other means, such as through parliamentary inquiries, academic research, leaks or journalism. What are the factors that might be causing an increase in the use of non-binding instruments?

Non-binding instruments have always been used in bilateral dealings between States; there is nothing new about this. As Aust points out:

> Even when the subject is proper and lawful, diplomats know that it is not possible for all international deals to be embodied in treaties, whether or not they are on trivial or important matters. Yet the deal needs to be formalised on paper in some way.[30]

If there has been an increase in the overall number of non-binding arrangements between States over the past century, it seems likely that this is due to the increasing number of interactions between States, as modern life requires closer co-operation in ever more fields of human activity. In other words, the use of treaties and non-treaty instruments have both increased. Another factor could be the increasing tendency of domestic ministries to conduct international relations directly with their counterparts in other governments, without dealing through foreign ministries. This has undoubtedly resulted in more non-binding instruments now being concluded at agency level or between regional subdivisions of States, than was the case a few decades ago. But does this mean that there are correspondingly fewer treaties? In other words, if this trend continues, will governments or agencies use non-binding instruments to conduct their relations in situations that would have warranted a treaty in the past?

In multilateral forums, high-profile examples of non-binding instruments concluded in recent decades come readily to mind. This is especially so in the environmental field: the Declaration of the United Nations Conference on the Human Environment (Stockholm Declaration), 1972 and the Rio Declaration on Environment and Development, 1992 being perhaps the most significant. The human rights field is another where declarations proliferate, most famously the Universal Declaration on Human Rights, 1948. Some of these were concluded in circumstances in which a treaty could not have been: for

[28] See the section on 'Should Non-binding International Instruments Be Published?' in Chapter 3 at 113.

[29] See for example, A Aust, *Modern Treaty Law and Practice* (3rd edn, CUP 2013) 28. Aust refers to 'the relentless rise of the MOU (or political commitment)'.

[30] ibid.

example, it is inconceivable that in 1992 there could have been a global treaty on environment and development, or that one could be agreed upon now. On the other hand, some declarations have paved the way for later negotiations on a treaty with similar content: for example, the Universal Declaration on Human Rights laid the foundations for two human rights treaties (the International Covenants on Civil and Political Rights and on Economic, Social and Cultural Rights, 1966). In some situations, negotiating States decide that a non-binding text is their *preferred* outcome, while in other situations the same States argue in favour of a treaty but then settle for a non-binding outcome as a *compromise* with States that were reluctant to conclude any deal at all.

The ILC's gradual move away from producing draft treaties has been cited as an indicator of global trends. During the first decades of its work, the ILC's outputs were typically draft treaty provisions which then formed the basis of a global treaty adopted by States. By contrast, in recent decades most of the ILC's output has been in the form of studies, guides and other kinds of non-binding text. Views differ as to whether or not this is a positive development. It certainly illustrates the point that even when the topic is of high importance, States do not always consider that making a treaty is the best way to achieve their objectives. It does not follow however that treaty-making is *generally* considered less desirable; all one can say is that the particular topics chosen by the ILC in recent years did not attract consensus for a new treaty, and that the ILC has found other creative ways to contribute to the development of international law.

When there is no international consensus for a new treaty, or when an IO is deadlocked, it is only natural that the States that wish to proceed will talk to each other outside the formal process. The outcome may not take on any conventional institutional form. For example, the grouping known as the 'P5 + 1' negotiated with Iran and reached informal agreement on Iran's nuclear programme, paving the way for the Joint Comprehensive Plan of Action (the 'Iran nuclear deal') to be adopted by Iran, those six States and the EU.[31] When no treaty is possible, other ways of pinning down deals are found, and the result may be politically significant even if not legally binding. This has happened a number of times in the UN climate change process: between the adoption of the Kyoto Protocol 1997 and the Paris Agreement 2015 (both treaties), negotiations resulted in outcomes such as the Copenhagen Accord 2009 and the Cancun Agreements 2010 (not treaties, and largely non-binding, but nevertheless important). These examples illustrate some of the many

[31] On the adoption of the Joint Comprehensive Plan of Action in 2015, see US Department of State, 'Joint Comprehensive Plan of Action' www.state.gov/e/eb/tfs/spi/iran/jcpoa/ accessed 27 September 2018. On the US decision to withdraw in 2018, see UNSC, 'Joint Comprehensive Plan of Action on Iran Nuclear Issue at Crossroads 3 Years Later, Under-Secretary-General for Political Affairs Tells Security Council' (Press Release SC/13398, 27 June 2018) www.un.org /press/en/2018/sc13398.doc.htm accessed 27 September 2018.

advantages that States may see in sealing a deal without a treaty – speed, flexibility, informality and (for some) the avoidance of domestic parliamentary treaty procedures.

In certain regions, regional organisations have been established through the adoption of non-binding instruments. In Southeast Asia, ASEAN was originally founded by the ASEAN Declaration, 1967, a political document that aims to promote regional peace and stability, and strengthen regional co-operation and mutual assistance on matters of common interest.[32] The ASEAN Ministerial Meeting adopted another important non-binding instrument, the 'Declaration of ASEAN Concord, 1976', which laid the foundation for free trade and political co-operation in Southeast Asia.[33]

The Arctic is another region where the principal institutions for international governance were established by non-legal documents: starting with the Rovaniemi process in 1991 leading to the Ottawa Declaration, 1996, which established the Arctic Council and still governs it.[34] The Council is the leading intergovernmental forum promoting co-operation, co-ordination and interaction among the Arctic States, Arctic indigenous communities and other Arctic inhabitants on common Arctic issues. It has continued to function without a treaty basis, and, despite the proposals of some Arctic States and others for an Arctic Treaty, the majority of Arctic States, the USA in particular, prefer non-treaty status for this forum. There are a number of reasons for this, an important one being the unique consultative status accorded to the Arctic indigenous peoples as 'Permanent Participants' in the Council. There is no reason in principle why such a status could not be conferred by treaty, but it seems some of the Member States would be reluctant to do so. This illustrates yet another advantage that non-binding arrangements can have over treaties, in situations where non-State actors are essential – such as indigenous peoples, armed groups or corporations. The law of treaties, as it is today, precludes them from becoming a treaty party, but there is no legal reason why a treaty could not confer a lesser role for them in an institution or process. Politically however, States tend to be more comfortable to deal directly with such actors in a non-legal context, especially where recognition or legitimacy is an issue, and non-State actors may also prefer a more flexible process in which they could potentially be treated as equal partners.

However, a further look at these examples also shows that States may not remain satisfied with non-binding arrangements when circumstances become more serious. The need for global action to combat climate change is now widely acknowledged as urgent and compelling; so despite some initial

[32] The ASEAN Declaration (adopted 8 August 1967, entered into force 8 August 1967) 1331 UNTS 235.

[33] Declaration of ASEAN Concord (adopted 24 February 1976) https://asean.org/?static_post=declaration-of-asean-concord-indonesia-24-february-1976 accessed 27 September 2018.

[34] Declaration on Establishment of the Arctic Council (adopted 19 September 1996) 35 ILM 1387.

reluctance to conclude a treaty, views changed. The Paris Agreement 2015 took less than a year to enter into force and now has over 170 parties. In Southeast Asia, ASEAN leaders signed the ASEAN Charter in November 2007, formally laying the legal foundations for ASEAN to function as an IO. In the Arctic region, while the Arctic Council itself retains its non-legal status, since 2011 three new treaties have been concluded under its auspices by the Arctic States on, respectively, search and rescue, oil spills and scientific co-operation.[35] A similar pattern can be seen in recent developments in other forums. At the IMO, the two non-binding instruments on shipping in the Polar regions adopted in 2002 and 2009 were rapidly overtaken by a move to convert them into treaty texts, and this was achieved by the adoption of the mandatory Polar Code in 2014. In the sphere of international environmental law, it seemed after the turn of the century that the era of new treaties was over; yet the Minamata Convention on Mercury was concluded in 2013 to protect human health and the environment from the adverse effects of mercury, and already has over eighty parties. It has been suggested that it was the reality of climate change that was the driver behind these developments.[36] It is also evident that there are a range of reasons why States find it necessary to conclude a treaty: for example, when the need to act is urgent and they need reassurance that other States will comply; when implementation will impact the economy and States need to know that there will be a level playing field such that their economic competitors will not have an unfair advantage; when action needs to be taken by the private sector which needs domestic legislation and law enforcement on the basis of a treaty approved by the legislature; when legal certainty on the details is needed for forward planning. This applies, above all, to trade agreements, and in many other sectors such as the environment and energy, shipping and aviation, where the economic and human impacts are significant.

There does not seem to be any evidence that treaties will be less important in the future, and many indications to the contrary.[37] Whether the actual numbers of new treaties concluded each year goes up or down, whether the proportion of bilateral treaties to multilateral treaties changes, whether closed multilateral treaties increase in preference to universal treaties or vice versa, whether important States leave IOs and seek new bilateral treaties instead, or

[35] Agreement on Cooperation on Aeronautical and Maritime Search and Rescue in the Arctic (adopted 12 May 2011, entered into force 19 January 2013) 50 ILM 1119 (2011); Agreement on Cooperation on Marine Oil Pollution Preparedness and Response in the Arctic (adopted 15 June 2013, entered into force 25 February 2016) Arctic Council 2013 http://hdl.handle.net/11374/529 accessed 27 September 2018; and Agreement on Enhancing International Arctic Scientific Cooperation (adopted 11 May 2017, entered into force 23 May 2018) Arctic Council 2017 http://hdl.handle.net/11374/1916 accessed 27 September 2018.

[36] T Koivurova, 'Increasing Relevance of Treaties: The Case of the Arctic, (2014) 108 *AJIL Unbound* 52–56, 54–56.

[37] H Cantú-Rivera, 'The Expansion of International Law Beyond Treaties', (2014) 108 *AJIL Unbound* 70–73.

bask in splendid isolation for a while, it seems there will always be other States seeking to join those organisations, or to persuade others to join them in a new grouping. In addition, there is likely to be public demand for important alliances to be made in a treaty form that will be subject to parliamentary and public scrutiny. It follows that there will always be work for treaty lawyers and Treaty Offices, in the unmaking of treaties as well as their making, amending, re-forming and the routine engagement with treaty processes and rule-making within treaty bodies.

A trend that does seem to point the way towards the future is the growing complexity and variety in the ways that non-binding instruments and treaties are used, often in combination. Non-binding instruments sometimes pave the way for treaties. Treaties are sometimes supplemented with non-binding standards, codes, guidance and policy documents, at the same time, or over a period of time. An overarching non-binding institution can generate treaties on specific subjects; or an overarching treaty can act as a framework for more detailed implementing arrangements of a non-binding nature. Sometimes binding and non-binding provisions are found in the same document. All kinds of permutations and relationships between treaties and non-binding standards are possible, and no doubt more will be devised in the future. Sometimes the distinction between treaties and other kinds of instruments is blurred, and sometimes there is confusion about whether a particular text is binding at all, or on whom. The actors in the process of developing these interlocking legal and non-legal instruments may be different; for example, UNCLOS is a living treaty which sets a framework for development of the law of the sea by a wide variety of actors and processes outside of the treaty itself.[38] What this may mean for the work of treaty lawyers and Treaty Offices is explored below. While it is clear that they cannot, and will not need to be, involved in all of these non-treaty and non-legal processes, ever greater knowledge and professionalism on their part will be needed to identify and deal with the aspects that do require their attention.

Public Demands for Transparency, Accountability and Participation in Treaties

The demands of legislatures and the public for a greater say in the treaties that their governments participate in have been increasing for over a century, and it is unlikely that this trend will be reversed. On the contrary, it would seem that dissatisfaction is growing at as fast a rate as ever, and the ability of treaties and constitutions to evolve to accommodate this is under increasing

[38] J Barrett, 'UNCLOS: A "Living" Treaty?' in J Barrett and R Barnes (eds), *Law of the Sea: UNCLOS as a Living Treaty* (BIICL, London 2016) 5 and 15–36. See also R Barnes, 'The Continuing Vitality of UNCLOS' in ibid 467–71.

strain. This is manifest at both the international treaty and national constitutional levels.

Transparency and Participation at the International Treaty Level

The international law of treaties reflects the principle of transparency in one important respect, namely the requirement to register all treaties with the UN Secretary General. This is designed to avoid the existence of secret treaties, albeit without an effective enforcement mechanism. However it does not apply any principle of transparency in treaty negotiations or treaty ratification. Rather, the law of treaties provides the framework within which individual treaties may provide for participation by non-State actors, through their own specific provisions or by rules made under them. The UN system and a number of other IOs have created a role for representatives of civil society, including NGOs and private sector groups, to observe and participate in meetings.[39]

Multilateral treaties in the fields of human rights, environment, arms control and international humanitarian law have developed specific modes of participation by representatives of civil society, in ways that are customised to the needs of each particular treaty. This is not always provided for in the treaty itself; typically it has been developed later, through rules of procedure. This development can be seen in the principal human rights treaties, some of which set up an independent expert body to monitor treaty compliance, but do not make any provision for participation by civil society in that process. Rather, this has been developed later by the independent treaty monitoring bodies through their own rules of procedure. The monitoring body of the ICCPR, the Human Rights Committee, started in the 1980s to create opportunities for international and national NGOs to participate in its processes. It has gradually evolved to the point that the Committee considers that 'the cooperation, with the Committee, of domestic and international non-governmental organizations (NGOs) working on the promotion and protection of human rights is essential for the promotion and implementation of the International Covenant on Civil and Political Rights and its Optional Protocols'.[40]

Few treaties have addressed issues of transparency and participation in their own proceedings, on the face of the treaty. One of the few is the Convention on Access to Information, Public Participation in Decision-making and Access to Justice in Environmental Matters, 1998 (Aarhus Convention).[41] Although

[39] B K Woodward, *Global Civil Society in International Lawmaking and Global Governance: Theory and Practice* (Martinus Nijhoff, Leiden 2010).

[40] Human Rights Committee, 'The relationship of the Human Rights Committee with non-governmental organizations' (4 June 2012) CCPR/C/104/3, para 1.

[41] Convention on Access to Information, Public Participation in Decision-making and Access to Justice in Environmental Matters (adopted 25 June 1998, entered into force 30 October 2001) 2162 UNTS 447 (Aarhus Convention).

negotiated in the UN Economic Commission for Europe (UNECE), it is not restricted to States within Europe and now has nearly fifty parties. The subject of the Convention goes to the heart of the relationship between people and governments. The Convention is not only an environmental agreement, it is also about government accountability, transparency and responsiveness. It confers rights on the public and imposes on parties and public authorities corresponding obligations regarding access to information and public participation and access to justice. The Aarhus Convention is also forging a new process for public participation in the negotiation and implementation of international agreements.[42] It provides:

> Any non-governmental organization, qualified in the fields to which this Convention relates, which has informed the Executive Secretary of the Economic Commission for Europe of its wish to be represented at a meeting of the Parties shall be entitled to participate as an observer unless at least one third of the Parties present in the meeting raise objections.[43]

The Convention also provides that the arrangements for the review of compliance by parties 'shall allow for appropriate public involvement and may include the option of considering communications from members of the public on matters related to this Convention'.[44] The parties have said that they consider the enhancement of the role of civil society in international decision-making to be one of the greatest successes of the Aarhus Convention.[45]

Does the role played by civil society in the Aarhus Convention represent a model for the future – or a high-water mark? It seems that interest in the Convention beyond the geographic limits of the UNECE region is growing. It has already inspired processes in Asia and America. In the UN Economic Commission for Latin America and the Caribbean, a Regional Agreement on Access to Information, Public Participation and Justice in Environmental Matters in Latin America and the Caribbean has been adopted and was opened for signature in 2018.[46] It establishes a Committee to Support Implementation and Compliance whose role will be to review compliance and formulate

[42] UNECE, 'Introduction to the Convention' www.unece.org/env/pp/introduction.html accessed 27 September 2018.

[43] Aarhus Convention, art 10(5) and (6). Practical arrangements to manage admittance and terms for participation are addressed in rules of procedure.

[44] ibid art 15.

[45] UNECE, 'Nineteenth meeting of the Working Group of the Parties to the Aarhus Convention' (17–19 June 2015) www.unece.org/env/pp/aarhus/wgp19.html accessed 27 September 2018.

[46] Regional Agreement on Access to Information, Public Participation and Justice in Environmental Matters in Latin America and the Caribbean (adopted 4 March 2018, not yet in force) UNTC, Chapter XXVI, Environment, item 18. https://treaties.un.org/ accessed 27 September 2018. It is open for signature from 27 September 2018 to 26 September 2020. See also Economic Commission for Latin America and the Caribbean, 'Regional Agreement on Access to Information, Public Participation and Justice in Environmental Matters in Latin America and the Caribbean' www.cepal.org/en/taxonomy/term/8280 accessed 27 September 2018.

recommendations, 'ensuring the significant participation of the public and paying particular attention to the national capacities and circumstances of the Parties'. Unlike the Aarhus Convention, it contains no specific reference to civil societies or NGOs, so it is not yet clear whether any observer role will be provided for them in the compliance review process; this will depend upon the rules of procedure to be adopted by the COP.

Some NGOs have expressed the hope that the principles of the Aarhus Convention may help to promote transparency in other areas such as trade treaty negotiations.[47] It is too early to tell whether the Aarhus model will be followed in other regions or even in the European region in other fields. The experience that States have had in the Aarhus Convention bodies has certainly forced them to take more notice of the views of NGOs at the international level than ever before. Whether this might make them, or others, more cautious in the future about opening the door to more participation, or whether it might inspire confidence that any challenges can be managed, is beyond the scope of this Handbook to assess. What *is* clear is that there will be ever greater public demands for transparency and participation in international treaty bodies.[48] And that States and IOs *will* need to find innovative ways to respond and accommodate these aspirations, whether by building on the Aarhus model or otherwise.

Transparency and Participation at National Constitutional Level

At the national level there is naturally much greater variation in the demands made for transparency and participation in treaty processes, and in the responses by governments and legislatures. Most State constitutions dating from the mid-twentieth century onwards prescribe a formal role for the legislature in treaty ratification.[49] In the UK, calls for Parliament to have the opportunity to scrutinise the Executive's treaty-making date back to at least the late nineteenth century, resulting in the adoption of the constitutional practice known as the 'Ponsonby Rule' in 1924. Similar developments occurred throughout the twentieth century in other systems of parliamentary government. Such changes may evolve through custom and practice, in the absence of, or in addition to, constitutional provisions. They tend not to stand still for long, and legislatures have continued to push for a greater role; for example, demanding a say over a wider range of treaties, pre-signature scrutiny, inquiry

[47] See *UNECE* (n 45).

[48] UNECE, 'Governments and civil society looking to further transparency and public participation in the 2030 Agenda for Sustainable Development at Budva meetings' (3 July 2017) www.unece.org/info/media/presscurrent-press-h/environment/2017/governments-and-civil-society-looking-to-further-transparency-and-public-participation-in-the-2030-agenda-for-sustainable-development-at-budva-meetings/doc.html accessed 27 September 2018.

[49] See the section on 'Internal Preparations to Give Consent to Be Bound' especially on 'States: Constitutional and Legal Requirements' in Chapter 6 at 230–33.

by committee, delaying powers, examination of proposed reservations, and so on.

Parliamentary control over treaty-making by elected representatives has not sufficed to satisfy the general public in the case of politically controversial treaties. Civil society organisations have insisted upon their right to present their views directly to their national legislature on draft treaties that they believe will affect them. Trade agreements have been among the most controversial, with widespread protests and demands for parliaments to take account of public concerns. This has occurred not only in relation to national parliaments but also in the EU, where arrangements for democratic accountability for treaty negotiations are even more remote from the citizens concerned.

The issues could not be more clearly set out than in the 2015 report of an Australian Senate committee that conducted an inquiry into Australia's treaty-making process.[50] While the particulars are specific to Australia, the general issues it raises are relevant the world over. Major constitutional reform of treaty scrutiny in Australia in the late 1990s included the establishment of a new treaty committee within Parliament and an inquiry system in which members of the public could address the committee directly. Despite this, there were widespread protests in relation to Australia's negotiation of international trade agreements, including the TPP and several bilateral agreements. This prompted the Senate to set up an inquiry to consider further reforms to promote more transparency in the treaty process generally. It reported that:

> The committee is left in no doubt that in respect of the Commonwealth treaty-making process there is a groundswell for change backed by compelling evidence and practical suggestions for improvement. The committee received evidence from leading industry bodies, the union movement, academic experts and other stakeholders voicing frustration with the lack of effective consultation and parliamentary engagement during treaty negotiations.[51]

And the Committee made recommendations for reform, concluding that:

> Doing nothing is no longer an option. Treaty-making in Australia faces a number of challenges which cannot be met by continuing with the existing process unchanged. These challenges include the changing nature of Australia's international obligations and their intrusion into domestic law and regulation; new methods of consultation and negotiation adopted in overseas jurisdictions resulting in less secrecy; and ensuring that DFAT is adequately resourced with the knowledge and skills to negotiate, conclude and review complex free trade agreements.[52]

[50] Senate of Australia Foreign Affairs, Defence and Trade References Committee, *Blind Agreement: Reforming Australia's Treaty-making Process* (Senate Printing Unit, Canberra 2015).

[51] ibid 71, para 6.1. [52] ibid x.

Similar issues of transparency in treaty processes are troubling governments, legislatures, courts and civil society organisations on every continent. Balancing the power of the executive to act unilaterally and decisively in the national interest with the need for democratic deliberation through parliamentary oversight is a recurring theme. Another is whether, when and how direct democracy should interact with parliamentary democracy. Should citizens be given a vote on ratifying a treaty or withdrawing from a treaty, by means of a plebiscite or referendum? What happens when the outcome of a popular vote differs from the view of the legislature?

Responses to these issues naturally vary. The following examples show how the issues tend to persist, whichever approach is taken.

The Swiss Constitution has long provided for a referendum on a number of issues including treaty ratifications. Tensions have arisen between the views of voters expressed in a 2014 referendum on limiting immigration and the decision of the Swiss Government and Parliament in 2016 to sign a treaty with the EU to extend free movement to Croatian workers.[53] It remains unclear how this can be resolved.

In the case mentioned above of public concern in South Korea about the conclusion of a trade agreement with the USA, the RoK Government made no concessions to public opinion in 2011 but it remains to be seen how the treaty renegotiation will play out with Parliament and the public.

In the UK, the dust had barely settled on the 2010 statutory reform of parliamentary scrutiny of treaties when there was further legislation to require a referendum before certain EU treaty amendments could be made.[54] This was superseded six years later by a referendum vote to leave the EU, following which there has been controversy surrounding the role of Parliament in this process, and litigation by private citizens overturned the government's attempt to initiate treaty withdrawal without parliamentary authority.[55]

The EU Commission responded to dissatisfaction about transparency over its treaty negotiations, in particular the TTIP, by publishing a new policy on transparency of trade negotiations in November 2014, which sets out greater access to texts for members of the European Parliament. However, debate continues on how, in future treaty negotiations, the EU should take account of the views of civil society and national parliaments.[56]

[53] 'Swiss Lawmakers Back Croatia Free Movement Treaty', *Swiss Info* (26 April 2016) www.swissinfo.ch/eng/swiss-eu-relations_swiss-lawmakers-back-croatia-free-movement-treaty/42115118 accessed 27 September 2018 and 'Swiss Extend Free Movement to Croatia after Immigration Vote', Swiss Info (16 December 2016) www.swissinfo.ch/eng/new-immigration-law-clears-final-hurdle/42769316 accessed 27 September 2018.

[54] J Barrett, 'The United Kingdom and Parliamentary Scrutiny of Treaties: Recent Reforms', (2011) 60 *ICLQ* 225–45.

[55] *R (Miller) v Secretary of State for Exiting the European Union* [2017] UKSC 5.

[56] J Adriaensen, 'The Future of EU Trade Negotiations: What Has Been Learnt from CETA and TTIP?', European Politics and Policy, London School of Economics (29 November 2017) http://

The recent drive by the Indonesian Parliament to increase its role in relation to treaty-making is also illuminating. According to Indonesia's Law on International Agreements of 2000, the Government is required to obtain Parliament's approval to ratify certain categories of treaties on important matters.[57] The Parliament exercised its new power by withholding its approval for Indonesia's ratification of the ASEAN Charter due to public pressure in 2007–2008. The refusal was due to the Parliament's objection to the government's failure to consult it during the drafting and signing process. Furthermore, both the Indonesian public and Parliament expressed concerns about the survival of the consensus rule in the ASEAN Charter being detrimental to Indonesia's interest as the largest country in ASEAN, as well as the lack of meaningful human rights provisions.[58] Although the Parliament finally approved Indonesia's ratification of the Charter in late 2008, it launched an initiative to amend the Law on International Agreement in 2012 with the aim of expanding its own role in Indonesia's participation in international treaties.[59]

All over the world, demands for greater transparency and consultation in treaty-making have been increasing for decades, centuries in some cases, and there seems no likelihood that this trend will ever go into reverse.[60] But at the same time as demanding a greater say in treaties, parliaments often struggle to keep on top of scrutinising the texts already routinely sent to them. Some parliaments may lack the expertise to prioritise treaties that require in-depth scrutiny, while in others the problems may be inadequate institutional

blogs.lse.ac.uk/europpblog/2017/11/29/the-future-of-eu-trade-negotiations-what-has-been-learned-from-the-ceta-and-ttip-experiences/ accessed 27 September 2018.

57 Law 24 of 2000 on International Agreements, 23 October 2000, State Gazette 2000 No. 185, art 10. An unofficial translation of this law is provided by the Ministry of Foreign Affairs of Indonesia and on file with the authors. See also, Constitution of the Republic of Indonesia of 1945, 18 August 1945 (last amended in 2002) art 11(English version) (5th edn, Office of the Registrar and the Secretariat General of the Constitutional Court of the Republic of Indonesia, Jakarta 2015) www.mahkamahkonstitusi.go.id/public/content/infoumum/regulation/pdf/uud45%20eng.pdf accessed 26 September 2018.

58 'Legislators yet again Refuse to Ratify the ASEAN Charter', *Antara News* (Jakarta, 8 February 2008) (in Indonesian) www.antaranews.com/berita/92931/anggota-dpr-kembali-tolak-ratifikasi-asean-charter accessed 27 September 2018; Rizal Sukma, 'Commentary: To Be Responsible, Indonesia should not Ratify ASEAN Charter', *The Jakarta Post* (Jakarta, 22 July 2008) www.thejakartapost.com/news/2008/07/22/commentary-to-be-responsible-indonesia-should-not-ratify-asean-charter.html accessed 27 September 2018; and 'Opposition to ASEAN Charter Grows Following Lee's Remarks' *The Jakarta Post* (Jakarta, 25 July 2008) www.thejakartapost.com/news/2008/07/25/opposition-asean-charter-grows-following-lee039s-remarks.html accessed 27 September 2018.

59 The first Draft Law was concluded in 2012 but it has not yet been discussed by the Parliament. It is still listed in Parliament's National Legislation Programme 2015–2019. See House of Representatives of the Republic of Indonesia, 'National Legislation Programme 2015–2019 (in Indonesian) www.dpr.go.id/uu/prolegnas-long-list accessed 27 September 2018.

60 L Henkin, 'Treaties in a Constitutional Democracy' (1989) 10 *Michigan Journal of International Law* 406; A Thorp, 'Parliamentary Scrutiny of Treaties – up to 2010', SN/IA/4693 (25 September 2009) 30–37 https://researchbriefings.parliament.uk/ResearchBriefing/Summary/SN04693#fullreport accessed 26 September 2018.

mechanisms or resources, or insufficient co-operation among legislators of different political parties. Governments may be willing, in principle, to provide more transparency and consultation, but may also be mindful of the shortcomings of parliamentary procedures and reluctant to risk long delays and wrangles that could impede the efficient conduct of international treaty relations. Moreover, governments often lack imagination in devising innovative ways of managing public participation in treaty decisions, and may also have legitimate concerns about the interplay between this and the role of the legislature.

Future challenges are evident from the various trends outlined above – the overall increase in volume of treaties, the changes in patterns of international treaty relations, controversial treaty withdrawals, increase in rule-making within IOs and treaty bodies, increase in use of non-binding instruments instead of or as well as treaties, and changing technologies. Legislatures need to appraise the increasing amount of international law-making that is happening outside their purview, and decide whether they *should* have a role in relation to such items as mandatory Security Council resolutions, binding measures adopted by treaty bodies, treaty amendments adopted by tacit acceptance procedures, and treaty withdrawals, if they do not already. If they decide they should expand the scope or rigour of their scrutiny, this will inevitably require a review of the resources and institutional mechanisms they need to do so, as well as the additional information required from their government.

Technological Change: How Might It Affect Treaty Practice?

Technology has transformed office work and external communications in recent decades – from typewriter to word processor to computer, from letter, stamp and envelope to fax to email and social media, from printed gazettes to websites, from quill pen to ballpoint pen to electronic button, from buff folder tied with pink ribbon to e-documents on floppy disk to flash drive to cloud storage. Those who work with treaties are of course participants in this changing culture. Yet the law of treaties has not been amended to take account of these changes. Has treaty practice changed with the e-times? Will it need to in the future, and is it likely to reduce the work of Treaty Offices or increase it?

Technological changes in treaty practice have taken place at the UN level as well as regional and national levels. The UN Treaty Office updated its own practice with regard to use of electronic documents and notified this to all other parts of the UN Secretariat in 2001.[61] It also started publishing its treaty series and treaty status information online at around that time. The UN

[61] UNSG ST/SGB/2001/7, 'Secretary-General's bulletin: Procedures to be followed by the departments, offices and regional commissions of the United Nations with regard to treaties and international agreements' (28 August 2001).

Secretariat has proceeded more slowly where the changes impinge upon the service it provides directly to Member States. In 2010 the UN Legal Counsel informed Member States that:

> in light of the United Nations' effort to reduce paper consumption and to conserve energy and resources, the Treaty Section of the Office of Legal Affairs will discontinue the distribution of the Depositary notifications (CNs) on paper per 1 April 2010. The Depositary notifications will continue to be accessible electronically.[62]

Although the provision of this information is free of charge, it is obvious that this change may have been detrimental to States without adequate internet services. Such States could cope with this by having their New York missions print the online notifications and send them by bag to their foreign ministry, but this does of course transfer a resource burden to that State.

By contrast, the demands made by the UN Treaty Office on UN Member States to perform treaty actions by electronic means are more modest. The UN Treaty Handbook, which provides guidance to States on the UN's procedures, makes very little mention of digital technology. The 2012 edition has not changed substantially from previous editions in this regard. All requirements in the UN's Depositary procedures for 'signatures' on documents make clear that a physical signature on a paper document is still required. The few references to new technology are mostly in guidance which offers Member States an option to submit a copy of a document by electronic means, pending deposit of the signed paper original, rather than a mandatory requirement to use electronic means. This is unsurprising, as the UN's requirements need to accommodate States at all stages of technological development.

Most of the UN guidance is unspecific about the technological means which are normally used or permissible. Typically, it refers to 'communications' in a way that is neutral as to method. For example, with respect to declarations deposited at the time of signing or ratifying a treaty, the Handbook states that '[t]he Secretary-General simply communicates the text of the declaration to all States concerned by Depositary notification'[63] and with respect to registration, '[w]hen the Secretariat receives instruments for the purpose of registration'.[64] This wording is vague enough to cover sending a notification by post, email or by some other method yet to be devised. Likewise, other paragraphs which refer to requirements for certain notifications to be made 'in writing' are consistent with writing by hand, pen or any electronic means. In this sense, the UN guidance goes no further than the VCLT terms which do not refer to modes of communication. It does however leave it to Member States to interpret how the requirements might apply to new means of communications.

[62] UN Legal Counsel, UN Doc LA41TR/221/DepositaryNotifications/2010 (3 February 2010).
[63] Treaty Section of the Office of Legal Affairs, *Treaty Handbook* (2nd edn, UN 2012) 18, para 3.6.5.
[64] ibid 30 para 5.3.1.

One of the few parts of the UN Handbook to expressly request use of electronic means is on registration of treaties. Most of these procedures ask for a paper copy and an electronic one 'if available', for example: 'A party must submit ONE certified true and complete copy of **all** authentic text(s) in paper format and, if available, ONE electronic copy to the Secretariat for registration purposes.'[65] This is however followed by the more mandatory requirement: 'A paper and electronic copy of the treaty or international agreement in all the languages in which it was concluded must be submitted.' It is explained that: 'The Secretariat requires clear copies of treaties and international agreements for publication purposes as it publishes in electronic format the text of the treaty as submitted.'[66] As a bilateral treaty needs only to be registered by one party, this is not likely to present obstacles to registration in practice.

Regional organisations have greater leeway to update their communications technology and procedures at a pace to suit their Member States. The CoE for example started a new electronic procedure for Depositary notifications in 2006 after consultations with Member States. It is backed up by a monthly paper notification.[67] The ASEAN Secretariat continues to use traditional paper methods for its treaty notifications. When governments act as depositary for individual treaties, they may choose to adhere to traditional paper methods or offer electronic options to parties for certain purposes. For example, while some depositaries will accept an advanced scanned copy of the original instrument and take that as the date of deposit (on condition that the original is received promptly), the UK when acting as Depositary does not; only original paper documentation is accepted. The UK Treaty Section does however circulate Depositary communications electronically.

National Treaty Offices of course have to comply with the technological requirements of depositaries, in their dealings with them. In their bilateral treaty procedures they may use any means they agree upon, but when choosing novel means they will need to consider how the international law of treaties and the national laws and procedures of each State concerned will apply. When it comes to national publication of treaties and treaty information, States have discretion to use any methods that meet the needs of their national laws, legislature and public. In this area, there is already an enormous range of practice. Australia was the first State to start publishing its treaties and treaty information online in the 1990s. Most States and IOs now have some form of online treaty information, but there are considerable variations in the amount of information provided, its accuracy and searchability. Some States still do not have any such facility. States with public treaty websites typically still publish print versions of treaty texts and status information as well, and usually

[65] ibid 34, para 5.6. [66] ibid 38, para 5.7.4.

[67] CoE Director General of Legal Affairs letter to all Permanent Representatives of 20 February 2006, entitled 'Start of the new procedure for notifications relating to Council of Europe treaties'. A copy of the letter was kindly provided to Jill Barrett by the Council of Europe Treaty Office in December 2011, which she retains on file.

stipulate that only the official printed publication is the authoritative version. A few States, such as the Netherlands, have designated their treaty online publications as the official ones. In some cases it may be ambiguous which is authoritative. Given the propensity for electronic versions to become corrupted or detached from their original source, this can create challenges for the identification of accurate and authentic information.

Not all technological change is beneficial for treaty practice. Even in developed countries which have pioneered new methods of making treaty information more widely accessible, austerity measures can suddenly bite on government IT resources. For example, the UK Treaties Online website, first published by the FCO in 2010, was widely appreciated by its users both in and outside government, but when all ministries' websites were later merged into a single government resource, Treaties Online was scaled down and made less accessible. A similar merging of ministry websites occurred in the Netherlands, resulting in a single government website with less accessible treaty information. It is also common for problems to occur when one part of a government, ministry or organisation upgrades its IT systems but another part does not. It can result in what was once a fine treaty information service becoming a poor or unusable one, and, even worse, treaty records being irretrievable.

It is to be expected that, over the coming years, the disparity in the ability of national Treaty Offices to participate in new forms of digital technology will grow ever wider. This will present challenges for IOs, under pressure to save resources and speed up services, yet with a duty to ensure inclusiveness. It is foreseeable that there will in time be pressure to permit formal treaty documents such as Full Powers and ratification instruments to be signed digitally and sent electronically. When this occurs, there will be challenges for Treaty Offices in working out what the new procedural requirements should be, and how to cater at the same time for States which are able to use the new technology and those which are not, and the ensuing incompatibilities.

Governments and organisations may communicate in any way they choose when negotiating treaties. This makes the task of establishing what was agreed, and whether there was an intention to establish legal relations, ever more complex. The law of treaties provides flexibility as to the kind of 'instrument' or 'instruments' an international agreement is embodied in and the evidence required to establish that it was intended to be governed by international law. Deciding whether a set of bilateral email exchanges constitute a treaty may present different legal issues from an exchange of letters, and even more so when emails, letters and other kinds of communications are mixed together. The law of treaties has not been updated with reference to any particular technology and so there are no easy answers; international lawyers will need to apply general principles to ever more complex and novel forms of communications. Treaty Offices will need databases that can read, retrieve and cross-reference information across an increasingly fragmented range of media.

How Can Treaty Offices Prepare for the Challenges of the Future?

The challenges outlined above will engage those concerned with treaties across all State institutions and beyond. Some will concern policy-makers at the highest levels. Treaty Offices and treaty lawyers have important roles to play in alerting policy-makers and politicians to major new trends in treaty practice, anticipating problems and demands before they occur, wherever possible. They will need to provide up-to-date information and statistics about treaties that they deal with, as well as scan the horizon for new treaty developments that could be relevant. When policy-makers consider institutional change to meet new demands, the Treaty Office can provide indispensable support to this process by working out whether and how it could be implemented in practice, how it could affect other treaty stakeholders, how they could be consulted, any resource implications for the Treaty Office itself, and, not least, its compatibility with international and national legal obligations.

Many changes in treaty practice will affect the day-to-day work of Treaty Offices more than anyone else. They may be the first port of call for queries about whether this or that novel type of treaty-like instrument is or is not a treaty; whether it requires ratification, parliamentary scrutiny, publication or registration. They will need to acquire and master new technology to deal with new international requirements for digital treaty transactions, and find ways to make it work with existing and possibly incompatible systems across their administrations. They may be the first recipients of novel demands from parliament or the public for access to treaty negotiating texts or treaty information, and have to decide whether the existing rules require it, allow a discretion or need to be considered afresh.

The increasing need for expertise on treaty procedures within governments and IOs – for unmaking as well as making and managing treaties – added to the increasing demands for transparency from parliaments and the public show that the work of the Treaty Office will be vital for the future. In this Handbook we have presented the PLATO principles and shown how they underpin current good treaty practice in all its aspects.[68] We commend the same PLATO principles to guide the future strategy of treaty practice, to address the challenges that we can already foresee and have outlined above, and those that we cannot yet predict.

PROFESSIONAL	LEGAL	ASSURED	TRANSPARENT	ORGANISED

[68] The PLATO principles are introduced and explained in Chapter 1 at 14.

Box 10.1 Applying the PLATO principles to future challenges for treaty officials

PROFESSIONAL

Professional approach to treaty work by those who do it and by their organisation

The best way to ensure that a government or IO is equipped to cope with future challenges in treaty relations is for treaty practice to be recognised at the highest level as specialised work requiring knowledge, training and professional skills. The administration needs to plan for the future of the Treaty Office, providing adequate resources for recruitment, training, capacity-building, career development and retention of treaty officials, and knowledge management. The right mix of legal, IT, information management, administrative, communication, publishing and protocol skills are needed to enable the office to respond quickly to changing international treaty procedures and technologies, and to contribute creatively to the development of new practices to address them.

When the staff of the Treaty Office take a professional approach to their specialism, placing a high priority on learning, development and knowledge-sharing, this equips them to foresee changes and new challenges and take proactive steps to adapt to them. At its best, it motivates treaty professionals to create networks of contacts with those in equivalent roles in other governments and IOs. This can be one of the most effective ways to share knowledge of treaty procedures, benefit from the experience of others who have already dealt with a new type of problem, and be aware of changes on the horizon.

LEGAL

Legal requirements met– Lawyers fully engaged

The growing complexity of treaty relations, and the ways in which different kinds of treaty and non-treaty instruments interact, will make international law advice ever more indispensable in the future. In addition, the growing demands for constitutional reforms to give a greater role in treaty matters to national parliaments, regional and devolved authorities, and the public also requires constitutional law expertise. Lawyers who deal with treaties will therefore need to be experts in the area of law that is known in some jurisdictions as 'foreign relations law'. Treaty officials will need to work closely with international lawyers (if they are not international lawyers

Box 10.1 (cont.)

themselves) and develop 'legal awareness' as part of their professional training. With the increasing proliferation of international rule and policy-making under the auspices of treaty bodies, it is already a practical impossibility for all such material to pass through the hands of the Treaty Office. The Treaty Office will need international law expertise to navigate its way through, prioritise, distinguish between treaties and non-treaties, instruments that need ratifications, consultation, publication and registration and those that do not, and consider the wider implications of proposed new ways of working.

ASSURED

Reliable, dependable, trustworthy, guaranteed

Whatever changes may occur in the form and means of treaty negotiations and treaty acts, there will always be the same need to ensure that they are authorised and authentic. The current mix of paper and various digital and other formats of treaty records has already introduced scope for confusion. The availability of texts on the internet has also increased the scope for documents to be lost or corrupted, and for their source and status to be unclear. When treaty users use search engines to bring up a treaty text or treaty information, how can they tell which of numerous results is the authentic one, if any? The average treaty user may not distinguish between a draft and a final text, or between the authentic text as adopted versus an unofficial consolidated text. A trained treaty official will always know how to check these things, and will also make the status of any published versions clear to the reader. A good example of this is the Energy Charter website, which provides a 'Consolidated Version of the Energy Charter Treaty and Related Documents', pointing out that it is not a legal document and has been compiled by the Energy Charter Secretariat to facilitate work on the documents, but for legal analysis the reader is advised to refer to the authenticated/certified copies of the texts which are also provided on the website. Not all secretariat websites are as clear as this, but they ought to be.[69]

As technology changes the challenges will become greater, not only in distinguishing between authentic and non-authentic texts, but on a range of new problems such as how a treaty may be signed or ratified digitally,

[69] See sections on 'Managing Treaty Collections' and 'Setting Up a Treaty Database' in Chapter 4 at 132–39 and 139–49 respectively.

Box 10.1 (cont.)

how that digital signature is to be stored and how it can later be checked for authenticity. The need for professional treaty officials who specialise in these procedures and keep up to date with changing forms and practices can only increase in the future.

TRANSPARENT

Clear and easy to understand, available and accessible

Transparency is likely to be the area of greatest challenge in the future, to meet evolving public expectations. As discussed above, controversial treaties such as those on trade, investment or climate change, and, within the EU, EU constitutional reform treaties and the treaties needed to facilitate the UK's withdrawal from the EU, attract enormous political pressures from parliaments and public for access to negotiating texts and the right to participate. The response in such high-profile situations would normally be for politicians or high-level policy-makers. The principle of transparency is however one that should permeate the day-to-day work of the Treaty Office. There must be easy access to treaty procedures, practice guidance and information for all who need it for their work, and for others as appropriate. Publications of treaty texts should be widely and publicly accessible and user-friendly. Clarity is important in guidelines and standards for treaty officials, as well as information provided for the public. Treaty officials should actively disseminate practices and procedures within their organisation and beyond. They should provide sufficient information in sufficient time to the legislature to enable democratic oversight of the exercise of treaty-making powers and other treaty acts.

Treaty Offices that strive to improve transparency in their routine work, as a matter of habit, will be best placed to respond to new challenges in the future. They will also be able to support their political authorities in their efforts to respond to public demands for transparency and participation in treaty-making.

ORGANISED

Systematic, efficient, regular

The principles of good organisation of treaty procedures and information underpin every other principle of good treaty practice. Thought needs to be given to the organisation of treaty records systems to ensure that future generations of staff will be able to be access and use it. Treaty procedures and practices need to be written down, expressed in a way

Box 10.1 (cont.)

that will be understood by future staff with no personal memory of the practice in question.

With the increasing involvement in treaty work of a wider range of government officials from domestic ministries and agencies, having a central point of contact for treaty actions and procedures (such as a Treaty Section or Treaty Office) for all internal and external contacts will be ever more important. Likewise, a single central authority should have ultimate responsibility for the provision of authoritative treaty information across the government (or secretariat) and to the public. The more diffuse treaty work becomes, and the more varied the technological means for doing it, the more important it will be to have effective horizontal co-ordination, with all aspects of treaty procedure interlocking and working harmoniously together across the government (or IO).

Centralisation of treaty procedures does not mean that it all takes place within the Treaty Office. The more that treaty-related work is carried out in domestic ministries and agencies across government, the more treaty officials will need to *go out of the Treaty Office* in order to do their job of promoting awareness of treaty procedures to those who need it (but who may not yet realise that they do).

Concluding Remark

The importance of good treaty practice for the smooth conduct of international relations and for the avoidance of tension, misunderstandings and disputes leading to litigation, international and domestic, is not likely to change. Whatever the future form of treaty practices, we hope that the PLATO principles will endure as a useful guide. More fundamentally, we hope that by stimulating debate on what constitutes good treaty practice, this Handbook might help to generate more of it.

Annexes

Annex I
Examples of Final Clauses in a Single-instrument Bilateral Treaty

Agreement between the Government of the Kingdom of the Netherlands and the Government of the United Kingdom of Great Britain and Northern Ireland on the Reciprocal Holding of Stocks of Crude Oil and/or Petroleum Products[1]

Article 8

This Agreement shall enter into force on the first day of the second month after each Government has notified the other Government through the diplomatic channel of the completion of their respective procedures necessary for the entry into force of the Agreement.

Article 9

1. This Agreement may be terminated by either Government upon giving notice in writing, through the diplomatic channel to the other Government, not less than six months before the end of any calendar year. The Agreement shall cease to be in force from the first day of the following calendar year.
2. Neither Government shall exercise the power of termination in paragraph (1) of this Article without having informed the Commission of the European Communities of its intention to do so.

[1] Agreement between the Government of the Kingdom of the Netherlands and the Government of the United Kingdom of Great Britain and Northern Ireland on the Reciprocal Holding of Stocks of Crude Oil and/or Petroleum Products (adopted 26 June 2006, entered into force 1 June 2008) 2579 UNTS 201.

3. This Agreement may not be terminated during a supply crisis.

IN WITNESS whereof the undersigned, being duly authorised thereto by their respective Governments, have signed this Agreement.

DONE in two originals, at London, this 26th day of June 2006 in the English language only.

For the Government of the Kingdom of the Netherlands,
J.M.V.A. GRAAF DE MARCHANT ET D'ANSEMBOURG

For the Government of the United Kingdom of Great Britain and Northern Ireland,
MALCOLM WICKS

Agreement between the Government of the Republic of Latvia and the Government of the Republic of Korea on the Mutual Recognition and Exchange of Driving Licenses[2]

Article 10

1. This Agreement shall enter into force on the thirtieth (30th) day following the date of receipt of the last notification indicating the fulfillment by the Contracting Parties of all domestic requirements for its entry into force. It shall remain in force for an indefinite period of time.
2. Either Contracting Party may terminate this Agreement by giving the other Contracting Party written notice through diplomatic channels. In such case, termination shall take effect on the thirtieth (30th) day following the receipt of the notice by the other Contracting Party.
3. This Agreement may be modified or amended with the mutual written consent of the Contracting Parties. Such modification or amendment shall enter into force on a date mutually agreed upon by the Contracting Parties.

IN WITNESS WHEREOF, the undersigned, being duly authorized thereto by their respective Governments, have signed this Agreement.

DONE in duplicate at Riga on the 8th day of March, 2011, in the Latvian, Korean and English languages, all texts being equally authentic. In case of any divergence of interpretation, the English text shall prevail.

[2] Agreement between the Government of the Republic of Latvia and the Government of the Republic of Korea on the Mutual Recognition and Exchange of Driving Licenses (adopted 8 March 2011, entered into force on 28 May 2011) 2830 UNTS 79.

For the Government
of the Republic of Latvia

For the Government
of the Republic of Korea

Annex II
Examples of Final Clauses in a Multilateral Treaty

Convention on the Rights of the Child[3]

Part III
Article 46
The present Convention shall be open for signature by all States.

Article 47
The present Convention is subject to ratification. Instruments of ratification shall be deposited with the Secretary-General of the United Nations.

Article 48
The present Convention shall remain open for accession by any State. The instruments of accession shall be deposited with the Secretary-General of the United Nations.

Article 49
1. The present Convention shall enter into force on the thirtieth day following the date of deposit with the Secretary-General of the United Nations of the twentieth instrument of ratification or accession.
2. For each State ratifying or acceding to the Convention after the deposit of the twentieth instrument of ratification or accession, the Convention shall enter into force on the thirtieth day after the deposit by such State of its instrument of ratification or accession.

Article 50
1. Any State Party may propose an amendment and file it with the Secretary General of the United Nations. The Secretary-General shall thereupon communicate the proposed amendment to States Parties, with a request that they indicate whether they favour a conference of States Parties for the purpose of considering and voting upon the proposals.

[3] Convention on the Rights of the Child (adopted 20 November 1989, entered into force 2 September 1990) 1577 UNTS 3.

In the event that, within four months from the date of such communication, at least one third of the States Parties favour such a conference, the Secretary-General shall convene the conference under the auspices of the United Nations. Any amendment adopted by a majority of States Parties present and voting at the conference shall be submitted to the General Assembly for approval.

2. An amendment adopted in accordance with paragraph 1 of the present article shall enter into force when it has been approved by the General Assembly of the United Nations and accepted by a two-thirds majority of States Parties.
3. When an amendment enters into force, it shall be binding on those States Parties which have accepted it, other States Parties still being bound by the provisions of the present Convention and any earlier amendments which they have accepted.

Article 51

1. The Secretary-General of the United Nations shall receive and circulate to all States the text of reservations made by States at the time of ratification or accession.
2. A reservation incompatible with the object and purpose of the present Convention shall not be permitted.
3. Reservations may be withdrawn at any time by notification to that effect addressed to the Secretary-General of the United Nations, who shall then inform all States. Such notification shall take effect on the date on which it is received by the Secretary-General.

Article 52

A State Party may denounce the present Convention by written notification to the Secretary-General of the United Nations. Denunciation becomes effective one year after the date of receipt of the notification by the Secretary-General.

Article 53

The Secretary-General of the United Nations is designated as the depositary of the present Convention.

Article 54

The original of the present Convention, of which the Arabic, Chinese, English, French, Russian and Spanish texts are equally authentic, shall be deposited with the Secretary-General of the United Nations.

In witness thereof the undersigned plenipotentiaries, being duly authorized thereto by their respective Governments, have signed the present Convention.

Council of Europe Convention on Action against Trafficking in Human Beings[4]

Chapter X Final Clauses

Article 42 Signature and Entry into Force

1. This Convention shall be open for signature by the member States of the Council of Europe, the non-member States which have participated in its elaboration and the European Community.
2. This Convention is subject to ratification, acceptance or approval. Instruments of ratification, acceptance or approval shall be deposited with the Secretary General of the Council of Europe.
3. This Convention shall enter into force on the first day of the month following the expiration of a period of three months after the date on which 10 Signatories, including at least 8 member States of the Council of Europe, have expressed their consent to be bound by the Convention in accordance with the provisions of the preceding paragraph.
4. In respect of any State mentioned in paragraph 1 or the European Community, which subsequently expresses its consent to be bound by it, the Convention shall enter into force on the first day of the month following the expiration of a period of three months after the date of the deposit of its instrument of ratification, acceptance or approval.

Article 43 Accession to the Convention

1. After the entry into force of this Convention, the Committee of Ministers of the Council of Europe may, after consultation of the Parties to this Convention and obtaining their unanimous consent, invite any non-member State of the Council of Europe, which has not participated in the elaboration of the Convention, to accede to this Convention by a decision taken by the majority provided for in Article 20 *d* of the Statute of the Council of Europe, and by unanimous vote of the representatives of the Contracting States entitled to sit on the Committee of Ministers.
2. In respect of any acceding State, the Convention shall enter into force on the first day of the month following the expiration of a period of three months after the date of deposit of the instrument of accession with the Secretary General of the Council of Europe.

Article 44 Territorial Application

1. Any State or the European Community may, at the time of signature or when depositing its instrument of ratification, acceptance, approval or accession, specify the territory or territories to which this Convention shall apply.
2. Any Party may, at any later date, by a declaration addressed to the Secretary General of the Council of Europe, extend the application of this Convention

[4] Council of Europe Convention on Action against Trafficking in Human Beings (adopted 16 May 2005, entered into force 10 February 2008) CETS 197.

to any other territory specified in the declaration and for whose international relations it is responsible or on whose behalf it is authorised to give undertakings. In respect of such territory, the Convention shall enter into force on the first day of the month following the expiration of a period of three months after the date of receipt of such declaration by the Secretary General.

3. Any declaration made under the two preceding paragraphs may, in respect of any territory specified in such declaration, be withdrawn by a notification addressed to the Secretary General of the Council of Europe. The withdrawal shall become effective on the first day of the month following the expiration of a period of three months after the date of receipt of such notification by the Secretary General.

Article 45 Reservations

No reservation may be made in respect of any provision of this Convention, with the exception of the reservation of Article 31, paragraph 2.

Article 46 Denunciation

1. Any Party may, at any time, denounce this Convention by means of a notification addressed to the Secretary General of the Council of Europe.
2. Such denunciation shall become effective on the first day of the month following the expiration of a period of three months after the date of receipt of the notification by the Secretary General.

Article 47 Notification

The Secretary General of the Council of Europe shall notify the member States of the Council of Europe, any State signatory, any State Party, the European Community, to any State invited to sign this Convention in accordance with the provisions of Article 42 and to any State invited to accede to this Convention in accordance with the provisions of Article 43 of:

a. any signature;
b. the deposit of any instrument of ratification, acceptance, approval or accession;
c. any date of entry into force of this Convention in accordance with Articles 42 and 43;
d. any amendment adopted in accordance with Article 41 and the date on which such an amendment enters into force;
e. any denunciation made in pursuance of the provisions of Article 46;
f. any other act, notification or communication relating to this Convention;
g. any reservation made under Article 45.

In witness whereof the undersigned, being duly authorised thereto, have signed this Convention.

Done at Warsaw, this 16th day of May 2005, in English and in French, both texts being equally authentic, in a single copy which shall be deposited in the archives of the Council of Europe. The Secretary General of the Council of Europe shall transmit certified copies to each Member State of the Council of Europe, to the non-member States which have participated in the elaboration of this Convention, to the European Community and to any State invited to accede to this Convention.

Annex III
Example of an Exchange of Notes Constituting a Treaty

Exchange of Notes constituting an Agreement between the Government of the United Kingdom of Great Britain and Northern Ireland and the Government of the People's Republic of China concerning the Establishment of a Consulate-General of each Country in the other at Wuhan and Belfast[5]

No.1

Her Majesty's Embassy at Beijing to the Ministry of Foreign Affairs for the Government of the People's Republic of China

20 February 2014

Note No. 021/14

The Embassy of the United Kingdom of Great Britain and Northern Ireland in China presents its compliments to the Ministry of Foreign Affairs of the People's Republic of China and, on behalf of the Government of the United Kingdom of Great Britain and Northern Ireland, has the honour to propose that, with the common desire to further develop the friendly relations between the two countries, the Government of the United Kingdom of Great Britain and Northern Ireland and the Government of the People's Republic of China hereby agree to establish a Consulate-General of each country in the other as follows:

1. The Government of the People's Republic of China gives its consent to the Government of the United Kingdom of Great Britain and Northern Ireland to establish a Consulate-General at Wuhan, with the consular district comprising of Hubei Province.

2. The Government of the United Kingdom of Great Britain and Northern Ireland gives its consent to the Government of the People's Republic of China to establish a Consulate-General at Belfast, with the consular district comprising of Northern Ireland; and for the Consulate-General at Edinburgh to adjust its consular district to Scotland only, having been comprised of both Scotland and Northern Ireland previously. The parties agree that Article 2 of the exchange of notes on the mutual establishment of the Consulates-General of Guangzhou and Edinburgh has been duly amended.

[5] Exchange of Notes constituting an Agreement between the Government of the United Kingdom of Great Britain and Northern Ireland and the Government of the People's Republic of China Concerning the Establishment of a Consulate-General of each Country in the other at Wuhan and Belfast (signed 20 and 21 February 2014, entered into force 21 February 2014) UKTS 23 (2016). The reproduction of the excerpts of the said Exchange of Notes is made in accordance with and subject to the Open Government Licence for public sector information www.nationalarchives.gov.uk/doc/open-government-licence/version/1/open-government-licence.htm accessed 4 December 2018.

3. In accordance with the Vienna Convention on Consular Relations of April 24 1963 and relevant laws and regulations of their respective countries, the Government of the United Kingdom of Great Britain and Northern Ireland and the Government of the People's Republic of China shall each provide the other party with the necessary assistance for the establishment of the Consulates-General, and exercising their Consular functions.

If the above agreement is confirmed by the Ministry of Foreign Affairs of the People's Republic of China on behalf of the Government of the People's Republic of China, this note together with the reply from the Ministry of Foreign Affairs shall constitute an Agreement between the Government of Great Britain and Northern Ireland and the Government of the People's Republic of China which shall enter into force on the date of the latter's reply.

The Embassy of the United Kingdom of Great Britain and Northern Ireland in China avails itself of this opportunity to renew to the Ministry of Foreign Affairs of the People's Republic of China the assurances of its highest consideration.

No.2

Ministry of Foreign Affairs of the People's Republic of China to the Embassy of the United Kingdom of Great Britain and Northern Ireland in China

21 February 2014

Note No. (2014) 70

The Ministry of Foreign Affairs of the People's Republic of China presents its compliments to the Embassy of the United Kingdom of Great Britain and Northern Ireland in China and has the honour to acknowledge receipt of the latter's Note No.021/14 of 20 February 2014 which reads as follows:

[As in Note No.1]

On behalf of the Government of the People's Republic of China, the Ministry of Foreign Affairs of the People's Republic of China has the honour to confirm its agreement to the content of the above note.

The Ministry of Foreign Affairs of the People's Republic of China avails itself of this opportunity to renew to the Embassy of the United Kingdom of Great Britain and Northern Ireland in China the assurances of its highest consideration.

Annex IV
Examples of an Exchange of Letters Constituting a Treaty

A Example of Exchange of Letters A

Exchange of Letters Amending the Free Trade Agreement between the Government of New Zealand and the People's Republic of China[6]

Letter No. 1: Letter from the Government of New Zealand to the Government of the People's Republic of China (1st page)

Mr Gao Hucheng
Minister of Commerce
The People's Republic of China

20 November 2014

Your Excellency,

I have the honour to refer to the *Free Trade Agreement between the Government of New Zealand and the Government of the People's Republic of China* (the 'Agreement'), done at Beijing on 7 April 2008, and to the discussions that have taken place between representatives of our two Governments regarding television co-production.

Pursuant to those discussions, I now have the honour to propose, on behalf of the Government of New Zealand, that the Agreement be amended in accordance with Article 212 to include as Annex 15 the *Television Programmes Co-Production Agreement between the Government of New Zealand and the Government of the People's Republic of China* attached to this Letter (the 'Annex'). The Annex will hereafter form an integral part of the Agreement.

If the above proposal is acceptable to the Government of the People's Republic of China, I have the further honour to propose that this Letter together with your Letter in reply indicating such acceptance shall constitute an agreement between the two Governments, which shall enter into force sixty days from the date of your reply, in accordance with Article 212.

I take this opportunity to extend to you the assurances of my highest considerations.

Sincerely,

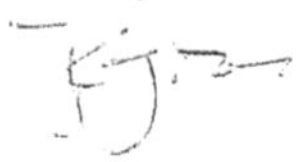

Hon Tim Groser
Minister of Trade

6 Exchange of Letters Amending the Free Trade Agreement between the Government of New Zealand and the People's Republic of China (signed 20 November 2014, entered into force 20 January 2015) NZTS 2015–01 B2014-14. The Annex referred to in each Letter, and attached to it, consists of a new Annex to the Free Trade Agreement, entitled 'Annex 15 the Television Programmes Co-Production Agreement between the Government of New Zealand and the Government of the People's Republic of China'. In this Annex, we have reproduced only the first page of New Zealand's Letter and the first and second pages of China's Letter. The original Exchange of Letters consists of twenty-three pages (in English and Chinese). Excerpts from the Exchange of Letters are reproduced with the kind permission of the Ministry of Foreign Affairs and Trade of New Zealand.

Letter No. 2: Letter from the Government of the People's Republic of China to the Government of New Zealand (first and second pages)

Hon Tim Groser

Minister of Trade

New Zealand

20 November 2014

Dear Minister,

I acknowledge the receipt of your letter of 20 November 2014, which reads as follows:

> "I have the honour to refer to the *Free Trade Agreement between the Government of New Zealand and the Government of the People's Republic of China* (the 'Agreement'), done at Beijing on 7 April 2008, and to the discussions that have taken place between representatives of our two Governments regarding television co-production.
>
> Pursuant to those discussions, I now have the honour to propose, on behalf of the Government of New Zealand, that the Agreement be amended in accordance with Article 212 to include as Annex 15 the *Television Programmes Co-Production Agreement between the Government of New Zealand and the Government of the People's Republic of China* attached to this Letter (the 'Annex'). The Annex will hereafter form an integral part of the Agreement.
>
> If the above proposal/s are acceptable to the Government of the People's Republic of China, I have the further honour to propose that this Letter together with your Letter in reply indicating such acceptance shall constitute an agreement between the two Governments, which shall enter into force sixty days from the date of your reply, in accordance with Article 212."

I have the honour to confirm the above proposal is acceptable to the Government of the People's Republic of China, and that your letter and this letter in reply will constitute an agreement between our two governments in the matter which will come into effect sixty days from the date of this letter in reply.

I take this opportunity to renew to you the assurances of my highest considerations.

Sincerely,

Mr Gao Hucheng

Minister of Commerce

People's Republic of China

B Example of Exchange of Letters B

Exchange of Letters amending the Agreement on a Working Holiday Scheme between the Government of New Zealand and the Government of the Argentine Republic[7]

Letter 1: Letter from the Government of the Argentine Republic to the Government of New Zealand

Ministro de Relaciones Exteriores, Comercio Internacional y Culto

(Non official translation)

Buenos Aires, November 5, 2010

Your Excellency,

I have the honour to refer to the "Agreement on a Working Holiday Scheme between the Government of the Argentine Republic and the Government of New Zealand", hereinafter, the "Agreement", signed in Buenos Aires on 22 November 2001.

In this regard, pursuant to Article 11 of the Agreement, I would like to propose, on behalf of the Argentine Government, the following amendments to the Agreement:

1. That Article 1(a) of the Agreement be amended to read as follows: "is a citizen of the Argentine Republic;"

2. That Article 1(c) of the Agreement be amended to read as follows: "is aged between eighteen (18) and thirty-five (35) years, both inclusive, at the time of application;"

H.E. Hon. Murray Mc Cully
Minister of Foreign Affairs of New Zealand
WELLINGTON

[7] Exchange of Letters amending the Agreement on a Working Holiday Scheme between the Government of New Zealand and the Government of the Argentine Republic (adopted 13 December 2010, entered into force 28 July 2011) NZTS 2011 No. 8 B2010/28. This copy was provided by the Ministry of Foreign Affairs and Trade of the Government of New Zealand and is

3. That Article 4 of the Agreement be amended to read as follows: "The Government of New Zealand shall require any citizen from the Argentine Republic who has entered New Zealand through the Scheme operating under this Agreement to comply with the laws and regulations of New Zealand and not to engage in employment that is contrary to the purpose of the Scheme. Participants in the Scheme shall not be permitted to engage in permanent employment during their stay in New Zealand. The Government of New Zealand shall allow any citizen from the Argentine Republic who has entered New Zealand through the Scheme to enrol in training or study courses not exceeding a total of six (6) months' duration during their stay in New Zealand."

4. That Article 5(a) of the Agreement be amended to read as follows: "is a citizen of New Zealand;"

5. That Article 5(c) of the Agreement be amended to read as follows: "is aged between eighteen (18) and thirty-five (35) years, both inclusive, at the time of application;"

6. That Article 7 of the Agreement be amended to read as follows: "Subject to Article 6, the Government of the Argentine Republic shall issue a special-purpose transitory visa to any New Zealand citizen who satisfies each of the requirements in Article 5. This transitory visa shall be granted by the consular office in New Zealand and shall be valid for a period of twelve (12) months from the date of entry into the Argentine Republic."

7. That Article 8 of the Agreement be amended to read as follows: "The Government of the Argentine Republic shall require any New Zealand citizen who has

reproduced here with kind permission. The text of the Agreement is published on New Zealand Treaties Online www.treaties.mfat.govt.nz/search/details/t/3742 accessed 5 December 2018.

entered the Argentine Republic through the Scheme operating under this Agreement to comply with the laws and regulations of the Argentine Republic and not to engage in employment that is contrary to the purpose of the Scheme. Participants in the Scheme shall not be permitted to engage in permanent employment during their stay in the Argentine Republic. The Government of the Argentine Republic shall allow any citizen from New Zealand who has entered the Argentine Republic through the Scheme to enrol in training or study courses not exceeding a total of six (6) months' duration during their stay in the Argentine Republic."

Should the foregoing be agreeable to the Government of New Zealand, I have the honour to propose that this Note and the Note from Your Excellency giving consent shall constitute an agreement between our two Governments amending the Agreement, which shall enter into force on the date of receipt of the last notice by which the Parties inform each other of the fulfilment of their internal procedural requirements for entry into force.

Please accept, your Excellency, the assurances of my highest consideration.

Letter 2: Letter from the Government of New Zealand to the Government of the Argentine Republic

Héctor Timerman

Minister of Foreign Affairs, International Trade and Worship of the Argentine Republic

13 December, 2010

Your Excellency,

I have the honour to refer to your Note of 5 November, 2010 regarding the "Agreement on a Working Holiday Scheme between the Government of the Argentine Republic and the Government of New Zealand", signed in Buenos Aires on 22 November 2001 (the "Agreement"), which reads as follows:

> *"H.E. Hon. Murray McCully*
> *Minister of Foreign Affairs of New Zealand*
> *WELLINGTON*
>
> *Buenos Aires, November 5, 2010*
>
> *Your Excellency,*
>
> *I have the honour to refer to the "Agreement on a Working Holiday Scheme between the Government of the Argentine Republic and the Government of New Zealand", hereinafter, the "Agreement", signed in Buenos Aires on 22 November 2001.*

In this regard, pursuant to Article 11 of the Agreement, I would like to propose, on behalf of the Argentine Government, the following amendments to the Agreement:

1. That Article 1(a) of the Agreement be amended to read as follows: "is a citizen of the Argentine Republic;"

2. That Article 1(c) of the Agreement be amended to read as follows: "is aged between eighteen (18) and thirty-five (35) years, both inclusive, at the time of application;"

3. That Article 4 of the Agreement be amended to read as follows: "The Government of New Zealand shall require any citizen from the Argentine Republic who has entered New Zealand through the Scheme operating under this Agreement to comply with the laws and regulations of New Zealand and not to engage in employment that is contrary to the purpose of the Scheme. Participants in the Scheme shall not be permitted to engage in permanent employment during their stay in New Zealand. The Government of New Zealand shall allow any citizen from the Argentine Republic who has entered New Zealand through the Scheme to enrol in training or study courses not exceeding a total of six (6) months' duration during their stay in New Zealand."

4. That Article 5(a) of the Agreement be amended to read as follows: "is a citizen of New Zealand;"

5. That Article 5(c) of the Agreement be amended to read as follows: "is aged between eighteen (18) and thirty-five (35) years, both inclusive, at the time of application;"

6. That Article 7 of the Agreement be amended to read as follows: "Subject to Article 6, the Government of the Argentine Republic shall issue a special-purpose transitory visa to any New Zealand citizen who satisfies each of the requirements in Article 5. This transitory visa shall be granted by the consular office in New Zealand and shall be valid for a period of twelve (12) months from the date of entry into the Argentine Republic."

7. That Article 8 of the Agreement be amended to read as follows: "The Government of the Argentine Republic shall require any New Zealand citizen who has entered the Argentine Republic through the Scheme operating under this Agreement to comply with the laws and regulations of the Argentine Republic and not to engage in employment that is contrary to the purpose of the Scheme. Participants in the Scheme shall not be permitted to engage in permanent employment during their stay in the Argentine Republic. The Government of the Argentine Republic shall allow any citizen from New Zealand who has entered the Argentine Republic through the Scheme to enrol in training or study courses not exceeding a total of six (6) months' duration during their stay in the Argentine Republic."

Should the foregoing be agreeable to the Government of New Zealand, I have the honour to propose that this Note and the Note from Your Excellency giving consent shall constitute an agreement between our two Governments amending the Agreement, which shall enter into force on the date of receipt of the last notice by which the Parties inform each other of the fulfilment of their internal procedural requirements for entry into force.

Please accept, your Excellency, the assurances of my highest consideration.

I am pleased to confirm that the proposed changes are acceptable to the Government of New Zealand, and that your Note, together with this Note in reply, shall constitute, between our two Governments, an agreement amending the Agreement, which shall enter into force on the date of receipt of the last notice by which the Parties inform each other of the fulfilment of their internal procedural requirements for entry into force.

I avail myself of this opportunity to renew to Your Excellency, the assurances of my highest consideration.

Murray McCully

Minister of Foreign Affairs of New Zealand

Annex V
United Nations Model Instrument of Full Powers[8]

ANNEX 3 – MODEL INSTRUMENT OF FULL POWERS

(To be signed by the Head of State, Head of Government or Minister for Foreign Affairs)

FULL POWERS

I, [name and title of the Head of State, Head of Government or Minister for Foreign Affairs],

HEREBY AUTHORIZE [name and title] to [sign *, ratify, denounce, effect the following declaration in respect of, etc.] the [title and date of treaty, convention, agreement, etc.] on behalf of the Government of [name of State].

Done at [place] on [date].

[Signature]

* Subject to the provisions of the treaty, one of the following alternatives is to be chosen: [subject to ratification] or [without reservation as to ratification].
Reservations made upon signature must be authorized by the full powers granted to the signatory.

[8] From *Treaty Handbook* (2nd ed) by the Treaty Section of the Office of Legal Affairs ©2002–2012 United Nations. Reprinted with the permission of the United Nations.

Annex VI
Examples of Full Powers

A Full Powers for Signing a Bilateral Treaty[9]

B2010/23

I, MURRAY STUART MCCULLY
Minister of Foreign Affairs
of New Zealand

do hereby certify that

NICHOLAS JOHN HURLEY
New Zealand High Commissioner to Samoa

is vested with full powers and authority to sign, on behalf of the Government of New Zealand, the *Agreement between the Government of New Zealand and the Government of Samoa for the Allocation of Taxing Rights with respect to Certain Income of Individuals and to Establish a Mutual Agreement Procedure in respect of Transfer Pricing Adjustments.*

IN WITNESS WHEREOF, I have signed and sealed these presents at Wellington, this 1st day of August 2010.

Hon Murray Stuart McCully
Minister of Foreign Affairs

[9] New Zealand Full Powers for the Agreement between the Government of New Zealand and the Government of Samoa for the Allocation of Taxing Rights with respect to Certain Income of Individuals and to Establish a Mutual Agreement Procedure in respect to Transfer Pricing Adjustments (signed 1 August 2010). Reprinted with the permission of the Ministry of Foreign Affairs and Trade of New Zealand.

B Full Powers for Signing a Multilateral Treaty[10]

FULL POWERS

I, George Yong-Boon Yeo, Minister for Foreign Affairs of the Republic of Singapore,

HEREBY AUTHORISE Lim Hng Kiang, Minister for Trade and Industry, to sign on behalf of the Government of the Republic of Singapore, the Agreement on Investment under the Framework Agreement on Comprehensive Economic Cooperation among the Governments of the Member Countries of the Association of Southeast Asian Nations and the Republic of Korea.

Done at the Republic of Singapore on Monday, the 18th day of May 2009.

GEORGE YONG-BOON YEO

[10] Singapore Full Powers for the Agreement on Investment under the Framework Agreement on Comprehensive Economic Cooperation among the Governments of the Member Countries of the Association of Southeast Asian Nations with the Republic of Korea (signed 18 May 2009). Reprinted with the permission of the Legal Services and Agreements Directorate of the ASEAN Secretariat. The signed original of the Full Powers is on file with the Secretariat and can be accessed on ARC – ASEAN Secretariat Resource Centre, 'The Archives of the ASEAN Legal Documents' http://arc-agreement.asean.org/file/doc/2015/02/full-power-to-lim-hng-kiang-to-the-agreement-on-investment-under-the-framework-agreement-on-comprehensive-economic-cooperation-among-the-governments-of-the-member-countries-of-the-association-of-southeast-asian-nations-and-the-republic-of.pdf accessed 2 November 2018.

Annex VII
United Nations Model Instrument of Ratification/Acceptance/Approval[11]

ANNEX 4 – MODEL INSTRUMENT OF RATIFICATION, ACCEPTANCE OR APPROVAL

(To be signed by the Head of State, Head of Government or Minister for Foreign Affairs)

[RATIFICATION / ACCEPTANCE / APPROVAL]

WHEREAS the [title of treaty, convention, agreement, etc.] was [concluded, adopted, opened for signature, etc.] at [place] on [date],

AND WHEREAS the said [treaty, convention, agreement, etc.] has been signed on behalf of the Government of [name of State] on [date],

NOW THEREFORE I, [name and title of the Head of State, Head of Government or Minister for Foreign Affairs] declare that the Government of [name of State], having considered the above-mentioned [treaty, convention, agreement, etc.], [ratifies, accepts, approves] the same and undertakes faithfully to perform and carry out the stipulations therein contained.

IN WITNESS WHEREOF, I have signed this instrument of [ratification, acceptance, approval] at [place] on [date].

[Signature]

[11] From *Treaty Handbook* (2nd ed) by the Treaty Section of the Office of Legal Affairs ©2002–2012 United Nations. Reprinted with the permission of the United Nations.

Annex VIII
Example of an Instrument of Ratification[12]

INSTRUMENT OF RATIFICATION

WHEREAS the Third Protocol Amending the Treaty of Amity and Cooperation in Southeast Asia ("Protocol") was opened for signature, at Ha Noi, Viet Nam, on 23 July 2010,

AND WHEREAS the said Protocol was signed by the Government of the Republic of Singapore on 23 July 2010,

AND WHEREAS Article 3 of the Protocol provides that it shall be subject to ratification,

NOW THEREFORE I, George Yong-Boon Yeo, Minister for Foreign Affairs of the Republic of Singapore declare that the Government of the Republic of Singapore, having considered the above mentioned Protocol, ratifies the same and undertakes faithfully to perform and carry out the stipulations therein contained.

IN WITNESS WHEREOF, I have signed this instrument of ratification at the Republic of Singapore on 11 October 2010.

MINISTRY OF FOREIGN AFFAIRS SINGAPORE

GEORGE YONG-BOON YEO
MINISTER FOR FOREIGN AFFAIRS
REPUBLIC OF SINGAPORE

[12] Singapore Instrument of Ratification of the Third Protocol Amending the Treaty of Amity and Cooperation in Southeast Asia (signed 11 October 2010). Reprinted with the permission of the Legal Services and Agreement Directorate of the ASEAN Secretariat. The signed original instrument of ratification is on file with the Secretariat a copy of which can be accessed on 'ASEAN Legal Instruments' http://agreement.asean.org/media/download/20140117144638.pdf accessed 2 November 2018.

Annex IX
United Nations Model Instrument of Accession[13]

ANNEX 5 – MODEL INSTRUMENT OF ACCESSION

(To be signed by the Head of State, Head of Government or Minister for Foreign Affairs)

ACCESSION

WHEREAS the [title of treaty, convention, agreement, etc.] was [concluded, adopted, opened for signature, etc.] at [place] on [date],

NOW THEREFORE I, [name and title of the Head of State, Head of Government or Minister for Foreign Affairs] declare that the Government of [name of State], having considered the above-mentioned [treaty, convention, agreement, etc.], accedes to the same and undertakes faithfully to perform and carry out the stipulations therein contained.

IN WITNESS WHEREOF, I have signed this instrument of accession at [place] on [date].

[Signature]

[13] From *Treaty Handbook* (2nd ed) by the Treaty Section of the Office of Legal Affairs ©2002–2012 United Nations. Reprinted with the permission of the United Nations.

Annex X
Example of an Instrument of Accession[14]

MINISTRY OF FOREIGN AFFAIRS
THE SOCIALIST REPUBLIC OF VIETNAM
ASEAN NATIONAL SECRETARIAT

Hanoi 10 March 1997

No: 104 ASVN/III/97

H.E. Mr. Michael Cheok
Director-General
ASEAN - Singapore
Singapore

Dear colleague,

I have the honour to inform you that on behalf of the Government of the Socialist Republic of Vietnam, H.E. Mr. Nguyen Manh Cam, Minister of Foreign Affairs, signed on 20 February 1997 the Instrument of Accession to the Agreement for the Facilitation of Search for Aircrafts in Distress and Rescue of Survivors of Aircraft Accidents signed in Singapore on 14 April 1972. (A copy of the Instrument is attached herewith).

The original copy of the Instrument will be sent to you for deposit with the Ministry of Foreign Affairs of Singapore by the Vietnamese Embassy in Singapore in due course.

With my best regards.

Yours sincerely,

NGUYEN MANH HUNG
Director General
ASEAN - Vietnam

CC: Secretary General of ASEAN
All ASEAN Directors-General
Vietnamese Embassy in Singapore

[14] Vietnam Instrument of Accession to the Agreement for the Facilitation of Search for Aircraft in Distress and Rescue of Survivors of Aircraft Accidents (signed 20 February 1997). Reprinted with the permission of the Treaty Legal Services and Agreements Directorate of the ASEAN Secretariat. The signed and stamped original instrument of accession is on file with the Secretariat a copy of which can be accessed on ARC – ASEAN Secretariat Resource Centre, 'The Archives of the ASEAN Legal Documents' http://arc-agreement.asean.org/file/doc/2014/02/instrument-of-accession-of-the-socialist-republic-of-viet-nam-for-the-agreement-for-the-facilitation-of-search-for-aircrafts-in-distress-and-rescue-of-supervisors-of-aircraft-accidents-.pdf accessed 2 November 2018.

11.MAR'97 10:39 ASEAN VIETNAM MOFA 008448435758 P.2/3

MINISTRY OF FOREIGN AFFAIRS
THE SOCIALIST REPUBLIC OF VIETNAM

INSTRUMENT OF ACCESSION

WHEREAS, the Agreement for the Facilitation of Search for Aircrafts in Distress and Rescue of Survivors of Aircraft Accidents was signed at Singapore on 14th April 1972 by the Governments of the Republic of Indonesia, Malaysia, the Republic of the Philippines, the Republic of Singapore and the Kingdom of Thailand being members of the Association of the Southeast Asian Nations (ASEAN) ;

WHEREAS, Article 8 of the said Agreement stipulates that the said Agreement shall be open for accession by any new Member of ASEAN by the deposit of an Instrument of Accession with the Ministry of Foreign Affairs of Singapore ;

NOW THEREFORE, the Government of the Socialist Republic of Vietnam being a State Member of the Association of Southeast Asian Nations (ASEAN) and of the International Civil Aviation Organization (ICAO) having considered the aforesaid Agreement hereby accedes to the Agreement for the Facilitation of Search for Aircrafts in Distress and Rescue of Survivors of Aircraft Accidents which was signed at Singapore on 14th April 1972, and undertakes faithfully to fulfill and carry out the stipulations therein contained.

2.

Upon accession to this Agreement, the Government of the Socialist Republic of Vietnam understands that, for the purpose of this Agreement, the term "territories" shall include mainland, islands, territorial waters and the above air space, as defined in the laws of the Socialist Republic of Vietnam and in accordance with international law including the 1982 United Nations Convention on the Law of the Sea.

IN WITNESS WHEREOF, the undersigned, being duly authorized thereto by the Government of the Socialist Republic of Vietnam, has signed and sealed this Instrument of Accession to the Agreement.

Done at Hanoi on the 20th day of February, One thousand nine hundred and ninety-seven.

NGUYEN MANH CAM
Minister of Foreign Affairs
Socialist Republic of Vietnam

Annex XI
United Nations Model Instrument of Reservation/Declaration[15]

ANNEX 6 – MODEL INSTRUMENT OF RESERVATION/DECLARATION

(To be signed by the Head of State, Head of Government or Minister for Foreign Affairs)

[RESERVATION / DECLARATION]

I, [name and title of the Head of State, Head of Government or Minister for Foreign Affairs],

HEREBY DECLARE that the Government of [name of State] makes the following [reservation / declaration] in relation to article(s) [---] of the [title and date of adoption of the treaty, convention, agreement, etc.]:

[Substance of reservation / declaration]

IN WITNESS WHEREOF, I have hereunto set my hand and seal.

Done at [place] on [date].

[Signature and title]

[15] From *Treaty Handbook* (2nd ed) by the Treaty Section of the Office of Legal Affairs ©2002–2012 United Nations. Reprinted with the permission of the United Nations.

Annex XII
Examples of an Instrument of Reservation

A Example of a Reservation Contained within an Instrument of Ratification[16]

(14)

WHEREAS a Sixth Protocol to the General Agreement on Privileges and Immunities of the Council of Europe was adopted by the Council of Ministers on 9 February 1996;

AND WHEREAS the said Protocol was signed on behalf of the Government of the United Kingdom of Great Britain and Northern Ireland on 27 October 1999;

NOW THEREFORE the Government of the United Kingdom of Great Britain and Northern Ireland, having considered the Protocol aforesaid, hereby confirm and ratify the same and undertake faithfully to perform and carry out all the stipulations therein contained, except that, until such time as the necessary legislation is enacted, the United Kingdom reserves the right not to apply Article 1 of the Sixth Protocol in respect of the spouses and minor children of judges.

[16] The Government of the United Kingdom's reservation to Article 1 of the Sixth Protocol to the General Agreement on Privileges and Immunities of the Council of Europe contained in its instrument of ratification of the Sixth Protocol to the General Agreement on Privileges and Immunities of the Council of Europe. The UK's ratification instrument was signed on 4 October 2001. A copy of this instrument was provided by the Treaty Section of the FCO and is reproduced here with kind permission. The reproduction of this instrument is made in accordance with and subject to the Open Government Licence for public sector information

In witness whereof this Instrument of Ratification is signed and sealed by Her Majesty's Principal Secretary of State for Foreign and Commonwealth Affairs.

Done at London the fourth day of October, Two thousand and one.

Jack Straw

www.nationalarchives.gov.uk/doc/open-government-licence/version/1/open-government-licence.htm accessed 4 December 2018.

B Example of an Instrument of Reservation Accompanying an Instrument of Ratification[17]

(6)

WHEREAS the Fourth Additional Protocol to the European Convention on Extradition was open for signature in Vienna on 20 September 2012;

AND WHEREAS the said Protocol was signed by the Government of the United Kingdom of Great Britain and Northern Ireland on 6 January 2014;

NOW THEREFORE the Government of the United Kingdom of Great Britain and Northern Ireland, having considered the Protocol aforesaid, hereby confirms and ratifies the same and undertakes faithfully to perform and carry out all the stipulations therein contained subject to the terms of the reservation and declarations contained in the accompanying Note.

[17] Reservation and declarations made by the Government of the UK on ratification of the Fourth Additional Protocol to the European Convention on Extradition. The UK's instrument of ratification and the accompanying instrument of reservation and declarations were signed on 3 September 2014. A copy of this instrument was provided by the Treaty Section of the FCO and is reproduced here with kind permission. The reproduction of this instrument is made in accordance with and subject to the Open Government Licence for public sector information www.nationalarchives.gov.uk/doc/open-government-licence/version/1/open-government-licence.htm accessed 4 December 2018.

In witness whereof this Instrument of Ratification is signed and sealed by Her Majesty's Principal Secretary of State for Foreign and Commonwealth Affairs.

Done at London the THIRD day of SEPTEMBER. Two thousand and fourteen.

3 September 2014

His Excellency, Thorbjorn Jagland
Secretary General of the Council of Europe
Strasbourg

I have the honour to refer to the European Convention on Extradition, ratified by the United Kingdom of Great Britain and Northern Ireland on 13 February 1991, (the 'Convention') and the United Kingdom of Great Britain and Northern Ireland's ratification of the Fourth Additional Protocol to the Convention (the 'Fourth Additional Protocol') and to inform you that the Government of the United Kingdom of Great Britain and Northern Ireland expresses its consent to be bound by the Fourth Additional Protocol, subject to the reservation and declarations below.

Reservation

In accordance with Article 6, paragraph 3, of the Fourth Additional Protocol, the Government of the United Kingdom of Great Britain and Northern Ireland declares that, for the purpose of Article 12 and Article 14, paragraph 1.a, of the Convention, it reserves the right to require the original or authenticated copy of a request and supporting documents.

Declarations

In accordance with Article 12, paragraph 1, of the Convention, as replaced by Article 2, paragraph 1, of the Fourth Additional Protocol, the Government of the United Kingdom of Great Britain and Northern Ireland designates the Home Office as its competent authority for the purpose of sending and receiving requests for extradition.

In accordance with Article 14, paragraph 3, of the Convention, as replaced by Article 3 of the Fourth Additional Protocol, the Government of the United Kingdom of Great Britain and Northern Ireland declares that a requesting Party may restrict the personal freedom of an extradited person in the circumstances set out in Article 14, paragraph 3, as replaced.

I avail myself of this opportunity to renew to your Excellency the assurances of my highest consideration.

PHILIP HAMMOND

Annex XIII
Example of a Note Confirming the Completion of Domestic Procedures[18]

ARG/NZ/2/3/1
LATAM/NZ/1/3/1

The Ministry of Foreign Affairs and Trade presents its compliments to the Embassy of Argentina and has the honour to refer to the *Exchange of Letters amending the Agreement on a Working Holiday Scheme between the Government of New Zealand and the Government of the Argentine Republic* signed on 5 November and 13 December 2010 and the Argentine Ministry of Foreign Affair's note number 27/11 dated 24 January 2011 advising, that the Argentine Republic has completed its internal requirements for the modification of the Agreement to enter into effect.

The Ministry of Foreign Affairs and Trade has the further honour to notify the Embassy of Argentina that New Zealand has completed its internal procedural requirements for the modification of the Agreement to enter into effect. In accordance with the Exchange of Letters, the modifications to the Agreement will enter into force on the date of receipt of this Note.

The Ministry of Foreign Affairs and Trade takes this opportunity to renew to the Embassy of Argentina the assurances of its highest consideration.

Ministry of Foreign Affairs and Trade

WELLINGTON

27 July 2011

[18] New Zealand Note dated 27 July 2011 confirming the completion of its domestic procedures and the date of entry into force of the Exchange of Letters amending the Agreement on a Working Holiday Scheme between the Government of New Zealand and the Government of the Argentine Republic. A copy of this note was provided by the Ministry of Foreign Affairs and Trade of New Zealand and is reproduced here with kind permission.

Annex XIV
Examples of a Depositary Notification of Ratification and Entry into Force

A Depositary Notification to a State of the Date of its Ratification and Entry into Force of the Treaty

New Zealand Depositary Notification informing Chile of the date of ratification by Chile of the Convention on the Conservation and Management of High Seas Fishery Resources in the South Pacific Ocean[19]

LGL/FISH/SPFO

The Ministry of Foreign Affairs and Trade presents its compliments to the Embassy of the Republic of Chile and has the honour to refer to the *Convention on the Conservation and Management of High Seas Fishery Resources in the South Pacific Ocean* ("the Convention") done at Auckland on 14 November 2009.

On behalf of the Government of New Zealand as Depositary for the Convention, the Ministry of Foreign Affairs and Trade has the honour to inform the Embassy of the Republic of Chile that 25 July 2012 has been formally recorded as the date of deposit of its Instrument of Ratification and that the other Contracting Parties have been duly notified. The Ministry of Foreign Affairs and Trade has the honour to attach a current status list for the Convention.

The Ministry of Foreign Affairs and Trade has the further honour to inform the Embassy of the Republic of Chile that the requirements of Article 38(1) have now been met. In accordance with that Article the Convention will enter into force on 24 August 2012, 30 days after the date of receipt of the Republic of Chile's Instrument of Ratification.

The Ministry of Foreign Affairs and Trade takes this opportunity to renew to the Embassy of the Republic of Chile the assurances of its highest consideration.

MINISTRY OF FOREIGN AFFAIRS & TRADE NEW ZEALAND

Ministry of Foreign Affairs and Trade

WELLINGTON

25 July 2012

[19] New Zealand Depositary Notification dated 25 July 2012 informing Chile of the date of ratification by Chile and entry into force of the Convention on the Conservation and Management of High Seas Fishery Resources in the South Pacific Ocean. A copy of this

B Depositary Notification to a State of the Date of its Ratification of the Treaty

New Zealand Depositary Notification on the Entry into Force of the Trans-Pacific Strategic Economic Partnership to Singapore[20]

M2005/03

LGL/BTE/FTA/TRI

The Ministry of Foreign Affairs and Trade of New Zealand presents its compliments to the Singapore High Commission and has the honour to refer to the *Trans-Pacific Strategic Economic Partnership* ("the Agreement") done at Wellington on 18 July 2005 and to which Singapore is a signatory state.

New Zealand wishes to advise that, in its capacity as Depositary for the Agreement, it received an Instrument of Ratification to the Agreement from the Government of New Zealand on 20 April 2006.

New Zealand further wishes to advise that, in its capacity as Depositary for the Agreement, it received an Instrument of Ratification to the Agreement from the Government of Singapore on 28 April 2006. The Government of New Zealand wishes to thank the Government of Singapore for the deposit of said Instrument.

The Instrument of Ratification to the Agreement from the Government of New Zealand states that the Agreement shall enter into force for New Zealand on 1 May 2006. The Instrument of Ratification to the Agreement from the Government of Singapore states that the Agreement shall enter into force for Singapore on 1 May 2006.

A current status list for the Agreement is attached for the Government of Singapore's reference.

Notification was provided by the Ministry of Foreign Affairs and Trade of New Zealand and is reproduced here with kind permission.

20 Depositary Notification dated 28 April 2006 to the Government of Singapore on the date ratification by Singapore of the Trans-Pacific Strategic Economic Partnership to Singapore, LGL/BTE/FTA/TRI. A copy of this note was provided by the Ministry of Foreign Affairs and Trade of New Zealand and is reproduced here with kind permission.

The Ministry of Foreign Affairs and Trade of New Zealand takes this opportunity to renew to the Singapore High Commission the assurances of its highest consideration.

Ministry of Foreign Affairs and Trade

WELLINGTON

28 April 2006

Encl 1

Annex XV
United Nations Model Certifying Statement for Registration or Filing and Recording[21]

ANNEX 9 – MODEL CERTIFYING STATEMENT FOR REGISTRATION OR FILING AND RECORDING

(Model for the certifying statement required under the General Assembly Regulations to give effect to Article 102 of the Charter)[1]

CERTIFYING STATEMENT

I, THE UNDERSIGNED [name of the authority], hereby certify that the attached text is a true and complete copy of [title of the agreement, name of the Parties, date and place of conclusion], that [it includes all reservations made by Signatories or Parties thereto], and that it was concluded in the following languages: [...]. *I further certify that the additional copy of this Agreement submitted on electronic media is a true and complete copy of [title of the agreement].*[2]

I FURTHER CERTIFY that the Agreement came into force on [date] by [method of entry into force], in accordance with [article or provision in the agreement], and that it was signed by [...] and [...].[3]

[Place and date of signature of certifying statement]

[Signature and title of certifying authority]

---

[1] For the text of the Regulations adopted by General Assembly resolution 97 (I) of 14 December 1946 and later amended by General Assembly resolutions 364B (IV) of 1 December 1949, 482 (V) of 12 December 1950 and 33/141 of 19 December 1978, see United Nations *Treaty Series*, vol. 859/860, p. VIII, 1973. See also General Assembly resolution 52/153 of 15 December 1997; *Repertory of Practice of United Nations Organs* (vol. V, New York, 1955, Articles 92-111, and Supplements 1 to 7).

[2] The language in italics must be included when additional copies of a treaty are provided on an electronic medium.

[3] For multilateral agreements, a complete list of contracting States or organizations with the date of deposit of the instruments of ratification, accession, etc., and the date of entry into force of the agreement for each party must be provided.

[21] From *Treaty Handbook* (2nd ed) by the Treaty Section of the Office of Legal Affairs ©2002–2012 United Nations. Reprinted with the permission of the United Nations.

Annex XVI
Example of an Official Publication of a Treaty[22]

REPUBLIC OF SINGAPORE

GOVERNMENT GAZETTE

TREATIES SUPPLEMENT

Published by Authority

NO. 1] **FRIDAY, JUNE 8** **[2007**

First published in the Government *Gazette*, Electronic Edition, on 4th June 2007 at 5.00 pm.

No. T 1

AGREEMENT

BETWEEN

THE GOVERNMENT OF THE REPUBLIC OF SINGAPORE

AND

THE GOVERNMENT OF THE REPUBLIC OF INDONESIA

ON

THE PROMOTION AND PROTECTION OF INVESTMENTS

The Government of the Republic of Singapore and the Government of the Republic of Indonesia (each hereinafter referred to as a "Contracting Party");

BEARING in mind the friendly and cooperative relations existing between the two countries and their peoples;

INTENDING to create favourable conditions for investments by investors of one Contracting Party in the territory of the other Contracting Party on the basis of sovereign equality and mutual benefit;

RECOGNIZING that the Agreement on the Promotion and Protection of Investments (hereinafter referred to as "the Agreement") will be conducive to the stimulation of investment activities in both countries pursuant to prevailing laws and regulations of the respective countries;

HAVE AGREED AS FOLLOWS:

[22] Republic of Singapore Government Gazette No. 1 [2007] 8 June 2007. In this Annex we have reproduced only the first and final pages of this issue of the Singapore Government Gazette.

IN WITNESS WHEREOF, the undersigned, duly authorized thereto by their respective Governments, have signed this Agreement.

Done in duplicate at Singapore on 16th February 2005 in the Indonesian and English languages, both texts being equally authentic. If there is any divergence concerning interpretation, the English text shall prevail.

For the Government of the Republic of Singapore	For the Government of the Republic of Indonesia
LIM HNG KIANG Minister for Trade and Industry	DR. N. HASAN WIRAJUDA Minister for Foreign Affairs

Annex XVII
Examples of Treaty Provisions on Continuing Obligations after Withdrawal or Termination

A Examples of Continuing Obligations Provisions in Bilateral Treaties

Agreement Between the Government of the Republic of Latvia and the Government of the Republic of Estonia on the Exchange and Mutual Protection of Classified Information[23]

Article 17(3)

Each Party may terminate this Agreement through diplomatic channels at any time. In such a case, the Agreement shall expire six months after the receipt of the termination notice by the other Party. In the case of termination, Classified Information transmitted or generated within the application of this Agreement shall continue to be protected under the provisions of this Agreement.

Agreement on Trade and Technical Cooperation between the Government of the Republic of Turkey and the Government of the Oriental Republic of Uruguay[24]

Article VIII

[...]

The Present Agreement shall remain in force for a period of three years and thereafter its validity shall be automatically extended for successive periods of one year, unless a written notice of termination is given by either Contracting Party three months prior to its expiration.

Article IX

In the event of the termination of this Agreement, its provisions shall continue to apply in respect of any unfulfilled obligations of the commercial contracts and business arrangements concluded during the period of its validity.

23 Agreement between the Government of the Republic of Latvia and the Government of the Republic of Estonia on the exchange and mutual protection of classified information (adopted 6 June 2011, entered into force 20 July 2011) 2830 UNTS 11.

24 Agreement on Trade, Economic and Technical Cooperation between the Government of the Republic of Turkey and the Government of the Oriental Republic of Uruguay (signed 30 April 2009, entered into force 25 October 2011) 2830 UNTS 51.

Agreement between the Government of the United Kingdom of Great Britain and Northern Ireland and the Government of the Russian Federation on Co-operation in the Peaceful Uses of Nuclear Energy[25]

Article 9

1. This Agreement shall enter into force on the ninetieth day following the day of signature and remain in force for a period of fifteen years. Thereafter it shall remain in force unless either Party shall have given the other one year's notice of termination in writing.
2. Termination of this Agreement shall not affect any co-operation initiated in the period of validity of the Agreement and not completed at the time of its termination.

Agreement on Encouragement and Reciprocal Protection of Investments between the Kingdom of the Netherlands and the Republic of Kazakhstan[26]

Article 14

1. The present Agreement shall enter into force on the first day of the second month following the day on which the Contracting Parties have notified each other in writing through diplomatic channels that the required domestic procedures have been complied with. The Agreement shall remain in force for a period of fifteen years.
2. Unless written notice of termination has been given by either Contracting Party at least six months before the date of expiry of its validity, the present Agreement shall be extended tacitly for periods of ten years, whereby each Contracting Party reserves the right to terminate the Agreement upon notice of at least six months before the date of expiry of the current period of validity.
3. In respect of investments made before the date of the termination of the present Agreement, the provisions of the foregoing articles of this Agreement shall continue to be effective for a further period of fifteen years from that date.

[25] Agreement between the Government of the United Kingdom of Great Britain and Northern Ireland and the Government of the Russian Federation on Co-operation in the Peaceful Uses of Nuclear Energy (done 3 September 1996, entered into force 3 December 1996) UKTS No. 107 (1996).

[26] Agreement on Encouragement and Reciprocal Protection of Investments between the Kingdom of the Netherlands and the Republic of Kazakhstan (done 27 November 2002, entered into force 1 August 2007) 2877 UNTS 49.

B Examples of Continuing Obligations Provisions in Multilateral Treaties

Convention for the Protection of Human Rights and Fundamental Freedoms[27]

Article 58 Denunciation

2. Such a denunciation shall not have the effect of releasing the High Contracting Party concerned from its obligations under this Convention in respect of any act which, being capable of constituting a violation of such obligations, may have been performed by it before the date at which the denunciation became effective.

United Nations Convention on the Law of the Sea[28]

Article 317 Denunciation

2. A State shall not be discharged by reason of the denunciation from the financial and contractual obligations which accrued while it was a Party to this Convention, nor shall the denunciation affect any right, obligation or legal situation of that State created through the execution of this Convention prior to its termination for that State.

International Agreement Regarding the Maintenance of Certain Lights in the Red Sea[29]

Article 12(1)

[...] Denunciation shall take effect at the end of the financial year following that in which notice is given and a contributing Government shall remain liable for a contribution incurred before its denunciation takes effect.

[27] Convention for the Protection of Human Rights and Fundamental Freedoms (as amended by Protocols No. 11 and No. 14) 1950 ETS 5.

[28] UNCLOS (adopted 10 December 1982, entered into force 16 November 1994) 1988 UNTS 3.

[29] International Agreement regarding the Maintenance of Certain Lights in the Red Sea (adopted 20 February to 19 August 1962, entered into force 28 October 1966) UKTS 8 (1967).

International Coffee Agreement, 2000[30]

Article 52 Duration and Termination

(2) (3) … Notwithstanding the termination of this Agreement, the Council shall remain in being for as long as necessary to take such decisions as are needed during the period of time required for the liquidation of the Organization, settlement of its accounts and disposal of its assets.

[30] International Coffee Agreement (adopted 28 September 2000, entered into force 17 May 2005) 2161 UNTS 308.

Glossary

acceptance or approval A means to express a State's consent to be bound to a treaty that has the same legal effect as ratification, unless the treaty provides otherwise. Most treaties that provide for acceptance or approval require a prior signature. (Article 14(2) VCLT 1969 and Article 14(3) VCLT 1986).

accession A means to express a State's consent to be bound to a treaty, as provided by that treaty. However, unlike ratification, acceptance or approval, accession is a one-step procedure that only requires a State or an IO to deposit an instrument of accession.

Accession is usually only available for States and IOs that have not signed the treaty. Some treaties provide accession as an option only after the treaty is closed for signatures. (Article 15 VCLT 1969 and Article 15 VCLT 1986).

adoption A treaty is created when its text is adopted. A bilateral treaty is adopted when both parties formally agree that the text is concluded, in the sense that it is final. A multilateral treaty is adopted when all parties participating in its negotiation are agreed on a final text, whether by consensus or by vote. At this point the obligations in it are not binding; States and IOs that wish to become party have to consent to be bound and bring it into force, according to the procedures applicable to that treaty.

bilateral treaty A treaty with two parties (two States, two IOs or one State and one IO).

certified true copies Exact copies of the treaty that have been signed. Certification is normally shown by the signature of the Head of Treaty Office or a senior legal official, and the pages are bound and sealed.

Conferences of Parties The principle policy-making body for some multilateral treaties. The Conference's functions and powers are normally set by the treaty itself. It is typically tasked with meeting periodically to take stock of the implementation of the treaty and to consider future action.

(expressing) consent to be bound A unilateral treaty act by which an individual State or IO formally commits itself to all the obligations in the treaty, which will become binding upon it when the treaty enters into force according to its terms (which will depend upon the equivalent unilateral act being done by others). The act is irreversible, in the sense that once a party has expressed its consent to be bound, it is committed, unless it can withdraw in a manner provided for in the treaty. But it does not necessarily by itself bring a treaty into force.

denunciation (or withdrawal) A situation in which one party leaves the treaty, that is, ceases to be a party. The terms 'withdrawal' and 'denunciation' are interchangeable.

depositary The depositary of a treaty is the custodian of the original text of the treaty, whose other functions are provided under the treaty. It is mainly responsible for ensuring the proper execution of all treaty actions to that treaty. The depositary's duties are international in character, and the depositary is under an obligation to act impartially in the performance of those duties. A depositary can be one or more States, an IO or the chief administrative officer of an IO (Article 77 VCLT 1969 and the UN Treaty Handbook).

domestic law of treaties In relation to a State, it consists of the national rules that determine who in that State has the power to conclude a treaty, how and when, and what effect the treaty has in the national legal system. These rules are usually considered to be part of constitutional law, and the most important ones may be set out in the national constitution.

The domestic law of treaties of an IO consists of the provisions of its constitution or founding documents, and any other internal rules, that define the capacity of the IO to conclude treaties, as well as who in the IO has the power to perform treaty acts, and who in the IO has the responsibility to carry out treaty obligations.

entry into force Occurs when the conditions specified in the treaty are met; it requires enough consents to be bound (two for a bilateral treaty; for a multilateral it could be all or a minimum number of negotiating parties) plus any other conditions specified in the treaty such as elapse of a specified time. A bilateral treaty is either in force for both parties or neither. A multilateral treaty enters into force for all who have consented to be bound when its threshold is met. Thereafter, it will enter into force for any new party when it consents to be bound and the conditions are met (Article 24 VCLT 1969 and Article 24 VCLT 1986).

exchange of instruments constituting a treaty A treaty may be formed by an exchange of instruments, such as notes verbales or letters. Bilateral treaties are commonly made in this form. The consent of the parties to be bound is expressed by the exchange of instruments, when those instruments specify that they are to have such effect, or the parties have agreed that this shall be the effect. The exchange may take place simultaneously, or by each party delivering its instrument to the other consecutively, in which case the second delivery completes the exchange (Article 13 VCLT 1969 and Article 13 VCLT 1986).

Final Act The record of a meeting at which a treaty text was formally adopted. The text of the treaty is normally set out in or appended to the Final Act. It may also contain statements made by the parties, individually or collectively, about the text and other related material (Articles 9 and 10 VCLT 1969 and VCLT 1986).

final clauses Treaty provisions, normally placed at or near the end of a treaty, that set out how the treaty is to operate. At the minimum, they need to specify which States or IOs are eligible to be party (for multilateral treaties), how they may express their consent to be bound and how the treaty will enter into force. A multilateral treaty needs to designate a depositary.

In addition, it is usually desirable to have provisions on some or all of the following matters: relationship of the treaty to other treaties, settlement of disputes, amendment and review, status of annexes, duration, termination or denunciation, provisional application, territorial application, reservations, obligations of the depositary, registration and authentic texts.

Full Powers A document that shows that a named person has authority to perform a specified treaty act or class of acts, on behalf of a State or an IO.

Expressed more precisely, it is a document emanating from the competent authority of a State or from the competent authority of an organ of an IO designating a person or persons to represent the State or the IO for negotiating, adopting or authenticating the text of a treaty, for expressing the consent of the State or IO to be bound by a treaty, or for accomplishing any other act with respect to a treaty (Article 2(1)(c) VCLT 1969 and VCLT 1986).

instruments of ratification, acceptance, approval or accession The document by which a State or an IO ratifies, accepts, approves or accedes to a treaty. To be effective, the instrument must be deposited with or delivered to the other party or parties or the depositary (Article 16 VCLT 1969 and VCLT 1986).

international law of treaties The rules of public international law about treaties that govern how treaties are made, brought into force, implemented, operated, interpreted, wound up and so on. The rules are part of customary international law, and the most important ones are contained in the VCLT 1969 and VCLT 1986.

international organisation Intergovernmental organisation (Article 2(1) VCLT 1969 and VCLT 1986).

limited membership multilateral treaty A multilateral treaty that is open to named States and/or IOs only, and/or a defined category of States and/or IOs, such as those within a particular geographical region or which are members of a particular IO, or those which meet any other criteria such as engaging in a particular industry or activity.

multilateral treaty A treaty with three or more parties.

PLATO principles Five generic principles for good treaty practice: P: Professional (professional approach to treaty work by those who do it and by the organisation). L: Legal (legal requirements met; lawyers fully engaged). A: Assured (accuracy, authenticity and authority are assured). T: Transparent (clear, communicated, available and accessible in practice). O: Organised (systematic, efficient, regular).

plurilateral treaty A limited membership multilateral treaty that is open only to the negotiating States or IOs that are named in the treaty. Such a treaty may have several parties or as few as three.

Protocol Normally used to denote a treaty which is supplementary to an existing treaty.

ratification A means to express consent to be bound to a treaty that is provided in most multilateral treaties and some bilateral treaties. Ratification is normally the second part of a two-step procedure for expressing consent to be bound, where the first step is signature. It usually has the same legal effect as an act of formal confirmation, acceptance or approval, where these are provided as alternatives (Article 14 VCLT 1969 and VCLT 1986).

reservation A unilateral statement, however phrased or named, made by a State or by an IO when signing, ratifying, accepting, approving or acceding to a treaty, whereby it purports to exclude or to modify the legal effect of certain provisions of the treaty in their application to that State (Article 2(1)(d) VCLT 1969 and VCLT 1986).

signature The first commonly used step to participate in a treaty is signing that treaty. There are two types of signature:

- *Definitive signature*: the signature is effective, by itself, to bind a State or an IO to a treaty.
- *Signature subject to ratification*: the signature is not sufficient by itself to bind a State or an IO to a treaty, but is rather the first step of a two-step procedure, the second part of which is to be completed at a later date (Article 12 VCLT 1969 and VCLT 1986).

signature, exchange of instruments constituting a treaty, ratification, act of formal confirmation, acceptance, approval or accession Means by which a State or IO may establish its consent to be bound by a treaty on the international plane, as provided for in the treaty or otherwise agreed by the negotiating parties (VCLT 1969, Articles 2(1)(b) and 11 and VCLT 1986, Articles 2(1)(b), 2(1)(b bis), 2(1)(b ter) and 11).

sunset clause A provision in a treaty which prescribes a fixed period of time and/or other condition(s) after which the treaty will expire. The effect of such a provision is usually that when the specified period of time has expired or the specified condition(s) is/are met, this triggers the automatic termination of the treaty.

termination The treaty ceases to be in force, for all parties.

testimonium The last formal part of a treaty. A testimonium usually forms the lines below which the signatories sign and contains information on the date and place of adoption or signature.

treaty An international agreement concluded between States, or between IOs, or between any combination thereof, in written form and governed by international law, whether embodied in a single instrument or in two or more related instruments and whatever its particular designation (Article 2(1)(a) VCLT 1969 and VCLT 1986).

treaty collection The whole set of treaty documents, records and information (internal and published) held by a government or an IO.

treaty law The rights and obligations set out in treaties or arising under treaties. It is concerned with the *contents* of *particular* treaties. (Note however that 'treaty law' is used by some people as convenient shorthand for 'the international law of treaties', so care should be taken to interpret these words in the sense in which they were meant.)

treaty-like instruments Any kind of international document that is not a treaty but might bear some resemblance to one. From a legal point of view, there are broadly three categories which a treaty-like instrument may fall into:

- instruments which are binding under international law;
- instruments which are binding under national law; and
- instruments which are not binding under any system of law.

Treaty Office A unit within a government or IO dedicated to the handling of treaty procedures and treaty information for the whole government or IO. In some contexts, in this Handbook, 'Treaty Office' also includes reference to any officials whose functions include treaty procedures, whether or not in a unit dedicated to treaties.

treaty practice Refers to the procedures and practices followed by States and IOs in the creation and handling of treaties, and acts relating to treaties. Strictly speaking, 'treaty practice' refers only to the handling of treaties and does not include the handling of other kinds of international instruments such as declarations, understandings and arrangements.

treaty stakeholders All categories of people involved in the handling of treaties or affected by them. Treaty stakeholders include both treaty actors and treaty users, as these categories are not mutually exclusive.

universal treaty A multilateral treaty that is open to all States, and may also be open to IOs.

withdrawal (or denunciation) A situation in which one party leaves the treaty, that is, ceases to be a party. The terms 'withdrawal' and 'denunciation' are interchangeable.

Suggested Further Reading

Books

Aust A, *Modern Treaty Law and Practice* (3rd edn, CUP 2013).

Cannizzaro E (ed), *The Law of Treaties Beyond the Vienna Convention* (OUP 2011).

Corten O and Klein P (eds), *The Vienna Convention on the Law of Treaties: A Commentary* (OUP 2011).

Gardiner R, *Treaty Interpretation* (2nd edn, OUP 2015).

Hollis D (ed), *The Oxford Guide to Treaties* (OUP 2012).

et al. (eds), *National Treaty Law and Practice: Dedicated to the Memory of Monroe Leigh* (Brill 2005).

Polakiewicz J, *Treaty-making in the Council of Europe* (Council of Europe Publishing 1999).

Roberts I (ed), *Satow's Diplomatic Practice* (7th edn, OUP 2016), Book VII Treaties and Treaty-Making.

Sinclair I, *The Vienna Convention and the Law of Treaties* (2nd edn, Melland Schill Studies, Manchester University Press 1984).

Wolfrum R and Röben V (eds), *Developments of International Law in Treaty Making* (Springer 2005).

Zidar A and Gauci J (eds), *The Role of Legal Advisers in International Law* (Brill 2017).

Journal Articles and Book Chapters

Harrington J, 'Redressing the Democratic Deficit in Treaty Law Making: (Re)Establishing a Role for Parliament' (2005) 50 *McGill Law Journal* 465.

Mason D, '"Deliberative Democratising" of Australian Treaty Making: Putting into Context the Significance of Online Access to the Treaty Process' (2016) 24(2) *Journal of Law, Information & Science* 1.

Peters A, 'Treaty Making Power' in R Wolfrum (ed), *Max Planck Encyclopedia of Public International Law* (OUP 2012).

Kohona P, 'Some Notable Developments in the Practice of the UN Secretary-General as Depositary of Multilateral Treaties: Reservations and Declarations', (2005) 99 *American Journal of International Law* 433.

Publications by Governments and International Organisations

Council of Europe, 'The Treaty Office in a Nutshell', PDF booklet. Source: Treaty Office on http://conventions.coe.int (General Information).

Council of Europe, Committee of Legal Advisers on Public International Law, 'Database on the Organisation and Functions of the Office of the Legal Adviser in the Ministry of Foreign Affairs'. Source: www.coe.

New Zealand Government, Ministry of Foreign Affairs and Trade, 'International Treaty Making: Guidance for government agencies on practice and procedures for concluding international treaties and arrangements', PDF booklet, August 2018 edition. Source: www.mfat.govt.nz/en/about-us/who-we-are/treaties/.

United Kingdom Government, FCO, Legal Directorate, Treaty Section, 'Treaties and Memoranda of Understanding (MOUs): Guidance on practice and procedures' (2nd edn, FCO, updated March 2014), PDF, Source: www.gov.uk.

United Nations, International Law Commission, 'Guide to Practice on Reservations to Treaties' *Yearbook of the International Law Commission* (vol II, 2011, Part Two).

United Nations, Treaty Section of the Office of Legal Affairs, *Treaty Handbook* (2nd edn, UN 2012).

United Nations, Treaty Section of the Office of Legal Affairs, *Summary of Practice of the Secretary-General as Depositary of Multilateral Treaties* (ST/LEG/7/Rev.1, UN 1994).

United Nations, *International Law Handbook: Collection of Instruments* (UN 2017), Book One, Chapters 1 and 2.

United Nations, *Final Clauses of Multilateral Treaties: Handbook* (UN 2003).

Index

Introductory Note

In the interests of usability, where concepts are referred to very frequently, either the relevant entries are split into a number of subheadings or an effort has been made to list only the most significant discussions. As the whole work is about 'treaty law', use of this term (and certain others which occur throughout the book) as an entry point has been restricted. Information will be found under the relevant detailed entries.